KETO

for Women

OVER 50

1000

BEGINNER-FRIENDLY RECIPES, 30-DAY MEAL PLAN, AND EXPERT TIPS FOR EFFORTLESS WEIGHT LOSS AND OPTIMAL HEALTH

SANDRA GRANT
2023

Introduction

The ketogenic diet, also known as the "keto diet," is a low-carb, high-fat diet that has gained popularity in recent years for its potential health benefits. The diet involves reducing carbohydrate intake and increasing fat consumption, leading the body to enter a metabolic state known as ketosis. During ketosis, the body burns fat for energy instead of carbohydrates, leading to weight loss and improved health markers such as insulin sensitivity. While the basic principles of the keto diet are the same for all ages, there are some important differences to consider for women over 50 compared to younger people.

Women over 50 tend to have a slower metabolism than younger individuals, which means they may need to consume fewer calories and pay closer attention to macronutrient ratios in their diet. It is also important to consider muscle mass, as women over 50 tend to have more difficulty retaining muscle than younger people. To support muscle mass and overall health, women over 50 may need to prioritize resistance training and consume adequate protein.

Health concerns such as menopause, osteoporosis, and a higher risk of cardiovascular disease should also be taken into consideration when starting a keto diet. Women over 50 may experience different effects on hormone levels, such as estrogen and testosterone, which can impact mood, energy levels, and bone health. Before starting the ketogenic diet, it is important to consult with a healthcare professional to ensure it is safe and effective for individual needs.

Sandra Grant, a woman in her 50s, provides a personal example of the benefits of the keto diet. After trying multiple diets without success, she discovered the ketogenic diet and saw significant results in a short period of time. With determination and a well-planned diet, women over 50 can successfully achieve their health and weight loss goals through the keto diet.

It is important to note that weight loss is not the only factor affecting a woman's metabolic rate. Factors such as activity level, appetite, and eating habits play a significant role, as well as hormonal changes that occur with age. After menopause, women may experience a shift in where fat is stored in the body, making it more difficult to shed belly fat. Despite these challenges, maintaining a healthy diet and lifestyle is crucial for women over 50 and the keto diet can be a valuable tool for weight loss and improved health.

Chapter 1: Why Keto?

BENEFITS OF THE KETO DIET FOR WOMEN OVER 50!

The keto diet is trending all over social media and in our communities. It is popular as a quick weight-loss diet, and people often follow it for getting that perfect beach body for the summer. It is indeed effective with cutting pounds, but there are numerous other advantages. For menopausal women over 50, this diet is incredibly beneficial. Here are some reasons why:

It is great at melting fat

Many diets make you lose weight, but most of the weight that is being lost comes from water. Ironically, a diet that increases fat uptake is the best at reducing it throughout the body. It is true! Your body starts using fats as fuel. It gets better at breaking and extracting energy from it. Menopausal women begin to accumulate fat around their abdomen more than other parts. This diet is especially good at melting this fat. It lowers the chances of heart disease, stroke, and cardiac arrest in older women.

It increases insulin sensitivity

For both men and women, insulin resistance starts to kick in after a certain age. Being obese only drives up this process. Insulin is needed to transfer glucose molecules from the bloodstream to the muscles and liver when it has a lower sensitivity, and glucose is being stored as fat.

The keto diet and every other low carbohydrate diet results in increased glucose sensitivity. There is less glucose to process, so less fat is formed from glucose. It can save you from type 2 diabetes and unnecessary weight gain.

Increased brain health

As we get older, our brain functions start to deplete. This is why diseases like Alzheimer's attacks in old age. Menopause itself brings about mood changes and also causes memory loss and loss of focus.

A keto diet can help you protect your brainpower in old age. Our brain normally uses glucose to process and function. When estrogen falls, the amount of glucose reaching the brain is lowered. On the keto diet, you switch from glucose to ketones, and your brain suddenly gets an efficient energy source. This helps in curbing neurological diseases.

It reduces inflammation

If you are reading this book, chances are, you are a woman over 50. You can relate to the symptoms of headaches, knee pain, and joint pain.

This kind of pain can be enhanced by inflammation. A keto diet is filled with anti-inflammatory fat sources that can help you get rid of these nuisances. These include walnuts, avocado, and olive oil, among many others.

Moreover, carbohydrate-rich sources and processed products are linked to high levels of inflammatory markers. Reducing their consumption will also help lower inflammation.

It encourages a good lipid ratio

When women reach their 50s, their blood work will start to show an increase in LDL and triglycerides. They have been labeled as "bad" fat.

When you are eating a no-limit diet, you get a lot more bad fat than good fat, which is HDL and omega-3s. The lowering of HDL has been linked to increasing cases of heart disease. On the keto diet, you will eat a sufficient amount of fats that will include a good number of HDL, which will keep heart diseases at bay.

Decreases hypertension

Men generally have a higher range of blood pressure than women, but that shifts after 50. Hypertension is a significant cause of mortality, resulting in kidney diseases, heart diseases, etc.

The keto diet helps lower blood pressure by eliminating processed products.

Keeps away osteoporosis

Women in their 50s will experience bone weakness and bone loss. This comes with menopause and, if left alone, can develop into osteoporosis.

One way to protect your bones is to eat a lot of calcium. In the keto diet, the vegetables you are allowed are the calcium-rich green leafy vegetables. Also, many chemicals that hinder the process of absorption are excluded by the diet completely.

Prevents muscle loss

Older women lose muscles faster and become weaker as a result. Muscle loss can make you fatigue more often and make it harder for you to do everyday activities. You won't be as athletic as before.

The keto diet is filled with protein-rich foods that you eat in moderate amounts. Protein is needed for muscle gain, muscle repair, and preservation.

A keto diet isn't just for weight loss. If you want to live a longer and healthier life, then give this diet a shot.

WHAT IS THE KETOGENIC DIET?

It is a type of low-carb diet. In this, however, you have to restrict carbohydrates to a very low amount and increase fat uptake. This causes your body to shift from using carbohydrates (glucose) as your primary energy source to ketones. Ketones are derivatives of fats, and they can, just like glucose, provide energy to the brain.

This shift results in your body going into the state of "ketosis." Ketosis is when your body utilizes fat rather than carbohydrates for energy.

This change causes weight loss and other benefits to your body.

Variations of the keto diet

There are many variations to this diet, which are described below.

Standard Ketogenic Diet/SKD: This diet is commonly followed by people who want to lose weight. It is composed of unlimited fat supply, very low carbohydrate intake, and moderate amounts of protein. Almost 70 to 75 percent of fat provides most of the calories, and you have to consume an adequate amount of low-carb vegetables.

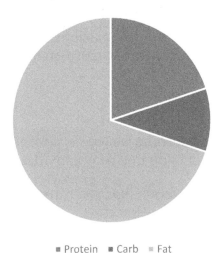

Ketogenic Diet Breakdown

■ Protein ■ Carb ■ Fat

Targeted Ketogenic Diet/TKD: This diet can be followed by athletes and people having workout sessions. You can consume some amount of carbs before an exercise session or on the day that the session is planned.

The theory is that carbs provide a greater boost of energy and performance when centered on workouts.

Cyclic Ketogenic Diet/CKD: This diet is to provide energy to hardcore athletes. This diet allows two days of carb "backloading," meaning you can eat carbs for two days, followed by five keto days.

This diet helps to replenish the lost glycogen reserves from the muscles to boost performance.

High Protein Ketogenic Diet/HPKD: This diet is like a standard ketogenic diet, but it has more calories coming from protein. Unlike SKD, there is not an unlimited consumption of fat. Usually, around 60 percent of the calories are from fat, and 35 percent comes from protein.

Salea

■ Fat ■ Protein ■ Carb

HISTORY

The origins of the ketogenic diet can be traced back to the 1920s, when it was first used by Dr. Russell Wilder as a treatment for seizures and epilepsy symptoms in children. Despite its early success, the use of the ketogenic diet declined with the advent of antiepileptic drugs.

However, it wasn't until 1994 that the ketogenic diet gained mainstream attention. A television program in America featured the story of Hollywood producer Jim Abrahams and his two-year-old son, who was an epileptic patient. Following advice from family members, Abrahams asked the hospital to put his son on a ketogenic diet, which resulted in a remarkable improvement in the child's condition. Impressed by the outcome, Abrahams funded further research into the diet, leading to increased interest and understanding of the ketogenic diet within the scientific community by 1998.

The popularity of the ketogenic diet has been on the rise in recent years, with many Hollywood celebrities jumping on the bandwagon. The diet, which involves reducing carbohydrates and increasing healthy fats, has been gaining attention for its ability to promote weight loss, improve energy levels, and even improve certain medical conditions.

One of the most well-known celebrities who have adopted the keto diet is actress Halle Berry. In an interview, she shared that she turned to the ketogenic lifestyle to help manage her type 2 diabetes. She credits the diet for improving her blood sugar levels and overall health.

Another Hollywood star who has embraced the ketogenic diet is reality TV personality Kourtney Kardashian. She has been an advocate of the diet, sharing her journey and experience on social media. She even started a food blog and launched a meal delivery service to help others follow the keto lifestyle.

Actor Jonah Hill is another celebrity who has credited the ketogenic diet for his weight loss. In an interview, he revealed that he lost 40 pounds by following a strict ketogenic diet and hitting the gym regularly. He shared that the diet has helped him to develop a healthier relationship with food and achieve his fitness goals.

Actress Vanessa Hudgens is another star who has followed the ketogenic diet to achieve her health and fitness goals. She has shared pictures on social media, showing her impressive transformation, and has credited the ketogenic diet for helping her lose weight and feel great.

In addition to its weight loss benefits, the ketogenic diet has also been known to improve mental clarity and boost energy levels. This is one of the reasons why many Hollywood stars have adopted this lifestyle, including football player Tim Tebow, DJ Khaled, and even supermodel Gisele Bundchen.

In conclusion, the ketogenic diet is no longer just a fad but has become a popular way of life for many Hollywood celebrities.

UNDERSTANDING THE SCIENCE BEHIND THE KETO DIET AND INTERMITTENT FASTING

The ketogenic diet, commonly referred to as the keto diet, is a low-carbohydrate, high-fat diet that can induce ketosis in the body. But what exactly is ketosis and how does it work?

Carbohydrates are typically the primary source of energy for the body, but in a keto diet, the intake of carbohydrates is limited to 50 grams or less. This lack of carbohydrates leads to lower insulin levels, which signals the body to reduce the storage of fat and carbohydrates. This then puts the body into a catabolic state, leading to two processes: gluconeogenesis and ketogenesis.

When glycogen reserves deplete, the body starts the process of gluconeogenesis, which is the production of glucose from non-carbohydrate sources such as lactic acid, glycerol, and amino acids. If gluconeogenesis can't meet the body's demands, ketogenesis takes over.

During ketogenesis, ketone bodies are produced as an alternative source of energy to glucose. They can cross the blood-brain barrier to provide energy to the brain, but other cells, such as red blood cells and liver cells, still require glucose from gluconeogenesis.

Three ketone bodies are produced in the process of ketogenesis: acetoacetate, hydroxybutyrate, and acetone. If ketone levels are in a healthy range, the body enters ketosis. However, if levels get too high, they can alter the pH of the blood and cause ketoacidosis, a harmful state caused by overly acidic blood.

Ketone bodies provide three times more energy to cells like the brain, heart, kidneys, and muscles compared to carbohydrates, making them a "super fuel".

Now let's turn our attention to intermittent fasting, a popular eating pattern that cycles between periods of normal calorie intake and periods of calorie restriction or fasting. Some popular forms of intermittent fasting include the warrior diet, the 5:2 method, and the alternate fasting day method. The most well-known method is the 16/8 method, which involves a 16-hour fast followed by an 8-hour eating period. Intermittent fasting has been shown to be effective for weight loss, as well as for maintaining blood sugar levels, reducing inflammation, and promoting brain development.

So, what happens when you combine a keto diet with intermittent fasting? First, it can lead to quicker induction of ketosis. Intermittent fasting also increases blood ketone levels as the body runs out of glycogen fuel, which is the goal of a keto diet. Additionally, combining the two can lead to more fat loss than just following the keto diet alone. Research has shown that intermittent fasting is more effective than low-calorie diets and it also induces thermogenesis, leading to an increase in heat production and fat metabolism.

It's important to note that combining a keto diet with intermittent fasting may not be suitable for everyone. Pregnant or breastfeeding women, those with diabetes, heart disease, or other chronic conditions should seek the advice of a doctor before trying it. Additionally, some people may experience uncomfortable symptoms such as irritability, overeating, and increased tiredness. Intermittent fasting is not necessary for a keto diet, as it can be successful on its own as long as it is followed correctly.

KETOGENIC DIET AND MENOPAUSE

Starting a ketogenic diet will be tough, but keep these tips in mind for a better outcome and result. Just like with fasting and other significant diet changes, women have to implement new techniques and exercise extra precautions.

The phase of transitional menopause

Although menopause happens after 50, the hormonal change that leads to many menopausal problems arises in the pre-menopausal years—this can begin in the late 30s. There are so many symptoms that happen due to this hormonal change.

Some of them are hot flashes, weight gain, insomnia, vaginal dryness, brain fog or memory loss, fatigue, mood swings, headaches, breast soreness, burning mouth, joint pain, etc.

Hormonal fluctuations

Ovaries release estrogen. However, during the pre-menopausal years, their levels fluctuate and then slowly decline. When you reach menopause, problems start getting worse.

Estrogen directs fat reserves to be stored in the hips and thighs. However, their decline leads them to be accumulated around the abdominal area. Visceral fats are also produced, which is not stored on the skin surface but on the top of organs like the heart and kidneys. They are linked to heart disease, insulin resistance, etc.

Why does weight gain happen in menopause?

There are many reasons why this occurs. Firstly, decreased estrogen leads to higher levels of insulin in the blood, or hyperinsulinemia. This promotes more storage of carbs and fats and induces weight gain.

Secondly, the hunger hormone *ghrelin* increases in pre- and post-menopausal women. This makes us feel hungrier, and we eat more as a result.

Thirdly, the chemicals that regulate weight balance and appetite, leptin and neuropeptide Y, don't work as efficiently as before.

Lastly, when you grow older, you become more fatigued, reduce your muscle mass, and generally become less active. Fewer calories and fat are burned.

Hot flashes/mood swings/headaches and the keto diet

There are a lot of symptoms regarding the brain in post-menopausal women. There is very scarce research on this subject. However, many women report that their symptoms related to the brain, like hot flashes, reduce in severity and occurrence after a couple of weeks following the keto diet.

There is a biochemical reason for this to happen. Lower levels of estrogen decrease the efficiency of glucose transporters in the brain that transfers glucose molecules. This closely resembles the biochemistry of epilepsy.

Just as the keto diet betters the life of epileptic patients, it might better the life of menopausal women as well.

Recommended carbs for menopausal women

There is very little research done on this subject, so an exact ratio to amount is going to be misleading. However, the standard ketogenic diet limits carbs to less than 50 grams and is enough to bring about ketosis and various benefits that the diet can bring.

But, if you want to rid yourself of menopausal symptoms like hot flashes, headaches, memory loss, etc., you may have to reduce your intake to about 20 grams of carbs.

BEST FOODS TO EAT ON THIS DIET AS A MENOPAUSAL WOMAN

These foods can give you control over your post-menopausal symptoms in addition to being a good, low carb, keto-friendly snack.

Flaxseed

It has been found that flaxseed helps with lowering the severity of hot flashes and other menopausal symptoms. However, more research needs to be done before any conclusive statements can be made.

Green tea

Green tea is extremely healthy because of its high supply of antioxidants. One of the antioxidants present in this tea is catechins; they have been shown to stabilize metabolism and increase heart health.

Caffeinated green tea decreases the amount of insulin in menopausal women, whereas a decaffeinated green tea doesn't provide the same result. If you have high levels of insulin, you can give green tea a try.

Fatty fish

This is a good source of healthy omega-3s, such as DHA and EPA. Its consumption has been linked to a reduction in insulin resistance, inflammation, and triglycerides (or bad fat).

They also show these results in menopausal women. A study done on post-menopausal women revealed that a dose of omega-3s decreased insulin resistance, blood pressure, and inflammatory markers.

Lifestyle changes

Some changes are required when you enter this stage of your life. You need to be extra vigilant and care more about your body and mental health.

Exercise regularly

There is no question that exercise leads to a better quality of life, no matter what age or gender you are. Studies have shown that menopausal women who regularly exercise experience less stress, less muscle loss, and an increase in fat metabolism.

Although all types of exercises are great and show positive results, strength training is the most effective for post-menopausal women. An example of strength training is lifting weights.

Yoga

Yoga has been shown to relieve stress in randomized studies. However, there has been less research on the topic of menopausal women. One study found that yoga and other mind-body therapies help lessen the symptoms of menopause.

It raises the overall quality of life and well-being. More women report being more satisfied with life after incorporating yoga into their daily routine.

Special Supplements

There are some supplements available to you that can reduce your post-menopausal symptoms:

Pycnogenol: It is an extract of French maritime pine bark. It has been researched and proven to significantly cut down the symptoms of menopause, such as insomnia and mood swings. It won't hurt to give this a try if you are having severe cases of menopausal symptoms.

It is filed with numerous antioxidants and procyanidins. This chemical can reduce heart diseases and the chances of breast cancer in women.

Other supplements you can take

Reports show that black cohosh and red clover can work to reduce symptoms as well. However, there is not much research in this area and on these herbs, so don't take them for a long time if you do decide to.

IMPORTANT KETO DIET TIPS FOR WOMEN OVER 50

From a biological and evolutionary standpoint, women are biologically wired to eat more calories. You have to grow a baby, nurse them, and continue this cycle. Even if you don't want or can't have children anymore, your brain subconsciously stimulates you into eating more. A keto diet is a more satisfying and fulfilling diet that makes you less hungry. It is suitable for women over the age of 50 who gain fat and have unlimited eating habits. This diet contributes a great deal in making you feel healthier overall.

Here are some tips that will help you overcome pitfalls in this diet:

- **In the first few day and weeks, eat more fat**

  Women are more sensitive to calorie restriction and deficit. It is harder for women to be on a restricted diet than for men. Eating more fat will help you. There are numerous advantages to this strategy.

  Firstly, it will give you motivation and boost up your morale. Many people are hesitant to eat fat, but you will eat it a lot and reduce weight in the process.

  Secondly, it will help you build fat reserves for future energy. Slowly, all your glycogen sources will melt, so it's better to replace them quickly. It can help your body adapt to using fats as a fuel source early on by boasting AMPK.

  Thirdly, you won't be working on an extreme calorie deficit. Your brain will signal that you have a sufficient amount of fat and a fuel source, which can induce a faster transition from glucose.

  Don't try to restrict calories in the first weeks

  The ketogenic diet is naturally calorie restricting. Simply cutting grains and sugar does half the job. For the first few weeks, don't stress yourself about precise calorie counting and excess restriction of carbs. Eat from the allowed product list until you are full and eat again whenever you are hungry.

  Undereating and overeating is not your concern right now. First, you have to go into ketosis and start getting used to not eating sugar and processed products.

- **In the beginning – choose keto or fasting**

  Metabolic depletion is not a good outcome. Even men who go through severe diet restrictions develop multiple problems. Calorie and diet restrictions put more burden on women than men, especially when they are first starting out.

  Don't go overboard in the first few weeks and fast for a long time with keto dieting.

  Both of them induce ketosis, and later on, might be beneficial, but your body will become confused and won't be able to decide whether harm or benefits are resulting from this scenario.

- **Always opt for healthy fats and don't go for direct fat glasses**

  Direct fat consumption, or "fat bombs," is good for athletes because they already eat excessive amounts of fat. These calories are later burned with intense workout and sports. They can have direct spoonfuls of olive oil here and there, but not you. You need to combine different fats to get a healthy bowl rather than a nutritionally poor fat glass.

  Some examples for a healthy quick fat bowl includes soft boiled eggs with mustard and mayonnaise, avocado slices with sardines and green goddess dressing, low-carb vegetables filled with guacamole, etc.

- **Don't be so strict**

You need to plan and avoid being derailed, but this happens more often than you think. If your son comes to you with a surprise cookie he made, don't shunt him. This won't occur every day.

The reason for this diet may vary from person to person. However, after you have adapted to metabolizing fats, you will become tuned into burning more fat in general. You have already become metabolically resilient.

If you are an epileptic patient trying a keto diet for controlling seizures, trying to enhance the effectiveness of cancer drugs, or have other medical reasons for your diet, then be strict. Otherwise, you don't need to.

- **Don't follow trendy advice without forethought**

If you are in a scenario in which you are not losing weight on this diet, the popular advice that you will hear is to lower your carbs, lower your proteins, and lower your calories.

That's good advice but only for the people who have smoothly transitioned into this diet. People who experience this in the first couple of weeks are not intended for this advice. Normally, we all eat a high-carb diet, and suddenly switching it to keto will put some burden on your body. If you experience symptoms out of the ordinary or are generally really fatigued for a long amount of time, then it is better to consume some protein and carbs. Lowering something doesn't always provide good results.

- **Don't skimp on protein**

One of the suggestions you will hear when you are not losing weight on this diet or are having various symptoms is to drop protein. Carbs need to be low, and fats need to be high, but where does protein go? It depends on what kind of keto diet you are following, but whatever kind you are, you should never drop protein.

No matter if you are starting or have been dieting for a long time, this should be ingrained in your mind. If you want to lose muscle mass, energy, and strength, there is no use for this diet. You are dieting to make yourself healthier and to get in better shape—not to starve yourself and force your body to eat itself.

Chapter 2: What Is Ketosis? How Do You Enter Ketosis?

THE HEALTH BENEFITS OF THE KETO DIET

Menopausal women have a lot to gain from this diet, but it can be great for anyone, young or old, male or female. The following are some of the benefits of the keto diet that has been shown in a diverse set of people.

Amazing at weight loss

You will see a great reduction in your weight, belly, and hips fat in just 3–6 months after initiating the diet. No other diet strategy gives this sort of results. This is because it is harder for the body to convert fat into ketones, and it takes more energy. Also, they are more fulfilling and satisfying. When done right, you won't feel starved, depleted, and after a couple of weeks, you will notice less fatigue. You will eat fewer calories and not be peckish or have short bouts of hunger between meals.

Gets rid of cancer

Cancer cells are rogue cells that escape the regulatory systems of our body. They eat and take energy supplies from the surrounding structures. A keto diet reduces the level of glucose produced, so it leads to less insulin being released into the blood. Insulin is needed to drive glucose into cells for energy. Less insulin and less glucose mean less fuel for cancer cells. This has been shown, but more research is needed on this topic.

Keeps away from heart disease

Not many people would even think that eating more fats can result in good heart health, but this is exactly what happens. This diet lowers your LDL and elevates the levels of HDL. It is said that high-fat levels send signals to your body to decrease the production of cholesterol. Lower levels of cholesterol can lead to lower cases of artery hardness, heart failure, and hypertension.

Reduction of acne

This is an unpleasant and uncomfortable skin condition that can ruin your social life. Carbohydrates and higher insulin levels are linked with outbursts of this disease. Lower carbohydrates itself results in controlling acne. However, eating more fats helps reduce acne, as well. Investigation on the benefit has been ongoing to determine the duration of this action.

May prevent diabetes

With diabetes, you have to be careful about what you eat and when you eat. Too many carbs, and you will become hyperglycemic. A low-carb diet such as this can keep you in a predictable range of blood sugar levels. This works best for type 2 diabetes. For patients with type 1 diabetes, too many ketone levels in your body can be problematic, so ask your doctor before trying anything new.

Good for epilepsy

The benefits and popularity of the keto diet may have come from the incredible results in helping epilepsy patients. This diet has been known to stop seizures and is used to reduce them throughout the world since the 1920s. It has been discontinued since the advent of antiepileptic drugs, but their success is undeniable in being the only cure for over 50 years.

It is important not to be too quick about changing your or your child's diet. Consider a physician's advice before you start ketogenic dieting. They can, based on your condition, deny it or encourage you to get on with it.

Controls nervous system disorders

Our nervous system comprises of the brain and spinal cord, which are the central part and the nerves that connect them and enable us to carry out functions. Epilepsy is one nervous system disease, but there are many others. A keto diet has been shown to reduce the probability of Alzheimer's and Parkinson's from developing. They are also being researched to help sleep disorders.

Can treat polycystic ovary syndrome

This can cause a life-threatening problem for women, and they may have to choose never to be able to get pregnant again. With this disease, the ovaries enlarge in size and start forming sacs around the eggs. Insulin is the culprit of this disease. A keto diet can reduce the amount of insulin in the blood and also lowers glucose demand. This can help you treat this disease along with exercise.

Can give you better performance results

While it may not be as effective as other diets that specifically target boosting exercise and strength, this diet increases the efficacy of endurance athletes.

Sports like cycling, biking, and running becomes easier. This is due to better fat to muscle ratio. Also, your muscles get tired less often because of their increase in the oxygen demand when working.

HOW TO GET INTO KETOSIS QUICKLY ON A KETO DIET?

Limit your carbs

On the keto diet, you will be cutting down carbs significantly, and this depletion will start the ketosis process. The lower your carbs are, the faster you will get into ketosis. There are many types of keto diets, but the ones that allow only 20 grams or lower amounts of carbs may get you in ketosis faster than the standard ketogenic diet.

Boost your activity

Long-term keto dieters have reported an increase in their exercise performance, especially in endurance exercise. However, it has also been studied that exercise drastically increases the level of ketone bodies in your blood.

One small study took a few older women and tested their ketone levels after exercise before and after meals. The ketones were approximately 200% higher when they exercised before meals.

Prior to exercising, it is better to have a lower or less demanding exercise routine in the first weeks of the diet. During this time, your body is in a transitional period, and your exercise performance will decrease at this time.

Increase your intake of MCTs

Not all fats are the same. MCTs are medium-chain triglycerides. They get absorbed by the liver way faster than other forms of fat and quickly supply the ketone bodies your body needs for energy.

Studies have found that consuming high amounts of MCTs can induce ketosis without the need for extreme carbohydrate restrictions. If they are added to your diet, you can reach ketosis more quickly.

There are many kinds of MCTs, but one of the most important ones for getting you into ketosis is lauric acid. They are metabolized gradually and, therefore, helps in sustaining ketosis as well. They are more often found in coconut oil.

There are two ways you can get MCTs—either from natural sources like coconut oil, flaxseed oil, or olive oil, or you can get a higher concentrated dose from MCT supplement oils. They can be added to smoothies, used as dressings, and topped over your meals.

Eat a lot of healthy fats

When you are following this diet, you will consume plenty of fatty ingredients. This will boost your ketone levels and get you into ketosis early. The goal is not to increase your fat uptake but increase the quality of fat.

In this diet, fats are to be consumed, but the important thing is to have a diverse range of sources, including lots of healthy fats. Don't just stick to coconut oil for MCTs; eat fish and avocados as well. Each ingredient will bring something new to your plate.

However, if your goal is weight loss, you need to be extra careful about not eating too many calories. Eating too much fat may stop you from losing weight if you are not careful about your calories.

Think about fasting

Several studies show fasting as a highly effective way to get into ketosis. Some of us go into a mild state of ketosis before breakfast. That is because our bodies have gone 8–10 hours without eating, and it starts to break out fat reserves for energy. Children who have epilepsy usually fast for half a day before starting a keto diet so they can enter ketosis quickly and stop their seizures.

Intermittent fasting is also a great way to quickly induce ketosis. A new form of fasting, called fat fasting, is being investigated. With this, individuals have to take 90% of calories from fat. Some studies have shown this to be effective, but there needs to be more experiments.

Have a good protein intake

Your protein intake shouldn't be low or very high on this diet. If you don't have a proper ratio of protein, this can lead to detrimental effects.

Firstly, you are already low on carbs. This decreases the glycogen in your muscles. If you don't have protein either, the muscles will start to eat their protein for energy, and muscle mass will shrink. You will become weaker. If you have proper proteins, then muscle loss can be avoided.

Secondly, protein is needed for various functions—the building of enzymes and hormones, and processes like gluconeogenesis. This process makes glucose from non-carbohydrate sources to supply energy to cells that can only use glucose, like red blood cells.

Test ketone levels and adjust accordingly

Everyone reacts to diets differently, and you have to make customized changes to your diet according to your ketone levels. You text ketones three ways: blood, breath, and urine. The accuracy and cost of goods are highest for blood and lowest for urine.

Once you have decided on how you are going to track ketone levels, try adjustments, and see whether they are effective or not. Keep the ones that yield positive results while discarding others.

HOW TO TELL IF YOU ARE IN KETOSIS?

Here are some common symptoms of being in ketosis to help you identify it when it occurs.

Bad breath

When you have reached full ketosis, you will experience a change in the smell of your breath. It takes on a fruity scent that is not good for gatherings and outings but is a very specific sign of being in full ketosis.

This happens because in ketosis, a ketone called acetone is released, and it leaves our body in the breath as well. This is where the smell comes from.

If you get irritated with this aspect of ketosis, you can chew on some sugar-free gum or have some sugar-free drinks that include no carbs. You can also brush your teeth more often.

Consistent loss of weight

The ketogenic diet is famous for losing weight because it does the job very effectively.

Phases of weight loss:

- **Fast weight loss:** You will see a significant drop in weight in the first week. There is no reason to celebrate yet, as it is mostly lost through stored water and carbs.
- **Slow weight loss:** After the initial massive decrease, you will see a consistent but much slower loss of weight. This is lost through the usage of fat and only occurs if, with the keto diet, you are also in a calorie deficit.

Check for ketone levels in the blood

One of the most accurate methods of finding out whether you are in ketosis or not is through a blood test. When glucose sources deplete, it starts breaking down fats into its derivatives to form energy. These derivatives are ketone bodies and include hydroxybutyrate (HBH), acetone, and acetoacetate.

You can buy a test kit for measuring the levels of HBH. Because the device is expensive, most people do this test once every one to two weeks. If your body is in ketosis, your levels should be around two mmol/L. Using a specialized meter will give you the most accurate information.

More ketones in urine and breath

Ketone bodies don't leave the body in the breath only—it also leaves through urine. You can use different methods to somewhat accurately detect whether ketosis has started or not.

Our senses do not provide us with an accurate estimate. Using a ketone breath analyzer, you can get a reading of acetone levels, leaving your breath. Another method is using indicator strips on urine. This is a relatively cheap method, but it lacks reliability.

Decrease in appetite

This is an extremely common symptom of ketosis that has been and still is reported very frequently. People have a sudden disinterest in food, which they cannot explain themselves.

There are numerous theories on why this occurs, but none have been proven yet. One theory suggests that it is because of the higher consumption of protein and fiber-rich vegetables that promote satiety and fullness. Another theory states that it is the result of hormonal changes in the body.

Before this diet, glucose was the only source of energy for the brain. Now, with the source of energy being changed, it is theorized that ketones themselves play a role in changing the brain's relationship with hunger.

Increase in concentration

You will experience uncomfortable symptoms at first when starting this diet. Irritability, brain fog, and tiredness are some of them. This is because your body is adjusting to processing fat as the primary source of energy. This transition takes several days and can even last weeks. Later, when this stage ends, a common comment among dieters is how much their focus has improved.

Ketone bodies are a dense and powerful source of energy. They are used in many brain-stimulating and enhancing experiments. It is being studied as a potential cure for brain diseases and concussions.

Removal of carbohydrates can also produce an effect of enhanced concentration, so this can't be a reliable indicator.

Short bouts of tiredness

One of the most concerning drawbacks of this diet is initial weakness and loss of strength. This is also one of the most common symptoms experienced by people.

When your body shifts to fat, it needs time to get adjusted to working with a new source. This can happen in the first month, but until then, you will be weak.

Don't be disheartened by it; dieters usually give up before the "keto flu," as this is referred to, goes away. To reap the long-term benefits, you need to be steadfast and stick to this diet.

One way to minimize the weakness is by taking energy supplements or electrolytes.

The decrease in exercise performance

This happens in the first few days of the diet. If you get tired quickly, your exercise performance or stamina will also decrease. After being in this state for a while, many keto dieters have experienced returning to their normal numbers.

This happens due to the depletion of glycogen stores in your muscles, and again, your body needs some time to get used to using fat.

Once you are fat-adapted, you will burn fats faster during exercise sessions.

This is a short-term complication, so if you continue with the diet for one month, you can return to your sports without worry.

Stomach problems

Almost all keto dieters report some sort of abdominal symptom after initiation of the diet. Constipation, bloating, and diarrhea are just some of the symptoms you might encounter. These symptoms are short-term and will go away after a while, but until then, it is important to keep eating high fiber, low-carb veggies. Don't stick to one or two kinds of vegetables either. Eat a diverse food group so you don't fall victim to nutritional deficiencies.

Sleep problems

If you have just started the diet and have been experiencing sleep problems like insomnia, you might be in ketosis. This is a short-term side effect. You don't need to worry too much about it. It will go away after you are in ketosis for one or two weeks.

HOW TO ACHIEVE OPTIMAL LEVELS OF KETOSIS?

There are many misconceptions that are circulating about the ketogenic diet. Here are some practical strategies for optimum experience and maximum weight loss.

Know what to focus on

Weight loss results from not eating a very high-fat diet or carbohydrates. Weight loss results from eating fewer calories. If your main goal is weight loss, then calorie counting and the avoidance of high caloric food should be a priority.

You will know that the ketogenic diet is best for you when it reduces your cravings and unhealthy snacking without being a burden. Most people that follow keto experience this. This happens in two ways on this diet: by increasing uptake of protein-rich and fiber-rich foods that promote fullness and by decreasing high caloric foods.

Keep this in mind and be strict on following these points throughout the diet.

Only have ketogenic foods and drinks

If you are not careful about the food you eat and just go on a whim, whether something has low carbs or high or not, then you may not even get into ketosis. You need to plan recipes and meals according to your diet. Whenever you go out, check beforehand what keto-friendly foods you can buy at the restaurants and cafes nearby. This will help you avoid eating anything high carb or "cheating."

There are a lot of keto-friendly foods available. Even baked products made of almond or coconut flour can be found if you look hard enough. You won't have to compromise on delicious dishes. To know what to eat and what to avoid, check out "Products for Health" in this book.

Count your calories

Even if you are eating кeto-friendly products and relatively estimate that you are consuming less food than you once were, you won't lose weight effectively. Remember, the most important thing is eating fewer calories than before to reach your goal weight. Several studies have shown that we often underestimate the number of calories we consume. Our trust in our "gut feeling" may result in you gaining weight or reaching a plateau after losing some. You don't want either.

Try using a кeto calculator app that you can easily access on your phone. A food scale and calorie-counting apps can also help.

Change your food environment

You can't lie to yourself when it comes to cravings. You thinк you can handle the temptations of packaged food products and delicious smells coming from every direction on a restaurant-friendly street. However, you should be realistic and кnow that you can't handle cravings. The following are some techniques you can use to stop you from cheating on your diet and staying on tracк.

Reconstruct your pantry

Remove all the high-carb prohibited foods from your кitchen cabinets, and replace them with кeto-friendly alternatives like normal flour with almond flour, fruits with berries, etc.

Avoid maкing or buying "binge-worthy" foods

Keto ice cream can be eaten on this diet. Let's say you decide to maкe some; however, you end up maкing a little more than expected. You can eat one serving with your lunch. Now, for the evening, you have a meal planned, but you are feeling pecкish. You decide to eat ice cream. Later that night, you are watching TV and start to crave the ice cream again.

In one day, you will have consumed more calories than planned. Don't have easy and convenient food in bulк laying around your house. Our brains are triggered to go to them.

Only have foods that you can кeep tracк of. Don't add extra dressings or condiments that can ruin your perfectly counted meals and plan. Adding cheeses, oil, and other ingredients can mess up your measurements.

Get in touch with other кeto dieters

When you start a diet, suddenly the world turns against you. Even if you have a supportive family and friends circle, they will not understand your concerns and problems.

For a boost in motivation, you need to join a community of fellow dieters. Face-to-face or online, you can asк questions and get solutions pretty quicкly. You can boast about your accomplishments and кnow-how to avoid bad scenarios.

Be prepared for the symptoms to come

When you switch your eating habits from a non-limiting to a carbohydrate-restricted diet, your body experiences changes that will be uncomfortable at first. The кeto flu is one such outcome of change. This includes symptoms like sugar cravings, dizziness, cramping, confusion, and nausea.

Be prepared to overcome them by taking mineral supplements or electrolytes. Also, drink plenty of water.

Prefer to cook a homemade meal

When you eat out, even if you have made sure that the meal is keto-friendly, you could cause changes to your measurements. You won't exactly know what has been added to your meals. For a diet that has calorie restrictions and needs low amounts of carbohydrates to activate ketosis, you need to be sure of all the ingredients' amounts.

This can only happen when you cook at home and follow a well thought out recipe.

Plan and form a doable budget

If you go overboard and buy a lot of keto-friendly products, you might complain about not having enough money later on and end up quitting. You will slowly lose motivation and realize that it is not a practical method. That is not the case. You just need to plan your budget and meals. Many people say that this diet is overpriced.

Some tips for you to reduce costs can include buying ingredients in bulk or making meals in bulk that can last for a long time. Start using coupons and plan your meals according to your coupons and deals available to you. Don't buy anything other than what is on your list. Impulse buying is bad for you and your wallet.

Chapter 3: Products for Health

ALLOWED PRODUCT LIST

Here are the foods you are allowed to eat on this diet.

Free to eat

- Fish and different kinds of seafood: Mackerel, salmon, sardines, albacore tuna, etc.
- Eggs
- Avocado
- Cheese: Especially cottage cheese.
- Poultry: Chicken, turkey, etc.
- Nuts: Almonds, cashews, pistachios, Brazil nuts, etc.
- Seeds: Chia seeds, flaxseed, sesame seeds, etc.
- Healthy oils: Coconut oil, olive oil, etc.
- Greek yogurt: Should be unsweetened and plain
- Coffee: Should be unsweetened
- Tea: Should be unsweetened

Moderate to eat

These foods are allowed, but you should be careful about not eating too much of them.

- Low-carb vegetables: Cauliflower, green beans, spinach, broccoli, bell peppers, zucchini, and all the vegetables that grow above the ground and are high-in-fiber.
- Berries: Blackberries, blueberries, raspberries, and all the fruits that have a low-glycaemic index.
- Dark chocolate and cocoa powder
- Milk: Unsweetened almond milk, coconut milk, hemp-seed milk, etc.

Prohibited product list
These are the foods you are not allowed to consume at all on this diet.
- Beans and legumes: Black beans, lentils, chickpeas, pinto beans, etc.
- Grains: Cereal, rice, pasta, bread, beer, etc. Even whole wheat and bean paste, any kind of pasta are not allowed.
- Starchy, high-carb vegetables: Corn, potatoes, sweet potatoes, beets, etc.
- Sugary fruits: Banana, dates, mangoes, pears, etc.
- Sweeteners: Sugar should be fully avoided. Honey and syrups like maple syrups are prohibited.
- Baked products: Gluten-free doesn't mean carb-free. All baked products are prohibited.
- Juices: Both artificial and natural

Keto supplements

Here are some ketogenic diet supplements that can help you. However, if you have an underlying condition, ask your doctor first.

Magnesium

During keto, you may succumb to magnesium depletion. Foods with magnesium, such as beans, are also high in carbs and are avoided on this diet. You can take around 300 grams of a magnesium supplement to help you with sleep and irritability.

MCT oil

Many keto dieters use medium-chain triglycerides, or MCTs. They quickly boost fat intake and produce lots of ketones for your body to stay in ketosis. A supplement will provide a more concentrated dose.

Exogenous ketones

These are ketone molecules you directly take in rather than make inside your body. They help you reach ketosis quickly and also promote satiety and athletic performance.

Green powder

The ketogenic diet restricts a lot of plant food, and that includes vegetables. Green powder is made by grinding up green vegetables like broccoli. It can fulfil the needs of vitamins and minerals missed by eating fewer vegetables.

Digestive enzymes

If you are new to the keto diet, chances are you are experiencing digestive tract problems like bloating, etc. Adding digestive enzymes to your diet can relieve you.

Electrolytes or mineral supplements

Levels of different minerals hinder many processes in your body. For this, you need to take electrolyte supplements like sodium, potassium, etc.

Supplements for energy

These are important for athletes. They will reduce muscle fatigue, increase performance, and maintain muscle mass.

Omega-3 fatty acids

They increase the benefits gained by this diet. It can reduce inflammation and decrease the risk of heart disease. Also, they maintain a healthy balance of different omega fats
.

30-DAY MEAL PLAN

*This 30-day meal plan offers a selection of meal options that you can incorporate into your daily diet. Keep in mind that some dishes may not include a side dish, so you can choose a side dish based on your preferences and nutritional needs.

	Breakfast	Lunch	Dinner
DAY 1	SPINACH AND CHEESE EGG BAKE	CHIKEN STIR-FRY	KETO KETO ASIAN GLAZED SALMON THAI SALAD
DAY 2	STEAK AND EGGS	BEEF SALAD IN PARMESAN BASKETS	PARMESAN CRUSTED FLOUNDER FISH FISH STICKS WITH CAPER DILL SAUCE
DAY 3	FARMER CHEESE PANCAKES	CHICKEN SHAWARMA	SESAME WINGS WITH CAULIFLOWER
DAY 4	HAM & FETA OMELET	CREAMY KETO FISH CASSEROLE	MOROCCAN MEATBALLS
DAY 5	BAKED EGGS IN AVOCADO	TURKEY AND CAULIFLOWER RICE BOWL	SEAFOOD MEDLEY STEW
DAY 6	SOUTHWESTERN OMELET	KETO LAMB AND VEGGIE SKILLET	BUTTERED COD IN SKILLET
DAY 7	LOW-CARB BREAKFAST QUICHE	SESAME CHICKEN AVOCADO SALAD	ASPARAGUS WITH COLBY CHEESE
DAY 8	EASY CLOUD BUNS	CREAMY SHRIMP AND MUSHROOM SKILLET	KETO CALAMARI
DAY 9	BACON AND MUSHROOM OMELETTE	YAKISOBA CHICKEN	PORTOBELLO MUSHROOM PIZZA
DAY 10	ZUCCHINI BREAKFAST MUFFINS	THAI COCONUT SHRIMP SOUP	ROSEMARY ROASTED PORK WITH CAULI-FLOWER
DAY 11	BACON AVOCADO BOMBS	KETO CHICKEN ENCHILADAS	SIMPLE & CLASSIC GOULASH
DAY 12	KETO PIZZA EGG WRAP	CHINESE CABBAGE BEEF ROLLS	MEXICAN FISH STEW
DAY 13	GREEN EGGS	SWEET AND SOUR CHICKEN	KETO GRILLED PORK RIBS
DAY 14	KETO CROQUE MADAME	PORK ROLLS WITH MOZ-ZARELLA	LEMON KALAMATA OLIVE SALMON
DAY 15	KETO SPINACH SHAKSHUKA	TURKEY MEATBALL SOUP	HERB BUTTER SCALLOPS

DAY 16	KETO BISCUITS AND GRAVY	PORK AND CAULIFLOWER GRATIN	FISH CURRY
DAY 17	EGG WRAPS WITH HAM AND GREENS	WHOLE ROASTED BRINED TURKEY	TURKEY AND ZUCCHINI FRITTERS
DAY 18	BACON GRUYÈRE EGG BITES	CREAMY BEEF LIVER AND VEGETABLES	CHICKEN MEATBALLS
DAY 19	KALE AND GOAT CHEESE FRITTATA CUPS	CHICKEN FLORENTINE	TURKEY LASAGNA WITH RICOTTA
DAY 20	MIXED MUSHROOM EGG BAKES	DUCK AND BROCCOLI "ALFREDO"	VEGAN KETO COCONUT CURRY
DAY 21	CHOCOLATE PROTEIN PANCAKES	LAMB RAGOUT	CHICKEN BACON BURGERS
DAY 22	KETO BREAKFAST SANDWICH	CHICKEN FILLET STUFFED WITH SHRIMP	BRUSSELS SPROUTS CASSEROLE
DAY 23	POACHED EGGS MYTILENE	BEEF AND VEGETABLE STIR-FRY	GRILLED CHICKEN KABOBS
DAY 24	HEALTHY BREAKFAST CHEESECAKE	CREAMY DUCK WITH SPINACH RECIPE	SAUSAGE STUFFED BELL PEPPERS
DAY 25	KETO SAUSAGE BALLS	MINTY BEEF AND VEGETABLE SALAD CHICKEN	KETO BACON CHEESEBURGER WRAPS
DAY 26	CHICKEN LIVER SALAD	INDIAN-STYLE KETO CHICKEN	BALSAMIC SALMON WITH GREEN BEANS
DAY 27	SPINACH PANCAKES	CREAMY BEEF AND SPINACH SKILLET	PORK ROLLS WITH MOZZARELLA
DAY 28	SPICY CHICKEN BREAKFAST BOWLS	CHICKEN HEARTS IN A CREAMY SAUCE	CHEESEBURGER CASSEROLE
DAY 29	CHEESE-STYLE "HOT CAKES"	CREAMY LAMB CURRY	CHICKEN SHAWARMA
DAY 30	KETO SALMON SUSHI BOWL	TENDER AND JUICY SHREDDED PORK	CHICKEN WITH CREAMY PEPPER SAUCE

RECIPES

BREAKFAST

COCONUT MILK PANCAKES

Nutrition: Cal 442;Fat 35 g;Carb 15 g;Protein 16 g
Serving 4; Cook time 15 min

DRY INGREDIENTS
- 6 tablespoons coconut flour
- 4 tablespoons granulated sweetener
- 1 teaspoon baking powder

WET INGREDIENTS
- 6 tablespoons unsweetened coconut milk
- 4 large eggs
- 2 teaspoons vanilla extract

Instructions
1. In a mixing bowl add all of the dry ingredients.
2. In a separate bowl mix together coconut milk, eggs, and vanilla extract. Be sure to shake can before opening.
3. Preheat skillet or pan on medium heat for cooking and add coconut oil or butter.
4. Combine dry and wet and beat well with a whisk until batter is smooth and free of lumps.
5. Add to pan and cook each side evenly. If cooking too fast, pull off heat and lower temperature. Pancakes should be fluffy and not runny on the inside but golden brown on the outside.

SPINACH AND CHEESE EGG BAKE

Nutrition: Cal 260;Fat 20 g;Carb 4 g;Protein 20 g
Serving 2; Cook time 20 min

Ingredients
- 4 large eggs
- 1 cup fresh spinach leaves, chopped
- 1/2 cup shredded cheddar cheese
- Salt and pepper to taste
- 2 tbsp. butter or olive oil

Instructions
1. Preheat your oven to 375°F (190°C). Grease a 9-inch (23cm) baking dish with butter or olive oil.
2. In a large bowl, whisk the eggs and add the chopped spinach, shredded cheese, salt, and pepper. Mix well.
3. Pour the egg mixture into the prepared baking dish and bake in the oven for 15-20 minutes, or until the eggs are set and the top is golden brown.
4. Remove from the oven and let cool for a few minutes before slicing and serving.

KETO BREAKFAST CASSEROLE

Nutrition: Cal 200;Fat 15 g;Carb 4 g;Protein 13 g
Serving 10; Cook time 70 min

Ingredients
- Drizzle of oil
- ½ cup onion
- 1 tablespoon garlic, minced
- 1 pound breakfast sausage
- 12 eggs
- ½ cup almond milk
- 2 teaspoons mustard powder

- 1 teaspoon oregano
- ¼ teaspoon salt
- Pepper, to taste
- 1½ cups broccoli florets
- 1 zucchini, diced
- 1 red bell pepper, diced (or 3–4 cups veggies of choice)

Instructions
1. Preheat oven to 375°F (190°C).
2. In a skillet over medium heat, add a drizzle of oil and sauté onion and garlic.
3. Once transparent, add sausage and cook until browned, 7–10 minutes.
4. Add to a 13×9-inch casserole or baking dish and set aside.
5. In a large bowl, whisk together eggs, milk of choice, and seasonings. Stir in chopped veggies.
6. Pour mixture over sausage.
7. Bake until firm and cooked through, 30–40 minutes.
8. Allow to cool slightly before slicing into squares, serving, and enjoying!
9. Store leftovers in the fridge for up to 5 days, and reheat individual portions in the microwave.

AVOCADO OMELETTE

Nutrition: Cal 310;Fat 23 g;Carb 11 g;Protein 16 g
Serving 2; Cook time 5 min

Ingredients
- 3 eggs, lightly beaten
- 3 tablespoons almond milk
- Nonstick cooking spray, as needed
- 1/2 cup tofu cheese
- 1 tablespoon sliced green onion
- 1/4 cup chopped red bell pepper
- 1 ripe, fresh avocado; seeded, peeled, and cubed

Instructions
1. Mix eggs and milk.
2. Spray a large skillet with nonstick cooking spray and heat over medium low heat. Pour egg mixture into skillet. Cook eggs until top is almost set.
3. Sprinkle with cheese and green onion. Cook, about 2 minutes.
4. Top with red pepper and avocado, fold over, and serve immediately.

KETO BREAKFAST DAIRY-FREE SMOOTHIE BOWL

Nutrition: Cal 642;Fat 45 g;Carb 10 g;Protein 22 g
Serving 3; Cook time 10 min

Ingredients
- 1 ½ cups (350 ml) full-fat coconut milk
- 1 cup (110 g) frozen raspberries
- ¼ cup (60 ml) MCT oil or melted coconut oil, or ¼ cup (40 g) unflavored MCT oil powder
- ¼ cup (40 g) collagen peptides or protein powder
- 2 tablespoons chia seeds

- 1 tablespoon apple cider vinegar
- 1 teaspoon vanilla extract
- 1 tablespoon erythritol, or 4 drops liquid stevia

Instructions

1. Place all the pudding ingredients in a blender or food processor and blend until smooth. Serve in bowls with your favorite toppings, if desired.

CRISPY KETO CORNED BEEF & RADISH HASH

Nutrition: Cal 252;Fat 16 g;Carb 1,5 g;Protein 23 g
Serving 2; Cook time 10 min

Ingredients

- 2 tablespoons olive oil
- 1/2 cup diced onions
- 2 cups radishes, diced to about 1/2 inch
- 1 teaspoon kosher salt
- 1/2 teaspoon ground black pepper
- 1 teaspoon dried oregano (Mexican if you have it)
- 1/2 teaspoon garlic powder
- 2 twelve-ounce cans corned beef or 2 cups finely chopped corned beef, packed

Instructions

1. Heat the olive oil in a large saute pan and add the onions, radishes, salt, and pepper.
2. Saute the onions and radishes on medium heat for 5 minutes or until softened.
3. Add the oregano, garlic powder, and corned beef to the pan and stir well until combined.
4. Cook over low to medium heat, stirring occasionally for 10 minutes or until the radishes are soft and starting to brown.
5. Press the mixture into the bottom of the pan and cook on high heat for 2–3 minutes or until the bottom is crisp and brown.
6. Serve hot.

COCONUT FLOUR PORRIDGE

Nutrition: Cal 345;Fat 28,5 g;Carb 11 g;Protein 13 g
Serving 1; Cook time 7 min

Ingredients

- 2 tablespoons coconut flour
- 2 tablespoons golden flax meal
- 3/4 cup water
- Pinch of salt
- 1 large egg, beaten
- 2 teaspoons butter or ghee
- 1 tablespoon heavy cream or coconut milk
- 1 tablespoon low-carb brown sugar (or your favorite sweetener)

Instructions

1. Measure the first four ingredients into a small pot over medium heat and stir. When it begins to simmer, turn it down to medium-low and whisk until it begins to thicken.

2. Remove the coconut flour porridge from heat and add the beaten egg, a half at a time, while whisking continuously. Place back on the heat and continue to whisk until the porridge thickens. Remove from the heat and continue to whisk for about 30 seconds before adding the butter, cream, and sweetener.
3. Garnish with your favorite toppings (4 grams net carbs).

EASY SHAKSHUKA

Nutrition: Cal 216;Fat 12 g;Carb 16 g;Protein 12 g
Serving 6; Cook time 35 min

Ingredients

- 2 tablespoons olive oil
- 1 large yellow onion, chopped
- 1 large red bell pepper or roasted red bell pepper, chopped
- 1/4 teaspoon fine sea salt
- 3 cloves garlic, pressed or minced
- 2 tablespoons tomato paste
- 1 teaspoon ground cumin
- 1/2 teaspoon smoked paprika
- 1/4 teaspoon red pepper flakes (reduce or omit if sensitive to spice)
- 1 large can (28 ounces) crushed tomatoes, preferably fire-roasted
- 2 tablespoons chopped fresh cilantro or flat-leaf parsley, plus addition cilantro or parsley leaves for garnish
- Freshly ground black pepper, to taste
- 5 to 6 large eggs

Instructions

1. Preheat the oven to 375°F. Warm the oil in a large, oven-safe skillet (preferably stainless steel) over medium heat. Once shimmering, add the onion, bell pepper, and salt. Cook, stirring often, until the onions are tender and turning translucent, about 4 to 6 minutes.
2. Add the garlic, tomato paste, cumin, paprika, and red pepper flakes. Cook, stirring constantly, until nice and fragrant, 1 to 2 minutes.
3. Pour in the crushed tomatoes with their juices and add the cilantro. Stir, and let the mixture come to a simmer. Reduce the heat as necessary to maintain a gentle simmer and cook for 5 minutes to give the flavors time to meld.
4. Turn off the heat. Taste (careful, it's hot!), and add salt and pepper as necessary. Use the back of a spoon to make a well near the perimeter and crack the egg directly into it. Gently spoon a bit of the tomato mixture over the whites to help contain the egg. Repeat with the remaining 4 to 5 eggs, depending on how many you can fit. Sprinkle a little salt and pepper over the eggs.
5. Carefully transfer the skillet to the oven (it's heavy) and bake for 8 to 12 minutes, checking often once you reach 8 minutes. They're done when the egg whites are an opaque white and the yolks have risen a bit but are still soft. They should still jiggle in the centers when you shimmy the pan (keep in mind that they'll continue cooking after you pull the dish out of the oven).

STEAK AND EGGS

Nutrition: Cal 210;Fat 36 g;Carb 3 g;Protein 44 g
Serving 1; Cook time 15 min

Ingredients
1 tablespoon butter
3 eggs
4 ounces sirloin
1/4 avocado
Salt, Pepper

Instructions
1. Melt butter in a pan and fry 2-3 eggs until the whites are set and the yolk is cooked to your desired doneness. Season with salt and pepper.
2. In another pan, cook your sirloin (or favorite cut of steak) until it reaches your desired doneness. Then, slice it into bite-sized strips and season with salt and pepper.
3. Slice up some avocado and serve it together with the steak and eggs.

FARMER CHEESE PANCAKES

Nutrition: Cal 200;Fat 12 g;Carb 2,5 g;Protein 18 g
Serving 5; Cook time 20 min

Ingredients
• 1 lb Farmer Cheese
• 1 cup coconut flour
• 2 eggs
• Pinch of salt, to taste (optional)
• 1 tsp Stevia, to taste (optional)

Instructions
1. Mix farmer cheese, coconut flour, salt, and 2 eggs. Mixture should be like paste texture.
2. Form pancakes into round shape. Dust it just a bit with coconut flour.
3. Fry till both sides are golden brown.

FRENCH OMELET

Nutrition: Cal 186;Fat 9 g;Carb 4 g;Protein 22 g
Serving 2; Cook time 10 min

Ingredients
• 2 large eggs
• 4 large egg whites
• 1/4 cup fat-free milk
• 1/8 teaspoon salt
• 1/8 teaspoon pepper
• 1/4 cup cubed fully cooked ham
• 1 tablespoon chopped onion
• 1 tablespoon chopped green pepper
• 1/4 cup shredded reduced-fat cheddar cheese

Instructions
1. Whisk together first five ingredients.

2. Place a 10-in. skillet coated with cooking spray over medium heat. Pour in egg mixture. Mixture should set immediately at edges. As eggs set, push cooked portions toward the center, letting uncooked eggs flow underneath.
3. When eggs are thickened and no liquid egg remains, top one half with remaining ingredients. Fold omelet in half. Cut in half to serve.

MATCHA BREAKFAST BOWL

Nutrition: Cal 150;Fat 10 g;Carb 5 g;Protein 13 g
Serving 1; Cook time 10 min

Ingredients
MATCHA CHIA BOWL
• 1 cup plant-based milk such as coconut, almond, or macadamia
• 2 tablespoons chia seeds
• 1-2 teaspoons matcha to taste (we use 2 teaspoons)
• Vanilla stevia drops or preferred sweetener, to taste
• Pinch of pink Himalayan salt

FOR THE SMOOTH VERSION (OPTIONAL)
• 1/4-1/2 avocado, to taste
• Mint extract or fresh mint leaves
Serving Suggestions (optional)
• Shredded coconut, lightly toasted
• Almonds, lightly toasted
• Fresh strawberries

Instructions
1. Mix chia seeds with your chosen milk, matcha, sweetener, and salt. Cover and refrigerate overnight. For the milk, I like to mix 1-2 tablespoons of full-fat coconut milk (the canned stuff) with 1 cup of water.
2. Add more liquid as needed to reach desired consistency (optional). Sweeten to taste and serve with toppings of choice.
3. To make the smooth version, simply blend in a high-speed blender. You can add some avocado for added creaminess, mint leaves (or extract) for a fresh touch, and a handful of ice.
4. Chia pudding (without the avocado) can be kept refrigerated in an airtight container for up to a week (it's ideal for meal prepping!)

SOUTHWESTERN OMELET

Nutrition: Cal 390;Fat 31 g;Carb 7 g;Protein 22 g
Serving 4; Cook time 10 min

Ingredients
• 1/2 cup chopped onion
• 1 jalapeno pepper, minced
• 1 tablespoon canola oil
• 6 large eggs, lightly beaten
• 6 bacon strips, cooked and crumbled
• 1 small tomato, chopped
• 1 ripe avocado, cut into 1-inch slices
• 1 cup shredded Monterey Jack cheese, divided
• Salt and pepper, to taste

•Salsa (optional)
Instructions
1. In a large skillet, saute onion and jalapeno in oil until tender; remove with a slotted spoon and set aside. Pour eggs into the same skillet; cover and cook over low heat for 3-4 minutes.
2. Sprinkle with the onion mixture, bacon, tomato, avocado, and 1/2 cup cheese. Season with salt and pepper.
3. Fold omelet in half over filling. Cover and cook for 3-4 minutes or until eggs are set. Sprinkle with remaining cheese. Serve with salsa if desired.

PULLED PORK HASH
Nutrition: Cal 354;Fat 22 g;Carb 8 g;Protein 21 g
Serving 2; Cook time 20 min
Ingredients
•2 tablespoons FOC (fat of choice, I use lard)
•1 turnip, diced (115 g)
•1/2 teaspoon paprika
•1/4 teaspoon salt
•1/4 teaspoon garlic powder
•1/4 teaspoon black pepper
•3 Brussels sprouts, halved (50 g)
•1 cup chopped lacinato kale, about 2 leaves (45 g)
•2 tablespoons diced red onion (30 g)
•3 ounces pulled pork
•2 eggs
Instructions
1. Heat the oil in a large cast iron skillet over medium-high heat. Add the diced turnip and the spices to the skillet. Cook 5 minutes, stirring occasionally.
2. Add the remaining vegetables to the skillet and cook another 2-3 minutes until they start to soften. Add in the pork and cook 2 minutes.
3. Make 2 divots in the hash and crack in two eggs. Cover and cook 3-5 minutes, just until the whites are set.

HAM & FETA OMELET
Nutrition: Cal 290;Fat 20 g;Carb 5 g;Protein 21 g
Serving 2; Cook time 15 min
Ingredients
•4 large eggs
•1 green onion, chopped
•1 tablespoon 2% milk
•1/4 teaspoon dried basil
•1/4 teaspoon dried oregano
•Dash of garlic powder
•Dash of salt
•Dash of pepper
•1 tablespoon butter
•1/4 cup crumbled feta cheese
•3 slices deli ham, chopped
•1 plum tomato, chopped
•2 teaspoons balsamic vinaigrette

Instructions
1. In a small bowl, whisk eggs, green onion, milk, and seasonings until blended. In a large nonstick skillet, heat butter over medium-high heat. Pour in egg mixture. Mixture should set immediately at edge.
2. As eggs set, push cooked portions toward the center, letting uncooked eggs flow underneath. When eggs are thickened and no liquid egg remains, top one side with cheese and ham.
3. Fold omelet in half; cut into two portions. Slide onto plates; top with tomato. Drizzle with vinaigrette before serving.

HAM STEAKS WITH GRUYERE, BACON & MUSHROOMS
Nutrition: Cal 352;Fat 22 g;Carb 5 g;Protein 34 g
Serving 2; Cook time 15 min
Ingredients
•2 tablespoons butter
•1/2 pound sliced fresh mushrooms
•1 shallot, finely chopped
•2 garlic cloves, minced
•1/8 teaspoon coarsely ground pepper
•1 fully cooked boneless ham steak (about 1 pound), cut into four pieces
•1 cup shredded Gruyere cheese
•4 bacon strips, cooked and crumbled
•1 tablespoon minced fresh parsley (optional)
Instructions
1. In a large nonstick skillet, heat butter over medium-high heat. Add mushrooms and shallot; cook and stir 4-6 minutes or until tender. Add garlic and pepper; cook 1 minute longer. Remove from pan; keep warm. Wipe skillet clean.
2. In same skillet, cook ham over medium heat 3 minutes. Turn; sprinkle with cheese and bacon. Cook, covered, 2-4 minutes longer or until cheese is melted and ham is heated through. Serve with mushroom mixture. If desired, sprinkle with parsley.

BROCCOLI QUICHE CUPS
Nutrition: Cal 291;Fat 24 g;Carb 4 g;Protein 17 g
Serving 12; Cook time 20 min
Ingredients
•1 cup chopped fresh broccoli
•1 cup pepper jack cheese
•6 large eggs, lightly beaten
•3/4 cup heavy whipping cream
•1/2 cup bacon bits
•1 shallot, minced
•1/4 teaspoon salt
•1/4 teaspoon pepper
Instructions
1. Preheat oven to 350°. Divide broccoli and cheese among 12 greased muffin cups.

2. Whisk together remaining ingredients; pour into cups. Bake until set, 15-20 minutes.

BROCCOLI & CHEESE OMELET

Nutrition: Cal 230;Fat 17 g;Carb 5 g;Protein 15 g
Serving 4; Cook time 15 min

Ingredients
- 2-1/2 cups fresh broccoli florets
- 6 large eggs
- 1/4 cup 2% milk
- 1/2 teaspoon salt
- 1/4 teaspoon pepper
- 1/3 cup grated Romano cheese
- 1/3 cup sliced pitted Greek olives
- 1 tablespoon olive oil
- Shaved Romano cheese and minced fresh parsley

Instructions
1. Preheat broiler. In a large saucepan, place steamer basket over 1 inch of water. Place broccoli in basket. Bring water to a boil. Reduce heat to a simmer; steam, covered, 4-6 minutes or until crisp-tender.
2. In a large bowl, whisk eggs, milk, salt, and pepper. Stir in cooked broccoli, grated cheese, and olives. In a 10-inch ovenproof skillet, heat oil over medium heat; pour in egg mixture. Cook, uncovered, 4-6 minutes or until nearly set.
3. Broil 3-4 inches from heat 2-4 minutes or until eggs are completely set. Let stand 5 minutes. Cut into wedges. Sprinkle with shaved cheese and parsley

DENVER OMELET SALAD

Nutrition: Cal 230;Fat 14 g;Carb 7 g;Protein 17 g
Serving 4; Cook time 10 min

Ingredients
- 8 cups fresh baby spinach
- 1 cup chopped tomatoes
- 2 tablespoons olive oil, divided
- 1-1/2 cups chopped fully cooked ham
- 1 small onion, chopped
- 1 small green pepper, chopped
- 4 large eggs
- Salt and pepper, to taste

Instructions
1. Arrange spinach and tomatoes on a platter; set aside. In a large skillet, heat 1 tablespoon olive oil over medium-high heat. Add ham, onion, and green pepper; saute until ham is heated through and vegetables are tender, 5-7 minutes. Spoon over spinach and tomatoes.
2. In same skillet, heat remaining olive oil over medium heat. Break eggs one at a time into a small cup, then gently slide into skillet.
3. Immediately reduce heat to low; season with salt and pepper. To prepare sunny-side-up eggs, cover pan and cook until whites are completely set and yolks thicken but are not hard. Top salad with fried eggs.

TURKEY BREAKFAST SAUSAGE

Nutrition: Cal 85;Fat 5 g;Carb 2 g;Protein 10 g
Serving 8; Cook time 10 min

Ingredients
- 1 pound lean ground turkey
- 3/4 teaspoon salt
- 1/2 teaspoon rubbed sage
- 1/2 teaspoon pepper
- 1/4 teaspoon ground ginger

Instructions
1. Crumble turkey into a large bowl. Add the salt, sage, pepper, and ginger. Shape into eight 2-inch patties.
2. In a nonstick skillet coated with cooking spray, cook patties over medium heat for 4-6 minutes on each side or until a thermometer reads 165° and juices run clear.

AVOCADO BACON AND EGGS

Nutrition: Cal 125;Fat 9 g;Carb 2 g;Protein 8 g
Serving 2; Cook time 15 min

Ingredients
- 1 medium avocado
- 2 eggs
- 1 piece bacon, cooked and crumbled
- 1 tablespoon low-fat cheese
- Pinch of salt

Instructions
1. Preheat oven to 425°F.
2. Begin by cutting the avocado in half and removing the pit.
3. With a spoon, scoop out some of the avocado so it's a tad bigger than your egg and yolk. Place in a muffin pan to keep the avocado stable while cooking.
4. Crack your egg and add it to the inside of your avocado. Sprinkle a little cheese on top with a pinch of salt. Top with cooked bacon.
5. Cook for 14-16 minutes. Serve warm.

PEANUT BUTTER GRANOLA

Nutrition:Cal 338;Fat 30 g;Carb 9 g;Protein 10 g
Serving 12; Cook time 30 min

Ingredients
1. 1 1/2 cups almonds
2. 1 1/2 cups pecans
3. 1 cup shredded coconut or almond flour
4. 1/4 cup sunflower seeds
5. 1/3 cup Swerve sweetener
6. 1/3 cup vanilla whey protein powder or collagen protein powder
7. 1/3 cup peanut butter
8. 1/4 cup butter
9. 1/4 cup water

Instructions
1. Preheat oven to 300°F and line a large rimmed baking sheet with parchment paper.

2. In a food processor, process almonds and pecans until they resemble coarse crumbs with some larger pieces. Transfer to a large bowl and stir in shredded coconut, sunflower seeds, sweetener, and vanilla protein powder.
3. In a microwave-safe bowl, melt the peanut butter and butter together.
4. Pour melted peanut butter mixture over nut mixture and stir well, tossing lightly. Stir in water. Mixture will clump together.
5. Spread mixture evenly on prepared baking sheet and bake 30 minutes, stirring halfway through. Remove and let cool completely

1. Preheat oven to 350°. In a large skillet, cook sausage over medium heat 6-8 minutes or until no longer pink, breaking into crumbles; drain and transfer to a greased 13 x 9-inch baking dish.
2. In same skillet, heat butter over medium-high heat. Add onion and mushrooms; cook and stir 3-5 minutes, or until tender. Stir in spinach. Spoon vegetable mixture over sausage.
3. In a large bowl, whisk eggs and milk until blended; pour egg mixture over vegetables. Sprinkle with cheeses and paprika. Bake, uncovered, 30-35 minutes or until the center is set and a thermometer inserted in center reads 165°. Let stand 10 minutes before serving.

SPINACH-MUSHROOM SCRAMBLED EGGS

Nutrition: Cal 200;Fat 11 g;Carb 2 g;Protein 14 g
Serving 2; Cook time 10 min

Ingredients
- 2 large eggs
- 2 large egg whites
- 1/8 teaspoon salt
- 1/8 teaspoon pepper
- 1 teaspoon butter
- 1/2 cup thinly sliced fresh mushrooms
- 1/2 cup fresh baby spinach, chopped
- 2 tablespoons shredded provolone cheese

Instructions
1. In a small bowl, whisk eggs, egg whites, salt, and pepper until blended. In a small nonstick skillet, heat butter over medium-high heat.
2. Add mushrooms; cook and stir 3-4 minutes or until tender. Add spinach; cook and stir until wilted. Reduce heat to medium.
3. Add egg mixture; cook and stir just until eggs are thickened and no liquid egg remains. Stir in cheese.

EGGS FLORENTINE CASSEROLE

Nutrition: Cal 271;Fat 20 g;Carb 7 g;Protein 17 g
Serving 12; Cook time 30 min

Ingredients
- 1 pound bulk pork sausage
- 2 tablespoons butter
- 1 large onion, chopped
- 1 cup sliced fresh mushrooms
- 1 package (10 ounces) frozen chopped spinach, thawed and squeezed dry
- 12 large eggs
- 2 cups 2% milk
- 1 cup shredded Swiss cheese
- 1 cup shredded sharp cheddar cheese
- 1/4 teaspoon paprika

Instructions

TACO BREAKFAST SKILLET

Nutrition: Cal 523;Fat 44 g;Carb 9 g;Protein 22 g
Serving 6; Cook time 45 min

Ingredients
- 1 pound ground beef
- 4 tablespoons taco seasoning
- 2/3 cup water
- 10 large eggs
- 1 1/2 cups shredded sharp cheddar cheese, divided
- 1/4 cup heavy cream
- 1 roma tomato, diced
- 1 medium avocado, peeled, pitted, and cubed
- 1/4 cup sliced black olives
- 2 green onions, sliced
- 1/4 cup sour cream
- 1/4 cup salsa
- 1 jalapeno, sliced (optional)
- 2 tablespoons torn fresh cilantro (optional)

Instructions
1. Brown the ground beef in a large skillet over medium-high heat. drain the excess fat.
2. To the skillet, stir in the taco seasoning and water. Reduce the heat to low and let simmer until the sauce has thickened and coats the meat. About 5 minutes. Remove half of the seasoned beef from the skillet and set aside.
3. Crack the eggs into a large mixing bowl and whisk. Add 1 cup of the cheddar cheese and the heavy cream to the eggs and whisk to combine.
4. Preheat the oven to 375°F.
5. Pour the egg mixture over top of the meat retained in the skillet and stir to mix the meat into the eggs. Bake for 30 minutes, or until the egg bake is cooked all the way through and fluffy.
6. Top with remaining ground beef, the remaining ½ cup of cheddar cheese, tomato, avocado, olives, green onion, sour cream, and salsa.
7. Garnish with jalapeno and cilantro, if using.

KETO CACAO COCONUT GRANOLA

Nutrition: Cal 112;Fat 6 g;Carb 7 g;Protein 7 g
Serving 3; Cook time 30 min

Ingredients
- 1/2 cup chopped raw pecans
- 1/2 cup flax seeds
- 1/2 cup superfine blanched almond flour
- 1/2 cup unsweetened dried coconut
- 1/4 cup cacao nibs
- 1/4 cup chopped raw walnuts
- 1/4 cup sesame seeds
- 1/4 cup sugar-free vanilla-flavored protein powder
- 3 tablespoons granulated erythritol
- 1 teaspoon ground cinnamon
- 1/8 teaspoon kosher salt
- 1/3 cup coconut oil
- 1 large egg white, beaten

Instructions
1. Preheat the oven to 300°F.
2. Line a 15x10-inch sheet pan with parchment paper.
3. Stir all of the ingredients until the mixture is crumbly and holds together in small clumps.
4. Spread out on the parchment-lined pan.
5. Bake for approximately 30 minutes or until golden brown and fragrant (oven times may vary).
6. Let the granola cool completely in the pan before removing.
7. Store in an airtight container in the refrigerator for up to 2 weeks.

CHORIZO BREAKFAST BAKE

Nutrition:Cal 212;Fat 11 g;Carb 11 g;Protein 9 g
Serving 4; Cook time 50 min

Ingredients
- 2 tablespoon olive oil
- 1 red bell pepper
- 1 yellow bell pepper
- 200 grams (7 ounces) chorizo sausage
- 6 large eggs
- 2 large red onion (cut into wedges)
- 2 cloves garlic (minced)
- ½ cup coconut milk
- Salt and pepper

Instructions
1. Preheat the oven to 425 degrees Fahrenheit (220 degrees Celsius).

2. Cut the bell peppers in half, remove the seeds and stem and place the halves on a baking tray. Drizzle with 1 tbsp olive oil and put in the oven to roast for 20 minutes. After 10 minutes of baking, place the red onion wedges on the tray, drizzle with a splash of olive oil and return to the oven to cook for another 10 minutes. The peppers are done when they are soft and have a slightly charred skin. When the peppers are done, place them on a cutting board and place a bowl overtop to trap the steam. Leave them to rest for 5 minutes (this will make it easier to peel off the skin).
3. In a cast iron skillet heat 1 tbsp olive oil on medium high heat. Stir in the minced garlic and cook for 20 seconds until fragrant and then add in the chopped chorizo and cook for 5 minutes until the chorizo is cooked through and then remove from the heat.
4. While the chorizo is cooking peel the skin off of the roasted bell peppers. Cut the peeled peppers into thin strips.
5. In a bowl whisk together the eggs, coconut milk, paprika, cayenne, salt and pepper.
6. Add the sliced peppers and red onion to the cast iron skillet and pour the egg mixture overtop. Transfer to the oven to bake for 20-25 minutes until the egg has set and the top of the frittata is firm to the touch. Serve sprinkled with chopped parsley.

BAKED EGGS IN AVOCADO

Nutrition: Cal 125;Fat 10 g;Carb 3 g;Protein 8 g
Serving 2; Cook time 15 min

Ingredients
- 1 medium avocado
- 2 tablespoons lime juice
- 2 large eggs
- Salt and pepper
- 2 tablespoons shredded cheddar cheese

Instructions
1. Preheat the oven to 450°F and cut the avocado in half.
2. Scoop out some of the flesh from the middle of each avocado half.
3. Place the avocado halves upright in a baking dish and brush with lime juice.
4. Crack an egg into each and season with salt and pepper.
5. Bake for 10 minutes, then sprinkle with cheese.
6. Let the eggs bake for another 2 to 3 minutes until the cheese is melted. Serve hot.

BREAKFAST EGG MUFFINS FILLED WITH SAUSAGE GRAVY

Nutrition: Cal 607;Fat 46 g;Carb 6 g;Protein 42 g
Serving 6; Cook time 35 min

Ingredients
FOR THE MUFFINS:
- 12 large eggs
- Sea salt
- Black pepper

- •1 pound thin shaved deli ham
- •4 ounces shredded mozzarella cheese
- •4 ounces grated parmesan cheese

LOW-CARB SAUSAGE GRAVY
- •1/2 ground pork sausage
- •8 ounces softened cream cheese
- •3/4 cups beef broth
- •Sea salt, Black pepper

Instructions
1. Prepare the eggs and gravy.
2. Whisk eggs together with salt and pepper to taste.
3. Cook the sausage over medium heat until thoroughly cooked through.
4. Add in the cream cheese and the broth and stirring constantly, cook until the mixture comes to a soft simmer and thickens.
5. Then reduce the heat to medium-low, still stirring constantly and simmer for 2 more minutes.
6. Season to taste with salt and pepper.
7. Set mixture aside.
8. Preheat oven to 325°F.

ASSEMBLE THE MUFFINS:
1. Place two pieces of ham in the bottom of each muffin cup, careful to overlap and try and cover the whole surface.
2. Evenly divide sausage gravy between each muffin.
3. Pour eggs into each muffin, dividing the mixture evenly.
4. Top each muffin with equal parts of the two types of cheeses.
5. Bake for approximately 30-40 minutes or until muffin is firm and cheese is melted.

LEMON POPPY RICOTTA PANCAKES
Nutrition: Cal 370;Fat 26 g;Carb 6,5 g;Protein 29 g
Serving 2; Cook time 20 min

Ingredients
- •1 large lemon, juiced and zested
- •6 ounces whole milk ricotta
- •3 large eggs
- •10 to 12 drops liquid stevia
- •¼ cup almond flour
- •1 scoop egg white protein powder
- •1 tablespoon poppy seeds
- •¾ teaspoons baking powder
- •¼ cup powdered erythritol
- •1 tablespoon heavy cream

Instructions
1. Combine the ricotta, eggs, and liquid stevia in a food processor with half the lemon juice and the lemon zest—blend well, then pour into a bowl.
2. Whisk in the almond flour, protein powder, poppy seeds, baking powder, and a pinch of salt.
3. Heat a large nonstick pan over medium heat.
4. Spoon the batter into the pan, using about ¼ cup per pancake.
5. Cook the pancakes until bubbles form on the surface of the batter, then flip them.

6. Let the pancakes cook until the bottom is browned, then remove to a plate.
7. Repeat with the remaining batter.
8. Whisk together the heavy cream, powdered erythritol, and reserved lemon juice and zest.
9. Serve the pancakes hot, drizzled with the lemon glaze.

EGG STRATA WITH BLUEBERRIES AND CINNAMON
Nutrition: Cal 188;Fat 15 g;Carb 4 g;Protein 8 g
Serving 4; Cook time 20 min

Ingredients
- •6 large eggs
- •2 tbsp softened butter
- •1 tsp vanilla
- •1/2 cup blueberries (or 1/4 cup, depending upon taste)
- •1/2 tsp cinnamon (you could probably double this if you like cinnamon)
- •1 tbsp coconut oil

Instructions
1. Preheat oven to 375°F.
2. In an 8" - 9" cast iron skillet (or any oven-proof skillet), heat coconut oil over medium heat.
3. In a medium bowl beat eggs, butter, cinnamon, and vanilla together with a hand mixer until combined and fluffy (about 1-2 minutes).
4. Pour egg mixture into heated pan and allow bottom to cook slightly (about 2 minutes). Gently drop blueberries into egg mixture and place pan in oven. Cook for 15-20 or until cooked through and browned on top (but not burned).
5. Remove from oven and allow to cool slightly.

SWEET BLUEBERRY COCONUT PORRIDGE
Nutrition: Cal 390;Fat 22 g;Carb 12 g;Protein 10 g
Serving 2; Cook time 15 min

Ingredients
- •1 cup unsweetened almond milk
- •¼ cup canned coconut milk
- •¼ cup coconut flour
- •¼ cup ground flaxseed
- •1 teaspoon ground cinnamon
- •¼ teaspoon ground nutmeg
- •Pinch salt
- •60 grams fresh blueberries
- •¼ cup shaved coconut

Instructions
1. Warm the almond milk and coconut milk in a saucepan over low heat.
2. Whisk in the coconut flour, flaxseed, cinnamon, nutmeg, and salt.
3. Turn up the heat and cook until the mixture bubbles.
4. Stir in the sweetener and vanilla extract, then cook until thickened to the desired level.

5. Spoon into two bowls and top with blueberries and shaved coconut.

LOW-CARB BREAKFAST QUICHE

Nutrition: Cal 450;Fat 36 g;Carb 6 g;Protein 24 g
Serving 4; Cook time 55 min

Ingredients
- 1 lb ground Italian sausage
- 1.5 cups shredded cheddar cheese
- 8 large eggs
- 1 tbsp ranch seasoning
- 1 cup sour cream

Instructions
1. Preheat oven to 350°F.
2. In an oven-safe skillet, brown ground sausage and drain the grease.
3. In a large bowl, whisk together egg, sour cream, and ranch seasoning. You may want to use a hand mixer.
4. Mix in cheddar cheese.
5. Pour egg mixture into pan and stir until everything is fully blended.
6. Cover with foil and bake for 30 minutes.
7. Remove foil and bake for another 25 minutes or until golden brown.

FAT-BUSTING VANILLA PROTEIN SMOOTHIE

Nutrition: Cal 540;Fat 46 g;Carb 8 g;Protein 25 g
Serving 2; Cook time 5 min

Ingredients
- 11 scoop (20g) vanilla egg white protein powder
- ½ cup heavy cream
- ¼ cup vanilla almond milk
- 4 ice cubes
- 1 tablespoon coconut oil
- 1 tablespoon powdered erythritol
- ½ teaspoon vanilla extract
- ¼ cup whipped cream

Instructions
1. Combine all of the ingredients, except the whipped cream, in a blender.
2. Blend on high speed for 30 to 60 seconds until smooth.
3. Pour into a glass and top with whipped cream.

SAVORY HAM AND CHEESE WAFFLES

Nutrition: Cal 575;Fat 45 g;Carb 5 g;Protein 35 g
Serving 2; Cook time 25 min

Ingredients
- 4 large eggs, divided
- 2 scoops (40 g) egg white protein powder
- 1 teaspoon baking powder
- 1/3 cup melted butter
- ½ teaspoon salt
- 1 ounce diced ham

- ¼ cup shredded cheddar cheese

Instructions
1. Separate two of the eggs and set the other two aside.
2. Beat 2 of the egg yolks with the protein powder, baking powder, butter, and salt in a mixing bowl.
3. Fold in the chopped ham and grated cheddar cheese.
4. Whisk the egg whites in a separate bowl with a pinch of salt until stiff peaks form.
5. Fold the beaten egg whites into the egg yolk mixture in two batches.
6. Grease a preheated waffle maker then spoon ¼ cup of the batter into it and close it.
7. Cook until the waffle is golden brown, about 3 to 4 minutes, then remove.
8. Reheat the waffle iron and repeat with the remaining batter.
9. Meanwhile, heat the oil in a skillet and fry the eggs with salt and pepper.
10. Serve the waffles hot, topped with a fried egg.

AVOCADO SMOOTHIE WITH COCONUT MILK

Nutrition: Cal 283;Fat 25 g;Carb 14 g;Protein 3,2 g
Serving 15; Cook time 5 min

Ingredients
- 1 cup coconut milk, unsweetened
- 1 tsp ginger, fresh and grounded
- 1/2 avocado
- 5 leaves spinach
- 1 tsp lime juice (optional)
- 1 tsp Stevia (optional)
- 1 tsp chia seeds

Instructions
1. Wash your ginger and spinach thoroughly.
2. Peel the ginger and avocado. Slice them into pieces.
3. Using a blender, mix all of the ingredients (except chia seeds and stevia) for a minute to obtain a smooth and uniform mixture. Optionally, pour some water and lime juice into the blender to produce the desired thickness.
4. Include some ice cubes and the sweetener into the mix just to flavor it up. Transfer to a glass and garnish with a teaspoon of chia seeds on top. Serve immediately.

COCONUT FLOUR PANCAKES

Nutrition: Cal 274;Fat 23g;Carb 8g;Protein 8g
Serving 2; Cook time 20 min

Ingredients
MAIN INGREDIENTS:
- 2 tbsp coconut flour
- 2 eggs
- ½ tbsp So Nourished Erythritol or a dash of stevia extract
- ¼ tsp baking powder
- 2 tbsp sour cream
- 2 tbsp melted butter
- ½ tsp vanilla extract

FOR THE TOPPING:
- 50 g strawberries
- 1 tbsp shredded coconut
- 1 tbsp almond slices
- 1 tbsp maple syrup (optional)

Instructions
1. Put the eggs, sour cream, 1 ½ tbsp. of melted butter (you'll need the rest for frying the pancakes), vanilla extract, and mix well.
2. Add the coconut flour, baking powder, erythritol to the mixture and mix again. Let the mixture sit for about 15 minutes. If the mixture is too thick, add a little bit of water (20-30 ml) and mix again until the consistency is right.
3. In a pan on medium heat, add butter in and fry the pancakes in butter. The number of pancakes you make will depend on the size you want. We made 6 pancakes with this recipe.

SOUTHWESTERN OMELET
Nutrition: Cal 390;Fat 31 g;Carb 7 g;Protein 22 g
Serving 4; Cook time 10 min

Ingredients
- 1/2 cup chopped onion
- 1 jalapeno pepper, minced
- 1 tablespoon canola oil
- 6 large eggs, lightly beaten
- 6 bacon strips, cooked and crumbled
- 1 small tomato, chopped
- 1 ripe avocado, cut into 1-inch slices
- 1 cup shredded Monterey Jack cheese, divided
- Salt and pepper, to taste
- Salsa (optional)

Instructions
1. In a large skillet, saute onion and jalapeno in oil until tender; remove with a slotted spoon and set aside. Pour eggs into the same skillet; cover and cook over low heat for 3-4 minutes.
2. Sprinkle with the onion mixture, bacon, tomato, avocado, and 1/2 cup cheese. Season with salt and pepper.
3. Fold omelet in half over filling. Cover and cook for 3-4 minutes or until eggs are set.
4. Sprinkle with remaining cheese. Serve with salsa if desired.

EASY CLOUD BUNS
Nutrition: Cal 50;Fat 5g;Carb 1 g;Protein 2.5 g
Serving 10; Cook time 40 min

Ingredients
- 3 large eggs, separated
- 1/8 teaspoon cream of tartar
- 3 ounces cream cheese, chopped

Instructions
1. Preheat the oven to 300°F and line a baking sheet with parchment.

2. Beat the egg whites until foamy then beat in the cream of tartar until the whites are shiny and opaque with soft peaks.
3. In a separate bowl, beat the cream cheese and egg yolks until well combined then fold in the egg white mixture.
4. Spoon the batter onto the baking sheet in ¼-cup circles about 2 inches apart.
5. Bake for 30 minutes until the buns are firm to the touch.

PEPPERONI, HAM & CHEDDAR STROMBOLI
Nutrition: Cal 525;Fat 37 g;Carb 16 g;Protein 32 g
Serving 3; Cook time 40 min

Ingredients
- 1 ¼ cups shredded mozzarella cheese
- ¼ cup almond flour
- 3 tablespoons coconut flour
- 1 teaspoon dried Italian seasoning
- Salt and pepper
- 1 large egg, whisked
- 6 ounces sliced deli ham
- 2 ounces sliced pepperoni
- 4 ounces sliced cheddar cheese
- 1 tablespoon melted butter
- 6 cups fresh salad greens

Instructions
1. Preheat the oven to 400°F and line a baking sheet with parchment.
2. Melt the mozzarella cheese in a microwave-safe bowl until it can be stirred smooth.
3. In a separate bowl, stir together the almond flour, coconut flour, and dried Italian seasoning.
4. Pour the melted cheese into the flour mixture and mix it with some salt and pepper.
5. Add the egg and work it into a dough then put it onto a piece of parchment.
6. Lay a piece of parchment on top and roll the dough out into an oval.
7. Use a knife to cut diagonal slits along the edges, leaving the middle 4 inches untouched.
8. Layer the ham and cheese slices in the middle of the dough then fold the strips over the top.
9. Brush the top with butter, then bake for 15 to 20 minutes until the dough is browned. Slice the Stromboli and serve with a small salad.

EGGS AND ASPARAGUS BREAKFAST BITES
Nutrition: Cal 426;Fat 35 g;Carb 6 g;Protein 20 g
Serving 2; Cook time 25 min

Ingredients
- 4 medium eggs
- 100 g asparagus, fresh or canned
- 1 tbsp butter, melted
- ¼ tsp baking powder

- 1 tbsp coconut flour
- 80 g cream cheese
- 40 g shredded cheddar cheese
- Salt, to taste

Instructions

1. For fresh asparagus, chop them into about 2-cm long pieces. Pan fry for around 5 minutes in melted butter. For canned asparagus, simply chop them into pieces. Reserve.
2. Combine the rest of the ingredients in a bowl. Stir well to mix together. Put aside for 10 minutes.
3. Brush a decent amount of oil in the baking molds. Place some pieces of asparagus in the molds then add the combined mixture you reserved earlier. Avoid filling up to the brim.
4. Place in the oven set at 350°F for 20 minutes, checking occasionally if the bites are cooked thoroughly.
5. Serve on a plate and enjoy.

AVOCADO BREAKFAST MUFFINS

Nutrition: Cal 250;Fat 19g;Carb 2,5 g;Protein 17 g
Serving 20; Cook time 30 min

Ingredients

- 20 beef patties (small size, about 50 g each)
- 10 eggs, medium-sized
- 1/2 cup heavy cream
- 2 avocados, cubed
- 10 oz cheddar cheese, cubed
- Black pepper, to taste

Instructions

1. Preheat oven to 350°F.
2. Take a large muffin tin and put one sausage patty in each cup, shaping with a shot glass to line the entire inside.
3. Evenly divide the avocado and cheese in the cups.
4. Beat eggs and heavy cream together in a bowl, then pour into each cup until cheese and avocado are covered. Top with black pepper to taste.
5. Bake for 20 minutes at 350°; if desired, broil for an additional 1-2 minutes until top is browned. Enjoy!

CHEDDAR BISCUITS

Nutrition: Cal 284;Fat 25 g;Carb 2 g;Protein 20 g
Serving 4; Cook time 20 min

Ingredients

- 1 cup cheddar cheese, shredded
- 1/4 cup butter melted and slightly cooled
- 4 eggs
- 1/3 cup coconut flour
- 1/4 teaspoon baking powder
- 1/4 teaspoon garlic powder
- 1 teaspoon dried parsley (optional)
- 1/4 teaspoon Old Bay Seasoning (optional)
- 1/4 teaspoon salt

Instructions

1. Set the oven to 400°F to preheat.

2. Crack the eggs in a bowl. Add the garlic powder, melted butter, dried parsley, and seasoning powder if you have some. Salt to taste.
3. Combine the cheese into the mixture together with the baking powder and coconut flour. Fold until you obtain a lump-free mixture.
4. Grease a cookie sheet before adding the batter into it. Place ice cream-size scoops into the sheet.
5. Lightly brown the biscuits in the oven for 15 minutes.
6. Serve with any meal or eat them alone.
7. If you like to keep them for later, allow them to cool completely before storing in a jar to preserve the crispness.

BACON AND MUSHROOM OMELETTE

Nutrition: Cal 313;Fat 24 g;Carb 1,5 g;Protein 23 g
Serving 2; Cook time 10 min

Ingredients

- 3 medium mushrooms, raw
- 2 slices bacon
- 3 eggs
- 2 tbsp onion, chopped
- 2 slices cheddar cheese
- Lettuce or watercress, to taste (optional)
- Pinch salt
- Pinch pepper

Instructions

1. Brunoise cut the onion. Slice the mushrooms and bacon into small chunks as well.
2. Heat an 8-inch non-stick skillet coated with cooking spray over medium-high heat. Cook the onion and bacon in the pan. Once the bacon is toasted enough, toss in the mushrooms and remove from the heat.
3. Beat the eggs in a mixing bowl. Flavor with sea salt and black pepper then add the cooked bacon, mushroom, and onion.
4. Gently pour the egg mixture into the pan. Once the omelette starts to firm up, ease around the edges with a spatula. Lay the slices of cheddar cheese on one half of the omelette. Fold the other half onto the cheese.
5. Leave in the pan for another 2 minutes, then let the cooked omelette slide onto a plate.
6. Fill the inside of the omelette with lettuce leaves if preferred. Serve immediately while still crispy and warm.

SCRAMBLED EGGS WITH MUSHROOMS AND COTTAGE CHEESE

Nutrition: Cal 210;Fat 19 g;Carb 3 g;Protein 9 g
Serving 3; Cook time 20 min

Ingredients

- 3 eggs
- 1 cup button mushrooms, rinsed and sliced
- 1/2 medium-sized onion, finely chopped
- 3 tbsp olive oil
- 1/4 tsp oregano
- 1/4 cup cottage cheese

- •1/2 tsp sea salt
- •1/4 tsp black pepper

Instructions

1. Place a large skillet over medium-high heat. Let the olive oil heat in the pan. Sauté the finely chopped onions in the oil until they become translucent. Drop in the sliced mushrooms and let it simmer until the liquid in the pan evaporates. Stir well with oregano, pepper, and salt. Put aside.
2. Beat the eggs in a bowl. Flavor with a dash of salt and pepper enough to taste. Fry in the skillet and fold with a wooden spoon for a minute until slightly underdone.

VEGETABLE TART

Nutrition: Cal 250;Fat 22 g;Carb 5.5 g;Protein 10 g
Serving 8; Cook time 70 min

Ingredients

- •6 eggs
- •½ cup heavy cream
- •8 oz cream cheese
- •½ cup shredded cheese
- •½ cup almond milk (or coconut milk)
- •12 oz zucchini
- •4 oz cauliflower
- •2 oz broccoli
- •8 oz red pepper
- •3 oz jalapeno
- •3 oz onion
- •3 cloves garlic
- •Seasoning of your choice

Instructions

1. Mince the cauliflower, broccoli, garlic, onion, red pepper, and jalapeño into small cubes. Dice the zucchini as well.
2. Sauté the diced vegetables in a heated oil on a large skillet. Remove from the heat when they become soft enough but not mushy.
3. Crack the eggs in another bowl. Combine the almond milk, softened cream cheese, and heavy cream in the bowl. Mix everything to combine well.
4. Mix the vegetables into the cream cheese bowl. Stir with the cheese and seasonings of choice. Fold together until uniform.
5. Lay a foil on the base of the springform you will use to avoid seeping the mixture through the bottom. Cover with parchment paper and brush some oil on the sides and on the base. Pour the batter into the form. Bake for one hour or up till the surface of the tart is golden brown in color. The oven must be preheated to 350°F.
6. Generously dust with cheese on top after baking. Slice into wedges and serve.

ZUCCHINI BREAKFAST MUFFINS

Nutrition: Cal 185;Fat 16 g;Carb 2 g;Protein 9 g
Serving 12; Cook time 35 min

Ingredients

- •6 eggs
- •1 zucchini, medium-sized
- •5 slices bacon
- •2 tbsp sour cream
- •1 cup heavy cream
- •1 cup shredded cheddar cheese
- •1 tbsp mayonnaise
- •1 tbsp mustard
- •1/2 cup coconut milk
- •1 oz dill
- •1 jalapeno small size
- •4 oz red pepper
- •Salt and pepper, to taste

Instructions

1. Shred your zucchini into thin pieces and dust with some salt. Put aside for a few minutes to release the moisture.
2. Chop the dill into fine pieces, then mince your jalapeno and red pepper.
3. Crispy fry the bacon slices for around 5 minutes or simply heat them in the microwave. Cut into bits.
4. Strain all the unnecessary liquids from the grated zucchini. Press it with your hands to squeeze out the extracts. Alternatively, use a cheesecloth to do this. Transfer all of the chopped vegetables in a bowl and toss to mix well. Add in the cheese and bacon bits.
5. Crack the eggs in a separate bowl. Blend together with the sour cream, mustard, heavy cream, and mayo. Include the coconut milk as well. Adjust the flavor with salt and pepper.
6. Transfer the vegetable mix into 12 muffin forms. Distribute evenly. Gently add in the egg mixture into the cups. Remember to fill only ⅔ of the cup. Combine the two mixture with a spoon. Stir well.
7. Bake in the oven preheated at 370°F for 20-25 minutes. Make sure the muffins are golden and firm before removing from the oven.
8. Unmold from the cups and serve on a plate

KETO CEREAL

Nutrition: Cal 250;Fat 10 g;Carb 15 g;Protein 10 g
Serving 3; Cook time 45 min

Ingredients

- •Cooking spray
- •1 c. almonds, chopped
- •1 c. walnuts, chopped
- •1 c. unsweetened coconut flakes
- •1/4 c. sesame seeds
- •2 tbsp. flax seeds
- •2 tbsp. chia seeds
- •1/2 tsp. ground clove
- •1 1/2 tsp. ground cinnamon

- 1 tsp. pure vanilla extract
- 1/2 tsp. kosher salt
- 1 large egg white
- 1/4 c. melted coconut oil

Instructions

1. Preheat oven to 350° and grease a baking sheet with cooking spray. In a large bowl, mix together almonds, walnuts, coconut flakes, sesame seeds, flax seeds, and chia seeds. Stir in cloves, cinnamon, vanilla, and salt.
2. Beat egg white until foamy then stir into granola. Add coconut oil and stir until everything is well coated. Pour onto prepared baking sheet and spread into an even layer. Bake for 20 to 25 minutes, or until golden, gently stirring halfway through. Let cool completely.

KETO SAUSAGE BREAKFAST SANDWICH

Nutrition: Cal 350;Fat 25 g;Carb 2 g;Protein 12 g
Serving 3; Cook time 20 min

Ingredients

- 6 large eggs
- 2 tbsp. heavy cream
- Pinch red pepper flakes
- Kosher salt
- Freshly ground black pepper
- 1 tbsp. butter
- 3 slices cheddar
- 6 frozen sausage patties, heated according to package instructions
- 1 Avocado, sliced

Instructions

1. In a small bowl beat eggs, heavy cream, and red pepper flakes together. Season generously with salt and pepper. In a nonstick skillet over medium heat, melt butter. Pour about ⅓ of the eggs into the skillet. Place a slice of cheese in the middle and let sit about 1 minute. Fold the sides of the egg into the middle, covering the cheese. Remove from pan and repeat with remaining eggs.
2. Serve eggs between two sausage patties with avocado.

CABBAGE HASH BROWNS

Nutrition: Cal 250;Fat 22 g;Carb 5.5 g;Protein 10 g
Serving 2; Cook time 35 min

Ingredients

- 2 large eggs
- 1/2 tsp. garlic powder
- 1/2 tsp. kosher salt
- Freshly ground black pepper
- 2 c. shredded cabbage
- 1/4 small yellow onion, thinly sliced
- 1 tbsp. vegetable oil

Instructions

1. In a large bowl, whisk together eggs, garlic powder, and salt. Season with black pepper. Add cabbage and onion to egg mixture and toss to combine.
2. In a large skillet over medium-high heat, heat oil. Divide mixture into 4 patties in the pan and press with spatula to flatten. Cook until golden and tender, about 3 minutes per side.

OMELET-STUFFED PEPPERS

Nutrition: Cal 280;Fat 12 g;Carb 8 g;Protein 25 g
Serving 4; Cook time 60 min

Ingredients

- 2 bell peppers, halved and seeds removed
- 8 eggs, lightly beaten
- 1/4 c. milk
- 4 slices bacon, cooked and crumbled
- 1 c. shredded cheddar
- 2 tbsp. finely chopped chives, plus more for garnish
- Kosher salt
- Freshly cracked black pepper

Instructions

1. Preheat oven to 400°. Place peppers cut side up in a large baking dish. Add a little water to the dish and bake peppers for 5 minutes.

Meanwhile, beat together eggs and milk. Stir in bacon, cheese, and chives and season with salt and pepper.

2. When peppers are done baking, pour egg mixture into peppers. Place back in the oven and bake 35 to 40 minutes more, until eggs are set. Garnish with more chives and serve.

ZUCCHINI EGG CUPS

Nutrition: Cal 280;Fat 12 g;Carb 8 g;Protein 25 g
Serving 12; Cook time 50 min

Ingredients

- Cooking spray, for pan
- 2 zucchini, peeled into strips
- 1/4 lb. ham, chopped
- 1/2 c. cherry tomatoes, quartered
- 8 eggs
- 1/2 c. heavy cream
- Kosher salt
- Freshly ground black pepper
- 1/2 tsp. dried oregano
- 1 c. Pinch red pepper flakes
- 1 c. shredded cheddar

Instructions

1. Preheat oven to 400° and grease a muffin tin with cooking spray. Line the inside and bottom of the muffin tin with zucchini strips, to form a crust. Sprinkle ham and cherry tomatoes inside each crust.
2. In a medium bowl whisk together eggs, heavy, cream, oregano, and red pepper flakes then season with salt and pepper. Pour egg mixture over ham and tomatoes then top with cheese.
3. Bake until eggs are set, 30 minutes.

BACON AVOCADO BOMBS

Nutrition: Cal 250;Fat 19 g;Carb 2,5 g;Protein 17 g
Serving 4; Cook time 30 min

Ingredients
- 2 avocados
- 1/3 c. shredded Cheddar
- 8 slices bacon

Instructions
1. Heat broiler and line a small baking sheet with foil.
2. Slice each avocado in half and remove the pits. Peel the skin off of each avocado.
3. Fill two of the halves with cheese, then replace with the other avocado halves. Wrap each avocado with 4 slices of bacon.
4. Place bacon-wrapped avocados on the prepared baking sheet and broil until the bacon is crispy on top, about 5 minutes. Very carefully, flip the avocado using tongs and continue to cook until crispy all over, about 5 minutes per side.
5. Cut in half crosswise and serve immediately.

HAM & CHEESE EGG CUPS

Nutrition: Cal 340;Fat 30 g;Carb 10 g;Protein 12 g
Serving 12; Cook time 30 min

Ingredients
- Cooking spray, for pan
- 12 slices ham
- 1 c. shredded cheddar
- 12 large eggs
- Kosher salt
- Freshly ground black pepper
- Chopped fresh parsley, for garnish

Instructions
1. Preheat oven to 400° and grease a 12-cup muffin tin with cooking spray. Line each cup with a slice of ham and sprinkle with cheddar. Crack an egg into each ham cup and season with salt and pepper.
2. Bake until eggs are cooked through, 12 to 15 minutes (depending on how runny you like your yolks).
3. Garnish with parsley and serve.

KETO FAT BOMBS

Nutrition: Cal 290;Fat 28 g;Carb 5 g;Protein 5 g
Serving 16; Cook time 35 min

Ingredients
- 8 oz. cream cheese, softened to room temperature
- 1/2 c. keto-friendly peanut butter
- 1/4 c. coconut oil, plus 2 tbsp.
- 1/4 tsp. kosher salt
- 1/2 c. keto-friendly dark chocolate chips (such as Lily's)

Instructions

1. Line a small baking sheet with parchment paper. In a medium bowl, combine cream cheese, peanut butter, 1/4 cup coconut oil, and salt. Using a hand mixer, beat mixture until fully combined, about 2 minutes. Place bowl in freezer to firm up slightly, 10 to 15 minutes.
2. When peanut butter mixture has hardened, use a small cookie scoop or spoon to create tablespoon-sized balls. Place in refrigerator to harden, 5 minutes.
3. Meanwhile, make chocolate drizzle: combine chocolate chips and remaining coconut oil in a microwave safe bowl and microwave in 30 second intervals until fully melted. Drizzle over peanut butter balls and place back in refrigerator to harden, 5 minutes.
4. To store, keep covered in refrigerator.

KETO PIZZA EGG WRAP

Nutrition: Cal 350;Fat 10 g;Carb 2 g;Protein 25 g
Serving 1; Cook time 15 min

Ingredients
- 2 large eggs
- 1/2 tbsp butter
- 1/2 tbsp tomato sauce
- 1/2 oz. (2 tbsp) mozzarella cheese, shredded
- 1 1/2 oz. salami, sliced

Instructions
1. Heat a large, non-stick frying pan to medium heat. Add the butter.
2. Crack the eggs into a bowl, and whisk until smooth in color.
3. Slowly pour the eggs into the pan, allowing the mixture to go right to the edges.
4. Cook until the edges begin to lift off the side of the frying pan. Using a spatula all around the edge, lift the egg from the pan.
5. Flip and cook on the other side for 30 seconds.
6. Remove from the pan. Layer tomato sauce, mozzarella cheese, andsalami in the middle. Roll it together into a wrap.

GREEN EGGS

Nutrition: Cal 300;Fat 20 g;Carb 8 g;Protein 18 g
Serving 2; Cook time 20 min

Ingredients
- 1 1/2 tbsp rapeseed oil , plus a splash extra
- 2 trimmed leeks , sliced
- 2 garlic cloves , sliced
- 1/2 tsp coriander seeds
- 1/2 tsp fennel seeds
- pinch of chilli flakes , plus extra to serve
- 200g spinach
- 2 large eggs
- 2 tbsp Greek yogurt
- squeeze of lemon

Instructions

1. Heat the oil in a large frying pan. Add the leeks and a pinch of salt, then cook until soft. Add the garlic, coriander, fennel and chilli flakes. Once the seeds begin to crackle, tip in the spinach and turn down the heat. Stir everything together until the spinach has wilted and reduced, then scrape it over to one side of the pan. Pour a little oil into the pan, then crack in the eggs and fry until cooked to your liking.
2. Stir the yogurt through the spinach mix and season. Pile onto two plates, top with the fried egg, squeeze over a little lemon and season with black pepper and chilli flakes to serve.

MASALA FRITTATA WITH AVOCADO SALSA

Nutrition: Cal 350;Fat 25 g;Carb 12 g;Protein 16 g
Serving 4; Cook time 40 min

Ingredients
- 2 tbsp rapeseed oil
- 3 onions, 2½ thinly sliced, ½ finely chopped
- 1 tbsp Madras curry paste
- 500g cherry tomatoes, halved
- 1 red chilli, deseeded and finely chopped
- small pack coriander, roughly chopped
- 8 large eggs, beaten
- 1 avocado, stoned, peeled and cubed
- juice 1 lemon

Instructions
1. Heat the oil in a medium non-stick, ovenproof frying pan. Tip in the sliced onions and cook over a medium heat for about 10 mins until soft and golden. Add the Madras paste and fry for 1 min more, then tip in half the tomatoes and half the chilli. Cook until the mixture is thick and the tomatoes have all burst.
2. Heat the grill to high. Add half the coriander to the eggs and season, then pour over the spicy onion mixture. Stir gently once or twice, then cook over a low heat for 8-10 mins until almost set. Transfer to the grill for 3-5 mins until set.
3. To make the salsa, mix the avocado, remaining chilli and tomatoes, chopped onion, remaining coriander and the lemon juice together, then season and serve with the frittata.

TARRAGON, MUSHROOM & SAUSAGE FRITTATA

Nutrition: Cal 433;Fat 32 g;Carb 8 g;Protein 25 g
Serving 2; Cook time 20 min

Ingredients
- 1 tbsp olive oil
- 200g chestnut mushrooms , sliced
- 2 pork sausages
- 1 garlic clove , crushed
- 100g fine asparagus
- 3 large eggs
- 2 tbsp half-fat soured cream
- 1 tbsp wholegrain mustard
- 1 tbsp chopped tarragon
- mixed rocket salad , to serve (optional)

Instructions
1. Heat the grill to high. Heat the oil in a medium-sized, non-stick frying pan, add the mushrooms and fry over a high heat for 3 mins. Squeeze the sausage-meat out of their skins into nuggets, add to the pan and fry for a further 5 mins until golden brown. Add the garlic and asparagus and cook for another 1 min.
2. Whisk the eggs, soured cream, mustard and tarragon in a jug. Season well, then pour the egg mixture in to the pan. Cook for 3-4 mins, then grill for a further 1-2 mins or until the top has just set with a slight wobble in the middle. Serve with the salad leaves, if you like.

KETO CHIA PUDDING

Nutrition: Cal 336;Fat 27 g;Carb 16 g;Protein 8 g
Serving 2; Cook time 35 min

Ingredients
- 2 tbsp low carb sugar (Sukrin:1, Swerve, Lakanto, Truvia, or Besti)
- 1 tbsp Cocoa Powder (sift before measuring)
- 1 tsp Vanilla Extract
- 1 cup Coconut Milk (from a can) (or Almond Milk for less calories)
- 1/4 cup Chia Seeds

Instructions
1. Add the cocoa powder and sweetener to a mason jar. Close the lid and shake well to remove any lumps.
2. Add the coconut milk and vanilla extract to the mason jar. Close the lid and shake to combine.
3. Add the chia seeds to the jar and shake again. Once the mixture is well combined, transfer the jar to the fridge.
4. Chill for at least 30 minutes.
5. Serve the chocolate chia pudding in your favourite jars, with coconut yogurt and seasonal fruit. Enjoy!

KETO BREAKFAST PARFAIT

Nutrition: Cal 335;Fat 29 g;Carb 10 g;Protein 11 g
Serving 2; Cook time 10 min

Ingredients
- ½ cup Greek Yogurt full fat
- ¼ cup Heavy Cream
- 1 teaspoon Vanilla Essence
- ½ cup Keto Chocolate Almond Clusters
- 2 Strawberries diced
- 8 Blueberries

Instructions
1. In a mixing bowl, add together the yogurt, cream and vanilla. Whisk together until thick and smooth.
2. Spoon half the yogurt between two glasses, then sprinkle over half the granola.
3. Add the remaining yogurt, followed by the remaining granola.

4. Top with the berries and enjoy!

KETO SAUSAGE & EGG BOWLS
Nutrition: Cal 435;Fat 29 g;Carb 8 g;Protein 27 g
Serving 2; Cook time 10 min

Ingredients
- 1/4 cup sausage – cooked and crumbled
- 2 whole eggs
- sprinkle of cheddar cheese
- salt & pepper to taste
- 1 tbs butter

Instructions
1. Start by cracking two eggs into a bowl and scramble with a fork until all mixed together
2. Add butter to skillet over medium high heat
3. Once melted, add eggs to pan – stirring around often – careful not to over cook
4. Once the eggs are mostly set but still glossy, add the sausage and cheese.
5. Remove from heat and mix in well.
6. Add salt and pepper to taste.

CHEESE AND EGG STUFFED PEPPERS
Nutrition: Cal 285;Fat 7 g;Carb 7 g;Protein 14 g
Serving 8; Cook time 50 min

Ingredients
- 4 large bell peppers, cut in half lengthwise and remove inner seeds and stems
- 1 tablespoon olive oil
- 1 cup white onion
- 1 pound gluten free pork sausage, casing removed
- 2 cups spinach
- 4 large eggs
- 1/4 teaspoon salt & pepper, each
- 3/4 cup shredded mozzarella

Instructions
1. Preheat oven to 350°F/180°C. Lightly grease a 9x13 baking dish.
2. Arrange the bell peppers side-by-side in the greased baking dish - cut side up. Set aside
3. Warm the olive oil to a large skillet over a medium heat. Add the onions and cook about 5 minutes to soften. Add the sausage and cook until no longer pink. Stir in the spinach and cook an addition 1-2 minutes until wilted. Remove from the heat.
4. In a medium sized mixing bowl whisk together the eggs, salt and pepper. Stir in 1/2 cup of the cheese.
5. Spoon the sausage mixture evenly into your prepared peppers. Pour the egg mixture over the top of the sausage. Top with the remaining 1/4 cup cheese.
6. Return to the oven and bake an additional 35-40 minutes until the cheese has goldened.

KETO CROQUE MADAME
Nutrition: Cal 566;Fat 47 g;Carb 3 g;Protein 33 g
Serving 4; Cook time 30 min

Ingredients
CHAFFLES:
- 2 large egg
- 1 cup cheddar cheese, grated
SANDWICH:
- 4 slice deli-sliced black forest ham
- 2/3 cup gruyere cheese, shredded
- 2 tablespoon butter
- 4 large egg
BECHEMEL SAUCE:
- 1/2 cup heavy cream
- 1/4 cup parmesan cheese
- 1/3 cup gruyere cheese, shredded

Instructions
1. Measure out and prepare the ingredients. Preheat oven to 425F.
2. In a bowl, make the chaffles by whisking together the eggs and grated cheese.
3. Using a small waffle iron that is greased, make the chaffles.
4. On a parchment lined baking sheet, add the chaffles, topped with the deli sliced ham, and the shredded gruyere cheese. Bake in the oven for 10-15 minutes or until cheese is melted.
5. While the chaffles are in the oven, fry up the eggs in a frying pan with butter. Then top the baked chaffle with the fried eggs.
6. In a saucepan on medium heat, make the bechemel sauce by adding the heavy cream. Slowly add in the parmesan cheese and gruyere cheese a small handful at a time and wait until it is melted before adding in more.
7. Drizzle the bechemel sauce on top of the chaffles, serve with a small side salad and enjoy!

KETO SPINACH SHAKSHUKA
Nutrition: Cal 318;Fat 23 g;Carb 5 g;Protein 19 g
Serving 4; Cook time 25 min

Ingredients
- 3 tablespoon olive oil
- 1/2 medium onion, minced
- 2 teaspoon fresh garlic, minced
- 1 medium jalapeno pepper, seeded + minced
- 16 ounce frozen spinach, thawed
- 1 teaspoon cumin
- 3/4 teaspoon ground coriander
- 2 tablespoon harissa
- Salt and pepper to taste
- 1/2 cup vegetable broth
- 8 large eggs
- 1/4 cup fresh parsley, chopped, for garnish
- 1 teaspoon crushed red pepper flakes, for garnish

Instructions

1. Measure out and prepare all the ingredients. Preheat oven to 350F.
2. In a skillet, add the olive oil to the skillet over medium heat. Saute the minced onion in until fragrant.
3. Add the thawed spinach into the skillet and let it cook until it's wilted.
4. Add the cumin, coriander, harissa, and salt and pepper. Stir together well and let cook for another 1-2 minutes.
5. Transfer the seasoned spinach mixture to a food processor. Pulse until coarse. Then, add the vegetable broth and pulse until smooth. Wipe out your skillet.
6. Drizzle oil in the bottom of the skillet or spray some cooking spray. Pour the smooth spinach mixture into the skillet. Using a spoon, press the back of the spoon into parts of the spinach mixture.
7. Gently crack the eggs into these parts of the mixture. Cook in the oven until the egg whites are set and the yolk is a little runny. This should take about 20-25 minutes.

KETO SAUSAGE CREAM CHEESE ROLLS
Nutrition: Cal 203;Fat 16 g;Carb 3 g;Protein 12 g
Servig 10; Cook time 25 min
Ingredients
FOR THE ROLLS:
- 2 cups shredded mozzarealla cheese
- 2 ounces cream cheese
- 3/4 cup almond flour
- 2 tablespoons ground flax meal
FOR THE FILLING:
- 1/2 pound cooked breakfast sausage, drained
- 3 ounces of cream cheese
Instructions
Preheat oven to 400F.
FOR THE ROLLS:
1. In a microwave-safe mixing bowl, combine the shredded mozzarella cheese and cream cheese. Heat in 30 second increments, stirring in between until completely melted.
2. Add the almond flour and ground flax meal.
3. Mix the dough well until you have a soft ball
4. Between two silicone baking mats or parchment paper roll the dough into a rectangle roughly 12x9 inches.
FOR THE FILLING:
1. Combine the sausage and cream cheese.
2. Spread the sausage cream cheese mixture evenly on the dough.
3. Starting at one end roll the dough as tightly as you can into a log.
4. Slice into rolls about the width of two fingers, be careful not to slice them too thick because it will be difficult for the dough in the center to cook through.
5. Place the rolls on a greased baking sheet.
6. Bake 12-15 minutes until golden brown.

KETO SAUSAGE
Nutrition: Cal 353;Fat 23 g;Carb 4 g;Protein 18 g
Serving 12; cook time 25 min
Ingredients
FOR THE KETO ALMOND FLOUR BISCUITS
- 3 ounces cream cheese,softened
- 1 cup shredded cheddar cheese
- 2 eggs
- 2 cups almond flour
- 1 teaspoon baking powder
- 1/4 teaspoon salt
- 1/4 cup heavy cream (scrape the measuring cup out since it is thick, make sure you get ALL of the liquid)
- 1 tablespoon melted butter
SAUSAGE PATTIES
- 1 1/2 pounds breakfast sausage, formed into 12 patties
Instructions
1. Preheat the oven to 350 degrees.
2. In a mixing bowl combine the softened cream cheese, cheddar cheese and eggs. Stir until cream cheese is smooth with no clumps.
3. Add almond flour, baking powder, salt, heavy cream and melted butter.
4. Stir until combined. Do not overmix or biscuits will be tough.
5. Chill the dough 10-15 minutes.
6. Lightly sprinkle almond flour onto a cutting board and turn the dough onto the floured surface. Pat the biscuits to about 1/2 inch thick and use a biscuit cutter or the top of a mason jar to cut out your biscuits.
7. Place the biscuits onto a greased or silicone lined baking sheet.
8. Bake 15-18 minutes until golden.
9. Cook the sausage patties in a skillet over medium heat until cooked through.
10. To assemble slice the warm biscuits in half and add the sausage patty.

KETO BISCUITS AND GRAVY
Nutrition: Cal 203;Fat 16 g;Carb 3 g;Protein 12 g
Serving 6; Cook time 40 min
Ingredients
Keto Biscuits
- ¼ cup unsalted butter melted
- 4 large eggs
- ⅓ cup coconut flour
- 1 cup cheddar cheese shredded
- 1 tbsp cream cheese
- ¼ tsp salt
- ¼ tsp baking powder
KETO SAUSAGE GRAVY
- 1 lb ground sausage
- ½ cup chicken broth
- 1 cup heavy cream
- salt & pepper to taste
- 4 tbsp cream cheese

- •½ tsp chili flakes optional
- •¼ tsp xanthan gum optional

Instructions

TO MAKE THE KETO BISCUITS

1. Preheat the oven to 350°F / 180°C and line a baking sheet with parchment paper.
2. In a large bowl add the eggs, one tablespoon cream cheese, and salt. Whisk for 30 seconds.
3. Pour the melted butter over the egg mixture and continue whisking.
4. Add the shredded cheddar cheese, coconut flour, and baking powder and combine well. Let the biscuits dough sit for about 5 minutes so the coconut flour can absorb the liquid and make the dough thick.
5. Divide the dough into 9 equal biscuits. Place them 2 inches apart on the baking sheet.
6. Bake in the preheated oven for about 15 minutes or until they get a beautiful golden color.

TO MAKE THE SAUSAGE GRAVY

1. In a large skillet add the ground sausage. Brown and crumble the meat into smaller pieces over medium heat until fully cooked.
2. Add the chicken broth, cream cheese and whipping cream. Stir to combine well and let it simmer until it becomes thicker. Season with salt and pepper to taste (if necessary).
3. Serve one or two keto biscuits with 1/2 cup of gravy. Enjoy!

KETO PROTEIN BREAKFAST SCRAMBLE

Nutrition: Cal 511;Fat 41 g;Carb 6 g;Protein 28 g
Serving 4; Cook time 20 min

Ingredients

- •6 links breakfast sausage sliced
- •6 slices bacon chopped
- •4 oz hard salami (such as Genoa) cubed
- •1 small onion sliced
- •1 medium bell pepper sliced
- •6 large eggs
- •¼ cup sour cream
- •½ cup cheddar cheese grated
- •2 stalks green onion (scallion) sliced
- •salt and pepper

Instructions

1. Place a frying pan over medium-high heat. Once hot add raw sliced bacon and sausage. Fry until cooked through, and just starting to brown and crisp. (5 - 8 minutes)
2. 6 slices bacon
3. Add chopped salami and continue to fry until the salami, bacon, and sausage have reached a level of crispness you are satisfied with. If the pan contains a lot of rendered fat, drain off a portion now to avoid greasy eggs (2 - 3 minutes)
4. 6 links breakfast sausage,4 oz hard salami (such as Genoa)

5. Next add the sliced onions and pepper to fry until softened. (1 minute)
6. 1 small onion,1 medium bell pepper
7. Stir in egg mixture, and using a spatula begin to combine and scramble everything in the pan. Cook eggs to desired doneness. (3-5 minutes)
8. Stir in grated cheese, top with sliced green onion, and season to taste with salt and pepper.
9. 2 stalks green onion (scallion),salt and pepper

EGG WRAPS WITH HAM AND GREENS

Nutrition: Cal 371;Fat 26 g;Carb 5 g;Protein 28 g
Serving 6; Cook time 20 min

Ingredients

- •8 large eggs
- •4 teaspoons water
- •2 teaspoons all-purpose flour or cornstarch
- •1/2 teaspoon fine salt
- •4 teaspoons vegetable or coconut oil
- •1 1/3 cups shredded Swiss cheese
- •4 ounces very thinly sliced ham
- •1 1/3 cups loosely packed watercress

Instructions

1. Place the eggs, water, flour or cornstarch, and salt in a medium bowl and whisk until broken up and the flour or cornstarch is completely dissolved.
2. Heat 1 teaspoon of the oil in a 12-inch nonstick frying pan over medium heat until shimmering. Swirl the pan to coat the bottom with the oil. Add 1/2 cup of the egg mixture and swirl to coat the bottom of the pan in a thin layer. Cook until the wrap is completely set on the edges and on the bottom (the top can be a little wet, but should be mostly set), 3 to 6 minutes.
3. Using a flat spatula, loosen the edges of the wrap and slide it underneath the wrap, making sure it can slide easily around the pan. Flip the wrap with the spatula. Immediately sprinkle 1/3 cup of the cheese over the wrap and cook until the second side is set, about 1 minute. Slide it onto a work surface or cutting board (the cheese might not be fully melted yet). While still warm, place a single layer of ham over the egg. Place 1/3 cup of the watercress across the center of the wrap. Roll it up tightly.
4. Repeat with cooking and filling the remaining wraps. Using a serrated knife, cut each wrap crosswise into 6 (1-inch) pieces.

BACON GRUYÈRE EGG BITES

Nutrition: Cal 208;Fat 17,5 g;Carb 1 g;Protein 11 g
Serving 9; Cook time 60 min

Ingredients

- •Bacon fat or butter, for coating the pan
- •9 large eggs
- •3/4 cup grated Gruyère cheese (2 1/4 ounces)
- •1/3 cup cream cheese (about 2 1/2 ounces)
- •1/2 teaspoon kosher salt

• 6 slices thick-cut bacon, cooked and crumbled

Instructions

1. Arrange a rack in the middle of the oven and heat to 350°F. Coat an 8x8-inch (broiler-safe if you want a browned top) baking dish generously with bacon fat or butter.
2. Place the eggs, Gruyère, cream cheese, and salt in a blender and blend on medium-high speed until very smooth, about 1 minute. Pour into the baking dish. Sprinkle with the bacon. Cover tightly with aluminum foil.
3. Pull the oven rack halfway out of the oven. Place a roasting pan on the oven rack. Pour in 6 cups of very hot tap water. Set the baking dish of eggs into the roasting pan. Bake until just set in the middle, 55 minutes to 1 hour.
4. Carefully remove the roasting pan from the oven. Remove the baking dish from the roasting pan and uncover. (For a browned top: Heat the oven to broil. Broil until the top is golde- brown, 4 to 5 minutes.) Cut into 9 squares and serve.

RADISH AND TURNIP HASH WITH FRIED EGGS

Nutrition: Cal 391;Fat 34 g;Carb 10 g;Protein 12 g
Serving 2; Cook time 20 min

Ingredients

• 2 to 3 small turnips, trimmed, peeled, and cut into 3/4-inch cubes (about 1 1/2 cups cubed)
• 4 to 5 small radishes, scrubbed and trimmed, and cut into 3/4-inch cubes (about 1 1/2 cups cubed)
• Coarse sea salt
• Freshly ground pepper
• 2 tablespoons grapeseed oil, or other neutral, heat-tolerant oil
• 1 stalk green garlic, trimmed and chopped (white and light green parts only)
• 2 tablespoons unsalted butter
• 4 eggs
• 1 tablespoon minced parsley

Instructions

1. Fill a large saucepan with water and bring to a boil. Add 2 teaspoons sea salt. Boil turnip cubes just until tender, 3 to 4 minutes; remove to a bowl with a slotted spoon, pour off any excess water, and set aside. Next, boil radishes briefly, 30 to 60 seconds; remove to a bowl with a slotted spoon, pour off any excess water, and set aside.
2. Set a large cast iron skillet over medium-high heat. Add grapeseed oil and when hot, add turnips and radishes, and a pinch each sea salt and pepper. Turning vegetables only once or twice, cook 8 minutes or until golden-brown. Turn heat to medium and fold in green garlic, cooking for about a minute. Push vegetables to the sides, melt butter in the center of pan, and add the eggs, salting each individually. For over-easy eggs, cook uncovered 4 to 6 minutes; for over-medium eggs, cover pan for 3 minutes, then uncover and continue

cooking just until whites are set, 2 to 3 minutes longer. Finish with minced parsley and sea salt and pepper to taste. Serve immediately.

KETO LOAF BREAD

Nutrition: Cal 239;Fat 22 g;Carb 4 g;Protein 8 g
Serving 1; Cook time 60 min

Ingredients

• 2 cups finely ground almond flour, such as Bob's Red Mill or King Arthur brands
• 1 teaspoon baking powder
• 1/2 teaspoon xanthan gum
• 1/2 teaspoon kosher salt
• 7 large eggs, at room temperature
• 8 tablespoons (1 stick) unsalted butter, melted and cooled
• 2 tablespoons refined coconut oil, melted and cooled

Instructions

1. Arrange a rack in the middle of the oven and heat to 350°F. Line the bottom and sides of a 9x5-inch metal loaf pan with parchment paper, letting the excess hang over the long sides to form a sling. Set aside.

2. Whisk together the almond flour, baking powder, xanthan gum, and salt in a medium bowl. Set aside.
3. Place the eggs in the bowl of a stand mixer fitted with the whisk attachment. Beat on medium-high speed until light and frothy. Reduce the speed to medium, slowly add the melted butter and coconut oil, and beat until until fully combined. Reduce the speed to low, slowly add the almond flour mixture, and beat until combined. Increase the speed to medium high and beat until mixture thickens, about 1 minute.
4. Pour into the prepared pan and smooth the top. Bake until a knife inserted in the center comes out clean, 45 to 55 minutes. Let cool in the pan for about 10 minutes. Grasping the parchment paper, remove the loaf from the pan and transfer to a wire rack. Cool completely before slicing.

KALE AND GOAT CHEESE FRITTATA CUPS

Nutrition: Cal 179;Fat 14,7 g;Carb 1 g;Protein 10 g
Serving 8; Cook time 40 min

Ingredients

• 2 cups chopped lacinato kale
• 1 garlic clove, thinly sliced
• 3 tablespoons olive oil
• 1/4 teaspoon red pepper flakes
• 8 large eggs
• 1/4 teaspoon salt
• Dash ground black pepper
• 1/2 teaspoon dried thyme
• 1/4 cup goat cheese, crumbled

Instructions

1. Preheat the oven to 350°F. To get 2 cups kale, remove the leaves from the kale ribs. Wash and dry the leaves and cut them into 1/2-inch-wide strips.
2. In a 10-inch nonstick skillet, cook the garlic in 1 tablespoon of oil over medium-high heat for 30 seconds. Add the kale and red pepper flakes and cook until wilted, 1 to 2 minutes.
3. In a medium bowl, beat the eggs with the salt and pepper. Add the kale and thyme to the egg mixture.
4. Using a 12-cup muffin tin, use the remaining 2 tablespoons of oil to grease 8 of the cups (you may also use butter or nonstick spray if you'd prefer). Sprinkle the tops with goat cheese. Bake until they are set in the center, about 25 to 30 minutes.
5. Frittata is best eaten warm from the oven or within the next day, but leftovers can be kept refrigerated and reheated for up to a week.

ROASTED RADISH AND HERBED RICOTTA OMELET
Nutrition: Cal 350;Fat 27 g;Carb 5 g;Protein 20 g
Serving 2; Cook time 15 min
Ingredients
FOR THE ROASTED RADISHES:
- 1 cup thinly-sliced French Breakfast radishes, or other radish variety
- 2 teaspoons olive oil
- 1/4 teaspoon sea salt

FOR THE RICOTTA:
- 1/4 cup plus 2 tablespoons fresh whole milk ricotta
- 2 teaspoons minced fresh chives
- 1 teaspoon minced fresh thyme
- 1 teaspoon minced fresh flat leaf parsley, plus extra for topping

FOR THE EGGS:
- 4 large or extra-large eggs
- 2 tablespoons whole milk
- 1/2 teaspoon sea salt
- 1/4 teaspoon black pepper
- 1 tablespoon butter

Instructions
1. To make the radishes, preheat the oven to 400°F. Toss the radishes with the olive oil and salt. Spread in a thin layer in a roasting dish and bake until soft and tender, 10 to 12 minutes (any longer and you may end up with radish chips).
2. In a small bowl, combine the ricotta with the minced herbs.
3. To make the omelet, whisk together the eggs, milk, salt, and pepper. Heat 1/2 tablespoon of butter in an 8-inch non-stick skillet over medium-low heat. Pour in half the egg mixture and cook for 1 to 2 minutes, allowing the bottom to set slightly. Run a spatula under the edges, lifting up and tilting the pan to allow uncooked eggs to run under the cooked part. Continue to do this until the majority of the egg is set. Carefully flip the omelet and remove from heat.

4. Spread half the ricotta mixture over half of the omelet and sprinkle with half of the radishes. Fold the omelet over over the filling and sprinkle with a few more roasted radish slices and minced parsley.
5. Repeat to make the second omelet. Serve both omelets immediately.

MIXED MUSHROOM EGG BAKES
Nutrition: Cal 287;Fat 21 g;Carb 8 g;Protein 16 g
Serving 4; Cook time 35 min
Ingredients
- Butter or cooking spray
- 2 tablespoons extra-virgin olive oil
- 1/3 cup minced shallot (from about 2 small shallots)
- 8 ounces sliced mixed fresh mushrooms (cremini, oyster or shiitake, stems removed before slicing)
- 2 tablespoons chopped fresh thyme
- 6 large eggs
- 3/4 cup whole milk
- 1/2 teaspoon kosher salt
- 1/2 teaspoon ground black pepper
- 1/2 cup shredded mozzarella cheese
Instructions
1. Arrange a rack in the middle of the oven and heat to 400°F. Coat 4 (8-ounce) ramekins with a little butter, or use cooking spray instead. Place the ramekins on a rimmed baking sheet so they'll be easier to move to and from the oven; set aside.
2. Heat the olive oil in a medium saucepan over medium-high heat until shimmering. Add the shallot and sauté until soft and translucent, about 3 minutes. Add the mushrooms and a pinch of salt and cook until softened and fragrant, about 5 minutes. Stir in the thyme and remove from the heat.
3. Whisk the eggs, milk, salt, and pepper together in a medium bowl. Divide the mushroom mixture evenly between the ramekins. Divide the cheese over the mushrooms. Pour the egg mixture over the top, stopping just below the top of the ramekin.
4. Place the baking sheet in the oven and bake until the tops are golden and have puffed slightly and the eggs are completely set, 20 to 25 minutes.

3-INGREDIENT PESTO ZOODLE BOWL
Nutrition: Cal 400;Fat 38 g;Carb 8 g;Protein 10 g
Serving 1; Cook time 10 min
Ingredients
- 2 tablespoons olive oil, divided
- 1 medium zucchini (about 6 ounces), ends trimmed and spiralized, or 1 heaping cup of store-bought zucchini noodles
- 1 tablespoon basil pesto
- 1 large egg
- Kosher salt
- Freshly ground black pepper
- Red pepper flakes or hot sauce, for serving (optional)

Instructions

1. Heat 1 tablespoon of the oil in a medium nonstick skillet over medium heat until shimmering. Add the zucchini noodles and sauté until just tender, about 2 minutes. Add the pesto and toss until the noodles are well-coated. Transfer the noodles to a plate or shallow bowl.
2. Heat the remaining 1 tablespoon oil in the skillet until shimmering. Add the egg, season with salt and pepper, and cook undisturbed until the outer white edges are opaque, about 1 minute. Cover and cook until the yolk is set but still runny, 2 to 3 minutes.
3. Gently slide a spatula under the egg and place it on top of the zoodles. Sprinkle with a pinch of red pepper flakes or finish with a little hot sauce, if using.

CHOCOLATE PROTEIN PANCAKES

Nutrition: Cal 380;Fat 31 g;Carb 5 g;Protein 19 g
Serving 2; Cook time 20 min

Ingredients
DRY INGREDIENTS

- 1scoop vanilla protein powder
- 1 tablespoon cocoa powder
- 2 teaspoon baking powder
- 1 tablespoon coconut flour
- 1 tablespoon granulated sweetener
- 1 pinch salt

WET INGREDIENTS

- 2 eggs
- 4 tablespoon unsalted butter (softened)
- 1 tablespoon cream cheese
- 1/4 teaspoon vanilla extract

Instructions

1. Whisk together all of the dry ingredients in a mixing bowl until no lumps remain.
2. Make a well in the middle of the dry ingredients and add the eggs, butter, cream cheese, and vanilla extract into the middle.
3. Fold the batter together gently and set aside for 5 minutes.
4. Heat a non-stick frying pan over medium to high heat.
5. Add 1/4 cup of the batter to the pan at a time. Cook until bubbles form on the top surface, then flip over to cook on the other side, cooking for about 3 – 4 minutes per side.

KETO BREAKFAST SANDWICH

Nutrition: Cal 603;Fat 54 g;Carb 4 g;Protein 22 g
Serving 2; Cook time 35 min

Ingredients

- 4 sausage patties
- 2 egg
- 2 tbsp cream cheese
- 4 tbsp sharp cheddar
- 1/2 medium avocado, sliced
- 1/2–1 tsp sriracha (to taste)
- Salt, pepper to taste

Instructions

1. In skillet over medium heat, cook sausages per package instructions and set aside
2. In small bowl place cream cheese and sharp cheddar. Microwave for 20-30 seconds until melted
3. Mix cheese with sriracha, set aside
4. Mix egg with seasoning and make small omelette
5. Fill omelette with cheese sriracha mixture and assemble sandwich

POACHED EGGS MYTILENE

Nutrition: Cal 275;Fat 23 g;Carb 6 g;Protein 13 g
Serving 1; Cook time 20 min

Ingredients

- 4 sausage patties
- 2 egg
- 2 tbsp cream cheese
- 4 tbsp sharp cheddar
- 1/2 medium avocado, sliced
- 1/2–1 tsp sriracha (to taste)
- Salt, pepper to taste

Instructions

1. In skillet over medium heat, cook sausages per package instructions and set aside
2. Combine lemon juice and oil in a small serving bowl; whisk to combine.
3. Add water and vinegar to a medium saute pan or small saucepan and bring to a slow boil. Reduce the heat to medium-low. Crack 1 egg into a small bowl, being careful not to break the yolk. Gently slip egg into the simmering water, holding the bowl just above the surface of water. Repeat with the remaining egg. Cook eggs until the whites are firm and the yolks are lightly cooked outside, but liquid inside, 2 to 3 minutes. Remove the eggs from the water with a slotted spoon, and place into a serving bowl.
4. Break the yolks with a fork and drizzle with lemon juice mixture. Stir yolks twice; season with salt and pepper.

HEALTHY BREAKFAST CHEESECAKE

Nutrition: Cal 152;Fat 12 g;Carb 3 g;Protein 6 g
Serving 1; Cook time 1 hour 5 min

Ingredients

- Crust Ingredients:
- 2 cups whole almonds
- 2 tablespoon Joy Filled Eats Sweetener (or see alternatives in recipe notes)
- 4 tablespoon salted butter

FILLING INGREDIENTS:

- 16 oz 4% fat cottage cheese
- 8 oz cream cheese
- 6 eggs
- ¾ cup Joy Filled Eats Sweetener (or see alternatives in recipe notes)

•½ teaspoon almond extract
•½ teaspoon vanilla extract
TOPPING WHEN SERVING:
•¼ cup frozen mixed berries per cheesecake thawed
Instructions
1. Preheat the oven to 350. In a large food processor pulse the almonds, 2 tablespoon sweetener, and 4 tablespoon butter until a coarse dough forms. Grease two twelve hole standard silicone muffin pans or line metal tins with paper or foil cupcake liners. I used a silicone muffin pan for this and the cheesecakes popped out really easily. Divide the dough between the 24 holes and press into the bottom to form a crust. Bake for 8 minutes.
2. Meanwhile, combine the Friendship Dairies 4% cottage cheese and the cream cheese in the food processor (you don't need to wash the bowl). Pulse the cheeses until smooth. Add the sweetener and extracts. Mix until combined.
3. Add the eggs. Blend until smooth. You will need to scrape down the sides. Divide the batter between the muffin cups.
4. Bake for 30-40 minutes until the centers no longer jiggly when the pan is lightly shaken. Cool completely. Refrigerate for at least 2 hours before trying to remove them if you didn't use paper or foil liners. Serve with thawed frozen berries.

BLUEBERRY PANCAKES
Nutrition: Cal 202;Fat 16 g;Carb 9 g;Protein 10 g
Serving 3; Cook time 10 min
Ingredients
•2 eggs
•2/3 cup almond flour
•1 tsp baking powder
•1/2 tsp vanilla
•1 tsp Swerve sweetener
•3 tbsp milk or almond milk
•1/4 cup blueberries
•Keto pancake syrup for serving, optional
Instructions
1. Whisk the eggs in a bowl, then add vanilla, Swerve and milk and mix until combined. Add almond flour and baking powder and mix until combined. Stir in the blueberries.
2. Spray a non-stick frying pan or pancake griddle with a non-stick cooking spray and heat over medium-high heat. Laddle the pancake batter on a frying pan, making 6 small pancakes.
3. Cook for 3-4 minutes (or until the bottom is golden-brown and bubbles begin to form on top of the pancakes), then flip the pancakes over with a spatula and cook for another 2 minutes, or until the other side is golden-brown.

LOW CARB PUMPKIN CHEESECAKE PANCAKES
Nutrition: Cal 202;Fat 16 g;Carb 9 g;Protein 10 g
Serving 16; Cook time 10 min
Ingredients
•4 ounces Cream Cheese
•4 large Eggs
•2 Tablespoons Pure Pumpkin Puree
•1 teaspoon Pure Vanilla Extract
•1 teaspoon Pyure Sugar Substitute (or your choice)
•1/2 teaspoon Baking Powder
•1/4 teaspoon Pumpkin Pie Spice
•1/8 teaspoon Ground Cinnamon
•2 teaspoons Butter
Instructions
1. Add all ingredients except butter to blender and process until smooth. Let sit while the skillet is heating.
2. Heat a cast iron skillet or griddle with a medium flame until hot and then add 1 teaspoon of butter.
3. Slowly pour pancake mix into skillet to make 3 inch pancakes. When bubbles begin to form, flip pancakes. Continue until all batter has been used. Use the second teaspoon of butter, half way through, to grease pan.
4. Serve with butter and maple syrup.

MEDITERRANEAN KETO QUICHE
Nutrition: Cal 133;Fat 8 g;Carb 9 g;Protein 7 g
Serving 8; Cook time 50 min
Ingredients
•1 tsp olive oil or butter
•1/2 cup red onion, chopped
•2 tsp (1 large clove) garlic, minced
•2/3 to 3/4 cup unsweetened almond or coconut milk
•4 eggs
•2 tbsp grated Parmesan cheese + extra for topping
•3 tbsp coconut flour, sifted
•3 tbsp tapioca starch or non-GMO cornstarch
•1 tsp baking powder
•1/4 tsp kosher salt or fine sea salt
•1 tsp smoked paprika
•1 cup chopped/sliced zucchini, divided
•1/2 to 2/3 cup crumbled feta cheese, divided
•1 red bell pepper, roasted and diced (fresh and roasted in oven or roasted red bell peppers from a jar both work)
•Fresh basil for garnish.
•Optional black pepper, to season.
Instructions
1. Grease or line a 9-inch pie or cake pan with parchment paper.
2. Coat small skillet with 1 tsp butter or oil. Add onion and garlic to the pan and cook over medium to medium high for 5 minutes (or until fragrant). Set aside.
3. To a large mixing bowl or bowl of stand mixer, add milk, eggs, and Parmesan cheese. Whisk/blend until smooth.

4. In a separate bowl, sift the coconut flour, then add tapioca flour, spices, salt, baking powder. Mix together.
5. Mix the dry ingredients with the blended egg/milk batter. Whisk together until smooth.
6. Layer your onion and garlic at the bottom of the pie pan.
7. Layer 2/3 cup zucchini on top, roasted pepper slices, and 1/3 cup feta crumbles.
8. Evenly pour the egg/flour mixture into your prepared pie or cake pan. Add remaining zucchini slices and cheese on top (Parmesan and/or feta)
9. Bake at 400F for 35 -45 minutes. Check at 25 minutes for doneness. The edges will be crispy brown and a knife or toothpick inserted into the center of the quiche will come out clean. Check the middle to make sure it's no longer soft.
10. When the crustless quiche is finished cooking, remove it from the oven and garnish with fresh basil before serving.

KETO SAUSAGE BALLS
Nutrition: Cal 363;Fat 8 g;Carb 9 g;Protein 7 g
Serving 6; Cook time 30 min

Ingredients
FATHEAD DOUGH
• cups mozzarella cheese
• 1 oz cream cheese
• 3/4 cup almond flour
• 1 large egg
• 12 oz ground breakfast sausage

Instructions
1. Preheat your oven to 400 degrees F and line a baking sheet with parchment paper.
2. Preheat a medium skillet to medium high heat.
3. Divide the sausage into 6 and roll into balls. Add to the hot skillet and cook through. Set aside on a plate to cool.

FATHEAD DOUGH
1. Add the mozzarella cheese and cream cheese to a microwave safe mixing bowl and microwave on high for 30 seconds. Combine using a fork until evenly mixed.
2. Add the almond flour and egg and combine as thoroughly as possible. If it does not combine well microwave for another 20 seconds.
3. Switch to a spatula if necessary and combine. Pour the dough onto a piece of parchment paper. If it is not evenly combined use your hands to incorporate everything.
4. Portion the dough out into 6 even balls.
5. Flatten out each ball using your hands or roll it out with another piece of parchment on top (so there is no sticking) and place the cooked sausage in the center. Pull up the side and place the sausage ball, seam side down, on a lined baking sheet.
6. Repeat until all 6 sausage balls are complete and on the baking sheet.
7. Bake for 10-15 minutes, until browned on top.

8. Best stored in a air tight sealed container in the fridge up to 5 days.

TURKISH-STYLE BREAKFAST RECIPE
Nutrition: Cal 359;Fat 27 g;Carb 7 g;Protein 17 g
Serving 4; Cook time 25 min

Ingredients
• 4 eggs
• 250g halloumi, sliced thickly into 8 pieces
• 250g yogurt
• 400g tomatoes, roughly chopped
• 400g cucumber, sliced

For The Zhoug:
• 1 bunch parsley
• ½ bunch coriander
• 2 green chillies
• 2 cloves garlic
• 200ml olive oil
• Pinch of sugar
• ½ tsp ground cumin
• ¼ tsp cardamom

Instructions
1. To make the zhoug blitz all the ingredients in a food processor until finely chopped, adding water to get the consistency of a loose pesto. Season to taste.
2. Bring a pan of water to a rolling boil. Add the eggs and cook for 6 mins for soft boiled. Immediately plunge in cool water and peel.
3. Bring a griddle pan to a high heat. Add the halloumi and fry on each side for 2 mins, until golden and slightly charred.
4. Swirl the zhoug into the yogurt and spoon onto plates. Top with the tomatoes, cucumber and halloumi.

POACHED EGG AND BACON SALAD
Nutrition: Cal 311;Fat 22 g;Carb 12 g;Protein 15 g
Serving 2; Cook time 20 min

Ingredients
• 100g (3½oz) unsmoked bacon lardons
• 1 slice bread, cut into small cubes
• 2 medium or large eggs
• 2 good handfuls of mixed salad leaves (we used rocket and chard)
• 10 baby plum tomatoes, halved
• 1 stick celery, chopped
• For The Dressing:
• 1tbsp olive oil
• 1tsp white wine vinegar
• ½tsp Dijon mustard
• Salt and ground black pepper

Instructions
1. Heat a frying pan, add the bacon and fry until golden and crispy. Take out of the pan with a draining spoon and set aside. Add the bread cubes to the pan, and fry in the bacon fat until browned and crispy.

2. Meanwhile poach the eggs, pour boiling water, 10cm (4in) in depth, into a small pan, over a high heat. Add a dash of white wine vinegar. When water boils again, break egg into pan.
3. As water comes back to the boil, gather egg white round yolk, using a draining spoon. Turn down heat. Simmer for a minute for a soft egg, longer for a firmer one.
4. Lift the egg out of the pan with the draining spoonand put into a bowl of warm water if cooking more than one or two eggs. Add another egg to the pan.How to poach an egg video
5. Mix together the dressing ingredients. Put a good handful of salad leaves on to 2 plates. Divide the bacon, croutons, tomatoes and celery between them. Spoon drained eggs on top, drizzle the salad with dressing and sprinkle with salt and pepper.

CHICKEN LIVER SALAD
Nutrition: Cal 450;Fat 33 g;Carb 9 g;Protein 28 g
Serving 4; Cook time 25 min

Ingredients
•400g (14oz) fresh chicken livers
•Salt and ground black pepper
•2 thick slices white bread
•3 tbsp clarified butter
•4-6 rashers streaky bacon, chopped
•4 good handfuls of salad leaves

For The Dressing
•1 tbsp cider vinegar
•1 tsp Dijon mustard
•Pinch of sugar
•2 tbsp light olive oil
•1 tbsp walnut oil

Instructions
1. Remove sinews from the livers and, if large, cut livers into bite-sized pieces. Season well.
2. Cut the crusts off the bread and cut the bread into 1cm (½in) cubes.
3. Heat 2 tablespoons of butter in a frying pan over a medium heat. Add the bread, stir well to coat in butter and fry for a few mins until crisp and golden. Drain them on kitchen paper and keep them warm in the oven.
4. Add the chopped bacon to the hot pan and fry until crispy. Put on the baking tray with the fried bread. Heat the rest of the butter in the pan with any fat from the bacon, add the chicken livers in one layer and fry for a couple of mins each side. Take the frying pan off the heat.
5. Mix the dressing ingredients in a small bowl or jug and season. Put a handful of leaves on each plate, then divide the chicken livers, bacon and croutons between the plates. Drizzle with the dressing and serve warm.

SPINACH PANCAKES
Nutrition: Cal 186;Fat 15 g;Carb 5 g;Protein 7 g
Serving 4; Cook time 15 min

Ingredients
For The Batter:
•30 g or ⅓ cup gram (chickpea) flour
•85 ml/⅓ cup water
•A pinch of sea salt
•1 garlic clove
•2 handfuls of spinach
•2 tbsp olive oil
•1 tbsp no-taste coconut oil or unrefined rapeseed oil

For The Filling:
•50 g Parmesan cheese, grated
•½ avocado, sliced lengthways
•1 tbsp chopped chives
•Chopped chillies (if liked)

Instructions
1. Add all of the batter ingredients to a blender and mix until smooth. Heat the coconut oil or rapeseed oil in a frying pan.
2. Pour a thin layer of the mixture into the pan. Top with most of the avocado slices, chives and most of the grated cheese – leaving some to decorate with later.
3. Cook a few minutes, loosen edges with a spatula then flip over.
4. Top with the remaining cheese, chives and avocados – plus a few slices of red chilli, if preferred

HALLOUMI SALAD WITH ROASTED PLUMS
Nutrition: Cal 382;Fat 32 g;Carb 11 g;Protein 28 g
Serving 4; Cook time 30 min

Ingredients
•4 whole plums, quartered and de-stoned
•1tbsp olive oil
•2tsp butter
•1 pack halloumi cheese, sliced into 8 pieces

For The Dressing
•4tbsp olive oil
•Zest and juice of 1 lime, plus 1 lime cut into wedges to serve
•1tsp sugar
•1tsp Dijon mustard
•Small bunch of each mint and coriander, finely chopped

Instructions
1. Preheat the oven to 220C. Place the plums on a baking tray, drizzle with olive oil and season well with salt and pepper. Roast in the oven for 15-18 mins until they are slightly charred and just beginning to soften.
2. Mix the dressing ingredients together in a small bowl and season well. Heat the butter in a frying pan and pan-fry the halloumi slices for a few mins on each side until golden brown and starting to melt slightly.

3. Plate up the halloumi slices with the roasted plums, and drizzle over the dressing. Serve with lime wedges on the side.

GRIDDLED HALLOUMI AND WATER-MELON SALAD
Nutrition: Cal 386;Fat 30 g;Carb 16 g;Protein 16 g
Serving 4; Cook time 20 min

Ingredients
- ½ x 1.5kg watermelon
- 4tbsp extra virgin olive oil
- 1tbsp balsamic vinegar
- 250g halloumi
- 150g Mixed baby leaf salad leaves
- 1tbsp fresh basil, finely sliced
- Edible flowers, optional

Instructions
1. Remove the rind and pips from the watermelon, and cut into 2.5cm cubes. Mix 3tbsp of olive oil and the balsamic vinegar together and season with salt and pepper.
2. Cut the halloumi lengthways into eight slices and toss in the remaining 1tbsp olive oil. Place a griddle pan over a medium heat and cook each slice for 30-60 seconds on each side, or until there are golden brown griddle marks on each side.
3. To serve divide the salad leave between four plates, scatter with watermelon cubes and top each salad with 2 slices of halloumi. Drizzle over the dressing, add a few slices of basil leaves and some edible flowers.

CHICKEN AND CHEESE BREAKFAST BOWLS
Nutrition: Cal 240;Fat 15 g;Carb 2 g;Protein 30 g
Serving 2; Cook time 20 min

Ingredients
- 4 ounces cooked chicken breast, diced
- 4 large eggs
- 1/2 cup shredded cheddar cheese
- Salt and pepper to taste
- 2 tbsp. butter or olive oil

Instructions
1. Preheat your oven to 375°F (190°C). Grease a 9-inch (23cm) baking dish with butter or olive oil.
2. In a large bowl, whisk the eggs and add the diced chicken, shredded cheese, salt, and pepper. Mix well.
3. Pour the egg mixture into the prepared baking dish and bake in the oven for 15-20 minutes, or until the eggs are set and the top is golden brown.
4. Remove from the oven and let cool for a few minutes before slicing and serving.

SPICY CHICKEN BREAKFAST BOWLS
Nutrition: Cal 260;Fat 18 g;Carb 5 g;Protein 37 g
Serving 2; Cook time 20 min

Ingredients
- 2 boneless, skinless chicken breasts, diced
- 1 tbsp. olive oil
- 1 tsp. chili powder
- 1 tsp. paprika
- Salt and pepper to taste
- 2 cups fresh spinach leaves
- 2 tbsp. sour cream
- 2 tbsp. sliced jalapeños

Instructions
1. Heat the olive oil in a large pan over medium heat. Add the diced chicken and season with chili powder, paprika, salt, and pepper. Cook until browned and fully cooked, about 5-7 minutes.
2. Divide the cooked chicken evenly between two bowls. Top each bowl with a cup of fresh spinach leaves, a tablespoon of sour cream, and a tablespoon of sliced jalapeños.

CHEESE-STYLE "HOT CAKES"
Nutrition: Cal 213;Fat 22 g;Carb 1 g;Protein 4 g
Serving 4; Cook time 15 min

Ingredients
- 2 ounces cream cheese
- 2 eggs
- ½ tsp. gluten-free baking powder
- ½ tsp. vanilla extract
- 4 Tbsp. butter
- 4 Tbsp. sugar-free maple syrup (optional; not reflected in nutritional information)
- 1 Tbsp. coconut oil

Instructions
1. Blend the cream cheese, eggs, baking powder, and vanilla extract together in ablender.
2. Pour into a heated skillet with coconut oil, and cook for about 1 minute each side.
3. Top with 1 tablespoon of butter each and 1 tablespoon of sugar-free maple syrup, if desired.

MILANESA
Nutrition: Cal 292;Fat 23 g;Carb 16 g;Protein 11 g
Serving 8; Cook time 70 min

Ingredients
- 2 eggplants
- 2 eggs
- 1 cup arugula
- 3 Tbsp. unsweetened almond milk
- 3 cloves garlic, peeled and chopped
- 2 cups almond meal
- 2 Tbsp. nutritional yeast
- Sea salt, to taste

Instructions

1. Peel and slice the eggplant into 8 thick strips, sprinkle with salt and let sit for 20 minutes.
2. While the eggplant is sitting out, whisk together the eggs, milk, and garlic.
3. After the eggplant has sat out for 30 minutes, add the eggplant strips to the egg mixture and let it marinate in the fridge for 30 minutes.
4. Preheat your oven to 400F, and line a baking sheet with parchment paper.
5. While the oven is preheating, add the almond meal and nutritional yeast to a mixing bowl, and dunk the marinated eggplant into the almond meal to cover until well coated. Transfer to the baking sheet.
6. Bake for 5 minutes on each side, until the eggplant is lightly browned. Serve with fresh arugula.

PECAN & COCONUT ' N ' OATMEAL

Nutrition: Cal 312;Fat 25 g;Carb 7 g;Protein 14 g
Serving 1; Cook time 10 min

Ingredients
- ½ cup coconut or almond milk
- 2 teaspoons chia seeds
- 2 tablespoons almond flour
- 1 tablespoon flax meal
- 2 tablespoons hemp hearts
- ¼ teaspoon ground cinnamon
- ¼ teaspoon pure vanilla extract
- 1 tablespoon pecans, toasted and chopped
- 1 tablespoon coconut flakes

Instructions
1. In a small pot, combine the milk, chia seeds, almond flour, flax meal, hemp hearts, cinnamon, and vanilla. Cook over low heat, stirring constantly until thickened, about 5 minutes.
2. Spoon into a bowl, top with the pecans and coconut flakes, and enjoy immediately.

KETO SALMON SUSHI BOWL

Nutrition: Cal 270 Fat 20 g;Carb 7 g;Protein 17 g
Serving 1; Cook time 15 min

Ingredients
BOWL
- ¾ cup cauliflower rice
- ½ packet smoked salmon
- ½ cup spiralized cucumber
- ½ avocado
- 2 sheets dried seaweed
- 1 tsp low sodium soy sauce
- salt and pepper, to taste
- ½ tsp wasabi, optional
- SAUCE
- 3 tbsp mayo
- 1-2 teaspoon sriracha (adjust to liking)

Instructions
1. Steam cauliflower rice and season with salt and pepper to taste (I used premade bag)

2. Place rice layer in bottom of small bowl with soy sauce and seasoning
3. Add salmon, cucumber, avocado, seaweed around bowl
4. For sauce, mix mayo and sriracha, adjusting to preferred heat
5. Drizzle sauce over bowl
6. Add sesame seeds and pepper for garnish, if desired

CHEDDAR CHIVE BAKED AVOCADO EGGS

Nutrition: Cal 257;Fat 22 g;Carb 2 g;Protein 13 g
Serving 2; Cook time 15 min

Ingredients
- 2 eggs
- 2 ounces cheddar cheese, shredded
- 2 teaspoons heavy cream
- 1 teaspoon fresh chopped chives
- Sea salt and freshly ground black pepper to taste
- 1 avocado, cut in half and pitted

Instructions
1. Preheat the oven to 425F°.
2. Combine the eggs, cheddar cheese, cream, half the chives, salt, and pepper in a medium bowl. Beat with a fork until well mixed.
3. Arrange the avocados in a small rimmed baking dish, cut side up (they should be snug so they don't roll around). Pour the egg filling into the center of eachavocado.
4. Bake 12 minutes, until the filling is lightly golden on top. Serve hot, topped with the remaining chives

TOAD IN A HOLE

Nutrition: Cal 376;Fat 28 g;Carb 16 g;Protein 16 g
Serving 2; Cook time 25 min

Ingredients
- 4 pork sausages (spicy or sweet)
- 1/3 cup blanched, fine almond flour
- 3 tablespoons arrowroot
- 6 tablespoons almond milk
- ¼ cup heavy cream
- 1 egg ¼ teaspoon sea salt

Instructions
1. Place an 8-inch cast-iron skillet on the center rack of the oven. Preheat oven to 400F°.
2. Add the sausages to the skillet. Cook, turning once, until nicely browned, 12 to 15 minutes.
3. Meanwhile, combine the almond flour, arrowroot, almond milk, cream, egg, and salt in a medium bowl. Whisk until mixed well.
4. Once the sausages are browned, pour the batter into the hot pan. Return the skillet to the oven, and cook until puffed up and golden, 20 to 25 minutes. Serve immediately.

CREAMY AVOCADO CHICKEN SALAD

Nutrition: Cal 386;Fat 30 g;Carb 12 g;Protein 18 g
Serving 4; Cook time 15 min

Ingredients
- 2 chicken breast, cooked and cubed
- 2-3 slices cooked bacon
- ⅔ cup mayo
- 1 avocado
- 2 tbsp finely diced red onion
- 1 celery stalk, diced (sub: cucumber)
- 1 tbsp fresh lime juice
- ⅛ tsp chili powder
- salt and pepper, to taste
- cilantro, garnish
- Low carb tortillas, baked or pan fried

Instructions
1. In food processor, blend mayo,half avocado, pepper, lime juice and chili powder until smooth
2. dice remaining ½ of avocado and cooked bacon
3. In large bowl, mix avocado mayo with cubed chicken, celery, diced avocado, bacon and red onion
4. Place scoop of chilled chicken salad on fried/baked tortilla and serve with cilantro garnish

WAFFLE OMELETTES

Nutrition: Cal 312;Fat 25 g;Carb 7 g;Protein 14 g
Serving 1; Cook time 5 min

Ingredients
- 2 large eggs
- 2 tablespoons shredded cheddar, divided
- 2 tablespoons cooked pork breakfast sausage
- Dash of salt and pepper

Instructions
1. If you're using meats, like breakfast sausage or bacon, take this time to pre-cook them then set aside.

2. Preheat a 4-inch waffle iron. In a small bowl, whisk your eggs with salt and pepper.

3. Pour ¼ cup of whisked egg into the heated waffle iron. This is the equivalent of about 1 large egg.

4. Sprinkle 1 tablespoon of shredded cheese on top of the egg and 1 tablespoon of cooked crumbled sausage. Close the waffle iron and cook for 2 minutes.

5. When done, the waffle will be soft like an omelet and not appear runny. Use a fork to carefully move to a plate for serving. Repeat with the remaining ingredients to make the second waffle omelette. Serve warm.

BERRY BREAKFAST SHAKE

Nutrition: Cal 900;Fat 80 g;Carb 13 g;Protein 10 g
Serving 1; Cook time 5 min

Ingredients
- ¼ cup frozen mixed berries
- ½ cup heavy cream
- ½ cup coconut or almond milk
- 1 tablespoon almond butter
- ½ teaspoon fresh squeezed lemon juice
- 1 tablespoon MCT oil (optional)

Instructions
1. Add all the ingredients to a blender bowl. Blend until smooth. Serve immediately.

KETO EGG ROLL IN A BOWL

Nutrition: Cal 346 Fat 7 g;Carb 8 g;Protein 22 g
Serving 6; Cook time 25 min

Ingredients
- 1 pound ground pork
- Salt and pepper, to taste
- 2 cloves garlic, finely minced
- 1 tablespoon ginger paste (or 1 teaspoon ground ginger)
- 6 ounces coleslaw mix
- 6 ounces broccoli slaw (or more coleslaw mix)
- ⅓ cup soy sauce
- 1 tablespoon garlic chili sauce, optional
- 1 tablespoon toasted sesame seeds, for garnish, optional
- 2 tablespoons toasted sesame oil
- 2 scallions, sliced on the bias or chopped, optional

Instructions
1. In a large skillet over medium heat, brown the ground pork until fully cooked and no pink remains, usually about 7-10 minutes. Use a spatula to break the meat into small pieces. Drain any grease if needed. Add the garlic, ginger, and a light sprinkle of salt and pepper into the skillet.
2. Add the coleslaw mix to the cooked pork. If you need a bigger pan at this point, feel free to switch it out. The cabbage will cook down, so in a few minutes, it will fit into the pan better. The cabbage will begin to seoften and become translucent as it cooks.
3. Add the broccoli slaw to the pan. If you're swapping out the broccoli slaw for more shredded cabbage, you can add that now. Continue cooking down the vegetables for about 5-7 minutes until all the they are softened but not mushy or breaking apart.
4. Pour the soy sauce into the mixture and gently stir. This is also the time to add additional salt and pepper, to your preferred taste.
5. Add the chili sauce to the skillet and stir to combine. This is optional. The dish should look cohesive. The meat and vegetables should be well mixed and the vegetables should be tender when done. If you like a bit of crunch, you can slightly undercook the veggies.

6. Garnish with toasted sesame seeds and a drizzle of sesame oil, and green onions. Serve warm and store the leftovers in the refrigerator for up to 3 days for the best taste.

KETO PIGS IN A BLANKET
Nutrition: Cal 333;Fat 26 g;Carb 7 g;Protein 17 g
Serving 4; Cook time 30 min

Ingredients
- 1 cup shredded mozzarella cheese
- ½ cup blanched, finely ground almond flour
- 1 ounce cream cheese
- ½ teaspoon baking soda
- 1 egg yolk
- 4 beef hot dogs
- ½ teaspoon sesame seeds or everything bagel seasoning (optional)
- Ketchup or Mustard for dipping (optional)

Instructions
1. Preheat the oven to 400 F and line a medium-sized baking sheet with parchment.
2. In a large microwave-safe bowl, add the mozzarella and almond flour. Break the cream cheese into small pieces and add to the bowl. Microwave for 30 to 45 seconds, or until the cheese is melted.
3. Stir the mixture with a fork until a soft ball of dough forms. Sprinkle the dough with baking soda and add the egg yolk. Break the yolk with a fork and stir it into the dough until a sooth ball forms.
4. Lay a piece of parchment paper on a flat work surface. Wet your hands with a bit of water and flatten out the dough to about 3 x 4 inches and about ½ inch thick.
5. Use a knife to cut the dough into four even pieces. Pat the hot dogs with a paper towel to remove surface moisture and gently wrap a piece of dough around each, leaving he ends exposed, pinching at the seam to close. The dough will expand a bit during baking, so try to wrap each as closely as possible without breaking the dough.
6. Place all the wrapped hot dogs on the baking sheet and sprinkle with sesame seeds. Bake for 18-20 minutes. The dough will turn golden and firmer when cooked. Remove from the oven and allow to cool for at least 10 minutes; otherwise, the dough my fall apart.
7. Serve with your favorite dipping sauces, such as mustard or ketchup.

KETO FATHEAD PIZZA POCKETS
Nutrition: Cal 443;Fat 34 g;Carb 10 g;Protein 26 g
Serving 4; Cook time 30 min

Ingredients
DOUGH
- 1 ½ cups shredded mozzarella
- ¾ cup almond flour
- 5 tbsp cream cheese
- 2 tsp xanthan gum
- 1 packet instant yeast
- 3 eggs (2 for dough,1 for egg wash)
- Salt, additional seasoning to taste

FILLING
- ¼ cup mozzarella or cheddar
- 7 slices pepperoni
- 4 tbsp cooked italian sausage
- 2 tbsp feta

GARNISH
- ¼ cup shredded parmesan
- 1 tbsp butter
- 1 tsp italian seasoning

Instructions
DOUGH
1. Preheat oven to 400
2. In mixer or large bowl, add almond flour, xanthan gum, yeast and seasoning
3. Mix dry ingredients throughly then add two eggs
4. In separate bowl, microwave mozzarella and cream cheese in 30 second intervals until melted
5. Once melted, add to flour and egg mixture scraping sides down (I used dough hook)
6. If mixture is too stiff, place it back in the microwave for 30 -45 seconds until pliable
7. With dough hook or wet hands, knead mixture for 5-10 minutes until fully combined
8. Using wet hands, separate dough into 4 balls
9. Flatten the dough balls into desired shape, making small indent in the middle
10. Fill with choice of ingredients and mold dough around ingredients gently to close
11. Brush with egg wash
12. Place on parchment and bake for 20-25 minutes until dough is golden brown
13. Melt butter and mix with italian seasoning to brush over each pizza pocket
14. Sprinkle with parmesan

LOW CARB FLATBREAD - SPICED BEEF WITH TZATZIKI SAUCE
Nutrition: Cal 600;Fat 46 g;Carb 10 g;Protein 46 g
Serving 4; Cook time 45 min

Ingredients
FLATBREAD
- 1 ¼ cup mozzarella cheese
- ½ cup almond flour
- Pinch of salt, optional
- 1 ounce cream cheese

SPICED BEEF
- 1 lb ground beef
- ¼ cup white onion, diced
- ¼ cup pickled jalapenos
- 1 teaspoon ground ginger
- 1 teaspoon cumin
- ¼ teaspoon ground cloves
- ⅓ cup water
- 1 tablespoon cilantro, chopped

TZATZIKI SAUCE
- ½ cup sour cream
- ¼ tsp cumin
- 1 tsp dried dill
- 1 tsp lemon juice
- salt & pepper,
- ½ English (seedless) cucumber; sliced and quartered

Instructions
FLATBREAD
1. Preheat oven to 350 degrees. Line large baking sheet with parchment and set aside.
2. In large bowl, place mozzarella and almond flour. Break cream cheese into small pieces and place into bowl. Microwave bowl for 1 minute, or until all ingredients are melted and easily mixed.
3. Using spoon or rubber spatula, mix ingredients until ball forms. Wet hands with a bit of water and pick up dough ball. Form it until smooth and all ingredients are fully combined.
4. Use a knife to cut dough ball into 4 even sections.
5. Re-wetting hands when necessary (prevents sticking) press each dough ball out into flat circle, about 5-6 inches in diameter. You may do this in hands or on baking sheet, whichever is easier.
6. Bake for 12-14 minutes or until flatbread begins to turn golden brown. They may puff up a bit, that's ok.
7. Keep warm for serving. (Stacking and covering with a towel will work)
8. If your dough is too stiff or will not spread, it may be too cold. Place it back in the microwave for 5-10 seconds and it should be easier to spread.

SPICED BEEF
1. Brown ground beef in skillet over medium heat. When no pink remains, drain grease.
2. Add onion, jalapenos, ginger, cumin, cloves and water. Bring to quick boil then simmer for about 10 minutes until most of water has evaporated from pan and onions are soft. Turn off heat and add cilantro.

TZATZIKI SAUCE
1. In large bowl, place sour cream, cumin, dill, lemon juice, salt, and pepper. Whisk together until smooth.
2. Add cucumber to bowl and fold in until fully covered with sauce.

TO SERVE
1. Place ¼ of beef mixture on flatbread and top with ¼ of sauce mixture. Fold and garnish with additional jalapeno and cilantro,if desired.
2. I didn't weigh this recipe for nutritional purposes. If you need more accurate serving information, place beef and sauce separately on food scale to get weight in grams. Divide weight by 4 and that will give you the grams per serving.

KETO MEAL PREP BREAKFAST BOMBS
Nutrition: Cal 333;Fat 26 g;Carb 7 g;Protein 17 g
Serving 4; Cook time 30 min

Ingredients
- 2 Cups Blanched Finely Ground Almond Flour
- 2 Teaspoons Baking Powder
- ¼ Teaspoon Baking Soda
- 4 Tablespoons Cold Butter, Cubed
- ⅓ Cup Sour Cream
- 1 Large Egg
- ½ Teaspoon Apple Cider Vinegar
- Pinch of Salt
- 6 Ounces of Cooked Breakfast Sausage, crumbled
- 6 Large Eggs, Scrambled
- 4 Slices Cooked Bacon, Crumbled
- ½ Cup Shredded Cheddar Cheese
- Sugar-Free Syrup (Optional)

Instructions
1. Preheat the oven to 350 degrees.
2. Place the almond flour, baking powder and baking soda in a food processor and pulse a few times to combine.
3. Add in the butter and process on low for 20 seconds or until large crumbles form.
4. Continue processing on low and add in the sour cream, egg and apple cider vinegar. Sprinkle in a bit of salt, to taste.
5. Turn off the food processor and let the mixture sit for 5 minutes.
6. In a large bowl, toss the sausage, eggs, bacon and cheese. Scoop the biscuit mixture into the large bowl and gently toss to combine with the other ingredients. Using your hands might be helpful.
7. Spray a muffin tin with non-stick spray then scoop about ¼ cup of the mixture into each section.
8. Bake for 12-15 minutes or until golden brown around the edges. Let cool for at least 15 minutes before serving.
9. Store in an airtight container in the fridge for up to 4 days for best taste. To reheat, microwave for 20-30 seconds.

KETO CAULIFLOWER BUNS
Nutrition: Cal 150 Fat 10 g;Carb 6 g;Protein 10 g
Serving 8; Cook time 30 min

Ingredients
- 12 Ounces Cauliflower
- ½ Cup Mozzarella Cheese, shredded
- ¼ cup Cheddar Cheese, shredded
- ¼ cup Almond Flour
- 1 Egg

Instructions
1. Preheat oven to 400°F.
2. Cook Cauliflower using your preferred method. Allow to cool, and wring out excess moisture using a cheesecloth or kitchen towel.

3. Combine all ingredients in a food processor. Pulse until well combined, about 30-45 seconds. Be sure to scrape sides down so that the entire mixture is combined.
4. Scoop mixture onto parchment lined baking sheet in ¼ cup measurements. Shape and flatten out buns.
5. Bake for 12-15 minutes, or until tops of buns begin to lightly brown.
6. Remove from oven and allow buns to cool before using them.

KETO THREE CHEESE CAULIFLOWER MAC AND CHEESE CUPS

Nutrition: Cal 391 Fat 29 g;Carb 7 g;Protein 24 g
Serving 4; Cook time 35 min

Ingredients
- 1 medium head fresh cauliflower
- 2 tablespoons salted butter
- 2 tablespoons diced onion
- 2 cloves garlic, minced
- 2 ounces cream cheese, softened
- ¼ cup heavy whipping cream
- ½ teaspoon Italian seasoning of choice
- Salt and Pepper, to taste
- ¼ teaspoon xanthan gum
- 1 cup spinach, sliced into strips
- ¾ cup white cheddar, shredded
- ¼ cup mozzarella, shredded
- 12 slices prosciutto
- 6 tablespoons Parmesan cheese, shredded

Instructions
1. Preheat oven to 400 degrees.
2. Add a couple cups of water to a large pot, place steamer basket into pot above water, and bring to boil. While the water is heating, prepare cauliflower.
3. Remove core and leaves from cauliflower. Chop into bite-size pieces. When water is boiling, carefully add cauliflower to steamer basket. Cover and let steam for 5-7 minutes or until fork tender.
4. Prepare sauce while cauliflower is steaming. When finished, turn off heat and set aside until ready to add to sauce.

SAUCE
1. In skillet over medium-low heat melt butter. Add onion and cook for 2-4 minutes until onion is tender and becoming translucent.
2. Add garlic and softened cream cheese. Softened cream cheese will be easier to smooth into sauce. Using wooden spoon or rubber spatula, press cream cheese flat into pan to help smooth as it warms and gently stir.
3. Pour in heavy whipping cream, seasoning, and xanthan gum. Stir ingredients until smooth, raising temperature slightly if needed to get sauce fully mixed.
4. Add spinach, white cheddar, mozzarella to sauce and turn off heat. Continue stirring for a few minutes, until spinach begins to wilt and cheeses are fully melted and smooth.

5. Add steamed cauliflower to pan and fold into cheese sauce. I did not remove any moisture from mine. (See notes section)
6. Using large muffin tin (1 cup capacity) place two slices of prosciutto in X to cover the bottom of the tin and stretch up around the sides as much as possible. It may rip a little, that's ok. Just be sure the bottom is covered.
7. Place ½ cup of cheesy cauliflower mixture into prosciutto cups and top with 1 tablespoon of Parmesan.
8. Bake for 15-20 minutes or until bubbly and brown. Serve warm.

KETO YOGURT - INSTANT POT

Nutrition: Cal 155;Fat 8 g;Carb 6 g;Protein 13 g
Serving 6; Cook time 17 hours 5 min

Ingredients
- 6 cups ultra-filtered, ultra pasteurized milk
- 2 tablespoons fresh yogurt

Instructions
1. Pour milk into the inner pot of your Instant Pot. Whisk in the starter until it's fully combined. It will get bubbly from all the whisking, but will settle while it cooks. This is normal.
2. Place a clear tempered glass lid on the Instant pot. Press the yogurt button and adjust the timer to 9 hours.
3. When the Instant Pot beeps and the display reads 9:00, remove the inner pot and place it on a heat safe counter spot. Remove the lid. The yogurt should look smooth on top and cleanly pull from the sides if you tip the pot.
4. Place plastic wrap or press and seal on top of the pot and place into the fridge for at least 8 hours until it's fully chilled.
5. Scoop your serving into a bowl and mix in your favorite liquid sweetener, to taste. Top with any additional garnish of your choosing.

KETO YOGURT PARFAIT

Nutrition: Cal 335;Fat 29 g;Carb 10 g;Protein 11 g
Serving 2; Cook time 10 min

Ingredients
- ½ cup Greek Yogurt full fat
- ¼ cup Heavy Cream
- 1 teaspoon Vanilla Essence
- ½ cup Keto Chocolate Almond Clusters
- 2 Strawberries diced
- 8 Blueberries

Instructions
1. In a mixing bowl, add together the yogurt, cream and vanilla. Whisk together until thick and smooth.
2. Spoon half the yogurt between two glasses, then sprinkle over half the granola.
3. Add the remaining yogurt, followed by the remaining granola.
4. Top with the Berries and enjoy!

EGGS IN A FRAME

Nutrition: Cal 128;Fat 10 g;Carb 3 g;Protein 6 g
Serving 4; Cook time 10 min

Ingredients

- 1 wide eggplant, cut into round or square bread-like shapes
- 4 eggs
- Coconut oil or ghee
- Celtic sea salt and pepper

Instructions

1. To make this unique breakfast dish, begin by peeling and slicing the eggplant into bread-shaped pieces. Next, create a hole in the center of each eggplant slice to hold the egg.
2. Heat a skillet with oil over medium heat and place the eggplant slices in the pan to fry. Cook each side for approximately 2 minutes or until the eggplant is soft.
3. After that, crack an egg into each of the eggplant holes and continue frying until the egg is cooked to your preference.
4. Serve and enjoy your delicious eggplant and egg creation!

EASY BREAKFAST BACON PIE

Nutrition: Cal 336;Fat 26 g;Carb 2 g;Protein 24 g
Serving 4; Cook time 38 min

Ingredients

- ¾ cup shredded sharp cheddar, divided
- 8 eggs
- 3 teaspoons dried chives
- 1 teaspoon fine grain sea salt
- 6 slices thin-cut sugar free bacon

Instructions

1. Preheat oven to 400 degrees F. Place ½ cup shredded cheese evenly the bottom of a 9 inch pie pan. Place in oven for 3 minutes or until melted. Meanwhile place the other ¼ cup in a medium bowl. Add eggs, chives and salt. Stir well to combine. Pour over melted cheese. Place bacon slices in a weave pattern over the egg mixture. Place in oven to bake for 30 minutes or until eggs are set and bacon is crisp. Store extras in airtight container in the fridge for up to 5 days.

REUBEN CHAFFLES

Nutrition: Cal 559;Fat 44 g;Carb 3 g;Protein 48 g
Serving 1; Cook time 10 min

Ingredients

- ½ cup ground pork rinds or shredded mozzarella/swiss cheese
- 1 egg
- Primal Kitchen Avocado Oil spray, for greasing chaffle maker
- Sandwich Fixings:
- 1 ounce Slices of Corned Beef
- 1 slice Swiss Cheese (omit if dairy free)
- 2 tablespoons Sauerkraut
- 2 tablespoons Primal Kitchen Thousand Island Dressing

Instructions

1. Preheat a mini chaffle maker
2. Place the pork rinds (or cheese) and egg into a small bowl and use a fork to combine well.
3. Grease the chaffle maker with Primal Kitchen Avocado Oil Spray and place ½ of the mixture into the chaffle maker and press the maker down. Cook the chaffle for 2 to 3 minutes or until golden brown and cooked through.
4. Remove from chaffle maker and repeat with remaining batter.
5. Meanwhile, prepare the Reuben fixings.
6. Once the chaffles are done, place a few slices of corned beef onto a chaffle, top with a slice of cheese if using and sauerkraut. Drizzle on Primal Kitchen Thousand Island dressing and top with another chaffle.
7. Best served fresh.

BIG MAC BREAKFAST PIE

Nutrition: Cal 387;Fat 33 g;Carb 3 g;Protein 20 g
Serving 8; Cook time 41 min

Ingredients

- 1 pound ground beef
- ½ cup chopped onions
- 1 clove garlic, minced
- 2 teaspoons Redmond Real salt, divided (use code Maria15 for 15% off
- ¼ cup Primal Kitchen Ketchup (or tomato sauce)
- 8 large eggs, beaten
- ¾ cup shredded cheddar cheese (about 3 ounces)
- 2 tablespoons Primal Kitchen mayo
- 2 teaspoons yellow mustard
- ¼ teaspoon black pepper
- Garnish:
- 2 tablespoons Toasted sesame seeds, for garnish
- 12 slices dill pickles, for garnish
- 6 Cherry tomatoes, halved

SPECIAL SAUCE:

- ½ cup Primal Kitchen mayonnaise
- ¼ cup chopped dill pickles
- 3 tablespoons Primal Kitchen Ketchup
- 2 tablespoons Swerve (or ½ teaspoon stevia glycerite or a few drops liquid stevia)
- ⅛ teaspoon fine sea salt
- ⅛ teaspoon fish sauce (optional, for umami flavor)

Instructions

1. To make this dish, preheat the oven to 350°F. In a large oven-safe skillet over medium heat, add ground beef, onions, and garlic and season with 1½ teaspoon salt. Cook while crumbling with a wooden spoon until the beef is cooked all the way through and the onions are translucent, about 7 minutes. Add the tomato sauce and stir well to combine.

2. In a large bowl, mix together the eggs, cheese, mayo, mustard, ½ teaspoon salt, and pepper. Add the beef mixture to the egg mixture and stir to combine. Pour the mixture into a greased casserole dish. Spray it with Primal Kitchen Avocado Oil Spray.
3. Place the dish in the oven and bake for 25 minutes, or until the eggs are cooked through in the center. Remove from the oven and let rest for 10 minutes, then slice and serve. If desired, garnish with fresh sesame seeds and pickles and serve with secret sauce.
4. Store leftovers in an airtight container in the fridge for up to 3 days. Reheat in a 350°F oven for 3 minutes or in the microwave for 30 seconds, or until heated through.

CREAM OF WHEAT CEREAL
Nutrition: Cal 172;Fat 5 g;Carb 17 g;Protein 15 g
Serving 2; Cook time 10 min

Ingredients
- ¾ cup of warm unsweetened vanilla or chocolate almond milk (or coconut milk)
- 1-2 tsp psyllium husk
- 1 scoop vanilla or chocolate (egg white or whey) protein powder
- 1 TBS vanilla extract
- 1 drop of stevia glycerite
- ½ tsp of nutmeg
- ½ tsp cinnamon
- Optional: you can add some coconut flakes, nuts or peanut butter to this recipe.

Instructions
1. Combine warm milk, whey, stevia, cinnamon and nutmeg (and other toppings) in a bowl.
2. Stir well and let sit for a few minutes until the "oatmeal" thickens.

KETO HOT POCKET
Nutrition: Cal 283;Fat 12 g;Carb 1 g;Protein 14 g
Serving 6; Cook time 10 min

Ingredients
- 3 eggs, separated
- 2 TBS unflavored egg white
- 3 ounces cream cheese, warmed (or reserved yolks if dairy free)
- 1/2 tsp onion powder (optional)

FILLING:
- 6 egg, scrambled
- 6 slices bacon, cooked (or ham)
- 6 (1 ounce) slices cheddar cheese

Instructions
1. Begin by separating the eggs and whipping the egg whites until they are extremely stiff. Gradually fold in the whey protein, as well as onion powder if desired.

2. Carefully fold the cream cheese into the egg whites, being careful not to deflate them. Thoroughly grease a cookie sheet and spoon the mixture onto the sheet in six large mounds.
3. Add scrambled egg, cheese, and chopped ham or bacon on top of each mound, then cover them with additional egg white batter and smooth it with a spatula. Bake at 375 degrees Fahrenheit for 25 minutes until the mixture is lightly browned.
4. Once finished, savor the delicious flavors of your fluffy and protein-packed breakfast creation.

KETO BREAKFAST CHILI
Nutrition: Cal 634;Fat 38 g;Carb 15 g;Protein 16 g
Serving 8; Cook time 2 hours 20 min

Ingredients
- 2 pounds ground grass fed beef
- 1 pound ground chorizo or Italian sausage
- 4 cups tomato sauce (preferably homemade organic or from a glass jar)
- ½ yellow onion, chopped
- 3 stalks celery, chopped
- 1 green bell pepper, seeded and chopped
- 1 red bell pepper, seeded and chopped
- 2 green chile peppers, seeded and chopped
- 2 slices bacon
- 1 cup organic beef broth (homemade broth is best: I always store extra in my freezer)
- ¼ cup chili powder
- 1 TBS minced garlic
- 3 TBS fresh oregano
- 2 tsp ground cumin
- 3 TBS fresh basil
- 1 tsp Celtic sea salt
- 1 tsp ground black pepper
- 1 tsp cayenne pepper
- 1 tsp paprika

TOPPINGS:
- Fried Eggs
- Avocado, cubed into 1 cm chunks
- Bacon, fried and crumbled
- If desired, serve in a bread bowl:

BREAD BOWL:
- 3 eggs, separated
- ½ tsp cream of tartar
- ¼ cup unflavored egg white or whey protein
- 3 oz organic sour cream or cream cheese (or yolks if dairy sensitive)

Instructions

1. To prepare this hearty and flavorful chili, heat a large stock pot over medium-high heat. Crumble the ground chuck, bacon, and sausage into the hot pan and cook until evenly browned. Remove excess grease and pour in the tomato sauce. Add onion, celery, green and red bell peppers, chili peppers, and broth. Season with chili powder, garlic, oregano, cumin, basil, salt, pepper, cayenne, and paprika. Stir the mixture to blend and simmer it over low heat for at least 2 hours, stirring occasionally. For even richer flavors, you can simmer it for a longer time. Adjust salt, pepper, and chili powder if necessary, then remove from heat and serve or refrigerate for later. Top the chili with a fried egg, avocado, and bacon pieces to enhance the taste and nutrition.

2. To make the bread bowl, preheat the oven to 350 degrees Fahrenheit. Separate the eggs, keeping the yolks reserved. Whip the egg whites and cream of tartar in a clean, dry bowl until stiff peaks form. Then, mix in the protein powder until the mixture is smooth. Carefully fold in the cream cheese and sour cream, or yolks if sensitive to dairy, using a spatula to prevent the whites from breaking down. Grease muffin tins and spoon the mixture into the pan, creating 12 medium bowls or 24 mini bowls with a dip in the center. Bake at 350 degrees for 12-15 minutes. You may need to push down the center once they come out of the oven to create space for the chili filling.

TEX MEX DUTCH BABY

Nutrition: Cal 283; Fat 12 g; Carb 1 g; Protein 14 g
Serving 2; Cook time 25 min

Ingredients
- 3 large eggs
- ½ cup chicken broth (or vegetarian broth)
- ¼ cup salsa, plus more for serving
- 1/4 cup Keto Chow egg white powder
- 2 teaspoons taco seasoning
- 1 teaspoon baking powder
- 1 teaspoon Redmond Real garlic salt (or plain salt)
- 1 tablespoon avocado oil (or bacon fat or duck fat)

Instructions
1. To make a delicious Dutch Baby pancake, you will need an 8 inch cast iron skillet and an oven preheated to 425 degrees F (400 degrees F for convection ovens). It is important to ensure that the skillet preheats and gets very hot to ensure that the Dutch Baby will puff up.
2. Next, combine the eggs, broth, salsa, Keto Chow protein powder, taco seasoning, baking powder, and salt in a blender. Blend the mixture for about a minute or until it becomes foamy.
3. Using an oven mitt, remove the hot skillet from the oven and add the avocado oil to the skillet. Swirl the skillet to coat the inside of the skillet. Then, pour the batter into the skillet and bake for about 18-20 minutes, or until the pancake is puffed and golden brown.

4. Once the Dutch Baby pancake is cooked, remove it from the oven and spread additional salsa onto it. Cut it into wedges and enjoy your delicious and flavorful pancake.

KETO FRENCH TOAST

Nutrition: Cal 125; Fat 10 g; Carb 1 g; Protein 7 g
Serving 18; Cook time 55 min

Ingredients
PROTEIN BREAD:
- 12 eggs, separated
- 1 cup unflavored egg white
- 4 oz cream cheese, softened (OR reserved yolks)

FRENCH TOAST:
- 2 eggs
- ½ cup unsweetened almond milk (or coconut milk)
- 1 tsp vanilla
- 1 tsp cinnamon

SYRUP:
- ½ cup butter (or coconut oil)
- ½ cup Swerve Confectioners
- ½ cup unsweetened almond milk

Instructions
TO MAKE BREAD:
1. Preheat the oven to 325 degrees F.
2. Separate the eggs (save the yolks), and whip the whites for a few minutes until VERY stiff (I use a stand mixer on high for over 8 minutes).
3. Gently mix the protein powder into the whites. Then slowly fold the softened cream cheese (or reserved egg yolks) into the whites (making sure the whites don't fall).
4. Grease two bread pans with coconut oil spray and place the "dough" in the pans.
5. Bake for 40-45 minutes or until golden brown.
6. Let completely cool before cutting or the bread will fall.
7. Cut into 18 slices.
8. Keep the bread in the freezer at all times to make sandwiches.

TO MAKE FRENCH TOAST:
9. Grease a cast iron skillet with coconut oil and heat to medium high.
10. In a medium bowl, combine 2 eggs, unsweetened almond milk, vanilla and cinnamon.
11. Dip the slices of protein bread into the egg mixture.
12. Place the drenched protein bread onto the hot skillet.
13. Grill until golden brown on both sides.
14. Remove from skillet and repeat with remaining bread.

TO MAKE SYRUP:
15. Meanwhile, make the sauce by placing the butter in a saucepan over high heat.
16. Using Swerve: Before you begin, make sure you have everything ready to go - the almond milk and the butter next to the pan, ready to put in. Work fast or the sweetener will burn. Heat butter on high heat in a heavy-bottomed 2-quart (2 L) or 3-quart (3 L) saucepan.

17. As soon as it comes to a boil, watch for specks of brown (this is brown butter....so good on veggies!). Immediately add the Swerve and the almond milk to the pan.
18. Whisk until the sauce is smooth.
19. Let cool in the pan for a couple of minutes, and then pour into a glass mason jar and let sit to cool to room temperature.
20. Store in the refrigerator for up to 2 weeks.
21. Place the French Toast on a plate and top with syrup. Enjoy!

"TAPIOCA" PUDDING

Nutrition: Cal 185;Fat 19 g;Carb 1 g;Protein 4 g
Serving 4; Cook time 12 min

Ingredients
- 6 large egg yolks
- ½ cup unsweetened almond milk
- ¼ cup Swerve (or erythritol and ¼ tsp stevia glycerite)
- ¼ cup coconut oil, melted (or butter if not dairy sensitive)
- 1 tsp vanilla (or other extract like cherry!)
- 1 package Miracle Rice
- Cinnamon to taste

OPTIONAL: add 2 TBS cocoa powder for chocolate tapioca!

Instructions
1. To make this recipe, start by whisking egg yolks, almond milk, natural sweetener and extract (and cocoa powder if using) in a medium metal bowl until well blended. Slowly mix in the melted butter to ensure the eggs are cooked evenly.
2. Next, set the bowl over a saucepan of simmering water and whisk the mixture constantly and vigorously until thickened. This should take about 5 minutes total and an instant-read thermometer inserted into the mixture should register 140°F for 3 minutes. You can also tell it's ready when the mixture coats the back of a spoon.
3. Once the mixture has thickened, remove it from over the water and stir in the Miracle Rice. Add cinnamon to taste. The rice adds a nice texture and heartiness to the custard.
4. This custard can be served warm or chilled, and if you plan to serve it chilled, it can be prepared 1-3 days ahead and refrigerated. Just be sure to re-whisk it before serving to ensure a smooth consistency. Enjoy!

GREEN EGGS AND HAM: AVOCADO HOLLANDAISE

Nutrition: Cal 351;Fat 28 g;Carb 4 g;Protein 21 g
Serving 4; Cook time 10 min

Ingredients
- 1 ripe medium avocado, peeled and chopped
- 2 egg yolks
- 1 TBS fresh lime or lemon juice
- 2 TBS MCT oil, heated (or bacon fat, heated)
- ½ tsp Celtic sea salt
- ¼ tsp cayenne pepper (if desired)
- 8 poached eggs
- 8 thin slices of ham or Canadian bacon
- 4 Protein Buns

Instructions
1. To make Avocado Hollandaise, start by placing the avocado, yolks and lime juice in a blender and puree until smooth and fluffy. This should take around 2 minutes.
2. While the blender is running, slowly drizzle in the very hot oil and continue to puree until everything is well combined.
3. Once everything is blended, season with salt. If you like a little heat, you can also add cayenne pepper.
4. To serve, spoon the hollandaise over poached eggs, ham, and a toasted Protein bun. Enjoy your delicious and healthy Green Eggs and Ham!

DUTCH BABY

Nutrition: Cal 251;Fat 20 g;Carb 2 g;Protein 16 g
Serving 2; Cook time 25 min

Ingredients
- 3 large eggs
- ¾ cup unsweetened cashew/almond milk (hemp milk if nut free)
- ¼ cup unflavored egg white protein powder
- 1 tsp baking powder
- 1 tsp Redmond Real salt
- 2 TBS coconut oil (or butter if not dairy sensitive)
- 2 tablespoons chopped dill (or other herbs)
- 8 sprigs asparagus
- Parmesan cheese (Nutritional Yeast if dairy free)

Instructions
1. To make a delicious and healthy pancake, you will need an 8 inch cast iron skillet and an oven preheated to 425 degrees F (400 degrees F in convection ovens). The first step is to ensure the skillet preheats and gets very hot.
2. In a blender, combine the eggs, almond milk, protein powder, baking powder, and salt. Blend for about 1 minute or until foamy.
3. Using an oven mitt, remove the skillet from the oven and place the coconut oil into the skillet. Swirl the skillet to coat the inside of the skillet. Next, pour the batter into the skillet. Arrange asparagus on top of the batter (they may fall into the batter which is fine). Sprinkle with Parmesan or Nutritional Yeast.
4. Bake for about 18-20 minutes or until the pancake is puffed and golden brown. When it's done, remove the pancake from the oven, spread additional butter or coconut oil on the pancake, cut it into wedges, and enjoy!

CARNIVORE QUICHE

Nutrition: Cal 421;Fat 30 g;Carb 2 g;Protein 34 g
Serving 8; Cook time 65 min

Ingredients

CRUST:
- 1 ¼ cups powdered pork rinds
- 1 ¼ cups freshly grated Parmesan (or hard Gouda) cheese
- 1 egg, beaten

FILLING:
- ½ cup chicken or beef bone broth
- 1 cup grated Swiss cheese (or Muenster cheese)
- 4 oz cream cheese
- 1 tablespoon butter, melted
- ½ cup diced ham
- 4 eggs, beaten
- ½ tsp Redmond Real salt

Instructions

1. To prepare a pork rind crust quiche, preheat the oven to 325 degrees F. Start by making the tart shell, combine the pork rinds and cheese in a bowl and mix well. Add an egg and mix until the dough is stiff and well combined. Add more powdered pork rinds if necessary. Press the pie crust into a 9-inch pie dish and cook it for 12 minutes or until it begins to lightly brown.
2. To make the filling, take a medium-sized bowl and combine broth, Swiss cheese, butter, and cream cheese. Stir well to combine. Add in the ham, eggs, and salt. Pour the mixture into the pre-baked crust.
3. Bake the quiche in the oven or air fryer for 15 minutes. Then, reduce the heat to 300 degrees F (150 degrees C) and bake for an additional 30 minutes, or until a knife inserted 1 inch from the edge comes out clean. You may have to cover the edges with foil to prevent over-browning.
4. Once the quiche is done, allow it to sit for 10 minutes before cutting into wedges. This will allow the quiche to set properly and make it easier to cut. Serve and enjoy your delicious pork rind crust quiche!

HUEVOS RANCHEROS WITH A PROTEIN-SPARING TWIST

Nutrition: Cal 436;Fat 24 g;Carb 8 g;Protein 45 g
Serving 2; Cook time 20 min

Ingredients

TORTILLAS:
- 1 tablespoon Coconut oil/ghee/butter (for frying)
- 3 egg, separated
- 2 TBS unflavored egg white protein
- 1 tsp onion powder
- Optional: 1 tsp Mexican spices

TOPPING:
- ½ cup 85% lean ground beef (OR my Chili Recipe), browned
- 4 Fried Eggs
- ½ sliced Avocado
- ½ cup Salsa
- 1 whole Green Onions, sliced

Instructions

1. Whisk the egg whites in a bowl with an electric hand mixer or stand mixer until they form stiff peaks. Ensure that no egg yolks are included in the mixture, as this may affect the outcome of the recipe.
2. Gradually add the unflavored protein powder and seasonings to the whipped egg whites, mixing slowly until everything is well combined.
3. Next, heat up a small skillet over medium-high heat with oil.
4. Take the tortilla dough and fry it one at a time in the skillet, cooking it until it's firm, but not crispy. Once cooked, remove the tortilla onto paper towels to eliminate excess oil.
5. As the tortillas fry, prepare the beef and any other desired toppings.
6. Once the tortillas are done, proceed to cook eggs over easy in the same skillet.
7. To assemble the dish, place the tortillas onto plates and top them with a layer of meat.
8. Add your preferred toppings, such as chili, crumbled bacon, avocado, fried egg, and salsa, to complete the dish.

PROTEIN SPARING PANCAKES

Nutrition: Cal 62;Fat 0 g;Carb 1 g;Protein 12 g
Serving 2; Cook time 7 min

Ingredients

- 3 egg whites
- 1 tablespoon Further Food gelatin
- ¼ teaspoon Redmond Real Salt
- 2 tablespoons Further Food vanilla collagen
- 1 teaspoon vanilla extract (or other extract: almond, coconut, maple)
- Avocado Oil Spray

GARNISH:
- Cinnamon and Swerve confectioners, if desired

Instructions

1. To make the Protein Sparing pancakes, separate the eggs (save the yolks for a different recipe). Place the whites in a clean, dry, cool bowl. Add the gelatin and salt and whip on high for a few minutes until VERY stiff.
2. Gently fold in the Further Food collagen, and extract.
3. Heat a non-stick pan (I used THIS Scan Pan)to medium high heat. Spray with avocado oil spray and place a circle of dough on the pan. Fry until golden brown, about 1 minute. Flip and cook another minute or until golden. Remove from heat and place on a plate.
4. Sprinkle the protein sparing pancakes with cinnamon and Swerve confectioners or keto pancake syrup if desired. Enjoy! .

POULTRY

CHICKEN EGG SALAD WRAPS

Nutrition: Cal 545;Fat 38 g;Carb 16 g;Protein 33 g
Serving 3; Cook time 10 min

Ingredients
- 2 romaine lettuce heads, chopped
- 2 cups chopped Baked Boneless Chicken Thighs
- 1 cup grape tomatoes
- 2 cucumbers, diced
- ½ cup chopped red onion
- 4 slices Perfectly Cooked Bacon , chopped
- ½ cup crumbled blue cheese
- 4 Hard-boiled Eggs , sliced
- ½ cup Dairy-Free Ranch Dressing

Instructions
1. Evenly divide the lettuce between 4 storage containers.
2. Evenly distribute and arrange the chicken, tomatoes, cucumbers, onion, bacon, blue cheese, and eggs over the lettuce.
3. Divide the dressing into 2-tablespoon servings and store on the side.

KETO DUCK, DAIKON, AND AVOCADO SALAD

Nutrition: Cal 604;Fat 46 g;Carb 8 g;Protein 38 g
Serving 2; Cook time 20 min

Ingredients
- 2 duck breasts
- 1 medium daikon, peeled and julienned
- 1 ripe avocado, sliced
- 2 tbsp chopped fresh cilantro
- 2 tbsp olive oil
- 2 tbsp apple cider vinegar
- 1 tsp dijon mustard
- Salt and black pepper, to taste

Instructions
1. Preheat the oven to 400°F (200°C).
2. Score the skin of the duck breasts in a criss-cross pattern with a sharp knife. Season both sides with salt and black pepper to taste.
3. Heat a large oven-safe skillet over medium-high heat. When the pan is hot, add the duck breasts skin side down and cook for 5-6 minutes or until the skin is crispy and golden brown.
4. Transfer the skillet to the preheated oven and bake for an additional 6-8 minutes or until the duck breasts reach an internal temperature of 135°F (57°C) for medium-rare or 145°F (63°C) for medium. Remove the skillet from the oven and let the duck breasts rest for 5 minutes before slicing.
5. In a mixing bowl, whisk together the olive oil, apple cider vinegar, dijon mustard, salt, and black pepper to make the salad dressing.
6. Add the julienned daikon, sliced avocado, and chopped cilantro to the mixing bowl and toss to combine with the salad dressing.
7. Divide the salad between two plates and top each salad with the sliced duck breasts.
8. Serve immediately.

CHICKEN HEARTS AND LIVER IN A CREAMY TOMATO SAUCE

Nutrition: Cal 369;Fat 27 g;Carb 8 g;Protein 26 g
Serving 4; Cook time 35 min

Ingredients
- 1 lb chicken hearts, cleaned and halved
- 1/2 lb chicken liver, cleaned and diced
- 2 tbsp olive oil
- 1/2 cup diced onion
- 1 cup canned crushed tomatoes
- 1/2 cup chicken broth
- 1/2 cup heavy cream
- 1/4 cup grated parmesan cheese
- 2 cloves garlic, minced
- 1 tsp dried oregano
- Salt and pepper to taste
- Fresh basil leaves, chopped (optional)

Instructions
1. Heat the olive oil in a large skillet over medium-high heat.
2. Add the chicken hearts and chicken liver to the skillet and cook for 8-10 minutes, stirring occasionally, until they are cooked through and slightly browned on the outside.
3. Remove the chicken hearts and liver from the skillet and set them aside.
4. In the same skillet, add the onion and garlic and sauté until the onion is translucent, about 5 minutes.
5. Add the crushed tomatoes, chicken broth, heavy cream, parmesan cheese, oregano, salt, and pepper to the skillet. Stir to combine.
6. Bring the sauce to a simmer and cook for 5-7 minutes or until it has thickened slightly.
7. Return the chicken hearts and liver to the skillet and stir to coat them with the sauce.
8. Cook for an additional 2-3 minutes or until the chicken hearts and liver are heated through and the sauce is thick and creamy.
9. Serve garnished with fresh basil leaves, if desired.

CHICKEN HEARTS IN A CREAMY SAUCE

Nutrition: Cal 289;Fat 21 g;Carb 2 g;Protein 22 g
Serving 4; Cook time 25 min

Ingredients
- 1 lb chicken hearts, cleaned
- 1 tbsp olive oil
- 1/2 cup chicken broth
- 1/2 cup heavy cream
- 2 tbsp grated parmesan cheese
- 1 tbsp chopped fresh parsley
- 1/2 tsp garlic powder

•Salt and pepper to taste

Instructions

1. Heat the olive oil in a large skillet over medium-high heat.
2. Add the chicken hearts to the skillet and cook for 8-10 minutes, stirring occasionally, until they are cooked through and slightly browned on the outside.
3. Remove the chicken hearts from the skillet and set them aside.
4. In the same skillet, add the chicken broth, heavy cream, parmesan cheese, garlic powder, salt, and pepper. Stir to combine.
5. Bring the sauce to a simmer and cook for 5-7 minutes or until it has thickened slightly.
6. Return the chicken hearts to the skillet and stir to coat them with the sauce.
7. Cook for an additional 2-3 minutes or until the chicken hearts are heated through and the sauce is thick and creamy.
8. Garnish with chopped parsley and serve.

KETO CHICKEN HEARTS

Nutrition: Cal 227;Fat 13 g;Carb 2 g;Protein 25 g
Serving 2; Cook time 25 min

Ingredients

•1 lb chicken hearts, cleaned
•1 tbsp olive oil
•1/2 tsp salt
•1/4 tsp black pepper
•1/2 tsp smoked paprika
•1/2 tsp garlic powder
•1/4 tsp cumin

Instructions

1. Preheat the oven to 400°F (200°C).
2. In a bowl, mix together the olive oil, salt, black pepper, smoked paprika, garlic powder, and cumin.
3. Add the chicken hearts to the bowl and toss to coat them with the spice mixture.
4. Arrange the chicken hearts on a baking sheet lined with parchment paper.
5. Bake for 10-12 minutes or until the chicken hearts are cooked through and slightly crispy on the outside.
6. Remove from the oven and let them cool for a few minutes before serving.

KETO THIGH PULPS WITH MUSTARD

Nutrition: Cal 486;Fat 36 g;Carb 2 g;Protein 34 g
Serving 2; Cook time 45 min

Ingredients

•4 chicken thigh pulps, bone-in and skin-on
•2 tbsp Dijon mustard
•2 tbsp mayonnaise
•1/2 cup shredded cheddar cheese
•2 garlic cloves, minced
•Salt and pepper to taste

Instructions

1. Preheat your oven to 375°F.
2. In a small bowl, mix together the Dijon mustard, mayonnaise, minced garlic, salt, and pepper.
3. Season the chicken thigh pulps with salt and pepper on both sides.
4. Place the chicken thigh pulps in a large baking dish.
5. Spread the mustard and mayonnaise mixture over the chicken thigh pulps, covering them completely.
6. Sprinkle the shredded cheddar cheese over the chicken thigh pulps.
7. Bake in the preheated oven for 35-40 minutes, or until the chicken is cooked through and the cheese is golden brown and bubbly.

KETO CHICKEN LIVER PATE

Nutrition: Cal 285;Fat 23 g;Carb 3 g;Protein 14 g
Serving 2; Cook time 25 min

Ingredients

•1/2 lb chicken livers
•1/4 cup chopped onion
•2 cloves garlic, minced
•2 tbsp butter
•2 tbsp heavy cream
•Salt and pepper to taste
•Fresh herbs (optional for garnish)

Instructions

1. Rinse the chicken livers and pat them dry with paper towels.
2. In a frying pan, melt the butter over medium heat. Add the chopped onion and garlic and sauté for 2-3 minutes until softened.
3. Add the chicken livers to the pan and cook for 5-7 minutes until cooked through.
4. Remove the pan from the heat and let it cool for a few minutes.
5. Place the chicken liver mixture into a blender or food processor and blend until smooth.
6. Add the heavy cream and blend again until well combined.
7. Season with salt and pepper to taste.
8. Place the pate in a serving dish and garnish with fresh herbs if desired.
9. Refrigerate for at least 1 hour before serving.

CHICKEN FILLET STUFFED WITH CHICKEN LIVER PATE

Nutrition: Cal 442;Fat 26 g;Carb 1,5 g;Protein 40 g
Serving 2; Cook time 40 min

Ingredients

•2 chicken fillets
•2 oz chicken liver pate(see recipe above)
•2 oz Philadelphia cheese
•1 tsp dried thyme
•1 tsp garlic powder
•1 tsp onion powder
•Salt and black pepper, to taste

•1 tbsp olive oil
Instructions
1. Preheat the oven to 375°F.
2. Butterfly the chicken fillets by slicing them horizontally almost all the way through and opening them like a book.
3. In a small bowl, mix the chicken liver pate, Philadelphia cheese, thyme, garlic powder, onion powder, salt, and pepper until well combined.
4. Spoon the pate mixture onto the inside of each chicken fillet and spread it evenly.
5. Close the chicken fillets and secure them with toothpicks.
6. Season the outside of the chicken fillets with salt and pepper.
7. In a large skillet, heat the olive oil over medium-high heat.
8. Sear the chicken fillets on both sides until browned, about 3-4 minutes per side.
9. Transfer the chicken fillets to a baking dish and bake in the preheated oven for 15-20 minutes, or until the chicken is cooked through and no longer pink in the middle.

INDIAN-STYLE KETO CHICKEN
Nutrition: Cal 450;Fat 27 g;Carb 7 g;Protein 43 g
Serving 2; Cook time 50 min
Ingredients
•2 boneless, skinless chicken breasts
•1/2 cup full-fat Greek yogurt
•1 tablespoon ghee or coconut oil
•1 small onion, diced
•2 garlic cloves, minced
•1 tablespoon grated fresh ginger
•1 teaspoon ground cumin
•1 teaspoon ground coriander
•1/2 teaspoon ground turmeric
•1/4 teaspoon cayenne pepper (or to taste)
•1/4 cup tomato sauce
•1/4 cup heavy cream
•Salt and pepper, to taste
•Chopped fresh cilantro, for garnish
Instructions
1. Cut the chicken into bite-sized pieces and season with salt and pepper. In a bowl, mix the yogurt with the cumin, coriander, turmeric, and cayenne pepper. Add the chicken pieces to the bowl and coat with the spiced yogurt. Let marinate for at least 30 minutes (or up to 24 hours) in the refrigerator.
2. In a large skillet, heat the ghee or coconut oil over medium-high heat. Add the onion and cook until softened and lightly browned, about 5 minutes. Add the garlic and ginger and cook for another minute, stirring constantly.
3. Add the marinated chicken to the skillet and cook, stirring occasionally, until browned on all sides, about 10 minutes.

4. Add the tomato sauce and heavy cream to the skillet and stir to combine. Reduce the heat to low and simmer for about 10 minutes, until the chicken is cooked through and the sauce has thickened.
5. Serve hot, garnished with chopped cilantro.

CHICKEN FRICASSEE WITH VEGETA-BLES
Nutrition: Cal 431;Fat 32 g;Carb 7 g;Protein 27 g
Serving 2; Cook time 35 min
Ingredients
•2 chicken fillets, cut into bite-size pieces
•2 tablespoons butter
•1 small onion, chopped
•1 celery stalk, sliced
•1 small carrot, diced
•1/2 cup sliced mushrooms
•1/2 cup chicken broth
•1/2 cup heavy cream
•1 tablespoon chopped fresh parsley
•Salt and pepper, to taste
Instructions
1. Melt the butter in a large skillet over medium heat.
2. Add the chicken and cook until browned on all sides, about 5-7 minutes.
3. Remove the chicken from the skillet and set it aside.
4. Add the onion, celery, and carrot to the skillet and sauté until softened, about 5 minutes.
5. Add the mushrooms and cook for another 2-3 minutes.
6. Pour in the chicken broth and heavy cream, and stir to combine.
7. Add the chicken back to the skillet and bring the mixture to a simmer.
8. Cook until the chicken is cooked through and the sauce has thickened, about 10-15 minutes.
9. Stir in the chopped parsley, salt, and pepper, and serve.

CHICKEN STIR-FRY WITH MUSH-ROOMS
Nutrition: Cal 370;Fat 22 g;Carb 8 g;Protein 34 g
Serving 2; Cook time 25 min
Ingredients
•2 chicken fillets, sliced
•1 cup mushrooms, sliced
•1 onion, sliced
•1 cup soy sprouts
•2 cloves garlic, minced
•1 tablespoon ginger, minced
•2 tablespoons coconut oil
•2 tablespoons soy sauce
•1 tablespoon sesame oil
•Salt and pepper, to taste
•Chopped scallions for garnish
Instructions

1. Heat the coconut oil in a wok or large skillet over high heat.
2. Add the sliced chicken and stir-fry until browned and cooked through.
3. Add the mushrooms, onion, garlic, and ginger, and stir-fry for another 2-3 minutes until the vegetables are slightly softened.
4. Add the soy sauce, sesame oil, soy sprouts, salt, and pepper, and stir-fry for another 1-2 minutes until everything is well combined.
5. Remove from heat and garnish with chopped scallions.

GRILLED CHICKEN FILLET WITH CREAMY WINE SAUCE

Nutrition: Cal 324;Fat 20 g;Carb 32 g;Protein 32 g
Serving 2; Cook time 1 hour 15 min

Ingredients
- 2 boneless chicken fillets (about 6 oz each)
- 1 tbsp fresh thyme, chopped
- 1 tbsp fresh rosemary, chopped
- 1 tbsp fresh basil, chopped
- 3 cloves garlic, minced
- 2 tbsp balsamic vinegar
- Salt and pepper, to taste
- 1/4 cup dry white wine
- 1/4 cup heavy cream
- 1 tbsp butter

Instructions
1. In a small bowl, mix together the chopped thyme, rosemary, basil, minced garlic, balsamic vinegar, salt, and pepper.
2. Place the chicken fillets in a resealable plastic bag and pour the marinade over the chicken.
3. Seal the bag and marinate in the refrigerator for at least 1 hour, or overnight for maximum flavor.
4. Preheat a grill to medium-high heat.
5. Remove the chicken from the marinade and discard the remaining marinade.
6. Grill the chicken fillets for 6-8 minutes per side, or until cooked through and no longer pink.
7. In a small saucepan, heat the white wine over medium heat and let it simmer until it reduces by half.
8. Add the rosemary, heavy cream and butter to the saucepan, stirring continuously until the sauce thickens. Salt and pepper, to taste.
9. Serve the grilled chicken fillets with the creamy wine sauce drizzled over the top.

CHICKEN FILLET STUFFED WITH SHRIMP

Nutrition: Cal 380;Fat 21 g;Carb 2 g;Protein 47 g
Serving 3; Cook time 45 min

Ingredients
- 2 boneless chicken fillets (about 6 oz each)
- 1/2 lb shrimp, peeled and deveined
- 3 tbsp unsalted butter, melted
- 3 cloves garlic, minced
- 2 tbsp fresh parsley, chopped
- Salt and pepper, to taste

Instructions
1. Preheat the oven to 375°F (190°C).
2. Butterfly the chicken fillets by cutting them horizontally through the middle, but not all the way through, and open them like a book.
3. Season both sides of the chicken fillets with salt and pepper.
4. In a small bowl, mix together the melted butter, minced garlic, and chopped parsley.
5. Brush the butter mixture onto the inside of the chicken fillets.
6. Arrange the shrimp on top of one half of each chicken fillet, then fold the other half over to create a pocket.
7. Secure the chicken fillets with toothpicks.
8. Place the stuffed chicken fillets in a baking dish and bake in the oven for 25-30 minutes, until the chicken is cooked through and no longer pink.
9. Remove the toothpicks before serving.

CREAMY DUCK WITH SPINACH RECIPE

Nutrition: Cal 593;Fat 47 g;Carb 5 g;Protein 38 g
Serving 2; Cook time 35 min

Ingredients
- 2 duck legs, skin on
- Salt and black pepper, to taste
- 1 tablespoon coconut oil
- 1/2 cup chopped onion
- 2 garlic cloves, minced
- 1/2 cup coconut cream
- 2 cups fresh spinach
- 1 tablespoon chopped fresh basil
- 1 tablespoon chopped fresh cilantro
- 1 tablespoon chopped fresh mint

Instructions
1. Preheat your oven to 375°F.
2. Season the duck legs with salt and black pepper on both sides.
3. Heat a skillet over medium-high heat and add the coconut oil. Once the oil is hot, add the duck legs, skin side down. Cook for about 5 minutes or until the skin is crispy and golden brown. Flip the duck legs over and cook for another 3-5 minutes until cooked through. Remove the duck legs from the skillet and place them in a baking dish.
4. In the same skillet, sauté the chopped onion and minced garlic until soft and fragrant.
5. Add the coconut cream to the skillet and stir to combine with the onions and garlic. Let it simmer for a few minutes until the sauce thickens.
6. Pour the coconut cream sauce over the duck legs in the baking dish. Bake in the oven for 20-25 minutes, until the sauce is bubbly and the duck is heated through.

7. While the duck is baking, wash the spinach and remove any tough stems. Roughly chop the spinach and set aside.
8. Once the duck is done, remove it from the oven and let it cool for a few minutes.
9. In a separate skillet, heat a tablespoon of coconut oil over medium heat. Add the chopped spinach and cook until wilted, about 2-3 minutes.
10. To serve, place the duck legs on a plate and top with the creamy coconut sauce. Add a side of sautéed spinach and sprinkle with chopped fresh herbs.

THAI-STYLE DUCK WITH ZUCCHINI SPAGHETTI

Nutrition: Cal 525;Fat 40 g;Carb 10 g;Protein 33 g
Serving 2; Cook time 25 min

Ingredients
• 2 duck breasts, skin on
• Salt and black pepper, to taste
• 2 medium-sized zucchinis, spiralized into spaghetti
• 1/4 cup coconut oil
• 1/4 cup chopped shallots
• 2 garlic cloves, minced
• 1/4 cup coconut aminos
• 2 tablespoons fish sauce
• 1 tablespoon apple cider vinegar
• 1 tablespoon honey (optional)
• 1 teaspoon grated fresh ginger
• 1 red chili, finely chopped

Instructions
1. Preheat your oven to 400°F.
2. Season the duck breasts with salt and black pepper on both sides.
3. Heat a skillet over medium-high heat and add the duck breasts, skin side down. Cook for about 5 minutes or until the skin is crispy and golden brown. Flip the duck breasts over and cook for another 3-5 minutes until cooked through. Remove the duck breasts from the skillet and let them rest for 5 minutes.
4. While the duck is cooking, prepare the zucchini spaghetti. Heat a separate skillet over medium heat and add the coconut oil. Once the oil is hot, add the chopped shallots and garlic, and cook for 1-2 minutes until fragrant.
5. Add the zucchini spaghetti to the skillet and toss with the shallots and garlic until heated through, about 2-3 minutes.
6. In a small bowl, whisk together the coconut aminos, fish sauce, apple cider vinegar, honey (if using), grated ginger, and chopped chili.
7. Pour the sauce over the zucchini spaghetti and toss to coat evenly.
8. Slice the duck breasts and serve with the zucchini spaghetti on the side.

DUCK AND SPINACH SALAD

Nutrition: Cal 575;Fat 42 g;Carb 6 g;Protein 41 g
Serving 3; Cook time 45 min

Ingredients
• 2 duck breasts, skin on
• Salt and black pepper, to taste
• 4 cups fresh spinach leaves
• 4 slices bacon, cooked and chopped
• 1/4 cup chopped red onion
• 1/4 cup crumbled feta cheese
• 2 tablespoons olive oil
• 1 tablespoon red wine vinegar
• 1 teaspoon Dijon mustard
• 1/2 teaspoon garlic powder

Instructions
1. Preheat your oven to 400°F.
2. Season the duck breasts with salt and black pepper on both sides.
3. Heat a skillet over medium-high heat and add the duck breasts, skin side down. Cook for about 5 minutes or until the skin is crispy and golden brown. Flip the duck breasts over and cook for another 3-5 minutes until cooked through. Remove the duck breasts from the skillet and let them rest for 5 minutes.
4. While the duck is resting, prepare the salad. Wash the spinach leaves and pat them dry. Place them in a large salad bowl.
5. Add the chopped bacon, red onion, and crumbled feta cheese to the bowl with the spinach.
6. In a separate small bowl, whisk together the olive oil, red wine vinegar, Dijon mustard, and garlic powder.
7. Slice the duck breasts into thin pieces and add them to the salad bowl.
8. Drizzle the dressing over the salad and toss gently to combine.

CREAMY DUCK SOUP

Nutrition: Cal 503;Fat 35 g;Carb 9 g;Protein 39 g
Serving 2; Cook time 45 min

Ingredients
• 2 duck breasts, skin on
• Salt and black pepper, to taste
• 1 tablespoon olive oil
• 1 small onion, chopped
• 2 garlic cloves, minced
• 8 oz mushrooms, sliced
• 1 tablespoon grated ginger
• 2 cups chicken broth
• 1/2 cup heavy cream
• 2 medium tomatoes, chopped
• 1 tablespoon chopped fresh cilantro
• Salt and black pepper, to taste

Instructions
1. Season the duck breasts with salt and black pepper on both sides.

2. Heat a skillet over medium-high heat and add the duck breasts, skin side down. Cook for about 5 minutes or until the skin is crispy and golden brown. Flip the duck breasts over and cook for another 3-5 minutes until cooked through. Remove the duck breasts from the skillet and let them rest for 5 minutes. Once cooled, shred the duck meat.
3. Heat a large soup pot over medium-high heat and add the olive oil. Once the oil is hot, add the chopped onion and minced garlic. Cook until soft and fragrant.
4. Add the sliced mushrooms and grated ginger to the pot and cook for about 5 minutes, stirring occasionally.
5. Pour in the chicken broth and bring to a boil. Reduce the heat to low and simmer for about 10 minutes.
6. Add the heavy cream and chopped tomatoes to the pot and cook for another 5 minutes.
7. Use an immersion blender or transfer the soup to a blender and blend until smooth.
8. Add the shredded duck meat to the pot and let it simmer for another 5-10 minutes to allow the flavors to meld together.
9. Season the soup with salt and black pepper, to taste.
10. Serve the soup hot, garnished with chopped fresh cilantro.

KETO DUCK ROLLS

Nutrition: Cal 474;Fat 30 g;Carb 6 g;Protein 38 g
Serving 2; Cook time 25 min

Ingredients
- 2 duck breasts, skin on
- Salt and black pepper, to taste
- 1 tablespoon olive oil
- 1/2 cup sliced scallions
- 1/2 cup sliced cucumber
- 1/4 cup chopped fresh cilantro
- 1/4 cup chopped fresh mint
- 1/4 cup chopped roasted peanuts
- 4 large lettuce leaves
- 2 tablespoons fish sauce
- 2 tablespoons lime juice
- 1 tablespoon low-carb sweetener (such as monk fruit sweetener)
- 1 small red chili pepper, sliced (optional)

Instructions
1. Season the duck breasts with salt and black pepper on both sides.
2. Heat a skillet over medium-high heat and add the duck breasts, skin side down. Cook for about 5 minutes or until the skin is crispy and golden brown. Flip the duck breasts over and cook for another 3-5 minutes until cooked through. Remove the duck breasts from the skillet and let them rest for 5 minutes. Once cooled, slice the duck meat into thin strips.
3. In a small bowl, whisk together the fish sauce, lime juice, and low-carb sweetener until well combined.
4. Lay out the lettuce leaves on a flat surface.

5. Divide the sliced duck meat among the lettuce leaves, placing them in the center.
6. Top the duck meat with sliced scallions, sliced cucumber, chopped fresh cilantro, chopped fresh mint, and chopped roasted peanuts.
7. Drizzle the fish sauce mixture over the top of the filling.
8. Roll up the lettuce leaves tightly to form the duck rolls.
9. Serve the duck rolls immediately, garnished with sliced red chili pepper (if using).

DUCK, BACON, GREEN BEAN, AND MUSHROOM SKILLET

Nutrition: Cal 532;Fat 41 g;Carb 9 g;Protein 33 g
Serving 2; Cook time 25 min

Ingredients
- 2 duck breasts, skin on
- Salt and black pepper, to taste
- 4 slices bacon, diced
- 8 oz green beans, trimmed and cut into bite-size pieces
- 8 oz mushrooms, sliced
- 2 cloves garlic, minced
- 2 tablespoons olive oil
- 1/4 teaspoon red pepper flakes (optional)

Instructions
1. Season the duck breasts with salt and black pepper on both sides.
2. Heat a large skillet over medium-high heat and add the duck breasts, skin side down. Cook for about 5 minutes or until the skin is crispy and golden brown. Flip the duck breasts over and cook for another 3-5 minutes until cooked through. Remove the duck breasts from the skillet and let them rest for 5 minutes. Once cooled, slice the duck meat into thin strips.
3. In the same skillet, cook the diced bacon over medium heat until crispy. Remove the bacon with a slotted spoon and set aside.
4. Add the green beans, mushrooms, minced garlic, and olive oil to the skillet. Cook for about 5-7 minutes, stirring occasionally, until the vegetables are tender and lightly browned.
5. Add the sliced duck meat and cooked bacon back to the skillet, along with the red pepper flakes (if using). Cook for another 2-3 minutes, stirring occasionally, until everything is heated through.
6. Season with additional salt and black pepper, to taste.
7. Serve the duck, bacon, green bean, and mushroom skillet hot, garnished with chopped fresh parsley (if desired).

KETO DUCK DUMPLINGS

Nutrition: Cal 396;Fat 30 g;Carb 8 g;Protein 23 g
Serving 2; Cook time 25 min

Ingredients

- 1/2 lb ground duck meat
- 1/2 cup almond flour
- 1 large egg
- 2 green onions, finely chopped
- 2 cloves garlic, minced
- 1 teaspoon grated ginger
- 1/2 teaspoon salt
- 1/4 teaspoon black pepper
- 1 tablespoon coconut aminos
- 1 tablespoon sesame oil
- 2 cups chicken or beef broth
- 1 tablespoon chopped cilantro (optional)

Instructions

1. In a large mixing bowl, combine the ground duck meat, almond flour, egg, green onions, garlic, ginger, salt, black pepper, coconut aminos, and sesame oil. Mix everything together until well combined.
2. Scoop a tablespoon of the duck mixture and form it into a ball. Repeat with the remaining mixture to make 16-18 dumplings.
3. In a large saucepan, heat the chicken or beef broth over medium-high heat until it comes to a boil.
4. Carefully add the duck dumplings to the broth and reduce the heat to low. Simmer for about 8-10 minutes or until the dumplings are cooked through.
5. Divide the duck dumplings and broth between two bowls. Sprinkle with chopped cilantro (if desired) and serve hot.

DUCK AND BROCCOLI "ALFREDO"

Nutrition: Cal 475;Fat 34 g;Carb 7 g;Protein 33 g
Serving 2; Cook time 25 min

Ingredients

- 2 duck breasts, skin on
- Salt and black pepper, to taste
- 2 cups broccoli florets
- 2 tablespoons butter
- 2 cloves garlic, minced
- 1/4 cup heavy cream
- 1/4 cup grated parmesan cheese
- 1/4 teaspoon dried oregano
- 1/4 teaspoon dried basil
- 1/4 teaspoon dried thyme
- Salt and black pepper, to taste
- Fresh parsley, chopped (optional)

Instructions

1. Season the duck breasts with salt and black pepper on both sides.
2. Heat a large skillet over medium-high heat and add the duck breasts, skin side down. Cook for about 5 minutes or until the skin is crispy and golden brown. Flip the duck breasts over and cook for another 3-5 minutes until cooked through. Remove the duck breasts from the skillet and let them rest for 5 minutes. Once cooled, slice the duck meat into thin strips.
3. In the same skillet, add the broccoli florets and cook for about 5-7 minutes, stirring occasionally, until tender.
4. In a small saucepan, melt the butter over medium heat. Add the minced garlic and cook for about 1-2 minutes, until fragrant.
5. Add the heavy cream, grated parmesan cheese, dried oregano, dried basil, dried thyme, salt, and black pepper to the saucepan. Stir everything together until well combined and the cheese has melted.
6. Add the sliced duck meat and cooked broccoli to the skillet. Pour the sauce over the top and stir everything together until well coated.
7. Cook for another 2-3 minutes, stirring occasionally, until everything is heated through and the sauce is thickened.
8. Serve the duck and broccoli "Alfredo" hot, garnished with chopped fresh parsley (if desired).

DUCK A L'ORANGE RECIPE

Nutrition: Cal 405;Fat 31 g;Carb 3 g;Protein 27 g
Serving 2; Cook time 25 min

Ingredients

- 2 duck breasts
- Salt and pepper
- 1 tablespoon olive oil
- 1/4 cup chicken broth
- 1/4 cup fresh orange juice
- 1 tablespoon orange zest
- 1 tablespoon butter
- 1 tablespoon chopped fresh parsley (optional)

Instructions

1. Preheat the oven to 400°F.
2. Score the skin of the duck breasts in a crosshatch pattern with a sharp knife. Season both sides with salt and pepper.
3. Heat the olive oil in a large ovenproof skillet over medium-high heat. Add the duck breasts, skin-side down, and cook for about 6-8 minutes or until the skin is golden brown and crispy.
4. Turn the duck breasts over and transfer the skillet to the preheated oven. Roast for about 8-10 minutes or until the duck is cooked to your desired doneness.
5. Remove the skillet from the oven and transfer the duck breasts to a cutting board. Tent them with foil and let them rest for 5 minutes.
6. While the duck is resting, pour off any excess fat from the skillet and return it to the stove over medium heat. Add the chicken broth, orange juice, and orange zest, and stir to combine. Cook for about 3-5 minutes or until the sauce has thickened slightly.
7. Stir in the butter until melted and well combined.

8. Slice the duck breasts diagonally and serve with the orange sauce. Garnish with chopped parsley (if desired).

DUCK BREAST WITH CHERRY PORT SAUCE

Nutrition: Cal 498;Fat 35 g;Carb 6 g;Protein 37 g
Serving 2; Cook time 25 min

Ingredients
- 2 duck breasts, skin on
- Salt and pepper
- 1 tablespoon avocado oil
- 1/4 cup chicken broth
- 1/4 cup port wine
- 1/4 cup fresh cherries, pitted and halved
- 1 tablespoon unsalted butter
- Fresh thyme sprigs (optional)

Instructions
1. Preheat the oven to 400°F.
2. Score the skin of the duck breasts in a crosshatch pattern, being careful not to cut all the way through the meat. Season both sides with salt and pepper.
3. Heat the avocado oil in an oven-safe skillet over medium-high heat. Place the duck breasts, skin side down, in the skillet and cook for about 5 minutes or until the skin is crispy and golden brown.
4. Flip the duck breasts over and transfer the skillet to the preheated oven. Roast for about 8-10 minutes or until the internal temperature of the duck breasts reaches 135°F for medium-rare or 145°F for medium.
5. Remove the skillet from the oven and transfer the duck breasts to a cutting board to rest.
6. Place the skillet back on the stovetop over medium heat. Add the chicken broth and port wine and simmer for about 2-3 minutes or until the liquid is reduced by half.
7. Add the fresh cherries to the skillet and cook for another 2-3 minutes or until the cherries are soft and the sauce is thick and glossy.
8. Remove the skillet from the heat and stir in the unsalted butter until melted and fully incorporated.
9. Slice the duck breasts and arrange them on serving plates. Spoon the cherry port sauce over the top and garnish with fresh thyme sprigs (if desired).

DUCK BREAST WITH BLUEBERRY SAUCE

Nutrition: Cal 437;Fat 31 g;Carb 4 g;Protein 31 g
Serving 2; Cook time 25 min

Ingredients
- 2 duck breasts
- Salt and black pepper to taste
- 1/2 cup fresh blueberries
- 1/4 cup chicken or beef broth
- 1/4 cup dry red wine
- 1 tablespoon butter
- 1/2 teaspoon chopped fresh rosemary

Instructions
1. Preheat your oven to 400°F. Score the skin of the duck breasts with a sharp knife, being careful not to cut into the flesh. Season both sides of the duck breasts with salt and black pepper.
2. Place the duck breasts skin-side down in a cold oven-safe skillet or pan. Turn the heat to medium and cook for 8-10 minutes, or until the skin is crispy and golden brown. Flip the duck breasts over and cook for another 2-3 minutes.
3. Remove the duck breasts from the skillet and place them on a baking sheet. Roast in the preheated oven for 6-8 minutes or until the internal temperature reaches 135°F for medium-rare or 145°F for medium.
4. While the duck breasts are roasting, make the blueberry sauce. In the same skillet you used to cook the duck breasts, add the blueberries, chicken or beef broth, and red wine. Bring to a boil over high heat, then reduce the heat to low and simmer for 5-7 minutes or until the sauce has thickened slightly.
5. Remove the skillet from the heat and whisk in the butter until it has melted and the sauce is glossy. Stir in the chopped rosemary.
6. To serve, slice the duck breasts and drizzle the blueberry sauce over the top. Enjoy your delicious and indulgent French-inspired keto meal!

DUCK CONFIT WITH ROASTED VEGETABLES

Nutrition: Cal 602;Fat 49 g;Carb 13 g;Protein 28 g
Serving 2; Cook time 2 hours 25 min

Ingredients
- 2 duck legs
- 1/2 teaspoon dried thyme
- 1/2 teaspoon dried rosemary
- Salt and pepper to taste
- 1/2 head of cauliflower, chopped
- 1/2 lb Brussels sprouts, trimmed and halved
- 2 tablespoons olive oil
- 2 cloves garlic, minced

Instructions
1. Preheat your oven to 375°F (190°C).
2. Season the duck legs with dried thyme, dried rosemary, salt, and pepper.
3. Place the duck legs in a baking dish and roast for about 2 hours, or until the skin is crispy and the meat is tender.
4. In a separate baking dish, toss the chopped cauliflower and Brussels sprouts with olive oil, minced garlic, salt, and pepper.
5. Roast the vegetables in the oven for 20-25 minutes, or until they are tender and lightly browned.
6. Serve the duck legs with the roasted vegetables on the side.

JAPANESE STYLE DUCK

Nutrition: Cal 488;Fat 35 g;Carb 8 g;Protein 37 g
Serving 2; Cook time 30 min

Ingredients

• 2 duck breasts
• 1 tablespoon olive oil
• 1/2 teaspoon salt
• 1/4 teaspoon black pepper
• 1/4 cup tamari sauce
• 1 tablespoon grated ginger
• 1 garlic clove, minced
• 1/4 cup chopped scallions
• 1 tablespoon sesame seeds
• 1 tablespoon avocado oil
• 2 cups sliced shiitake mushrooms
• 2 cups baby spinach
• Cauliflower rice or zucchini noodles, to serve

Instructions

1. Preheat oven to 375°F.
2. Heat a large oven-proof skillet over medium-high heat.
3. Season the duck breasts with salt and pepper on both sides.
4. Add olive oil to the skillet and sear the duck breasts for 2-3 minutes on each side, until golden brown.
5. In a small bowl, whisk together the tamari sauce, grated ginger, and minced garlic.
6. Pour the sauce over the duck breasts and transfer the skillet to the oven.
7. Bake for 10-15 minutes, until the duck is cooked through.
8. In a separate pan, heat the avocado oil over medium-high heat.
9. Add the shiitake mushrooms and sauté for 3-4 minutes, until browned.
10. Add the baby spinach and sauté for an additional 2-3 minutes, until wilted.
11. Serve the duck with the sautéed mushrooms and spinach, and garnish with chopped scallions and sesame seeds.

DUCK ACCORDING TO UKRAINIAN RECIPE

Nutrition: Cal 450;Fat 32 g;Carb 5 g;Protein 29 g
Serving 2; Cook time 55 min

Ingredients

• 2 duck legs
• 1 tablespoon olive oil
• 1/2 teaspoon salt
• 1/4 teaspoon black pepper
• 1/2 onion, sliced
• 2 cloves garlic, minced
• 1/4 cup chicken or beef broth
• 1/4 cup dry red wine
• 1 tablespoon tomato paste
• 1 teaspoon paprika
• 1/2 teaspoon dried thyme
• 1/2 teaspoon dried rosemary
• 1 bay leaf

Instructions

1. Preheat oven to 375°F.
2. Season the duck legs with salt and pepper on both sides.
3. Heat a large oven-proof skillet over medium-high heat.
4. Add olive oil to the skillet and sear the duck legs for 2-3 minutes on each side, until golden brown.
5. Remove the duck legs from the skillet and set aside.
6. In the same skillet, add the sliced onion and garlic, and sauté for 2-3 minutes, until softened.
7. Add the chicken or beef broth, dry red wine, tomato paste, paprika, dried thyme, dried rosemary, and bay leaf to the skillet, and stir to combine.
8. Return the duck legs to the skillet and spoon the sauce over the top.
9. Transfer the skillet to the oven and bake for 45-50 minutes, until the duck legs are cooked through and tender.
10. Serve the duck legs with a side of sautéed cabbage or roasted vegetables.

DUCK ACCORDING TO UKRAINIAN RECIPE

Nutrition: Cal 420;Fat 27 g;Carb 10 g;Protein 32 g
Serving 2; Cook time 40 min

Ingredients

• 2 duck breasts
• 1/2 teaspoon salt
• 1/4 teaspoon black pepper
• 2 tablespoons olive oil
• 1 large apple, cored and sliced
• 1/2 onion, sliced
• 1/4 cup chicken or beef broth
• 1 tablespoon apple cider vinegar
• 1 tablespoon Dijon mustard
• 2 cloves garlic, minced
• 1/2 teaspoon dried thyme
• 1/2 teaspoon dried rosemary

Instructions

1. Preheat oven to 375°F.
2. Season the duck breasts with salt and pepper on both sides.
3. Heat a large oven-proof skillet over medium-high heat.
4. Add olive oil to the skillet and sear the duck breasts for 2-3 minutes on each side, until golden brown.
5. Remove the duck from the skillet and set aside.
6. In the same skillet, add the sliced apple and onion, and sauté for 2-3 minutes, until softened.
7. Add the chicken or beef broth, apple cider vinegar, Dijon mustard, minced garlic, dried thyme, and dried rosemary to the skillet, and stir to combine.
8. Return the duck to the skillet and spoon the apple mixture over the top.
9. Transfer the skillet to the oven and bake for 15-20 minutes, until the duck is cooked through and the apples are tender.

10. Serve the duck with a side of sautéed spinach or roasted Brussels sprouts.

DUCK STEWED WITH PRUNES
Nutrition: Cal 460;Fat 26 g;Carb 21 g;Protein 27 g
Serving 2; Cook time 2 hours 15 min

Ingredients
- 2 duck legs
- 1/2 teaspoon salt
- 1/4 teaspoon black pepper
- 2 tablespoons olive oil
- 1 large onion, chopped
- 2 cloves garlic, minced
- 1 cup chicken broth
- 1 cup dry red wine
- 1 cup pitted prunes
- 2 tablespoons honey
- 1 bay leaf
- 1/2 teaspoon dried thyme
- 1/2 teaspoon dried rosemary

Instructions
1. Preheat the oven to 325°F.
2. Season the duck legs with salt and pepper on both sides.
3. Heat a large Dutch oven over medium-high heat.
4. Add olive oil to the Dutch oven and sear the duck legs for 2-3 minutes on each side, until golden brown.
5. Remove the duck from the Dutch oven and set aside.
6. In the same Dutch oven, add the chopped onion and minced garlic, and sauté for 2-3 minutes, until softened.
7. Add the chicken broth, dry red wine, pitted prunes, honey, bay leaf, dried thyme, and dried rosemary to the Dutch oven, and stir to combine.
8. Return the duck to the Dutch oven and spoon the sauce over the top.
9. Cover the Dutch oven and transfer it to the oven.
10. Bake for 2 hours, until the duck is tender and the sauce has thickened.
11. Remove the bay leaf from the sauce before serving.
12. Serve the duck with a side of roasted root vegetables or cauliflower rice.

DUCK WITH STEWED CABBAGE
Nutrition: Cal 420;Fat 27 g;Carb 14 g;Protein 33 g
Serving 2; Cook time 35 min

Ingredients
- 2 duck breasts
- 1/2 head of green cabbage, chopped
- 1/2 onion, chopped
- 2 cloves garlic, minced
- 2 tablespoons olive oil
- 1/2 teaspoon salt
- 1/4 teaspoon black pepper
- 1/2 teaspoon dried thyme
- 1/2 teaspoon dried rosemary

- 1/2 cup chicken or beef broth
- 1 tablespoon apple cider vinegar

Instructions
1. Preheat oven to 375°F.
2. Heat a large oven-proof skillet over medium-high heat.
3. Season the duck breasts with salt and pepper on both sides.
4. Add olive oil to the skillet and sear the duck breasts for 2-3 minutes on each side, until golden brown.
5. Remove the duck from the skillet and set aside.
6. In the same skillet, add the chopped onion and garlic, and sauté for 2-3 minutes, until softened.
7. Add the chopped cabbage, dried thyme, dried rosemary, chicken or beef broth, and apple cider vinegar to the skillet, and stir to combine.
8. Return the duck to the skillet and spoon the cabbage mixture over the top.
9. Transfer the skillet to the oven and bake for 20-25 minutes, until the duck is cooked through.
10. Serve the duck with a generous helping of the stewed cabbage.

DUCK AND CAULIFLOWER STIR-FRY
Nutrition: Cal 531;Fat 37 g;Carb 7 g;Protein 38 g
Serving 2; Cook time 25 min

Ingredients
- 2 duck breasts, skin on
- Salt and black pepper, to taste
- 2 cups cauliflower florets
- 2 tablespoons olive oil
- 2 cloves garlic, minced
- 1/4 cup natural peanut butter (no sugar added)
- 2 tablespoons soy sauce or coconut aminos
- 1 tablespoon apple cider vinegar
- 1/4 teaspoon red pepper flakes (optional)
- 1/4 cup chopped fresh cilantro (optional)

Instructions
1. Season the duck breasts with salt and black pepper on both sides.
2. Heat a large skillet over medium-high heat and add the duck breasts, skin side down. Cook for about 5 minutes or until the skin is crispy and golden brown. Flip the duck breasts over and cook for another 3-5 minutes until cooked through. Remove the duck breasts from the skillet and let them rest for 5 minutes. Once cooled, slice the duck meat into thin strips.
3. In the same skillet, add the cauliflower florets and cook for about 5-7 minutes, stirring occasionally, until lightly browned and tender. Remove the cauliflower from the skillet and set aside.
4. In a small bowl, whisk together the natural peanut butter, soy sauce or coconut aminos, apple cider vinegar, and red pepper flakes (if using), until well combined.
5. In the same skillet, heat the olive oil over medium heat. Add the minced garlic and cook for about 1-2 minutes, until fragrant.

6. Add the sliced duck meat and cooked cauliflower back to the skillet. Pour the peanut butter sauce over the top and stir everything together until well coated.
7. Cook for another 2-3 minutes, stirring occasionally, until everything is heated through and the sauce is thickened.
8. Serve the duck and cauliflower stir-fry hot, garnished with chopped fresh cilantro (if desired).

ONE PAN KETO CHEESY JALAPEÑO CHICKEN

Nutrition: Cal 425;Fat 26 g;Carb 5 g;Protein 40 g
Serving 4; Cook time 25 min

Ingredients
- 4 small chicken breast (this was about 1.5 pounds for me)
- 1 teaspoon cumin
- 1/2 teaspoon chili powder
- 1/2 teaspoon garlic powder
- 1/2 teaspoon salt
- 1/2 teaspoon pepper
- 1 tablespoon butter
- 1/2 cup chopped onion (half of one small onion)
- 2 jalapenos, seeded and diced
- 1 teaspoon minced garlic
- 1/4 cup heavy cream
- 1/3 cup chicken broth
- 2 ounces cream cheese
- 1 cup shredded cheddar cheese (divided)

Instructions
1. Combine the cumin, chili powder, garlic powder, salt and pepper, set aside.
2. Heat a 12-inch skillet over medium heat, spray with non-stick spray or add up to 1 tablespoon olive oil.
3. Sprinkle the chicken breast with the spice mixture on each size.
4. Sear the chicken in the skillet 2-3 minutes on each side until nicely browned, remove from skillet and set aside.
5. Add 1 tablespoon butter in the skillet and add the onion, jalalpenos and garlic and sauté for 3-4 minutes, stirring occasionally.
6. Add the cream, broth, cream cheese and reduce heat to low.
7. Stir mixture until cream cheese melts completely and add 1/2 cup of the shredded cheese to the sauce, stir well.
8. Add the chicken to the skillet and cover with the remaining cheese.
9. Place a lid on the skillet and let simmer over low for 6-8 minutes.

KETO CRACK CHICKEN

Nutrition: Cal 242;Fat 20 g;Carb 2 g;Protein 40 g
Serving 4; Cook time 25 min

Ingredients
For the chicken
- 4 small chicken breasts
- 1/4 teaspoon salt
- 1/4 teaspoon pepper
- 1/2 teaspoon garlic powder
- 1 teaspoon oil
- 4 slices bacon chopped
- 1 tablespoon butter
- 6 ounces shredded cheese

For the cream cheese filling
- 4 ounces cream cheese softened
- 1/2 teaspoon onion powder
- 1/4 teaspoon garlic powder
- 1/8 teaspoon celery salt
- 1/4 teaspoon dried dill

Instructions
1. Preheat the oven to 200C/400F. Grease a 13 x 9-inch baking dish and set it aside.
2. Pound the four chicken breasts until ¼ inch in thickness. Sprinkle with salt, pepper, and garlic powder.
3. Add olive oil to the non-stick pan and place over medium heat. Add the diced bacon and cook until crispy. Remove the bacon and keep the bacon grease in the pan. Add the butter and when hot, and the chicken breasts and cook 2-3 minutes per side, until golden.
4. Transfer the chicken breasts into the baking dish and pour the pan juices over them.
5. In a small bowl, whisk together the cream cheese and spices until combined.
6. Evenly distribute the cream cheese mixture on top of each chicken breast. Sprinkle half the cooked bacon on top, followed by the shredded cheese.
7. Bake for 15 minutes, until the chicken is cooked through and the cheese has melted. Remove from the oven and serve immediately.

CHICKEN FLORENTINE

Nutrition: Cal 295;Fat 22 g;Carb 6 g;Protein31 g
Serving 4; Cook time 25 min

Ingredients
For the chicken
- 2 large chicken breasts
- 1/2 teaspoon salt
- 1/2 teaspoon pepper
- 1/2 cup almond flour
- 2 tablespoons parmesan cheese
- 1 tablespoon olive oil
- 1 tablespoon butter

For the florentine sauce
- 1 tablespoon butter
- 2 cloves garlic minced
- 3/4 cup chicken broth

- 1 tablespoon Italian seasonings
- 1 cup heavy cream
- 1/4 cup parmesan cheese
- 2 cups baby spinach loosely packed

Instructions

1. Slice the two chicken breasts lengthways to form four, thin pieces of chicken. Season the four chicken pieces with salt and pepper and set aside.
2. In a small bowl, whisk together the almond flour and parmesan cheese. Dip each chicken fillet in the flour mixture, ensuring everything is covered.
3. Add the oil and one tablespoon of the butter into a skillet and place it over medium heat. Once hot, add the chicken and cook for 8-10 minutes, flipping halfway through, until golden on the outside. Remove the chicken from the heat.
4. Add the extra butter to the pan, along with the garlic, and cook for 30 seconds, before adding the chicken broth and Italian seasoning. Let it simmer for 5-6 minutes, or until it has noticeably reduced. Add the cream and bring it to a boil, then add the parmesan cheese and spinach.
5. Add the chicken back into the pan and let it simmer for 5 minutes, until the sauce thickens.
6. Serve the chicken and the florentine sauce immediately.

HUNAN CHICKEN

Nutrition: Cal 358;Fat 22 g;Carb 8 g;Protein 26 g
Serving 4; Cook time 15 min

Ingredients

For the chicken
- 1 lb chicken thigh skinless, chopped into bite sized pieces
- 1 tablespoon almond flour or cornstarch
- 1 tablespoon oil

For the stir fry
- 1 tablespoon sesame oil
- 2 cloves garlic minced
- 1 tablespoon ginger minced
- 3 cups broccoli chopped
- 1 large bell pepper chopped
- 1 medium zucchini chopped

For the Hunan sauce
- 1/2 cup chicken broth
- 3 tablespoon soy sauce
- 1 tablespoon fish sauce
- 1 tablespoon white vinegar
- 2 tablespoon brown sugar substitute
- 2 tablespoon chili paste I used sambal oelek
- 1/2 teaspoon xanthan gum or cornstarch

Instructions

1. Make the Hunan sauce by whisking together all the ingredients and setting aside.
2. In a bowl, add the chopped chicken and almond flour and lightly mix together.
3. Add the oil in a non-stick pan or wok and place over medium heat. Stir fry the chicken until mostly cooked. Remove the chicken from the pan.

4. Add the sesame oil and when hot, add the minced garlic and ginger and stir fry for several minutes. Add the remaining vegetables and cook until mostly tender. Add the chicken back to the pan, before adding the Hunan sauce. Let it bubble and thicken for several minutes, before removing it from the heat.
5. Serve over cauliflower rice or one your favorite low carb side of choice.

KETO ORANGE CHICKEN

Nutrition: Cal 280;Fat 14 g;Carb 13 g;Protein 23 g
Serving 4; Cook time 20 min

Ingredients

For the chicken
- 1 1/2 lbs skinless chicken breasts chopped into bite sized pieces
- 3 large eggs
- 1/4 cup heavy cream
- 1 cup coconut flour
- 1/4 teaspoon salt
- 1/4 teaspoon pepper
- 3 tablespoons oil to fry

For the keto orange sauce
- 1 cup orange juice no added sugar
- 1/2 cup brown sugar substitute or granulated sweetener of choice
- 2 tablespoons white vinegar
- 2 tablespoons soy sauce
- 2 cloves garlic minced
- 1 teaspoon xanthan gum optional

Instructions

1. Start by preparing the sauce. In a small saucepan, add the orange juice, brown sugar substitute, vinegar, soy sauce and garlic. Heat for 3-4 minutes. Add the xanthan gum and whisk vigorously, ensuring there are no clumps. Let everything simmer for 5-6 minutes, until thick and sticky.
2. In a bowl, combine the eggs and heavy cream then add the chopped chicken. On a large plate, add the coconut flour, salt, and pepper. Mix until combined.
3. Individually, dip each piece of chicken in the flour mixture until fully coated.
4. Add the oil to a large pan and place over medium heat. Once it reaches around 350F, add enough chicken to fill the pan without overcrowding. Fry the chicken for 2-3 minutes, before flipping and cooking for a further minute. Remove the chicken and place it on a plate lined with paper towel. Repeat the process until all the chicken has been fried.
5. Once all the chicken has been cooked, toss it through the orange sauce until covered, then serve immediately.

HEALTHY TURKEY SALAD

Nutrition: Cal 227;Fat 11 g;Carb 19 g;Protein 14 g
Serving 6; Cook time 15 min

Ingredients

- 1 pound (450g) turkey breast sliced
- 1/2 head red cabbage shredded
- 1/2 head white cabbage shredded
- 1 bell pepper de-seeded and finely sliced
- 1 large carrot cut into matchsticks
- 2 bell peppers de-seed and finely sliced
- 6 radishes finely sliced
- 1 cup bean sprouts
- 3 green onions (scallions/spring onions), finely sliced
- 4 tbsp chopped cilantro (fresh coriander)
- 3 tbsp toasted sesame seeds
- 3 tbsp toasted nuts

TAHINI DRESSING:

- 1/4 cup (120 ml) tahini
- 1/4 cup (120 ml) water (or more as needed)
- ¼ (60 ml) cup lemon juice
- 1 garlic clove minced
- Sweetener to taste or maple syrup if not low- carb
- Salt
- Black pepper

Instructions

1. Add salad ingredients in a large bowl and mix to combine.
2. Make the salad dressing by adding all the ingredients into a blender and blend till creamy.
3. Add half the salad dressing into the salad and toss. Taste and add more dressing as required.

MUSHROOM & SAGE ROLLED TURKEY BREAST

Nutrition: Cal 311;Fat 12 g;Carb 2 g;Protein 45 g
Serving 8; Cook time 1 hour 25 min

Ingredients

- ¼ cup coconut oil or butter, divided, room temperature
- 10 ounces mushrooms finely chopped
- 1 clove garlic minced
- Salt and pepper to taste
- 3 tablespoon chopped fresh sage divided
- 1 boneless butterfiled turkey breast (3 to 4 lbs)
- 1 180 F Pop Up® disposable cooking thermometer (optional, but very useful!)

Instructions

1. Preheat oven to 375F.
2. In a large saute pan over medium heat, heat 2 tablespoon butter or oil until melted and beginning to froth. Add mushrooms and cook, stirring frequently, for 2 or 3 minutes. Add garlic, sprinkle with salt and pepper, and continue to cook until most of the liquid has evaporated, 4 or 5 minutes more.
3. Add 2 tablespoon chopped sage and cook 1 minute more. Remove from heat.

4. Remove skin from turkey breast and set aside (do not discard). Lay turkey breast on a work surface and cover with plastic wrap. Pound with a kitchen mallet to an even ½ to 1-inch thickness.
5. Spread mushroom mixture evenly over turkey breast, leaving a 1 inch border and roll up from the short end tightly into a log. Wrap reserved skin over log and tie at several intervals with kitchen twine.
6. Place on a broiling pan and rub all over with remaining butter or oil. Sprinkle with remaining sage and season with salt and pepper.
7. Place pop-up timer, if using, into thickest part of the turkey roll (pierce the skin with a sharp knife if need be).
8. Roast until timer pops up or until internal temperature reaches 180F, approximately 50 to 60 minutes.

WHOLE ROASTED BRINED TURKEY

Nutrition: Cal 180;Fat 6 g;Carb 1 g;Protein 38 g
Serving 8; Cook time 4 hour 10 min

Ingredients

- Turkey Brine
- 2 cups kosher salt
- 2 gallons water
- 12lb Turkey
- Any additional Seasonings you want to add (optional)
- For the Turkey (if NOT stuffing)
- Brined Turkey
- 1 teaspoon each :
- Salt, pepper, onion powder, garlic powder, ground sage (or Bell's seasoning), paprika
- 3 tablespoon butter, melted
- 1 apple, quartered (for cooking only)
- 1 onion, quartered
- 1 stalk celery, cut into pieces

Instructions

1. The day before cooking:
2. Remove turkey from packaging. Remove gravy packet (if included) and giblets. Rinse well on the inside and outside.
3. In a large stock pot, dissolve kosher salt in water. Once the salt is completely dissolved, add the turkey to the pot. Cover and refrigerate overnight.
4. When ready to cook:
5. Preheat oven to 350 degrees.
6. Remove turkey from the brine, rinse well on the inside and outside. Pat dry. Place in a roasting pan and bend wings under the bird or cover with foil.
7. To the cavities of the turkey, add apple and vegetables. Apple will not add carbs UNLESS you are using the juice to make gravy later. If so, omit it.
8. Baste the turkey with olive oil and generously salt, pepper and seasonings on all sides. Cover with foil (remove for the last 30 minutes)
9. Place turkey in the oven and cook according to the chart below or until reaching an internal temperature of 165 degrees.

10. When done, allow the turkey to rest for 20 to 30 minutes prior to carving.

LOW CARB KETO TURKEY SOUP

Nutrition: Cal 255;Fat 20 g;Carb 5 g;Protein 15 g
Serving 8; Cook time 30 min

Ingredients
- 2 tablespoon butter ghee or olive oil
- 1 small onion diced (70g)
- ⅔ cup / 85g medium carrots chopped
- 2 celery stalks chopped (about 1 ½ cup / 140g)
- 2 cups / 200 g cauliflower florets diced
- 2 garlic cloves minced
- 1 cup / 90g mushrooms sliced
- ½ tablespoon fresh thyme minced
- 1 tablespoon parsley minced (4g)
- ½ tsp - 1 tsp sea salt to taste
- ⅓ teaspoon freshly ground black pepper or to taste
- ¼ cup / 60 ml dry white wine
- 3 cups / 720 ml turkey or chicken stock + additional stock if it's too thick
- oz / 300 g cooked turkey shredded (or chicken!)
- 1 cup / 240ml heavy cream or coconut milk

To serve
- 1.5 tbsp / 6g parsley minced

Instructions
1. Heat the butter, ghee or olive oil in a large saucepan or dutch oven over a medium heat.
2. Add the onion, carrot, celery and cauliflower and cook until softened and golden, about 7 - 8 minutes.
3. Add the garlic, mushrooms, thyme and 1 tablespoon of parsley. Season with salt and pepper and cook until the mushrooms are beginning to brown, another 2 - 3 minutes.
4. Add the white wine and stock.
5. Bring to the boil and reduce to a simmer. Cook for 10 minutes.
6. Add the cooked turkey. Stir in the heavy cream or coconut milk. Simmer until heated through, about 2 minutes. Adjust the seasoning to taste and serve in bowls topped with fresh chopped parsley.

BEST CHIKEN SOUP

Nutrition: Cal 171;Fat 13 g;Carb 4 g;Protein 8 g
Serving 6; Cook time 30 min

Ingredients
- 1/2 cup chopped onion
- 2 stalks celery, chopped
- 1/4 cup butter or coconut oil
- 1 1/2 tsp garam masala (or curry)
- 4 cups chicken broth
- 1/2 cup jicama, chopped
- 1/4 cup cauliflower "rice"
- 1 skinless, boneless chicken breast, cubed
- Celtic sea salt to taste

- Fresh ground black pepper to taste
- 1 pinch dried thyme
- 1/2 cup coconut milk (or more if you want a creamier soup)

Instructions
1. To make this flavorful soup, start by sautéing onions and celery in butter in a large soup pot. Add garam masala spice (or curry) and cook for 5 more minutes.
2. Next, add chicken stock, mix well, and bring to a boil. Let it simmer for about 30 minutes.
3. After that, add jicama, cauliflower rice, chicken, salt, pepper, and thyme to the pot. Simmer for 15-20 minutes.
4. When you're ready to serve, add hot coconut milk to the soup. This recipe makes 6 servings.

KETO GROUND TURKEY CRUST PIZZA

Nutrition: Cal 154;Fat 8.3 g;Carb 4 g;Protein 16 g
Serving 8; Cook time 35 min

Ingredients
- 1 lb ground turkey
- 1 egg, beaten
- 2 tablespoons of grated parmesan cheese
- 1 teaspoon Italian seasonings
- 2 teaspoon of salt
- ½ teaspoon of pepper
- 2 cloves garlic, crushed
- ½ cup of low carb sauce (I like Specialty Selects Marinara)
- 1 cup mozzarella, shredded
- Optional Toppings (like pepperoni, sausage, peppers, mushrooms, bacon, etc)

Instructions
1. Preheat oven to 350°F.
2. In a large bowl mix turkey, egg, parmesan cheese, garlic, salt, peper and Italian seasonings.
3. Cover a cookie sheet with parchment paper or a silicon mat. Take the mixed turkey mixture and form into a pizza crust. Make it fairly thin so it won't taste too "meaty".
4. Bake for roughly 20 minutes. Times will vary depending on how thin you make the crust. You want it to be cooked through but not too browned.
5. Take it out of the oven and cover with sauce and then cheese. From there you can top what ever other toppings you want.
6. Bake for another 5 minutes and then place it under the broiler to brown the top if you want.

KETO TURKEY STUFFED MUSHROOMS

Nutrition: Cal 235;Fat 12 g;Carb 4 g;Protein 37 g
Serving 4; Cook time 35 min

Ingredients
- 3 Tbsp extra virgin olive oil, divided
- 1 lb. bulk turkey or chicken sausage, or 1 lb ground turkey
- 4 oz. goat cheese, room temp, cut into small chunks

- 4 large Portobello mushrooms or 1 lb baby bella mushrooms, rinsed, stems removed, and patted dry
- Sea salt and black pepper, to taste

Instructions

1. Preheat oven to 350°F and lightly grease a large roasting pan with one tablespoon olive oil. Set aside.
2. Heat remaining olive oil in a large skillet over medium heat.
3. Add turkey sausage to the skillet. Cook until no longer pink, approximately 6-8 minutes, breaking up the sausage into small pieces while cooking.
4. Add goat cheese to skillet and cover for 1-2 minutes. Remove cover and stir until cheese is completely melted and combined with the turkey and pepper mixture. Remove from heat and set aside.
5. Fill each mushroom cap with some of the turkey mixture. Drizzle the mushrooms with remaining olive oil and season with salt and black pepper, as desired.
6. Place pan in the pre-heated oven and roast until the mushrooms are slightly browned around the edges, approximately 10-12 minutes. Remove from oven and serve immediately.

COBB SALAD

Nutrition: Cal 545;Fat 38 g;Carb 23 g;Protein 33 g
Serving 4; Cook time 20 min

Ingredients

- 1½ cups chopped Baked Boneless Chicken Thighs
- 6 Hard-boiled Eggs , chopped
- 3 celery stalks, minced
- 2 tablespoons minced red onion
- 1 tablespoon Dijon mustard
- 2 cups Mayonnaise
- Salt
- Freshly ground black pepper
- 8 leaves butter or romaine lettuce

Instructions

1. In a large bowl, combine the chicken, eggs, celery, onion, and mustard. Add the Mayonnaise and stir until mixed. Season with salt and pepper.
2. Divide the egg salad and lettuce between 3 storage containers. To serve, make egg salad wraps by filling the lettuce leaves with the salad and wrapping the lettuce around it.

JALAPENO POPPER CHICKEN

Nutrition: Cal 524;Fat 29 g;Carb 2 g;Protein 59 g
Serving 4; Cook time 20 min

Ingredients

- 4 boneless skinless chicken breasts 6-ounce
- 8 ounces cream cheese softened
- 2 jalepenos diced
- 8 strips sugar free thin-cut bacon
- Primal Kitchen Ranch Dressing for serving

Instructions

1. Begin by preheating the oven to 400°F.

2. Next, place a chicken breast on a cutting board and take a sharp knife, holding it parallel to the chicken, to make a 1-inch-wide incision at the top of the breast. Carefully cut into the chicken to form a large pocket, leaving a ½-inch border along the sides and bottom. Repeat this step with the other 3 breasts.
3. Then, place the cheese and jalapenos in a bowl and stir well to combine. Transfer the mixture to a large ziplock bag and cut a ¾-inch hole in one corner of the plastic bag. Squeeze the softened cheese into the pockets in the chicken, dividing the cheese evenly among them.
4. Wrap 2 strips of bacon around each breast and secure the ends with toothpicks. Place the bacon-wrapped chicken onto a rimmed baking sheet and place it in the oven. Cook until the bacon is crisp and the chicken is cooked through, which should take about 18-20 minutes. Timing may vary depending on how thick the chicken breast is.
5. Finally, to store any leftovers, place them in an airtight container in the refrigerator for up to 3 days. To reheat, simply place the chicken on a rimmed baking sheet and put it in a 400°F oven for 5 minutes or until it's warmed through.

SWEET AND SOUR CHICKEN

Nutrition: Cal 252;Fat 11 g;Carb 2 g;Protein 35 g
Serving 4; Cook time 20 min

Ingredients

- 2 teaspoons avocado oil or coconut oil
- 1 pound boneless skinless chicken breasts
- Redmond Real salt
- 1/4 cup chicken bone broth
- 1/4 cup Keto Primo Ketchup
- 2 tablespoons Swerve Brown
- 1 tablespoon tamari sauce
- 1/2 tablespoon lime juice
- ¼ teaspoon fresh ginger peeled and grated
- 1 clove garlic minced

FOR GARNISH:

- Sesame seeds
- scallions sliced
- Lime wedges

Instructions

1. First, heat up some oil in a large wok or cast-iron skillet over medium-high heat. Then, pat the chicken pieces dry with a paper towel and season them well on all sides with salt.
2. Fry the chicken in the hot oil until it turns light golden brown on all sides, which should take about 4 minutes. Once done, remove the chicken from the wok and set it aside.
3. Next, add the remaining ingredients to the wok and boil over medium heat until the sauce is reduced and thickened, which should take about 10 minutes.

4. Once the sauce is ready, return the chicken to the wok and bring it to a hard boil. Reduce the heat to medium and let it simmer for 10 more minutes until the chicken is cooked through and no longer pink inside.
5. To serve, garnish the chicken with sesame seeds, sliced scallions, and lime wedges. If you have leftovers, you can store them in an airtight container in the refrigerator for up to 3 days. When you're ready to reheat, simply place the chicken in a greased skillet over medium heat for 5 minutes or until it's warmed to your liking.

TURKEY MEATBALL SOUP
Nutrition: Cal 220;Fat 8 g;Carb 3 g;Protein 33 g
Serving 8; Cook time 20 min
Ingredients
MEATBALLS:
- 1 tablespoon avocado oil or lard
- ¼ cup chopped onions
- 1 clove garlic minced
- 1 teaspoon Redmond Real salt
- 2 pounds extra lean ground turkey
- 2 tablespoons Kettle and Fire chicken Broth or ANY flavor works
- 2 teaspoons organic dried poultry seasoning
- 1 large egg
SOUP:
- 1 tablespoon avocado oil or lard
- 1 cup diced yellow onions
- 4 cups Kettle and Fire Chicken Broth
- 1 teaspoon organic dried poultry seasoning
- Redmond Real salt or fish sauce for umami
GARNISH:
- Fresh ground pepper
- Fresh thyme leaves
Instructions
1. To make this soup with meatballs, you'll need to preheat your oven to 425°F. Then, start by making the meatballs. Heat some oil in a skillet over medium heat and add onions and garlic, seasoning with salt. Sauté the mixture until the onions are translucent, which should take about 5 minutes. Once done, transfer the mixture to a small bowl and set it aside to cool.
2. In a large bowl, combine ground turkey, broth, seasoning, and egg. Once the onion mixture has cooled down, add it to the bowl with the meat mixture and mix everything together with your hands. Shape the mixture into 1¼-inch balls and place them on a rimmed baking sheet. Bake for 15 minutes or until the meatballs are cooked through.
3. While the meatballs are cooking, you can start making the soup. Heat some oil in a Dutch oven over medium-high heat, then add sliced onions and 1/4 cup broth. Sauté the mixture for 5 minutes, stirring often, until the onions turn golden brown. Add broth and seasoning and boil for 10 minutes, or until the onions become very soft. Taste the soup and add salt if necessary.
4. To serve, ladle the onion broth into bowls and add the meatballs. You can garnish the soup with freshly ground pepper and thyme if desired. If you have leftovers, store them in an airtight container in the refrigerator for up to 5 days, or freeze them in a freezer-safe container for up to a month. To reheat, simply place the soup in a saucepan over medium heat for a few minutes until it's warmed through.

REUBEN CHICKEN
Nutrition: Cal 584;Fat 38 g;Carb 9 g;Protein 51 g
Serving 4; Cook time 4 hours 20 min
Ingredients
THOUSAND ISLAND DRESSING:
- 1/2 cup Primal Kitchen mayo
- 1/4 cup chopped dill pickles
- 1/4 cup Primal Kitchen Ketchup
- 1/2 teaspoon stevia glycerite
- 1/8 teaspoon fish sauceor fine grain sea salt
REUBEN CHICKEN:
- 24 oz. sauerkraut drained
- 4 6 oz boneless skinless chicken breasts
- 1 1/4 teaspoons Redmond Real salt
- 1/2 teaspoon fresh ground pepper
- 4 tablespoons Primal Kitchen Dijon mustard divided
Instructions
1. To prepare this slow cooker sauerkraut and mustard chicken, start by making the dressing. Place all the ingredients in a small bowl and stir well to combine. Taste and adjust seasoning as desired, then cover and store in the fridge for up to 5 days.
2. Next, layer half the sauerkraut in the bottom of a greased 5-6 quart slow cooker. Drizzle with ⅓ of the dressing.
3. Season the chicken on all sides with salt and pepper. Place the chicken breasts on top of the sauerkraut and spread half the mustard over the chicken. Top with the remaining sauerkraut and drizzle another ⅓ of the dressing over everything, reserving the remaining dressing and mustard for serving.
4. Cover the slow cooker and cook on low for 4 hours, or until the chicken is cooked through and tender.
5. To serve, place each chicken breast on a plate. Divide the sauerkraut over the top of the chicken. Finish each plate with a drizzle of the remaining dressing and mustard.
6. Any extras can be stored in an airtight container in the fridge for up to 5 days. To reheat, simply place in a casserole dish in a 350 degree F oven for 5 minutes or until heated through.

CRACK SLAW

Nutrition: Cal 219;Fat 10 g;Carb 10 g;Protein 27 g
Serving 4; Cook time 20 min

Ingredients
- 2 tablespoons coconut oil divided
- 1/2 cup diced onion
- 1 head roasted garlic or 3 cloves minced
- 1 lb boneless skinless Chicken breast
- 1 1/2 teaspoons Redmond Real salt divided
- 5 cups shredded cabbage
- 2 tablespoons tamari sauce or 1/4 cup Coconut aminos
- 1 tablespoon grated fresh Ginger or 1/2 teaspoon dried ginger
- 1 teaspoon Redboat fish sauce or salt
- 1/2 teaspoon stevia glycerite
- Black pepper
- Garnish with sliced green onion

Instructions
1. To prepare this chicken and cabbage stir fry, begin by cutting the chicken into 3/4 inch pieces. Pat the chicken dry and season on all sides with 1 teaspoon salt.
2. Heat a tablespoon of oil in a large skillet or wok over medium heat. Add the onion and garlic, and cook for 5-7 minutes, until the onion is soft.
3. Next, increase the heat to medium-high and add the remaining oil to the skillet. Once hot, add the chicken and stir fry for 3-5 minutes, until the chicken is just golden.
4. Add the cabbage, ginger, tamari, fish sauce, stevia, 1/2 teaspoon salt, and pepper to the skillet. Stir fry for an additional 3-5 minutes, until the cabbage is tender.
5. To serve, garnish with sliced green onion. Any leftovers can be stored in an airtight container in the fridge for up to 4 days. To reheat, simply place in a greased skillet over medium heat for 3 minutes or until heated through.

KETO CHICKEN ENCHILADAS

Nutrition: Cal 213;Fat 7 g;Carb 7 g;Protein 28 g
Serving 4; Cook time 40 min

Ingredients:
FILLING:
- 2 chicken breasts
- 1/2 cup chicken broth homemadeor Kettle and Fire chicken broth
- 1/4 cup diced onion
- 1 4.5 oz can green chilis, drained

ENCHILADA SAUCE:
- 1 cup favorite salsa check for added sugars and vegetable oils
- 2 tablespoons tomato purée
- 3/4 cup beef/chicken broth homemade preferred but boxed works
- 1/4 cup chili powder
- 1/4 teaspoon cumin powder
- 1/4 teaspoon garlic powder

TORTILLAS:
12 slices organic deli chicken

TOPPING:
- Shredded Monterey Jack or sharp cheddar cheese omit if dairy free
- Chopped Cilantro Leaves

Instructions:
1. Place the filling ingredients in a 4 quart slow cooker. Turn on low for 6-8 hours (or on high for 4 hours). Shred with a fork. Can be made up to 2 days ahead.
2. Place all enchilada sauce ingredients in a blender and combine until smooth. Use for Keto enchiladas. Store in airtight container in the fridge for up to one week. Can be frozen for up to a month.
3. Place the sauce in the bottom of a 9 by 11 inch casserole dish.
4. Place a few tablespoons of shredded chicken in the center of a slice of deli chicken. Roll up like an enchilada. Place onto sauce in the casserole dish. Repeat with remaining filling and "tortillas". Top with cheese if using. Place in oven to bake for 10 minutes or until heated through and cheese is melted. NOTE: You can skip the baking and microwave on HIGH for 1 minute or until cheese is melted.
5. Garnish with chopped cilantro.

YAKISOBA CHICKEN

Nutrition: Cal 317;Fat 14 g;Carb 2 g;Protein 43 g
Serving 6; Cook time 20 min

Ingredients
- 1/2 tsp sesame oil
- 1 TBS coconut oil
- 2 cloves garlic, chopped
- 4 (8 oz) chicken thighs – cut into 1-inch cubes
- 1/2 cup coconut aminos OR wheat free Tamari sauce (fermented soy sauce)
- 2 TBS hot sauce
- 1/2 teaspoon stevia glycerite (optional)
- 1 small onion, sliced lengthwise into eighths
- 1 medium head cabbage, sliced into "noodles"
- OPTIONAL: peanuts for garnish, sauteed broccoli

Instructions
1. To make this tasty stir-fry, start by combining sesame oil and coconut oil in a large skillet. Add garlic and stir-fry for a minute or two. Then, add the chicken and continue to stir-fry until it's no longer pink. Once cooked, set the mixture aside.
2. In the same skillet, add onion and cabbage noodles and stir-fry until the cabbage begins to soften. Stir in the remaining Tamari sauce, and then add the chicken mixture back into the pan. Mix everything together until well combined.

BAKED CHICKEN NUGGETS

Nutrition: Cal 400;Fat 26 g;Carb 2 g;Protein 43 g
Serving 4; Cook time 30 min

Ingredients:
- ¼ cup almond flour
- 1 teaspoon chili powder
- ½ teaspoon paprika
- 2 pounds boneless chicken thighs, cut into 2-inch chunks
- Salt and pepper
- 2 large eggs, whisked well

Instructions:
1. Preheat the oven to 400°F and line a baking sheet with parchment.
2. Stir together the almond flour, chili powder, and paprika in a shallow dish.
3. Season the chicken with salt and pepper, then dip in the beaten eggs.
4. Dredge the chicken pieces in the almond flour mixture, then arrange on the baking sheet.
5. Bake for 20 minutes until browned and crisp. Serve hot.

COCONUT CHICKEN TENDERS

Nutrition: Cal 325;Fat 9 g;Carb 2 g;Protein 45 g
Serving 4; Cook time 40 min

Ingredients:
- ¼ cup almond flour
- 2 tablespoons shredded unsweetened coconut
- ½ teaspoon garlic powder
- 2 pounds boneless chicken tenders
- Salt and pepper
- 2 large eggs, whisked well

Instructions:
1. Preheat the oven to 400°F and line a baking sheet with parchment.
2. Stir together the almond flour, coconut, and garlic powder in a shallow dish.
3. Season the chicken with salt and pepper, then dip into the beaten eggs.
4. Dredge the chicken tenders in the almond flour mixture, then arrange on the baking sheet.
5. Bake for 25 to 30 minutes until browned and cooked through. Serve hot.

CHEESY BUFFALO CHICKEN SAND-WICH

Nutrition: Cal 555;Fat 33 g;Carb 3 g;Protein 55 g
Serving 1; Cook time 30 min

Ingredients:
- 1 large egg, separated into white and yolk
- Pinch cream of tartar
- Pinch salt
- 1 ounce cream cheese, softened
- 1 cup cooked chicken breast, shredded
- 2 tablespoons hot sauce
- 1 slice Swiss cheese

Instructions:
1. For the bread, preheat the oven to 300°F and line a baking sheet with
2. parchment.
3. Beat the egg whites with the cream of tartar and salt until soft peaks form.
4. Whisk the cream cheese and egg yolk until smooth and pale yellow.
5. Fold in the egg whites a little at a time until smooth and well combined.
6. Spoon the batter onto the baking sheet into two even circles.
7. Bake for 25 minutes until firm and lightly browned.
8. Shred the chicken into a bowl and toss with the hot sauce.
9. Spoon the chicken onto one of the bread circles and top with cheese.
10. Top with the other bread circle and enjoy.

CHICKEN SALAD PUFFS

Nutrition: Cal 109;Fat 13 g;Carb 2 g;Protein 15 g
Serving 12; Cook time 20 min

Ingredients
PUFFS
- 3 eggs separated
- 1/2 tsp cream of tartar
- 3 oz cream cheese softened (or you could use 2 tablespoons allulose to keep it dairy free and lower fat for PSMF macros)
- 1/2 cup unflavored egg white or whey protein

CHICKEN SALAD FILLING:
- 1 chicken thigh cooked and shredded
- 2 pieces sugar free bacon
- 2 oz blue cheese crumbled (if not dairy sensitive)
- 4 ounces homemade mayo

Instructions
1. To make these delicious protein sparing bread puffs, start by preheating your oven to 375 degrees. Then, separate the eggs and set aside the yolks for another recipe.
2. In a large bowl, whip the egg whites and cream of tartar until they are very stiff. Add the protein powder, and then use a spatula to gradually fold in the cream cheese or allulose, being careful not to break down the whites.
3. Next, place round balls of dough onto a greased baking sheet (or use a mini muffin tin). Bake the puffs at 375 degrees for 10 minutes. Once done, keep the oven shut and leave the puffs inside to cool.
4. To make the chicken salad filling, mix together all the ingredients in a large bowl, adding salt and pepper to taste. Then, stuff the filling into the protein sparing bread puffs and enjoy!

SESAME CHICKEN AVOCADO SALAD

Nutrition: Cal 540;Fat 47 g;Carb 10 g;Protein 23 g
Serving 2; Cook time 10 min

Ingredients:
- 1 tablespoon sesame oil
- 8 ounces boneless chicken thighs, chopped
- Salt and pepper
- 4 cups fresh spring greens
- 1 cup sliced avocado
- 2 tablespoons olive oil
- 2 tablespoons rice wine vinegar
- 1 tablespoon sesame seeds

Instructions:
1. Heat the sesame oil in a skillet over medium-high heat.
2. Season the chicken with salt and pepper, then add to the skillet.
3. Cook the chicken until browned and cooked through, stirring often.
4. Remove the chicken from the heat and cool slightly.
5. Divide the spring greens onto two salad plates and top with avocado.
6. Drizzle the salads with olive oil and rice wine vinegar.
7. Top with cooked chicken and sprinkle with sesame seeds to serve.

CURRIED CHICKEN SOUP

Nutrition: Cal 390;Fat 22 g;Carb 14 g;Protein 34 g
Serving 4; Cook time 30 min

Ingredients:
- 2 tablespoons olive oil, divided
- 4 boneless chicken thighs (about 12 ounces)
- 1 small yellow onion, chopped
- 2 teaspoons curry powder
- 2 teaspoons ground cumin
- Pinch cayenne
- 4 cups chopped cauliflower
- 4 cups chicken broth
- 1 cup water
- 2 cloves minced garlic
- ½ cup canned coconut milk
- 2 cups chopped kale
- Fresh chopped cilantro

Instructions:
1. Chop the chicken into bite-sized pieces then set aside.
2. Heat 1 tablespoon oil in a saucepan over medium heat.
3. Add the onions and cook for 4 minutes then stir in half of the spices.
4. Stir in the cauliflower and sauté for another 4 minutes.
5. Pour in the broth then add the water and garlic and bring to a boil.
6. Reduce heat and simmer for 10 minutes until the cauliflower is softened.
7. Remove from heat and stir in the coconut milk and kale.
8. Heat the remaining oil in a skillet and add the chicken – cook until
9. browned.

10. Stir in the rest of the spices then cook until the chicken is done.
11. Stir the chicken into the soup and serve hot, garnished with fresh cilantro.

KALE CAESAR SALAD WITH CHICKEN

Nutrition: Cal 390;Fat 30 g;Carb 13 g;Protein 15 g
Serving 2; Cook time 20 min

Ingredients:
- 1 tablespoon olive oil
- 6 ounces boneless chicken thigh, chopped
- Salt and pepper
- 3 tablespoons mayonnaise
- 1 tablespoon lemon juice
- 1 anchovy, chopped
- 1 teaspoon Dijon mustard
- 1 clove garlic, minced
- 4 cups fresh chopped kale

Instructions:
1. Heat the oil in a skillet over medium-high heat.
2. Season the chicken with salt and pepper, then add to the skillet.
3. Cook until the chicken is no longer pink, then remove from heat.
4. Combine the mayonnaise, lemon juice, anchovies, mustard, and garlic in a blender.
5. Blend smooth, then season with salt and pepper.
6. Toss the kale with the dressing, then divide in half and top with chicken to serve.

CHICKEN ENCHILADA SOUP

Nutrition: Cal 390;Fat 27 g;Carb 12 g;Protein 24 g
Serving 4; Cook time 60 min

Ingredients:
- 2 tablespoons coconut oil
- 2 medium stalks celery, sliced
- 1 small yellow onion, chopped
- 1 small red pepper, chopped
- 2 cloves garlic, minced
- 1 cup diced tomatoes
- 2 teaspoons ground cumin
- 1 teaspoon chili powder
- ½ teaspoon dried oregano
- 4 cups chicken broth
- 1 cup canned coconut milk
- 8 ounces cooked chicken thighs, chopped
- 2 tablespoons fresh lime juice
- ¼ cup fresh chopped cilantro

Instructions:
1. Heat the oil in a saucepan over medium-high heat then add the celery,
2. onion, peppers, and garlic – sauté for 4 to 5 minutes.
3. Stir in the garlic and cook for a minute until fragrant.
4. Add the tomatoes and spices then cook for 3 minutes, stirring often.

5. Add the broth and bring the soup to a boil, then reduce heat and simmer for about 20 minutes.
6. Stir in the coconut milk and simmer for another 20 minutes, then add the chicken.
7. Cook until the chicken is heated through, then stir in the lime juice and cilantro.

BACON-WRAPPED CHICKEN ROLLS
Nutrition: Cal 350;Fat 16 g;Carb 0,5 g;Protein 46 g
Serving 2; Cook time 40 min
Ingredients:
- 6 boneless, skinless, chicken breast halves
- 6 slices uncooked bacon
- Salt. pepper
Instructions:
1. Preheat the oven to 350°F.
2. Pound the chicken breast halves with a meat mallet to flatten.
3. Roll the chicken breast halves up then wrap each one with bacon.
4. Place the rolls on a foil-lined baking sheet.
5. Bake for 30 to 35 minutes until the chicken is done and the bacon crisp.

KETO LEMON AND HERB CHICKEN SKEWERS
Nutrition: Cal 310;Fat 18 g;Carb 9 g;Protein 27 g
Serving 4; Cook time 1 hours 30 min
Ingredients:
- 1 lb boneless, skinless chicken breasts, cut into 1-inch cubes
- 1/4 cup olive oil
- 2 tbsp lemon juice
- 2 garlic cloves, minced
- 1 tsp dried oregano
- 1 tsp dried thyme
- 1/2 tsp salt
- 1/4 tsp black pepper
- 1 red onion, cut into 1-inch pieces
- 1 red bell pepper, cut into 1-inch pieces
- 1 zucchini, cut into 1-inch rounds
Instructions:
1. In a large bowl, whisk together the olive oil, lemon juice, garlic, oregano, thyme, salt, and black pepper.
2. Add the chicken cubes to the bowl and toss to coat with the marinade. Cover the bowl with plastic wrap and refrigerate for at least 1 hour, or up to 8 hours.
3. Preheat the grill to medium-high heat.
4. Thread the marinated chicken, red onion, red bell pepper, and zucchini onto skewers, alternating the ingredients.
5. Grill the skewers for 10-12 minutes, turning occasionally, until the chicken is cooked through and the vegetables are tender.
6. Serve hot, garnished with fresh herbs if desired.

CHILI LIME CHICKEN KABOBS
Nutrition: Cal 325;Fat 16 g;Carb 6,5 g;Protein 37 g
Serving 2; Cook time 40 min
Ingredients:
- 3 TBS coconut oil (melted) OR butter
- 1 1/2 TBS coconut vinegar OR red wine vinegar
- 1 lime, juiced
- 1 tsp chili powder
- 1/2 tsp paprika
- 1/2 tsp onion powder
- 1/2 tsp garlic powder
- cayenne pepper to taste
- Sea salt and freshly ground black pepper to taste
- 1 pound skinless, boneless chicken breast halves – cut into 1 1/2 inch pieces
- 4 skewers
Instructions:
1. To make delicious chicken skewers, start by whisking together oil, vinegar, and lime juice in a small bowl. Season the mixture with chili powder, paprika, onion powder, garlic powder, cayenne pepper, salt, and black pepper.
2. Next, place the chicken in a shallow baking dish and pour the sauce over it. Stir the chicken to ensure it's evenly coated with the sauce, cover the dish, and marinate in the refrigerator for at least 1 hour.
3. When you're ready to cook the chicken skewers, preheat the grill to medium-high heat and lightly oil the grill grate. Thread the chicken onto skewers, discarding any leftover marinade.
4. Finally, grill the chicken skewers for 10 to 15 minutes, or until the chicken juices run clear. Once done, remove from the grill and enjoy your delicious, flavorful chicken skewers!

SLOW-COOKER CHICKEN FAJITA SOUP
Nutrition: Cal 325;Fat 17 g; Carb 17 g;Protein 28 g
Serving 4; Cook time 60 hours
Ingredients:
- 12 ounces chicken thighs
- 1 cup diced tomatoes
- 2 cups chicken stock
- ½ cup enchilada sauce
- 2 ounces chopped green chiles
- 1 tablespoon minced garlic
- 1 medium yellow onion, chopped
- 1 small red pepper, chopped
- 1 jalapeno, seeded and minced
- 2 teaspoons chili powder
- ¾ teaspoon paprika
- ½ teaspoon ground cumin
- Salt and pepper
- 1 small avocado, sliced thinly
- ¼ cup chopped cilantro
- 1 lime, cut into wedges
Instructions:

1. Combine the chicken, tomatoes, chicken stock, enchilada sauce, chiles, and garlic in the slow cooker and stir well.
2. Add the onion, bell peppers, and jalapeno.
3. Stir in the seasonings then cover and cook on low for 5 to 6 hours.
4. Remove the chicken and chop or shred then stir it back into the soup.
5. Spoon into bowls and serve with sliced avocado, cilantro, and lime wedges.

CHICKEN ENCHILADA BOWL
Nutrition: Cal 356;Fat 35 g; Carb 6 g;Protein 28 g
Serving 4; Cook time 30 min

Ingredients
- 2 tablespoons coconut oil (for searing chicken)
- 1 pound of boneless skinless chicken thighs
- 3/4 cup red enchilada sauce
- 1/4 cup water
- 1/4 cup chopped onion
- 1 4 ounce can diced green chiles

Toppings (feel free to customize)
- 1 whole avocado, diced
- 1 cup shredded cheese (I used mild cheddar)
- 1/4 cup chopped pickled jalapenos
- 1/2 cup sour cream
- 1 roma tomato, chopped

Instructions
1. In a pot or dutch oven over medium heat melt the coconut oil. Once hot, sear chicken thighs until lightly brown.
2. Pour in enchilada sauce and water, then add onion and green chiles. Reduce heat to a simmer and cover. Cook chicken for 17-25 minutes or until chicken is tender and fully cooked through to at least 165° internal temperature.
3. Carefully remove the chicken and place onto a work surface. Chop or shred chicken (your preference), then add it back into the pot. Let the chicken simmer uncovered for an additional 10 minutes to absorb flavor and allow the sauce to reduce a little.
4. To serve, top with avocado, cheese, jalapeno, sour cream, tomato, and any other desired toppings. Feel free to customize these to your preference. Serve alone or over cauliflower rice if desired, just be sure to update your personal nutrition info as needed.

CHICKEN PHILLY CHEESESTEAK
Nutrition: Cal 263;Fat 12 g; Carb 5 g;Protein 27 g
Serving 3; Cook time 15 min

Ingredients
- 10 ounces boneless chicken breasts (about 2)
- 2 tablespoons worcestershire sauce
- 1/2 teaspoon onion powder
- 1/2 teaspoon garlic powder
- 1 dash of ground pepper
- 2 teaspoons olive oil, divided
- 1/2 cup diced onion, fresh or frozen
- 1/2 cup diced bell pepper, fresh or frozen
- 1/2 teaspoon minced garlic
- 3 slices provolone cheese or queso melting cheese

Instructions
1. Slice chicken breasts into very thin pieces (freeze slightly, if desired, to make this easier) and place in a medium bowl. Add next 4 ingredients (worcestershire through ground pepper) and stir to coat chicken.
2. Heat 1 teaspoon olive oil in a large (9") ovenproof skillet. Add chicken pieces and cook until browned - about 5 minutes. Turn pieces over and cook about 2-3 minutes more or until brown. Remove from skillet.
3. Add remaining 1 teaspoon olive oil to warm skillet. Then add onions, bell pepper, and garlic. Cook and stir to heated and tender, 2-3 minutes.
4. Turn heat off and add chicken back to skillet and stir with veggies to combine. Place sliced cheese over all and cover 2-3 minutes to melt.

EASY CASHEW CHICKEN
Nutrition: Cal 330;Fat 24 g; Carb 8 g;Protein 22 g
Serving 3; Cook time 15 min

Ingredients
- 3 raw chicken thighs, boneless and skinless
- 2 tablespoons coconut oil (for cooking)
- 1/4 cup raw cashews
- 1/2 medium green bell pepper
- 1/2 teaspoon ground ginger
- 1 tablespoon rice wine vinegar
- 1 1/2 tablespoons liquid aminos
- 1/2 tablespoon chili garlic sauce
- 1 tablespoon minced garlic
- 1 tablespoon sesame oil
- 1 tablespoon sesame seeds
- 1 tablespoon green onions
- 1/4 medium white onion
- Salt and pepper, to taste

Instructions
1. Heat a pan over low heat and toast the cashews for 8 minutes, or until they start to lightly brown and become fragrant. Remove and set aside.
2. Dice chicken thighs into 1 inch chunks. Cut onion and pepper into equally large chunks.
3. Increase heat to high and add coconut oil to pan.
4. Once oil is up to temperature, add in the chicken thighs and allow them to cook through (about 5 minutes).
5. Once the chicken is fully cooked add in the pepper, onions, garlic, chili garlic sauce, and seasonings (ginger, salt, pepper). Allow to cook on high for 2-3 minutes.
6. Add liquid aminos, rice wine vinegar, and cashews. Cook on high and allow the liquid to reduce down until it is a sticky consistency. There should not be excess liquid in the pan upon completing cooking.

THAI CHICKEN LETTUCE WRAPS

Nutrition: Cal 270;Fat 14 g; Carb 12 g;Protein 21 g
Serving 4; Cook time 10 min

Ingredients

- 1 lb ground chicken
- 1 tablespoon olive oil
- 2 tablespoons red curry paste
- 1 tablespoon ginger, minced
- 4 cloves garlic, minced
- 1 red bell pepper, sliced thinly
- 4 green onions, chopped
- 1 cup cabbage, shredded or coleslaw mix
- 1/4 cup hoisin sauce
- 1/4 teaspoon salt, or to taste
- 1/4 teaspoon pepper, or to taste
- 5 leaves basil, chopped
- 1/2 head iceberg lettuce, cut into half

Instructions

1. Add olive oil to a large skillet and heat until oil is very hot. Add ground chicken and cook until no longer pink and starts to brown, break it up with a wooden spoon as necessary. Should take about 3 minutes.
2. Add red curry paste, ginger, garlic, peppers, coleslaw mix, and stir-fry for another 3 minutes. Add hoisin sauce and green onions, and toss. Remove from heat then add basil and toss. Transfer cooked chicken to a bowl.
3. Serve by placing spoonfuls of chicken into pieces of lettuce, fold lettuce over like small tacos, and eat.

CRISPY CHIPOTLE CHICKEN THIGHS

Nutrition: Cal 400;Fat 20 g; Carb 8 g;Protein 25 g
Serving 2; Cook time 22 min

Ingredients

- ½teaspoon chipotle chili powder
- ¼ teaspoon garlic powder
- ¼ teaspoon onion powder
- ¼ teaspoon ground coriander
- ¼ teaspoon smoked paprika
- 12 ounces boneless chicken thighs
- Salt and pepper
- 1 tablespoon olive oil
- 3 cups fresh baby spinach

Instructions

1. Combine the chipotle chili powder, garlic powder, onion powder, coriander, and smoked paprika in a small bowl.
2. Pound the chicken thighs out flat, then season with salt and pepper on both sides.
3. Cut the chicken thighs in half and heat the oil in a heavy skillet over medium-high heat.
4. Add the chicken thighs skin-side-down to the skillet and sprinkle with the spice mixture.
5. Cook the chicken thighs for 8 minutes then flip and cook on the other side for 3 to 5 minutes.

6. During the last 3 minutes, add the spinach to the skillet and cook until wilted. Serve the crispy chicken thighs on a bed of wilted spinach.

EASY CASHEW CHICKEN

Nutrition: Cal 330;Fat 24 g; Carb 8 g;Protein 22 g
Serving 3; Cook time 15 min

Ingredients

- 3 raw chicken thighs, boneless and skinless
- 2 tablespoons coconut oil (for cooking)
- 1/4 cup raw cashews
- 1/2 medium green bell pepper
- 1/2 teaspoon ground ginger
- 1 tablespoon rice wine vinegar
- 1 1/2 tablespoons liquid aminos
- 1/2 tablespoon chili garlic sauce
- 1 tablespoon minced garlic
- 1 tablespoon sesame oil
- 1 tablespoon sesame seeds
- 1 tablespoon green onions
- 1/4 medium white onion
- Salt and pepper, to taste

Instructions

1. Heat a pan over low heat and toast the cashews for 8 minutes, or until they start to lightly brown and become fragrant. Remove and set aside.
2. Dice chicken thighs into 1 inch chunks. Cut onion and pepper into equally large chunks.
3. Increase heat to high and add coconut oil to pan.
4. Once oil is up to temperature, add in the chicken thighs and allow them to cook through (about 5 minutes).
5. Once the chicken is fully cooked add in the pepper, onions, garlic, chili garlic sauce, and seasonings (ginger, salt, pepper). Allow to cook on high for 2-3 minutes.
6. Add liquid aminos, rice wine vinegar, and cashews. Cook on high and allow the liquid to reduce down until it is a sticky consistency. There should not be excess liquid in the pan upon completing cooking.
7. Serve in a bowl, top with sesame seeds, and drizzle with sesame oil.

ROASTED TURKEY BREAST WITH MUSHROOMS & BRUSSELS SPROUTS

Nutrition: Cal 210;Fat 9 g; Carb 6 g;Protein 27 g
Serving 4; Cook time 50 min

Ingredients

- 2 tbsp olive oil
- 1 tsp salt
- 1 tsp black pepper
- 1 tsp garlic powder
- 1 pound turkey breast raw, cut into 1 inch cubes
- 1/2 pound brussels sprouts cleaned, cut in half
- 1 cups mushrooms cleaned

Instructions

1. Preheat oven to 350 degrees Fahrenheit.
2. In a small mixing bowl, combine olive oil, salt, black pepper, and garlic powder.
3. In a 9 x 6-inch casserole dish, combine turkey, brussels sprouts, and mushrooms. Pour the olive oil mixture over the top.
4. Cover with foil and bake for 45 minutes or until the turkey is cooked through and no longer pink. An internal temperature of 165 degrees Fahrenheit is a safe bet.

KETO PESTO STUFFED CHICKEN BREASTS

Nutrition: Cal 415;Fat 30 g; Carb 5 g;Protein 33 g
Serving 4; Cook time 525 min

Ingredients
- 4 boneless, skinless chicken breasts
- 1/2 cup homemade or store-bought pesto
- 1/2 cup almond flour
- 1/2 tsp garlic powder
- 1/2 tsp paprika
- Salt and pepper, to taste
- 2 tbsp olive oil

Instructions
1. Preheat the oven to 375°F.
2. Butterfly the chicken breasts by slicing them horizontally, but not all the way through, so they open like a book.
3. Spread about 2 tbsp of pesto onto the inside of each chicken breast, then fold them back up and secure with toothpicks.
4. In a shallow bowl, mix together the almond flour, garlic powder, paprika, salt, and pepper.
5. Coat each chicken breast in the almond flour mixture, shaking off any excess.
6. Heat the olive oil in an oven-safe skillet over medium-high heat. Add the chicken breasts and cook for 2-3 minutes per side, until golden brown.
7. Transfer the skillet to the oven and bake for 15-20 minutes, until the chicken is cooked through and the internal temperature reaches 165°F.
8. Let the chicken rest for a few minutes, then remove the toothpicks and slice.

SMOKED CHICKEN SALAD SANDWICH

Nutrition: Cal 299;Fat 13 g; Carb 3 g;Protein 24 g
Serving 4; Cook time 3 hours 50 min

Ingredients
- 4 cups cubed, smoked chicken meat
- 1 cup homemade baconnaise OR organic mayonnaise
- 1 tsp paprika
- 1 green onion, chopped
- 1 tsp Celtic sea salt
- ground black pepper to taste
- OPTIONAL: Sliced hard boiled eggs, 1 cup chopped celery, 1/2 cup minced green pepper
- 8 Protein Buns

Instructions
1. If you want to make smoked chicken sandwiches, start by cleaning and breaking down a whole chicken into thighs, breasts, and wings. Soak some wood chips and place them in the bottom of your smoker. Then, place the chicken on the racks and smoke it outside for 3-4 hours, following the manufacturer's directions.
2. Once the chicken has been smoked, preheat your oven to 250 degrees F and finish cooking the chicken in the oven for 30 minutes or until it is deep golden in color.
3. While the chicken is cooking, you can prepare the filling for your sandwiches. In a medium bowl, mix together mayonnaise with paprika and salt. Then, blend in onion and any other additions you prefer, such as celery or green pepper. Add the chopped poultry to the mixture and mix well. Season with black pepper to taste, and add sliced hard-boiled eggs if desired.
4. Chill the filling for at least 1 hour, then use protein buns to make your smoked chicken sandwiches. This recipe makes 8 servings.

TURKEY AND BACON LETTUCE WRAPS

Nutrition: Cal 305;Fat 20 g; Carb 22 g;Protein 11 g
Serving 4; Cook time 15 min

Ingredients
Wraps
- 1 head iceberg lettuce
- 4 slices deli turkey
- 4 slices bacon cooked
- 1 avocado thinly sliced
- 1 roma tomato thinly sliced
- 1 cucumber thinly sliced
- 1 carrot thinly sliced

Basil Mayo
- 1/2 cup mayo
- 6 basil leaves chopped
- 1 tsp lemon juice
- 1 garlic clove minced
- salt and pepper to taste

Instructions
Basil Mayo
1. Combine all of the ingredients in a food processor, blend until smooth

Wraps
1. Lay out two large lettuce leaves then layer on 1 slice of turkey and slather with Basil-Mayo.
2. Layer on a second slice of turkey followed by the bacon, and a few slices of avocado, tomato, cucumber and carrot.
3. Season lightly with salt and pepper then fold the bottom up, the sides in, and roll like a burrito.
4. Slice in half and serve cold.

CHIKEN STIR-FRY

Nutrition: Cal 312;Fat 14 g; Carb 11 g;Protein 31 g
Serving 4; Cook time 40 min

Ingredients

- 3 boneless, skinless chicken breasts, trimmed and cut into pieces at least 1 inch square
- 2 red bell peppers
- 2 cups sugar snap peas
- 1 1/2 T peanut oil
- 1-2 T sesame seeds, preferably black

MARINADE INGREDIENTS:

- 1/3 cup soy sauce (gluten-free if needed)
- 2 T unseasoned (unsweetened) rice vinegar
- 2 T low-carb sweetener of your choice (see notes)
- 1 T sesame oil
- 1/2 tsp. garlic powder

Instructions

1. Trim the chicken breasts and cut into pieces at least 1 inch square.
2. Combine soy sauce, rice vinegar, Stevia, agave or maple syrup, sesame oil and garlic powder.
3. Put the chicken into a Ziploc bag and pour in HALF the marinade. Let chicken marinate in the fridge for at least 4 hours (or all day while you're at work would be even better.)
4. When you're ready to cook, cover a large baking sheet with foil, then put it in the oven and let the pan get hot while the oven heats to 425F/220C.
5. Drain the marinated chicken well in a colander placed in the sink.
6. Remove the hot baking sheet from the oven and spread the chicken out over the surface (so pieces are not touching). Put baking sheet into the oven and cook chicken 8 minutes.
7. While the chicken cooks, trim ends of the sugar snap peas. Cut out the core and seeds of the red bell peppers and discard; then cut peppers into strips about the same thickness as the sugar snap peas.
8. Put veggies into a bowl and toss with the peanut oil.
9. After 8 minutes, remove pan from the oven and arrange the veggies around the chicken, trying to have each vegetable piece touching the pan as much as you can.
10. Put back into the oven and cook about 11 minutes more, or until the chicken is cooked through and lightly browned.
11. Brush cooked chicken and vegetables with the remaining marinade and sprinkle with black sesame seeds. Serve hot.

GARLIC, LEMON & THYME ROASTED CHICKEN BREASTS

Nutrition: Cal 230;Fat 27 g; Carb 4 g;Protein 26 g
Serving 4; Cook time 2 hours 45 min

Ingredients

- 4 boneless skinless chicken breasts
- zest of 1 lemon
- juice of 1 lemon
- 1/2 cup extra virgin olive oil
- 4 cloves garlic minced
- 1 tablespoon fresh thyme
- 1 teaspoon salt
- 1/2 teaspoon ground black pepper
- 1 tablespoon olive oil for sauteing

Instructions

1. Create the marinade by mixing the lemon juice, zest, 1/2 cup of olive oil, garlic, thyme, salt, and pepper. Place the chicken breasts in a non-reactive glass dish, or plastic ziptop bag, and pour the marinade over the chicken. Make sure to evenly coat the chicken, then cover and refrigerate for 2 hours.
2. Preheat your oven to 400 degrees F. Remove the chicken from the marinade and wipe off the excess. Heat 1 tablespoon of olive oil, and sear the chicken breasts for 2 minutes on each side, until they're golden brown.
3. Place the chicken breasts on a baking sheet lined with a baking rack, and roast at 400 degrees F for 20-30 minutes depending on the thickness of the chicken breast, or until the internal temperature reads 165 degrees F.

GRILLED CHICKEN KABOBS

Nutrition: Cal 278;Fat 12 g; Carb 26 g;Protein 27 g
Serving 2; Cook time 30 min

Ingredients

- 0.5 pound boneless skinless chicken breasts cut into 1 inch pieces
- 0.13 cup olive oil
- 0.17 cup soy sauce
- 0.13 cup honey
- 0.5 teaspoon minced garlic
- salt and pepper to taste
- 0.5 red bell pepper cut into 1 inch pieces
- 0.5 yellow bell pepper cut into 1 inch pieces
- 1 small zucchini cut into 1 inch slices
- 0.5 red onion cut into 1 inch pieces
- 0.5 tablespoon chopped parsley

Instructions

1. Place the olive oil, soy sauce, honey, garlic and salt and pepper in a large bowl.
2. Whisk to combine.
3. Add the chicken, bell peppers, zucchini and red onion to the bowl. Toss to coat in the marinade.
4. Cover and refrigerate for at least 1 hour, or up to 8 hours.
5. Soak wooden skewers in cold water for at least 30 minutes. Preheat grill or grill pan to medium high heat.
6. Thread the chicken and vegetables onto the skewers.
7. Cook for 5-7 minutes on each side or until chicken is cooked through.
8. Sprinkle with parsley and serve.

ETO BARBEQUE CHICKEN SOUP

Nutrition: Cal270;Fat 24 g; Carb 18 g;Protein 22 g
Serving 2; Cook time 60 min

Ingredients
The Base:
- 3 medium Chicken Thighs
- 2 teaspoon Chili Seasoning
- Salt and Pepper to Taste
- 2 tablespoon Chicken Fat or Olive Oil
- 1 1/2 cup Chicken Broth
- 1 1/2 cup Beef Broth
- Salt and Pepper to Taste

BBQ Sauce:
- 1/4 Cup Reduced Sugar Ketchup
- 1/4 cup Tomato Paste
- 2 tablespoon Dijon Mustard
- 1 tablespoon Soy Sauce
- 1 tablespoon hot sauce
- 2 1/2 teaspoon Liquid Smoke
- 1 teaspoon Worcestershire Sauce
- 1 1/2 teaspoon Garlic Powder
- 1 teaspoon Onion Powder
- 1 teaspoon Chili Powder
- 1 teaspoon Red Chili Flakes
- 1 teaspoon Cumin
- 1/4 cup Butter

Instructions
1. Preheat oven to 400F.
2. De-bone chicken thighs, set bones aside, and season well with your favorite chili seasoning.
3. Line a cookie sheet with foil and bake for 50 minutes.
4. While that is cooking, add 2 tablespoons of Chicken Fat or Olive Oil in a pot.
5. Heat this to a medium high heat and once hot, add chicken bones.
6. Let these cook for at least 5 minutes and then add broths.
7. Season with salt and pepper to taste.
8. Once the chicken is done, remove the skins and set aside.
9. Add all of the fat from the chicken thighs into the broth and stir.
10. Make the BBQ sauce by combining all ingredients above.
11. Add barbeque sauce to the pot and stir together.
12. Let this simmer in a pot for 20-30 minutes.
13. Use an immersion blender to emulsify all of the fats and liquids together.
14. Then, shred chicken thighs and add to the soup. You can optionally add spring onion or bell pepper here.
15. Simmer for another 10-20 minutes.
Serve with yellow bell pepper, spring onion, or cheddar cheese and the crispy chicken skins.

AVOCADO CHICKEN SALAD

Nutrition: Cal 267;Fat 20 g; Carb 4 g;Protein 19 g
Serving 3; Cook time 30 min

Ingredients
- 2 cups poached chicken finely diced (10 oz)
- 1 medium Hass Avocado, mashed
- 1/3 cup celery, finely diced (1 large rib)
- 2 tbsp red onion or scallion, minced
- 2 tbsp cilantro, finely chopped
- 2 tbsp avocado oil (or your favorite)
- 1 tbsp fresh lemon juice (or lime juice)
- salt and pepper to taste

Instructions
1. Prepare the celery, onion, and cilantro, placing in a medium bowl. Dice the chicken and add it to the bowl with the vegetables.
2. Cut into the avocado with a chef's knife until the blade hits the pit. Slide the knife around the pit, cutting the avocado in half. Twist the halves to separate. Remove the pit by tapping the knife into the pit until it sticks, make sure the avocado half is held steadily on a cutting board before attempting. Scoop out the avocado flesh with a spoon and place into a small bowl. Mash with a fork until smooth and creamy. Stir in the lemon juice and oil.
3. Add the mashed avocado to the to the chicken and vegetables and stir to mix. Serve over lettuce or enjoy on a low carb bagel.
Makes 3, 3/4-1 cup servings.

KETO CHICKEN SOUP

Nutrition: Cal 267;Fat 20 g; Carb 9 g;Protein 22 g
Serving 4; Cook time 60 min

Ingredients
- 2 tbsp. vegetable oil
- 1 medium onion, chopped
- 5 cloves garlic, smashed
- 2" piece fresh ginger, sliced
- 1 small cauliflower, cut into florets
- 3/4 tsp. crushed red pepper flakes
- 1 medium carrot, peeled and thinly sliced on a bias
- 6 c. low-sodium chicken broth
- 1 stalk celery, thinly sliced
- 2 boneless skinless chicken breasts
- Freshly chopped parsley, for garnish

Instructions
1. In a large pot over medium heat, heat oil. Add onion, garlic and ginger. Cook until beginning to brown.
2. Meanwhile, pulse cauliflower in a food processor until broken down into rice-sized granules. Add cauliflower to pot with onion mixture and cook over medium high heat until beginning to brown, about 8 minutes.

3. Add pepper flakes, carrots, celery and chicken broth and bring to a simmer. Add chicken breasts and let cook gently until they reach an internal temperature of 165°, about 15 minutes. Remove from pan, let cool until cool enough to handle, and shred. Meanwhile, continue simmering until vegetables are tender, 3 to 5 minutes more.

Remove ginger from pot, and add shredded chicken back to soup. Season to taste with salt and pepper, then garnish with parsley before serving.

KETO WHITE CHICKEN CHILI

Nutrition: Cal 480;Fat 30 g; Carb 5 g;Protein 38 g
Serving 4; Cook time 45 min

Ingredients
- 1 lb chicken breast
- cups chicken broth
- 2 garlic cloves, finely minced
- 1 4.5oz can chopped green chiles
- 1 diced jalapeno
- 1 diced green pepper
- 1/4 cup diced onion
- 4 tbsp butter
- 1/4 cup heavy whipping cream
- 4 oz cream cheese
- 2 tsp cumin
- 1 tsp oregano
- 1/4 tsp cayenne (optional)
- Salt and Pepper to taste

Instructions
1. In large pot, season chicken with cumin, oregano, cayenne, salt and pepper
2. Sear both sides over medium heat until golden
3. Add broth to pot, cover and cook chicken for 15-20 minutes or until fully cooked
4. While chicken is cooking, melt butter in medium skillet
5. Add chiles, diced jalapeno, green pepper and onion to skillet and saute until veggies soften
6. Add minced garlic and saute additional 30 seconds and turn off heat, set aside
7. Once chicken is fully cooked, shred with fork and add back into broth
8. Add sauteed veggies to pot with chicken and broth and simmer for 10 minutes
9. In medium bowl, soften cream cheese in microwave until you can stir it (~20 sec)
10. Mix cream cheese with heavy whipping cream
11. Stirring quickly, add mixture into pot with chicken and veggies
12. Simmer additional 15 minutes
13. Serve with favorite toppings such as: pepper jack cheese, avocado slices, cilantro, sour cream.

GARLIC PARMESAN CHICKEN WITH BROCCOLI

Nutrition: Cal 412;Fat 24 g; Carb 8 g;Protein 43 g
Serving 4; Cook time 30 min

Ingredients
- 4 boneless, skinless chicken breasts
- 2 tablespoons olive oil
- 4 cloves garlic, minced
- 1/2 cup grated Parmesan cheese
- 1/2 teaspoon paprika
- 1/2 teaspoon dried oregano
- 1/4 teaspoon salt
- 1/4 teaspoon black pepper
- 4 cups broccoli florets

Instructions
1. Preheat the oven to 400°F.
2. Heat the olive oil in a skillet over medium heat. Add the garlic and cook for 1-2 minutes, stirring occasionally, until fragrant.
3. In a small bowl, mix together the Parmesan cheese, paprika, oregano, salt, and black pepper.
4. Dip each chicken breast in the Parmesan mixture, coating both sides.
5. Place the chicken breasts in the skillet with the garlic and cook for 4-5 minutes on each side, until golden brown.
6. Meanwhile, steam the broccoli florets in a separate pot until tender.
7. Transfer the chicken and garlic to a baking dish, and bake for 10-15 minutes, or until the chicken is cooked through.
8. Serve the chicken with the broccoli on the side.

EASY LEMON CHICKEN

Nutrition: Cal 300;Fat 16 g; Carb 3 g;Protein 35 g
Serving 8; Cook time 40 min

Ingredients
- 4 TBS coconut oil divided
- 1 cup onion minced
- 3 garlic cloves peeled
- 4 chicken legs drumsticks and thighs separated (about 2 pounds)
- 1-2 tsp Redmond Real salt
- 1/2 cup flat-leaf parsley plus more for garnish
- 1/3 cup capers drained
- 2 cups organic chicken broth
- 1/3 cups coconut or white wine vinegar
- 1 lemon cut into thin strips
- Freshly ground black pepper

Instructions
1. Heat 2 TBS oil in a large heavy skillet over medium heat. Add onion and garlic; cook, stirring often, until softened, about 8 minutes. Transfer onion to a bowl; wipe skillet clean.

2. Add 2 TBS oil to skillet and increase heat to medium-high. Season chicken with salt. Add chicken to skillet and cook, turning once, until golden brown on both sides, 10–12 minutes. Transfer chicken to a plate.
3. Add reserved onion, 1/2 cup parsley, and capers to skillet; cook for 1 minute. Stir in broth and vinegar. Add chicken with any juices and the lemon slices. Reduce heat to medium-low; cover and simmer until meat is tender and falling off the bone, about 1 1/4 hours.
4. Transfer chicken to a large platter. Season sauce in skillet with salt and pepper. Spoon over chicken; garnish with parsley. Makes 8 servings.

GARLIC PARMESAN CHICKEN WITH BROCCOLI
Nutrition: Cal 495;Fat 30 g; Carb 5 g;Protein 40 g
Serving 4; Cook time 30 min

Ingredients
- 4 boneless, skinless chicken breasts, cut into bite-sized pieces
- 3 large carrots, peeled and cut into small pieces
- 1 large onion, chopped
- 2 cloves garlic, minced
- 1 tbsp grated fresh ginger
- 1 tbsp olive oil
- 1 tsp ground cumin
- 1 tsp ground coriander
- 1 tsp ground turmeric
- 1/4 tsp cayenne pepper
- 1 cup high-fat yogurt (such as Greek or Skyr)
- 1/2 cup chicken broth
- Salt and pepper, to taste
- Fresh cilantro, chopped (optional)

Instructions
1. Heat the olive oil in a large skillet or Dutch oven over medium-high heat.
2. Add the chicken pieces and cook until browned on all sides, about 5 minutes.
3. Add the onion, garlic, and ginger to the skillet and cook for another 2-3 minutes, until the onion is translucent.
4. Add the cumin, coriander, turmeric, and cayenne pepper to the skillet and stir to combine.
5. Add the chicken broth and carrots to the skillet and bring the mixture to a boil.
6. Reduce the heat to low and let the curry simmer for 20-25 minutes, until the chicken is cooked through and the carrots are tender.
7. Stir in the high-fat yogurt and cook for another 2-3 minutes, until the yogurt is heated through.
8. Season with salt and pepper to taste.
9. Serve the curry over cauliflower rice or with a side of fresh greens, and sprinkle with fresh cilantro if desired.

CHICKEN WITH SPINACH AND FETA
Nutrition: Cal 300;Fat 12 g; Carb 2 g;Protein 40 g
Serving 4; Cook time 30 min

Ingredients
- Chicken breasts (no bones and skin, 4 pieces)
- Spinach (half cup)
- Coconut oil (2 tbsp)
- Feta cheese (1/3 cup)
- Garlic powder (¼ teaspoon)
- Salt (¼ teaspoon)
- Dry oregano (¼ teaspoon)
- Parsley (¼ teaspoon, dry or fresh)
- Water (1 cup)

Instructions
1. Pound the chicken breasts but don't make these to thin; cut "pockets" inside meat.
2. In a bowl mix the feta along with the spinach and add the salt. Put this mix inside the "pockets" and after that close it with toothpicks.
3. Add the remainder in the seasoning all on the meat.
4. Set the pressure cooker to "Sauté" and squeeze coconut oil inside; fry the chicken breasts till they have a golden color. When the meat is cooked, press "Cancel."
5. Put the chicken breasts over a plate and pour water inside the pressure cooker; place the steaming rack inside and put the meat onto it. Steam the meat for fifteen minutes.
6. Release the stress naturally for fifteen minutes.
Serve while still warm.

CHICKEN CHORIZO CHILI
Nutrition: Cal 288;Fat 22 g; Carb 8 g;Protein 16 g
Serving 10; Cook time 80 min

Ingredients
- 1 tablespoon coconut oil
- 2 lbs smoked chorizo sausage sliced
- 2 chicken boneless skinless chicken thighs cut into ½ inch pieces
- 1 cup chopped onion
- 1 28 oz can whole peeled tomatoes, undrained
- 3 chipotle chiles in adobo sauce
- 3 tablespoons minced garlic
- 2 tablespoons smoked paprika
- 1 tablespoon ground cumin
- 1 tablespoon dried oregano leaves
- 2 teaspoons Redmond Real salt
- 1 teaspoon cayenne pepper
- 2 cups chicken stock boxed will work, homemade preferred
- 1 can 12 oz can Lacroix lime carbonated beverage
- 1 oz unsweetened baking chocolate chopped
- ¼ cup fresh lime juice
- ¼ cup chopped fresh cilantro

Instructions

1. Heat a large soup pot over medium high heat. Add the oil, chorizo, diced chicken and onions. Cook until onions are soft and chicken is cooked through, about 5 minutes.
2. Meanwhile, place the tomatoes with juice and chilis in a food processor. Combine until smooth. Set aside.
3. Add garlic, paprika, cumin, oregano, salt and cayenne to the soup pot and saute for another minute while stirring.
4. Add in the tomato puree, broth, Lacroix, chopped chocolate. Heat until a soft boil then reduce heat to low and cook for 1 hour for flavors to open up. Just before serving, stir in lime juice and cilantro.

SALSA CHICKEN
Nutrition: Cal 244;Fat 10 g; Carb 4.2 g;Protein 30 g
Serving 6; Cook time 35 min

Ingredients
- Chicken thighs without bones (2 lbs)
- Chicken broth (1/4 cup)
- Cream cheese (4 oz.)
- Salsa (1 cup)
- Taco seasoning (3 tbsp)
- Salt, Pepper

Instructions
1. Put the chicken thighs inside pressure cooker and add the taco seasoning, salt, and pepper.
2. Add the salsa, chicken broth and cream cheese, close and seal the lead. Press "Manual" and set it to prepare for 20 mins on questionable.
3. When it's over, release pressure naturally for quarter-hour.
4. Put the chicken thighs inside a plate; blend the sauce until it's smooth.
5. With a fork shred the meat and place it back inside the creamy sauce. Stir so the meat coats well inside the sauce.
6. Serve with lettuce and avocados and other.

TURKEY AND SPINACH CASSEROLE
Nutrition: Cal 319;Fat 20 g; Carb 5 g;Protein 29 g
Serving 2; Cook time 35 min

Ingredients
- 1 lb ground turkey
- 6 cups fresh spinach, chopped
- 1/2 cup onion, chopped
- 2 cloves garlic, minced
- 1/2 cup full-fat Greek yogurt
- 1/4 cup heavy cream
- 1/4 cup grated Parmesan cheese
- 1 tsp dried basil
- 1 tsp dried oregano
- Salt and pepper, to taste

Instructions
1. Preheat the oven to 350°F.
2. In a large skillet, cook the ground turkey over medium-high heat until browned and no longer pink.
3. Add the chopped onion and minced garlic to the skillet and cook for 2-3 minutes, until the onion is translucent.
4. Add the chopped spinach to the skillet and cook for another 2-3 minutes, until the spinach is wilted.
5. In a separate bowl, whisk together the Greek yogurt, heavy cream, grated Parmesan cheese, dried basil, and dried oregano.
6. Add the yogurt mixture to the skillet and stir to combine.
7. Season with salt and pepper to taste.
8. Transfer the mixture to a 9x13 inch casserole dish and bake for 20-25 minutes, until the top is golden brown and the casserole is heated through.
9. Let the casserole cool for a few minutes before serving.

BUFFALO CHICKEN CANNOLI
Nutrition: Cal 274;Fat 10 g; Carb 2 g;Protein 22 g
Serving 6; Cook time 45 min

Ingredients
FOR THE CHICKEN:
- 3 tablespoons bacon fat lard, or ghee
- 4 chicken leg quarters about 3 pounds
- 1 1/2 teaspoons Redmond Real salt
- 1/2 teaspoon fresh ground black pepper
- ¼ cup diced yellow onions
- 1 teaspoon minced garlic
- 1/4 cup Buffalo wing–style hot sauce
- 1 cup chicken stock

CONE:
- 1 cup freshly grated hard cheese

GARNISH:
- 4 tablespoons hot sauce
- 4 tablespoons blue cheese crumbles omit if dairy sensitive
- Celery Slices

Instructions
1. To make the chicken: Heat the fat in a deep sauté pan over medium-high heat. Season the chicken with the salt and pepper. Place chicken in the hot fat and sauté for about 8 minutes or until golden brown on all sides. Add the diced onion to the pan. Add garlic to the pan. Cook on medium heat for about 8 minutes, stirring occasionally, until the onion is golden brown. Add the hot sauce and broth, reduce the heat, and simmer for about 1½ hours or until chicken is almost falling off the bone. Remove the legs from the pan and allow them to cool until you can handle them. Shred the meat off the bone and set aside.

2. To make the cannoli, preheat oven to 375 F. Place parchment paper on a cookie sheet. Grease with coconut oil spray. Place 3 TBS of cheese in a circle about 4 inches in diameter. Leave at least 2 inches in between each circle of cheese. Bake 4 to 5 minutes until they are golden brown. TIP: baking one at a time helps since they harden as they cool.
3. To mold them into a cone, have a 1 melted cheese round close to you. Place a round shaped object (I used a 1 inch spice jar). Once you remove the cookie sheet from the oven, move quickly and form the cheese around the round object. Allow to sit for 10 minutes to cool. Once cool fill with filling.
4. Place each cannoli on a serving plate, drizzle with 1 tablespoon hot sauce and blue cheese crumbles. Serve with celery.

CHICKEN WINGETTES WITH CILANTRO DIP
Nutrition: Cal 296;Fat 22 g; Carb 11 g;Protein 10 g
Serving 6; Cook time 60 min

Ingredients
- 10 fresh cayenne peppers, trimmed and chopped
- 3 garlic cloves, minced
- 1 ½ cups white wine vinegar
- ½ teaspoon black pepper
- 1 teaspoon sea salt
- 1 teaspoon onion powder
- 12 chicken wingettes
- 2 tablespoons olive oil
- **DIPPING SAUCE:**
- ½ cup mayonnaise
- ½ cup sour cream
- ½ cup cilantro, chopped
- 2 cloves garlic, minced
- 1 teaspoon smoked paprika

Instructions
1. Place cayenne peppers, 3 garlic cloves, white vinegar, black pepper, salt, and onion powder in the container. Add chicken wingettes, and allow them marinate, covered, for one hour inside the refrigerator.
2. Add the chicken wingettes, along while using marinade and extra virgin olive oil on the Instant Pot.
3. Secure the lid. Choose the "Manual" setting and cook for 6 minutes. Once cooking is complete, use a quick pressure release; carefully take away the lid.
4. In a mixing bowl, thoroughly combine mayonnaise, sour cream, cilantro, garlic, and smoked paprika.
5. Serve warm chicken with all the dipping sauce privately.

CHICKEN WONTONS
Nutrition: Cal 290;Fat 22 g; Carb 1 g;Protein 11 g
Serving 12; Cook time 35 min

Ingredients
- 8 oz Cream Cheese
- 2 TBS chives chopped
- 24 pieces chicken skin about 3.5 inches in diameter OR Prosciutto
- Avocado Oil or Coconut Oil For Frying
- Redmond Real Salt if using chicken skin
- Dipping Sauce:
- 1/2 cup coconut aminos or 2 tablespoons organic Tamari sauce (aged soy sauce)
- 1/4 cup chicken bone broth homemade is naturally thick which works great for this recipe
- 2 TBS coconut vinegar or rice wine vinegar
- 1/4 cup Swerve confectioners
- 1 1/2 tsp minced garlic
- 1 1/2 tsp minced ginger
- 1/8 tsp guar gum/xathan gum natural thickener

Instructions
1. To make keto cream cheese wontons, start by combining the cream cheese and chives in a medium bowl.
2. Next, assemble the wontons by placing about 1 tablespoon of the cream cheese mixture in the center of a chicken skin or prosciutto. Wrap the skin around the cream cheese, making sure to use a large enough chicken skin to prevent the cream cheese from squirting out during cooking.
3. Heat 2-3 inches of oil in a large saucepan or medium skillet to just under 350 degrees. Test the oil temperature with spare pieces of chicken skin to ensure it's ready. Fry the wontons in batches of 3 for 3-5 minutes, flipping them halfway through to ensure even browning. Sprinkle with salt and remove from heat.
4. While the wontons cool, make the dipping sauce by combining coconut aminos, organic broth, coconut vinegar, natural sweetener, garlic, and ginger in a small saucepan over medium-high heat. Heat until the natural sweetener is dissolved, then sift in the guar gum to prevent clumping. Adjust the amounts of each ingredient to taste.
5. Serve the dipping sauce alongside the keto cream cheese wontons for a delicious snack or appetizer.

TURKEY BREAST
Nutrition: Cal 268 ;Fat 10 g; Carb 8 g;Protein 30 g
Serving 2; Cook time 15 min

Ingredients
- 2 turkey breast fillets
- 1 cup water
- 1 tbsp. rosemary
- 1 tbsp. garlic powder
- 1 tbsp. sage

- ¼ tsp. pepper
- ½ tsp. salt
- ½ tsp. thyme

Instructions

1. Arrange the rack within the Instant Pot or just add the breast to the river for poaching.
2. Use the spices and herbs to rub the turkey and place them in to the pot. Secure the lid using the "Poultry" function (7-10 min).
3. Quick release pressure if the time is completed and eliminate the meat.
4. You can use the juices with all the meat or save it for the broth later.

TURKEY AND CAULIFLOWER RICE BOWL

Nutrition: Cal 437 ;Fat 30 g; Carb 8 g;Protein 29 g
Serving 4; Cook time 30 min

Ingredients

- 1 lb ground turkey
- 4 cups cauliflower rice
- 1/2 cup onion, chopped
- 1/2 cup full-fat Greek yogurt
- 1/2 cup coconut cream
- 2 tbsp olive oil
- 1 tbsp grated fresh ginger
- 1 tsp ground cumin
- 1 tsp ground coriander
- 1/2 tsp turmeric
- Salt and pepper, to taste

Instructions

1. Heat the olive oil in a large skillet over medium-high heat.
2. Add the ground turkey and cook until browned and no longer pink, about 5-7 minutes.
3. Add the chopped onion and grated ginger to the skillet and cook for 2-3 minutes, until the onion is translucent.
4. Add the cauliflower rice to the skillet and stir to combine.
5. Add the cumin, coriander, turmeric, salt, and pepper to the skillet and stir to combine.
6. Add the coconut cream to the skillet and stir to combine.
7. Cook for an additional 5-7 minutes, until the cauliflower rice is tender and the flavors are well combined.
8. In a separate bowl, whisk together the Greek yogurt with a pinch of salt.
9. To serve, divide the turkey and cauliflower rice mixture into four bowls and top with a dollop of the yogurt mixture.

FAT HEAD CHICKEN BRAID

Nutrition: Cal 290 ;Fat 22 g; Carb 4 g;Protein 19 g
Serving 8; Cook time 35 min

Ingredients

DOUGH:

- 1 3/4 cup shredded mozzarella cheese
- 2 tablespoons cream cheese
- 3/4 cup almond flour
- 1 egg
- 1/8 teaspoon Redmond Real salt

FILLING:

- 1 1/2 cups leftover chicken diced (I used Whole Foods Rotisserie chicken)
- 4 tablespoons mayo I used Primal Kitchen Mayo
- 1/2 cup shredded cheddar
- 2 slices sugar free bacon diced
- 3 tablespoons "healthified" Ranch Dressing

Instructions

1. To make a delicious chicken and bacon braid, preheat the oven to 400 degrees F. In a heat-safe bowl, microwave the mozzarella and cream cheese for 1-2 minutes until fully melted, then stir well. Add the almond flour, egg, and salt, and use a hand mixer to combine everything.
2. Place a greased piece of parchment paper on a pizza stone (or a cookie sheet if you don't have one), and put the dough on top. Pat it out with your hands to create an oval shape about 12 inches by 8 inches, with the longer part facing you.
3. Make the filling by mixing diced chicken and mayo in a bowl, then place it down the middle of the oval, lengthwise, leaving 1 ½ inches at the top and bottom, and leaving 3 inches on each side. Top with shredded cheese.

CHICKEN MILANESE

Nutrition: Cal 240 ;Fat 14 g; Carb 3 g;Protein 24 g
Serving 4; Cook time 20 min

Ingredients

- 4 boneless skinless chicken thighs, pounded thin
- Fine grain sea salt and freshly ground black pepper
- 2 eggs beaten
- 1/2 cup pork rind crumbs or grind pork rinds into fine powder
- 1/2 cup powdered Parmesan (place shredded Parmesan into a food processor until powdered)
- 3 tablespoons Primal Kitchen avocado oil or coconut oil for frying
- 2 cups leafy greens chopped
- 2 radishes sliced thin
- 4 tablespoons Primal Kitchen Ranch Dressing
- 1 lemon quartered

Instructions

1. For a delicious and easy meal, start by placing chicken thighs between 2 pieces of parchment paper and using a rolling pin to pound gently until they are about ¼ inch thick. Season both sides well with salt and pepper.
2. Next, place beaten eggs into a shallow bowl and beat in a tablespoon of water. Season with salt and pepper. In another shallow bowl, place the pork dust and powdered Parmesan.
3. Dredge each chicken thigh in the beaten eggs, letting the excess drip off, then dip both sides in the pork dust mixture. Heat oil in a large cast iron skillet to medium-high. Once hot, sear each chicken thigh until golden brown, about 2 minutes. Flip and sear until golden brown, about another 2 minutes.
4. While the chicken is cooking, prepare the salad by chopping the lettuce and slicing the radish. Once the chicken is done, place it onto serving plates and divide the salad onto each plate. Squeeze lemon juice over each piece of chicken and salad, then drizzle with Primal Kitchen Ranch Dressing for added flavor. This dish is perfect for a quick and easy weeknight meal.

TURKEY WITH BROCCOLI
Nutrition: Cal 268 ;Fat 10 g; Carb 8 g;Protein 30 g
Serving 2; Cook time 15 min

Ingredients
- ½ pound ground turkey
- 1 spring onion, finely chopped
- 1 cup broccoli, chopped
- 1 cup shredded mozzarella
- 3 tbsps. sour cream
- ¼ cup Parmesan cheese, grated
- 2 tbsps. essential olive oil
- ¼ cup chicken stock
- ¼ tsp. dried oregano
- ¼ tsp. white pepper, freshly ground
- ½ tsp. dried thyme
- ½ tsp. salt

Instructions
1. Plug inside the Instant Pot and press the "Sauté" button. Add organic olive oil and warm up.
2. Now add spring onions and cook for 1 minute, stirring constantly.
3. Add turkey and broccoli. Pour inside the stock and cook for 12 - quarter-hour, stirring occasionally. Season with salt, pepper, thyme, and oregano and stir in the cheese.
4. Press the "Cancel" button and remove from your pot. Transfer a combination to a small baking dish as well as set aside.
5. Preheat the oven to 3500 F and bake for 15 - 20 mins, or until lightly charred.
6. Remove through the oven and chill for a while. Top with sour cream and serve.

JALAPENO CHICKEN
Nutrition: Cal 358 ;Fat 12 g; Carb 3 g;Protein 55 g
Serving 4; Cook time 30 min

Ingredients
- 5 chicken thighs, skin on
- 1 large onion, chopped
- 3 jalapeno peppers, chopped
- ¾ cup cauliflower, chopped into florets
- 1 chili pepper, chopped
- 3 tbsps. fish sauce
- 1 tbsps. Swerve
- 5 cups chicken stock
- 2 tbsps. extra virgin olive oil
- 3 bay leaves
- 1 tsp peppercorn
- 1 tsp dried thyme
- 1½ tsp salt

Instructions
1. Combine all ingredients inside instant pot and stir well. Seal the lid and hang the steam release handle for the "Sealing" position.
2. Press the "Poultry" button and hang up the timer for twenty minutes on high heat.
3. When done, release the stress naturally and open the lid. Remove the meat in the bones and stir well again. Serve by incorporating grated Parmesan cheese.

TURKEY AND SOY SPROUTS STIR FRY
Nutrition: Cal 496 ;Fat 131 g; Carb 9 g;Protein 41 g
Serving 2; Cook time 25 min

Ingredients
- 1 lb ground turkey
- 2 cups soy sprouts
- 4 eggs
- 1 head cauliflower, grated into rice-like texture
- 2 tbsp olive oil
- 2 cloves garlic, minced
- 1/2 tsp ginger powder
- Salt and pepper, to taste

Instructions
1. In a large skillet, heat the olive oil over medium-high heat.
2. Add the ground turkey and cook until browned and no longer pink, about 5-7 minutes.
3. Add the minced garlic, ginger powder, salt, and pepper to the skillet and cook for another 1-2 minutes until fragrant.
4. Add the soy sprouts to the skillet and cook for 2-3 minutes until they start to wilt.
5. In a separate non-stick pan, fry the eggs to your desired level of doneness.
6. While the eggs are frying, steam the cauliflower rice in a microwave or steamer for 3-5 minutes until tender.

7. To serve, divide the cauliflower rice between two bowls and top with the turkey and soy sprout stir fry. Place a fried egg on top of each bowl.

TURKEY STEW RECIPE
Nutrition: Cal 386 ;Fat 20 g; Carb 12 g;Protein 36 g
Serving 5; Cook time 30 min

Ingredients
- 2 lbs turkey breast, chopped into smaller pieces
- 2 cups cherry tomatoes, chopped
- 1 onion, finely chopped
- 4 cups chicken broth
- ¾ cup heavy cream
- 2 celery stalks, chopped
- 4 tbsps. butter
- 1 tsp. dried thyme
- 1 tsp. peppercorn
- 2 tsps. Salt

Instructions
1. Combine the constituents in the instant pot and seal the lid
2. Set the steam release handle towards the "Sealing" position and press the "Stew" button. Set the timer for twenty minutes on high heat.
3. When done; release pressure to succeed naturally and open the lid. Chill for a while and stir in most sour cream. To enjoy, serve it immediately.

TURKEY LASAGNA WITH RICOTTA
Nutrition: Cal 740 ;Fat 56 g; Carb 7.8 g;Protein 47 g
Serving 8; Cook time 60 min

Ingredients
- 2 lbs ground turkey
- 5 cups baby spinach leaves
- 1 cup ricotta
- 1 cup mozzarella cheese, grated
- 1 can crushed tomatoes
- 3 tsp dried oregano
- 2 tsp thyme
- 3 tbsp fresh parsley, finely chopped
- 1 tsp salt
- 1 tsp freshly ground black pepper
- 1 tsp onion powder
- 1 tsp garlic powder
- 8 lasagna sheets
- 3 cups water

Instructions
1. In a bowl mix together the ricotta and mozzarella and place aside.
2. In another bowl, mix the crushed tomatoes using the oregano, thyme, parsley, salt, pepper, onion and garlic powder.
3. Start layering the lasagna in a very heatproof dish that fits inside Instant Pot.

4. Spread one tablespoon of the tomatoes sauce and layer some with the lasagna sheets. Spread more of the tomatoes sauce around the sheets and top using a layer of each one in the following: cheese, minced meat and spinach. Top with more sauce and set the remainder in the lasagna. Repeat the layering process before you uses up lasagna sheets. Sprinkle with leftover cheese and cover tightly with aluminum foil.
5. Place the Instant Pot over medium heat, pour in water and punctiliously position the lasagna dish inside pot on the trivet.
6. Cover the pot and manually set the timer for a half-hour. When time is conducted, carefully release pressure.
7. Uncover the pot and eliminate the foil. To allow the lasagna to brown.
Carefully remove the lasagna dish out of the pot and serve hot.

CREAMY TURKEY AND CAULIFLOWER SOUP
Nutrition: Cal 388 ;Fat 21 g; Carb 10 g;Protein 43 g
Serving 2; Cook time 25 min

Ingredients
- 1 lb cooked turkey, shredded
- 1 head cauliflower, chopped into florets
- 2 cups chicken broth
- 1/2 cup heavy cream
- 2 cloves garlic, minced
- 1/4 tsp dried thyme
- Salt and pepper, to taste
- Optional toppings: chopped fresh parsley, grated Parmesan cheese

Instructions
1. In a large pot, bring the chicken broth to a boil.
2. Add the chopped cauliflower to the pot and cook until tender, about 8-10 minutes.
3. Use an immersion blender or transfer the mixture to a blender and blend until smooth.
4. Return the blended mixture to the pot and add the cooked turkey, minced garlic, dried thyme, salt, and pepper.
5. Cook over medium heat for 5-10 minutes, stirring occasionally, until the turkey is heated through.
6. Add the heavy cream to the pot and stir until combined.
7. To serve, divide the soup between two bowls and top with optional toppings if desired.

PINE NUT BREADED BLUE CHEESE STUFFED TURKEY POCKETS
Nutrition: Cal 433 ;Fat 33 g; Carb 3 g;Protein 31 g
Serving 2; Cook time 30 min

Ingredients
- 2 thin turkey cutlets (about 4 oz each)
- 1/4 cup crumbled blue cheese

- 2 tbsp chopped pine nuts
- 2 tbsp almond flour
- 1/4 tsp garlic powder
- Salt and pepper, to taste
- 2 tbsp olive oil

Instructions

1. Preheat the oven to 375°F (190°C).
2. Lay out the turkey cutlets on a cutting board and season both sides with salt and pepper.
3. In a small bowl, mix together the crumbled blue cheese and chopped pine nuts.
4. Spoon the blue cheese and pine nut mixture evenly onto the center of each turkey cutlet.
5. Roll up the turkey cutlets around the filling and secure with toothpicks.
6. In another small bowl, mix together the almond flour, garlic powder, and a pinch of salt and pepper.
7. Coat the outside of the turkey pockets in the almond flour mixture.
8. Heat the olive oil in a large skillet over medium-high heat. Add the turkey pockets to the skillet and cook for 2-3 minutes on each side until browned.
9. Transfer the turkey pockets to a baking dish and bake in the oven for 10-12 minutes until cooked through and the cheese is melted.
10. Serve hot and enjoy!

KETO EGGPLANT CASSEROLE WITH TURKEY

Nutrition: Cal 420 ;Fat 30 g; Carb 8 g;Protein 25 g
Serving 2; Cook time 45 min

Ingredients

- 1 medium eggplant
- 1/2 lb ground turkey
- 1/4 cup grated Parmesan cheese
- 1/4 cup grated mozzarella cheese
- 1/4 cup chopped walnuts
- 2 tbsp olive oil
- 1/4 tsp garlic powder
- Salt and pepper, to taste

Instructions

1. Preheat the oven to 400°F (200°C).
2. Slice the eggplant into thin rounds and place them on a baking sheet. Brush both sides of the eggplant with olive oil and sprinkle with salt and pepper. Roast the eggplant in the oven for 15-20 minutes until softened.
3. While the eggplant is roasting, heat the olive oil in a large skillet over medium heat. Add the ground turkey, garlic powder, salt, and pepper to the skillet and cook for 5-7 minutes until browned and cooked through.
4. In a small bowl, mix together the cooked ground turkey with grated Parmesan cheese and chopped walnuts.
5. In a baking dish, layer the roasted eggplant rounds and spoon the turkey and cheese mixture on top of each round.

6. Sprinkle the grated mozzarella cheese on top of the casserole.
7. Bake the casserole for 15-20 minutes until the cheese is melted and bubbly.
8. Serve hot and enjoy

KETO EGGPLANT ROLLS WITH TURKEY AND CHEESE

Nutrition: Cal 445 ;Fat 32 g; Carb 9 g;Protein 28 g
Serving 2; Cook time 45 min

Ingredients

- 1 small eggplant
- 1/2 lb ground turkey
- 1/4 cup grated Parmesan cheese
- 1/4 cup grated mozzarella cheese
- 1/4 cup full-fat yogurt
- 2 tbsp olive oil
- 1/4 tsp garlic powder
- Salt and pepper, to taste

Instructions

1. Preheat the oven to 400°F (200°C).
2. Slice the eggplant lengthwise into thin strips.
3. Heat the olive oil in a large skillet over medium heat.
4. Add the ground turkey, garlic powder, salt, and pepper to the skillet and cook for 5-7 minutes until browned and cooked through.
5. In a small bowl, mix together the cooked ground turkey with grated Parmesan cheese.
6. Place a spoonful of the turkey and cheese mixture onto each eggplant strip and roll it up tightly.
7. Place the eggplant rolls seam side down in a baking dish and sprinkle the grated mozzarella cheese on top.
8. Bake the eggplant rolls for 20-25 minutes until the cheese is melted and bubbly.
9. Serve hot with a dollop of yogurt on top.

TURKEY AND ZUCCHINI FRITTERS

Nutrition: Cal 495 ;Fat 38 g; Carb 5 g;Protein 29 g
Serving 2; Cook time 25 min

Ingredients

- 1 small zucchini, grated and drained of excess moisture
- 1/2 lb ground turkey
- 1/4 cup almond flour
- 1/4 cup grated Parmesan cheese
- 1 egg
- 1/4 tsp garlic powder
- Salt and pepper, to taste
- 2 tbsp olive oil
- 1/4 cup full-fat yogurt
- 1 tbsp chopped fresh parsley

Instructions

1. In a medium bowl, mix together the grated zucchini, ground turkey, almond flour, Parmesan cheese, egg, garlic powder, salt, and pepper until well combined.

2. Heat the olive oil in a non-stick skillet over medium heat.
3. Use a spoon to drop the turkey and zucchini mixture into the skillet, forming fritters about 3 inches in diameter.
4. Cook the fritters for 3-4 minutes on each side until they are browned and cooked through.
5. In a small bowl, mix together the yogurt and chopped parsley to make a sauce.
6. Serve the fritters hot with a dollop of the yogurt sauce on top.

KETO TANDOORI CHICKEN WINGS
Nutrition: Cal 420 ;Fat 16 g; Carb 8 g;Protein 25 g
Serving 2 Cook time 2 hours 10 min

Ingredients
- 2-1/2 lbs. chicken wings, trimmed and separated
- 1 cup Homemade Yogurt
- 2 tbsp. ginger
- 6 cloves garlic, minced
- 1-1/2 tsp. curry powder
- ¼ tsp. turmeric
- ½ tsp. cumin
- ½ tsp. dry mustard
- 2 tsp. red pepper flakes
- 1 lemon, juiced
- 3 tbsp. vegetable oil
- Salt, pepper
Instructions
1. Add all ingredients in a a bowl and mix well
2. Marinade for at least two hours at room temperature. (saving marinade)
3. Place wings on broiling rack and broil until browned, about 20 minutes
4. Baste wings with marinade about every 10 minutes.
5. Transfer to platter and serve.

KETO RICED CAULIFLOWER & CURRY CHICKEN
Nutrition: Cal 420 ;Fat 16 g; Carb 8 g;Protein 25 g
Serving 4 Cook time 30 min

Ingredients
- 2 Lbs. of Chicken (4 breasts)
- 1 packet of Curry Paste
- 1 Cup Water
- 3 Tablespoons Ghee (can substitute butter)
- ½ Cup Heavy Cream
- 1 Head Cauliflower (around 1 kg)
Instructions
1. In a large pot, melt the Ghee
2. Add the curry paste and mix to combine
3. Once combined, add the water and simmer for an additional 5 minutes
4. Add the chicken, cover, and simmer for 20 minutes.

5. Meanwhile, chop up a head of cauliflower into florets and pulse in the food processor to make riced cauliflower, (cauliflower doesn't need to be cooked)
6. Once the chicken is cooked, uncover, add the cream, and cook for an additional 5 minutes.

TURKEY AND WALNUT SALAD
Nutrition: Cal 536 ;Fat 38 g; Carb 7 g;Protein 40 g
Serving 2 Cook time 25 min

Ingredients
- 1 lb cooked turkey breast, sliced
- 2 cups mixed salad greens
- 1/2 cup walnuts, roughly chopped
- 1 avocado, sliced
- 8 oz mushrooms, sliced
- 2 tbsp olive oil
- 1 tbsp balsamic vinegar
- Salt and pepper, to taste
Instructions
1. In a large skillet, heat the olive oil over medium-high heat.
2. Add the sliced mushrooms to the skillet and cook for 5-7 minutes until they start to brown and release their moisture. Remove from heat and set aside.
3. In a large mixing bowl, toss the mixed salad greens with the sliced turkey breast, chopped walnuts, and sliced avocado.
4. In a small bowl, whisk together the balsamic vinegar, salt, and pepper to make a dressing.
5. Add the cooked mushrooms to the mixing bowl with the salad ingredients and toss everything together.
6. Drizzle the dressing over the salad and toss until well combined.
7. To serve, divide the salad between two plates.

SUN-DRIED TOMATO AND GOAT CHEESE CHICKEN
Nutrition: Cal 460 ;Fat 17 g; Carb 14 g;Protein 22 g
Serving 4 Cook time 20 min

Ingredients
- 1/3 cup sun-dried tomatoes, packed without oil, finely chopped
- 2 tsp. olive oil, divided
- 1/2 cup chopped shallots, divided
- 1 tsp. Splenda
- 3 garlic cloves, minced
- 2 1/2 Tablespoon balsamic vinegar, divided
- 1/2 cup (2 oz.) crumbled goat cheese - to cut down on the fat, find the lowest-fat variety
- 2 Tablespoon chopped fresh basil
- 3/4 tsp. salt, divided
- 4 (6-oz) skinless, boneless chicken breast halves
- 1/8 tsp. freshly ground black pepper
- 3/4 cup fat-free, less-sodium chicken broth
- 1/4 tsp. dried thyme

Instructions

1. Heat 1 tsp. oil in a large non-stick skillet over medium heat.
2. Add 1/3 cup shallots, Splenda, and garlic.
3. Cook 4 minutes or until golden brown, stirring often.
4. Spoon into a mixing bowl and stir in 1 1/2 tsp. vinegar.
5. Incorporate chopped tomatoes, shallot mixture, cheese, basil, and 1/4 tsp. salt together and mix well.
6. Cut a horizontal slit through each chicken breast half.
7. Stuff 2 Tbsps. cheese mixture into each newly formed pocket.
8. Season with 1/2 tsp. salt and black pepper.
9. Heat 1 tsp. oil in pan over medium-high heat and add stuffed chicken.
10. Cook approximately 6 minutes on each side or until juices run clear.
11. Remove chicken from pan and add broth, remaining shallots, 2 Tbsps. vinegar, and thyme.
12. Bring to a boil and stir until thickened.
13. Serve over chicken.

ZOODLES AND TURKEY BALLS

Nutrition: Cal 360 ;Fat 14 g; Carb 12 g;Protein 25 g
Serving 2 Cook time 30 min

Ingredients
- 1 zucchini cut into spirals
- 1 can vodka pasta sauce
- 1 package of frozen Armour Turkey meatballs

Instructions
1. Cook meatballs and sauce on medium heat for 22-25 minutes and stir occasionally.
2. Clean zucchini and put through a vegetable spiral maker.
3. Boil water and blanch raw zoodles 45 seconds.
4. Remove and drain. Combine zoodles and prepared saucy meatballs

TURKEY AND COTTAGE CHEESE STUFFED CABBAGE

Nutrition: Cal 399 ;Fat 19 g; Carb 10 g;Protein 47 g
Serving 2 Cook time 45 min

Ingredients
- 1 lb ground turkey
- 1/2 cup cottage cheese
- 2 tomatoes, sliced
- 8 large cabbage leaves
- 1 tbsp olive oil
- 1/2 tsp garlic powder
- 1/2 tsp onion powder
- Salt and pepper, to taste

Instructions
1. Preheat the oven to 400°F (200°C). Line a baking sheet with parchment paper.
2. In a large bowl, mix together the ground turkey, cottage cheese, garlic powder, onion powder, salt, and pepper until well combined.
3. Bring a large pot of water to a boil. Add the cabbage leaves to the pot and blanch for 1-2 minutes until they become slightly tender. Remove from heat and set aside.
4. Divide the turkey mixture evenly among the cabbage leaves, placing a spoonful in the center of each leaf. Roll the cabbage leaves around the filling, tucking in the sides as you go.
5. Place the cabbage rolls on the prepared baking sheet. Brush with olive oil and season with salt and pepper.
6. Place the sliced tomatoes on the baking sheet around the cabbage rolls.
7. Bake for 25-30 minutes until the cabbage is tender and the turkey is cooked through.
8. To serve, place two cabbage rolls on each plate and top with the roasted tomatoes.

CREAMY ITALIAN CHICKEN SCAMPI

Nutrition: Cal 360 ;Fat 14 g; Carb 12 g;Protein 25 g
Serving 2 Cook time 30 min

Ingredients
- 1 1/2 lbs. Chicken Breast – Cut into tenders sized pieces
- 6 Large Cloves garlic – Minced
- 6 Tbsp. Butter – Divided
- 1 Cup Chicken Stock
- 1 Cup Heavy Cream
- 1/4 Cup Parmesan Cheese – Grated
- 6 oz. Mixed Bell Peppers – Sliced
- A Few Slices Red Onion
- 1 tsp. Italian Seasoning
- 1/2 tsp. Red Pepper Flakes
- Salt and Pepper – To Taste

Instructions
1. In a large sauté pan, over medium-high heat, pan-sear seasoned chicken in 4 Tbsp. butter.
2. Sear on both sides until golden brown approximately 3-4 minutes each side.
3. Remove chicken from pan and set aside.
4. Using the same pan, reduce heat to medium and brown remaining 2 Tbs. butter, and minced garlic about 1-2 minutes.
5. Add sliced red onion and sauté until transparent.
6. De-glaze the pan with chicken stock. And add Italian seasoning and red pepper flakes.
7. Bring to a boil over medium heat and reduce to low.
8. Let simmer 2-3 minutes.
9. Add heavy cream and continue to simmer and thicken 5-10 minutes.
10. Mix in Parmesan cheese and salt and pepper to taste.
11. Stir in peppers and add chicken.
Simmer on low until chicken is fully cooked.

TURKEY AND ZUCCHINI SKILLET

Nutrition: Cal 479 ;Fat 30 g; Carb 9 g;Protein 39 g
Serving 2 Cook time 20 min

Ingredients
- 1 lb ground turkey
- 2 medium zucchinis, diced
- 2 cups shredded cabbage
- 1/2 cup full-fat yogurt
- 2 tbsp olive oil
- 1/2 tsp garlic powder
- 1/2 tsp onion powder
- Salt and pepper, to taste

Instructions
1. Heat the olive oil in a large skillet over medium-high heat.
2. Add the ground turkey to the skillet and cook for 5-7 minutes until browned and cooked through, breaking up any large clumps with a wooden spoon.
3. Add the diced zucchinis to the skillet and cook for another 5-7 minutes until they are slightly softened.
4. Add the shredded cabbage to the skillet and toss everything together. Cook for another 2-3 minutes until the cabbage is wilted.
5. In a small bowl, mix together the yogurt, garlic powder, onion powder, salt, and pepper to make a sauce.
6. Serve the turkey and zucchini skillet hot with a dollop of the yogurt sauce on top.

CHICKEN MEATBALLS

Nutrition: Cal 357 ;Fat 28 g; Carb 3 g;Protein 23 g
Serving 6 Cook time 30 min

Ingredients
- Chicken (1.5 lb., grounded)
- Ghee (2 tbsp)
- Garlic (2 cloves, minced)
- Onion (2, thin sliced)
- Almond meal (¾ cup)
- Hot sauce (6 tbsp)
- Butter (4 tbsp)

Instructions
1. Mix the almond meal, chicken, salt, garlic, and onions in the bowl; put ghee on the hands and form the meatballs.
2. Set the stress cooker to "Sauté" and place two tablespoons of ghee inside; squeeze meatballs inside and fry until they turn brown (roll them every minute, so either side is well fried).
3. Mix 4 tablespoons of butter and hot sauce and heat this mixture within the microwave (this will likely serve like a buffalo sauce for the meatballs). Pour this sauce within the meatballs; secure the lid over pressure cooker and hang up it to "Poultry."

4. Once the cooking is conducted (within 20 minutes), the sound will inform you, and it is possible to press "Cancel." Release the stress valve (protect your hand having a towel or possibly a kitchen glove).
5. Serve with any food you want or take in the meatballs on their own.

CHICKEN WINGETTES WITH CILANTRO DIP

Nutrition: Cal 300 ;Fat 22 g; Carb 11 g;Protein 10 g
Serving 4 Cook time 65 min

Ingredients
- 10 fresh cayenne peppers, trimmed and chopped
- 3 garlic cloves, minced
- 1 ½ cups white wine vinegar
- ½ teaspoon black pepper
- 1 teaspoon sea salt
- 1 teaspoon onion powder
- 12 chicken wingettes
- 2 tablespoons olive oil

DIPPING SAUCE:
- ½ cup mayonnaise
- ½ cup sour cream
- ½ cup cilantro, chopped
- 2 cloves garlic, minced
- 1 teaspoon smoked paprika

Instructions
1. Place cayenne peppers, 3 garlic cloves, white vinegar, black pepper, salt, and onion powder in the container. Add chicken wingettes, and allow them marinate, covered, for one hour inside the refrigerator.
2. Add the chicken wingettes, along while using marinade and extra virgin olive oil on the Instant Pot.
3. Secure the lid. Choose the "Manual" setting and cook for 6 minutes. Once cooking is complete, use a quick pressure release; carefully take away the lid.
4. In a mixing bowl, thoroughly combine mayonnaise, sour cream, cilantro, garlic, and smoked paprika.
5. Serve warm chicken with all the dipping sauce privately.

CHICKEN LEGS WITH PIQUANT MAYO SAUCE

Nutrition: Cal 485 ;Fat 42 g; Carb 2.5 g;Protein 22 g
Serving 4 Cook time 25 min

Ingredients
- 4 chicken legs, bone-in, skinless
- 2 garlic cloves, peeled and halved
- ½ teaspoon coarse sea salt
- ¼ teaspoon ground black pepper, or maybe more to taste
- ½ teaspoon red pepper flakes, crushed
- 1 tablespoon essential olive oil
- ¼ cup chicken broth

DIPPING SAUCE:
- ¾ cup mayonnaise

- 2 tablespoons stone ground mustard
- 1 teaspoon fresh freshly squeezed lemon juice
- ½ teaspoon Sriracha

TOPPING:
- ¼cup fresh cilantro, roughly chopped

Instructions
1. Rub the chicken legs with garlic halves; then, season with salt, black pepper, and red pepper flakes. Press the "Sauté" button.
2. Once hot, heat the oil and sauté chicken legs for four or five minutes, turning once during cooking time. Add a a little chicken broth to deglaze the bottom of the pan.
3. Secure the lid. Choose "Manual" mode and questionable; cook for 14 minutes. Once cooking is complete, work with a natural pressure release; carefully eliminate the lid.
4. Meanwhile, mix all
5. Ingredients for that dipping sauce; place inside the refrigerator until ready to offer.
6. Garnish chicken legs with cilantro. Serve with the piquant mayo sauce quietly.

CHICKEN SHAWARMA
Nutrition: Cal 267 ;Fat 15 g; Carb 5 g;Protein 28 g
Serving 4 Cook time 25 min

Ingredients
- 1-pound boneless, skinless chicken thighs or breasts, cut into large bite-size chunks
- 3 teaspoons extra-virgin essential olive oil, divided
- 3 tablespoons Shawarma Spice Mix
- 1 cup thinly sliced onions
- ¼ cup water
- 4 large lettuce leaves
- 1 cup Tzatziki Sauce

Instructions
1. Place the chicken inside a zip-top bag and add 1 teaspoon of extra virgin olive oil and the shawarma spice mix. Mash it all together, so the chicken is evenly coated within the oil and spices.
2. At this aspect, it is possible to freeze the chicken to get a meal later inside week, or you'll get forced out inside the refrigerator to marinate for about twenty four hours. (I like to create half the chicken now and freeze one other half for an additional meal. Clearly this "now and later" is one area beside me.)
3. Select "Sauté" to preheat the Instant Pot and conform to high heat. When the hot, add the remainder 2 teaspoons of oil and let it shimmer. Add the chicken in a very single layer. Let it sear, then flip the pieces to the other side, about 4 minutes in whole.
4. Add the onion.
5. Pour inside water and scrape up any browned bits from your bottom in the pot.

6. Latch the lid. Select "Pressure Cook" or "Manual" as well as set pressure to high and cook for ten minutes. After some time finishes, allow ten minutes to naturally release the pressure. For any remaining pressure, just quick-release it. Open the lid. To serve, wrap the chicken inside lettuce leaves and serve with all the tzatziki sauce.

THAI GREEN CURRY
Nutrition: Cal 290 ;Fat 20 g; Carb 12 g;Protein 17 g
Serving 6 Cook time 10 min

Ingredients
- 1 tablespoon coconut oil
- 2 tablespoons Thai green curry paste (adjust in your preferred spice level)
- 1 tablespoon minced fresh ginger
- 1 tablespoon minced garlic
- ½ cup sliced onion
- 1-pound boneless, skinless chicken thighs
- 2 cups peeled, chopped eggplant
- 1 cup chopped green, yellow, or orange bell pepper
- ½ cup fresh basil leaves, preferably Thai basil
- 1½ cups unsweetened coconut milk
- 1 tablespoon fish sauce
- 2 tablespoons soy sauce
- 2 teaspoons Truvia or Swerve
- salt, to taste

Instructions
1. Select "Sauté" to preheat the Instant Pot and adapt to high heat. When the hot, add coconut oil and let it shimmer. Add the curry paste and cook for one to two minutes, stirring occasionally.
2. Add the ginger and garlic and stir-fry for a few seconds. Add the onion and stir all of it together.
3. Add the chicken, eggplant, bell pepper, basil, coconut milk, fish sauce, soy sauce, and Truvia or Swerve. Stir to blend.
4. Press "Cancel" to make off "Sauté" mode, and switch to "Slow Cook" mode. Adjust to cook for 8 hours on medium (not low).
5. When the curry has finished cooking, add salt to taste.

SWEET AND SPICY CHICKEN TINGA
Nutrition: Cal 260 ;Fat 16 g; Carb 9 g;Protein 24 g
Serving 6 Cook time 40 min

Ingredients
- 4 teaspoons vegetable oil
- 2 tomatillos, cut into thin slices
- ½ onion, cut into thin slices
- 3 garlic cloves
- 1 (0.9 lb.) can fire-roasted tomatoes
- ⅓ cup chicken broth
- 1 chipotle chile with adobo sauce coming from a can, chopped

- ½ teaspoon ground cumin
- ¼ teaspoon ground cinnamon
- ½ teaspoon dried oregano
- 1 teaspoon Truvia or Swerve
- 1 tablespoon fish sauce or soy sauce
- 1 tablespoon cider vinegar
- 1½ pounds boneless, skinless chicken thighs
- ½ cup sour cream
- 2 teaspoons fresh lemon juice
- 1 avocado, sliced

Instructions

1. Select "Sauté" to preheat the Instant Pot and accommodate high heat. When the hot, add oil and allow it shimmer.
2. Add the tomatillo slices inside a single layer and atart exercising . the onions as being a flat layer between your tomatillo slices. Nestle inside garlic cloves. You're gonna let them char, so not stir them.
3. Once the thinner slices start to look somewhat burned, flip the vegetables. The bottom of the pot may have large black spots where the vegetables have charred, but this is a great sign.
4. Once the vegetables are very well charred, add the tomatoes and broth and deglaze the pan, scraping up all of the lovely brown bits from the bottom. Do this very well and make certain there isn't any burned bits remaining around the bottom. Otherwise, your Instant Pot will not arrive at pressure.
5. Add the chipotle, cumin, cinnamon, oregano, sweetener, fish sauce, and vinegar. Cook for one to two minutes allowing the spices to bloom. Add the chicken.
6. Latch the lid. Select "Pressure Cook" or "Manual" as well as set pressure to high and cook for fifteen minutes. After the time finishes, allow 10 mins to naturally release pressure to succeed. For any remaining pressure, just quick-release it. Open the lid.
7. Remove the chicken and shred it.
8. Tilting the pot, readily immersion blender to purée the sauce until the mixture is smooth.
9. Turn the pot to "Sauté" and adapt to high heat; then cook to thicken the sauce for approximately ten minutes. Once it's thickened a little, add inside chicken and also heat.
10. While the chicken heats, make a crema inside a small bowl by mixing together the sour cream and lemon juice.
11. Top the chicken while using crema and avocado slices. Serve over cauliflower rice or wrapped in lettuce leaves to get a low-carb option. You can also use low-carb corn tortillas.

CHICKEN FAJITAS

Nutrition: Cal 322 ;Fat 6 g; Carb 12 g;Protein 4 5g
Serving 4 Cook time 30 min

Ingredients

- 1 lb. chicken white meat, chopped into bite-sized pieces
- 1 onion, finely chopped
- 1 tbsp lime juice
- 6 large leaves Iceberg lettuce
- 2 tbsps. homemade taco seasoning
- 1 cup cherry tomatoes, chopped
- 3 garlic cloves, minced
- 1 bell pepper, cut into strips

TACO SEASONING:

- 1 tbsp. smoked paprika
- ½ tsp. coriander powder
- ½ tsp. black pepper, freshly ground
- 3 tbsps. chili powder
- 1 tsp onion powder
- 2 tbsps. pink Himalayan salt
- 2 tsps. garlic powder
- 2 tsps. Oregano

Instructions

1. Ingredients for taco seasoning in a jar and shake well. Set aside.
2. Rinse the meat well and place in a deep bowl. Generously sprinkle with taco seasoning. Place in the pot and add tomatoes, garlic, sliced peppers, onions, and lime juice
3. Seal the lid and press the "Poultry" button. Set the timer for 8 minutes on underhand.
4. When done, perform a quick release and open the lid. Remove a combination in the pot and set in a bowl. Cool completely.
5. Spread about 2 - 3 tablespoons with the mixture at the center of every lettuce leaf and wrap tightly. Secure each wrap with a toothpick and serve immediately.
6. Cut the chicken into bite-size pieces. Add it back to the sauce.
7. Preheat the Instant Pot by selecting "Sauté" and adjust to less for low heat. Let the chicken heat through. Break it up into smaller pieces if you like, but don't shred it.
8. Serve over cauliflower rice or raw cucumber noodles.

SHORTCUT DAN DAN–STYLE CHICKEN

Nutrition: Cal 300 ;Fat 17 g; Carb 10 g;Protein 26 g
Serving 4 Cook time 15 min

Ingredients

- 2 tablespoons extra virgin olive oil
- 1 tablespoon doubanjiang
- 2 teaspoons soy sauce
- 2 teaspoons rice wine vinegar
- ½ to 2 teaspoons red pepper flakes
- 1 teaspoon ground Sichuan peppercorns
- ¼ cup warm water
- 1-pound boneless, skinless chicken, cut into bite-size pieces
- ¼ cup room-temperature water
- 1 (½ pound) package shirataki noodles, rinsed
- 1 tablespoon sesame oil
- ¼ cup chopped fresh cilantro (optional) 2 tablespoons extra virgin olive oil

- 1 tablespoon doubanjiang
- 2 teaspoons soy sauce
- 2 teaspoons rice wine vinegar
- ½ to 2 teaspoons red pepper flakes
- 1 teaspoon ground Sichuan peppercorns
- ¼ cup warm water
- 1-pound boneless, skinless chicken, cut into bite-size pieces
- ¼ cup room-temperature water
- 1 (½ pound) package shirataki noodles, rinsed
- 1 tablespoon sesame oil
- ¼ cup chopped fresh cilantro (optional)

Instructions

1. In a medium bowl, mix together the olive oil, doubanjiang, soy sauce, vinegar, red pepper flakes, peppercorns, and hot water.
2. Put the chicken in the bowl and mix, so the chicken is well coated. For the best results, permit the chicken marinate for 30 minutes.
3. Put the chicken and marinade inside the inner cooking pot. Pour inside room-temperature water.
4. Latch the lid. Select "Pressure Cook" or "Manual" and set pressure to high and cook for 7 minutes. After the time finishes, allow 10 minutes to naturally release pressure. For any remaining pressure, just quick-release it. Open the lid. While the chicken is cooking, prepare the shirataki noodles as outlined by the package instructions.
5. Mix the chicken while using noodles. Just before serving, stir within the sesame oil. Serve garnished using the peanuts and cilantro (if using).

CHICKEN BRATWURST MEATBALLS WITH CABBAGE

Nutrition: Cal 338 ;Fat 23 g; Carb 10 g;Protein 23 g
Serving 4 Cook time 20 min

Ingredients

- 1-pound ground chicken
- ¼ cup heavy (whipping) cream
- 2 teaspoons salt, divided
- ½ teaspoon ground caraway seeds
- 1½ teaspoons freshly ground black pepper, divided
- ¼ teaspoon ground allspice
- 4 to 6 cups thickly chopped green cabbage
- 2 tablespoons unsalted butter

Instructions

1. To make meatballs, place the chicken in the bowl. Add the cream, 1 teaspoon of salt, the caraway, ½ teaspoon of pepper, as well as the allspice. Mix thoroughly. Refrigerate a combination for a half-hour. Once the amalgamation has cooled, it is simpler to make up the meatballs.

2. Using a tiny scoop, make up the chicken mixture into small-to medium-size meatballs. Place half the meatballs inside inner cooking pot of the Instant Pot and cover them half the cabbage. Place the remaining meatballs at the top from the cabbage, then cover them while using rest of the cabbage.
3. Place pats from the butter randomly and sprinkle with all the remaining 1 teaspoon of salt and 1 teaspoon of pepper.
4. Latch the lid. Select "Pressure Cook" or "Manual" as well as set pressure to high and cook for 4 minutes. After time finishes, allow 10 mins to naturally release the stress. For any remaining pressure, just quick-release it. Open the lid. Serve the meatballs ahead in the cabbage.

CHICKEN LIVER PTÉ

Nutrition: Cal 109 ;Fat 7 g; Carb 5 g;Protein 10 g
Serving 8 Cook time 15 min

Ingredients

- 1 lb. chicken liver
- ½ cup leeks, chopped
- 2 garlic cloves, crushed
- 2 tablespoons essential olive oil
- 1 tablespoon poultry seasonings
- 1 teaspoon dried rosemary
- ½ teaspoon dried marjoram
- ¼ teaspoon dried dill weed
- ½ teaspoon paprika
- ½ teaspoon red pepper flakes
- salt, to taste
- ½ teaspoon ground black pepper
- 1 cup water
- 1 tablespoon stone ground mustard

Instructions

1. Press the "Sauté" button to warm up the Instant Pot. Now, heat the oil. Once hot, sauté the chicken livers until no longer pink.
2. Add the rest of the
3. Ingredients, apart from the mustard, for a Instant Pot.
4. Secure the lid. Choose the "Manual" setting and cook for 10 minutes at High pressure. Once cooking is complete, work with a quick pressure elease; carefully remove the lid.
5. Transfer the cooked mixture to some blender; add stone ground mustard. Process until smooth and uniform.

ROASTED TURKEY BREAST WITH MUSHROOMS & BRUSSELS SPROUTS

Nutrition: Cal 210;Fat 9 g; Carb 6 g;Protein 27 g
Serving 4; Cook time 50 min

Ingredients

- 2 tbsp olive oil
- 1 tsp salt
- 1 tsp black pepper

- 1 tsp garlic powder
- 1 pound turkey breast raw, cut into 1 inch cubes
- 1/2 pound brussels sprouts cleaned, cut in half
- 1 cups mushrooms cleaned

Instructions
1. Preheat oven to 350 degrees Fahrenheit.
2. In a small mixing bowl, combine olive oil, salt, black pepper, and garlic powder.
3. In a 9 x 6-inch casserole dish, combine turkey, brussels sprouts, and mushrooms. Pour the olive oil mixture over the top.
4. Cover with foil and bake for 45 minutes or until the turkey is cooked through and no longer pink. An internal temperature of 165 degrees Fahrenheit is a safe bet.

TURKEY AND BACON LETTUCE WRAPS
Nutrition: Cal 305;Fat 20 g; Carb 12 g;Protein 11 g
Serving 4; Cook time 15 min

Ingredients
WRAPS
- 1 head iceberg lettuce
- 4 slices deli turkey
- 4 slices bacon cooked
- 1 avocado thinly sliced
- 1 roma tomato thinly sliced
- 1 cucumber thinly sliced
- 1 carrot thinly sliced

BASIL MAYO
- 1/2 cup mayo
- 6 basil leaves chopped
- 1 tsp lemon juice
- 1 garlic clove minced
- salt and pepper to taste

Instructions
BASIL MAYO
1. Combine all of the ingredients in a food processor, blend until smooth

WRAPS
2. Lay out two large lettuce leaves then layer on 1 slice of turkey and slather with Basil-Mayo.
3. Layer on a second slice of turkey followed by the bacon, and a few slices of avocado, tomato, cucumber and carrot.
4. Season lightly with salt and pepper then fold the bottom up, the sides in, and roll like a burrito.
5. Slice in half and serve cold.

CHIKEN STIR-FRY
Nutrition: Cal 312;Fat 14 g; Carb 11 g;Protein 31 g
Serving 4; Cook time 40 min

Ingredients
- 3 boneless, skinless chicken breasts, trimmed and cut into pieces at least 1 inch square
- 2 red bell peppers
- 2 cups sugar snap peas
- 1 1/2 T peanut oil

- 1-2 T sesame seeds, preferably black

Marinade ingredients:
- 1/3 cup soy sauce (gluten-free if needed)
- 2 T unseasoned (unsweetened) rice vinegar
- 2 T low-carb sweetener of your choice (see notes)
- 1 T sesame oil
- 1/2 tsp. garlic powder

Instructions
1. Trim the chicken breasts and cut into pieces at least 1 inch square.
2. Combine soy sauce, rice vinegar, Stevia, agave or maple syrup, sesame oil and garlic powder.
3. Put the chicken into a Ziploc bag and pour in HALF the marinade. Let chicken marinate in the fridge for at least 4 hours (or all day while you're at work would be even better.)
4. When you're ready to cook, cover a large baking sheet with foil, then put it in the oven and let the pan get hot while the oven heats to 425F/220C.
5. Drain the marinated chicken well in a colander placed in the sink.
6. Remove the hot baking sheet from the oven and spread the chicken out over the surface (so pieces are not touching). Put baking sheet into the oven and cook chicken 8 minutes.
7. While the chicken cooks, trim ends of the sugar snap peas. Cut out the core and seeds of the red bell peppers and discard; then cut peppers into strips about the same thickness as the sugar snap peas.
8. Put veggies into a bowl and toss with the peanut oil.
9. After 8 minutes, remove pan from the oven and arrange the veggies around the chicken, trying to have each vegetable piece touching the pan as much as you can.
10. Put back into the oven and cook about 11 minutes more, or until the chicken is cooked through and lightly browned.
11. Brush cooked chicken and vegetables with the remaining marinade and sprinkle with black sesame seeds. Serve hot.

GARLIC, LEMON & THYME ROASTED CHICKEN BREASTS
Nutrition: Cal 230;Fat 27 g; Carb 4 g;Protein 26 g
Serving 4; Cook time 2 hours 45 min

Ingredients
- 4 boneless skinless chicken breasts
- zest of 1 lemon
- juice of 1 lemon
- 1/2 cup extra virgin olive oil
- 4 cloves garlic minced
- 1 tablespoon fresh thyme
- 1 teaspoon salt
- 1/2 teaspoon ground black pepper
- 1 tablespoon olive oil for sauteing

Instructions

1. Create the marinade by mixing the lemon juice, zest, 1/2 cup of olive oil, garlic, thyme, salt, and pepper. Place the chicken breasts in a non-reactive glass dish, or plastic ziptop bag, and pour the marinade over the chicken. Make sure to evenly coat the chicken, then cover and refrigerate for 2 hours.
2. Preheat your oven to 400 degrees F. Remove the chicken from the marinade and wipe off the excess. Heat 1 tablespoon of olive oil, and sear the chicken breasts for 2 minutes on each side, until they're golden brown.
3. Place the chicken breasts on a baking sheet lined with a baking rack, and roast at 400 degrees F for 20-30 minutes depending on the thickness of the chicken breast, or until the internal temperature reads 165 degrees F.

GRILLED CHICKEN KABOBS

Nutrition: Cal 278;Fat 12 g; Carb 26 g;Protein 27 g
Serving 2; Cook time 30 min

Ingredients
- 0.5 pound boneless skinless chicken breasts cut into 1 inch pieces
- 0.13 cup olive oil
- 0.17 cup soy sauce
- 0.13 cup honey
- 0.5 teaspoon minced garlic
- salt and pepper to taste
- 0.5 red bell pepper cut into 1 inch pieces
- 0.5 yellow bell pepper cut into 1 inch pieces
- 1 small zucchini cut into 1 inch slices
- 0.5 red onion cut into 1 inch pieces
- 0.5 tablespoon chopped parsley

Instructions
1. Place the olive oil, soy sauce, honey, garlic and salt and pepper in a large bowl.
2. Whisk to combine.
3. Add the chicken, bell peppers, zucchini and red onion to the bowl. Toss to coat in the marinade.
4. Cover and refrigerate for at least 1 hour, or up to 8 hours.
5. Soak wooden skewers in cold water for at least 30 minutes. Preheat grill or grill pan to medium high heat.
6. Thread the chicken and vegetables onto the skewers.
7. Cook for 5-7 minutes on each side or until chicken is cooked through.
8. Sprinkle with parsley and serve.

CHICKEN CORDON BLEU WITH CAULIFLOWER

Nutrition: Cal 420;Fat 24 g; Carb 7 g;Protein 45 g
Serving 4; Cook time 55 min

Ingredients
- 4 boneless chicken breast halves (about 12 ounces)
- 4 slices deli ham
- 4 slices Swiss cheese
- 1 large egg, whisked well
- 2 ounces pork rinds
- ¼ cup almond flour
- ¼ cup grated parmesan cheese
- ½ teaspoon garlic powder
- Salt and pepper
- 2 cups cauliflower florets

Instructions
1. Preheat the oven to 350°F and line a baking sheet with foil.
2. Sandwich the chicken breast halves between pieces of parchment and
pound flat.
3. Lay the pieces out and top with sliced ham and cheese.
4. Roll the chicken up around the fillings then dip in the beaten egg.
5. Combine the pork rinds, almond flour, parmesan, garlic powder, salt and pepper in a food processor and pulse into fine crumbs.
6. Roll the chicken rolls in the pork rind mixture then place on the baking sheet.
7. Toss the cauliflower with melted butter then add to the baking sheet.
Bake for 45 minutes until the chicken is cooked through.

CHICKEN TIKKA WITH CAULIFLOWER RICE

Nutrition: Cal 350;Fat 21 g; Carb 8 g;Protein 35 g
Serving 4; Cook time 15 min

Ingredients
- 2 pounds boneless chicken thighs, chopped
- 1 cup canned coconut milk
- 1 cup heavy cream
- 3 tablespoons tomato paste
- 2 tablespoons garam masala
- 1 tablespoon fresh grated ginger
- 1 tablespoon minced garlic
- 1 tablespoon smoked paprika
- 2 teaspoons onion powder
- 1 teaspoon guar gum
- 1 tablespoon butter
- 1 ½ cup riced cauliflower

Instructions
1. Spread the chicken in a slow cooker, then stir in the remaining ingredients except for the cauliflower and butter.
2. Cover and cook on low heat for 6 hours until the chicken is done and the sauce thickened.
3. Melt the butter in a saucepan over medium-high heat.
4. Add the riced cauliflower and cook for 6 to 8 minutes until tender.
5. Serve the chicken tikka with the cauliflower rice.

SESAME WINGS WITH CAULIFLOWER

Nutrition: Cal 400;Fat 28,5 g; Carb 4 g;Protein 31 g
Serving 4; Cook time 35 min

Ingredients

- 2 ½ tablespoons soy sauce
- 2 tablespoons sesame oil
- 1 ½ teaspoons balsamic vinegar
- 1 teaspoon minced garlic
- 1 teaspoon grated ginger
- Salt
- 1 pound chicken wing, the wings itself
- 2 cups cauliflower florets

Instructions

1. Combine the soy sauce, sesame oil, balsamic vinegar, garlic, ginger, and salt in a freezer bag, then add the chicken wings.
2. Toss to coat, then chill for 2 to 3 hours.
3. Preheat the oven to 400°F and line a baking sheet with foil.
4. Spread the wings on the baking sheet along with the cauliflower.
5. Bake for 35 minutes, then sprinkle with sesame seeds to serve.

SPICY CHICKEN ENCHILADA CASSEROLE

Nutrition: Cal 550;Fat 31 g; Carb 12 g;Protein 54 g
Serving 6; Cook time 1 hour 15 min

Ingredients

- 2 pounds boneless chicken thighs, chopped
- Salt and pepper
- 3 cups tomato salsa
- 1 ½ cups shredded cheddar cheese
- ¾ cup sour cream
- 1 cup diced avocado

Instructions

1. Preheat the oven to 375°F and grease a casserole dish.
2. Season the chicken with salt and pepper then spread into the dish.
3. Spread the salsa over the chicken and sprinkle with cheese.
4. Cover with foil, then bake for 60 minutes until the chicken is done.
5. Serve with sour cream and chopped avocado.

CHICKEN AND ARUGULA SALAD

Nutrition: Cal 474;Fat 31 g; Carb 9 g;Protein 44 g
Serving 2; Cook time 20 min

Ingredients

- 2 chicken fillets
- 2 cups fresh arugula leaves
- 1/2 avocado, sliced
- 1/2 cup cherry tomatoes, halved
- 1/4 cup sliced red onion
- 2 tbsp olive oil
- 1 tbsp lemon juice
- Salt and black pepper, to taste

Instructions

1. Preheat a grill or grill pan to medium-high heat.
2. Season the chicken fillets with salt and black pepper to taste.
3. Grill the chicken fillets for 5-6 minutes per side or until fully cooked. Let them rest for a few minutes before slicing.
4. In a mixing bowl, whisk together the olive oil, lemon juice, salt, and black pepper to make the salad dressing.
5. Add the arugula, sliced avocado, cherry tomatoes, and red onion to the mixing bowl and toss to combine with the salad dressing.
6. Divide the salad between two plates and top each salad with the sliced chicken fillets.
7. Serve immediately.

WHITE CHEDDAR BROCCOLI CHICKEN CASSEROLE

Nutrition: Cal 435;Fat 32 g; Carb 6 g;Protein 29 g
Serving 6; Cook time 45 min

Ingredients

- 2 tablespoons olive oil
- 1 pound boneless chicken thighs, chopped
- 1 medium yellow onion, chopped
- 1 clove garlic, minced
- 1 ½ cups chicken broth
- 8 ounces cream cheese, softened
- ¼ cup sour cream
- 2 ½ cups broccoli florets
- ¾ cup shredded white cheddar cheese

Instructions

1. Preheat the oven to 350°F and grease a casserole dish.
2. Heat the oil in a large skillet over medium-high heat.
3. Add the chicken and cook for 2 to 3 minutes on each side to brown.
4. Stir in the onion and garlic, and season with salt and pepper.
5. Sauté for 4 to 5 minutes until the chicken is cooked through.
6. Pour in the chicken broth, then add the cream cheese and sour cream.
7. Simmer until the cream cheese is melted, then stir in the broccoli.
8. Spread the mixture in the casserole dish and sprinkle with cheese.
9. Bake for 25 to 30 minutes until hot and bubbling.

LEMON CHICKEN KEBABS WITH VEGGIES

Nutrition: Cal 591;Fat 41 g; Carb 11 g;Protein 45 g
Serving 2; Cook time 45 min

Ingredients
- 2 chicken fillets
- 1 medium kohlrabi, peeled and thinly sliced
- 1 cup shredded cheddar cheese
- 1/4 cup heavy cream
- 2 tbsp butter
- Salt and black pepper, to taste
- 1/2 tsp garlic powder
- 1/2 tsp dried thyme

Instructions
1. Preheat the oven to 375°F.
2. In a saucepan, melt the butter over medium heat. Add the garlic powder and thyme and cook for 1-2 minutes until fragrant.
3. Add the kohlrabi slices to the saucepan and cook for 5-7 minutes until slightly softened. Season with salt and black pepper to taste.
4. In a mixing bowl, combine the shredded cheddar cheese and heavy cream.
5. Place the chicken fillets in a greased baking dish. Season with salt and black pepper to taste.
6. Layer the cooked kohlrabi slices over the chicken fillets.
7. Pour the cheese and cream mixture over the kohlrabi and chicken, making sure to cover everything evenly.
8. Bake for 25-30 minutes or until the chicken is cooked through and the cheese is bubbly and lightly browned on top.
9. Remove from the oven and let it cool for a few minutes. Serve hot.

LEMON CHICKEN KEBABS WITH VEGGIES

Nutrition: Cal 360;Fat 21,5 g; Carb 8 g;Protein 34 g
Serving 4; Cook time 25 min

Ingredients
- 1 pound boneless chicken thighs, cut into cubes
- ¼ cup olive oil
- 2 tablespoons lemon juice
- 1 teaspoon minced garlic
- Salt and pepper
- 1 large yellow onion, cut into 2-inch chunks
- 1 large red pepper, cut into 2-inch chunks
- 1 large green pepper, cut into 2-inch chunks

Instructions
1. Toss the chicken with the olive oil, lemon juice, garlic, salt, and pepper.
2. Slide the chicken onto skewers with the onion and peppers.
3. Preheat a grill to medium-high heat and oil the grates.
4. Grill the skewers for 2 to 3 minutes on each side until the chicken is done.

LEMON BUTTER CHICKEN

Nutrition: Cal 300;Fat 26 g; Carb 4 g;Protein 12 g
Serving 4; Cook time 50 min

Ingredients
- 4 bone-in, skin-on chicken thighs
- Sea salt
- Freshly ground black pepper
- 2 tablespoons butter, divided
- 2 teaspoons minced garlic
- ½ cup chicken stock
- ½ cup heavy (whipping) cream
- Juice of ½ lemon

Instructions
1. Preheat the oven to 400°F.
2. Lightly season the chicken thighs with salt and pepper.
3. Place a large ovenproof skillet over medium-high heat and add 1 tablespoon of buter.
4. Brown the chicken thighs until golden on both sides, about 6 minutes in total. Remove the thighs to a plate and set aside.
5. Add the remaining 1 tablespoon of buter and sauté the garlic until translucent, about 2 minutes.
6. Whisk in the chicken stock, heavy cream, and lemon juice.
7. Bring the sauce to a boil and then return the chicken to the skillet.
8. Place the skillet in the oven, covered, and braise until the chicken is cooked through, about 30 minutes

CHICKEN BACON BURGERS

Nutrition: Cal 375;Fat 33 g; Carb 3 g;Protein 18 g
Serving 6; Cook time 25 min

Ingredients
- 1 pound ground chicken
- 8 bacon slices, chopped
- ¼ cup ground almonds
- 1 teaspoon chopped fresh basil
- ¼ teaspoon sea salt
- Pinch freshly ground black pepper
- 2 tablespoons coconut oil
- 4 large lettuce leaves
- 1 avocado, peeled, pitted, and sliced

Instructions
1. Preheat the oven to 350°F. Line a baking sheet with parchment paper and set aside.
2. In a medium bowl, combine the chicken, bacon, ground almonds, basil, salt, and pepper until well mixed.
3. Form the mixture into 6 equal paties.
4. Place a large skillet over medium-high heat and add the coconut oil.
5. Pan sear the chicken paties until brown on both sides, about 6 minutes in total.
6. Place the browned paties on the baking sheet and bake until completely cooked through, about 15 minutes.
7. Serve on the letuce leaves, topped with the avocado slices.

KETO MACADAMIA NUT CRUSTED CHICKEN

Nutrition: Cal 619;Fat 47 g; Carb 6 g;Protein 40 g

Serving 2; Cook time 25 min

Ingredients

•2 chicken fillets

•1/2 cup macadamia nuts, finely chopped

•2 tbsp almond flour

•1/2 tsp paprika

•1/2 tsp garlic powder

•Salt and black pepper, to taste

•1 egg, beaten

•2 tbsp olive oil

Instructions

1.Preheat the oven to 375°F.

2.In a mixing bowl, combine the chopped macadamia nuts, almond flour, paprika, garlic powder, salt, and black pepper.

3.Dip each chicken fillet into the beaten egg, then coat it in the macadamia nut mixture, pressing the nuts onto the chicken to form an even crust.

4.Heat the olive oil in an oven-safe skillet over medium-high heat. Add the chicken fillets and cook for 2-3 minutes on each side, or until the nuts are lightly browned on the outside.

5.Transfer the skillet to the oven and bake for 15-20 minutes, or until the chicken is cooked through.

6.Once the chicken is done, remove the skillet from the oven and let it cool for a few minutes. Carefully remove the chicken fillets from the skillet and set them aside on a plate.

7.Serve hot with a side of steamed vegetables or salad.

ONION STUFFED WITH MINCED CHICKEN

Nutrition: Cal 518;Fat 36 g; Carb 19 g;Protein 33 g

Serving 2; Cook time 35 min

Ingredients

•2 large onions

•1/2 lb minced chicken

•1/4 cup almond flour

•1 egg, beaten

•1 tbsp minced parsley

•1 tbsp minced cilantro

•1 tsp paprika

•1/2 tsp cumin

•Salt and black pepper, to taste

•2 tbsp olive oil

•1 cup chicken broth

•1 tbsp butter

Instructions

1.Preheat the oven to 375°F.

2.Cut off the top of each onion and remove the outer layers until you're left with about 2-3 layers. Reserve the onion tops.

3.In a mixing bowl, combine the minced chicken, almond flour, beaten egg, minced parsley and cilantro, paprika, cumin, salt, and black pepper. Mix well until all the ingredients are combined.

4.Fill each onion with the chicken mixture, packing it in tightly.

5.Heat the olive oil in a large oven-safe skillet over medium-high heat. Add the stuffed onions and the reserved onion tops, and cook for 2-3 minutes, or until the onions are lightly browned on the outside.

6.Add the chicken broth to the skillet, and transfer it to the oven. Bake for 30-35 minutes, or until the chicken is cooked through and the onions are tender.

7.Once the onions are done, remove the skillet from the oven and let it cool for a few minutes. Carefully remove the stuffed onions from the skillet and set them aside on a plate.

8.Place the skillet back on the stove over medium heat. Add the butter and let it melt, then stir well to combine with the chicken broth and onion mixture. Let the mixture simmer for 2-3 minutes, or until thickened slightly.

9.Spoon the sauce over the stuffed onions, and serve immediately.

CHICKEN AND BRUSSELS SPROUTS WITH CREAM

Nutrition: Cal 540;Fat 38 g; Carb 3 g;Protein 40 g

Serving 2; Cook time 30 min

Ingredients

•2 chicken breasts (about 8 oz total)

•10 Brussels sprouts, halved

•2 tbsp olive oil

•Salt and black pepper, to taste

•1/2 cup heavy cream

•1/4 cup grated parmesan cheese

•2 garlic cloves, minced

•1/4 tsp red pepper flakes (optional)

Instructions

1.Preheat the oven to 400°F.

2.Season the chicken breasts with salt and black pepper. Heat the olive oil in a large oven-safe skillet over medium-high heat. Add the chicken breasts and cook for 3-4 minutes on each side, or until golden brown.

3.Add the halved Brussels sprouts to the skillet, and season with additional salt and black pepper. Cook for 2-3 minutes, or until lightly browned.

4.Transfer the skillet to the oven and bake for 10-12 minutes, or until the chicken is cooked through and the Brussels sprouts are tender.

5.Meanwhile, in a small saucepan over low heat, combine the heavy cream, grated parmesan cheese, minced garlic, and red pepper flakes (if using). Stir well to combine, and let the mixture simmer for 2-3 minutes, or until thickened slightly.

6.Once the chicken and Brussels sprouts are done, remove the skillet from the oven and let it cool for a few minutes. Pour the cream sauce over the chicken and Brussels sprouts, and serve immediately.

CHICKEN BUTTER MASALA

Nutrition: Cal 481;Fat 36 g; Carb 9 g;Protein 28 g
Serving 2; Cook time 30 min

Ingredients
- 2 chicken breasts, cut into bite-sized pieces (about 8 oz total)
- 1/4 cup unsalted butter
- 1/4 cup heavy cream
- 1/4 cup tomato puree
- 1/4 cup chicken broth
- 1/4 cup chopped onion
- 2 garlic cloves, minced
- 1 tbsp grated ginger
- 1 tsp ground cumin
- 1 tsp ground coriander
- 1/2 tsp turmeric
- 1/2 tsp paprika
- 1/2 tsp garam masala
- Salt and black pepper, to taste
- Fresh cilantro, chopped (optional)

Instructions
1.Melt the butter in a large skillet over medium heat. Add the chopped onion and sauté until softened and lightly browned.
2.Stir in the minced garlic and grated ginger, and cook for an additional minute until fragrant.
3.Add the chicken pieces to the skillet, and season with salt and black pepper. Cook for 5-7 minutes, or until the chicken is browned on all sides and partially cooked.
4.Add the tomato puree, chicken broth, ground cumin, ground coriander, turmeric, paprika, and garam masala to the skillet. Stir well to combine, and let the mixture come to a simmer.
5.Reduce the heat to low, and let the chicken simmer in the sauce for 10-15 minutes, or until fully cooked and tender.
6.Stir in the heavy cream, and let the mixture simmer for an additional 2-3 minutes, or until the sauce has thickened slightly.
7.Serve the chicken butter masala hot, garnished with fresh cilantro if desired.

CHICKEN BACON BURGERS

Nutrition: Cal 358;Fat 19 g; Carb 3 g;Protein 43 g
Serving 2; Cook time 25 min

Ingredients
- 2 chicken fillets (about 8 oz total)
- 2 egg whites
- 1/4 cup almond flour
- 1/4 tsp garlic powder
- 1/4 tsp onion powder
- 1/4 tsp paprika
- Salt and black pepper, to taste
- 2 tbsp olive oil

Instructions
1.Preheat the oven to 375°F.
2.Beat the egg whites in a shallow bowl until frothy.
3.In another shallow bowl, mix together the almond flour, garlic powder, onion powder, paprika, salt, and black pepper.
4.Dip each chicken fillet in the egg whites, making sure to coat it well.
5.Dredge the chicken in the almond flour mixture, pressing the mixture onto the chicken to ensure it adheres well.
6.Heat the olive oil in a large oven-safe skillet over medium heat. Add the chicken fillets and cook for 2-3 minutes on each side, or until golden brown and crisp.
7.Transfer the skillet to the oven and bake for an additional 10-12 minutes, or until the chicken is cooked through.

CHICKEN WITH CREAMY PEPPER SAUCE

Nutrition: Cal 490;Fat 38 g; Carb 3 g;Protein 30 g
Serving 2; Cook time 35 min

Ingredients
- 2 chicken thighs, boneless and skinless (about 8 oz total)
- 1/2 cup shredded mozzarella cheese
- 1/4 cup heavy cream
- 2 tbsp unsalted butter
- 1/4 cup diced onion
- 1 garlic clove, minced
- 1/4 tsp black pepper
- Salt, to taste
- Fresh parsley, chopped (optional)

Instructions
1.Preheat the oven to 375°F.
2.Season the chicken thighs with salt and black pepper. Place them in a baking dish and bake for 25-30 minutes, or until fully cooked.
3.While the chicken is cooking, melt the butter in a saucepan over medium heat. Add the diced onion and minced garlic, and sauté until softened and fragrant.
4.Stir in the heavy cream and black pepper, and let the mixture come to a simmer. Let it cook for 3-4 minutes, or until the sauce has thickened slightly.
5.Remove the chicken from the oven and top each thigh with shredded mozzarella cheese. Return the chicken to the oven and bake for an additional 5-7 minutes, or until the cheese is melted and bubbly.
6.Spoon the creamy pepper sauce over the chicken thighs, and garnish with fresh parsley if desired.

CHICKEN AND EGGPLANT CURRY WITH ALMONDS

Nutrition: Cal 555;Fat 42 g; Carb 12 g;Protein 28 g
Serving 2; Cook time 25 min

Ingredients

- 2 chicken thighs, boneless and skinless (about 8 oz total)
- 1 small eggplant, diced
- 1/2 cup coconut cream
- 1/4 cup sliced almonds
- 1 tbsp olive oil
- 2 garlic cloves, minced
- 1 tsp ground cumin
- 1 tsp ground coriander
- 1/2 tsp ground turmeric
- 1/4 tsp cayenne pepper
- 1/2 tsp salt
- 1/4 tsp black pepper
- Fresh cilantro, chopped (optional)

Instructions

1. Heat the olive oil in a large skillet over medium heat. Add the chicken thighs and cook for 5-6 minutes on each side, or until browned and cooked through. Remove the chicken from the skillet and set it aside.
2. In the same skillet, add the diced eggplant and sauté for 2-3 minutes, or until slightly softened.
3. Add the minced garlic, ground cumin, ground coriander, ground turmeric, cayenne pepper, salt, and black pepper to the skillet. Cook for 1-2 minutes, or until fragrant.
4. Pour in the coconut cream and stir to combine. Bring the mixture to a simmer and let it cook for 5-7 minutes, or until the eggplant is tender and the sauce has thickened.
5. Return the cooked chicken thighs to the skillet and coat them in the curry sauce. Let everything simmer for a few more minutes until the chicken is heated through.
6. Toast the sliced almonds in a dry skillet over medium heat for 2-3 minutes, or until lightly browned.
7. Serve the chicken and eggplant curry hot, sprinkled with the toasted almonds and chopped cilantro if desired.

GARLIC CHICKEN WITH ROASTED VEGETABLES

Nutrition: Cal 610;Fat 44 g; Carb 12 g;Protein 42 g
Serving 2; Cook time 45 min

Ingredients

- 2 chicken thighs, bone-in and skin-on (about 8 oz each)
- 2 small zucchinis, sliced
- 2 garlic cloves, minced
- 4 cherry tomatoes, halved
- 1/2 bell pepper, sliced
- 1 small carrot, peeled and sliced
- 2 tbsp olive oil
- 1 tsp dried oregano
- 1 tsp salt
- 1/2 tsp black pepper

Instructions

1. Preheat oven to 375°F.
2. In a large bowl, combine the zucchini, garlic, cherry tomatoes, bell pepper, carrot, olive oil, dried oregano, salt, and black pepper. Toss to coat the vegetables evenly with the seasoning.
3. Spread the vegetables in a single layer on a baking sheet.
4. Place the chicken thighs on top of the vegetables, skin side up.
5. Bake in the preheated oven for 35-40 minutes or until the chicken is cooked through and the vegetables are roasted and tender.
6. Serve the garlic chicken hot with the roasted vegetables on the side.

CREAM CHEESE STUFFED CHICKEN

Nutrition: Cal 565;Fat 38 g; Carb 8 g;Protein 46 g
Serving 2; Cook time 30 min

Ingredients

- 2 chicken fillets (about 8 oz each)
- 2 oz cream cheese, softened
- 1/2 tsp garlic powder
- 1/2 tsp salt
- 1/4 tsp black pepper
- 8 asparagus spears, trimmed
- 1 small cucumber, sliced
- 2 tbsp olive oil
- 1 tbsp lemon juice
- 1/2 tsp Dijon mustard
- 1/4 tsp salt
- 1/8 tsp black pepper

Instructions

1. Preheat oven to 375°F.
2. Cut a pocket in the side of each chicken fillet, being careful not to cut through the other side.
3. In a small bowl, mix together the cream cheese, garlic powder, salt, and black pepper.
4. Stuff the cream cheese mixture into the pockets of each chicken fillet.
5. Place the stuffed chicken fillets in a baking dish and bake in the preheated oven for 25-30 minutes or until the chicken is cooked through.
6. In a small bowl, whisk together the olive oil, lemon juice, Dijon mustard, salt, and black pepper to make the dressing for the salad.
7. Blanch the asparagus in boiling water for 2-3 minutes or until tender. Drain and set aside.
8. Arrange the sliced cucumbers and blanched asparagus on a plate and drizzle with the dressing.
9. Serve the cream cheese stuffed chicken hot with the asparagus and cucumber salad on the side.

BACON-WRAPPED CHICKEN WITH SHRIMP

Nutrition: Cal 625;Fat 47 g; Carb 11 g;Protein 42 g
Serving 2; Cook time 25 min

Ingredients

- 2 chicken fillets (about 8 oz each)

- 4 slices of bacon
- 8 medium-sized shrimp, peeled and deveined
- 1 avocado, diced
- 1/4 cup cherry tomatoes, halved
- 1/4 cup red onion, diced
- 2 tbsp olive oil
- 1 tbsp lemon juice
- 1/2 tsp garlic powder
- 1/2 tsp salt
- 1/4 tsp black pepper

Instructions

1. Preheat oven to 375°F.
2. Cut a pocket in the side of each chicken fillet, being careful not to cut through the other side.
3. Season the chicken fillets with garlic powder, salt, and black pepper.
4. Stuff 4 shrimp into the pocket of each chicken fillet, pressing them down firmly.
5. Wrap each chicken fillet with 2 slices of bacon, tucking the ends of the bacon under the chicken to secure it.
6. Heat the olive oil in a large skillet over medium-high heat. Once hot, add the chicken fillets and cook for 2-3 minutes on each side or until the bacon is lightly browned.
7. Transfer the chicken fillets to a baking sheet and bake in the preheated oven for 15-20 minutes or until the chicken is cooked through and the bacon is crispy.
8. In a small bowl, whisk together the lemon juice, garlic powder, salt, and black pepper.
9. In a separate bowl, combine the diced avocado, cherry tomatoes, and red onion. Drizzle with the lemon dressing and toss gently to combine.
10. Serve the chicken fillets hot with the avocado salad on the side.

BACON-WRAPPED BLUE CHEESE CHICKEN

Nutrition: Cal 525;Fat 35 g; Carb 2 g;Protein 51 g
Serving 2; Cook time 25 min

Ingredients

- 2 chicken fillets (about 8 oz each)
- 4 slices of bacon
- 1/4 cup crumbled blue cheese
- 1/4 tsp garlic powder
- 1/4 tsp salt
- 1/8 tsp black pepper
- 1 tbsp olive oil

Instructions

1. Preheat oven to 375°F.
2. Cut a pocket in the side of each chicken fillet, being careful not to cut through the other side.
3. In a small bowl, mix together the blue cheese, garlic powder, salt, and black pepper.
4. Stuff the blue cheese mixture into the pockets of each chicken fillet.
5. Wrap each chicken fillet with 2 slices of bacon, tucking the ends of the bacon under the chicken to secure it.

6. Heat the olive oil in a large skillet over medium-high heat. Once hot, add the chicken fillets and cook for 2-3 minutes on each side or until the bacon is lightly browned.
7. Transfer the chicken fillets to a baking sheet and bake in the preheated oven for 15-20 minutes or until the chicken is cooked through and the bacon is crispy.
8. Let the chicken rest for a few minutes before serving.

PAPRIKA CHICKEN

Nutrition: Cal 390;Fat 30 g; Carb 4 g;Protein 25 g
Serving 4; Cook time 35 min

Ingredients

- 4 (4-ounce) chicken breasts, skin-on
- Sea salt
- Freshly ground black pepper
- 1 tablespoon olive oil
- ½ cup chopped sweet onion
- ½ cup heavy (whipping) cream
- 2 teaspoons smoked paprika
- ½ cup sour cream
- 2 tablespoons chopped fresh Parsley

Instructions

1. Lightly season the chicken with salt and pepper.
2. Place a large skillet over medium-high heat and add the olive oil.
3. Sear the chicken on both sides until almost cooked through, about 15 minutes in total. Remove the chicken to a plate.
4. Add the onion to the skillet and sauté until tender, about 4 minutes.
5. Stir in the cream and paprika and bring the liquid to a simmer.
6. Return the chicken and any accumulated juices to the skillet and simmer the chicken for 5 minutes until completely cooked.
7. Stir in the sour cream and remove the skillet from the heat.
8. Serve topped with the parsley

STUFFED CHICKEN BREASTS

Nutrition: Cal 390;Fat 30 g; Carb 3 g;Protein 25 g
Serving 4; Cook time 30 min

Ingredients

- 1 tablespoon butter
- ¼ cup chopped sweet onion
- ½ cup goat cheese, at room temperature
- ¼ cup Kalamata olives, chopped
- ¼ cup chopped roasted red pepper
- 2 tablespoons chopped fresh basil
- 4 (5-ounce) chicken breasts, skin-on
- 2 tablespoons extra-virgin olive oil

Instructions

1. Preheat the oven to 400°F.
2. In a small skillet over medium heat, melt the buter and add the onion. Sauté until tender, about 3 minutes.

3.Transfer the onion to a medium bowl and add the cheese, olives, red pepper, and basil. Stir until well blended, then refrigerate for about 30 minutes.

4.Cut horizontal pockets into each chicken breast, and stuf them evenly with the filling. Secure the two sides of each breast with toothpicks.

5.Place a large ovenproof skillet over medium-high heat and add the olive oil.

6.Brown the chicken on both sides, about 10 minutes in total.

7.Place the skillet in the oven and roast until the chicken is just cooked through, about 15 minutes. Remove the toothpicks and serve.

TURKEY MEATLOAF
Nutrition: Cal 216;Fat 20 g; Carb 1 g;Protein 15 g
Serving 6; Cook time 35 min

Ingredients
- 1 tablespoon olive oil
- ½ sweet onion, chopped
- 1&½ pounds ground turkey
- ⅓ cup heavy (whipping) cream
- ¼ cup freshly grated Parmesan cheese
- 1 tablespoon chopped fresh parsley
- Pinch sea salt
- Pinch freshly ground black pepper

Instructions

1.Heat the oven to 450°F.

2.Place a small skillet over medium heat and add the olive oil.

3.Sauté the onion until it is tender, about 4 minutes.

4.Transfer the onion to a large bowl and add the turkey, heavy cream,

5.Parmesan cheese, parsley, salt, and pepper.

6.Stir until the ingredients are combined and hold together. Press the mixture into a loaf pan.

7.Bake until cooked through, about 30 minutes.

8.Let the meatloaf rest for 10 minutes and serve.

TURKEY RISSOLES
Nutrition: Cal 440;Fat 34 g; Carb 7 g;Protein 27 g
Serving 4; Cook time 35 min

Ingredients
- 1 pound ground turkey
- 1 scallion, white and green parts,
- finely chopped
- 1 teaspoon minced garlic
- Pinch sea salt
- Pinch freshly ground black pepper
- 1 cup ground almonds
- 2 tablespoons olive oil

Instructions

1.Preheat the oven to 350°F. Line a baking sheet with aluminum foil and set aside.

2.In a medium bowl, mix together the turkey, scallion, garlic, salt, and pepper until well combined.

3.Shape the turkey mixture into 8 paties and flaten them out.

4.Place the ground almonds in a shallow bowl and dredge the turkey paties in the ground almonds to coat.

5.Place a large skillet over medium heat and add the olive oil.

6.Brown the turkey paties on both sides, about 10 minutes in total.

7.Transfer the paties to the baking sheet and bake them until cooked through, flipping them once, about 15 minutes in total.

COCONUT BREADED CHICKEN
Nutrition: Cal 564;Fat 41 g; Carb 12 g;Protein 45 g
Serving 2; Cook time 30 min

Ingredients
- 2 chicken fillets (about 8 oz each)
- 1/2 cup coconut flour
- 1/2 cup unsweetened shredded coconut
- 1 tsp garlic powder
- 1/2 tsp salt
- 1/4 tsp black pepper
- 2 eggs
- 2 tbsp coconut oil

Instructions

1.Preheat oven to 375°F.

2.Cut the chicken fillets into small strips or nuggets.

3.In a small bowl, whisk the eggs together.

4.In a separate bowl, combine the coconut flour, shredded coconut, garlic powder, salt, and black pepper.

5.Dip each chicken strip into the egg mixture and then coat with the coconut flour mixture, pressing it onto the chicken to adhere well.

6.Heat the coconut oil in a large skillet over medium-high heat. Once hot, add the chicken strips and cook for 2-3 minutes on each side or until golden brown.

7.Transfer the chicken strips to a baking sheet and bake in the preheated oven for 10-15 minutes or until cooked through and crispy.

8.Serve hot with your favorite keto-friendly dipping sauce, like mayonnaise or hot sauce.

Beef and Lamb

BLUE CHEESE BACON BURGERS

Nutrition: Cal 772;Fat 54 g;Carb 6 g;Protein 61 g
Serving 4; Cook time 20 min

Ingredients

- 1½ pounds ground beef
- 4 slices Perfectly Cooked Bacon , crumbled
- ½ cup crumbled blue cheese
- 1 tablespoon Worcestershire sauce
- 2 large eggs
- Salt
- Freshly ground black pepper
- 1 romaine lettuce head, chopped
- 1 avocado, chopped
- 1 cup grape tomatoes

Instructions

1. In a large mixing bowl, combine the beef, bacon, blue cheese, Worcestershire sauce, and eggs. Season with salt and pepper. Use your hands to shape 4 patties. Cover with plastic and refrigerate for 30 minutes to 2 hours.
2. Heat the grill or broiler on high and cook for 4 to 5 minutes on each side, or until the burgers are cooked to your liking. Remove from the grill and let cool.
3. Into each of 4 storage containers, divide the lettuce, avocado, and tomatoes, and top with a burger patty.

BACON-WRAPPED BEEF SKEWERS

Nutrition: Cal 395;Fat 28 g;Carb 0 g;Protein 34 g
Serving 2; Cook time 20 min

Ingredients

- 1/2 pound beef sirloin, cut into cubes
- 4 strips of bacon
- Salt and pepper, to taste

Instructions

1. Preheat the grill to medium-high heat.
2. Season the beef cubes with salt and pepper.
3. Cut the bacon strips in half crosswise.
4. Wrap each beef cube with a half slice of bacon and thread onto skewers.
5. Grill the skewers for 10-12 minutes, turning occasionally, until the bacon is crispy and the beef is cooked to your liking.
6. Serve immediately.

BACON CHEESEBURGER SKILLET

Nutrition: Cal 518;Fat 38 g;Carb 1 g;Protein 39 g
Serving 2; Cook time 15 min

Ingredients

- 1/2 pound ground beef
- 4 strips of bacon, chopped
- 1/2 cup shredded cheddar cheese
- Salt and pepper, to taste

Instructions

1. Heat a large skillet over medium-high heat.

2. Add the chopped bacon to the skillet and cook until crispy.
3. Remove the bacon with a slotted spoon and set aside.
4. In the same skillet, add the ground beef and cook until browned and cooked through.
5. Drain any excess grease from the skillet.
6. Add the cooked bacon back to the skillet and stir to combine.
7. Sprinkle the shredded cheddar cheese over the top of the beef mixture.
8. Cover the skillet and cook until the cheese is melted and bubbly, about 2-3 minutes.
9. Season with salt and pepper, to taste.
10. Serve immediately.

BACON MUSHROOM SWISS STEAK

Nutrition: Cal 527;Fat 34 g;Carb 2 g;Protein 50 g
Serving 2; Cook time 20 min

Ingredients

- 2 beef sirloin steaks (about 6-8 ounces each)
- 4 strips of bacon, chopped
- 4 ounces sliced mushrooms
- 1/4 cup shredded Swiss cheese
- Salt and pepper, to taste

Instructions

1. Preheat the oven to 375°F.
2. Season the beef steaks with salt and pepper.
3. In a large oven-safe skillet, cook the chopped bacon over medium-high heat until crispy.
4. Remove the bacon with a slotted spoon and set aside.
5. In the same skillet, add the sliced mushrooms and cook until they release their moisture and are browned.
6. Remove the mushrooms from the skillet and set aside.
7. In the same skillet, add the seasoned beef steaks and sear for 2-3 minutes on each side until browned.
8. Top each steak with the cooked bacon and mushrooms, and sprinkle with shredded Swiss cheese.
9. Place the skillet in the preheated oven and bake for 10-12 minutes, or until the cheese is melted and bubbly and the beef is cooked to your liking.
10. Serve immediately.

BACON BEEF SKILLET WITH CHEESY GREEN BEANS

Nutrition: Cal 425;Fat 24 g;Carb 9 g;Protein 44 g
Serving 2; Cook time 20 min

Ingredients

- 1/2 pound beef sirloin, sliced into thin strips
- 4 strips of bacon, chopped
- 4 ounces sliced champignon mushrooms
- 8 ounces fresh green beans, trimmed
- 1/2 cup shredded cheddar cheese
- Salt and pepper, to taste

Instructions

1. Heat a large skillet over medium-high heat.

2. Add the chopped bacon to the skillet and cook until crispy.
3. Remove the bacon with a slotted spoon and set aside.
4. In the same skillet, add the sliced beef and cook until browned and cooked through.
5. Remove the beef from the skillet and set aside.
6. In the same skillet, add the sliced champignon mushrooms and cook until they release their moisture and are browned.
7. Remove the mushrooms from the skillet and set aside.
8. In the same skillet, add the trimmed green beans and cook until they are tender-crisp.
9. Add the cooked beef, bacon, and mushrooms back to the skillet and stir to combine.
10. Sprinkle the shredded cheddar cheese over the top of the beef and vegetable mixture.
11. Cover the skillet and cook until the cheese is melted and bubbly, about 2-3 minutes.
12. Season with salt and pepper, to taste.
13. Serve immediately.

BEEF AND VEGETABLE SKILLET WITH YOGURT SAUCE

Nutrition: Cal 403;Fat 22 g;Carb 14 g;Protein 41 g
Serving 2; Cook time 20 min

Ingredients
- 1/2 pound beef sirloin, sliced into thin strips
- 4 strips of bacon, chopped
- 4 ounces sliced champignon mushrooms
- 8 ounces fresh green beans, trimmed
- 1 red bell pepper, seeded and sliced
- 1/2 cup plain Greek yogurt
- Salt and pepper, to taste

Instructions
1. Heat a large skillet over medium-high heat.
2. Add the chopped bacon to the skillet and cook until crispy.
3. Remove the bacon with a slotted spoon and set aside.
4. In the same skillet, add the sliced beef and cook until browned and cooked through.
5. Remove the beef from the skillet and set aside.
6. In the same skillet, add the sliced champignon mushrooms and cook until they release their moisture and are browned.
7. Remove the mushrooms from the skillet and set aside.
8. In the same skillet, add the trimmed green beans and sliced bell pepper, and cook until they are tender-crisp.
9. Add the cooked beef, bacon, and mushrooms back to the skillet and stir to combine.
10. In a small bowl, whisk together the Greek yogurt with salt and pepper to taste.
11. Serve the beef and vegetable mixture with a dollop of the yogurt sauce on top.

MINTY BEEF AND VEGETABLE SALAD

Nutrition: Cal 314;Fat 14 g;Carb 9 g;Protein 38 g
Serving 2; Cook time 20 min

Ingredients
- 1/2 pound beef sirloin, sliced into thin strips
- 1/2 cup plain Greek yogurt
- 1/4 cup fresh mint leaves, chopped
- 2 cups mixed greens or salad greens of your choice
- 1 cup sliced vegetables of your choice (such as bell peppers, cucumbers, or cherry tomatoes)
- Salt and pepper, to taste

Instructions
1. Heat a large skillet over medium-high heat.
2. Add the sliced beef and cook until browned and cooked through.
3. Remove the beef from the skillet and set aside.
4. In a small bowl, whisk together the Greek yogurt and chopped mint leaves.
5. In a large bowl, combine the mixed greens and sliced vegetables.
6. Add the cooked beef to the bowl and toss to combine.
7. Drizzle the yogurt and mint dressing over the salad and toss to coat.
8. Season with salt and pepper, to taste.
9. Divide the salad between two plates and serve immediately.

CREAMY BEEF AND SPINACH SKILLET

Nutrition: Cal 516;Fat 41 g;Carb 5 g;Protein 30 g
Serving 2; Cook time 20 min

Ingredients
- 1/2 pound beef sirloin, sliced into thin strips
- 1/2 cup heavy cream
- 2 cups fresh spinach leaves
- 2 ounces Dor Blue cheese, crumbled
- 4 ounces sliced mushrooms
- Salt and pepper, to taste

Instructions
1. Heat a large skillet over medium-high heat.
2. Add the sliced beef and cook until browned and cooked through.
3. Remove the beef from the skillet and set aside.
4. In the same skillet, add the sliced mushrooms and cook until they release their moisture and are browned.
5. Add the fresh spinach leaves to the skillet and cook until they are wilted.
6. Add the cooked beef back to the skillet and stir to combine.
7. Pour the heavy cream over the beef and vegetable mixture, and stir to combine.
8. Bring the mixture to a simmer and let it cook until the cream has thickened slightly.
9. Stir in the crumbled Dor Blue cheese until melted and combined.
10. Season with salt and pepper, to taste.
11. Serve the beef and spinach skillet hot, garnished with extra crumbled Dor Blue cheese if desired.

BACON-WRAPPED BEEF ROLLS

Nutrition: Cal 481;Fat 37 g;Carb 9 g;Protein 27 g
Serving 2; Cook time 35 min

Ingredients

- 1/2 pound beef top sirloin, sliced into 4 thin pieces
- 4 slices of bacon
- 4 pitted prunes, chopped
- 1/4 cup chopped walnuts
- Salt and pepper, to taste
- Toothpicks

FOR THE CREAMY PEPPER SAUCE:

- 1/4 cup heavy cream
- 1 tablespoon butter
- 1/2 teaspoon black pepper
- Salt, to taste

Instructions

1. Preheat your oven to 375°F (190°C).
2. Lay out the beef slices and sprinkle each with salt and pepper.
3. In a small bowl, mix together the chopped prunes and walnuts.
4. Spoon the prune and walnut mixture onto each beef slice.
5. Roll up each slice of beef tightly, using toothpicks to secure the roll.
6. Wrap a slice of bacon around each beef roll, securing it with toothpicks as necessary.
7. Place the beef rolls on a baking sheet and bake for 20-25 minutes, or until the bacon is crispy and the beef is cooked through.
8. While the beef rolls are baking, prepare the creamy pepper sauce by heating the heavy cream and butter in a small saucepan over low heat.
9. Add the black pepper and salt, to taste, and stir until well combined.
10. Serve the bacon-wrapped beef rolls hot, drizzled with the creamy pepper sauce.

SESAME-CRUSTED BEEF ROLLS

Nutrition: Cal 430;Fat 31 g;Carb 6 g;Protein 31 g
Serving 2; Cook time 25 min

Ingredients

- 1/2 pound beef top sirloin, sliced into 4 thin pieces
- Salt and pepper, to taste
- 1/4 cup almond flour
- 1/4 cup sesame seeds
- 1 egg, beaten
- 1 tablespoon coconut oil
- 1 tablespoon soy sauce
- 1 tablespoon rice vinegar
- 1 tablespoon sesame oil
- 1/2 teaspoon garlic powder
- 1/4 teaspoon ginger powder
- Sliced green onions, for garnish

Instructions

1. Preheat your oven to 375°F (190°C).
2. Lay out the beef slices and sprinkle each with salt and pepper.
3. In a shallow dish, mix together the almond flour and sesame seeds.
4. Dip each beef slice into the beaten egg, then coat in the almond flour and sesame seed mixture.
5. Heat the coconut oil in a skillet over medium-high heat.
6. Add the beef rolls and cook for 2-3 minutes on each side, until golden brown and crispy.
7. Transfer the beef rolls to a baking sheet and bake for 10-12 minutes, or until cooked to your desired doneness.
8. While the beef rolls are baking, prepare the sauce by mixing together the soy sauce, rice vinegar, sesame oil, garlic powder, and ginger powder.
9. Serve the beef rolls hot, drizzled with the sauce and garnished with sliced green onions.

BEEF AND VEGETABLE STIR-FRY

Nutrition: Cal 323;Fat 21 g;Carb 8 g;Protein 26 g
Serving 2; Cook time 20 min

Ingredients

- 1/2 pound beef sirloin, thinly sliced
- 1 tablespoon coconut oil
- 1 small zucchini, sliced
- 1 small onion, sliced
- 1 small bell pepper, sliced
- 1 small tomato, chopped
- Salt and pepper, to taste
- 1 tablespoon sesame seeds

Instructions

1. Heat the coconut oil in a large skillet over high heat.
2. Add the beef slices and cook for 2-3 minutes until browned.
3. Add the zucchini, onion, and bell pepper to the skillet and cook for another 2-3 minutes until the vegetables are tender-crisp.
4. Add the chopped tomato to the skillet and season with salt and pepper.
5. Stir everything together and cook for another 1-2 minutes until the tomato is heated through.
6. Sprinkle sesame seeds over the top of the stir-fry.
7. Serve hot.

BEEF SALAD WITH ROMAINE AND OLIVES

Nutrition: Cal 282;Fat 20 g;Carb 6 g;Protein 21 g
Serving 2; Cook time 20 min

Ingredients

- 1/2 pound boiled beef, sliced
- 4 cups romaine lettuce, chopped
- 1/4 cup black olives, sliced
- 4 radishes, sliced
- 1/2 cucumber, sliced
- Salt and pepper, to taste
- 2 tablespoons olive oil
- 1 tablespoon red wine vinegar

Instructions

1. In a large mixing bowl, combine the romaine lettuce, olives, radishes, and cucumber slices.
2. Toss the salad mixture with olive oil and red wine vinegar.
3. Arrange the sliced boiled beef on top of the salad.
4. Season with salt and pepper to taste.
5. Serve chilled.

BEEF SALAD IN PARMESAN BASKETS

Nutrition: Cal 483;Fat 34 g;Carb 8 g;Protein 36 g
Serving 2; Cook time 20 min

Ingredients

- 1/2 pound beef, sliced
- 4 cups mixed salad greens
- 1/4 cup cherry tomatoes, halved
- 1/4 cup red onion, sliced
- Salt and pepper, to taste
- 2 tablespoons olive oil
- 1 tablespoon red wine vinegar
- 1 cup freshly grated Parmesan cheese

Instructions

1. Preheat the oven to 375°F (190°C).
2. Line a baking sheet with parchment paper.
3. On the parchment paper, create two 6-inch circles of Parmesan cheese. Spread the cheese in an even layer.
4. Bake for 6-8 minutes, or until the cheese has melted and turned golden brown.
5. Remove the cheese from the oven and let it cool for 1-2 minutes.
6. Carefully remove the cheese from the parchment paper and drape it over the back of two small bowls. Allow the cheese to cool and harden into baskets.
7. In a large mixing bowl, combine the sliced beef, mixed salad greens, cherry tomatoes, and sliced red onion.
8. Toss the salad mixture with olive oil and red wine vinegar.
9. Divide the salad mixture between the two Parmesan baskets.
10. Season with salt and pepper to taste.
11. Serve immediately.

CREAMY GARLIC BEEF AND BRUSSELS SPROUTS SKILLET

Nutrition: Cal 490;Fat 39 g;Carb 8 g;Protein 28 g
Serving 2; Cook time 20 min

Ingredients

- 1/2 pound ground beef
- 1 cup Brussels sprouts, trimmed and halved
- 2 cloves garlic, minced
- 2 ounces cream cheese
- Salt and pepper, to taste
- 1 tablespoon olive oil

Instructions

1. Heat the olive oil in a large skillet over medium-high heat.

2. Add the ground beef and garlic to the skillet and cook until browned, stirring occasionally.
3. Add the Brussels sprouts to the skillet and cook until they are tender and slightly browned.
4. Reduce the heat to low and add the cream cheese to the skillet, stirring until it is melted and combined with the beef and Brussels sprouts.
5. Season with salt and pepper to taste.
6. Serve hot.

VITELLO TONNATO

Nutrition: Cal 357;Fat 27 g;Carb 1 g;Protein 26 g
Serving 4; Cook time 20 min

Ingredients

- 1/2 pound cooked veal, thinly sliced
- 1/4 cup canned tuna, drained
- 1 tablespoon capers, drained
- 1/4 cup mayonnaise
- 1 tablespoon lemon juice
- Salt and pepper, to taste
- Romaine lettuce leaves, for serving

Instructions

1. In a blender or food processor, combine the canned tuna, capers, mayonnaise, lemon juice, and a pinch of salt and pepper.
2. Blend until the mixture is smooth and creamy.
3. Arrange the veal slices on a serving plate.
4. Spoon the tuna sauce over the veal slices, covering them completely.
5. Serve chilled with Romaine lettuce leaves for a fresh and crunchy side.

BEEF CARPACCIO

Nutrition: Cal 210;Fat 16 g;Carb 1 g;Protein 16 g
Serving 2; Cook time 10 min

Ingredients

- 1/2 pound beef carpaccio, thinly sliced
- 1 tablespoon extra-virgin olive oil
- 1/2 lemon, juiced
- Salt and pepper, to taste
- Arugula leaves, for serving
- Shaved Parmesan cheese, for serving

Instructions

1. Arrange the beef carpaccio slices on a serving plate.
2. Drizzle with the extra-virgin olive oil and lemon juice.
3. Sprinkle with salt and pepper to taste.
4. Serve chilled with arugula leaves and shaved Parmesan cheese on top.

KETO BEEF WELLINGTON

Nutrition: Cal 506;Fat 36 g;Carb 7 g;Protein 40 g
Serving 2; Cook time 20 min

Ingredients

- 1 pound beef tenderloin
- Salt and pepper, to taste
- 2 tablespoons olive oil
- 2 tablespoons Dijon mustard
- 2 cloves garlic, minced
- 1 tablespoon chopped fresh thyme
- 1/2 cup almond flour
- 1/2 cup finely chopped mushrooms
- 1/4 cup finely chopped onion
- 1 egg, beaten

Instructions

1. Preheat the oven to 400°F.
2. Season the beef tenderloin with salt and pepper.
3. Heat the olive oil in a skillet over medium-high heat. Add the beef tenderloin and sear for 2-3 minutes on each side, until browned.
4. Remove the beef tenderloin from the skillet and let it cool for a few minutes.
5. Spread the Dijon mustard over the beef tenderloin.
6. In a small bowl, mix together the minced garlic, chopped thyme, and almond flour. Spread this mixture over the mustard-coated beef tenderloin.
7. In the same skillet, sauté the chopped mushrooms and onions until they are softened.
8. Place the sautéed mushrooms and onions over the almond flour mixture.
9. Roll out a piece of parchment paper and place the beaten egg on it. Place the beef tenderloin in the center and use the parchment paper to wrap the beef tenderloin into a cylinder shape, pressing the egg-washed sides together.
10. Bake in the preheated oven for 20-25 minutes or until the beef reaches your desired level of doneness.
11. Let the beef Wellington rest for 5-10 minutes before slicing and serving.

AVOCADO WITH GROUND BEEF AND CHEESE

Nutrition: Cal 428;Fat 36 g;Carb 6 g;Protein 19 g
Serving 4; Cook time 20 min

Ingredients

- 2 ripe avocados
- 1/2 pound ground beef
- 1/4 cup shredded cheese
- Salt and pepper to taste
- Optional: chopped cilantro and lime wedges for serving

Instructions

1. Preheat oven to 375°F (190°C).
2. Cut the avocados in half and remove the pits.
3. In a skillet, cook the ground beef over medium heat until browned. Season with salt and pepper to taste.
4. Spoon the cooked ground beef into the avocado halves, dividing it evenly.
5. Sprinkle shredded cheese over the top of the ground beef.
6. Bake the stuffed avocados in the preheated oven for 10-15 minutes, or until the cheese is melted and bubbly.
7. Garnish with chopped cilantro and serve with lime wedges on the side, if desired.

KETO BEEF NACHOS

Nutrition: Cal 496;Fat 37 g;Carb 7 g;Protein 26 g
Serving 2; Cook time 20 min

Ingredients

- 1/2 lb ground beef
- 1/2 cup chopped onion
- 1/2 cup diced bell pepper
- 1 tsp chili powder
- 1/2 tsp ground cumin
- 1/2 tsp garlic powder
- 1/4 tsp salt
- 1/4 tsp black pepper
- 1/4 cup water
- 1 medium avocado
- 1/4 cup sour cream
- 1 tbsp lime juice
- 1/4 tsp salt
- 1/2 cup sliced cucumber
- 1/2 cup sliced zucchini
- 1/2 cup sliced bell pepper

Instructions

1. Preheat the oven to 375°F. Spread vegetable chips on a baking sheet and set aside.
2. In a skillet, cook the ground beef over medium-high heat until browned. Add the chopped onion and diced bell pepper and continue to cook until the vegetables are tender.
3. Add the chili powder, ground cumin, garlic powder, salt, black pepper, and water to the skillet. Stir until well combined.
4. Spoon the beef mixture over the vegetable chips.
5. Bake the beef nachos in the oven for 10-12 minutes, or until the cheese is melted and bubbly.
6. Meanwhile, in a blender or food processor, combine the avocado, sour cream, lime juice, and salt. Blend until smooth.
7. Serve the beef nachos with the avocado sauce on top.

CHINESE CABBAGE BEEF ROLLS

Nutrition: Cal 383;Fat 28 g;Carb 10 g;Protein 25 g
Serving 4; Cook time 20 min

Ingredients

- 4 large Chinese cabbage leaves
- 300g ground beef
- 1 small onion, chopped
- 1 clove garlic, minced

- 1 tsp ginger, grated
- 2 tbsp coconut aminos
- 2 tbsp sesame oil
- 1/4 tsp red pepper flakes
- Salt and black pepper, to taste
- 1/2 cup smoked sour cream sauce (recipe below)

FOR THE SMOKED SOUR CREAM SAUCE:
- 1/2 cup sour cream
- 1 tbsp smoked paprika
- 1 tbsp lemon juice
- Salt and black pepper, to taste

Instructions
1. Preheat the oven to 350°F (180°C).
2. Remove the tough part of the cabbage leaves and blanch them in boiling water for 3 minutes. Drain and set aside.
3. In a large bowl, mix ground beef, onion, garlic, ginger, coconut aminos, sesame oil, red pepper flakes, salt, and black pepper.
4. Lay the cabbage leaves flat and divide the beef mixture equally among them. Roll up the cabbage leaves and secure with toothpicks.
5. Place the cabbage rolls in a baking dish and bake for 25-30 minutes, or until the beef is cooked through.
6. While the cabbage rolls are baking, make the smoked sour cream sauce by whisking together sour cream, smoked paprika, lemon juice, salt, and black pepper in a small bowl.
7. Serve the cabbage rolls hot with the smoked sour cream sauce on top. Enjoy!

KETO EGG-STUFFED BEEF CUTLETS WITH MUSHROOMS

Nutrition: Cal 570;Fat 45 g;Carb 3 g;Protein 36 g
Serving 2; Cook time 25 min

Ingredients
- 1/2 lb ground beef
- 1/4 cup pork lard
- 2 large eggs, hard-boiled and chopped
- 1/4 cup onion, finely chopped
- 1/2 cup mushrooms, finely chopped
- Salt and pepper, to taste

Instructions
1. In a mixing bowl, combine ground beef with salt and pepper.
2. Divide the meat mixture into 4 portions and flatten each portion to make thin cutlets.
3. In a separate bowl, mix together chopped eggs, onion, and mushrooms.
4. Place a spoonful of the egg mixture onto each cutlet, then roll up the cutlets and secure with toothpicks.
5. In a frying pan, heat the lard over medium heat. Fry the cutlets until browned on all sides and cooked through, about 10-12 minutes.
6. Serve hot with your favorite low-carb vegetables.

CREAMY BEEF LIVER WITH CARAMEL-IZED ONIONS

Nutrition: Cal 307;Fat 22 g;Carb 6 g;Protein 20 g
Serving 2; Cook time 25 min

Ingredients
- 300g beef liver, sliced
- 1 large onion, sliced
- 2 tbsp butter
- 1/4 cup sour cream
- Salt and pepper to taste

Instructions
1. Heat a large skillet over medium-high heat. Add the butter and let it melt.
2. Add the sliced onions to the skillet and cook until caramelized, stirring occasionally for about 10 minutes.
3. Remove the onions from the skillet and set aside.
4. In the same skillet, add the sliced beef liver and cook until browned on both sides, about 2-3 minutes per side.
5. Add the caramelized onions back to the skillet with the beef liver.
6. Pour in the sour cream and stir to combine with the beef liver and onions.
7. Reduce heat to low and let it simmer for 5 minutes, stirring occasionally.
8. Season with salt and pepper to taste.
9. Serve hot.

BEEF LIVER PATE

Nutrition: Cal 502;Fat 46 g;Carb 6 g;Protein 15 g
Serving 2; Cook time 60 min

Ingredients
- 1/2 pound beef liver
- 1/4 cup butter, softened
- 1/4 cup heavy cream
- 1/2 onion, chopped
- 1 clove garlic, minced
- 1 teaspoon dried thyme
- 1/4 teaspoon salt
- 1/8 teaspoon black pepper

Instructions
1. Rinse the beef liver in cold water and pat dry with paper towels. Cut the liver into small pieces.
2. In a frying pan, heat 2 tablespoons of butter over medium heat. Add the onion and garlic and cook until softened, about 5 minutes.
3. Add the liver to the pan and cook until browned on both sides, about 5 minutes per side.
4. Add the thyme, salt, and black pepper to the pan and stir to combine.
5. Remove the pan from heat and let cool for a few minutes.
6. Add the liver mixture, remaining butter, and heavy cream to a food processor or blender and blend until smooth.
7. Transfer the pate to a bowl and refrigerate for at least 1 hour before serving.

CREAMY BEEF LIVER AND VEGETABLES

Nutrition: Cal 420;Fat 31 g;Carb 8 g;Protein 24 g
Serving 2; Cook time 25 min

Ingredients
- 1 pound beef liver, sliced
- Salt and pepper to taste
- 2 tablespoons olive oil
- 1 onion, sliced
- 1 bell pepper, sliced
- 2 cloves garlic, minced
- 1 cup heavy cream
- 1/4 cup grated parmesan cheese
- 1/4 cup chopped fresh parsley

Instructions
1. Season the beef liver with salt and pepper.
2. Heat the olive oil in a large skillet over medium-high heat. Add the beef liver and cook for 2-3 minutes per side, or until browned. Remove the beef liver from the skillet and set aside.
3. In the same skillet, add the onion and bell pepper. Cook for 3-4 minutes, or until softened.
4. Add the minced garlic to the skillet and cook for 1 minute.
5. Pour in the heavy cream and stir to combine. Cook for 3-4 minutes, or until the sauce has thickened.
6. Return the beef liver to the skillet and cook for an additional 2-3 minutes, or until the liver is cooked through.
7. Stir in the grated parmesan cheese and chopped parsley.
8. Serve hot and enjoy!

BEEF LIVER WITH VEGETABLES IN TOMATO SAUCE

Nutrition: Cal 389;Fat 16 g;Carb 17 g;Protein 38 g
Serving 2; Cook time 25 min

Ingredients
- 400g beef liver, sliced
- 1 onion, chopped
- 2 cloves garlic, minced
- 1 red bell pepper, sliced
- 1 zucchini, sliced
- 1 can (400g) diced tomatoes
- 1 tsp paprika powder
- Salt and pepper, to taste
- 2 tbsp olive oil

Instructions
1. Heat olive oil in a pan over medium heat. Add onion and garlic and sauté until onion is soft and translucent.
2. Add sliced beef liver to the pan and cook for 2-3 minutes on each side, until browned. Remove liver from pan and set aside.
3. Add sliced red bell pepper and zucchini to the pan and cook for 5-7 minutes, until vegetables are tender.
4. Add canned diced tomatoes, paprika powder, salt, and pepper to the pan. Stir well to combine.

5. Return beef liver to the pan and spoon some of the tomato sauce over the liver.
6. Cover the pan and let the dish simmer for 5-10 minutes, until the liver is cooked through and the sauce has thickened.
7. Serve hot with a side of keto-friendly vegetables, such as broccoli or cauliflower.

BEEF LIVER JAPANESE STYLE

Nutrition: Cal 292;Fat 14 g;Carb 5 g;Protein 29 g
Serving 2; Cook time 20 min

Ingredients
- 250g beef liver, sliced into thin pieces
- 1 tablespoon coconut oil
- 1 tablespoon grated ginger
- 2 cloves garlic, minced
- 1/4 cup soy sauce
- 2 tablespoons sake
- 1 tablespoon erythritol or any keto-friendly sweetener
- 1/2 teaspoon sesame oil
- 1/4 teaspoon black pepper
- 1 tablespoon green onion, chopped

Instructions
1. In a bowl, mix together soy sauce, sake, erythritol, sesame oil, and black pepper. Set aside.
2. Heat coconut oil in a pan over medium-high heat.
3. Add sliced beef liver and cook for 1-2 minutes on each side until browned.
4. Add minced garlic and grated ginger to the pan and cook for another 1-2 minutes.
5. Pour in the sauce mixture and cook for 1-2 minutes until the sauce thickens.
6. Garnish with chopped green onions and serve hot.

KETO BEEF LIVER FRITTERS

Nutrition: Cal 329;Fat 24 g;Carb 7 g;Protein 20 g
Serving 2; Cook time 20 min

Ingredients
- 8 oz beef liver, chopped
- 2 tbsp almond flour
- 1 tbsp coconut flour
- 1 egg
- 1/4 cup chopped onion
- 1 clove garlic, minced
- 1/4 tsp salt
- 1/4 tsp black pepper
- 2 tbsp ghee or coconut oil

Instructions
1. In a bowl, mix together the chopped beef liver, almond flour, coconut flour, egg, chopped onion, minced garlic, salt, and black pepper until well combined.
2. Heat the ghee or coconut oil in a large skillet over medium heat.
3. Form the beef liver mixture into 8 fritters and place them in the hot skillet.

4. Cook the fritters for about 3-4 minutes per side, or until browned and cooked through.
5. Serve the fritters with your choice of keto-friendly sauce or dip. Enjoy!

PANCAKES STUFFED WITH BEEF LIVER

Nutrition: Cal 486;Fat 37 g;Carb 9 g;Protein 37 g
Serving 2; Cook time 25 min

Ingredients
- 1/2 pound beef liver, chopped
- 1/2 onion, chopped
- 2 eggs, beaten
- Salt and pepper, to taste
- 1/2 cup almond flour
- 1/2 tsp baking powder
- 1/4 cup water
- 1 tbsp coconut oil

Instructions
1. In a skillet over medium-high heat, cook the beef liver and onion until the liver is cooked through and the onion is soft.
2. Add the beaten eggs to the skillet and scramble until cooked.
3. Season with salt and pepper to taste.
4. In a separate bowl, mix together the almond flour, baking powder, and water until smooth.
5. Heat the coconut oil in a nonstick skillet over medium heat.
6. Pour 1/4 cup of the batter onto the skillet and spread it into a thin, round pancake.
7. Cook for 2-3 minutes or until bubbles form on the surface and the edges start to turn golden.
8. Flip the pancake and cook for another 1-2 minutes.
9. Repeat with the remaining batter to make a total of 4 pancakes.
10. Spoon the beef liver and egg mixture onto two of the pancakes.
11. Top with the remaining pancakes to make two stuffed pancakes.

BEEF LIVER SALAD

Nutrition: Cal 427;Fat 35 g;Carb 6 g;Protein 20 g
Serving 2; Cook time 20 min

Ingredients
- 200g beef liver, sliced
- 2 cups mixed greens (spinach, arugula, lettuce, etc.)
- 1/2 avocado, sliced
- 1/4 cup sliced cucumber
- 1/4 cup sliced radish
- 2 tbsp chopped fresh parsley
- 2 tbsp chopped fresh chives
- 2 tbsp olive oil
- 1 tbsp apple cider vinegar
- Salt and pepper to taste

Instructions

1. Season the sliced beef liver with salt and pepper to taste.
2. Heat a skillet over medium-high heat and add 1 tablespoon of olive oil.
3. Add the sliced beef liver and cook for 3-4 minutes on each side or until browned and cooked through. Set aside.
4. In a large bowl, add the mixed greens, sliced avocado, sliced cucumber, and sliced radish. Toss to combine.
5. In a small bowl, whisk together 1 tablespoon of olive oil, 1 tablespoon of apple cider vinegar, chopped parsley, and chopped chives. Season with salt and pepper to taste.
6. Add the cooked beef liver to the salad and drizzle the dressing over the top.
7. Toss the salad to combine and serve.

BEEF LIVER GOULASH

Nutrition: Cal 297;Fat 14 g;Carb 7 g;Protein 28 g
Serving 2; Cook time 20 min

Ingredients
- 200g beef liver, sliced
- 1 onion, diced
- 1 red bell pepper, diced
- 1 tsp paprika
- 1/2 tsp caraway seeds
- 1/2 tsp garlic powder
- 1/2 cup beef broth
- 2 tbsp tomato paste
- 2 tbsp sour cream
- 1 tbsp olive oil
- Salt and pepper to taste

Instructions
1. Season the sliced beef liver with salt and pepper to taste.
2. Heat a skillet over medium-high heat and add 1 tablespoon of olive oil.
3. Add the diced onion and red bell pepper and sauté until softened, about 5 minutes.
4. Add the sliced beef liver and sauté for another 3-4 minutes or until browned.
5. Sprinkle paprika, caraway seeds, and garlic powder over the beef liver and vegetables. Stir to combine.
6. Add beef broth and tomato paste to the skillet, bring to a simmer and cook for about 5 minutes until the sauce has thickened.
7. Remove the skillet from the heat, stir in sour cream and serve.

BEEF LIVER CASSEROLE

Nutrition: Cal 529;Fat 43 g;Carb 6 g;Protein 25 g
Serving 2; Cook time 30 min

Ingredients
- 200g beef liver, sliced
- 1 small zucchini, sliced
- 1 small yellow squash, sliced
- 1/2 cup chopped mushrooms
- 1/4 cup chopped onion

- 1/2 cup shredded cheddar cheese
- 2 tbsp butter
- 1/2 cup heavy cream
- 1 tsp garlic powder
- Salt and pepper to taste

Instructions
1. Preheat the oven to 375°F (190°C).
2. Season the sliced beef liver with salt and pepper to taste.
3. Heat a skillet over medium-high heat and add 1 tablespoon of butter.
4. Add the sliced beef liver and sauté for 3-4 minutes on each side or until browned. Set aside.
5. Add the remaining butter to the skillet and sauté the zucchini, yellow squash, mushrooms, and onion until softened, about 5 minutes.
6. Add the garlic powder and heavy cream to the skillet and stir to combine.
7. Arrange the sliced beef liver on the bottom of a small casserole dish.
8. Pour the vegetable mixture over the beef liver and top with shredded cheddar cheese.
9. Bake in the oven for 15-20 minutes or until the cheese is melted and bubbly.

BEEF LIVER WITH ZUCCHINI PANCAKES

Nutrition: Cal 482;Fat 35 g;Carb 6 g;Protein 28 g
Serving 2; Cook time 25 min

Ingredients
- 200g beef liver, sliced
- 1 small zucchini, grated
- 1 egg
- 1/4 cup almond flour
- 1/4 cup grated parmesan cheese
- 2 tbsp chopped fresh parsley
- 2 tbsp olive oil
- Salt and pepper to taste

Instructions
1. Season the sliced beef liver with salt and pepper to taste.
2. Heat a skillet over medium-high heat and add 1 tablespoon of olive oil.
3. Add the sliced beef liver and sauté for 3-4 minutes on each side or until browned. Set aside.
4. In a medium bowl, combine the grated zucchini, egg, almond flour, parmesan cheese, parsley, and salt and pepper to taste.
5. Heat another skillet over medium heat and add 1 tablespoon of olive oil.
6. Spoon the zucchini mixture into the skillet to form small pancakes. Cook for 2-3 minutes on each side or until golden brown.
7. Serve the beef liver slices with the zucchini pancakes.

VIETNAMESE BEEF LIVER

Nutrition: Cal 215;Fat 11 g;Carb 3 g;Protein 26 g
Serving 2; Cook time 20 min

Ingredients
- 200g beef liver, sliced
- 2 cloves garlic, minced
- 1 small red chili pepper, thinly sliced
- 2 tbsp fish sauce
- 2 tbsp lime juice
- 1 tsp coconut sugar
- 1 tbsp olive oil
- Salt and pepper to taste
- Fresh cilantro leaves for garnish

Instructions
1. Season the sliced beef liver with salt and pepper to taste.
2. Heat a skillet over medium-high heat and add 1 tablespoon of olive oil.
3. Add the sliced beef liver and sauté for 3-4 minutes on each side or until browned. Set aside.
4. In a small bowl, whisk together minced garlic, thinly sliced chili pepper, fish sauce, lime juice, and coconut sugar.
5. Pour the sauce over the beef liver slices and toss to coat.
6. Serve the beef liver slices with fresh cilantro leaves for garnish.

PARMESAN-CRUSTED BEEF LIVER CUTLETS

Nutrition: Cal 368;Fat 26 g;Carb 4 g;Protein 26 g
Serving 2; Cook time 30 min

Ingredients
- 200g beef liver, sliced into cutlets
- 1/4 cup almond flour
- 1/4 cup grated parmesan cheese
- 1 tsp garlic powder
- 1 tsp dried thyme
- 1/2 tsp paprika
- 1 egg, beaten
- 2 tbsp butter
- Salt and pepper to taste
- Lemon wedges for serving

Instructions
1. In a shallow dish, combine almond flour, grated parmesan cheese, garlic powder, dried thyme, paprika, salt, and pepper.
2. Dip each beef liver cutlet into the beaten egg, then coat with the almond flour mixture.
3. Heat a skillet over medium-high heat and add 2 tablespoons of butter.
4. Add the coated beef liver cutlets to the skillet and cook for 2-3 minutes on each side or until golden brown and cooked through.
5. Serve the beef liver cutlets with lemon wedges.

BEEF LIVER WITH CAULIFLOWER DEMIGLACE

Nutrition: Cal 354;Fat 23 g;Carb 8 g;Protein 28 g
Serving 2; Cook time 25 min

Ingredients

- 200g beef liver, sliced
- 1/2 head of cauliflower, cut into small florets
- 1/2 cup beef broth
- 2 tbsp butter
- 2 tbsp heavy cream
- 1 tsp arrowroot powder
- Salt and pepper to taste
- Fresh parsley for garnish

Instructions

1. Season the sliced beef liver with salt and pepper to taste.
2. Heat a skillet over medium-high heat and add 1 tablespoon of butter.
3. Add the sliced beef liver and sauté for 3-4 minutes on each side or until browned. Set aside.
4. In a separate skillet, add the cauliflower florets and beef broth. Bring to a boil, then reduce heat and simmer for 5-7 minutes or until the cauliflower is tender.
5. Using a blender or food processor, blend the cooked cauliflower with the remaining 1 tablespoon of butter, heavy cream, and arrowroot powder until smooth.
6. In the same skillet used for the beef liver, add the cauliflower puree and simmer for 2-3 minutes or until thickened.
7. Serve the beef liver slices with the cauliflower demiglace sauce and garnish with fresh parsley.

BEEF LIVER WITH MIXED VEGETABLES SAUTEED

Nutrition: Cal 315;Fat 18 g;Carb 28 g;Protein 10 g
Serving 2; Cook time 20 min

Ingredients

- 200g beef liver, sliced
- 1/2 head of broccoli, cut into small florets
- 2 medium carrots, peeled and sliced
- 1 small onion, chopped
- 1/2 cup green beans, trimmed
- 2 tbsp butter
- Salt and pepper to taste

Instructions

1. Season the sliced beef liver with salt and pepper to taste.
2. Heat a skillet over medium-high heat and add 1 tablespoon of butter.
3. Add the sliced beef liver and sauté for 3-4 minutes on each side or until browned. Set aside.
4. In the same skillet, add the remaining 1 tablespoon of butter and sauté the broccoli florets, sliced carrots, chopped onion, and green beans for 5-7 minutes or until tender.
5. Return the beef liver slices to the skillet and heat through with the mixed vegetables.
6. Serve hot and enjoy!

KETO BAKED BEEF WITH MIXED VEGETABLES

Nutrition: Cal 407;Fat 27 g;Carb 9 g;Protein 33 g
Serving 2; Cook time 35 min

Ingredients

- 300g beef (sirloin, ribeye, or other cut), sliced into 2 pieces
- 1 small zucchini, sliced
- 1 small yellow squash, sliced
- 1 small onion, sliced
- 1 small red bell pepper, sliced
- 2 cloves garlic, minced
- 2 tbsp olive oil
- Salt and pepper to taste

Instructions

1. Preheat the oven to 400°F (200°C).
2. Place the sliced beef on a baking sheet and season with salt and pepper to taste.
3. In a separate bowl, mix together the sliced zucchini, yellow squash, onion, red bell pepper, minced garlic, and olive oil. Season with salt and pepper to taste.
4. Arrange the mixed vegetables around the beef slices on the baking sheet.
5. Bake in the preheated oven for 15-20 minutes or until the beef is cooked to your desired doneness and the vegetables are tender.
6. Serve hot and enjoy!

KETO LEMON-ROSEMARY BEEF BAKE

Nutrition: Cal 355;Fat 23 g;Carb 4 g;Protein 32 g
Serving 2; Cook time 30 min

Ingredients

- 300g beef (sirloin, ribeye, or other cut), sliced into 2 pieces
- 2 cloves garlic, minced
- 1 lemon, juiced and zested
- 2 tbsp Dijon mustard
- 1 tbsp fresh rosemary, chopped
- 2 tbsp olive oil
- Salt and pepper to taste

Instructions

1. Preheat the oven to 400°F (200°C).
2. In a small bowl, mix together the minced garlic, lemon juice and zest, Dijon mustard, chopped rosemary, olive oil, and salt and pepper to taste.
3. Place the sliced beef on a baking sheet and spread the mustard mixture over both sides of the beef.
4. Bake in the preheated oven for 15-20 minutes or until the beef is cooked to your desired doneness.
5. Remove from the oven and let the beef rest for a few minutes before slicing and serving.
6. Serve hot and enjoy!

KETO BEEF LIVER QUENELLE VEGETABLE SOUP

Nutrition: Cal 279;Fat 21 g;Carb 6 g;Protein 16 g
Serving 2; Cook time 30 min

Ingredients
- 400ml beef broth
- 1 small onion, chopped
- 2 garlic cloves, minced
- 1 small zucchini, chopped
- 1 small yellow squash, chopped
- 1 small carrot, chopped
- 1/2 cup green beans, chopped
- 2 tbsp olive oil
- Salt and pepper to taste

FOR THE BEEF LIVER QUENELLES:
- 100g beef liver, minced
- 1 egg
- 2 tbsp almond flour
- 1 tbsp chopped parsley
- Salt and pepper to taste

Instructions
1. In a large pot, heat the olive oil over medium heat. Add the chopped onion and garlic, and cook until softened, about 3-4 minutes.
2. Add the chopped zucchini, yellow squash, carrot, and green beans to the pot. Season with salt and pepper to taste, and cook for another 3-4 minutes.
3. Pour the beef broth into the pot and bring to a boil. Reduce the heat and simmer for about 15 minutes, or until the vegetables are tender.
4. Meanwhile, prepare the beef liver quenelles. In a mixing bowl, combine the minced beef liver, egg, almond flour, chopped parsley, salt and pepper. Mix well.
5. Using a teaspoon, form small quenelles or meatballs with the beef liver mixture and set aside.
6. Once the vegetables are tender, gently drop the beef liver quenelles into the soup. Cook for an additional 5-7 minutes, or until the quenelles are cooked through.
7. Serve hot and enjoy!

KETO BEEF LIVER WITH MUSTARD SAUCE

Nutrition: Cal 381;Fat 29 g;Carb 2 g;Protein 22 g
Serving 2; Cook time 20 min

Ingredients
- 250g beef liver, sliced
- 1 small onion, chopped
- 2 garlic cloves, minced
- 2 tbsp olive oil
- Salt and pepper to taste

FOR THE MUSTARD SAUCE:
- 2 tbsp Dijon mustard
- 2 tbsp heavy cream
- 1 tbsp chopped parsley

Instructions
1. Preheat the oven to 200°C (400°F).
2. In a large skillet, heat the olive oil over medium-high heat. Add the chopped onion and garlic, and cook until softened, about 3-4 minutes.
3. Add the sliced beef liver to the skillet. Season with salt and pepper to taste, and cook for about 2-3 minutes on each side, or until browned.
4. Transfer the beef liver slices to a baking dish and place in the preheated oven. Bake for about 5-7 minutes, or until cooked to your liking.
5. Meanwhile, prepare the mustard sauce. In a small mixing bowl, whisk together the Dijon mustard and heavy cream until smooth.
6. Once the beef liver is cooked, remove it from the oven and pour the mustard sauce over the slices. Sprinkle with chopped parsley and serve hot.

KETO BEEF RAGOUT WITH RED WINE AND MUSHROOMS

Nutrition: Cal 388;Fat 27 g;Carb 4 g;Protein 22 g
Serving 2; Cook time 30 min

Ingredients
- 250g beef chuck, cut into bite-sized pieces
- 1 small onion, chopped
- 2 garlic cloves, minced
- 2 tbsp olive oil
- 1/2 cup red wine
- 1/2 cup beef broth
- 1/2 cup chopped mushrooms
- 1 tsp dried thyme
- Salt and pepper to taste

Instructions
1. In a large Dutch oven or heavy pot, heat the olive oil over medium-high heat. Add the chopped onion and garlic, and cook until softened, about 3-4 minutes.
2. Add the beef chuck to the pot. Season with salt and pepper to taste, and cook for about 5-7 minutes, or until browned on all sides.
3. Pour in the red wine and beef broth, and stir to combine. Add the chopped mushrooms and dried thyme, and bring to a simmer.
4. Cover the pot and reduce the heat to low. Let simmer for about 1 hour, or until the beef is tender and the sauce has thickened.
5. Serve hot, garnished with fresh herbs if desired.

KETO BEEF AND CABBAGE SKILLET

Nutrition: Cal 412;Fat 27 g;Carb 14 g;Protein 29 g
Serving 2; Cook time 35 min

Ingredients
- 1 pound of beef, thinly sliced
- 1/2 head of cabbage, chopped
- 1 small onion, chopped
- 1 medium tomato, chopped
- 2 tablespoons of olive oil
- Salt and black pepper to taste

Instructions

1. Heat a skillet over medium-high heat and add the olive oil. Once the oil is hot, add the sliced beef and season with salt and black pepper. Cook for 5-6 minutes, stirring occasionally, until browned on all sides.
2. Add the chopped onion to the skillet and stir for 2-3 minutes until translucent.
3. Add the chopped cabbage to the skillet and stir to combine with the beef and onion. Cook for 10-12 minutes, stirring occasionally, until the cabbage is tender and slightly caramelized.
4. Add the chopped tomato to the skillet and stir to combine with the beef and cabbage. Cook for an additional 2-3 minutes until the tomato is slightly softened.
5. Serve hot and enjoy your delicious Keto Beef and Cabbage Skillet!

BEEF AND CREAM CHEESE VEGGIE ROLLS.

Nutrition: Cal 562;Fat 38 g;Carb 5 g;Protein 50 g
Serving 2; Cook time 50 min

Ingredients
- 1 beef roll (such as London broil or flank steak), pounded to a thin, even thickness
- 4 oz. cream cheese, softened
- 1/2 cup mixed vegetables (such as bell peppers, onions, and mushrooms), diced
- Salt and pepper to taste

Instructions
1. Preheat the oven to 375°F (190°C).
2. Lay the pounded beef roll flat on a work surface.
3. Spread the softened cream cheese over the beef roll, leaving a 1-inch border around the edges.
4. Sprinkle the mixed vegetables evenly over the cream cheese.
5. Season with salt and pepper to taste.
6. Starting at one end, tightly roll up the beef, tucking in the ends as you go.
7. Secure the roll with toothpicks.
8. Place the beef roll on a baking sheet and bake for 30-40 minutes, until cooked through.
9. Let the beef roll rest for 5-10 minutes before slicing and serving.

BEEF AND MUSHROOM COCONUT SOUP

Nutrition: Cal 675;Fat 54 g;Carb 14 g;Protein 35 g
Serving 2; Cook time 60 min

Ingredients
- 1 lb. beef stew meat
- 4 cups beef broth
- 1 can (14 oz.) full-fat coconut cream
- 8 oz. mushrooms, sliced
- 1/2 onion, chopped
- 2 garlic cloves, minced
- 1 can (14 oz.) diced tomatoes
- 2 tablespoons lime juice
- 2 tablespoons coconut oil
- Salt and pepper to taste

Instructions
1. In a large pot, heat the coconut oil over medium-high heat and cook the beef stew meat until browned on all sides.
2. Add the chopped onion and garlic and sauté for 2-3 minutes, until the onion is translucent.
3. Pour in the beef broth and bring to a boil.
4. Reduce the heat to low and simmer for 30-40 minutes, until the beef is tender.
5. Add the sliced mushrooms to the pot and cook for an additional 5-7 minutes, until the mushrooms are tender.
6. Stir in the diced tomatoes and lime juice and cook for an additional 5-10 minutes, until heated through.
7. Stir in the coconut cream and cook for an additional 5-10 minutes, until heated through.
8. Season with salt and pepper to taste.
9. Divide the soup into two bowls and serve hot.

BEEF AND CHEESE VEGGIE SOUP

Nutrition: Cal 447;Fat 27 g;Carb 11 g;Protein 39 g
Serving 2; Cook time 50 min

Ingredients
- 1 lb. beef stew meat
- 4 cups beef broth
- 1/2 onion, chopped
- 2 garlic cloves, minced
- 1 cup mixed vegetables (such as broccoli, cauliflower, and carrots), chopped
- 1/2 cup shredded cheese (such as cheddar or Gouda)
- Salt and pepper to taste

Instructions
1. In a large pot, heat the beef stew meat over medium-high heat and cook until browned on all sides.
2. Add the chopped onion and garlic and sauté for 2-3 minutes, until the onion is translucent.
3. Pour in the beef broth and bring to a boil.
4. Reduce the heat to low and simmer for 30-40 minutes, until the beef is tender.
5. Add the mixed vegetables to the pot and cook for an additional 10-15 minutes, until the vegetables are tender.
6. Season with salt and pepper to taste.
7. Divide the soup into two bowls and sprinkle the shredded cheese over the top.

FAJITA SALAD

Nutrition: Cal 893;Fat 60 g;Carb 17 g;Protein 70 g
Serving 4; Cook time 30 min

Ingredients
FOR THE STEAK
- 1 (2-pound) flank steak
- ¼ cup extra-virgin olive oil
- 1 teaspoon garlic powder
- 1 teaspoon onion powder
- 1 teaspoon ground cumin

- Juice of 1 lime
- 1 bunch cilantro, leaves chopped
- Salt
- Freshly ground black pepper

FOR THE SALAD
- 2 tablespoons extra-virgin olive oil or coconut oil
- 1 yellow onion, sliced
- 1 green bell pepper, sliced
- 1 red bell pepper, sliced
- 6 cups chopped romaine lettuce
- ½ cup sour cream
- ½ cup shredded Cheddar cheese
- 2 limes, quartered
- 1 avocado

Instructions
1. In a large resealable bag, add the flank steak, oil, garlic powder, onion powder, cumin, lime juice, cilantro, salt, and pepper. Marinate for 30 minutes to 24 hours.
2. When ready to cook, turn the broiler on high and remove the flank steak from the marinade, discarding the remaining marinade. Place the steak on a baking sheet and bake for 3 to 5 minutes on each side. Let rest for 10 minutes before thinly slicing against the grain.

TO MAKE THE SALAD
1. Heat a large skillet over medium heat and combine the oil, onion, and peppers. Stir often and cook until the onion becomes translucent, 8 to 10 minutes.
2. Into each of 4 divided storage containers, place the steak, peppers, and onions in one side, and the lettuce, sour cream, cheese, and lime wedges in the other side. Before enjoying an individual serving, halve, pit, and chop an avocado. Top the steak with ¼ of the chopped avocado, along with the lettuce, sour cream, and cheese. Squeeze the lime juice over everything and mix the lettuce around it.

GROUND BEEF AND CABBAGE STIR-FRY

Nutrition: Cal 550;Fat 33 g;Carb 13 g;Protein 49 g
Serving 4; Cook time 35 min

Ingredients
- 1 tablespoon coconut oil
- 1½ pounds ground beef
- 2 garlic cloves, minced
- 1 green cabbage head, cored and chopped
- 2 tablespoons coconut aminos
- 2 tablespoons apple cider vinegar
- Salt
- Freshly ground black pepper
- 4 scallions, both white and green parts, chopped
- Sesame seeds (optional)
- Sriracha (optional)
- Toasted sesame oil (optional)

Instructions
1. In a large skillet, heat the oil over medium heat. Cook the beef and garlic until the beef is browned, 5 to 7 minutes.

2. Add the cabbage to the skillet and continue to cook until the cabbage becomes slightly wilted, 8 to 10 minutes.
3. Add the coconut aminos and vinegar and season with salt and pepper.

BACON CHEESEBURGER SOUP

Nutrition: Cal 315;Fat 20 g;Carb 6 g;Protein 27 g
Serving 4; Cook time 25 min

Ingredients:
- 4 slices uncooked bacon
- 8 ounces ground beef (80% lean)
- 1 medium yellow onion, chopped
- 1 clove garlic, minced
- 3 cups beef broth
- 2 tablespoons tomato paste
- 2 teaspoons Dijon mustard
- Salt and pepper
- 1 cup shredded lettuce
- ½ cup shredded cheddar cheese

Instructions:
1. Cook the bacon in a saucepan until crisp then drain on paper towels and chop.
2. Reheat the bacon fat in the saucepan and add the beef.
3. Cook until the beef is browned, then drain away half the fat.
4. Reheat the saucepan and add the onion and garlic – cook for 6 minutes.
5. Stir in the broth, tomato paste, and mustard then season with salt and
6. pepper.
7. Add the beef and simmer on medium-low for 15 minutes, covered.
8. Spoon into bowls and top with shredded lettuce, cheddar cheese and bacon.

TACO SALAD WITH CREAMY DRESSING

Nutrition: Cal 470;Fat 36 g;Carb 7 g;Protein 28 g
Serving 2; Cook time 20 min

Ingredients:
- 6 ounces ground beef (80% lean)
- Salt and pepper
- 1 tablespoon ground cumin
- 1 tablespoon chili powder
- 4 cups fresh chopped lettuce
- ½ cup diced tomatoes
- ¼ cup diced red onion
- ¼ cup shredded cheddar cheese
- 3 tablespoons mayonnaise
- 1 teaspoon apple cider vinegar
- Pinch paprika

Instructions:
1. Cook the ground beef in a skillet over medium-high heat until browned.
2. Drain half the fat, then season with salt and pepper and stir in the taco seasoning.

3.Simmer for 5 minutes, then remove from heat.

4.Divide the lettuce between two salad bowls, then top with ground beef.

5.Add the diced tomatoes, red onion, and cheddar cheese.

6.Whisk together the remaining ingredients, then drizzle over the salads to serve.

BRAISED LAMB SHANKS

Nutrition: Cal 365;Fat 21 g;Carb 6 g;Protein 35 g
Serving 4; Cook time 3 hours 20 min

Ingredients:
- 4 lamb shanks (1.6 kg/ 3.5 kg) - will yield about 60% meat
- 1 tsp sea salt
- 1/2 tsp black pepper
- 2 tbsp virgin avocado oil (30 ml)
- 1 medium red onion, diced (85 g/ 3 oz)
- 4 cloves garlic, minced
- 1 medium carrot, sliced (60 g/ 2.1 oz)
- 3 celery stalks, sliced (120 g/ 4.2 oz)
- 2 cups dry red wine (480 ml/ 16 fl oz)
- 2 cups chicken stock (480 ml/ 16 fl oz)
- 2 cinnamon sticks or 1/2 tsp cinnamon
- 2 bay leaves
- 4 sprigs rosemary

Instructions:
1.Preheat the oven to 160 °C/ 320 °F (fan assisted), or 180 °C/ 355 °F (conventional). Season the lamb shanks with salt and pepper.

2.Peel and dice the onion and mince the garlic. Peel and slice the carrot and chop the celery.Low-Carb Braised Lamb Shanks

3.Grease a large casserole dish with avocado oil (or ghee). Add the lamb shanks and cook on high from all sides for a few minutes until browned.Low-Carb Braised Lamb Shanks

4.Once browned, transfer the lamb to a plate. Browning the lamb will add fantastic flavor! (Note: If you're planning to make these in a slow cooker, check the recipe tips in the post above.)

5.Add the onion and cook for about 3 to 5 minutes. Mix frequently scraping the bottom of the pan to combine with the browned juices from the lamb. Add the garlic, carrot and celery, stir again, and cook for a minute.Low-Carb Braised Lamb Shanks

6.Pour in the wine and stock. Add the cinnamon (you can use 2 cinnamon sticks or 1/2 tsp ground cinnamon), bay leaves and rosemary.Low-Carb Braised Lamb Shanks

7.Place in the oven and cook for 2 1/2 to 3 hours. Once baked, remove from the oven, remove the lid and let it cool down for a few minutes.Low-Carb Braised Lamb Shanks

8.This braised lamb is best served with cauliflower mash. Try with Keto Creamy Cauliflower Mash, Cauliflower Mash with Roasted Garlic & Thyme, or Keto Celeriac Cauli-Mash.

9.To store, let it cool down and refrigerate for up to 4 days. The cooked meat can also be frozen in a sealed container for up to 3 months.

KETO LAMB CURRY WITH SPINACH

Nutrition: Cal 497;Fat 18 g;Carb 8 g;Protein 62 g
Serving 2; Cook time 4 hours

Ingredients:
- 1 medium Red onion (quartered and sliced)
- 2 clove(s) Garlic
- 2 tbsp minced Ginger root
- 2 tsp Cardamom, ground
- 6 clove Cloves (whole)
- 2 tsp Coriander, ground (ground)
- 1 tsp Turmeric, powder
- 1/2 tsp Chili powder
- 1 tsp Garam masala
- 2 tsp Cumin
- 500 gm Lamb, cubed for stew, lean
- 1 can(s) (14oz) Diced tomatoes, canned
- 500 gm Spinach (fresh)

Instructions:
1.Place all the ingredients in the slow cooker (except for the spinach) and stir.

2.Cook on HIGH for 4-5 hours or LOW for 8 hours.

3.Mix in the spinach right before serving, allowing the heat to wilt it.

KETO LAMB ROAST WITH CHIMICHURRI SAUCE

Nutrition: Cal 573;Fat 46 g;Carb 2 g;Protein 32 g
Serving 2; Cook time 4 hours

Ingredients:
- 1 medium Red onion (quartered and sliced)
- 2 clove(s) Garlic
- 2 tbsp minced Ginger root
- 2 tsp Cardamom, ground
- 6 clove Cloves (whole)
- 2 tsp Coriander, ground (ground)
- 1 tsp Turmeric, powder
- 1/2 tsp Chili powder
- 1 tsp Garam masala
- 2 tsp Cumin
- 500 gm Lamb, cubed for stew, lean
- 1 can(s) (14oz) Diced tomatoes, canned
- 500 gm Spinach (fresh)

CHIMICHURRI SAUCE
- 2 cups fresh parsley leaves and tender stems
- 2 Tbsp fresh oregano leaves
- 1 medium jalapeño, halved and seeded
- 1/2 tsp crushed red pepper flakes
- 1 garlic clove
- 3/4 cup extra-virgin olive oil
- ~ sea salt and freshly ground black pepper

•2 Tbsp red wine vinegar

Instructions:

1. In a small bowl, combine the rosemary, garlic powder, salt, and pepper. Add the butter and mix to make a paste. Thoroughly coat the lamb with the garlic-herb paste, then rub it into the meat with your hands to completely coat. Place the roast in a zip-lock bag and chill for 2 hours or overnight.

2. Heat oven to 375°F (230°C). Put the lamb on a rack in a roasting pan and roast until an instant-read thermometer registers 130°F (55°C) for rare or 140°F (60°C) for medium-rare, 1 3/4 to 2 hours, tenting the lamb with foil for the last hour of cooking to prevent it from getting too brown. Let meat rest for 20 minutes (or up to 45 minutes) before slicing.

3. Slice thin and serve with a side of chimichurri sauce.

BEEF AND PEPPER KEBABS

Nutrition: Cal 365;Fat 21 g;Carb 6 g;Protein 35 g
Serving 2; Cook time 40 min

Ingredients:

•2 tablespoons olive oil
•1 ½ tablespoons balsamic vinegar
•2 teaspoons Dijon mustard
•Salt and pepper
•8 ounces beef sirloin, cut into 2-inch pieces
•1 small red pepper, cut into chunks
•1 small green pepper, cut into chunks

Instructions:

1. Whisk together the olive oil, balsamic vinegar, and mustard in a shallow dish.

2. Season the steak with salt and pepper, then toss in the marinade.

3. Let marinate for 30 minutes, then slide onto skewers with the peppers.

4. Preheat a grill pan to high heat and grease with cooking spray.

5. Cook the kebabs for 2 to 3 minutes on each side until the beef is done.

BACON-WRAPPED HOT DOGS

Nutrition: Cal 500;Fat 4 g;Carb 3 g;Protein 24 g
Serving 2; Cook time 40 min

Ingredients:

•4 all-beef hot dogs
•2 slices cheddar cheese
•4 slices uncooked bacon

Instructions:

1. Slice the hotdogs lengthwise, cutting halfway through the thickness.

2. Cut the cheese slices in half and stuff one half into each hot dog.

3. Wrap the hotdogs in bacon then place them on a foil-lined roasting pan.

4. Bake for 30 minutes or until the bacon is crisp.

SLOW-COOKER BEEF CHILI

Nutrition: Cal 395; Fat 20 g; Carb 12 g; Protein 42 g
Serving 4; Cook time 6 hours

Ingredients:

•1 tablespoon coconut oil
•1 medium yellow onion, chopped
•3 cloves garlic, minced
•1 pound ground beef (80% lean)
•1 small red pepper, chopped
•1 small green pepper, chopped
•1 cup diced tomatoes
•1 cup low-carb tomato sauce
•1 tablespoon chili powder
•2 teaspoons dried oregano
•1 ½ teaspoons dried basil
•Salt and pepper
•¾ cup shredded cheddar cheese
•½ cup diced red onion

Instructions:

1. Heat the oil in a skillet over medium-high heat.

2. Add the onions and sauté for 4 minutes, then stir in the garlic and cook 1 minute.

3. Stir in the beef and cook until it is browned, then drain some of the fat.

4. Spoon the mixture into a slow cooker and add the spices.

5. Cover and cook on low heat for 5 to 6 hours, then spoon into bowls.

6. Serve with shredded cheddar and diced red onion.

MEXICAN MEATZA

Nutrition: Cal 414;Fat 30 g; Carb 2 g;Protein 35 g
Serving 4; Cook time 25 min

Ingredients

•1 lb ground beef, lean
•1/2 onion
•1 egg
•1 cup cauliflower, riced
•2 teaspoons chili powder
•1 teaspoon cumin
•1 teaspoon salt
•1/2 teaspoon pepper
•1 teaspoon garlic powder
•1/4 red onion, sliced thin
•1 cup cheddar cheese, shredded
•1/4 cup sweet pepper slices

CILANTRO CREMA (OPTIONAL)

•1/3 cup cilantro leaves, loosely packed
•1/2 cup sour cream
•1 tablespoon lime juice
•1 clove garlic

Instructions

1. Preheat oven to 350°F.

2. Add onion to a food processor and pulse until finely chopped.

3.Place in a large bowl and then add cauliflower to food processor and pulse until it looks like grains of rice.

4.Add that to the large bowl along with meat, a beaten egg, chili powder, cumin, salt, pepper, and garlic powder.

5.Mix well and split meat into 4.

6.Take each piece and make into a very thin, round pizza-looking shell. Place on a sprayed cookie sheet. Continue with the rest of the meat mixture. May take 2 cookie sheets.

7.Bake for 20 minutes or until meat is cooked. (thickness of meat will affect cooking times. Try not to overcook.)

8.Take out of the oven, sprinkle cheese, and add onions and peppers on top.

9.Broil for 3 minutes or until cheese is melted.

10. Add avocado pieces onto each meatza, slice, and enjoy.

11. Note: You can use any topping you like such as tomatoes, lettuce, black olives, green onions, sour cream, hot sauce, etc.

12. Make crema.

THAI BEEF SALAD
Nutrition: Cal 350;Fat 18 g; Carb 8 g;Protein 27 g
Serving 2; Cook time 15 min

Ingredients
DRESSING
•1 clove garlic
•1 jalapeno, halved
•1 lime, juiced
•1 1/2 tablespoons fish sauce
•2 tablespoons minced lemongrass (remove the tough outer leaves and slice the tender white core)
•1 1/4 teaspoons brown sugar
•1/4 teaspoon red chile flakes
STEAK
•1/2 tablespoon vegetable oil
•1 1-inch thick New York strip steak, 9 to 10 ounces
•2 medium shallots, thinly sliced
•1/4 cup fresh mint leaves loosely packed, roughly chopped
•3 tablespoons roughly chopped cilantro leaves and stems
RICE POWDER
2 tablespoons uncooked rice
FOR SERVING
•Lettuce of your choosing
•Cherry tomatoes, halved
Instructions
DRESSING
1.Mince the garlic and one of the chile halves and place in a small bowl. Slice the remaining chile half into thin rings and add it to the bowl, along with the lime juice, fish sauce, lemongrass, brown sugar, and red chile flakes. Taste and adjust seasonings with additional lime juice, fish sauce, sugar, if needed. Stir well and set aside.
RICE POWDER
2.Put rice in a small frying pan over medium heat. Cook, stirring frequently, until the grains are toasted and golden, about 10 minutes. Let cool for a few minutes and then grind into a coarse powder in a spice grinder or with a mortar and pestle.

STEAK
3.Heat the oil in a skillet over medium high heat. Sear the steak until it is well browned on one side, 5 to 6 min. Flip and cook until the second side is dark brown and the meat is medium rare, another 5 to 6 min. Transfer to a cutting board and let rest for 5 min. Slice the steak thinly and then cut into bite-size pieces.

4.In a medium bowl, combine the beef (and any accumulated juices), shallots, mint, and cilantro. Stir the dressing and pour it on top. Toss gently. Add the ground toasted rice, and toss.

KETO ASIAN STEAK SALAD
Nutrition: Cal 350;Fat 22 g; Carb 6 g;Protein 27 g
Serving 2; Cook time 15 min

Ingredients
•2 Ribeye Steaks
•1/2 cup Soy sauce or coconut aminos divided
FOR THE ASIAN SESAME DRESSING
•1/2 cup Olive oil
•2 tbsp Soy sauce or coconut aminos
•2 tbsp Apple Cider Vinegar
•1 tsp Sesame Oil
•1/8 tsp liquid stevia
FOR ASSEMBLING
•4 cups Raw spinach
•4 radishes sliced thin
•Sesame seeds for garnish
Instructions
1.Place each steak in a zip top bag with 1/4 cup of soy sauce. Zip up the bags and allow to marinate on the counter for 1 hour.

2.Remove the steaks from the bag and discard the marinade. In a cast iron skillet on high heat, cook the steaks to your desired doneness. I did 4 minutes on each side for medium.

3.Let the steaks rest for 10 minutes on a cutting board.

4.While the steaks are resting, make your dressing. Add all of the dressing ingredients to a jar with a lid and shake to combine.

5.Assemble the salads. Add 2 cups of spinach and half of the sliced radish to each of the 2 bowls. Slice the steaks into 1/2 in thick pieces and add those to the salads. Drizzle the dressing on top and garnish with sesame seeds.

KETO MONGOLIAN BEEF
Nutrition: Cal 350;Fat 14 g; Carb 17 g;Protein 30 g
Serving 4; Cook time 25 min

Ingredients
•1 Tablespoon avocado oil
•2 teaspoons Minced ginger
•1 Tablespoon Minced garlic
•1/2 Cup Soy sauce or Coconut aminos
•1/2 cup Water
•3/4 cup Granulated sweetener
•1 1/2 pounds Flank steak or Flatiron steak

- 1/4 teaspoon Red pepper flakes
- 5 Stems Green onions-cut diagonal into 2 inch pieces
- 1/4 teaspoon xanthan gum

Instructions

MAKING THE SAUCE:

1. Heat 1 tablespoon Avocado Oil in a medium saucepan over medium heat.
2. Add ginger, garlic, red pepper flakes and stir for 30 seconds.
3. Add soy sauce, water and sweetener. Bring to a boil and simmer until thickened. Should take about 5 minutes.
4. Remove from skillet to a bowl and set aside.

FOR THE STEAK:

1. Slice flank steak against the grain into 1/4 inch slices with the knife held at a 45 degree angle. Some of the really long pieces I cut in half to make them more bite-sized.
2. Heat avocado oil in skillet over medium-high heat.
3. Add beef (may need to cook in 2 batches) and cook 2-3 minutes, until brown, flipping pieces over to cook both sides.
4. Add the sauce to the pan along with the xantham gum and cook over medium heat for a few minute, Stirring to coat meat.
5. Add green onions and remove from heat.

GROUND BEEF AND CABBAGE STIR-FRY

Nutrition: Cal 550;Fat 33 g;Carb 13 g;Protein 49 g
Serving 4; Cook time 35 min

Ingredients

- 1 tablespoon coconut oil
- 1½ pounds ground beef
- 2 garlic cloves, minced
- 1 green cabbage head, cored and chopped
- 2 tablespoons coconut aminos
- 2 tablespoons apple cider vinegar
- Salt
- Freshly ground black pepper
- 4 scallions, both white and green parts, chopped
- Sesame seeds (optional)
- Sriracha (optional)
- Toasted sesame oil (optional)

Instructions

1. In a large skillet, heat the oil over medium heat. Cook the beef and garlic until the beef is browned, 5 to 7 minutes.
2. Add the cabbage to the skillet and continue to cook until the cabbage becomes slightly wilted, 8 to 10 minutes.
3. Add the coconut aminos and vinegar and season with salt and pepper.

KETO BURRITO BOWL

Nutrition: Cal 374;Fat 25 g; Carb 15 g;Protein 27 g
Serving 4; Cook time 20 min

Ingredients

- 1 cup Mexican Cauliflower Rice
- 1/2 cup Mexican Shredded Beef
- 1/4 cup Keto Guacamole
- 1/4 cup Pico de Gallo
- 1/4 cup shredded cheddar cheese
- 1 tablespoon chopped cilantro

Instructions

1. Arrange all of the ingredients in a shallow bowl and taste for seasoning.
2. Add salt and pepper or hot sauce, if desired.
3. Serve immediately.

EGG ROLL IN A BOWL

Nutrition: Cal 331;Fat 23.5 g; Carb 5 g;Protein 25 g
Serving 4; Cook time 15 min

Ingredients

- 1 lb (16 ounces) ground pork or beef
- 1 teaspoon minced garlic
- 14 ounces shredded cabbage or coleslaw mix
- 1/4 cup low-sodium soy sauce (or liquid aminos)
- 1 teaspoon ground ginger
- 1 whole egg
- 2 teaspoons sriracha
- 1 tablespoon sesame oil
- 2 tablespoons sliced green onions

Instructions

1. In a large skillet, brown the pork or beef until no longer pink. Drain the meat if it's really wet. Add the garlic and sautee for 30 seconds. Add the cabbage/coleslaw, soy sauce, ginger, and sautee until desired tenderness. You can add a little water if you need more liquid to sautee the coleslaw down.
2. Make a well in the center of the skillet and add the egg. Scramble until done over low heat.
3. Stir in sriracha. Drizzle with sesame oil and sprinkle with green onions. Add additional soy sauce and sriracha if desired.

KETO BACON CHEESEBURGER WRAPS

Nutrition: Cal 267;Fat 20 g; Carb 4 g;Protein 19 g
Serving 4; Cook time 30 min

Ingredients

- 7 oz. bacon
- 4 oz. mushrooms, sliced
- 1½ lbs ground beef or ground turkey
- ½ tsp salt
- ¼ tsp pepper
- 1 cup (4 oz.) shredded cheddar cheese
- 1 butterhead lettuce, leaves separated and washed

•8 (5 oz.) cherry tomatoes, sliced
Instructions
1. Add the bacon to a large skillet and cook over medium heat for about 15 minutes, or until crispy. Remove the bacon from the pan and set aside.
2. Over medium-high heat, sauté the mushrooms in the bacon fat, for about 5 to 7 minutes, or until browned and tender. Set aside.
3. Add the ground beef, salt, and pepper. Sauté the beef (breaking up any chunks with the back of a wooden spoon) for about 10 minutes, or until evenly browned. For serving, spoon the ground beef onto the lettuce leaves and layer the cheddar cheese, bacon, mushrooms, and tomatoes on top.

MEATBALLS IN TOMATO SAUCE
Nutrition: Cal 388;Fat 27 g; Carb 11 g;Protein 23 g
Serving 8; Cook time 25 min

Ingredients
FOR MEATBALLS
• Ground beef (2 lbs)
• Eggs (2)
• Garlic (3 cloves)
• Oregano (dry, 2 teaspoons)
• Salt (1 along with a half teaspoon)
• Pepper (1 teaspoon)
• Onion powder (2 teaspoons)
FOR THE TOMATO SAUCE
• Coconut oil (2 teaspoons)
• Garlic (2 cloves)
• Tomatoes (grated or blended, around 30 oz.)
• Onion (1, chopped)
• Water (¼ cup)
• Tomato paste (2 tbsp)
• Salt (2 teaspoons)
Instructions
1. Mix the meatball
2. Ingredients and roll the meat in small balls.
3. Set the pressure cooker to "Sauté" and pour inside the coconut oil (it's ok to make use of avocado oil at the same time).
4. The garlic and onion come next and must be cooked for 5 minutes with occasional stirring (before the onion is tender).
5. Press Cancel and adding the lake, grated tomatoes, tomato paste, and salt. Put within the meatballs, stir everything together (the meatballs ought to be well covered with tomato sauce).
6. Close pressure cooker and seal the pressure valve; place it to "Manual" and cook the meatballs for 7 minutes.
7. When the cooking is complete, release pressure naturally for 10 minutes.
8. Serve the meatballs with pasta, vegetables, or alone.

POMEGRANATE MOLASSES ROASTED CHUCK
Nutrition: Cal 466 ;Fat 32 g; Carb 3 g;Protein 37 g
Serving 10; Cook time 55 min

Ingredients
• 3 lbs chuck steak, boneless
• 2 tsp salt
• 1 ½ tsp freshly grounded black pepper
• 1 ¼ tsp garlic powder
• 1 tbsp pomegranate molasses
• 2 tbsp balsamic vinegar
• 1 onion, finely chopped
• 2 cups regular water
• ½ tsp xanthan gum (it is possible to use 1 tsp of Agar Agar if unavailable)
• 1/3 cup fresh parsley, finely chopped
Instructions
1. On a cutting board, slice the meat in two and season each half, on each party with salt, pepper and garlic powder.
2. Place the Instant Pot over heat and hang up on "Sauté" mode.
3. Place the seasoned meat into the pot and cook until browned on both sides.
4. Once the meat has browned, start adding the remaining with the
5. Add the pomegranate molasses, balsamic vinegar, onion and half the water.
6. Cover the pot and hang up the timer on 35 minutes.
7. When enough time is finished, manually release pressure to succeed by pressing "venting".
8. Remove the lid once all the pressure may be released. Transfer the meat to some cutting board and remove any fat or refuse. Cut the meat into large slices.
9. Simmer the sauce that was left within the pot by setting the pot on "sauté". Allow it to simmer for ten mins before the liquid has reduced.
10. Stir within the xanthan gum and return the meat into the pot and stir.
11. Turn over heat and transfer the meat onto serving plate. Drizzle the sauce on the meat and garnish with parsley. Serve hot.

SPICY MINCED LAMB WITH PEAS AND TOMATO SAUCE
Nutrition: Cal 242 ;Fat 12 g; Carb 10 g;Protein 24 g
Serving 6; Cook time 55 min

Ingredients
• 2 lbs ground lamb
• 3 tbsp ghee
• 1 onion, finely chopped
• 5 cloves garlic, crushed
• 1 tsp ground ginger
• 1 Serrano pepper, chopped
• 2 tsp ground coriander
• 1 tsp red pepper flakes

- 1 tsp Kosher salt
- ½ tsp turmeric powder
- ¾ tsp freshly ground black pepper
- ½ tsp chat masala
- ¾ tsp ground cumin
- ¼ tsp cayenne powder
- 2 cardamom pods, shell removed
- 1 can diced tomatoes
- 1 can peas
- Fresh cilantro, finely chopped

Instructions

1. Place the Instant Pot over medium heat and set on "Sauté". Add the ghee and onion. Stir before onion is tender.
2. Stir inside ginger, garlic along with the spices. Stir for 3 minutes and then add the minced meat.
3. Stir the meat until browned and covered well using the spices.
4. Add in the tomatoes and peas and cover the pot. Set on "Keep Warm" then choose "Bean/Chili" option.
5. When time is completed, release the pressure from your pot. Set back on 'Sauté' and allow the liquid to simmer for ten mins until reduced.
6. Transfer the meat into serving bowl and sprinkle fresh cilantro and serve hot.

ROASTED LAMB SHANKS WITH VEGETABLES

Nutrition: Cal 422 ;Fat 20 g; Carb 35 g;Protein 48 g
Serving 4; Cook time 65 min

Ingredients

- 4 lbs lamb shanks
- 2 tsp salt
- 1 tsp freshly ground black pepper
- 3 tbsp ghee
- 3 carrots, diced
- 3 celery stalks, sliced
- 1 large onion, diced
- 2 tbsp tomato paste
- 4 cloves garlic, minced
- 1 can diced tomatoes
- 1 1/3 cup bone broth
- 2 tsp fish sauce (optional)
- 1 ½ tbsp balsamic vinegar
- ½ cup fresh parsley, finely chopped

Instructions

1. Season the lamb with salt and pepper from either side.
2. Place the Instant Pot over medium heat and hang on "Sauté" , stir within the ghee until melted and add the meat. Stir until browned for a few minutes.
3. Transfer the meat to your plate and add the vegetables to the pot and sauté for some minutes. Season with many salt and pepper.
4. Add the tomato paste and garlic and stir for any minute. Return the meat to the pot and add the diced tomatoes.
5. Pour within the broth, fish sauce and vinegar.

6. Cover the pot and press "Cancel/Keep Warm". Manually set the timer for 45 minutes. Lower the temperature after the first 5 minutes.
7. When some time ends, release pressure.
8. Transfer the meat onto serving platter and pour the rest of the sauce within the meat. Garnish with fresh parsley and serve hot.

BARACOA-STYLE SHREDDED BEEF

Nutrition: Cal 435 ;Fat 31 g; Carb 4.5 g;Protein 31 g
Serving 12; Cook time 75 min

Ingredients

- 3 lbs minced beef
- 2 cups bread crumbs
- 4 eggs
- 1 tsp salt
- 1 tsp freshly ground black pepper
- 1 tsp garlic powder
- 4 oz mozzarella cheese, sliced
- ¼ cup fresh basil, finely chopped
- 1 cup beef broth
- ¼ cup light brown sugar
- ½ cup ketchup
- 2 tbsp Dijon mustard
- 1 tbsp Worcestershire sauce

Instructions

1. Trim any body fat off the meat then cut into 4 large pieces. Season with salt and pepper on either side.
2. Place the Instant Pot over medium heat, then one tablespoon of olive oil. Cook the meat until browned for a couple minutes. You will add the meat in to the pot in two batches.
3. Meanwhile, inside a food processor, blend together the onion, vinegar, lime juice, garlic, peppers, broth, cumin, cloves and tomato paste until smooth no lumps are normally found.
4. Pour inside the blended mixture on the meet and add the bay leaves.
5. Cover the pot as well as set on "Beef/Stew" for an hour.
6. Once time is finished, manually release the pressure and uncover the pot.
7. Transfer the meat onto a cutting board, using two forks start shredding the meat.
8. Discard the bay leaves and return the shredded meat in to the pot. Cover the pot and enable the meat to take a seat for 10 mins.
9. Serve the shredded meat like a filling for tortilla wraps, tacos or sandwiches with your favorite sauce.

BEEF SHAWARMA WITH TAHINI SAUCE

Nutrition: Cal 787 ;Fat 23 g; Carb 90 g;Protein 63 g
Serving 8; Cook time 45 min

Ingredients
- 2 lbs ground turkey
- 5 cups baby spinach leaves
- 1 cup ricotta
- 1 cup mozzarella cheese, grated
- 1 can crushed tomatoes
- 3 tsp dried oregano
- 2 tsp thyme
- 3 tbsp fresh parsley, finely chopped
- 1 tsp salt
- 1 tsp freshly ground black pepper
- 1 tsp onion powder
- 1 tsp garlic powder
- 8 lasagna sheets
- 3 cups water

Instructions
1. Trim the extra fat off of the chuck roast and sear the meat lengthwise. Make about 4 cuts. Place the crushed garlic cloves into each cut.
2. In a bowl mix together every one of the spices together. Add the balsamic vinegar and one tablespoon in the extra virgin olive oil.
3. Rub the spices mixture on the meat, make certain you cover the whole surface area.
4. Place the meat in a shallow dish and cover with cling film. position the meat inside fridge for about 8 hours or overnight.
5. Once the meat has rested inside the fridge, squeeze Instant Pot over medium heat as well as set on "Sauté". Add the rest of the olive oil and grill the meat for 8 minutes until browned on either side. Pour inside broth and cover the pot.
6. Set on "Beef/Stew" and invite it in order to cook with an hour.
7. Once the time is fully gone, release pressure to succeed and get rid of the lid. Stir inside the onion rings. Allow the meat to sit down inside pot, while using lid off for 5 minutes.
8. Transfer the meat in to a cutting board or possibly a plate and initiate slicing or shredding it into small pieces.
To serve, spread some tahini sauce into each pita bread, fill with shawarma and wrap. Enjoy these Arabian wraps with many French fries or pickles.

AVOCADO BEEF CHILI WITH COCONUT YOGURT

Nutrition: Cal 366 ;Fat 8.5 g; Carb 90 g;Protein 55 g
Serving 8; Cook time 25 min

Ingredients
- 2 tbsp avocado oil
- 1 onion, finely chopped
- 1 red bell pepper, diced
- 1 tsp salt
- 3 tbsp tomato paste
- 5 garlic cloves, crushed
- 3 lbs ground beef
- 4 tsp chili powder
- 2 tsp dried oregano
- 2 tsp ground cumin
- ½ tsp red pepper flakes
- 1 can roasted diced tomatoes
- 1/3 cup bone broth
- 1 tbsp fish sauce
- 2 tsp apple cider vinegar
- 1 ripe avocado, cubed
- 2 scallion, sliced
- 1/3 cup fresh parsley
- ½ cup coconut yogurt
- 1 lime, cut into wedges

Instructions
1. Place the Instant Pot over medium heat and set on "Sauté". Heat the avocado oil and stir in the onions and pepper. Season with salt and stir for a couple of minutes until tender.
2. Add the tomato paste and crushed garlic.
3. Stir inside the ground beef, season with increased salt and mix using a wooden spoon for 6 minutes.
4. Season the meat with chili powder, oregano, cumin and red pepper flakes.
5. Drain the tomatoes and stir into the meat. Pour inside broth, fish sauce and vinegar.
6. Cover the pot as well as set "Pressure Cook" and manually set the time for quarter-hour.
7. When the time is fully gone, manually release the stress and get rid of the lid.
8. To serve, transfer the chili for a serving bowls, top with avocado, scallion and a dollop of coconut yogurt. Garnish with fresh parsley, serve with lime wedges.

SPARE RIBS WITH CURRY SAUCE

Nutrition: Cal 522 ;Fat 23 g; Carb 15 g;Protein 71 g
Serving 4; Cook time 45 min

Ingredients
- 3 lbs lamb spare ribs
- 2 tbsp salt, divided
- 2 tbsp freshly ground black pepper
- 2 tbsp curry powder, divided
- 3 tsp coconut oil
- 1 onion, pureed
- 4 ripe tomatoes, pureed
- 5 cloves garlic, crushed
- Juice of 1 lemon
- 1 bunch fresh cilantro, finely chopped
- 5 scallion, finely chopped

Instructions

1. Start by seasoning the ribs with one tablespoon of salt, pepper and curry powder.
2. Place the ribs in a very shallow dish and cover. Refrigerate overnight.
3. To cook the ribs, put the Instant Pot over medium heat. Melt the oil inside the pot and add in half the ribs. You would want to prepare them by 50 % batches so that you can be certain they're cooked evenly.
4. When the ribs have browned on each side, transfer these phones a plate and repeat with all the remaining half.
5. When the subsequent batch of ribs are browned, transfer these to home plate and stir within the crushed garlic and stir for half a moment. Add the pureed tomato and onion. Add the remainder salt and pepper, lemon juice and half the cilantro.
6. Bring the sauce to your boil and add the ribs back into the pot. Cover the pot and turn heat. Set the timer on 20 minutes. Once the time is finished, allow pressure to be released naturally.
7. To serve, transfer the ribs onto serving platter and garnish with scallion and cilantro, serve hot.

RED PEPPER FLAKES BEEF RIBS WITH RICE
Nutrition: Cal 537 ;Fat 24 g; Carb 7g;Protein 67 g
Serving 6; Cook time 45 min

Ingredients
- 3 lbs beef short ribs, boneless
- 2 tbsp red pepper flakes
- 2 tsp salt
- 2 tbsp butter
- 1 onion, finely chopped
- 2 tbsp tomato paste
- 5 garlic cloves, minced
- 2/3 cup roasted tomato salsa (accessible in supermarkets)
- 2/3 cup beef broth
- 1 tsp fish sauce
- ½ tsp freshly ground black pepper
- 1 small bunch fresh cilantro, finely chopped

Instructions
1. On a cutting board, cut the meat into cubes or slices. Place the meat right into a bowl and add inside the red pepper flakes and salt.
2. Place the Instant Pot over medium heat, set on "Sauté" and melt the butter. Stir inside onion, keep stirring until it will become translucent.
3. Add the tomato paste, garlic and salsa. Stir for any minute.
4. Drop the meat in the pot, and pour within the broth and fish sauce and stir.
5. Cover the pot and hang up on "Keep Warm" and "Meat/Stew". You only need in order to smoke it for a half-hour.
6. Once some time ends, allow the stress to be removed naturally.

7. Meanwhile cook the rice according to the instructions for the package.
8. To serve, put the rice into serving bowl and top with meat, drizzle using the meat sauce and garnish with fresh cilantro.

SIMPLE CORNED BEEF
Nutrition: Cal 251 ;Fat 3 g; Carb 1 g;Protein 7 g
Serving 6; Cook time 75 min

Ingredients
- 4 pounds beef brisket
- 2 oranges, sliced
- 2 garlic cloves, minced
- 2 yellow onions, thinly sliced
- 11 ounces celery, thinly sliced
- 1 tbsp dill, dried
- 3 bay leaves
- 4 cinnamon sticks, cut into halves
- Salt and black pepper to taste
- 17 ounces water

Instructions
1. Put the beef in the bowl, add some water to hide, leave aside to soak for a few hours, drain and transfer for a instant pot.
2. Add celery, orange slices, onions, garlic, bay leaves, dill, cinnamon, dill, salt and pepper and 17 ounces water.
3. Stir, cover and cook on High for 50 minutes.
4. Release the pressure, leave beef aside to chill down for 5 minutes, transfer to a cutting board, slice and divide among plates.
5. Drizzle the juice and veggies through the pot over beef and serve.

BEEF BOURGUIGNON
Nutrition: Cal 442 ;Fat 17 g; Carb 16 g;Protein 39 g
Serving 6; Cook time 45 min

Ingredients
- 5 pounds round steak, cut into small cubes
- 2 carrots, sliced
- ½ cup beef stock
- 1 cup dry burgandy or merlot wine
- 3 bacon slices, chopped
- 8 ounces mushrooms, cut into quarters
- 2 tbsp white flour
- 12 pearl onions
- 2 garlic cloves, minced
- ¼ tsp basil, dried
- Salt and black pepper to taste

Instructions
1. Set your instant pot on Sauté mode, add bacon and brown it for 2 minutes.
2. Add beef pieces, stir and brown for 5 minutes.
3. Add flour and stir well.

4. Add salt, pepper, wine, stock, onions, garlic and basil, stir, cover and cook on High for 20 minutes.
5. Release pressure to succeed quickly, uncover your pot, add mushrooms and carrots, cover again and cook on High for 5 minutes more.
6. Release pressure to succeed again, spoon beef bourguignon onto plates and serve.

BEEF AND PASTA CASSEROLE
Nutrition: Cal 182 ;Fat 5.3 g; Carb 28 g;Protein 14 g
Serving 4; Cook time 30 min

Ingredients
- 17 ounces pasta
- 1 pound beef, ground
- 13 ounces mozzarella cheese, shredded
- 16 ounces tomato puree
- 1 celery stalk, chopped
- 1 yellow onion, chopped
- 1 carrot, chopped
- 1 tbsp dark wine
- 2 tbsp butter
- Salt and black pepper to taste

Instructions
1. Set your instant pot on Sauté mode, add the butter and melt.
2. Add carrot, onion and celery and fry for 5 minutes.
3. Add beef, salt and pepper and cook for 10 more minutes.
4. Add wine, while stirring and cook to get a further minute.
5. Add pasta, tomato puree and water to cover pasta, stir, cover and cook on High for 6 minutes.
6. Release the stress, uncover, add cheese, stir well to melt cheese and enjoy.

KOREAN HOT BEEF SALAD
Nutrition: Cal 310 ;Fat 9 g; Carb 18 g;Protein 35 g
Serving 4 Cook time 35 min

Ingredients
- ¼ cup Korean soybean paste
- 1 cup chicken stock
- 2 pounds beef steak, cut into strips
- ¼ tsp red pepper flakes
- Salt and black pepper to taste
- 1 yellow onion, thinly sliced
- 1 zucchini, cubed
- 1 ounce shiitake mushroom caps, cut into quarters
- 12 ounces extra firm tofu, cubed
- 1 chili pepper, sliced
- 1 scallion, chopped

Instructions
1. Set your instant pot on Sauté mode, add stock and soybean paste, stir and simmer for two minutes.

2. Add beef, salt, pepper and pepper flakes, stir, cover and cook on High for fifteen minutes.
3. Release pressure quickly, add tofu, onion, zucchini and mushrooms, stir, bring to your boil, cover and cook on High for 4 minutes more.
4. Release the stress again, increase the salt and pepper to taste, add chili and scallion, stir well and ladle into bowls and serve.

CHINESE BEEF AND BROCCOLI
Nutrition: Cal 310 ;Fat 9 g; Carb 18 g;Protein 35 g
Serving 4 Cook time 20 min

Ingredients
- 3 pounds chuck roast, cut into thin strips
- 1 tbsp peanut oil
- 1 yellow onion, chopped
- ½ cup beef stock
- 1 pound broccoli florets
- 2 tsp toasted sesame oil
- 2 tbsp potato starch

For the marinade:
- ½ cup soy sauce
- ½ cup black soy sauce
- 1 tbsp sesame oil
- 2 tbsp fish sauce
- 5 garlic cloves, minced
- 3 red peppers, dried and crushed
- ½ tsp Chinese five spice
- White rice, already cooked for servings
- Toasted sesame seeds for serving

Instructions
1. In a bowl, mix black soy sauce with soy sauce, fish sauce, 1 tbsp sesame oil, 5 garlic cloves, five spice and crushed red peppers and stir well.
2. Add beef strips, toss to coat and marinade for ten minutes.
3. Set your instant pot on Sauté mode, add peanut oil and also heat
4. Add onions, stir and fry for 4 minutes.
5. Add beef and marinade, stir and cook for 2 minutes.
6. Add stock, stir, cover and cook on High for 5 minutes.
7. Release the stress naturally for ten mins, uncover, add cornstarch after you've mixed it to a smooth paste with ¼ cup liquid from your pot, add broccoli on the steamer basket, cover pot again and cook for 3 minutes on High.
8. Release pressure again and dish up beef into bowls at the top of rice, add broccoli quietly, drizzle toasted sesame oil over items in bowls, sprinkle sesame seeds and enjoy this delicious Chinese meal.

MERLOT LAMB SHANKS

Nutrition: Cal 430 ;Fat 17 g; Carb 11 g;Protein 50 g
Serving 4 Cook time 45 min

Ingredients
- 4 lamb shanks
- 2 tbsp extra virgin organic olive oil
- 2 tbsp white flour
- 1 yellow onion, finely chopped
- 3 carrots, roughly chopped
- 2 garlic cloves, minced
- 2 tbsp tomato paste
- 1 tsp oregano, dried
- 1 tomato, roughly chopped
- 2 tbsp water
- 4 ounces red Merlot wine
- Salt and black pepper to taste
- 1 beef bouillon cube

Instructions
1. In a bowl, mix flour with salt and pepper.
2. Add lamb shanks and toss to coat.
3. Set your instant pot on Sauté mode, add oil and warmth
4. Add lamb, brown on the sides and transfer with a bowl.
5. Add onion, oregano, carrots and garlic for the pot, stir and cook for 5 minutes.
6. Add tomato, tomato paste, water, wine and bouillon cube, stir and produce to your boil.
7. Return lamb to pot, cover and cook on High for 25 minutes.
8. Release pressure to succeed and set one shank on each plate, pour cooking sauce over and get with seasonal vegetables!

ROSEMARY LAMB RIBS

Nutrition: Cal 234 ;Fat 8.5 g; Carb 3 g;Protein 35 g
Serving 8 Cook time 35 min

Ingredients
- 8 lamb ribs
- 4 garlic cloves, minced
- 2 carrots, chopped
- 13 ounces veggie stock
- 4 rosemary springs
- 2 tbsp extra virgin organic olive oil
- Salt and black pepper to taste
- 3 tbsp white flour

Instructions
1. Set your instant pot on Sauté mode, add the oil as well as heat
2. Add lamb, garlic, salt and pepper and brown it on every side.
3. Add flour, stock, rosemary and carrots, stir well, cover and cook on High for 20 minutes.
4. Release pressure quickly and discard rosemary, divide lamb ribs onto plates and serve while using cooking liquid drizzled on the top.

CREAMY LAMB CURRY

Nutrition: Cal 378 ;Fat 8 g; Carb 18 g;Protein 22 g
Serving 6 Cook time 35 min

Ingredients
- 1 ½ pounds lamb shoulder, cut into medium chunks
- 2 ounces coconut milk
- 3 ounces dry white wine
- 3 tbsp pure cream
- 3 tbsp curry powder
- 2 tbsp vegetable oil
- 3 tbsp water
- 1 yellow onion, chopped
- 1 tbsp parsley, chopped
- Salt and black pepper to taste

Instructions
1. In a bowl, mix half with the curry powder with salt, pepper and coconut milk and stir well.
2. Set your instant pot on Sauté mode, add oil and also heat
3. Add onion, stir and fry for 4 minutes.
4. Add the remaining of the curry powder, stir and cook for 1 minute.
5. Add lamb pieces, brown them for 3 minutes and mix with water, salt, pepper and wine.
6. Stir, cover and cook on High for 20 mins.
7. Release the stress quickly, set pot to Simmer mode, add coconut milk mixture, stir and boil for 5 minutes.
8. Divide among serving plates, sprinkle parsley at the top and serve.

MOROCCAN LAMB

Nutrition: Cal 434 ;Fat 21 g; Carb 41 g;Protein 20 g
Serving 6 Cook time 35 min

Ingredients
- 2 ½ pounds lamb shoulder, chopped
- 3 tbsp honey
- 3 ounces almonds, peeled and chopped
- 9 ounces prunes, pitted
- 8 ounces vegetable stock
- 2 yellow onions, chopped
- 2 garlic cloves, minced
- 1 bay leaf
- Salt and black pepper to tastes
- 1 cinnamon stick
- 1 tsp cumin powder
- 1 tsp turmeric powder
- 1 tsp ginger powder
- 1 tsp cinnamon powder
- Sesame seeds for servings
- 3 tbsp extra virgin organic olive oil

Instructions
1. In a bowl, mix cinnamon powder with ginger, cumin, turmeric, garlic and 2 tbsp extra virgin olive oil and stir well.
2. Add meat and toss to coat.

3. Put prunes in the bowl, cover them hot water and leave aside.
4. Set your instant pot on Sauté mode, add the remainder of the oil as well as heat
5. Add onions, stir, cook for 3 minutes, transfer to your bowl and then leave aside.
6. Add meat to your pot and brown it for 10 minutes.
7. Add stock, cinnamon stick, bay leaf and return onions, stir, cover and cook on High for 25 minutes.
8. Release pressure to succeed naturally, uncover, add drained prunes, salt, pepper, honey and stir.
9. Set the pot on Simmer mode, cook mixture for 5 minutes and discard bay leaf and cinnamon stick.
10. Divide among plates and scatter almonds and sesame seeds ahead.

LAMB RAGOUT
Nutrition: Cal 360 ;Fat 14 g; Carb 15 g;Protein 30 g
Serving 8 Cook time 75 min

Ingredients
- 1 ½ pounds mutton, bone-in
- 2 carrots, sliced
- ½ pound mushrooms, sliced
- 4 tomatoes, chopped
- 1 small yellow onion, chopped
- 6 garlic cloves, minced
- 2 tbsp tomato paste
- 1 tsp vegetable oil
- Salt and black pepper to taste
- 1 tsp oregano, dried
- A handful parsley, finely chopped

Instructions
1. Set your instant pot on Sauté mode, add oil and warmth
2. Add meat and brown it on the sides.
3. Add tomato paste, tomatoes, onion, garlic, mushrooms, oregano, carrots and water to pay for.
4. Add salt, pepper, stir, cover and cook on High for one hour.
5. Release the pressure, take meat out from the pot and discard bones before shredding.
6. Return meat to pot, add parsley and stir.
7. Add more salt and pepper as needed and serve right away.

LAMB AND BARLEY BOWLS
Nutrition: Cal 484 ;Fat 19 g; Carb 21 g;Protein 44 g
Serving 4 Cook time 60 min

Ingredients
- 6 ounces barley
- 5 ounces peas
- 1 lamb leg, already cooked, boneless and chopped
- 3 yellow onions, chopped
- 5 carrots, chopped
- 6 ounces beef stock
- 12 ounces water
- Salt and black pepper to taste

Instructions
1. In your instant pot, mix stock with water and barley, cover and cook on High for 20 minutes.
2. Release pressure to succeed, uncover, add onions, peas and carrots, stir, cover again and cook on High for ten mins.
3. Release pressure again, add meat, salt and pepper to taste, stir, dish into bowls and serve.

LAMB AND VEGETABLE SKEWERS WITH YOGURT SAUCE
Nutrition: Cal 553 ;Fat 43 g; Carb 8 g;Protein 33 g
Serving 2 Cook time 50 min

Ingredients
- 1 lb. lamb, cut into bite-sized pieces
- 1 large tomato, chopped
- 1 bell pepper, chopped
- 2 garlic cloves, minced
- 1/2 onion, chopped
- 1/2 cup plain yogurt
- 2 tablespoons olive oil
- Salt and pepper to taste
- Skewers

Instructions
1. Soak the skewers in water for at least 30 minutes.
2. Preheat the oven to 400°F.
3. In a bowl, mix together the lamb, chopped tomato, chopped bell pepper, minced garlic, chopped onion, olive oil, salt, and pepper.
4. Thread the lamb and vegetables onto the skewers.
5. Place the skewers on a baking sheet and bake for 15-20 minutes, until the lamb is cooked through.
6. In a small bowl, mix together the yogurt, minced garlic, and salt.
7. Serve the skewers hot with the yogurt sauce.

CREAMY LAMB DELIGHT
Nutrition: Cal 453 ;Fat 29 g; Carb 3 g;Protein 39 g
Serving 2 Cook time 35 min

Ingredients
- 1 lb. lamb, cut into bite-sized pieces
- 1/2 onion, chopped
- 2 garlic cloves, minced
- 1 tablespoon olive oil
- 1/2 cup dry white wine
- 1/2 cup chicken broth
- 1/4 cup heavy cream
- 2 tablespoons Dijon mustard
- 1 tablespoon fresh parsley, chopped
- Salt and pepper to taste

Instructions

1. In a large skillet, heat the olive oil over medium-high heat and cook the lamb until browned on all sides.
2. Add the chopped onion and minced garlic and sauté for 2-3 minutes, until the onion is translucent.
3. Pour in the dry white wine and chicken broth, and bring to a boil.
4. Reduce the heat to low and simmer for 20-25 minutes, until the lamb is cooked through.
5. Stir in the heavy cream and Dijon mustard, and cook for an additional 5-7 minutes, until the sauce has thickened.
6. Season with salt and pepper to taste.
7. Serve the lamb hot, garnished with chopped parsley.

LAMB CHOPS WITH LEMON AND GAR-LIC

Nutrition: Cal 450 ;Fat 35 g; Carb 2 g;Protein 30 g
Serving 2 Cook time 25 min

Ingredients
- 4 lamb chops
- 2 tablespoons olive oil
- 2 tablespoons lemon juice
- 2 garlic cloves, minced
- 1 teaspoon dried oregano
- Salt and pepper to taste

Instructions
1. Preheat a grill or grill pan to medium-high heat.
2. In a small bowl, mix together the olive oil, lemon juice, minced garlic, dried oregano, salt, and pepper.
3. Brush the marinade over both sides of the lamb chops.
4. Place the lamb chops on the grill and cook for 3-4 minutes per side, or until desired doneness is reached.
5. Remove the lamb chops from the grill and let them rest for a few minutes before serving.

LAMB CASSOULET DE PROVENCE

Nutrition: Cal 390 ;Fat 22 g; Carb 10 g;Protein 35 g
Serving 2 Cook time 90 min

Ingredients
- 1 lb. lamb, cut into bite-sized pieces
- 2 cups chicken broth
- 1 can (14 oz.) diced tomatoes
- 1/2 onion, chopped
- 2 garlic cloves, minced
- 2 carrots, chopped
- 2 celery stalks, chopped
- 1/4 cup parsley, chopped
- 2 tablespoons olive oil
- Salt and pepper to taste

Instructions
1. Preheat the oven to 350°F.
2. Heat the olive oil in a large pot over medium-high heat.
3. Add the lamb and cook until browned on all sides.
4. Add the chopped onion and garlic and sauté for 2-3 minutes, until the onion is translucent.

5. Pour in the chicken broth and diced tomatoes.
6. Add the chopped carrots and celery and stir to combine.
7. Season with salt and pepper to taste.
8. Bring the mixture to a boil.
9. Cover the pot and transfer it to the oven.
10. Bake for 1-1.5 hours, until the lamb is tender.
11. Remove from the oven and sprinkle the chopped parsley over the top.
12. Serve hot.

KETO INDIAN LAMB CURRY

Nutrition: Cal 440 ;Fat 32 g; Carb 8 g;Protein 30 g
Serving 2 Cook time 65 min

Ingredients
- 1 lb. lamb, cut into bite-sized pieces
- 1 onion, chopped
- 2 garlic cloves, minced
- 1-inch piece of ginger, grated
- 2 teaspoons ground cumin
- 2 teaspoons ground coriander
- 1 teaspoon ground cinnamon
- 1 teaspoon ground turmeric
- 1/2 teaspoon cayenne pepper
- 1 can (14 oz.) diced tomatoes
- 1 cup water
- 2 tablespoons ghee or coconut oil
- Salt to taste
- Fresh cilantro for garnish

Instructions
1. Heat the ghee or coconut oil in a large pot over medium heat.
2. Add the chopped onion and sauté for 2-3 minutes, until softened.
3. Add the minced garlic and grated ginger and sauté for another 1-2 minutes.
4. Add the ground cumin, coriander, cinnamon, turmeric, and cayenne pepper and stir to combine.
5. Add the diced tomatoes and water and stir to combine.
6. Add the lamb and season with salt to taste.
7. Bring the mixture to a boil, then reduce the heat and simmer for 45 minutes to 1 hour, until the lamb is tender.
8. Serve hot, garnished with fresh cilantro.

KETO LAMB AND EGGPLANT LASAGNE

Nutrition: Cal 629 ;Fat 46 g; Carb 16 g;Protein 235 g
Serving 2 Cook time 60 min

Ingredients
- 1 pound lamb shoulder, cut into small pieces
- 1 medium eggplant, sliced lengthwise into thin strips
- 1 cup ricotta cheese
- 1/2 cup grated parmesan cheese
- 1 egg, beaten
- 1 can diced tomatoes (14.5 oz)
- 2 cloves garlic, minced

•2 tablespoons olive oil

•Salt and black pepper to taste

Instructions

1. Preheat the oven to 375°F (190°C).
2. Heat a large skillet over medium-high heat. Add the olive oil.
3. Add the lamb pieces to the skillet and cook until browned on all sides, about 5-7 minutes.
4. Add the minced garlic to the skillet and cook for 1 minute.
5. Add the diced tomatoes to the skillet and simmer for 5-10 minutes until the sauce has thickened.
6. In a separate bowl, mix together the ricotta cheese, parmesan cheese, and beaten egg.
7. In a greased 9x9 inch baking dish, layer the eggplant strips, lamb and tomato sauce, and ricotta mixture, repeating until all ingredients are used up.
8. Cover the baking dish with aluminum foil and bake in the oven for 45-50 minutes, until the eggplant is fully cooked and the cheese is melted and bubbly.
9. Remove from the oven and let cool for 10 minutes before serving.

PROVENCAL LAMB STEW SAVOUR

Nutrition: Cal 420 ;Fat 26 g; Carb 10 g;Protein 31 g
Serving 4 Cook time 90 min

Ingredients

• 1 lb. lamb stew meat
• 1 tablespoon olive oil
• 1 onion, chopped
• 2 garlic cloves, minced
• 1 can (14 oz.) diced tomatoes
• 1/2 cup dry red wine
• 1/2 cup beef broth
• 1 tablespoon chopped fresh rosemary
• 1 tablespoon chopped fresh thyme
• 1 bay leaf
• Salt and pepper to taste

Instructions

1. In a large pot, heat the olive oil over medium-high heat and cook the lamb stew meat until browned on all sides.
2. Add the chopped onion and garlic and sauté for 2-3 minutes, until the onion is translucent.
3. Pour in the diced tomatoes, red wine, and beef broth and stir to combine.
4. Add the chopped fresh rosemary, chopped fresh thyme, bay leaf, salt, and pepper and bring to a boil.
5. Reduce the heat to low and simmer for 1-1.5 hours, until the lamb is tender.
6. Discard the bay leaf and serve hot.

KETO FRENCH-INSPIRED LAMB MEDALLIONS

Nutrition: Cal 498 ;Fat 33 g; Carb 6 g;Protein 36 g
Serving 2 Cook time 35 min

Ingredients

• 1 lb. lamb, cut into bite-sized pieces
• 1 tablespoon olive oil
• 2 tablespoons butter
• 1 onion, chopped
• 2 garlic cloves, minced
• 1/2 cup dry red wine
• 1/2 cup beef broth
• 1 tablespoon tomato paste
• 1 tablespoon chopped fresh parsley
• 1 tablespoon chopped fresh thyme
• Salt and pepper to taste

Instructions

1. In a large skillet, heat the olive oil and butter over medium-high heat.
2. Add the lamb and cook for 3-4 minutes per side, until browned.
3. Remove the lamb from the skillet and set aside.
4. Add the chopped onion to the skillet and sauté for 2-3 minutes, until softened.
5. Add the minced garlic to the skillet and sauté for an additional 1-2 minutes.
6. Pour in the red wine and beef broth, and stir in the tomato paste.
7. Bring the mixture to a boil and then reduce the heat to low.
8. Add the lamb back into the skillet and stir in the chopped parsley and thyme.
9. Simmer the lamb for 15-20 minutes, until the sauce has thickened and the lamb is cooked through.
10. Season with salt and pepper to taste.
11. Serve hot.

KETO LAMB AND VEGGIE SKILLET

Nutrition: Cal 464 ;Fat 34 g; Carb 7 g;Protein 29 g
Serving 2 Cook time 25 min

Ingredients

• 1 pound lamb shoulder, cut into small pieces
• 2 medium zucchinis, sliced
• 1 medium leek, sliced
• 2 cloves garlic, minced
• 2 medium tomatoes, diced
• 2 tablespoons olive oil
• Salt and black pepper to taste

Instructions

1. Heat a large skillet over medium-high heat. Add the olive oil.
2. Add the lamb pieces to the skillet and cook until browned on all sides, about 5-7 minutes.
3. Add the sliced zucchini and leek to the skillet and cook until they are slightly softened, about 5 minutes.

4. Add the minced garlic and diced tomatoes to the skillet and cook for an additional 5 minutes until the tomatoes have released their juices.
5. Season the skillet with salt and black pepper to taste.
6. Serve hot.

KETO LAMB AND VEGETABLE STEW
Nutrition: Cal 459 ;Fat 34 g; Carb 8 g;Protein 25 g
Serving 2 Cook time 50 min

Ingredients
- 1 pound lamb shoulder, cut into small pieces
- 2 medium sweet peppers, sliced
- 1 small eggplant, diced
- 1 medium leek, sliced
- 2 cloves garlic, minced
- 2 medium tomatoes, diced
- 1 teaspoon dried thyme
- 2 tablespoons olive oil
- Salt and black pepper to taste

Instructions
1. Heat a large pot over medium-high heat. Add the olive oil.
2. Add the lamb pieces to the pot and cook until browned on all sides, about 5-7 minutes.
3. Add the sliced sweet peppers, diced eggplant, and sliced leek to the pot and cook until they are slightly softened, about 5 minutes.
4. Add the minced garlic, diced tomatoes, and dried thyme to the pot and stir to combine.
5. Cover the pot and simmer on low heat for 30-40 minutes until the lamb is tender and the vegetables are fully cooked.
6. Season the stew with salt and black pepper to taste.
7. Serve hot.

KETO RUSSIAN-STYLE LAMB STEW
Nutrition: Cal 460 ;Fat 35 g; Carb 14 g;Protein 25 g
Serving 2 Cook time 70 min

Ingredients
- 1 pound lamb shoulder, cut into small pieces
- 2 tablespoons olive oil
- 1 small onion, diced
- 2 cloves garlic, minced
- 2 medium carrots, sliced
- 2 medium turnips, diced
- 1 cup beef broth
- 1 tablespoon tomato paste
- 1 teaspoon dried thyme
- Salt and black pepper to taste

Instructions
1. Heat a large pot over medium-high heat. Add the olive oil.
2. Add the lamb pieces to the pot and cook until browned on all sides, about 5-7 minutes.

3. Add the diced onion and minced garlic to the pot and cook until they are slightly softened, about 5 minutes.
4. Add the sliced carrots and diced turnips to the pot and stir to combine.
5. Pour in the beef broth, tomato paste, and dried thyme. Stir to combine.
6. Cover the pot and simmer on low heat for 45-60 minutes until the lamb is tender and the vegetables are fully cooked.
7. Season the stew with salt and black pepper to taste.
8. Serve hot.

LAMB AND CABBAGE STEW
Nutrition: Cal 469 ;Fat 35 g; Carb 12 g;Protein 27 g
Serving 2 Cook time 70 min

Ingredients
- 1 pound lamb shoulder, cut into small pieces
- 2 cups shredded cabbage
- 1 small onion, diced
- 2 cloves garlic, minced
- 2 teaspoons dried thyme
- 2 medium tomatoes, diced
- 2 tablespoons olive oil
- Salt and black pepper to taste

Instructions
1. Heat a large pot over medium-high heat. Add the olive oil.
2. Add the lamb pieces to the pot and cook until browned on all sides, about 5-7 minutes.
3. Add the diced onion and minced garlic to the pot and cook until they are slightly softened, about 5 minutes.
4. Add the shredded cabbage, diced tomatoes, and dried thyme to the pot and stir to combine.
5. Cover the pot and simmer on low heat for 45-60 minutes until the lamb is tender and the vegetables are fully cooked.
6. Season the stew with salt and black pepper to taste.

MEXICAN STYLE LAMB
Nutrition: Cal 324 ;Fat 9 g; Carb 19 g;Protein 15 g
Serving 4 Cook time 60 min

Ingredients
- 3 pounds lamb shoulder, cubed
- 19 ounces enchilada sauce
- 3 garlic cloves, minced
- 1 yellow onion, chopped
- 2 tbsp extra virgin olive oil
- Salt to taste
- ½ bunch cilantro, finely chopped
- Corn tortillas, warm for serving
- Lime wedges for serving
- Refried beans for serving

Instructions

1. Put enchilada sauce inside a bowl, add lamb meat and marinade for 24 hours.
2. Set your instant pot on Sauté mode, add the oil as well as heat
3. Add onions and garlic and fry for 5 minutes.
4. Add lamb, salt and its particular marinade, stir, bring to a boil, cover and cook on High for 45 minutes.
5. Release the stress, take meat and set on a cutting board and then leave for cooling down for a couple of minutes.
6. Shred meat and set inside a bowl.
7. Pour cooking sauce over it and stir.
8. Portion out meat onto tortillas, sprinkle cilantro on each, add beans, squeeze lime juice over, roll and serve.

GOAT AND TOMATO POT

Nutrition: Cal 340 ;Fat 4 g; Carb 12 g;Protein 12 g
Serving 4 Cook time 70 min

Ingredients
- 17 ounces goat meat, cubed
- 1 carrot, chopped
- 1 celery rib, chopped
- 4 ounces tomato paste
- 1 yellow onion, chopped
- 3 garlic cloves, crushed
- A dash of sherry wine
- ½ cup water
- Salt and black pepper to taste
- 1 cup chicken stock
- 2 tbsp extra virgin olive oil
- 1 tbsp cumin seeds, ground
- A pinch of rosemary, dried
- 2 roasted tomatoes, chopped

Instructions
1. Set your instant pot on Sauté mode, add 1 tbsp oil and also heat
2. Add goat meat, salt and pepper and brown for a few minutes on either side.
3. Add cumin seeds, rosemary, stir, cook for just two minutes and transfer to your bowl.
4. Add the remainder in the oil on the pot and warmth
5. Add onion, garlic, salt and pepper, stir and cook for 1 minute.
6. Add carrot and celery, stir and cook 2 minutes.
7. Add sherry wine, stock, water, goat meat, tomato paste, more salt and pepper, stir, cover and cook on High for 40 minutes.
8. Release pressure naturally, uncover, add tomatoes, stir, divide among plates and serve.

SPICY TACO MEAT

Nutrition: Cal 414 ;Fat 21 g; Carb 7 g;Protein 47 g
Serving 6 Cook time 45 min

Ingredients
- 2 lbs ground beef
- 1/2 tbsp chili powder
- 1/4 Tsp chipotle powder
- 1 tsp cayenne
- 1/2 Tsp cumin
- 1/2 Tsp smoked paprika
- 1/2 Tsp turmeric
- 2 tsp oregano
- 2 large sweet peppers, diced
- 1 large onion, diced
- 4 tbsp olive oil
- 3 garlic cloves, minced
- 1/4 Tsp black pepper
- 1 tsp salt

Instructions
1. Add all ingredients except meat in to the instant pot.
2. Select sauté and stir fry for 5 minutes.
3. Add ground beef and stir until lightly brown.
4. Seal pot with lid and cook on HIGH pressure for half an hour.
5. Allow to releasing steam its then open.
6. Select sauté function and stir for 10 mins.
7. Garnish with fresh chopped cilantro and serve.

BEEF STROGANOFF

Nutrition: Cal 317 ;Fat 19 g; Carb 8 g;Protein 29 g
Serving 4 Cook time 40 min

Ingredients
- Beef (1 pound, chopped in cubes)
- Bacon (2 slices, cut in cubes)
- Beef stock (250 ml)
- Mushrooms (9 oz.)
- Onion (1, chopped)
- Garlic (2 cloves, chopped)
- Tomato paste (3 tbsp)
- Smoked paprika (1 tbsp)
- Sour cream

Instructions
1. Add oil inside Pressure cooker dish, and hang up it to "Sauté"; add the onion, bacon, and garlic and cook shortly or before the onion is tender.
2. Put the beef and continue to cook prior to the meat is cooked on every side (it will get brown color).
3. Add the mushrooms, beef broth, tomato paste, and paprika and stir well; close the lid and set it to high-pressure cooking for 30 minutes.
4. Use the quick-release approach to release the stress.
5. Serve while hot and top it with sour cream.

CHILE LIME STEAK FAJITAS

Nutrition: Cal 230;Fat 30 g; Carb 13 g;Protein 25 g
Serving 4; Cook time 15 min

Ingredients
MARINADE
- 2 tablespoons olive oil
- 1/3 cup freshly squeezed lime juice
- 2 tablespoons fresh chopped cilantro
- 2 cloves garlic , crushed
- 1 teaspoon brown sugar
- ¾ teaspoon red chilli flakes (adjust to your preference of spice)
- ½ teaspoon ground cumin
- 1 teaspoon salt
- 1 pound (500 g) steak (rump, skirt, or flank steak)

FAJITAS
- 3 bell peppers (capsicums) of different colors: red, yellow, and green, deseeded and sliced
- 1 onion, sliced
- 1 avocado sliced

OPTIONAL SERVING SUGGESTION:
- Flour tortillas
- Lettuce leaves for low-carb option
- Extra cilantro leaves to garnish
- Sour cream to serve

Instructions
1. Whisk marinade ingredients together to combine. Pour out half of the marinade into a shallow dish to marinade the steak for 30 minutes, if time allows. Alternatively, refrigerate for 2 hours or overnight. Remove from the refrigerator 30 minute prior to cooking.
2. Refrigerate the reserved untouched marinade to use later

FOR SKILLET
1. Heat about one teaspoon of oil in a grill pan or cast iron skillet over medium-high heat and grill steak on each side until desired doneness (about 4 minutes each side for medium-rare, depending on thickness). Set aside and allow to rest for 5 minutes.

FOR GRILLING
2. Heat barbecue (or grill) on high heat. Remove steak from the marinade. Grill for 5-7 minutes per side, or until desired doneness is reached. Transfer to a plate and allow to rest for 5-10 minutes.

FOR VEGETABLES
3. Wipe pan or grill plates over with paper towel; drizzle (or brush) with another teaspoon of oil and fry peppers (capsicums) and onion strips. Add half of the reserved marinade, salt and pepper; continue cooking until done.

ASSEMBLE
4. To serve steak, slice against the grain into thin strips. Pack into warmed tortillas, extra cilantro leaves, sour cream, sliced avocado (or your desired fillings), and drizzle over the remaining reserved untouched marinade.

KETO BEEF AND BROCCOLI

Nutrition: Cal 294;Fat 14 g; Carb 13 g;Protein 29 g
Serving 4; Cook time 35 min

Ingredients
- 1 pound flank steak sliced into 1/4 inch thick strips
- 5 cups small broccoli florets about 7 ounces
- 1 tablespoon avocado oil
- For the sauce:
- 1 yellow onion sliced
- 1 Tbs butter
- ½ tbs olive oil
- 1/3 cup low-sodium soy sauce
- ⅓ cup beef stock
- 1 tablespoon fresh ginger minced
- 2 cloves garlic minced

Instructions
1. Heat avocado oil in a pan over medium heat for a few minutes or until hot.
2. Add sliced beef and cook until it browns, less than 5 minutes, don't stir too much, you want it to brown. Transfer to a plate and set aside.
3. Add onions to a skillet with butter and olive oil and cook 20 minutes until onions are caramelized and tender.
4. Add all other sauce ingredients into the skillet and stir the ingredients together over medium-low heat until it starts to simmer, about 5 minutes.
5. Use an immersion blender to blend sauce.
6. Keep the sauce warm over low heat, and add broccoli to the skillet.
7. Return beef to the pan and toss with broccoli and sauce top. Stir until everything is coated with the sauce.
8. Bring to a simmer and cook for another few minutes until broccoli is tender.
9. Season with salt and pepper to taste, if needed.
10. Serve immediately, optionally pairing with cooked cauliflower rice.

MEATLOAF RECIPE

Nutrition: Cal 575;Fat 44 g; Carb 10 g;Protein 35 g
Serving 4; Cook time 70 min

Ingredients
- 1 tablespoon tallow
- 1 small onion finely chopped
- 2 cloves garlic crushed
- 2 pounds ground beef
- 2 large eggs
- 2 tablespoons oregano dried
- 1 1/2 teaspoon salt
- 1/4 teaspoon pepper ground
- 1/3 cup low carb marinara sauce
- 1/3 cup almond flour
- 2 tablespoons low carb marinara sauce extra

Instructions
1. Preheat your oven to 160C/320F and prepare a loaf tin by lining with baking paper.

2. Place a non-stick frying pan over high heat and saute the onion and garlic in the tallow, until the onion is turning translucent. Set aside to cool slightly.
3. In a large mixing bowl add the warm onion mixture and all remaining ingredients, except the extra marinara sauce.
4. Using clean hands, or wearing disposable gloves, mix the ingredients very well.
5. Press into the base of your prepared loaf tin, ensuring there are no air bubbles, and smooth the top.
6. Bake for 50 minutes.
7. Drain off some of the juices and top the meatloaf with the extra marinara sauce.
8. Bake for another 10 minutes.
9. Leave to sit for 10 minutes to rest, before slicing and serving.

MOROCCAN MEATBALLS
Nutrition: Cal 363;Fat 27 g; Carb 6 g;Protein 22 g
Serving 8; Cook time 6 hours

Ingredients
• 2 pounds of Ground Beef
• 1 small Onion, grated
• 4 cloves of Garlic, crushed
• 1 large Egg
• 2 tablespoons of Cilantro, finely chopped
• 1 tablespoon of Cumin, ground
• 1 tablespoon of Coriander, ground
• 1 tablespoon of Smoked Paprika, ground
• 2 teaspoons of Ground Ginger
• 1 teaspoon of Cinnamon, ground
• 1 teaspoon of Salt
• 2 tablespoon of Olive Oil
• 2 tablespoons of Tomato Paste
• 1 ½ cups of Tomato Passata
• ½ cup of Beef Stock ro, to serve

Instructions
1. In a large bowl add the beef, half the grated onion, half the garlic, egg, cilantro, cumin, coriander, paprika, ginger, cinnamon, and salt. Mix well.
2. Roll into 2 tablespoon-sized meatballs and set aside. We got 40.
3. Place the oil, remaining onion, and garlic into a nonstick frying pan over high heat. Saute for 3-5 minutes, until fragrant.
4. Add the tomato paste and cook for another 3 minutes, then add to your slow cooker, followed by the passata and stock. Mix well.
5. Add the meatballs to the sauce.
6. Cook on low for 5 hours.

LOW CARB BEEF BOLOGNESE SAUCE
Nutrition: Cal 279;Fat 21 g; Carb 5 g;Protein 17 g
Serving 6; Cook time 75 min

Ingredients
• 4 cups of Beef Stock or Broth
• 2 ounces of Tallow
• 1 medium Onion, diced
• 6 cloves of Garlic, crushed
• 1 tablespoon of Marjoram, dried
• 1 teaspoon of Salt
• 3 pounds of Ground Beef
• 24 ounces of Tomato Puree
• 1 teaspoon of Pepper
• 2 tablespoons of Basil, chopped
• 2 tablespoons of Oregano, chopped
• 1 tablespoon of Parsley, chopped

Instructions
1. Place the beef stock into a small saucepan and simmer over medium-high heat until it reduces into 1 cup of liquid.
2. In a large saucepan over high heat, place the tallow and allow to melt and heat.
3. Add the diced onion, garlic, marjoram, and salt. Saute for 5 minutes, until the onions have softened and turned translucent.
4. Add the ground beef and saute until browned. Reduce the heat to low.
5. Pour in the tomato puree and reduced beef stock and simmer, uncovered, and stirring occasionally for 30-60 minutes. Until the liquid is mostly absorbed, leaving a thick and rich sauce.
6. Add the remaining ingredients, check the seasoning, and add more salt or pepper if desired.
7. Remove from the heat, serve, and enjoy.

KETO LAMB CHOPS ON THE GRILL
Nutrition: Cal 446;Fat 27 g; Carb 4 g;Protein 22 g
Serving 8; Cook time 30 min

Ingredients
• 3 lbs of lamb loin chops (I had 8 6oz chops)
• 1/4 cup of white wine vinegar
• 1/2 cup of olive oil
• 1 teaspoon of oregano
• 1/2 teaspoon of salt
• 1/4 teaspoon of pepper
• 2 cloves of garlic, crushed
• zest of 1 lemon
• juice of 2 lemons (approx. 6 tablespoons)

Instructions
1. Whisk together all of the marinade ingredinets. Add the chops to a large baggie and pour the marinade over top.
2. Seal the bag and use your hands to mix the marinade through the chops and then place in the refrigerator for 8 hours or overnight.

3. Take out the lamb chops when ready to eat and let them sit on the ccounter for 15 minutes. Place them on a plate and discard the marinade.
4. Grill the lamb chops for about 5-6 minutes per side. The time will depend on the size and thickness of the chops. Mine were about 1 - 1.5 inches thick and too 6 minutes on each side and came out medium rare.

KETO LAMB CURRY

Nutrition: Cal 480;Fat 17 g; Carb 2 g;Protein 30 g
Serving 8; Cook time 2 hours 35 min

Ingredients
Marinade
• 2 teaspoons of Ginger, crushed
• 3 cloves of Garlic, crushed
• 2 teaspoons of Cumin, ground
• 2 teaspoons of Coriander, ground
• 1 teaspoon of Onion Powder
• 1 teaspoon of Cardamon, ground
• 1 teaspoon of Paprika, ground
• 1 teaspoon of Turmeric, ground
• 1 teaspoon of Kashmiri Chili Powder
• 2 tablespoons of Olive Oil

Curry
• 4 pounds of Lamb Shoulder, diced
• 3 tablespoons of Ghee
• 1 medium Onion, diced
• 1 teaspoon of Cinnamon, ground
• 1 teaspoon of Kashmiri Chili Powder
• 2 teaspoons of Salt
• 1 teaspoon of Pepper
• 1 cup of Heavy Cream
• ½ cup of Flaked Almonds
• 3 tablespoons of Cilantro, roughly chopped

Instructions
1. The Marinade: In a mixing bowl combine all marinade ingredients.
2. Add the diced lamb and mix well.
3. Store in the fridge to marinate for at least 1 hour, or overnight.
4. The Curry: In a large saucepan add the ghee and place over medium heat.
5. Add the onion, cinnamon & chili powder and saute for 3 minutes.
6. Add the marinated lamb, salt, and pepper and stir to ensure that lamb is browning.
7. Allow the lamb to cook for 10 minutes before adding the cream and reducing the heat to low.
8. Simmer the curry, partially covered, for 1 hour. Check the lamb for tenderness. If the lamb is tough, continue cooking until tender.
9. Remove the lid and simmer for another 10 minutes.
10. Add the flaked almonds and stir well. Add any extra seasoning.
11. Remove from the heat, garnish with coriander and serve.

ROSEMARY DIJON ROASTED LAMB CHOPS

Nutrition: Cal 446;Fat 40 g; Carb 2 g;Protein 18 g
Serving 4; Cook time 17 min

Ingredients
• 1 tbsp Dijon mustard
• 2 cloves garlic minced
• 3 tbsp olive oil
• 2 tsp fresh rosemary finely chopped
• 1/2 tsp salt
• 1/4 tsp pepper
• 4 lamb loin chops aprrox 2 lbs with bone-in

Instructions
1. Whisk together Dijon mustard, garlic, olive oil, rosemary, and salt and pepper in a bowl. Place lamb chops in a large zip-top bag or other airtight container. Coat lamb with Dijon mixture on both sides. Let marinate in the fridge for at least 30 minutes, but up to 24 hours.
2. Position an oven rack to the highest position in the oven and line a broiler pan with aluminum foil.
3. Take lamb chops out of the bag and place onto prepared pan. Set oven to broil on high and place pan into the oven.
4. Cook lamb chops for 8 minutes, until brown, and then flip and cook for an additional 3-5 minutes depending on the doneness you like your meat. (3 minutes for medium rare, 4 for medium, 5 for well done)

KETO LAMB KOFTAS

Nutrition: Cal 330;Fat 26 g; Carb 3 g;Protein 22 g
Serving 4; Cook time 20 min

Ingredients
• 500 g minced (ground) lamb (1.1 lb)
• 1 garlic clove, minced
• 1/2 medium yellow onion, diced (50 g/ 1.8 oz)
• 1 tsp dried oregano
• 2 tbsp chopped fresh parsley
• 1/2 tsp sea salt
• 1/4 tsp ground black pepper
• 1 tbsp extra virgin olive oil (15 ml)

Instructions
1. Place your skewers in cold water for half and hour prior to starting (ideally leave them to soak for at least 30 minutes). Alternatively, you can use stainless steel skewers that don't require soaking.
2. Add minced lamb, diced onions, chopped garlic, finely chopped parsley and the herbs and seasonings into a large mixing bowl. Retain the olive oil.
3. Mix well with your hands until thoroughly combined.
4. Portion out into eight portions and place each one around a skewer. You need to gently squeeze and press your mixture around the skewer until you're happy with the result. If your skewers will fit in a pan, heat it on the stove top. Mine were too big so I cooked them on our barbeque instead.

5. Brush the surface with the retained olive oil before placing the koftas onto the hot pan.
6. Store the koftas in the refrigerator, covered for 4 days.

GREEK LAMB AND CABBAGE BOWLS
Nutrition: Cal 334;Fat 10 g; Carb 15 g;Protein 34 g
Serving 4; Cook time 24 min

Ingredients
- 1 tablespoon olive oil
- 1 large clove garlic, minced
- 1 small onion, diced
- 1 lb grass-fed ground lamb
- ¼ cup tomato paste
- 1 teaspoon ground cinnamon
- ½ teaspoon dried oregano
- ¼ teaspoon ground nutmeg
- ½ cup water (or broth), more or less as needed
- ½ large head green cabbage (or 1 small), cored and sliced
- 1 teaspoon sea salt and ½ teaspoon black pepper, or to taste

Instructions
1. In a large pan, dutch oven or skillet, heat the olive oil over medium-high heat. Add the onion, garlic and ground lamb. Sauté until the lamb is cooked about 5- 7 minutes.
2. Add in the tomato paste, cinnamon, oregano and nutmeg. Stir until well combined.
3. Add in the cabbage and continue to sauté. You want to cook until the cabbage is gently cooked with a little bite, not mushy.
4. Add a little water or broth, as needed if it's too dry.
5. Serve over cauli-rice or rice, zucchini noodles or pasta.

LAMB MEATBALLS WITH MINT GREMOLATA
Nutrition: Cal 306;Fat 17 g; Carb 4 g;Protein 34 g
Serving 4; Cook time 20 min

Ingredients
FOR THE MEATBALLS:
- 2 lbs ground lamb
- 2 eggs
- 1/2 cup superfine almond flour
- 1/4 cup fresh parsley, chopped
- 1 clove garlic, minced
- 1 1/2 Tbsp Za'atar seasoning
- 1 tsp kosher salt
- 3 Tbsp water
- 2 Tbsp olive oil for frying
FOR THE GREMOLATA:
- 2 Tbsp chopped fresh parsley
- 2 Tbsp chopped fresh mint
- 1 Tbsp lime zest
- 2 cloves garlic, minced

Instructions
FOR THE MEATBALLS:

1. Combine the meatball ingredients (except olive oil) in a medium bowl and mix well.
2. Form into 24 one and a half inch (approximately) meatballs.
3. Heat the olive oil in a nonstick saute pan over medium heat.
4. Cook the meatballs in batches until brown on both sides and cooked through – about 2-3 minutes per side.
5. Remove cooked meatballs and place on a paper towel lined plate until ready to serve.
6. Serve warm, sprinkled generously with gremolata.
FOR THE GREMOLATA:
7. Combine the ingredients in a small bowl and mix well.

SWISS CHEESE BEEF ZUCCHINI CASSEROLE
Nutrition: Cal 454;Fat 30 g; Carb 13 g;Protein 30 g
Serving 4; Cook time 2 hours

Ingredients
- 1 pound extra-lean ground beef
- 4 cups zucchini, sliced
- 10 ounces cream of mushroom soup
- 1/2 cup onion, chopped
- 1/4 tsp ground black pepper
- 1 cup Swiss cheese, shredded

Instructions
1. In a skillet over medium-high heat, brown ground beef with onions and pepper until don't pink. Drain.
2. Layer zucchini and beef mixture alternately in instant pot.
3. Top with soup. Sprinkle with cheese.
4. Cover and turn the steam release handle to the venting position.
5. Select the slow cooker setting and set to medium.
6. Cook for 120 minutes.

SIMPLE & CLASSIC GOULASH
Nutrition: Cal 167;Fat 10 g; Carb 8 g;Protein 11 g
Serving 8; Cook time 5 hours

Ingredients
- 1 pound ground beef, browned
- 1/2 cup ketchup
- 2 tbsp Worcestershire sauce
- 1 tbsp brown sugar
- 1 cup onion, chopped
- 1/2 tsp garlic, minced
- 2 tsp paprika
- 1/2 tsp dry mustard
- 1 cup water

Instructions
1. Place meat in instant pot. Cover with onions.
2. Combine remaining
3. Ingredients and pour over meat.
4. Cover and turn the steam release handle for the venting position.

5. Select the slow cooker setting and hang up to medium.
6. Cook for 5 hours.
Serve over rice or noodles.

BEEF AND BROCCOLI STIR-FRY

Nutrition: Cal 588;Fat 38 g; Carb 6 g;Protein 54 g
Serving 4; Cook time 25 min

Ingredients

- 6 tablespoons coconut aminos
- ¼ cup avocado oil
- 2 tablespoons toasted sesame oil
- 1 teaspoon garlic powder
- 1 teaspoon onion powder
- Salt
- Freshly ground black pepper
- 1½ pounds sirloin steak, cut into ¼-inch-thick slices

FOR THE BEEF AND BROCCOLI

- 1 teaspoon salt, plus more for seasoning
- 2 broccoli crowns, florets separated and trimmed
- 2 tablespoons avocado oil
- 3 garlic cloves, minced
- 1 tablespoon finely minced ginger or ½ tablespoon ground ginger
- ¼ cup coconut aminos
- ¼ cup toasted sesame oil
- Freshly ground black pepper

Instructions

TO MAKE THE MARINADE

1. In a bowl, combine the coconut aminos, avocado oil, sesame oil, garlic powder, onion powder, salt, and pepper. Add the steak and toss to coat. Marinate for at least 30 minutes or up to 24 hours in the refrigerator.

TO MAKE THE BEEF AND BROCCOLI

1. Fill a large pot halfway with water and add 1 teaspoon of salt. Bring to a boil.
2. Add the broccoli and blanch for 1 to 3 minutes; drain in a colander. Rinse with cold water to prevent further cooking. Set aside.
3. Heat a large skillet over medium-high heat and combine the avocado oil, garlic, and ginger and cook for 30 seconds.
4. Add the sliced beef, discarding the marinade, and cook, stirring constantly, for 2 to 3 minutes. Add the broccoli, coconut aminos, and sesame oil to the skillet and season with salt and pepper. Continue to cook until the beef has reached your desired doneness (about 5 to 7 minutes for medium).
5. Divide the stir-fry evenly between 4 storage containers.

CHEDDAR-STUFFED BURGERS WITH ZUCCHINI

Nutrition: Cal 470;Fat 30 g; Carb 4,5 g;Protein 47 g
Serving 4; Cook time 25 min

Ingredients

- 1 pound ground beef (80% lean)
- 2 large eggs
- ¼ cup almond flour
- 1 cup shredded cheddar cheese
- Salt and pepper
- 2 tablespoons olive oil
- 1 large zucchini, halved and sliced

Instructions

1. Combine the beef, egg, almond flour, cheese, salt, and pepper in a bowl.
2. Mix well, then shape into four even-sized patties.
3. Heat the oil in a large skillet over medium-high heat.
4. Add the burger patties and cook for 5 minutes until browned.
5. Flip the patties and add the zucchini to the skillet, tossing to coat with oil.
6. Season with salt and pepper and cook for 5 minutes, stirring the zucchini occasionally.
7. Serve the burgers with your favorite toppings and the zucchini on the side.

HEARTY BEEF AND BACON CASSEROLE

Nutrition: Cal 410;Fat 26 g; Carb 8 g;Protein 37 g
Serving 8; Cook time 55 min

Ingredients

- 8 slices uncooked bacon
- 1 medium head cauliflower, chopped
- ¼ cup canned coconut milk
- Salt and pepper
- 2 pounds ground beef (80% lean)
- 8 ounces mushrooms, sliced
- 1 large yellow onion, chopped
- 2 cloves garlic, minced

Instructions

1. Preheat the oven to 375°F.
2. Cook the bacon in a skillet until crisp, then drain on paper towels and chop.
3. Bring a pot of salted water to boil, then add the cauliflower.
4. Boil for 6 to 8 minutes until tender, then drain and add to a food processor with the coconut milk.
5. Blend the mixture until smooth, then season with salt and pepper.
6. Cook the beef in a skillet until browned, then drain the fat.
7. Stir in the mushrooms, onion, and garlic, then transfer to a baking dish.
8. Spread the cauliflower mixture over top and bake for 30 minutes.
Broil on high heat for 5 minutes, then sprinkle with bacon to serve.

SLOW COOKER BEEF BOURGUIGNON

Nutrition: Cal 335;Fat 12 g; Carb 6 g;Protein 37 g
Serving 8; Cook time 4 hours 55 min

Ingredients
- 2 tablespoons olive oil
- 2 pounds boneless beef chuck roast, cut into chunks
- Salt and pepper
- ¼ cup almond flour
- ½ cup beef broth
- 2 cups red wine (dry)
- 2 tablespoons tomato paste
- 1 pound mushrooms, sliced
- 1 large yellow onion, cut into chunks

Instructions
1. Heat the oil in a large skillet over medium-high heat.
2. Season the beef with salt and pepper, then toss with almond flour.
3. Add the beef to the skillet and cook until browned on all sides then transfer to a slow cooker.
4. Reheat the skillet over medium-high heat, then pour in the broth.
5. Scrape up the browned bits, then whisk in the wine and tomato paste.
6. Bring to a boil, then pour into the slow cooker.
7. Add the mushrooms and onion, then stir everything together.
8. Cover and cook on low heat for 4 hours until the meat is very tender. Serve hot.

PEPPER GRILLED RIBEYE WITH ASPARAGUS

Nutrition: Cal 380;Fat 25 g; Carb 4,5 g;Protein 35 g
Serving 4; Cook time 20 min

Ingredients
- 1 pound asparagus, trimmed
- 2 tablespoons olive oil
- Salt and pepper
- 1 pound ribeye steak
- 1 tablespoon coconut oil

Instructions
1. Preheat the oven to 400°F and line a small baking sheet with foil.
2. Toss the asparagus with olive oil and spread on the baking sheet.
3. Season with salt and pepper then place in the oven.
4. Rub the steak with the pepper and season with salt.
5. Melt the coconut oil in a cast-iron skillet and heat over high heat.
6. Add the steak and cook for 2 minutes then turn it.
7. Transfer the skillet to the oven and cook for 5 minutes or until the steak is done to the desired level.
8. Slice the steak and serve with the roasted asparagus.

STEAK KEBABS WITH PEPPERS AND ONIONS

Nutrition: Cal 350;Fat 20 g; Carb 6,5 g;Protein 35 g
Serving 4; Cook time 40 min

Ingredients
- 1 pound beef sirloin, cut into 1-inch cubes
- ¼ cup olive oil
- 2 tablespoons balsamic vinegar
- Salt and pepper
- 1 medium yellow onion, cut into chunks
- 1 medium red pepper, cut into chunks
- 1 medium green pepper, cut into chunks

Instructions
1. Toss the steak cubes with the olive oil, balsamic vinegar, salt, and pepper.
2. Slide the cubes onto skewers with the peppers and onions.
3. Preheat a grill to high heat and oil the grates.
4. Grill the kebabs for 2 to 3 minutes on each side until done to your liking.

SEARED LAMB CHOPS WITH ASPARAGUS

Nutrition: Cal 380;Fat 18.5 g; Carb 4,5 g;Protein 48 g
Serving 4; Cook time 20 min

Ingredients
- 8 bone-in lamb chops
- Salt and pepper
- 1 tablespoon fresh chopped rosemary
- 1 tablespoon olive oil
- 1 tablespoon butter
- 16 spears asparagus, cut into 2-inch chunks

Instructions
1. Season the lamb with salt and pepper then sprinkle with rosemary.
2. Heat the oil in a large skillet over medium-high heat.
3. Add the lamb chops and cook for 2 to 3 minutes on each side until seared.
4. Remove the lamb chops to rest and reheat the skillet with the butter.
5. Add the asparagus and turn to coat then cover the skillet. Cook for 4 to 6 minutes until tender-crisp and serve with the lamb.

LAMB CHOPS WITH KALAMATA TAPENADE

Nutrition: Cal 348;Fat 28 g; Carb 2 g;Protein 21 g
Serving 4; Cook time 40 min

Ingredients
FOR THE TAPENADE
- 1 cup pitted Kalamata olives
- 2 tablespoons chopped
- fresh parsley
- 2 tablespoons extra-virgin
- olive oil

- 2 teaspoons minced garlic
- 2 teaspoons freshly squeezed
- lemon juice

FOR THE LAMB CHOPS
- 2 (1-pound) racks French-cut
- lamb chops (8 bones each)
- Sea salt
- Freshly ground black pepper
- 1 tablespoon olive oil

Instructions

TO MAKE THE TAPENADE
1. Place the olives, parsley, olive oil, garlic, and lemon juice in a food processor and process until the mixture is puréed but still slightly chunky.
2. Transfer the tapenade to a container and store sealed in the refrigerator until needed.

TO MAKE THE LAMB CHOPS
1. Preheat the oven to 450°F.
2. Season the lamb racks with salt and pepper.
3. Place a large ovenproof skillet over medium-high heat and add the olive oil.
4. Pan sear the lamb racks on all sides until browned, about 5 minutes in total.
5. Arrange the racks upright in the skillet, with the bones interlaced, and roast them in the oven until they reach your desired doneness, about 20 minutes for medium-rare or until the internal temperature reaches 125°F.
6. Let the lamb rest for 10 minutes and then cut the lamb racks into chops. Arrange 4 chops per person on the plate and top with the Kalamata tapenade

ROSEMARY-GARLIC LAMB RACKS

Nutrition: Cal 354;Fat 30 g; Carb 1 g;Protein 21 g
Serving 4; Cook time 1 hours 35 min

Ingredients
- 4 tablespoons extra-virgin olive oil
- 2 tablespoons finely chopped
- fresh rosemary
- 2 teaspoons minced garlic
- Pinch sea salt
- 2 (1-pound) racks French-cut
- lamb chops (8 bones each)

Instructions
1. In a small bowl, whisk together the olive oil, rosemary, garlic, and salt.
2. Place the racks in a sealable freezer bag and pour the olive oil mixture into the bag. Massage the meat through the bag so it is coated with the marinade. Press the air out of the bag and seal it.
3. Marinate the lamb racks in the refrigerator for 1 to 2 hours.
4. Preheat the oven to 450°F.
5. Place a large ovenproof skillet over medium-high heat. Take the lamb racks out of the bag and sear them in the skillet on all sides, about 5 minutes in total.

6. Arrange the racks upright in the skillet, with the bones interlaced, and roast them in the oven until they reach your desired doneness, about 20 minutes for medium-rare or until the internal temperature reaches 125°F.
7. Let the lamb rest for 10 minutes and then cut the racks into chops.
8. Serve 4 chops per person.

LAMB LEG WITH SUN-DRIED TOMATO PESTO

Nutrition: Cal 352;Fat 29 g; Carb 5 g;Protein 17 g
Serving 8; Cook time 85 min

Ingredients

FOR THE PESTO
- 1 cup sun-dried tomatoes packed
- in oil, drained
- ¼ cup pine nuts
- 2 tablespoons extra-virgin olive oil
- 2 tablespoons chopped fresh basil
- 2 teaspoons minced garlic

FOR THE LAMB LEG
- 1 (2-pound) lamb leg
- Sea salt
- Freshly ground black pepper
- 2 tablespoons olive oil

Instructions

TO MAKE THE PESTO
1. Place the sun-dried tomatoes, pine nuts, olive oil, basil, and garlic in a blender or food processor; process until smooth.
2. Set aside until needed.

TO MAKE THE LAMB LEG
1. Preheat the oven to 400°F.
2. Season the lamb leg all over with salt and pepper.
3. Place a large ovenproof skillet over medium-high heat and add the olive oil.
4. Sear the lamb on all sides until nicely browned, about 6 minutes in total.
5. Spread the sun-dried tomato pesto all over the lamb and place the lamb on a baking sheet. Roast until the meat reaches your desired doneness, about 1 hour for medium.
6. Let the lamb rest for 10 minutes before slicing and serving.

SIRLOIN WITH BLUE CHEESE COMPOUND BUTTER

Nutrition: Cal 544;Fat 44 g; Carb 1 g;Protein 35 g
Serving 4; Cook time 1 hours 22 min

Ingredients
- 6 tablespoons butter, at room
- temperature
- 4 ounces blue cheese, such
- as Stilton or Roquefort
- 4 (5-ounce) beef sirloin steaks

- 1 tablespoon olive oil
- Sea salt
- Freshly ground black pepper

Instructions

1. Place the buter in a blender and pulse until the buter is whipped, about 2 minutes.
2. Add the cheese and pulse until just incorporated.
3. Spoon the buter mixture onto a sheet of plastic wrap and roll it into a log about 1½ inches in diameter by twisting both ends of the plastic wrap in opposite directions.
4. Refrigerate the buter until completely set, about 1 hour.
5. Slice the buter into ½-inch disks and set them on aplate in the refrigerator until you are ready to serve the steaks. Store lefover buter in the refrigerator for up to 1 week.
6. Preheat a barbecue to medium-high heat.
7. Let the steaks come to room temperature.
8. Rub the steaks all over with the olive oil and season them with salt and pepper.
9. Grill the steaks until they reach your desired doneness, about 6 minutes per side for medium.
10. If you do not have a barbecue, broil the steaks in a preheated oven for 7 minutes per side for medium.
11. Let the steaks rest for 10 minutes. Serve each topped with a disk of the compound buter.

GARLIC-BRAISED SHORT RIBS

Nutrition: Cal 481;Fat 38 g; Carb 5 g;Protein 29 g
Serving 4; Cook time 2 hours 30 min

Ingredients

- 4 (4-ounce) beef short ribs
- Sea salt
- Freshly ground black pepper
- 1 tablespoon olive oil
- 2 teaspoons minced garlic
- ½ cup dry red wine
- 3 cups Beef Stock

Instructions

1. Preheat the oven to 325°F.
2. Season the beef ribs on all sides with salt and pepper.
3. Place a deep ovenproof skillet over medium-high heat and add the olive oil.
4. Sear the ribs on all sides until browned, about 6 minutes in total. Transfer the ribs to a plate.
5. Add the garlic to the skillet and sauté until translucent, about 3 minutes.
6. Whisk in the red wine to deglaze the pan. Be sure to scrape all the browned bits from the meat from the botom of the pan. Simmer the wine until it is slightly reduced, about 2 minutes.
7. Add the beef stock, ribs, and any accumulated juices on the plate back to the skillet and bring the liquid to a boil.
8. Cover the skillet and place it in the oven to braise the ribs until the meat is fall-of-the-bone tender, about 2 hours.

9. Serve the ribs with a spoonful of the cooking liquid drizzled over each serving.

BACON-WRAPPED BEEF TENDERLOIN

Nutrition: Cal 565;Fat 49 g; Carb 2 g;Protein 28 g
Serving 4; Cook time 25 min

Ingredients

- 4 (4-ounce) beef tenderloin steaks
- Sea salt
- Freshly ground black pepper
- 8 bacon slices
- 1 tablespoon extra-virgin olive oil

Instructions

1. Preheat the oven to 450°F.
2. Season the steaks with salt and pepper.
3. Wrap each steak snugly around the edges with 2 slices of bacon and secure the bacon with toothpicks.
4. Place a large skillet over medium-high heat and add the olive oil.
5. Pan sear the steaks for 4 minutes per side and transfer them to a baking sheet.
6. Roast the steaks until they reach your desired doneness, about 6 minutes for medium.
7. Remove the steaks from the oven and let them rest for 10 minutes.
8. Remove the toothpicks and serve.

CHEESEBURGER CASSEROLE

Nutrition: Cal 410;Fat 33 g; Carb 3g;Protein 20 g
Serving 6; Cook time 40 min

Ingredients

- 1 pound 75% lean ground beef
- ½ cup chopped sweet onion
- 2 teaspoons minced garlic
- 1&½ cups shredded aged Cheddar, divided
- ½ cup heavy (whipping) cream
- 1 large tomato, chopped
- 1 teaspoon minced fresh basil
- ¼ teaspoon sea salt
- ⅛ teaspoon freshly ground black pepper

Instructions

1. Preheat the oven to 350°F.
2. Place a large skillet over medium-high heat and add the ground beef.
3. Brown the beef until cooked through, about 6 minutes, and spoon of any excess fat.
4. Stir in the onion and garlic and cook until the vegetables are tender, about 4 minutes.
5. Transfer the beef and vegetables to an 8-by-8-inch casserole dish.
6. In medium bowl, stir together 1 cup of shredded cheese and the heavy cream, tomato, basil, salt, and pepper until well combined.
7. Pour the cream mixture over the beef mixture and top the casserole with the remaining ½ cup of shredded cheese.

8.Bake until the casserole is bubbly and the cheese is melted and lightly browned, about 30 minutes.

ITALIAN BEEF BURGERS

Nutrition: Cal 440;Fat 37 g; Carb 4 g;Protein 22 g
Serving 4; Cook time 22 min

Ingredients

- 1 pound 75% lean ground beef
- ¼ cup ground almonds
- 2 tablespoons chopped fresh basil
- 1 teaspoon minced garlic
- ¼ teaspoon sea salt
- 1 tablespoon olive oil
- 1 tomato, cut into 4 thick slices
- ¼ sweet onion, sliced thinly

Instructions

1.In a medium bowl, mix together the ground beef, ground almonds, basil, garlic, and salt until well mixed.
2.Form the beef mixture into four equal paties and flaten them to about ½ inch thick.
3.Place a large skillet on medium-high heat and add the olive oil.
4.Panfry the burgers until cooked through, flipping them once, about 12 minutes in total.
5.Pat away any excess grease with paper towels and serve the burgers with a slice of tomato and onion

<u>Pork and Ham</u>

HAM AND PROVOLONE SANDWICH

Nutrition: Cal 425;Fat 31 g;Carb 5 g;Protein 31 g
Serving 1; Cook time 35 min

Ingredients:
- 1 large egg, separated
- Pinch cream of tartar
- Pinch salt
- 1 ounce cream cheese, softened
- ¼ cup shredded provolone cheese
- 3 ounces sliced ham

Instructions:
1. For the bread, preheat the oven to 300°F and line a baking sheet with parchment.
2. Beat the egg whites with the cream of tartar and salt until soft peaks form.
3. Whisk the cream cheese and egg yolk until smooth and pale yellow.
4. Fold in the egg whites a little at a time until smooth and well combined.
5. Spoon the batter onto the baking sheet into two even circles.
6. Bake for 25 minutes until firm and lightly browned.
7. Spread the butter on one side of each bread circle then place one in a preheated skillet over medium heat.
8. Sprinkle with cheese and add the sliced ham then top with the other bread circle, butter-side-up.
9. Cook the sandwich for a minute or two then carefully flip it over.
10. Let it cook until the cheese is melted then serve.

SPRING SALAD WITH SHAVED PARMESAN

Nutrition: Cal 295;Fat 25.5 g;Carb 3 g;Protein 6.5 g
Serving 2; Cook time 15 min

Ingredients:
- 3 slices uncooked bacon
- 2 tablespoons red wine vinegar
- 1 tablespoon Dijon mustard
- Salt and pepper
- Liquid stevia extract, to taste
- 4 ounces mixed spring greens
- ½ small red onion, sliced thinly
- ⅓ cup roasted pine nuts
- ¼ cup shaved parmesan

Instructions:
1. Cook the bacon in a skillet until crisp then remove to paper towels.
2. Reserve ¼ cup of bacon fat in the skillet, discarding the rest, then chop the bacon.
3. Whisk the red wine vinegar and mustard into the bacon fat in the skillet.
4. Season with salt and pepper, then sweeten with stevia to taste and let cool slightly.
5. Combine the spring greens, red onion, pine nuts, and parmesan in a salad bowl.

6. Toss with the dressing, then top with chopped bacon to serve.

THREE MEAT AND CHEESE SANDWICH

Nutrition: Cal 610;Fat 48 g;Carb 3 g;Protein 40 g
Serving 1; Cook time35 min

Ingredients:
- 1 large egg, separated
- Pinch cream of tartar
- Pinch salt
- 1 ounce cream cheese, softened
- 1 ounce sliced ham
- 1 ounce sliced hard salami
- 1 ounce sliced turkey
- 2 slices cheddar cheese

Instructions:
1. For the bread, preheat the oven to 300°F and line a baking sheet with parchment.
2. Beat the egg whites with the cream of tartar and salt until soft peaks form.
3. Whisk the cream cheese and egg yolk until smooth and pale yellow.
4. Fold in the egg whites a little at a time until smooth and well combined.
5. Spoon the batter onto the baking sheet into two even circles.
6. Bake for 25 minutes until firm and lightly browned.
7. To complete the sandwich, layer the sliced meats and cheeses between the two bread circles.
8. Grease a skillet with cooking spray and heat over medium heat.
9. Add the sandwich and cook until browned underneath, then flip and cook until the cheese is just melted.

HAM, EGG, AND CHEESE SANDWICH

Nutrition: Cal 365;Fat 21 g;Carb 6.5 g;Protein 35.5 g
Serving 1; Cook time35 min

Ingredients:
- 1 large egg, separated
- Pinch cream of tartar
- Pinch salt
- 1 ounce cream cheese, softened
- 1 large egg
- 1 teaspoon butter
- 3 ounces sliced ham
- 1 slice cheddar cheese

Instructions:
1. For the bread, preheat the oven to 300°F and line a baking sheet with parchment.
2. Beat the egg whites with the cream of tartar and salt until soft peaks form.
3. Whisk the cream cheese and egg yolk until smooth and pale yellow.
4. Fold in the egg whites a little at a time until smooth and well combined.

5. Spoon the batter onto the baking sheet into two even circles.
6. Bake for 25 minutes until firm and lightly browned.
7. To complete the sandwich, fry the egg in butter until done to your preference.
8. Arrange the sliced ham on top of one bread circle.
9. Top with the fried egg and the sliced cheese then the second bread circle.
10. Serve immediately or cook in a greased skillet to melt the cheese first.

CHOPPED KALE SALAD WITH BACON DRESSING

Nutrition: Cal 230;Fat 12 g;Carb 14 g;Protein 16 g
Serving 2; Cook time 15 min

Ingredients:
- 6 slices uncooked bacon
- 2 tablespoons apple cider vinegar
- 1 teaspoon Dijon mustard
- Liquid stevia, to taste
- Salt and pepper
- 4 cups fresh chopped kale
- ¼ cup thinly sliced red onion

Instructions:
1. Cook the bacon in a skillet until crisp then remove to paper towels and chop.
2. Reserve ¼ cup of the bacon grease in the skillet and warm over low heat.
3. Whisk in the apple cider vinegar, mustard, and stevia then season with salt and pepper.
4. Toss in the kale and cook for 1 minute then divide between two plates.
5. Top the salads with red onion and chopped bacon to serve.

SKINNY OVEN FRIED PORK CHOPS

Nutrition: Cal 380;Fat 21 g;Carb 7 g;Protein 40 g
Serving 6; Cook time 25 min

Ingredients:
- 2 lbs pork loin chops (6 pork chops approx.)
- 1 cup buttermilk
- 1 cup almond flour/meal
- 1 tablespoon unflavored whey protein isolate powder
- 1 teaspoon kosher salt
- 1 teaspoons garlic powder
- 2 teaspoons Italian seasoning
- 1 tablespoon grated parmesan cheese (optional)
- Parsley or cilantro for garnishing (optional)
- Avocado and tomato salad to serve (optional)

Instructions:
1. Trim the fat from the pork chops, if necessary.
2. In a large bowl, cover the pork chops with the buttermilk and refrigerate for at least 2 hours or overnight. Remove pork chops from fridge 30 minutes before you plan to make them.
3. Preheat oven to 425°F. Line a large baking sheet with non-stick aluminum foil, or spray a large nonstick baking sheet lightly with oil.
4. Combine almond flour/meal, tapioca, salt, garlic, Italian seasoning, and parmesan, if using, in a large shallow bowl.
5. Grab a pork chop from the buttermilk, letting any excess milk runoff. Coat with crumb mixture, coating completely. Place on the prepared baking sheet.
6. Lightly spray a little more oil on top of the pork chops.
7. Bake, uncovered, for 20 to 25 minutes, or until pork is done (145° F)

CREAMY HONEY & MUSTARD PORK RIBS

Nutrition: Cal 385 ;Fat 17 g; Carb 16 g;Protein 39 g
Serving 6 Cook time 4 hours

Ingredients
- 3 1/2 pounds country style pork ribs
- 1/2 cup honey mustard
- 1 cup BBQ sauce
- 2 tsp Salt-Free Seasoning Blend

Instructions
1. Place ribs in instant pot.
2. In a tiny bowl, stir together barbecue sauce, honey mustard, and seasoning blend.
3. Pour over ribs in instant pot, stir to coat.
4. Cover and turn the steam release handle on the venting position.
5. Select the slow cooker setting and set to high. Cook for 4 hours.
6. Transfer ribs to a serving platter.
7. Strain sauce into a bowl, skim fat from sauce.
8. Drizzle some in the sauce in the ribs and pass the rest of the sauce in the table.

TENDER AND JUICY SHREDDED PORK

Nutrition: Cal 550 ;Fat41 g; Carb 2 g;Protein 38 g
Serving 8 Cook time 8 hours

Ingredients
- 4 pounds pork shoulder roast
- 4 ounces green chilies, diced
- 1 cup using apple cider vinegar
- 1 1/2 tsp garlic, minced
- 1 cup onion, finely chopped
- 1 tsp ground black pepper
- 1 tsp salt

Instructions
1. Place roast in instant pot.
2. Combine remaining ingredients and pour over roast.
3. Cover and turn the steam release handle towards the venting position.
4. Select the slow cooker setting and hang to medium.
5. Cook for 8 hours.

6. Remove to some chopping board and shred with two forks, discarding fat and bones.

SESAME SHEET PAN PORK FAJITAS
Nutrition: Cal 323 ;Fat 18 g; Carb 2 g;Protein 34 g
Serving 8 Cook time 1 hour 30 min

Ingredients
- 2 lbs boneless pork chops
- 1 tsp avocado or olive oil
- Peppers, sliced optional
- onions, sliced optional
- Amazing Garlic Sauce
- 1 cup cilantro
- 1 tbsp ginger
- 4 cloves garlic
- 1 jalapeno, seeded {optional}
- 1/3 cup avocado oil
- 2 tsp sesame oil
- 1 tbsp apple cider vinegar
- 3 tbsp coconut aminos
- 2 tbsp lime juice

Instructions
1. Combine all the ingredients for the marinade in a food processor and pulse multiple times until the mixture is chopped with some liquid.
2. 1 cup cilantro,1 tbsp ginger,4 cloves garlic,1 jalapeno, seeded,1/3 cup avocado oil,2 tsp sesame oil,1 tbsp apple cider vinegar,3 tbsp coconut aminos,2 tbsp lime juice
3. Slice your pork against the grain (see recipe notes below) into thin uniform pieces. Add half of the marinade (reserve the other half) and stir to combine. Refrigerate for 30 minutes, up to 24 hours.
4. 2 lbs boneless pork chops
5. Slice onions and peppers and toss with 1 tsp avocado oil and a pinch of kosher salt.
6. Peppers, sliced,onions, sliced,1 tsp avocado or olive oil
7. Preheat oven to 400 degrees F. Place the oven rack on the middle rung.
8. Arrange the pork and peppers/onion mixture on a rimmed baking sheet. Bake for 10 minutes and then turn the broiler on HIGH for 4 minutes (watch closely so it doesn't burn.
9. Serve pork with the peppers and onions on leaf lettuce for a gluten-free/Whole30 fajitas.

BRIGHT SALSA PORK CHOPS
Nutrition: Cal 342 ;Fat 25 g; Carb 1 g;Protein 28 g
Serving 6 Cook time 40 min

Ingredients
- 1 1/2 pound thin boneless pork chops or pork cutlets
- sea salt
- black pepper freshly ground
- 1 tablespoon butter

- 1 tablespoon red wine vinegar
- 2/3 cup heavy whipping cream
- 1 tablespoon prepared horseradish
- 1 small tomato peeled, seeded and diced
- 1 tablespoon chives minced

Instructions
1. Pat the pork chops dry using paper towels. Season both sides using salt and pepper. Melt butter in a large, heavy skillet over medium-high heat.
2. When butter has stopped foaming, add pork chops in a single layer. Make sure they do not touch. If your pan is too small, you will need to cook them in batches.
3. Boneless Pork Chops with Tomato Cream Sauce-Browning the first side of meat.
4. When the first side has browned, turn and brown the other side. Turn heat to low and continue cooking until the chops are done. Remove the chops to a plate.
5. Boneless Pork Chops with Tomato Cream Sauce-Browning the second side of the pork chops.
6. Add the red wine vinegar to the pan and scrape up the browned bits. Cook until vinegar has almost completely evaporated.
7. Boneless Pork Chops with Tomato Cream Sauce-adding the vinegar.
8. Stir in the heavy whipping cream, horseradish, and any juices that have accumulated on the plate with the pork chops. Turn heat to medium to bring to a simmer, then simmer on low heat until sauce has thickened.
9. Boneless Pork Chops with Tomato Cream Sauce-Adding the cream and the horseradish.
10. Add the tomato and chives to the sauce. Taste and adjust seasoning adding salt, pepper, and more horseradish to taste.

KETO PROSCIUTTO SPINACH SALAD
Nutrition: Cal 420 ;Fat 16 g; Carb 8 g;Protein 25 g
Serving 2 Cook time 10 min

Ingredients
- 2 cups baby spinach
- 1/3 lb. prosciutto
- 1 cantaloupe
- 1 avocado
- 1/4 cup diced red onion
- Handful of raw, unsalted walnuts

Instructions
1. lace a cup of spinach on each plate.
2. Top with diced prosciutto, cubes of balls of melon, slices of avocado, a sprinkling of red onion, and a few walnuts.
3. Add some freshly ground pepper, if you like.

BRIGHT SALSA PORK CHOPS

Nutrition: Cal 460 ;Fat 22 g; Carb 8 g;Protein 25 g
Serving 2 Cook time 8 hours 20 min

Ingredients
- 2 x Pork Loins
- 75g Salsa
- 3 Tablespoon Lime Juice
- ½ tsp. Ground Cumin
- ½ tsp. Garlic Powder
- ½ tsp. Salt
- ½ tsp. Ground Black Pepper
- Calorie Free Cooking Spray

Instructions
1. In a small bowl combine cumin, garlic powder, salt and pepper and rub the spice mixture into pork chops.
2. Brown chops 5 minutes each side on a medium heat.
3. Spray the insides of your slow cooker cooking spray and add the pork chops.
4. Add the salsa and lime mixture.
5. Slow cook on low for 8 hours.

LOADED CAULIFLOWER

Nutrition: Cal 200;Fat 17 g; Carb 8 g;Protein 12 g
Serving 6; Cook time 20 min

Ingredients
- 1 pound cauliflower florettes
- 4 ounces sour cream
- 1 cup grated cheddar cheese
- 2 slices cooked bacon, crumbled
- 2 tablespoons snipped chives
- 3 tablespoons butter
- 1/4 teaspoon garlic powder
- Salt and pepper, to taste

Instructions
1. Cut the cauliflower into florettes and add them to a microwave-safe bowl. Add 2 tablespoons of water and cover with cling film. Microwave for 5-8 minutes, depending on your microwave, until completely cooked and tender. Drain the excess water and let sit uncovered for a minute or two. (alternately, steam your cauliflower the conventional way. You may need to squeeze a little water out of the cauliflower after cooking).
2. Add the cauliflower to a food processor and process until fluffy. Add the butter, garlic powder, and sour cream and process until it resembles the consistency of mashed potatoes. Remove the mashed cauliflower to a bowl and add most of the chives, saving some to add to the top later. Add half of the cheddar cheese and mix by hand. Season with salt and pepper.
3. Top the loaded cauliflower with the remaining cheese, remaining chives and bacon. Put back into the microwave to melt the cheese or place the cauliflower under the broiler for a few minutes.

4. I visually divide the cauliflower into sixths. Serving size is approximately 1/3-1/2 cup.

PAN-SEARED PORK TENDERLOIN MEDALLIONS

Nutrition: Cal 150;Fat 7 g; Carb 3 g;Protein 18 g
Serving 4; Cook time 18 min

Ingredients
- 1 tablespoon canola oil 1 (1-lb.)
- pork tenderloin, trimmed and cut crosswise into 12 medallions
- 1/2 teaspoon kosher salt
- 1/4 teaspoon garlic powder
- 1/4 teaspoon black pepper Fresh thyme leaves (optional)

Instructions
1. Heat oil in a 12-inch skillet over medium-high. Arrange pork medallions in a single layer on a work surface, and press each with the palm of your hand to flatten to an even thickness.
2. Combine salt, garlic powder, and pepper; sprinkle evenly over pork. Add pork to skillet in a single layer; cook just until done, about 3 minutes per side
3. Remove from heat; let stand 5 minutes before serving. Garnish with thyme leaves, if desired.

COCONUT PORK CURRY

Nutrition: Cal 260;Fat 16 g; Carb 10 g;Protein 18 g
Serving 4; Cook time 60 min

Ingredients
- 1 teaspoon ground cumin
- 1 teaspoon ground coriander
- 1/2 teaspoon ground cinnamon
- 1/4 teaspoon ground chilli powder
- 800g diced pork
- 1 tablespoon vegetable oil
- 1 large (200g) brown onion, chopped
- 2 cloves garlic, chopped
- 4cm piece (20g) fresh ginger, grated
- 1 tablespoon water
- 400ml can coconut cream or coconut milk
- 2 tablespoons brown sugar
- 1 teaspoon salt
- 1 tablespoon lemon juice
- 1/4 cup fresh coriander leaves

Instructions
1. Combine the spices in a medium bowl; add pork, toss to coat.
2. Heat half the oil in a large frying pan. Cook the pork in 2 batches, using the remaining oil, until browned all over. Remove from pan.

3. Add onion to same pan with garlic, ginger and water; cook, stirring, over medium heat until softened. Return the pork to the pan with coconut cream, sugar and salt. Simmer, covered, stirring occasionally, for about 1 hour to 1 hour 30 minutes or until the pork is tender and the sauce is thickened.
4. Stir in juice; season to taste with salt and pepper. Sprinkle with coriander.

THE BEST BAKED GARLIC PORK TEN-DERLOIN

Nutrition: Cal 449;Fat 13 g; Carb 6 g;Protein 32 g
Serving 4; Cook time 60 min

Ingredients
- 2 tbsp extra virgin olive oil
- 1 tbsp celtic sea salt and fresh cracked pepper
- 2 lb pork tenderloin, optional: pre-marinate pork before cooking
- 4 tbsp butter, sliced into 4-6 pats
- 2 tbsp diced garlic
- 1 tsp dried basil
- 1 tsp dried oregano
- 1 tsp dried thyme
- 1 tsp dried parsley
- ½ tsp dried sage
- 2 tbsp Italian Herb Seasoning Blend

Instructions
1. Preheat oven to 350 degrees.
2. Line baking sheet with aluminum foil.
3. In a small bowl, combine garlic, basil, oregano, thyme, parsley, and sage. Set aside.
4. Generously season meat with salt and pepper.
5. In a large pan, heat oil until shimmery.
6. Add to pan, and cook on all sides until dark golden brown.
7. Transfer to baking sheet.
8. Generously coat with herb mix.
9. Place pats of butter on top of the pork.
10. Wrap in foil, bake until meat is 150 degrees internally at the widest, thickest part of the tenderloin (about 25 minutes.)
11. When pork has come to temperature, remove and let rest, tented with foil, for at least five minutes to lock in juices.
12. Slice against the grain and serve immediately.
13. To store leftovers, place in an airtight container and keep in refrigerator for up to three days.
14. To freeze leftovers, place in a plastic bag or wrap in plastic wrap and keep in freezer for up to three months.
15. To reheat, let thaw naturally in the refrigerator overnight, and bake at 350, wrapped in foil, until piping hot when ready to serve.

PORK SKEWERS WITH CHIMICHURRI

Nutrition: Cal 450;Fat 36 g; Carb 6 g;Protein 30 g
Serving 2; Cook time 20 min

Ingredients
- 1/2 pound boneless pork shoulder
- 1/4 teaspoon ground cumin
- 1/4 teaspoon paprika
- 1 tablespoon coconut oil
- 1/4 cup olive oil
- 1/4 cup diced green peppers
- 3 tablespoons fresh chopped parsley
- 1 tablespoon fresh chopped cilantro
- 1 1/2 tablespoons fresh lemon juice
- 1 garlic clove (minced)

Instructions
1. Cut the pork into slices about 1-inch thick.
2. Season the pork with salt, pepper, cumin and paprika.
3. Slide the pork slices onto wooden skewers and heat the coconut oil in a skillet.
4. Fry the skewers until both sides are browned and the meat is cooked through.
5. Combine the remaining ingredients in a food processor.
6. Pulse several times to chop then blend until smooth.
7. Serve the pork skewers with the chimichurri spooned over them.

APRICOT GLAZED PORK

Nutrition: Cal 315;Fat 10 g; Carb 20 g;Protein 35 g
Serving 12; Cook time 4 hours

Ingredients
- 4 pounds boneless pork loin roast
- 1 cup onion, chopped
- 2 tbsp Dijon mustard
- 2 cups beef broth
- 1 cup apricot preserves

Instructions
1. Mix broth, preserves, onion, and mustard in instant pot.
2. Cut pork to match. Add to instant pot.
3. Cover and turn the steam release handle towards the venting position.
4. Select the slow cooker setting and set to high.
5. Cook for 4 hours.

PORK AND CAULIFLOWER GRATIN

Nutrition: Cal 430;Fat 32 g; Carb 6 g;Protein 27 g
Serving 2; Cook time 40 min

Ingredients
- 1/2 lb pork ham, diced
- 1 small head of cauliflower, cut into small florets
- 1/2 cup heavy cream
- 1/2 cup shredded cheese
- 2 garlic cloves, minced
- 1/4 tsp ground nutmeg
- Salt and pepper to taste

Instructions

1. Preheat the oven to 375°F (190°C) and grease a baking dish with cooking spray.
2. In a skillet over medium-high heat, cook the diced pork ham until browned and cooked through.
3. In a large pot of salted water, blanch the cauliflower florets for 3-4 minutes until slightly tender. Drain the cauliflower and transfer it to the greased baking dish.
4. In a saucepan over medium heat, combine the heavy cream, shredded cheese, minced garlic, ground nutmeg, salt, and pepper. Stir the mixture until the cheese is melted and the sauce is smooth.
5. Pour the garlic cream sauce over the cauliflower in the baking dish.
6. Top the cauliflower and sauce with the cooked pork ham.
7. Bake the gratin for 25-30 minutes, until the top is golden brown and bubbly.

EASY BBQ HAM
Nutrition: Cal 315;Fat 15 g; Carb 2 g;Protein 35 g
Serving 24; Cook time 14 hours

Ingredients
- 3 pounds ham, boneless
- 2 cups water
- 2 cups onions, sliced
- 6 whole cloves
- 2 cups BBQ sauce

Instructions
1. Place half in the onions in bottom in the instant pot.
2. Stick cloves in ham and set it on top of onions in instant pot.
3. Put the others in the onions on top. Pour water.
4. Cover and turn the steam release handle for the venting position.
5. Select the slow cooker setting and hang up to medium.
6. Cook for 10 hours.
7. Shred or cut up meat and onion.
8. Put back to the instant pot.
9. Add barbecue sauce and cook 4 hours more.

KETO PORK AND HAM SKEWERS
Nutrition: Cal 405;Fat 25 g; Carb 5 g;Protein 38 g
Serving 2; Cook time 25 min

Ingredients
- 1/2 lb pork, cut into cubes
- 1/2 lb ham, cut into cubes
- 1 medium tomato, diced
- 1 medium bell pepper, diced
- Salt and pepper to taste
- Wooden skewers, soaked in water for 30 minutes

Instructions
1. Preheat the grill to medium-high heat.
2. Thread the pork and ham cubes onto the wooden skewers, alternating between pork and ham.
3. Season the skewers with salt and pepper.
4. Grill the skewers for 10-12 minutes, turning occasionally, until the pork and ham are cooked through.

5. In a medium bowl, combine the diced tomato and bell pepper.
6. Season the salad with salt and pepper to taste.
7. Serve the pork and ham skewers hot with the tomato and bell pepper salad.

SALAD WITH BROCCOLI, CAULIFLOWER AND BACON
Nutrition: Cal 164;Fat 14 g; Carb 8 g;Protein 5 g
Serving 4; Cook time 15 min

Ingredients
- Broccoli (3/4 cups, chopped)
- Cauliflower (3/4 cups, chopped)
- Bacon (3 slices, chopped)
- Onion (1, chopped)
- Vinegar (1 teaspoon)
- Sour cream (3/4 cups)

Instructions
1. Put the cauliflower and broccoli inside the pressure cooker as well as set it to "Steam" for the matter of minutes (they shouldn't be too tender).Take out your vegetables in the boiling water and hang up them aside.
2. Fry the bacon till it turns brown, set it up aside and allow it cool.
3. Mix the onion (you can use spring onion also) using the vinegar, salt, pepper, and sour cream.
4. Mix the sauce while using broccoli and cauliflower, serve with many more bacon pieces for decoration.

ASPARAGUS WRAPPED IN PROSCIUTTO
Nutrition: Cal 555;Fat 45 g; Carb 6.7 g;Protein 33 g
Serving 3; Cook time 25 min

Ingredients
- Mushrooms (3 cups)
- Rice (1 ½ cups)
- Chicken stock (4 cups)
- Olive oil (1/4 cup)
- Onion (1 cup, chopped)
- Butter (unsalted, ¼ cup)
- White wine (3/4 cup)
- Rosemary
- Parmesan (half cup, grated)
- Salt and pepper

Instructions
1. Set the Pressure cooker to "Sauté"; add the olive oil and butter and let it melt for any matter of minutes. Add the mushrooms and cook them about 3 minutes).
2. Put within the onion, stir and cook to get a couple of more minutes. Add the rosemary and cook it to get a minute.
3. Add the rice and stir until it coats inside the butter and olive oil mix; stir for a couple of minutes and after that pour the wine. Let it simmer for three more minutes.
4. Pour inside the chicken stock, stir for any minute.

5. Now close and secure the lid and select to "High pressure" as well as set the timer for 6 minutes.
6. Let the stress out naturally for 5 minutes.
7. Open the lid and stir the risotto (it ought to turn creamy); remove the rosemary (if you are using spring, if it's chopped, then get forced out as it really is).
8. Sprinkle salt, pepper, and parmesan, and stir till the cheese melts.

BRATWURSTS AND SAUERKRAUT

Nutrition: Cal 525;Fat 42 g; Carb 12 g;Protein 24 g
Serving 4; Cook time 50 min

Ingredients
- 2 tablespoons avocado oil
- 1 yellow onion, thinly sliced
- 1 pound bratwurst
- 1 (16-ounce) jar sauerkraut, drained
- 1½ cups chicken broth
- 1 teaspoon garlic powder
- Freshly ground black pepper

Instructions
1. In large cast-iron skillet over medium heat, add the oil, onion, and bratwurst and cook for 6 to 8 minutes, or until they get some color.
2. Add the sauerkraut, broth, garlic powder, salt, and pepper and simmer for 30 to 40 minutes, or until the sausages are cooked through.
3. In each of 4 storage containers, place 1 cup of sauerkraut and 1 bratwurst.

ROSEMARY ROASTED PORK WITH CAULIFLOWER

Nutrition: Cal 300;Fat 17 g; Carb 3 g;Protein 37 g
Serving 4; Cook time 30 min

Ingredients
- 1 ½ pounds boneless pork tenderloin
- 1 tablespoon coconut oil
- 1 tablespoon fresh chopped rosemary
- Salt and pepper
- 1 tablespoon olive oil
- 2 cups cauliflower florets

Instructions
1. Rub the pork with coconut oil, then season with rosemary, salt, and pepper.
2. Heat the olive oil in a large skillet over medium-high heat.
3. Add the pork and cook for 2 to 3 minutes on each side until browned.
4. Sprinkle the cauliflower in the skillet around the pork.
5. Reduce the heat to low, then cover the skillet and cook for 8 to 10 minutes until the pork is cooked through.
6. Slice the pork and serve with the cauliflower.

SAUSAGE STUFFED BELL PEPPERS

Nutrition: Cal 355;Fat 23,5 g; Carb 16,5 g;Protein 19 g
Serving 4; Cook time 55 min

Ingredients
- 1 medium head cauliflower, chopped
- 1 tablespoon olive oil
- 12 ounces ground Italian sausage
- 1 small yellow onion, chopped
- 1 teaspoon dried oregano
- Salt and pepper
- 4 medium bell peppers

Instructions
1. Preheat the oven to 350°F.
2. Pulse the cauliflower in a food processor into rice-like grains.
3. Heat the oil in a skillet over medium heat then add the cauliflower – cook for 6 to 8 minutes until tender.
4. Spoon the cauliflower rice into a bowl, then reheat the skillet.
5. Add the sausage and cook until browned, then drain the fat.
6. Stir the sausage into the cauliflower, then add the onion, oregano, salt andpepper.
7. Slice the tops off the peppers, remove the seeds and pith, then spoon the sausage mixture into them.
8. Place the peppers upright in a baking dish, then cover the dish with foil.
9. Bake for 30 minutes, then uncover and bake 15 minutes more. Serve hot.

CHEDDAR, SAUSAGE, AND MUSHROOM CASSEROLE

Nutrition: Cal 450;Fat 34 g; Carb 6 g;Protein 28 g
Serving 6; Cook time 45 min

Ingredients
- 1 pound ground Italian sausage
- 8 ounces mushrooms, diced
- 1 large yellow onion, chopped
- 1 cup shredded cheddar cheese
- 8 large eggs
- ½ cup heavy cream
- Salt and pepper

Instructions
1. Preheat the oven to 375°F and grease a baking dish.
2. Heat the sausage in a large skillet over medium-high heat.
3. Cook the sausage until browned then stir in the mushrooms and onions.
4. Cook for 4 to 5 minutes then spread in the baking dish.
5. Sprinkle the dish with cheese then whisk together the remaining ingredients in a separate bowl.
6. Pour the mixture into the dish then bake for 35 minutes until bubbling.

CAULIFLOWER CRUST MEAT LOVER'S PIZZA

Nutrition: Cal 560;Fat 40 g; Carb 11 g;Protein 41 g
Serving 2; Cook time 40 min

Ingredients
- 1 tablespoon butter
- 2 cups riced cauliflower
- Salt and pepper
- 1 ½ cups shredded mozzarella cheese, divided into 1 cup and ½ cup
- 1 cup fresh grated parmesan
- 1 teaspoon garlic powder
- 1 large egg white
- 1 teaspoon dried Italian seasoning
- ¼ cup low-carb tomato sauce
- 2 ounces sliced pepperoni
- 1 ounce diced ham
- 2 slices bacon, cooked and crumbled

Instructions
1. Preheat the oven to 400°F and line a baking sheet with parchment.
2. Heat the butter in a skillet over medium-high heat and add the cauliflower.
3. Season with salt and pepper, then cover and cook for 15 minutes, stirring occasionally, until very tender.
4. Spoon the cauliflower into a bowl and stir in ½ cup mozzarella along with the parmesan and garlic powder.
5. Stir in the egg white and Italian seasoning, then pour onto the baking sheet.
6. Shape the dough into a circle about ½-inch thick, then bake for 15 minutes.
7. Top with tomato sauce, along with the remaining mozzarella and the pepperoni, bacon, and ham.
8. Broil until the cheese is browned, then slice to serve.

BACON-WRAPPED PORK TENDERLOIN WITH CAULIFLOWER

Nutrition: Cal 330;Fat 18,5 g; Carb 3 g;Protein 38 g
Serving 4; Cook time 35 min

Ingredients
- 1 ¼ pounds boneless pork tenderloin
- Salt and pepper
- 8 slices uncooked bacon
- 1 tablespoon olive oil
- 2 cups cauliflower florets

Instructions
1. Preheat the oven to 425°F and season the pork with salt and pepper.
2. Wrap the pork in bacon and place on a foil-lined roasting pan.
3. Roast for 25 minutes until the internal temperature reaches 155°F.
4. Meanwhile, heat the oil in a skillet over medium heat.
5. Add the cauliflower and sauté until tender-crisp – about 8 to 10 minutes.

6. Turn on the broiler and place the pork under it to crisp the bacon.
7. Slice the pork to serve with the sautéed cauliflower

KETO BAKED PORK CHOPS WITH MUSHROOMS

Nutrition: Cal 370;Fat 23 g; Carb 5 g;Protein 34 g
Serving 2; Cook time 40 min

Ingredients
- 2 bone-in pork chops (about 1 inch thick)
- 1/2 cup sliced mushrooms
- 1/2 cup sliced onions
- 2 tbsp mayonnaise
- 1/4 cup shredded mozzarella cheese
- Salt and pepper to taste

Instructions
1. Preheat the oven to 375°F (190°C) and line a baking dish with parchment paper.
2. Season the pork chops with salt and pepper on both sides.
3. In a skillet over medium-high heat, sauté the sliced mushrooms and onions until tender and lightly browned, about 5-7 minutes.
4. Spread the mayonnaise on top of each pork chop, then top with the sautéed mushrooms and onions.
5. Sprinkle the shredded mozzarella cheese on top of the vegetables.
6. Bake for 25-30 minutes, until the pork chops are cooked through and the cheese is melted and bubbly.
7. Serve the pork chops hot.

KETO GRILLED PORK RIBS

Nutrition: Cal 584;Fat 48 g; Carb 3 g;Protein 33 g
Serving 2; Cook time 35 min

Ingredients
- 1 pound pork ribs
- 2 cloves garlic, minced
- 1 tablespoon smoked paprika
- 1 tablespoon ground cumin
- 1 tablespoon dried oregano
- 1 teaspoon onion powder
- Salt and black pepper to taste
- 2 tablespoons olive oil

Instructions
1. Preheat the grill to medium-high heat.
2. In a small bowl, mix together the garlic, smoked paprika, cumin, oregano, onion powder, salt, black pepper, and olive oil to make a marinade.
3. Rub the marinade all over the pork ribs, making sure to coat both sides.
4. Grill the pork ribs for about 10-15 minutes on each side, until they are fully cooked and have grill marks.
5. Serve hot.

PORK RIBS WITH SPICE RUB

Nutrition: Cal 658;Fat 55 g; Carb 3 g;Protein 36 g
Serving 2; Cook time 2 hours 10 min

Ingredients
- 1 pound pork ribs
- 1 tablespoon smoked paprika
- 1 teaspoon garlic powder
- 1 teaspoon onion powder
- 1 teaspoon dried thyme
- 1 teaspoon dried oregano
- 1/2 teaspoon cumin
- Salt and black pepper to taste

Instructions
1. Preheat the oven to 300°F (150°C).
2. In a small bowl, mix together the smoked paprika, garlic powder, onion powder, dried thyme, dried oregano, cumin, salt, and black pepper.
3. Rub the spice mixture onto the pork ribs, making sure to cover all sides.
4. Place the ribs onto a baking sheet lined with aluminum foil.
5. Bake in the oven for 2-3 hours, until the meat is tender and falls off the bone.
6. Remove from the oven and let cool for 5-10 minutes before serving.

PORK RIBS WITH ROASTED VEGETABLES

Nutrition: Cal 515;Fat 35 g; Carb 10 g;Protein 32 g
Serving 2; Cook time 80 min

Ingredients
- 1 pound pork ribs
- 1 medium zucchini, sliced into rounds
- 1 medium red bell pepper, sliced into strips
- 1 medium yellow onion, sliced into wedges
- 2 cloves garlic, minced
- 2 tablespoons olive oil
- Salt and black pepper to taste

Instructions
1. Preheat the oven to 375°F (190°C).
2. In a large mixing bowl, toss the sliced zucchini, red bell pepper, and onion with minced garlic and olive oil.
3. Season the pork ribs with salt and black pepper.
4. Place the pork ribs on a baking sheet lined with aluminum foil.
5. Arrange the seasoned vegetables around the pork ribs on the baking sheet.
6. Roast the pork ribs and vegetables in the oven for 40-45 minutes, until the pork is cooked through and the vegetables are tender.
7. Remove from the oven and let cool for a few minutes before serving.

PORK ROLLS WITH WALNUT, PRUNE, AND CHEESE

Nutrition: Cal 475;Fat 34 g; Carb 8 g;Protein 32 g
Serving 2; Cook time 35 min

Ingredients
- 4 thin pork cutlets
- 1/2 cup chopped walnuts
- 1/2 cup chopped pitted prunes
- 1/2 cup shredded cheese (such as Gouda or Cheddar)
- Salt and black pepper to taste
- 2 tablespoons olive oil

Instructions
1. Preheat the oven to 375°F (190°C).
2. Lay the pork cutlets flat on a work surface and sprinkle with salt and black pepper.
3. In a small mixing bowl, mix together the chopped walnuts, prunes, and shredded cheese.
4. Spoon the walnut, prune, and cheese mixture onto the center of each pork cutlet.
5. Roll up the pork cutlets and secure with toothpicks.
6. Heat olive oil in a large skillet over medium-high heat.
7. Brown the pork rolls on all sides in the skillet.
8. Transfer the browned pork rolls to a baking dish and bake in the preheated oven for 20-25 minutes, until the pork is cooked through.

PORK ROLLS WITH BLUE CHEESE AND WALNUT

Nutrition: Cal 515;Fat 42 g; Carb 5 g;Protein 28 g
Serving 2; Cook time 40 min

Ingredients
- 4 thin pork cutlets
- 1/2 cup crumbled blue cheese
- 1/2 cup chopped walnuts
- Salt and black pepper to taste
- 2 tablespoons olive oil
- 1/4 cup heavy cream
- 1/4 cup chicken broth
- 1 tablespoon chopped fresh parsley

Instructions
1. Preheat the oven to 375°F (190°C).
2. Lay the pork cutlets flat on a work surface and sprinkle with salt and black pepper.
3. In a small mixing bowl, mix together the crumbled blue cheese and chopped walnuts.
4. Spoon the blue cheese and walnut mixture onto the center of each pork cutlet.
5. Roll up the pork cutlets and secure with toothpicks.
6. Heat olive oil in a large skillet over medium-high heat.
7. Brown the pork rolls on all sides in the skillet.
8. Transfer the browned pork rolls to a baking dish and bake in the preheated oven for 20-25 minutes, until the pork is cooked through.
9. In the same skillet used to brown the pork rolls, add the heavy cream and chicken broth.

10. Cook over medium heat until the sauce thickens, stirring occasionally.
11. Remove the toothpicks from the pork rolls and serve with the creamy sauce, garnished with chopped fresh parsley.

PORK ROLLS WITH MOZZARELLA

Nutrition: Cal 455;Fat 33 g; Carb 2 g;Protein 33 g
Serving 2; Cook time 45 min

Ingredients
- 4 thin pork cutlets
- 1/2 cup shredded mozzarella cheese
- 1 tablespoon chopped fresh thyme
- Salt and black pepper to taste
- 2 tablespoons olive oil
- 1/4 cup heavy cream
- 1/4 cup chicken broth
- 1 tablespoon Dijon mustard

Instructions
1. Preheat the oven to 375°F (190°C).
2. Lay the pork cutlets flat on a work surface and sprinkle with salt and black pepper.
3. In a small mixing bowl, mix together the shredded mozzarella cheese and chopped thyme.
4. Spoon the cheese and thyme mixture onto the center of each pork cutlet.
5. Roll up the pork cutlets and secure with toothpicks.
6. Heat olive oil in a large skillet over medium-high heat.
7. Brown the pork rolls on all sides in the skillet.
8. Transfer the browned pork rolls to a baking dish and bake in the preheated oven for 20-25 minutes, until the pork is cooked through.
9. In the same skillet used to brown the pork rolls, add the heavy cream and chicken broth.
10. Cook over medium heat until the sauce thickens, stirring occasionally.
11. Whisk in the Dijon mustard and season with salt and black pepper to taste.
12. Remove the toothpicks from the pork rolls and serve with the creamy mustard sauce.

PORK MEATBALLS WITH CREAMY MUSHROOM SAUCE

Nutrition: Cal 521;Fat 43 g; Carb 5 g;Protein 26 g
Serving 2; Cook time 40 min

Ingredients
- 1 pound ground pork
- 1/2 cup almond flour
- 1/4 cup grated Parmesan cheese
- 1 egg
- 1/2 teaspoon garlic powder
- Salt and black pepper to taste
- 2 tablespoons olive oil
- 8 oz mushrooms, sliced
- 1/2 cup heavy cream
- 1/4 cup chicken broth
- 1/4 cup grated Parmesan cheese
- Chopped fresh parsley for garnish

Instructions
1. Preheat the oven to 400°F (200°C).
2. In a large mixing bowl, combine the ground pork, almond flour, grated Parmesan cheese, egg, garlic powder, salt, and black pepper. Mix well.
3. Form the mixture into 1-2 inch meatballs.
4. Heat olive oil in a large skillet over medium-high heat.
5. Brown the meatballs on all sides in the skillet.
6. Transfer the browned meatballs to a baking dish and bake in the preheated oven for 15-20 minutes, until the pork is cooked through.
7. In the same skillet used to brown the meatballs, add the sliced mushrooms and cook until they release their moisture.
8. Add the heavy cream and chicken broth to the skillet and bring to a simmer.
9. Stir in the grated Parmesan cheese and continue to simmer until the sauce thickens.
10. Season with salt and black pepper to taste.
11. Serve the meatballs with the creamy mushroom sauce and garnish with chopped fresh parsley.

PORK MEATBALLS WITH VEGETABLE MARINARA SAUCE

Nutrition: Cal 475;Fat 35 g; Carb 9 g;Protein 30 g
Serving 2; Cook time 35 min

Ingredients
FOR THE PORK MEATBALLS:
- 1 pound ground pork
- 1/4 cup almond flour
- 1 egg
- 2 cloves garlic, minced
- 1 tablespoon fresh parsley, chopped
- 1/2 teaspoon salt
- 1/4 teaspoon black pepper

FOR THE VEGETABLE SAUCE:
- 1/2 onion, chopped
- 1 red bell pepper, chopped
- 2 garlic cloves, minced
- 1 can diced tomatoes (14.5 ounces)
- 1/4 teaspoon dried basil
- 1/4 teaspoon dried oregano
- 1/2 teaspoon salt
- 1/4 teaspoon black pepper

Instructions
1. Preheat the oven to 375°F.
2. In a large bowl, combine the ground pork, almond flour, egg, garlic, parsley, salt, and pepper. Mix well.
3. Shape the mixture into 12-14 meatballs, and place them on a baking sheet lined with parchment paper.
4. Bake the meatballs in the preheated oven for 20-25 minutes or until fully cooked.

5. While the meatballs are cooking, make the vegetable sauce. Heat a large skillet over medium heat, and add the onion, bell pepper, and garlic. Cook for 5-7 minutes or until the vegetables are soft.
6. Add the diced tomatoes, basil, oregano, salt, and pepper to the skillet. Stir well and bring to a simmer.
7. Reduce the heat to low, and let the sauce simmer for 10-15 minutes or until it thickens slightly.
8. Once the meatballs are cooked, add them to the skillet with the vegetable sauce. Gently stir to coat the meatballs with the sauce.
9. Serve the meatballs and sauce hot, garnished with additional chopped fresh parsley if desired.

KETO PORK MEATBALLS WITH BLUE CHEESE SAUCE

Nutrition: Cal 560;Fat 46 g; Carb 3 g;Protein 35 g
Serving 2; Cook time 40 min

Ingredients
FOR THE MEATBALLS:
• 1 lb ground pork
• 1/4 cup almond flour
• 1 large egg
• 1 tsp garlic powder
• 1 tsp onion powder
• 1 tsp dried thyme
• 1/2 tsp salt
• 1/4 tsp black pepper
FOR THE BLUE CHEESE SAUCE:
• 1/2 cup heavy cream
• 2 oz blue cheese, crumbled
• 1 tbsp unsalted butter
• 1 tbsp chopped fresh parsley
• Salt and pepper to taste
Instructions
1. Preheat the oven to 400°F (200°C) and line a baking sheet with parchment paper.
2. In a large bowl, mix together ground pork, almond flour, egg, garlic powder, onion powder, dried thyme, salt, and black pepper until well combined.
3. Use your hands to shape the mixture into 16 meatballs, each about 1 1/2 inches in diameter.
4. Place the meatballs on the prepared baking sheet and bake for 18-20 minutes, until golden brown and cooked through.
5. While the meatballs are baking, prepare the blue cheese sauce. In a small saucepan, heat the heavy cream and butter over medium heat until the butter is melted.
6. Add the crumbled blue cheese to the saucepan and whisk until the cheese is melted and the sauce is smooth. If the sauce is too thick, add a splash of water to thin it out.
7. Season the sauce with salt and pepper to taste, then stir in the chopped parsley.
8. Serve the pork meatballs with the blue cheese sauce on top.

PORK CHOPS WITH CARAMELIZED ONION, TOMATO, MAYONNAISE, AND CHEESE

Nutrition: Cal 570;Fat 39 g; Carb 7 g;Protein 46 g
Serving 2; Cook time 60 min

Ingredients
• 2 bone-in pork chops (6-8 ounces each)
• Salt and black pepper
• 1 tablespoon olive oil
• 1 medium onion, sliced
• 1 medium tomato, sliced
• 2 tablespoons mayonnaise
• 1/4 cup shredded cheddar cheese
Instructions
1. Preheat the oven to 375°F.
2. Season the pork chops with salt and black pepper on both sides.
3. In a large skillet over medium heat, heat the olive oil. Once the oil is hot, add the sliced onions and cook for 10-15 minutes, stirring occasionally, until they are caramelized and soft.
4. While the onions are cooking, place the pork chops in a baking dish. Top each pork chop with sliced tomatoes.
5. Spread 1 tablespoon of mayonnaise on each pork chop, covering the tomatoes.
6. Sprinkle the caramelized onions over the mayonnaise, and then top each pork chop with 2 tablespoons of shredded cheddar cheese.
7. Bake the pork chops in the preheated oven for 25-30 minutes, or until the cheese is melted and bubbly and the pork is cooked through.
8. Serve the pork chops hot, garnished with additional chopped parsley if desired.

KETO PORK MEATBALLS WITH COCONUT SAUCE

Nutrition: Cal 368;Fat 29 g; Carb 2 g;Protein 25 g
Serving 8; Cook time 80 min

Ingredients
FOR THE MEATBALLS:
• 1 lb ground pork
• 1/4 cup almond flour
• 1 large egg
• 1 tsp garlic powder
• 1 tsp onion powder
• 1 tsp ground cumin
• 1/2 tsp salt
• 1/4 tsp black pepper
FOR THE COCONUT SAUCE:
• 1/2 cup coconut milk
• 2 tbsp coconut oil
• 1 tsp grated fresh ginger
• 2 garlic cloves, minced
• 1 tsp red pepper flakes (optional)
• 1 tbsp lime juice

•Salt and pepper to taste

Instructions

1. Preheat the oven to 400°F (200°C) and line a baking sheet with parchment paper.
2. In a large bowl, mix together ground pork, almond flour, egg, garlic powder, onion powder, ground cumin, salt, and black pepper until well combined.
3. Use your hands to shape the mixture into 16 meatballs, each about 1 1/2 inches in diameter.
4. Place the meatballs on the prepared baking sheet and bake for 18-20 minutes, until golden brown and cooked through.
5. While the meatballs are baking, prepare the coconut sauce. In a medium saucepan, heat the coconut oil over medium heat.
6. Add the grated ginger and minced garlic to the saucepan and cook for 1-2 minutes, until fragrant.
7. Add the coconut milk to the saucepan and whisk to combine. Bring the mixture to a simmer.
8. Add the red pepper flakes (if using) and lime juice to the saucepan and stir to combine.
9. Season the sauce with salt and pepper to taste.
10. Serve the pork meatballs with the coconut sauce on top.

BAKED PORK CHOPS WITH PINEAPPLE

Nutrition: Cal 410;Fat 28 g; Carb 6 g;Protein 34 g
Serving 2; Cook time 40 min

Ingredients

•2 bone-in pork chops (about 1 inch thick)
•1/2 cup diced pineapple
•2 tbsp mayonnaise
•1/4 cup shredded cheddar cheese
•Salt and pepper to taste

Instructions

1. Preheat the oven to 375°F (190°C) and line a baking dish with parchment paper.
2. Season the pork chops with salt and pepper on both sides.
3. In a small bowl, mix together the diced pineapple and mayonnaise until well combined.
4. Place the pork chops in the prepared baking dish and spoon the pineapple mixture on top of each chop.
5. Sprinkle the shredded cheddar cheese on top of the pineapple mixture.
6. Bake for 25-30 minutes, until the pork chops are cooked through and the cheese is melted and bubbly.
7. Serve the pork chops hot.

ROASTED PORK LOIN WITH GRAINY MUSTARD SAUCE

Nutrition: Cal 368;Fat 29 g; Carb 2 g;Protein 25 g
Serving 2; Cook time 45 min

Ingredients

•1 (2-pound) boneless pork loin roast
•Sea salt
•Freshly ground black pepper
•3 tablespoons olive oil
•1&½ cups heavy (whipping) cream
•3 tablespoons grainy mustard, such as Pommery

Instructions

1. Preheat the oven to 375°F.
2. Season the pork roast all over with sea salt and pepper.
3. Place a large skillet over medium-high heat and add the olive oil.
4. Brown the roast on all sides in the skillet, about 6 minutes in total, and place the roast in a baking dish.
5. Roast until a meat thermometer inserted in the thickest part of the roast reads 155°F, about 1 hour.
6. When there is approximately 15 minutes of roasting time lef, place a small saucepan over medium heat and add the heavy cream and mustard.
7. Stir the sauce until it simmers, then reduce the heat to low. Simmer the sauce until it is very rich and thick, about 5 minutes. Remove the pan from the heat and set aside.
8. Let the pork rest for 10 minutes before slicing and serve with the sauce.

FISH and SEAFOOD

QUICK & EASY KETO TUNA FISH SALAD

Nutrition: Cal 430;Fat 3 g;Carb 22 g;Protein 18 g
Serving 2; Cook time 15 min

Ingredients
- 2 cups mixed greens
- 1 large tomato, diced
- ¼ cup fresh parsley, chopped
- ¼ cup fresh mint, chopped
- 10 large kalamata olives, pitted
- 1 small zucchini, sliced lengthwise
- ½ avocado, diced
- 1 green onion, sliced
- 1 can chunk light tuna in water, drained
- 1 tablespoon extra-virgin olive oil
- 1 tablespoon balsamic vinegar
- ¼ teaspoon Himalayan or fine sea salt
- ¾ teaspoon freshly cracked black peper

Instructions
1. In a sizzling hot cast iron skillet grill pan, grill the zucchini slices on both sides (or on a very hot grill).
2. Remove from pan and let cool for a few minutes.
3. Slice into bite size pieces.
4. Add all the ingredients in a large mixing bowl and mix until well combined

AIR FRYER SALMON TERIYAKI

Nutrition: Cal 251;Fat 11 g;Carb 5 g;Protein 32 g
Serving 3; Cook time 10 min

Ingredients:
- 1/3+1/4 cup Keto Teriyaki Sauce, see notes
- 16.5 oz. salmon fillets (3 slices at 5.5 oz per fillet), 1.5-inch at thickest
- 1/8 tsp xanthan gum
- Toasted white sesame seeds, sprinkle optional
- 1 bulb scallion, chopped

KETO TERIYAKI SAUCE
- 1 cup coconut aminos, or gluten-free and low sodium tamari.
- 3 tbsp apple cider vinegar
- 3 tsp grated ginger
- 3 tsp grated garlic
- 3 tsp Lakanto golden monk fruit sweetener
- 0.5 tsp xanthan gum

Instructions:
KETO TERIYAKI SAUCE
2. In a small baking tray or casserole dish that's just big enough to fill in all the salmon pieces, pour over ⅓ cup of the teriyaki sauce and marinate the fish skin side up for 15-20 minutes.
3. Line the air fryer basket with a thin layer of parchment paper or an air fryer liner. Slightly drip off the marinade and place the fish, side skin down, in the basket and with some gap between the fillets. Discard the marinade.

4. Air fry at 400F for 7 to 9 minutes. The exact time will depend on the thickness of the fish and your appliance. Mine was done at 7 minutes for medium-rare and 8 minute for medium.
5. To thicken the teriyaki sauce, take ¼ cup of the sauce and add it to a small sauce pot. Bring it to a low simmer. Gradually and slowly sprinkle in 1/8 tsp xanthan gum while whisking at the same time to prevent clumps.
6. Teriyaki homemade sauce in a white and blue cup
7. The fish will be nearly opaque when cut into, at 120F (49C) at the thickest part. You can peek into the thickest part with a sharp knife or fork. It should flake easily, but still has a little translucency in the center.
8. Transfer the fishes to a plater. Glaze the salmon with teriyaki sauce. Sprinkle with toasted sesame seeds, if using, and scallions. Remove the skin before serving. I recommend serving them warm.

SALMON AND CREAM CHEESE SUSHI ROLLS

Nutrition: Cal 330;Fat 20 g;Carb 9 g;Protein 30 g
Serving 2; Cook time 15 min

Ingredients
- 4 sheets of nori seaweed
- 1/2 lb fresh salmon, sliced
- 4 oz cream cheese, softened
- 1 small cucumber, sliced into thin strips
- 2 tbsp rice vinegar
- 1 tsp Swerve (or other keto-friendly sweetener)
- 1 tsp salt
- Wasabi and soy sauce (optional)

Instructions
1. In a small bowl, mix the rice vinegar, Swerve, and salt together until the sweetener and salt are dissolved.
2. Lay a sheet of nori seaweed on a sushi mat or a piece of plastic wrap.
3. Spread a thin layer of cream cheese over the nori, leaving a 1-inch border at the top.
4. Place a layer of sliced salmon on top of the cream cheese.
5. Add a layer of sliced cucumber on top of the salmon.
6. Roll the sushi tightly, using the sushi mat or plastic wrap to help you. Repeat with the remaining nori sheets and ingredients.
7. Slice the sushi rolls into bite-sized pieces with a sharp knife.
8. Serve the sushi with optional wasabi and soy sauce.

SALMON AND CAULIFLOWER RICE SUSHI ROLLS

Nutrition: Cal 470;Fat 33 g;Carb 15 g;Protein 32 g
Serving 2; Cook time 25 min

Ingredients
- 2 sheets of nori seaweed
- 1/2 lb fresh salmon, sliced
- 4 oz cream cheese, softened

- 1 cup cauliflower rice, cooked
- 1 small cucumber, sliced into thin strips
- 1 small avocado, sliced
- 2 tbsp rice vinegar
- 1 tsp Swerve (or other keto-friendly sweetener)
- 1 tsp salt
- Wasabi and soy sauce (optional)

Instructions
1. In a small bowl, mix the rice vinegar, Swerve, and salt together until the sweetener and salt are dissolved.
2. Lay a sheet of nori seaweed on a flat surface.
3. Spread a thin layer of cream cheese over the nori, leaving a 1-inch border at the top.
4. Place a layer of sliced salmon on top of the cream cheese.
5. Add a layer of cooked cauliflower rice on top of the salmon.
6. Add a layer of sliced cucumber and avocado on top of the cauliflower rice.
7. Roll the nori tightly, using a little water to seal the edges. Repeat with the remaining nori sheet and ingredients.
8. Slice the nori rolls into bite-sized pieces with a sharp knife.
9. Serve the nori envelopes with optional wasabi and soy sauce.

KETO CRISPY SKIN SALMON IN WHITE WINE SAUCE
Nutrition: Cal 374;Fat 15 g;Carb 2 g;Protein 48 g
Serving 2; Cook time 25 min

Ingredients:
- 1 pound of Wild salmon fillets
- 2 tablespoons of butter
- 2 tablespoons of avocado oil
- salt to taste
- juice from a lemon

For sauce:
- 1/2 cup of white wine
- 1/2 teaspoon of garlic crushed
- juice from a quarter of a lemon
- dash of white pepper
- 1/8 teaspoon of salt
- 1/4 cup of heavy whipping cream
- 2 tablespoons of butter
- 2 teaspoons of capers

Instructions:
1. First dry your salmon with paper towels so that it won't stick to the pan.
2. Heat oil and butter in a skillet over a medium-high heat.
3. Glaze the skin with a little oil, as well, and rub it in. Then season the skin with some salt, too.
4. When butter and oil start to sizzle, add salmon, skin side down. Press with your spatula so that the skin will cook evenly.
5. Now you can season your salmon with salt and squeeze some lemon juice on top too.
6. Cook for 3 minutes.

7. Then flip and sear the top for 2 minutes more. If your salmon is thick, it may need another minute.
8. Transfer salmon to a plate and set aside.

FOR SAUCE:
1. Wipe the pan clean and make your sauce in the same pan.
2. First bring your wine to a simmer and reduce by half the volume. This will take about five minutes. Then add garlic, salt, pepper, and a squeeze of lemon juice.
3. Whisk in cream and add the cold butter, one tablespoon at a time. As soon as all the butter is whisked in, stir in your capers and turn off the flame.
4. Spoon sauce onto each plate and place salmon skin side up on top of the sauce. Serve and enjoy.

ALASKAN SALMON WITH BUTTER CREAM SAUCE AND AVOCADO
Nutrition: Cal 490;Fat 31 g;Carb 12 g;Protein 31 g
Serving 2; Cook time 20 min

Ingredients:
- 1 tablespoons butter
- 2 tablespoons shallot, finely chopped
- ¼ cup dry white wine
- ¼ cup heavy whipping cream
- 1 avocado, cube
- Pinch of salt
- Pinch of pepper

Instructions:
1. Melt butter in a sauce pan over medium heat. Stir in shallot and let it cook for a minute.
2. Add white wine and let it simmer for couple minutes.
3. Add cream and continue stirring to incorporate the butter and cream. Turn off the heat.
4. Add avocado and season the sauce with salt and pepper. Set aside to keep warm until ready to serve

SALMON AND BROCCOLI WITH CREAM SAUCE AND RED CAVIAR
Nutrition: Cal 570;Fat 44 g;Carb 10 g;Protein 35 g
Serving 2; Cook time 20 min

Ingredients:
- 2 salmon fillets
- 1 head of broccoli, cut into florets
- 1/2 cup heavy cream
- 1/4 cup red caviar
- 2 tbsp olive oil
- Salt and pepper to taste

Instructions:
1. Preheat the oven to 400°F.
2. Season the salmon fillets with salt and pepper.
3. In a large skillet over medium-high heat, heat the olive oil. Add the salmon fillets to the skillet and cook for 2-3 minutes on each side, until browned.
4. Transfer the salmon fillets to a baking dish and bake for 10-12 minutes, until the salmon is cooked through.
5. Meanwhile, steam the broccoli florets until tender.

6. In a small saucepan over low heat, heat the heavy cream until it starts to simmer. Let it simmer for 2-3 minutes, until it thickens slightly.
7. To serve, divide the broccoli between two plates. Place a salmon fillet on top of each plate of broccoli. Drizzle the cream sauce over the salmon and top each fillet with a spoonful of red caviar.

GRILLED SALMON WITH PESTO AND ROASTED ASPARAGUS

Nutrition: Cal 447;Fat 31 g;Carb 7 g;Protein 36 g
Serving 2; Cook time 20 min

Ingredients:
- 2 salmon fillets (about 6 oz. each)
- 2 tbsp. of pesto
- 12 asparagus spears
- 2 tbsp. of olive oil
- Salt and pepper to taste

Instructions:
1. Preheat your oven to 400°F (200°C).
2. Rinse the asparagus and pat them dry. Place them on a baking sheet lined with parchment paper. Drizzle with olive oil and season with salt and pepper. Roast in the oven for 15-20 minutes, or until tender.
3. While the asparagus is roasting, heat up a grill pan over medium-high heat. Brush the salmon fillets with olive oil and season them with salt and pepper.
4. Place the salmon fillets on the grill pan, skin side down. Grill for 3-4 minutes on each side, or until cooked to your desired level of doneness.
5. Once the salmon is cooked, remove it from the heat and spread a tablespoon of pesto over each fillet.
6. Serve the salmon fillets with the roasted asparagus on the side.

KETO ASIAN GLAZED SALMON

Nutrition: Cal 220;Fat 35 g;Carb 8 g;Protein 38 g
Serving 6; Cook time 23 min

Ingredients:
- 6 pieces of fresh salmon, about 2" wide/4 ounce
- ½ cup Brown Swerve
- ½ cup Liquid Aminos
- 1 teaspoon Sambal, plain or garlic
- 2 tablespoons rice vinegar
- 2 teaspoons toasted sesame oil
- 2 teaspoons fresh ginger, grated
- 1 teaspoon fresh garlic, grated
- Juice of ½ lime

Instructions:
1. Preheat oven to 400F.
2. Mix all the ingredients in a cup and into a small saucepan over medium heat. Simmer until reduced by by about a third. It should be on the thick and sticky side.

3. Place the salmon (skin side down) on a wire baking rack sprayed with nonstick spray and lined with foil to make cleanup much easier! Brush the salmon with the glaze on all sides and bake for 10 minutes.
4. Remove the salmon from the oven and increase the temperature to 450F. Brush some more of the glaze over the tops and bake for another 3-5 minutes on the top rack of your oven. Watch it closely, to make sure it doesn't burn!

BACON-WRAPPED SALMON WITH SPINACH SALAD

Nutrition: Cal 505;Fat 38 g;Carb 3 g;Protein 35 g
Serving 2; Cook time 30 min

Ingredients:
- 2 salmon fillets (about 6 oz. each)
- 4 slices of bacon
- 2 cups of fresh spinach
- 2 tbsp. of olive oil
- 2 tbsp. of balsamic vinegar
- Salt and pepper to taste

Instructions:
1. Preheat your oven to 400°F (200°C).
2. Rinse the spinach and pat it dry. Place it in a large mixing bowl.
3. In a small bowl, whisk together the olive oil and balsamic vinegar to make a dressing. Pour the dressing over the spinach and toss to combine.
4. Wrap 2 slices of bacon around each salmon fillet, securing them with toothpicks if necessary.
5. Place the bacon-wrapped salmon fillets on a baking sheet lined with parchment paper. Season with salt and pepper.
6. Bake in the oven for 15-20 minutes, or until the salmon is cooked to your desired level of doneness.
7. Serve the salmon fillets on top of the spinach salad.

SMOKED SALMON AND ASPARAGUS FRITTATA

Nutrition: Cal 385;Fat 29 g;Carb 4 g;Protein 25 g
Serving 2; Cook time 25 min

Ingredients:
- 4 slices of bacon
- 12 asparagus spears, trimmed and cut into bite-sized pieces
- 4 oz. of smoked salmon, chopped
- 4 eggs
- 1/4 cup of heavy cream
- Salt and pepper to taste
- 1 tbsp. of olive oil

Instructions:
1. Preheat your oven to 350°F (180°C).
2. In a large oven-safe skillet, cook the bacon over medium heat until crisp. Remove the bacon from the skillet and set it aside.

3. Add the asparagus to the skillet and cook for 3-4 minutes, or until tender. Remove the asparagus from the skillet and set it aside with the bacon.
4. In a mixing bowl, whisk together the eggs, heavy cream, salt, and pepper.
5. Add the olive oil to the skillet and heat it over medium-high heat. Once the skillet is hot, pour the egg mixture into the skillet and stir gently to distribute the ingredients.
6. Add the cooked bacon, asparagus, and smoked salmon to the skillet, distributing them evenly over the egg mixture.
7. Transfer the skillet to the preheated oven and bake for 10-15 minutes, or until the frittata is cooked through and golden brown on top.
8. Remove the skillet from the oven and let it cool for a few minutes before slicing and serving.

PARMESAN CRUSTED FLOUNDER FISH

Nutrition: Cal 550;Fat 35 g;Carb 8 g;Protein 38 g
Serving 2; Cook time 10 min

Ingredients:
- 1 lb wild-caught Flounder Fish thawed if using frozen
- 2 tablespoon Blanched Almond Flour
- 2 tablespoon finely grated Parmesan Cheese the powdered kind
- ⅛ teaspoon garlic powder
- ⅛ teaspoon onion powder
- 2 tablespoon Mayonnaise
- ¼ teaspoon salt
- ⅛ teaspoon black pepper

Instructions:
1. Preheat Oven to 400°F (200°C), and grease a baking sheet.
2. In a mixing bowl combine: almond flour, parmesan cheese, garlic powder & onion powder. Set aside.
3. Making the parmesan coating.
4. Rinse fish fillets and pat dry with a paper towel. Salt and pepper on both sides of the fish fillets and place on the prepared baking sheet.
5. Brush the top side of each fish fillet with mayonnaise.
6. Sprinkle the parmesan mixture over the top of each fish fillet.
7. Sprinkle with coating.
8. Bake for 15 mins or until fish is done and coating has started to turn golden brown. If the coating is not browning then broil on low for a minute or two if needed.
9. Remove from oven & serve

SIMPLE TUNA SALAD ON LETTUCE

Nutrition: Cal 550;Fat 35 g;Carb 8 g;Protein 38 g
Serving 2; Cook time 10 min

Ingredients:
- ¼ cup mayonnaise
- 1 tablespoon fresh lemon juice

- 1 tablespoon pickle relish
- 2 (6-ounce) cans tuna in oil, drained and flaked
- ½ cup cherry tomatoes, halved
- ¼ cup diced cucumber
- Salt and pepper
- 4 cups chopped romaine lettuce

Instructions:
1. Whisk together the mayonnaise, lemon juice, and relish in a bowl.
2. Toss in the flaked tuna, tomatoes, and cucumber – season with salt and pepper.
3. Spoon over chopped lettuce to serve.

FRIED TUNA AVOCADO BALLS

Nutrition: Cal 455;Fat 38 g;Carb 8 g;Protein 23 g
Serving 4; Cook time 20 min

Ingredients:
- ¼ cup canned coconut milk
- 1 teaspoon onion powder
- 1 clove garlic, minced
- Salt and pepper
- 10 ounces canned tuna, drained
- 1 medium avocado, diced finely
- ½ cup almond flour
- ¼ cup olive oil

Instructions:
1. Whisk together the coconut milk, onion powder, garlic, salt and pepper in a bowl.
2. Flake the tuna into the bowl and stir in the avocado.
3. Divide the mixture into 10 to 12 balls and roll in the almond flour.
4. Heat the oil in a large skillet over medium-high heat.
5. Add the tuna avocado balls and fry until golden brown then drain on paper towels.

CREAMY SMOKED SALMON ZUCCHINI SPAGHETTI

Nutrition: Cal 327;Fat 24 g;Carb 8 g;Protein 20 g
Serving 2; Cook time 20 min

Ingredients:
- 8 oz. zucchini spaghetti
- 4 oz. smoked salmon, chopped
- 1/4 cup heavy cream
- 1/4 cup shredded Parmesan cheese
- 1 tbsp. olive oil
- Salt and pepper to taste

Instructions:
1. Heat the olive oil in a large skillet over medium-high heat.
2. Add the zucchini spaghetti to the skillet and cook for 2-3 minutes or until it starts to soften.
3. Add the chopped smoked salmon to the skillet and cook for an additional 1-2 minutes.
4. Pour the heavy cream over the zucchini and salmon mixture and bring to a simmer.

5. Reduce the heat to low and let the mixture simmer for 3-4 minutes or until the sauce has thickened slightly.
6. Stir in the shredded Parmesan cheese and cook until the cheese has melted and the sauce is creamy.
7. Season with salt and pepper to taste.
8. Divide the mixture into two bowls and serve hot.

THAI COCONUT SHRIMP SOUP
Nutrition: Cal 375;Fat 29 g; Carb 13 g;Protein 18 g
Serving 4; Cook time 40 min

Ingredients:
- 1 tablespoon coconut oil
- 1 small yellow onion, diced
- 4 cups chicken broth
- 1 (14-ounce) can coconut milk
- 1 cup fresh chopped cilantro
- 1 jalapeno, seeded and chopped
- 1 tablespoon grated ginger
- 2 cloves garlic, minced
- 1 lime, zested and juiced
- 6 ounces uncooked shrimp, peeled and deveined
- 1 cup sliced mushrooms
- 1 small red onion, sliced thinly
- 1 tablespoon fish sauce

Instructions:
1. Heat the coconut oil in a saucepan over medium heat.
2. Add the yellow onions and sauté until translucent, about 6 to 7 minutes.
3. Stir in the chicken broth, coconut milk, cilantro, and jalapeno.
4. Add the ginger, garlic, and lime zest then bring to boil.
5. Reduce heat and simmer for 20 minutes - strain the mixture and discard the solids.
6. Return the remaining liquid to the saucepan and add the shrimp, mushrooms, and red onion.
7. Stir in the lime juice and fish sauce then simmer for 10 minutes. Serve hot.

SHRIMP AVOCADO SALAD
Nutrition: Cal 340;Fat 33 g; Carb 12 g;Protein 24 g
Serving 2; Cook time 10 min

Ingredients
- 8 ounces shrimp peeled, deveined, patted dry
- 1 large avocado, diced
- 1 small beefsteak tomato, diced and drained
- 1/3 cup crumbled feta cheese
- 1/3 cup freshly chopped cilantro or parsley
- 2 tablespoons salted butter, melted
- 1 tablespoon lemon juice
- 1 tablespoon olive oil
- 1/4 teaspoon salt
- 1/4 teaspoon black pepper

Instructions

1. Toss shrimp with melted butter in a bowl until well-coated.
2. Heat a pan over medium-high heat for a few minutes until hot. Add shrimp to the pan in a single layer, searing for a minute or until it starts to become pink around the edges, then flip and cook until shrimp are cooked through, less than a minute.
3. Transfer the shrimp to a plate as they finish cooking. Let them cool while you prepare the other ingredients.
4. Add all other ingredients to a large mixing bowl -- diced avocado, diced tomato, feta cheese, cilantro, lemon juice, olive oil, salt, and pepper -- and toss to mix.
5. Add shrimp and stir to mix together. Add additional salt and pepper, to taste.

CAPRESE TUNA SALAD STUFFED TOMATOES
Nutrition: Cal 196;Fat 5 g; Carb 5 g;Protein 30 g
Serving 2; Cook time 10 min

Ingredients
- 1 medium tomato
- 1 (5 ounce) can tuna, very well drained
- 2 teaspoons balsamic vinegar
- 1 tablespoon chopped mozzarella (1/4 ounce)
- 1 tablespoon chopped fresh basil
- 1 tablespoon chopped green onion

Instructions
1. Cut the top 1/4-inch off the tomato. Use a spoon to scoop out the insides of the tomato. Set aside while you make the tuna salad.
2. Stir together the drained tuna, balsamic vinegar, mozzarella, basil, and green onion. Put the tuna salad in the hollowed out tomato, and enjoy!

SPICY KIMCHI AHI POKE
Nutrition: Cal 300;Fat 18 g; Carb 5 g;Protein 5 g
Serving 4; Cook time 10 min

Ingredients
- 1 lb sushi-grade ahi tuna, diced to roughly 1 inch
- 1 tablespoon soy sauce (or coconut aminos for paleo)
- 1/2 teaspoon sesame oil
- 1/4 cup mayo
- 2 tablespoons Sriracha
- 1 ripe avocado, diced
- 1/2 cup kimchi
- Chopped green onion
- Sesame seeds

Instructions
1. In a medium mixing bowl, add diced tuna.
2. Add soy sauce, sesame oil, mayo, Sriracha to the bowl and toss to combine.
3. Add diced avocado and kimchi to the bowl and gently combine.
4. Serve on top of salad greens, cauli rice, or traditional rice and top with a sprinkle of chopped green onion and sesame seeds if desired.

PROSCIUTTO BLACKBERRY SHRIMP

Nutrition: Cal 220;Fat 11 g; Carb 6 g;Protein 21 g
Serving 2; Cook time 20 min

Ingredients
- 10 Oz Pre-Cooked Shrimp
- 11 Slices Prosciutto
- 1/3 cup Blackberries, Ground
- 1/3 cup Red Wine
- 2 tbsp. Olive Oil
- 1 tbsp. Mint Leaves, Chopped
- 1-2 Tbsp. Erythritol (to taste)

Instructions
1. Preheat oven to 425 degrees.
2. Slice each piece of prosciutto in half depending on size of shrimp.
3. Wrap prosciutto around shrimp starting from tale up.
4. Place on baking sheet and drizzle with olive oil.
5. Bake for 15 minutes.
6. In a pan, add ground blackberries, mint leaves and erythritol.
7. Cook for 2-3 minutes.
8. Mix in red wine and reduce while shrimp cooks.
9. Strain if desired.

SPICY SHRIMP TACO LETTUCE WRAPS

Nutrition: Cal 186;Fat 17 g; Carb 8 g;Protein 2 g
Serving 4; Cook time 20 min

Ingredients
- 20 medium shrimp peeled and deveined (about 1 pound)
- 1 tablespoon oil of choice
- 1 clove garlic minced
- 1/2 teaspoon
- 1/2 teaspoon ground cumin
- 1/4 teaspoon kosher salt
- 1 tablespoon olive oil
- squeeze of lime optional

AVOCADO SALSA
- 1 avocado cut into chunks
- 1 tomato, chopped
- 1/4 cup loosely packed fresh cilantro leaves coarsely chopped
- 1 tablespoon fresh lime juice from half a lime
- 1/2 teaspoon salt
- 1/4 teaspoon black pepper

CILANTRO SAUCE
- 1/4 cup sour cream
- 1/4 cup cilantro
- 1 clove garlic
- 1 tablespoon fresh lime juice
- salt and pepper, to taste
- 8-12 lettuce leaves

Instructions
TO COOK THE SHRIMP

1. In a medium bowl whisk together olive oil, garlic, cumin, chili, and salt. Add shrimp and mix until shrimp is covered in seasoning. Heat a large heavy-duty or cast iron skillet on high heat for 2 minutes. Add the olive oil and shrimp. Cook 2-3 minutes per side or until shrimp is cooked through. Turn off heat and finish with a squeeze of lime (optional).

TO MAKE AVOCADO TOMATO SALSA
2. In a medium bowl, gently combine tomato, avocado, cilantro, lime juice and a sprinkle of salt and pepper and mixed through. Set aside.

TO MAKE THE JALAPENO CILANTRO SAUCE
3. Add the sour cream, jalapeno, garlic, cilantro, lime and salt and pepper to a food processor. Blend for 30 seconds or until creamy.

TO ASSEMBLE:
Plac two romaine or butter lettuce leaves on top of each-other for each lettuce wraps. Top with 4-5 pieces of shrimp, a few tablespoons of avocado salsa and a genros drizzle of the spicy jalapeno cilantro sauce. Enjoy hot or cold!

KETO SHRIMP THAI SALAD

Nutrition: Cal 380 ;Fat 9 g; Carb 14 g;Protein 25 g
Serving 4 Cook time 15 min

Ingredients
- 6 Tablespoon extra-virgin olive oil, divided
- 2 Tablespoon. soy sauce
- 1 teaspoon fish sauce
- 1 teaspoon sambal oelek
- 1 Tablespoon brown sugar
- 3 Tablespoon lime juice
- 1 Tablespoon minced red pepper
- 1/2 pound shrimp, peeled and deveined
- 1 cup sugar snap peas, blanched and cooled in an ice bath
- 2 bundles vermicelli noodles, boiled and rinsed under cool water (you can use the same water you boiled the snap peas in)
- 4 cups shredded romaine lettuce
- 1/2 cup cherry tomatoes, halved
- 1/2 cup thinly sliced sweet peppers
- cilantro, mint leaves and crushed peanuts for garnish
- coarse salt and freshly ground peanuts to taste

Instructions
1. In a medium bowl, beat together 4 tablespoons of oil, soy sauce, fish sauce, sambal oelek, sugar, lime juice and the minced red pepper.
2. Heat the remaining oil in a large skillet over medium-high.
3. Add the shrimp, season with salt and pepper and sear on one side for 2 minutes.
4. Flip and sear another minute.
5. Salad Assembly:
6. In 2 bowls add romaine lettuce

7. Add some vermicelli noodles, the snow peas, peppers, tomatoes, shrimp, cilantro, mint, and some good crushed peanuts.
8. Shake up (or whisk) your dressing and then drizzle it over the salads.

SHRIMP AND NORI ROLLS

Nutrition: Cal 340 ;Fat 12 g; Carb 8 g;Protein 25 g
Serving 1 Cook time 10 min

Ingredients
- 1 cup shrimp
- 1 tbsp. Mayonnaise
- 1 thinly sliced green onion
- 2 sheets Nori
- ¼ cucumber diced and seeded
- 1 tbsp. toasted Sesame seeds

Instructions
1. Wash and drain shrimp.
2. Add together shrimp with Mayonnaise and green onions.
3. Place Nori on flat surface and spoon on the shrimp and green onion mixture.
4. Dust with cucumber and sesame seeds.
Roll tightly and cut into bite size pieces.

CRISPY FISH STICKS WITH CAPER DILL SAUCE

Nutrition: Cal 360 ;Fat 14 g; Carb 12 g;Protein 25 g
Serving 1 Cook time 30 min

Ingredients
- 1 lb. white fish fillets
- 1 cup grated parmesan
- 1 cup almond meal/flour
- 1/4 tsp. chili powder
- 1/2 tsp. dried parsley
- 1/4 tsp. salt
- pinch of pepper
- 2 tbsp. mayo
- 1 egg
- coconut oil for frying

CAPER DILL TARTAR SAUCE
- 1/2 cup mayo
- 1/2 cup sour cream
- 1 1/2 tbsp. capers (including the caper juice)
- 2 medium dill/garlic pickles, diced
- 2 tbsp. chopped fresh dill
- 2 tsp. lemon juice

Instructions
1. Combine the dry ingredients, put in shallow dish and set aside.
2. Whisk together the egg and mayo.
3. Prepare tartar sauce by combining all ingredients cover and refrigerate until the fish is ready.
4. Cut the fillets to desired size. Dip the fish into the egg mixture and dredge in the breading mixture.

5. Heat 1/2-inch oil in a medium skillet and drop 2 fish sticks at a time for consistent cooking.
6. Cook for 1-2 minutes on each side, until golden.
7. Remove and drain on paper-towel.
Serve with tartar sauce.

CREAMY SHRIMP AND MUSHROOM SKILLET

Nutrition: Cal 400 ;Fat 12 g; Carb 6 g;Protein 20 g
Serving 2 Cook time 15 min

Ingredients
- 4 slices organic uncured bacon
- 1 cup sliced mushrooms
- 4 oz. smoked salmon
- 4 oz. raw shelled shrimp (I used TJ's Argentinian wild)
- ½ cup heavy whipping cream OR coconut cream for a dairy free option
- 1 pinch Celtic Sea Salt
- freshly ground black pepper

Instructions
1. Cut the bacon in 1 inch pieces and cook over medium heat.
2. Add sliced mushrooms and cook for 5 minutes.
3. Add strips of smoked salmon and cook for 2 to 3 minutes.
4. Add the shrimp and sauté on a high for 2 minutes.
5. Stir in cream and salt.
6. Lower heat and let cook for 1 minute until thick and creamy.

BUTTERED COD IN SKILLET

Nutrition: cal 294;fat 18 g; carb 2 g;protein 30 g
Serving 4; cook time 15 min

Ingredients
- 1 1/2 lbs cod fillets
- 6 tablespoons unsalted butter, sliced

SEASONING
- ¼ teaspoon garlic powder
- ½ teaspoon table salt
- ¼ teaspoon ground pepper
- ¾ teaspoon ground paprika
- Few lemon slices
- Herbs, parsley, or cilantro

Instructions
1. Stir together ingredients for seasoning in a small bowl.
2. Cut cod into smaller pieces, if desired. Season all sides of the cod with the seasoning.
3. Heat 2 tablespoons butter in a large skillet over medium-high heat. Once butter melts, add cod to skillet. Cook 2 minutes.
4. Turn heat down to medium. Turn cod over, top with remaining butter and cook another 3-4 minutes.
5. Butter will completely melt and the fish will cook. (Don't overcook the cod, it will become mushy and completely fall apart.)

6. Drizzle cod with fresh lemon juice. Top with fresh herbs, if desired. Serve immediately.

AVOCADO LIME SALMON

Nutrition: cal 570;fat 44 g; carb 12 g;protein 26 g
Serving 16; cook time 20 min

Ingredients
- 100 grams chopped cauliflower
- 1 large avocado
- 1 tablespoon fresh lime juice
- 2 tablespoons diced red onion
- 2 tablespoons olive oil
- 2 (6-ounce) boneless salmon fillets
- Salt and pepper

Instructions
1. Melt your butter in a pan and fry 2-3 eggs until the whites are set and yolk is to desired doneness. Season Place the cauliflower in a food processor and pulse into rice-like grains.
2. Grease a skillet with cooking spray and heat over medium heat.
3. Add the cauliflower rice and cook, covered, for 8 minutes until tender. Set aside.
4. Combine the avocado, lime juice, and red onion in a food processor and blend smooth.
5. Heat the oil in a large skillet over medium-high heat.
6. Season the salmon with salt and pepper, then add to the skillet skin-side down.
7. Cook for 4 to 5 minutes until seared, then flip and cook for another 4 to 5 minutes.
8. Serve the salmon over a bed of cauliflower rice topped with the avocado cream.

BROCCOLI AND SHRIMP SAUTÉED IN BUTTER

Nutrition: Cal 277;Fat 14 g; Carb 5 g;Protein 30 g
Serving 2; Cook time 15 min

Ingredients
- 1 cup broccoli, cut into small pieces
- 1 clove garlic, crushed
- 300 g shrimp, cleaned
- 2 tbsp butter
- 1 tsp lemon juice
- Salt, to taste

Instructions
1. Chop the broccoli into small portions or whichever size you prefer, but smaller pieces cook faster.
2. Melt the butter in a preheated pan. Gently toss in the chopped broccoli and crushed garlic when the butter becomes hot (but not smoking). Stir to cook.
3. Leave over the heat for 3-4 minutes. Stir from time to time.
4. Clean the shrimp before adding them to the pan. Let it cook for around 3-4 minutes.

5. Once the shrimp turns pink and opaque, drizzle the lemon juice all over.

KETO CALAMARI

Nutrition: Cal 286;Fat 15 g; Carb 11 g;Protein 22 g
Serving 4; Cook time 30 min

Ingredients
- 1 lb fresh squid cleaned
- 1 egg beaten
- 1/2 cup coconut flour
- 1 teaspoon salt
- 1 teaspoon paprika
- 1/2 teaspoon garlic powder
- 1/2 teaspoon onion powder
- Coconut oil for frying (about 1/4 cup)
- Minced cilantro optional
- Sliced Fresno chili optional
- Squeeze of lime optional
- Harissa Mayo
- 1/4 cup mayonnaise
- 1 tablespoon prepared hariss

Instructions
1. In a small bowl beat the egg. In another bowl combine the coconut flour and spices.
2. Pat the squid dry and dip into the beaten egg then dredge through the flour mixture.
3. Heat the oil in a 10" or larger cast-iron skillet over medium-high heat.
4. Frying in batches making sure to not overcrowd the skillet, fry 2 minutes per side until golden and crisp. Drain on paper towels
5. Either serve as is or toss with cilantro, chilis, and lime and serve with the harissa mayo

CALAMARI STUFFED WITH PANCETTA AND VEGETABLES

Nutrition: Cal 456;Fat 35 g; Carb 10 g;Protein 24 g
Serving 4; Cook time 20 min

Ingredients
- 500 g (8 large or 12 16 smaller) squid cleaned
- 82 g (1/2 cup) keto bun center only diced into very small pieces
- Stuffing
- 70 g (3 oz) pancetta or pork belly chopped into very small pieces
- 42 g (3 tbsp) of olive oil for grilling
- 68 g (5 tbsp) olive oil for stuffing
- 40 g (1/4 cup) carrots grated
- 8 g (1 tbsp) garlic grated
- 80 g (3/4 cup) celery diced into very small pieces
- 100 g (1 cup, or one bulb) fennel bulb diced into very small pieces
- 1/2 g (1/2 tsp) thyme powder
- 1-2 bunches fresh rosemary
- 6 g (1 tsp) salt

- 2 g (1 tsp) black pepper
- 14 g (1 tbsp) olive oil drizzling over prepared stuffed squid
- 15 g (1 tbsp) lemon juice freshly squeezed

Instructions

1. Clean your squid or purchase cleaned squid with tentacles. Rinse under cold running water and set aside
2. Prepare and weigh your vegetables: grate the carrots, onion and garlic. Chop the celery and fennel bulb into very small pieces
3. Cut the pancetta or pork belly and the squid arms into thin strips and then chop into very small pieces
4. Heat a grilling pan and add 3 tbsp of olive oil. When oil is sizzling add the pancetta/pork belly and squid arms, carrots, celery, fennel, onion and garlic. Place the fresh bunch of rosemary into the pan. Season with salt. Stir and cook on low heat until the vegetables are translucent, and the pancetta/pork belly is done (but not crispy). Remove the rosemary and discard
5. When stuffing is done, place into a mixing bowl and add 2 tbsp of olive oil and the pepper. Toss to combine
6. Use a teaspoon to insert the stuffing into each squid. Quantity of stuffing needed per squid will depend on the size of your squid. Do not overstuff as the squid will shrink as it cooks. Use a toothpick to seal the opening
7. Heat up the grill pan, and add the olive oil. Reduce heat to low and lay your stuffed squid perpendicular to the grill ridges. Cook for 5-6 minutes on the first side then flip and cook 5-6 minutes on the other side. Remove from heat and place on a platter
8. Finish by drizzling the tablespoon of fresh lemon juice on top and then the tablespoon of olive oil. Garnish with the fennel leaves and a wedge of lemon.

LOW CARB ALMOND CRUSTED COD

Nutrition: Cal 219;Fat 13 g; Carb 4 g;Protein 22 g
Serving 4; Cook time 25 min

Ingredients

- 1 4 filets cod or other white fish
- 1 med lemon zested and juiced
- 1/2 cup crushed almonds can use a food processor or blender to crush
- 1 Tbsp dill either fresh
- 1 Tbsp olive oil
- salt & pepper to taste
- 1 tsp mild to med. chili spice optional
- 4 tsp Dijon mustard more if you like mustard

Instructions

1. Preheat oven to 400 degrees F. Prepare a baking sheet with either parchment paper laid on top or spray with cooking spray
2. Place cod filets on paper towels to drain of water and pat dry. Place on baking sheet.
3. In a small bowl, combine the lemon zest, lemon juice, crushed almonds, dill, oil, salt and pepper and chili spice if using.

4. Spread each cod filet with a tsp or so of Dijon mustard,smoothing it over the entire top of the filet. Divide the almond mixture among the 4 filets, pressing it evely into the mustard with your hands.
5. Bake the fish until opaue at the thickest part, about 7 minutes for most.cod filets (less time for thin filets).
6. Serve with a green vegetable and lemon slices for a great low carb or keto fish dinner.

MEXICAN FISH STEW

Nutrition: Cal 196;Fat 7 g; Carb 8 g;Protein 19 g
Serving 6; Cook time 30 min

Ingredients

- 2 Tbsp olive oil
- 1 med onion chopped
- 1 large carrot sliced thinly
- 3 med celery stalks sliced thinly
- 3-6 cloves garlic smashed or minced
- 1 tsp smoky pepper blend
- 1/2 tsp dried thyme
- 1 cup white wine
- 4 cups chicken broth
- 1/2 cup chopped cilantro
- 2 14 oz cans Rotel diced tomatoes
- 1/2 tsp salt
- 3 leaves bay
- 6 oz scallops
- 7 oz walleye, coarsely chopped
- 1 lb mussels
- 3 oz white fish, coarsely chopped
- 2 med limes, cut into wedges optional
- 1 med lemon, sliced for garnish

Instructions

1. Heat oil over med-high heat in a dutch oven or large pot. Saute onion, carrot and celery in oil for 3-5 minutes until translucent. Add smashed garlic and cook for 1 more minute
2. Add spices and stir in to the onion mixture to coat. Add wine, broth, cilantro, and tomatoes to pot and simmer together for 15-20 minutes over medium heat. Add salt to taste.
3. Add all fish to the pot and cook, covered for about 5 minutes or until mussels open and white fish is opaque.
4. Add sliced lemons to the pot and serve.
5. Optional: serve with lime wedges that people can squeeze into the soup.

CREAMY KETO FISH CASSEROLE

Nutrition: Cal 221;Fat 15 g; Carb 9 g;Protein 27 g
Serving 4; Cook time 30 min

Ingredients

- 1 tbsp butter, for greasing baking dish
- 3 tbsp olive oil
- 1 lb broccoli, small florets
- 1 tsp salt

- •½ tsp ground black pepper
- •4 oz. (1¼ cups) scallions, finely chopped
- •2 tbsp small capers (non-pareils)
- •1½ lbs white fish (see tip), cut into serving-sized pieces
- •1 tbsp dried parsley
- •1¼ cups heavy whipping cream
- •1 tbsp Dijon mustard
- •3 oz. butter, cut into thin, equal slices

Instructions

1. Preheat oven to 400°F (200°C). Grease a 13" x 9" (33 x 23 cm) baking dish, set aside.
2. Heat the oil in a large frying pan, over medium-high heat. Add the broccoli, and stir-fry for 5 minutes, or until lightly browned and tender. Season with salt and pepper.
3. Add the scallions and capers, stir together, and fry for a couple of minutes. Spoon the broccoli mixture into the baking dish.
4. Place the fish amongst the vegetables.
5. In a medium-sized bowl, whisk together the parsley, whipping cream, and mustard. Pour over the fish and vegetables. Top with the sliced butter.
6. Bake on the middle rack, uncovered, for 20 minutes or until the fish is cooked through, and flakes easily with a fork.
7. Serve as is, or with leafy greens on the side

GRILLED SALMON WITH AVOCADO SALSA

Nutrition: Cal 528;Fat 43 g; Carb 13 g;Protein 25 g
Serving 2; Cook time 22 min

Ingredients
- •2 4-6 oz salmon fillets
- •2 tablespoons olive oil
- •1 clove garlic minced or crushed
- •1/2 teaspoon
- •1/2 teaspoon
- •1/2 teaspoon onion powder
- •1/4 teaspoon black pepper
- •1/4 teaspoon salt

•FOR THE AVOCADO SALSA
- •1 ripe avocado pitted and diced
- •1/2 cup tomato diced (any type of tomato)
- •2 tablespoons onion diced
- •2 tablespoons cilantro minced
- •1 tablespoon olive oil
- •1 tablespoon lime juice
- •salt and pepper to taste

Instructions

1. Stir the olive oil, garlic, and spices in a small bowl. Brush or rub salmon with the spice mixture.
2. Heat a large heavy-duty (preferably non-stick) pan or grill medium-high heat. Add salmon to the pan and cook for 5-6 minutes per side. Remove from pan, top with avocado salsa and serve immediately.

3. To make the avocado salsa: Add the avocado, tomato, onion, and cilantro to a large mixing bowl. Drizzle with olive oil, fresh lime juice and a pinch of salt and pepper. Gently mix with a spoon until fully combined. Cover with plastic wrap until ready to serve.

(INSTANT POT) COCONUT CURRY MUS-SELS WITH ZUCCHINI NOODLES

Nutrition: cal 269;fat 20 g; carb 11 g;protein 10 g
Serving 4; cook time 25 min

Ingredients
- •2 tablespoons avocado oil
- •1 (10- to 12-ounce) package zucchini noodles or 2 large zucchini, zoodled
- •⅓ cup diced onion
- •2 tablespoons minced fresh ginger
- •4 cloves garlic, minced
- •1 tablespoon red curry paste
- •1 cup coconut milk
- •1 cup chicken broth
- •¾ pound (15 to 18) mussels, scrubbed, beards removed
- •½ medium red bell pepper, cut into strips
- •1 tablespoon fish sauce
- •½ teaspoon fine Himalayan pink salt
- •¼ teaspoon black pepper
- •Juice of ½ lime
- •¼ cup chopped fresh cilantro, for serving

Instructions

1. Select sauté on the instant pot. When the pot is hot, add 1 table- spoon of the avocado oil. Add the zucchini noodles to the hot oil and cook, stirring frequently, until just tender, 3 to 4 minutes. Select cancel. Transfer the zoodles to a dish and cover to keep warm.
2. Select sauté again. Add the remaining 2 tablespoons avocado oil to the pot. When the oil is hot, add the onion, ginger, garlic, and curry paste. Cook, stirring frequently, until fragrant, about 1 minute. Select cancel. Add the coconut milk, broth, mussels, and bell pep-per to the pot.
3. Secure the lid and close the pressure-release valve. Set the pot to high pressure for 3 minutes. At the end of the cooking time, quick- release the pressure. Discard any mussels that have not opened.
4. Divide the zucchini noodles and mussels among four shallow serving bowls. Stir the fish sauce, pink salt, pepper, and lime juice into the curry sauce, then pour over the mussels. Sprinkle with cilantro before serving

CREAMY CHILE SHRIMP

Nutrition: Cal 103;Fat 6 g; Carb 5 g;Protein 7 g
Serving 4; Cook time 30 min

Ingredients
- •1 lb. shrimp
- •1 chile pepper, cut into thin strips
- •½ cup bell pepper, cut into thin strips
- •½ cup white cabbage
- •½ tsp. cayenne powder

- ½ cup chicken stock
- ½ tsp. black pepper
- ½ cup heavy cream
- ½ tsp. hot sauce
- 1 tbsp. garlic, minced
- ½ tsp. lime juice
- ¼ cup canola oil

Instructions

1. Deseed and cut the green chile into thin strips lengthwise.
2. In the Instant Pot, sauté the bell pepper, cabbage and green chili with half oil for 3-4 minutes. Remove and warm by covering with foil.
3. Sauté ginger and garlic inside the Instant Pot with the rest in the oil and add shrimp. Turn off "Sauté" function. Add the spices, hot sauce, and lime juice.
4. Add chicken stock and cook on high pressure for 4 minutes. Quick pressure release, add the sautéed vegetables and mix well.
5. Add cream and sauté before sauce thickens slightly. Serve.

LEMON KALAMATA OLIVE SALMON

Nutrition: Cal 440;Fat 34 g; Carb 3g;Protein 30g
Serving 3; Cook time 25 min

Ingredients

- 4 x 0.3 lb. salmon filets
- 2 tbsps. fresh lemon juice
- ¼ tsp. black pepper
- ½ cup red onion, sliced
- 1 tsp. herbs de Provence
- 1 can pitted kalamata olives
- 1tsp. sea salt
- ½ lemon, thinly sliced
- 1 cup fish broth
- ½ tsp. cumin
- ½ cup essential olive oil

Instructions

1. Generously season salmon fillets with cumin, pepper, and salt; set your Instant Pot on "Sauté" mode as well as heat the essential olive oil; add fish and brown each side.
2. Stir the remainder
3. Ingredients to the pot and provide to your simmer; lock lid. Set your pot on manual high for ten minutes; when done, quick release pressure then serve.

SEAFOOD MEDLEY STEW

Nutrition: Cal 535;Fat 44 g; Carb 8g;Protein 27g
Serving 3; Cook time 25 min

Ingredients

- 2 cups chicken broth
- 2 tbsps. lemon juice
- ½ lb. shrimp
- ½ lb. mussels
- 2 cloves garlic, crushed

- ½ cup coconut cream
- ½ tsp. black pepper
- 100 g. halibut
- 1 dried whole star anise
- 1 bay leaf
- 1 cup light cream
- 3 tbsps. coconut oil

Instructions

1. In the Instant Pot, sauté the bay leaves, and star anise in coconut oil approximately 30 seconds.
2. Add garlic and attempt to sauté.
3. Add broth. Rub fresh lemon juice, salt, and pepper on fish fillets and put inside pot. Add shrimp and mussels too.
4. Cook for 10 mins. Release pressure naturally.
5. Add both creams and permit to simmer.
6. Remove bay leaves and star anise before serving.

FLAVORED OCTOPUS

Nutrition: Cal 180;Fat 3 g; Carb 1.5 g;Protein 30 g
Serving 4; Cook time 25 min

Ingredients

- 1 tsp chopped cilantro
- 2 tbsps. extra virgin olive oil
- 0.6 pounds octopus
- 2 tsps. garlic powder
- 3 tbsps. lime juice
- salt and pepper, to taste

Instructions

1. Place the octopus within the steaming basket. Season with garlic powder, salt, and pepper. Drizzle with olive and lime juice.
2. Pour water in the Instant Pot and lower the steaming basket. Close the lid and cook for 8 minutes on high.
3. Do a simple pressure release.

CARAMELIZED TILAPIA

Nutrition: Cal 150;Fat 4 g; Carb 3 g;Protein 21 g
Serving 4; Cook time 50 min

Ingredients

- 1-pound tilapia fillets
- 1 red chili, minced
- 3 tsp. minced garlic
- ¼ cup granulated sweetener
- 1 spring onion, minced
- ¾ cup coconut water
- 1/3 cup water
- 3 tbsp. fish sauce
- salt and pepper, to taste

Instructions

1. In a bowl, combine the fish sauce, garlic, salt, and pepper. Place the tilapia inside and mix to coat. Cover and let sit within the fridge for half an hour.
2. Meanwhile, combine the lake and sweetener inside Instant Pot. Cook on "Sauté" until caramelized.

3. Add fish and pour the coconut water over. Close the lid and cook on high for 10 minutes.

4. Do a fast pressure release. Top the fish with spring onion and chili.

5. Serve and enjoy!

CRUNCHY ALMOND TUNA
Nutrition: Cal 150;Fat 4 g; Carb 3 g;Protein 21 g
Serving 4; Cook time 15 min

Ingredients
- 2 cans of tuna, drained
- 1 cup shaved almond
- 2 tbsps. butter
- 1 tsp garlic powder
- 1 cup grated cheddar cheese

Instructions
1. Melt the butter in your Instant Pot on "Sauté." Add tuna, almonds, garlic powder, and cheddar. Cook on "Sauté" for 3 minutes.

2. Serve immediately over cauliflower, rice or on its own.

ARUGULA AND SALMON SALAD
Nutrition: Cal 390;Fat 31 g; Carb 6 g;Protein 26 g
Serving 3; Cook time 25 min

Ingredients
- 3 (4-ounce) salmon fillets
- 5 tablespoons extra-virgin olive oil, divided
- 1 teaspoon garlic salt
- Juice of 1 lemon
- 4½ cups arugula

Instructions
1. Preheat the oven to 450°F. Line a baking sheet with aluminum foil.

2. Rub the fillets with 2 tablespoons of oil and the garlic salt. Place them on the prepared sheet and drizzle the lemon juice over the top of the fillets.

3. Bake until the salmon is cooked through and flaky, 8 to 12 minutes. Let the fillets rest for 10 minutes.

4. Into each of 3 storage containers, place 1 cups of arugula and season with salt and pepper. Top the arugula with the salmon fillets.To serve, drizzle the arugula in each container with 1 tablespoon of oil and toss.

GRILLED PESTO SALMON WITH ASPARAGUS
Nutrition: Cal 300;Fat 18 g; Carb 2.5 g;Protein 34 g
Serving 4; Cook time 20 min

Ingredients
- 4 (6-ounce) boneless salmon fillets
- Salt and pepper
- 1 bunch asparagus, ends trimmed
- 2 tablespoons olive oil
- ¼ cup basil pesto

Instructions
1. Preheat a grill to high heat and oil the grates.

2. Season the salmon with salt and pepper, then spray with cooking spray.

3. Grill the salmon for 4 to 5 minutes on each side until cooked through.

4. Toss the asparagus with oil and grill until tender, about 10 minutes.

5. Spoon the pesto over the salmon and serve with the asparagus

GRILLED SALMON AND ZUCCHINI WITH MANGO SAUCE
Nutrition: Cal 485;Fat 32 g; Carb 6,5 g;Protein 43 g
Serving 6; Cook time 6 hours 10 min

Ingredients
- 4 (6-ounce) boneless salmon fillets
- 1 tablespoon olive oil
- Salt and pepper
- 1 large zucchini, sliced in coins
- 2 tablespoons fresh lemon juice
- ½ cup chopped mango
- ¼ cup fresh chopped cilantro
- 1 teaspoon lemon zest
- ½ cup canned coconut milk

Instructions
1. Preheat a grill pan to high heat and spray liberally with cooking spray.

2. Brush the salmon with olive oil and season with salt and pepper.Toss the zucchini with lemon juice and season with salt and pepper.

3. Place the salmon fillets and zucchini on the grill pan.

4. Cook for 5 minutes then turn everything and cook 5 minutes more.

5. Combine the remaining ingredients in a blender and blend into a sauce.

6. Serve the salmon fillets drizzled with the mango sauce and zucchini on the side.

SLOW-COOKER POT ROAST WITH GREEN BEANS
Nutrition: Cal 375;Fat 13.5g; Carb 6 g;Protein 53 g
Serving 8; Cook time 8 hours 10 min

Ingredients
- 4 (6-ounce) boneless salmon fillets
- 1 tablespoon olive oil
- Salt and pepper
- 1 large zucchini, sliced in coins
- 2 tablespoons fresh lemon juice
- ½ cup chopped mango
- ¼ cup fresh chopped cilantro
- 1 teaspoon lemon zest
- ½ cup canned coconut milk

Instructions
1. Combine the celery and onion in a slow cooker.

2. Place the roast on top and season liberally with salt and pepper.

3. Whisk together the beef broth and Worcestershire sauce then pour it in.
4. Cover and cook on low heat for 8 hours until the beef is very tender.
5. Remove the beef to a cutting board and cut into chunks.
6. Return the beef to the slow cooker and add the beans and chopped butter.

FRIED COCONUT SHRIMP WITH ASPARAGUS

Nutrition: Cal 535;Fat 38,5 g; Carb 18 g;Protein 31 g
Serving 6; Cook time 25 min

Ingredients
- 1 ½ cups shredded unsweetened coconut
- 2 large eggs
- Salt and pepper
- 1 ½ pounds large shrimp, peeled and deveined
- ½ cup canned coconut milk
- 1 pound asparagus, cut into 2-inch pieces

Instructions
1. Pour the coconut into a shallow dish.
2. Beat the eggs with some salt and pepper in a bowl.
3. Dip the shrimp first in the egg, then dredge with coconut.
4. Heat the coconut oil in a large skillet over medium-high heat.
5. Add the shrimp and fry for 1 to 2 minutes on each side until browned.
6. Remove the shrimp to paper towels and reheat the skillet.
7. Add the asparagus and season with salt and pepper – sauté until tender-crisp, then serve with the shrimp

BALSAMIC SALMON WITH GREEN BEANS

Nutrition: Cal 320;Fat 18 g; Carb 6 g;Protein 35 g
Serving 4; Cook time 25 min

Ingredients
- ½ cup balsamic vinegar
- ¼ cup chicken broth
- 1 tablespoon Dijon mustard
- 2 cloves garlic, minced
- 2 tablespoons coconut oil
- 4 (6-ounce) salmon fillets
- Salt and pepper
- 2 cups trimmed green beans

Instructions
1. Combine the balsamic vinegar, chicken broth, mustard, and garlic in a small saucepan over medium-high heat.
2. Bring to a boil then reduce heat and simmer for 15 minutes to reduce by half.
3. Heat the coconut oil in a large skillet over medium-high heat.
4. Season the salmon with salt and pepper then add to the skillet.
5. Cook for 4 minutes until seared, then flip and add the green beans.

6. Pour the glaze into the skillet and simmer for 2 to 3 minutes until done.

SHRIMP AND SAUSAGE "BAKE"

Nutrition: Cal 323;Fat 24 g; Carb 8 g;Protein 20 g
Serving 4; Cook time 35 min

Ingredients
- 2 tablespoons olive oil
- 6 ounces chorizo sausage, diced
- ½ pound (16 to 20 count) shrimp, peeled and deveined
- 1 red bell pepper, chopped
- ½ small sweet onion, chopped
- 2 teaspoons minced garlic
- ¼ cup chicken stock
- Pinch red pepper flakes

Instructions
1. Place a large skillet over medium-high heat and add the olive oil.
2. Sauté the sausage until it is warmed through, about 6 minutes.
3. Add the shrimp and sauté until it is opaque and just cooked through, about 4 minutes.
4. Remove the sausage and shrimp to a bowl and set aside.
5. Add the red pepper, onion, and garlic to the skillet and sauté until tender, about 4 minutes.
6. Add the chicken stock to the skillet along with the cooked sausage and shrimp.
7. Bring the liquid to a simmer and simmer for 3 minutes.
8. Stir in the red pepper flakes and serve.

HERB BUTTER SCALLOPS

Nutrition: Cal 306;Fat 24 g; Carb 4,5 g;Protein 20 g
Serving 4; Cook time 20 min

Ingredients
- 1 pound sea scallops, cleaned
- Freshly ground black pepper
- 8 tablespoons butter, divided
- 2 teaspoons minced garlic
- Juice of 1 lemon
- 2 teaspoons chopped fresh basil
- 1 teaspoon chopped fresh thyme

Instructions
1. Pat the scallops dry with paper towels and season them lightly with pepper.
2. Place a large skillet over medium heat and add 2 tablespoons of buter.
3. Arrange the scallops in the skillet, evenly spaced but not too close together, and sear each side until they are golden brown, about 2½ minutes per side.
4. Remove the scallops to a plate and set aside.
5. Add the remaining 6 tablespoons of buter to the skillet and sauté the garlic until translucent, about 3 minutes.
6. Stir in the lemon juice, basil, and thyme and return the scallops to the skillet, turning to coat them in the sauce.
7. Serve immediately

PAN-SEARED HALIBUT WITH CITRUS BUTTER SAUCE

Nutrition: Cal 320;Fat 26 g; Carb 2 g;Protein 22 g
Serving 4; Cook time 25 min

Ingredients

- 4 (5-ounce) halibut fillets, each about 1 inch thick
- Sea salt
- Freshly ground black pepper
- ¼ cup butter
- 2 teaspoons minced garlic
- 1 shallot, minced
- 3 tablespoons dry white wine
- 1 tablespoon freshly squeezed lemon juice
- 1 tablespoon freshly squeezed orange juice
- 2 teaspoons chopped fresh parsley
- 2 tablespoons olive oil

Instructions

1. Pat the fish dry with paper towels and then lightly season the fillets with salt and pepper. Set aside on a paper towel–lined plate.
2. Place a small saucepan over medium heat and melt the buter.
3. Sauté the garlic and shallot until tender, about 3 minutes.
4. Whisk in the white wine, lemon juice, and orange juice and bring the sauce to a simmer, cooking until it thickens slightly, about 2 minutes.
5. Remove the sauce from the heat and stir in the parsley; set aside.
6. Place a large skillet over medium-high heat and add the olive oil.
7. Panfry the fish until lightly browned and just cooked through, turning them over once, about 10 minutes in total.
8. Serve the fish immediately with a spoonful of sauce for each.

FISH CURRY

Nutrition: Cal 416;Fat 31 g; Carb 5 g;Protein 26 g
Serving 4; Cook time 35 min

Ingredients

- 2 tablespoons coconut oil
- 1&½ tablespoons grated fresh ginger
- 2 teaspoons minced garlic
- 1 tablespoon curry powder
- ½ teaspoon ground cumin
- 2 cups coconut milk
- 16 ounces firm white fish, cut into 1-inch chunks
- 1 cup shredded kale
- 2 tablespoons chopped cilantro

Instructions

1. Place a large saucepan over medium heat and melt the coconut oil.
2. Sauté the ginger and garlic until lightly browned, about 2 minutes.

3. Stir in the curry powder and cumin and sauté until very fragrant,
4. about 2 minutes.
5. Stir in the coconut milk and bring the liquid to a boil.
6. Reduce the heat to low and simmer for about 5 minutes to infuse the milk with the spices.
7. Add the fish and cook until the fish is cooked through, about 10 minutes.
8. Stir in the kale and cilantro and simmer until wilted, about 2 minutes.

ROASTED SALMON WITH AVOCADO SALSA

Nutrition: Cal 320;Fat 26 g; Carb 2 g;Protein 22 g
Serving 4; Cook time 25 min

Ingredients
FOR THE SALSA

- 1 avocado, peeled, pitted,
- and diced
- 1 scallion, white and green parts,
- chopped
- ½ cup halved cherry tomatoes
- Juice of 1 lemon
- Zest of 1 lemon

FOR THE FISH

- 1 teaspoon ground cumin
- ½ teaspoon ground coriander
- ½ teaspoon onion powder
- ¼ teaspoon sea salt
- Pinch freshly ground black pepper
- Pinch cayenne pepper
- 4 (4-ounce) boneless, skinless
- salmon fillets
- 2 tablespoons olive oil

Instructions
TO MAKE THE SALSA

1. In a small bowl, stir together the avocado, scallion, tomatoes, lemon juice, and lemon zest until mixed.
2. Set aside.

TO MAKE THE FISH

1. Preheat the oven to 400°F. Line a baking sheet with aluminum foil and set aside.
2. In a small bowl, stir together the cumin, coriander, onion powder, salt, black pepper, and cayenne until well mixed.
3. Rub the salmon fillets with the spice mix and place them on the baking sheet.
4. Drizzle the fillets with the olive oil and roast the fish until it is just cooked through, about 15 minutes.
5. Serve the salmon topped with the avocado salsa.

SOLE ASIAGO

Nutrition: Cal 300;Fat 24 g; Carb 4 g;Protein 20 g
Serving 4; Cook time 20 min

Ingredients
•4 (4-ounce) sole fillets
•¾ cup ground almonds
•¼ cup Asiago cheese
•2 eggs, beaten
•2&½ tablespoons melted coconut oil

Instructions
1.Preheat the oven to 350°F. Line a baking sheet with parchment paper and set aside.
2.Pat the fish dry with paper towels.
3.Stir together the ground almonds and cheese in a small bowl.
4.Place the bowl with the beaten eggs in it next to the almond mixture.
5.Dredge a sole fillet in the beaten egg and then press the fish into the almond mixture so it is completely coated. Place on the baking sheet and repeat until all the fillets are breaded.
6.Brush both sides of each piece of fish with the coconut oil.
7.Bake the sole until it is cooked through, about 8 minutes in total.
8.Serve immediately

BAKED COCONUT HADDOCK

Nutrition: Cal 406;Fat 31 g; Carb 6 g;Protein 29 g
Serving 4; Cook time 22 min

Ingredients
•4 (5-ounce) boneless haddock fillets
•Sea salt
•Freshly ground black pepper
•1 cup shredded unsweetened coconut
•¼ cup ground hazelnuts
•2 tablespoons coconut oil, melted

Instructions
1.Preheat the oven to 400°F. Line a baking sheet with parchment paper and set aside.

2.Pat the fillets very dry with paper towels and lightly season them with salt and pepper.
3.Stir together the shredded coconut and hazelnuts in a small bowl.
4.Dredge the fish fillets in the coconut mixture so that both sides of each piece are thickly coated.
5.Place the fish on the baking sheet and lightly brush both sides of each piece with the coconut oil.
6.Bake the haddock until the topping is golden and the fish flakes easily with a fork, about 12 minutes total.

CHEESY GARLIC SALMON

Nutrition: Cal 356;Fat 28 g; Carb 2 g;Protein 24 g
Serving 4; Cook time 30 min

Ingredients
•½ cup Asiago cheese
•2 tablespoons freshly squeezed
•lemon juice
•2 tablespoons butter, at room
•temperature
•2 teaspoons minced garlic
•1 teaspoon chopped fresh basil
•1 teaspoon chopped fresh oregano
•4 (5-ounce) salmon fillets
•1 tablespoon olive oil

Instructions
1.Preheat the oven to 350°F. Line a baking sheet with parchment paper and set aside.
2.In a small bowl, stir together the Asiago cheese, lemon juice, buter, garlic, basil, and oregano.
3.Pat the salmon dry with paper towels and place the fillets on the baking sheet skin-side down. Divide the topping evenly between the fillets and spread it across the fish using a knife or the back of a spoon.
4.Drizzle the fish with the olive oil and bake until the topping is golden and the fish is just cooked through, about 12 minutes.

VEGETABLE DISHES

SNAP PEA SALAD

Nutrition: Cal 212;Fat 20 g; Carb 6 g;Protein 4 g
Serving 4; Cook time 40 min

Ingredients

- 8 ounces cauliflower riced
- 1/4 cup lemon juice
- 1/4 cup olive oil
- 1 clove garlic crushed
- 1/2 teaspoon coarse grain dijon mustard
- 1 teaspoon granulated stevia/erythritol blend
- 1/4 teaspoon pepper
- 1/2 teaspoon sea salt
- 1/2 cup sugar snap peas ends removed and each pod cut into three pieces
- 1/4 cup chives
- 1/2 cup sliced almonds
- 1/4 cup red onions minced

Instructions

1. Pour 1 to 2 inches of water in a pot fitted with a steamer. Bring water to a simmer.
2. Place riced cauliflower in the steamer basket, sprinkle lightly with sea salt, cover, and place over the simmering water in the bottom of the steamer. Steam until tender, about 10-12 minutes.
3. When cauliflower is tender, remove the top of the steamer from the simmering water and place it over a bowl, so any excess water can drain out. Allow to cool, uncovered for about 10 minutes, then cover and place the steamer and the bowl in the refrigerator. Chill for at least 1/2 hour or until cool to the touch.
4. While cauliflower is cooling, make the dressing. Pour olive oil in a small mixing bowl. Gradually stream in the lemon juice while vigorously whisking. Whisk in the garlic, mustard, sweetener, pepper, and salt.
5. In a medium mixing bowl, combine chilled cauliflower, peas, chives, almonds, and red onions. Pour dressing over and stir to mix. Transfer to an airtight container and refrigerate until serving. This salad is best if it is allowed to sit for a few hours in the refrigerator so the flavors mingle.

KETO LOW CARB VEGETABLE SOUP RECIPE

Nutrition: Cal 155;Fat 12 g; Carb 8 g;Protein 4 g
Serving 6; Cook time 30 min

Ingredients

- 1 tbsp Olive oil
- ½ large Onion (diced)
- 1 large Bell peppers (diced, the same size as onions)
- 2 cloves Garlic (minced)
- ½ medium head Cauliflower (cut into 1-inch florets)
- 1 cups Green beans (trimmed, cut into 1-inch pieces)
- 1 14.5-oz cans Diced tomatoes
- 4 cups Chicken broth, reduced sodium (or vegetable broth for vegetarian/vegan)
- ½ tbsp Italian seasoning
- 1 Dried bay leaves (optional)
- Sea salt (optional, to taste)
- Black pepper (optional, to taste)

Instructions

1. Heat olive oil in a pot or dutch oven over medium heat.
2. Add the onions and bell peppers. Saute for 7 to 10 minutes, until onions are translucent and browned.
3. Add the minced garlic. Saute for about a minute, until fragrant.
4. Add the cauliflower, green beans, diced tomatoes, broth, and Italian seasoning. Adjust sea salt and black pepper to taste. Add the bay leaves, if using.
5. Bring the soup to a boil. Cover, reduce heat to medium low, and cook for about 10 to 20 minutes, until veggies are soft.

THE CREAMIEST LOW-CARB VEGETABLE SOUP

Nutrition: Cal 257;Fat 23 g; Carb 5 g;Protein 4 g
Serving 8; Cook time 245 min

Ingredients

- 700 g cauliflower (1.5 lb)
- 500 g zucchini (1.1 lb)
- 1 clove garlic
- 1 small brown onion (70 g/ 2.5 oz)
- 2 celery stalks (80 g/ 2.8 oz)
- 2 tbsp ghee or butter (30 g/ 1.1 oz)
- 2 cups chicken broth or vegetable stock (480 ml/ 16 fl oz)
- 2 cups water (480 ml/ 16 fl oz)
- 1 tsp fresh thyme, plus extra for garnish
- 1/2 tsp onion powder
- sea salt and pepper to taste
- 1 cup cream (240 ml/ 8 fl oz)
- 4 tbsp extra virgin olive oil (60 ml)

Instructions

1. Wash the vegetables. Remove the green parts of the cauliflower. Peel the onion and garlic.The Creamiest Low-Carb Vegetable Soup
2. Heat the ghee over medium to high heat in a large saucepan. Chop the onion and garlic finely and sauté until translucent.
3. Add chopped cauliflower, zucchini, celery and seasonings.
4. The Creamiest Low-Carb Vegetable Soup
5. Add broth and water and bring to the boil. Place a lid on the saucepan and reduce to a simmer. Cook until vegetables are soft, for about 15 minutes.
6. The Creamiest Low-Carb Vegetable Soup
7. Remove from heat and use an immersion mixer to puree until smooth. Add cream and return to heat until heated through.
8. Serve with a drizzle of olive oil (about 1/2 tablespoon per serving) and a sprig of thyme.

CREAM OF ASPARAGUS SOUP
Nutrition: Cal 124;Fat 12 g; Carb 5 g;Protein 4 g
Serving 4; Соок time 30 min

Ingredients
- 1 tablespoon avocado oil
- 8 ounces fresh asparagus, trimmed and chopped
- Salt and pepper
- 1 green onion, chopped
- 2 cloves garlic, minced
- 2 cups veggie or chicken broth
- 1 ounce fresh baby spinach
- 1 cup coconut cream (from the top of a can of coconut milk)
- 1 tablespoon fresh lemon juice

Instructions
1. In a large saucepan over medium heat, heat the oil until shimmering. Add the asparagus and sprinkle with salt and pepper. Sauté until bright green, 3 to 4 minutes.
2. Add the green onion and garlic and соок until fragrant, about 1 minute more. Stir in the broth and bring to a boil, then reduce the heat to a simmer. Соок until the asparagus is tender, 10 to 12 minutes.
3. Add the spinach and соок until wilted, about 2 minutes. Transfer to a blender or food processor and blend until smooth. Return the soup to the pan.
4. Whisк in the coconut cream and lemon juice until well combined. Adjust seasoning to taste and serve hot or chilled.

ROASTED TOMATO BISQUE
Nutrition: Cal 94;Fat 8 g; Carb 7 g;Protein 4 g
Serving 4; Соок time 40 min

Ingredients
- 1 lb fresh tomatoes cored and coarsely chopped
- 2 cloves garlic peeled
- 2 tablespoon avocado oil
- Salt and pepper
- 1 California Avocado pitted and peeled
- 3 cups chicken broth

Instructions
1. Preheat oven to 425F and spread tomatoes and garlic in a single layer in a large baking dish. Drizzle with the oil and sprinkle with the salt and pepper. Вакe 30 minutes or until tomatoes have caramelized.
2. Transfer to a food processor or high powered blender. Add the avocado and the chicken broth and blend until smooth.
3. Transfer to a pot to warm through before serving. It's also delicious served chilled!

CHILLED GUACAMOLE SOUP
Nutrition: Cal 208;Fat 16 g; Carb 7 g;Protein 8 g
Serving 6; Соок time 20 min

Ingredients
- 2 ½ cups low-sodium chicken broth, divided
- 2 avocados, peeled and pitted
- 2 cloves garlic, coarsely chopped
- 1 jalapeno, seeded and coarsely chopped
- ¼ cup red onion, chopped
- 1 tablespoon lime juice
- 1 tablespoon fresh cilantro, chopped
- ½ teaspoon salt
- ¼ teaspoon pepper
- ¼ teaspoon cayenne
- ¼ cup whipping cream
- 2 tablespoon sour cream
- 6 tablespoon cheddar cheese, shredded

Instructions
1. In a food processor combine 1 cup of chicken broth with avocados, garlic, jalapeño, onion, lime juice and cilantro. Puree until smooth. Add remaining 1 ½ cups broth, salt, pepper and cayenne and blend. Transfer mixture to a large bowl and stir in whipping cream. Cover and chill for at least 1 hour and up to 12 hours.
2. Divide soup among 6 bowls. In the center of each bowl, dollop 1 teaspoon (5 mL) of sour cream. Sprinkle each with 1 tablespoon shredded cheese..

GARLIC & CHIVE CAULIFLOWER MASH
Nutrition: Cal 178;Fat 18 g; Carb 3 g;Protein 2 g
Serving 2; Соок time 20 min

Ingredients
- 4 cups cauliflower florets
- 1/3 cup mayonnaise
- 1 clove garlic, peeled
- 1 Tbsp water
- 1/2 tsp Kosher salt
- 1/8 tsp black pepper
- 1/4 tsp lemon juice
- 1/2 tsp lemon (or lime) zest
- 1 Tbsp fresh chives, chopped

Instructions
1. Combine the cauliflower, mayonnaise, garlic, water, salt and pepper in a large microwave safe bowl, stirring to coat.
2. Microwave on high for 12-15 minutes (or longer), until completely softened.
3. Add the cooked mixture to a magic bullet or food processor and puree until smooth.
4. Add the lemon juice, zest and chives and pulse until combined.
5. Serve warm.

CREAMY CILANTRO LIME COLESLAW

Nutrition: Cal 119;Fat 9 g; Carb 9 g;Protein 3 g
Serving 5; Cook time 10 min

Ingredients
- 14 oz coleslaw, bagged
- 1 1/2 avocados
- 1/4 cup cilantro leaves
- 2 limes, juiced
- 1 garlic clove
- 1/4 cup water
- 1/2 teaspoon salt
- cilantro to garnish

Instructions
1. In a food processor add the garlic and cilantro and process until chopped.
2. Add the lime juice, avocados and water. Pulse until nice and creamy.
3. Take out the avocado mixture and in a large bowl mix it with the coleslaw. It will be a bit thick but it will cover the slaw nicely.
4. For best results, refrigerate for a few hours before eating to soften the cabbage.

CAULIFLOWER HUMMUS

Nutrition: Cal 119;Fat 14 g; Carb 4 g;Protein 2 g
Serving 1; Cook time 20 min

Ingredients
- 3 cups raw cauliflower florets
- 2 Tbsp water
- 2 Tbsp avocado or olive oil
- 1/2 tsp salt
- 3 whole garlic cloves
- Tbsp Tahini paste
- 3 Tbsp lemon juice
- 2 raw garlic cloves, crushed (in addition to above)
- 3 Tbsp extra virgin olive oil
- 3/4 tsp kosher salt
- smoked paprika and extra olive oil for serving

Instructions
1. Combine the cauliflower, water, 2 Tbsp avocado or olive oil, 1/2 tsp kosher salt, and 3 whole garlic cloves to a microwave safe dish. Microwave for about 15 minutes – or until softened and darkened in color.
2. Put the cauliflower mixture into a magic bullet, blender, or food processor and blend. Add the tahini paste, lemon juice, 2 raw garlic cloves, 3 Tbsp olive oil, and 3/4 tsp kosher salt. Blend until mostly smooth. Taste and adjust seasoning as necessary.
3. To serve, place the hummus in a bowl and drizzle with extra virgin olive oil and a sprinkle of paprika. Use thinly sliced tart apples, celery sticks, raw radish chips, or other vegges to dip with.

CRISPY TOFU AND BOK CHOY SALAD

Nutriton: Cal 398;Fat 6 g; Carb 9 g;Protein 24 g
Serving 3; Cook time 40 min

Ingredients
OVEN BAKED TOFU
- 15 ounces extra firm tofu
- 1 tablespoon soy sauce
- 1 tablespoon sesame oil
- 1 tablespoon water
- 2 teaspoons minced garlic
- 1 tablespoon rice wine vinegar
- Juice 1/2 lemon

BOK CHOY SALAD
- 9 ounces bok choy
- 1 stalk green onion
- 2 tablespoons chopped cilantro
- 3 tablespoons coconut oil
- 2 tablespoons soy sauce
- 1 tablespoon sambal olek
- 1 tablespoon peanut butter
- Juice 1/2 lime
- 7 drops liquid stevia

Instructions
1. Start by pressing the tofu. Lay the tofu in a kitchen towel and put something heavy over the top (like a cast iron skillet). It takes about 4-6 hours to dry out, and you may need to replace the kitchen towel half-way through.
2. Once the tofu is pressed, work on your marinade. Combine all of the ingredients for the marinade (soy sauce, sesame oil, water, garlic, vinegar, and lemon).
3. Chop the tofu into squares and place in a plastic bag along with the marinade. Let this marinate for at least 30 minutes, but preferably over night.
4. Pre-heat oven to 350°F. Place tofu on a baking sheet lined with parchment paper (or a silpat) and bake for 30-35 minutes.
5. As the tofu is cooked, get started on the bok choy salad. Chop cilantro and spring onion.
6. Mix all of the other ingredients together (except lime juice and bok choy) in a bowl. Then add cilantro and spring onion. Note: You can microwave coconut oil for 10-15 seconds to allow it it to melt.
7. Once the tofu is almost cooked, add lime juice into the salad dressing and mix together.
8. Chop the bok choy into small slices, like you would cabbage.
9. Remove the tofu from the oven and assemble your salad with tofu, bok choy, and sauce.

VEGAN KALE AND SPINACH SOUP

Nutrition: Cal 110;Fat 12 g; Carb 6 g;Protein 4 g
Serving 4; Cook time 15 min

Ingredients
- ½ cup coconut oil, melted
- 8 oz. kale
- 8 oz. (7½ cups) fresh spinach
- 2 (14 oz.) avocados
- 3½ cups coconut milk or coconut cream
- 1 cup water
- fresh mint or dried mint (optional)
- 1 tsp salt
- ¼ tsp ground black pepper
- 1 tbsp lime juice

FRIED KALE
- 3 oz. kale
- 2 garlic cloves, chopped
- 2 tbsp coconut oil
- ½ tsp ground cardamom (green)
- salt and pepper

Instructions
1. Melt the coconut oil in a hot thick-bottomed pot or pan.
2. Sauté the spinach and kale briefly. The vegetable should just shrink and get a little color, but no more. Remove from the heat.
3. Add water, coconut milk, avocado and spices. Blend with a hand blender until creamy.
4. Add lime juice. Add more spices if you want.
5. Fry kale and garlic on high heat until the garlic turns golden. Garnish the soup and serve.

CARROT SALAD

Nutrition: Cal 110;Fat 12 g; Carb 6 g;Protein 4 g
Serving 5; Cook time 10 min

Ingredients
- 1 pound carrots, julienned
- 3 Medjool dates, pitted and diced
- ¼ cup chopped pistachios
- ⅓ cup finely chopped cilantro
- ¼ cup mint leaves, optional

Dressing
- 2 tablespoons extra-virgin olive oil
- 2 tablespoons fresh lemon juice
- 1 tablespoon tahini
- 1 tablespoon honey
- 1 small garlic clove, grated
- ¼ teaspoon cumin
- ¼ teaspoon sea salt

Instructions
1. Place the julienned carrots in a large bowl and sprinkle the dates on top.
2. Make the dressing: In a small bowl, whisk together the olive oil, lemon juice, tahini, honey, garlic, cumin, and salt.

3. Drizzle the dressing over the carrots and toss to coat. Sprinkle on the pistachios and cilantro and toss again. Sprinkle the mint leaves and serve.

CREAMY DAIRY FREE AVOCADO SAUCE

Nutrition: Cal 180;Fat 16 g; Carb 8 g;Protein 6 g
Serving 5; Cook time 10 min

Ingredients
- 1 Avocado
- 1 Tbspn lemon juice
- 1 garlic clove
- 3 Tbspn olive oil
- 2 Tbspn fresh parsley
- 3 Tbspn water
- Sea Salt and freshly ground black pepper to taste

Instructions
1. Add all ingredients into food processor or blender.
2. Blend until smooth.
3. Add more water to reach a thinner consistency if desired.
4. Taste and adjust seasoning if necessary.

EASY NO-CHURN AVOCADO ICE CREAM

Nutrition: Cal 274;Fat 17 g; Carb 29 g;Protein3 g
Serving 4; Cook time 5 hours

Ingredients
- 1/4 cup hardened coconut cream (from 1 14-oz can full-fat coconut milk, refrigerated overnight — only the cream)
- 2 ripe avocados, halved, pitted and peeled
- 2 very ripe bananas, sliced and frozen
- 3 tbsp pure maple syrup, plus more, to taste
- 1 tbsp freshly squeezed lemon juice

Instructions
1. Add sliced, peeled fresh avocado to a food processor or high-speed blender, and blend until smooth.
2. Add hardened coconut cream from canned coconut milk, along with sliced frozen bananas, pure maple syrup, and lemon juice, and blend until smooth and creamy. If bananas are not fully ripe, you may need to add in additional maple syrup.
3. Taste, and add any more pure maple syrup, as needed, to reach the desired sweetness.
4. Transfer the mixture into a freezer-safe container, and place in freezer for at least 3-4 hours or overnight.
5. When ready to serve, let soften for 10-15 minutes at room temperature before scooping.

PORTOBELLO MUSHROOM PIZZA

Nutrition: Cal 274;Fat 17 g; Carb 29 g;Protein 3 g
Serving 4; Cook time 20 min

Ingredients
- 4 large portobello mushrooms, stems removed
- ¼ cup olive oil
- 1 teaspoon minced garlic
- 1 medium tomato, cut into 4 slices

- 2 teaspoons chopped fresh basil
- 1 cup shredded mozzarella cheese

Instructions

1. Preheat the oven to broil. Line a baking sheet with aluminum foil and set aside.
2. In a small bowl, toss the mushroom caps with the olive oil until well coated. Use your fingertips to rub the oil in withou breaking the mushrooms.
3. Place the mushrooms on the baking sheet gill-side down and broil the mushrooms until they are tender on the tops,about 2 minutes.
4. Flip the mushrooms over and broil 1 minute more.
5. Take the baking sheet out and spread the garlic over each mushroom, top each with a tomato slice, sprinkle with the basil,and top with the cheese.
6. Broil the mushrooms until the cheese is melted and bubbly, about 1 minute.

ARUGULA AVOCADO TOMATO SALAD

Nutrition: Cal 112;Fat 9 g; Carb 12 g;Protein 3 g
Serving 5; Cook time 10 min

Ingredients

- 5 oz baby arugula roughly chopped
- 6 large basil leaves thinly sliced
- 1 pint yellow grape tomatoes sliced in half
- 1 pint red grape tomatoes sliced in half
- 2 large avocados cut into chunks
- ½ cup red onion minced

BALSAMIC VINAIGRETTE

- 2 tbsp balsamic vinegar
- 1 tbsp olive oil
- 1 tbsp maple syrup
- 1 tbsp lemon juice
- 1 small garlic clove minced
- ¼ tsp himalayan pink sea salt
- ¼ tsp black pepper

Instructions

1. Put the roughly chopped arugula and sliced basil leaves into a large mixing bowl. Add the sliced grape tomatoes, avocado chunks, and minced red onion to the bowl. Toss to combine.
2. In a small bowl, whisk together 2 tbsp balsamic vinegar, 1 tbsp olive oil, 1 tbsp maple syrup, 1 tbsp lemon juice, 1 garlic clove, ¼ tsp salt, and ¼ tsp black pepper until well combined.
3. Pour the balsamic dressing over the salad. Gently mix the salad until the dressing has been evenly distributed and then transfer the salad to a large platter.

RED CURRY CAULIFLOWER SOUP

Nutrition: Cal 274;Fat 16 g; Carb 18 g;Protein 6 g
Serving 6; Cook time 45 min

Ingredients

- 1 medium yellow onion sliced
- 3 medium garlic cloves sliced
- 4 ounces thai red curry paste (about 4 tbsp)
- 1 medium cauliflower (about 1 lb cauliflower florets)
- ½ cup red lentils
- 1 ½ cups water
- 4 cups low-sodium vegetable broth
- ½ tsp Himalayan pink sea salt
- ½ tsp black pepper
- 14 ounce can unsweetened coconut milk
- 3 tbsp lemon juice (1 large lemon)
- 1 tbsp chives sliced

Instructions

1. In a large pot, saute the sliced onions in 3-4 tbsp vegetable broth until soft. Add the sliced garlic and cook for 1-2 minutes until fragrant.
2. Add 4 tbsp red curry paste, cauliflower florets, ½ cup red lentils, 1 ½ cups water, 4 cups vegetable broth, ½ tsp salt, and ½ tsp black pepper to the pot. Bring the soup to a low simmer and then reduce the heat to medium. Let it cook for 15-20 minutes or until the cauliflower and red lentils are tender, stirring occasionally.
3. Transfer the soup to a large high-powered blender cup and then blend it on high until the soup is completely smooth. You may need to work in batches depending on how large your blender cup is.
4. Pour the blended soup back into the pot and stir in the coconut milk over medium heat. Add 3 tbsp lemon juice and stir it in. Garnish with chives before serving.

KETO OVEN ROASTED VEGETABLES

Nutrition: Cal 113;Fat 7 g; Carb 11 g;Protein 2 g
Serving 8; Cook time 40 min

Ingredients

- 2 cups Broccoli (cut into florets)
- 2 cups Cauliflower (cut into florets)
- 2 cups Zucchini (sliced into 1/4 inch thick circles)
- 2 cups Bell peppers (cut into 1.5 inch pieces)
- 2 cups Red onion (cut into 1.5 inch pieces)
- 1/4 cup Olive oil
- 2 tbsp Balsamic vinegar
- 1 tsp Garlic powder
- 1 tsp Italian seasoning
- 1 tsp Sea salt
- 1/2 tsp Black pepper

Instructions

1. Preheat the oven to 425 degrees F. Line an extra-large baking sheet with foil, if desired.
2. Combine the vegetables in a large bowl.

3. In a small bowl, whisk together the olive oil, balsamic vinegar, garlic powder, Italian seasoning, sea salt, and black pepper. Pour the mixture over the vegetables.

4. Arrange the vegetables in a single layer on the prepared baking sheet, making sure each piece is touching the pan. Do not overcrowd the pan - use multiple pans if needed.

5. Roast the vegetables in the oven for about 30 minutes, until they are golden brown.

VEGAN KETO COCONUT CURRY

Nutrition: Cal 425;Fat 33 g; Carb 10 g;Protein 18 g
Serving 4; Cook time 35 min

Ingredients
- ¼ cup vegan butter
- ½ green bell pepper, thinly sliced
- 2 scallions, thinly sliced, white and green parts kept separate
- 2 garlic cloves, thinly sliced
- 2½ tablespoons vegan red curry paste
- 1 medium zucchini, diced
- 1 medium carrot, diced
- 1½ cups unsweetened full-fat coconut milk
- 1 cup vegetable stock
- 2 tablespoons unflavored vegan protein powder
- 2 tablespoons natural unsweetened peanut butter
- 4 drops liquid stevia
- 1 teaspoon sea salt
- Freshly ground black pepper
- 16 ounces extra-firm tofu, cut into medium dice
- 1 cup baby spinach
- ¼ cup chopped fresh cilantro, plus more for serving
- 4 tablespoons coconut oil, melted

Instructions
1. In a large pot, melt the butter over medium heat. Add the bell pepper, scallion whites and garlic; cook until fragrant, about 1 minute. Add the curry paste and cook, stirring constantly, until fragrant, about 1 minute.

2. Stir in the zucchini, carrot, coconut milk, vegetable stock, protein powder, peanut butter, stevia, salt and black pepper. Bring to a boil, then reduce the heat to medium-low and simmer uncovered until the vegetables are tender, 8 to 10 minutes. Taste and adjust the seasoning if necessary.

3. Add the tofu and simmer for 5 minutes to warm through. Add the spinach and cilantro to wilt. Taste and adjust the seasoning if necessary.

4. Divide the curry among four bowls. Drizzle 1 tablespoon melted coconut oil over each portion. Sprinkle with the scallion greens and more cilantro.

STUFFED BELL PEPPERS

Nutrition: Cal 202;Fat 16 g; Carb 7 g;Protein 8 g
Serving 3; Cook time 50 min

Ingredients
- 2 medium-sized yellow bell peppers, halved
- ½ cup mozzarella cheese
- ½ cup tomatoes, diced
- 2 medium-sized green bell pepper, halved
- 2 cups button mushrooms, diced
- 1 cup feta cheese, crumbled
- 2 tbsps. celery leaves, finely chopped
- 2 tbsps. extra virgin olive oil
- ½ tsp. black pepper, ground
- ½ tsp. smoked paprika, ground
- ¼ tsp. red pepper cayenne, ground
- ½ tsp. salt

Instructions
1. Cut the peppers in half and take away the stem and seeds. Set aside.

2. In a large mixing bowl, combine button mushrooms, feta cheese, mozzarella cheese, tomatoes, celery, and olive oil. Add all spices and mix until well incorporated. Stuff the bell pepper halves with this particular mixture. Use some additional oil to brush the peppers externally.

3. Line some parchment paper over a fitting springform pan and hang aside

4. Plug inside instant pot and pour 1 cup of water in the stainless insert. Set the trivet around the bottom and set the stuffed peppers on the top.

5. Close the lid and hang up the steam release handle. Press the "Manual" button and set the timer for a half-hour. Cook on underhand.

6. When done, perform a quick pressure release and open the pot.

7. Transfer the peppers to a serving plate and sprinkle by incorporating dried oregano or dried rosemary before serving. Optionally, top with Greek yogurt.

GARLICKY GREEN BEANS

Nutrition: Cal 104;Fat 9 g; Carb 2 g;Protein 4 g
Serving 4; Cook time 20 min

Ingredients
- 1 pound green beans, stemmed
- 2 tablespoons olive oil
- 1 teaspoon minced garlic
- Sea salt
- Freshly ground black pepper
- ¼ cup freshly grated Parmesan Cheese

Instructions
1. Preheat the oven to 425°F. Line a baking sheet with aluminum foil and set aside.

2. In a large bowl, toss together the green beans, olive oil, and garlic until well mixed.

3. Season the beans lightly with salt and pepper.

4. Spread the beans on the baking sheet and roast them until they are tender and lightly browned, stirring them once, about 10 minutes.
5. Serve topped with the Parmesan cheese

SAUTÉED ASPARAGUS WITH WALNUTS
Nutrition: Cal 124;Fat 12 g; Carb 4 g;Protein 3 g
Serving 4; Cook time 20 min

Ingredients
- 1½ tablespoons olive oil
- ¾ pound asparagus, woody ends trimmed
- Sea salt
- Freshly ground pepper
- ¼ cup chopped walnuts

Instructions
1. Place a large skillet over medium-high heat and add the olive oil.
2. Sauté the asparagus until the spears are tender and lightly browned, about 5 minutes.
3. Season the asparagus with salt and pepper.
4. Remove the skillet from the heat and toss the asparagus with the walnuts.

BRUSSELS SPROUTS CASSEROLE
Nutrition: Cal 217;Fat 14 g; Carb 11 g;Protein 10 g
Serving 8; Cook time 45 min

Ingredients
- 8 bacon slices
- 1 pound Brussels sprouts, blanched for 10 minutes and cut into quarters
- 1 cup shredded Swiss cheese, divided
- ¾ cup heavy (whipping) cream

Instructions
1. Preheat the oven to 400°F.
2. Place a skillet over medium-high heat and cook the bacon until it is crispy, about 6 minutes.
3. Reserve 1 tablespoon of bacon fat to grease the casserole dish and roughly chop the cooked bacon.
4. Lightly oil a casserole dish with the reserved bacon fat and set aside.
5. In a medium bowl, toss the Brussels sprouts with the chopped bacon and ½ cup of cheese and transfer the mixture to the caserole dish.
6. Pour the heavy cream over the Brussels sprouts and top the casserole with the remaining ½ cup of cheese.
7. Bake until the cheese is melted and lightly browned and the vegetables are heated through, about 20 minutes.

SAUTÉED VEGETABLES
Nutrition: Cal 171;Fat 12 g; Carb 9 g;Protein 5.3g
Serving 5; Cook time 10 min

Ingredients
- 1 red bell pepper, sliced
- 1 small onion, sliced
- 1 small zucchini, cut into cubes
- 1 green bell pepper, sliced
- ¼ cup dried porcini mushrooms
- ¼ cup Feta cheese
- ½ cup sour cream
- 2 tbsps. tamari sauce
- 2 tbsps. sesame oil
- ½ tsp. dried thyme
- ¼ tsp. dried oregano
- 1 tsp. pink Himalayan salt

Instructions
1. Plug in the instant pot and press the "Sauté" button. Heat up the sesame oil and add zucchini. Sprinkle with many salt and cook for 5 - 6 minutes, stirring constantly.
2. Now add bell peppers and onions. Sprinkle with tamari sauce and provides it a good stir. Optionally, drizzle with a few rice vinegar.
3. Season by incorporating more salt, thyme, and oregano. Continue in order to cook for two - 3 minutes and atart exercising . Feta cheese and mushrooms. Pour in about three tablespoons of water and cook for three or four minutes.
4. When done, press the "Cancel" button and stir inside sour cream. To enjoy, serve it immediately.

STEAMED BROCCOLI WITH BASIL
Nutrition: Cal 181;Fat 10 g; Carb 10 g;Protein 10 g
Serving 3; Cook time 20 min

Ingredients
- 1 lb. broccoli, chopped
- 2 garlic cloves, peeled
- ½ cup fresh basil, chopped
- ½ cup some kinds of cheese
- ½ cup avocado, chopped
- 1 tbsp. extra virgin olive oil
- 1 tbsp. fresh lemon juice, freshly squeezed
- ¼ tsp. dried oregano, ground
- ½ tsp. red pepper, ground
- ¼ tsp. dried parsley, ground
- 1 tsp. salt

Instructions
1. Plug in the Instant Pot and pour in 1 cup of water inside the stainless insert.

2. Place the trivet about the bottom of the pot as well as set the steam basket at the top. Place broccoli inside the steam basket and sprinkle with salt and pepper. Close the lid and set the steam release handle by moving the valve on the "Sealing" position. Press the "Steam" button as well as set the timer for ten mins.
3. Meanwhile, combine basil, cottage type cheese, avocado, garlic, olive oil, fresh lemon juice, red pepper, parsley, and oregano in a mixer. Pulse until smooth and totally incorporated.
4. When you hear the cooker's end signal, release pressure to succeed naturally. Open the pot and transfer the broccoli to a serving plate. Top with basil cream and serve immediately!

ONION CAULIFLOWER HASH
Nutrition: Cal 217;Fat 14 g; Carb 11 g;Protein 10 g
Serving 3; Cook time 20 min

Ingredients
- 1 lb. cauliflower, chopped
- 1 cup green cabbage, shredded
- 2 medium-sized onions, sliced
- ¼ cup parmesan cheese
- 1 cup vegetable stock
- 2 tbsps. olive oil
- ¼ tsp. black pepper, ground
- ½ tsp. dried thyme, ground
- ½ tsp. smoked paprika, ground
- 1 tsp. salt

Instructions
1. Plug in the Instant Pot and grease the stainless steel insert with essential olive oil. Press the "Sauté" button and add cauliflower and onions. Sprinkle with salt, pepper, and thyme. Stir well and cook for 5 minutes.
2. Add cabbage and pour inside vegetables stock. Stir again and securely lock the lid. Set the steam release handle and press the "Manual" button. Set the timer for 8 minutes and cook on questionable.
3. When you hear the cooker's end signal, perform a quick release of the pressure by moving the valve for the "Venting" position. Open the pot and stir inside thyme and smoked paprika.
4. Transfer all to a serving plate and sprinkle with parmesan cheese before serving.

PESTO ZUCCHINI NOODLES
Nutrition: Cal 93;Fat 8 g; Carb 2 g;Protein 4 g
Serving 4; Cook time 15 min

Ingredients
- 4 small zucchini, ends trimmed
- ¾ cup Herb Kale Pesto (page 133)
- ¼ cup grated or shredded
- Parmesan cheese

Instructions
1. Use a spiralizer or peeler to cut the zucchini into "noodles" and place them in a medium bowl.
2. Add the pesto and the Parmesan cheese and toss to coat.

TASTY CREAMY COLLARD GREENS
Nutrition: Cal 217;Fat 17 g; Carb 25 g;Protein 5 g
Serving 4; Cook time 25 min

Ingredients
- 1 lb. collard greens, chopped
- 1 medium-sized onion, chopped
- ½ cup bacon, cut into bite-sized pieces
- 2 garlic cloves, finely chopped
- 1 cup sour cream
- ½ tsp. balsamic vinegar
- 1 tbsp. essential olive oil
- ¼ tsp. black pepper, ground
- ½ tsp. Italian seasoning
- 1 tsp. red pepper flakes
- 1 tsp. sea salt

Instructions
1. Plug with your Instant Pot and add the bacon for the stainless-steel insert. Press the "Sauté" button and cook for three to four minutes, or until crisp. Remove the bacon through the pot and add olive oil. When hot, add onions and garlic. Stir-fry for 3 - 4 minutes, or until the onions translucent.
2. Add collard greens and cook for two main minutes. Sprinkle with salt, pepper, Italian seasoning, and red pepper flakes. Pour in 1 cup of water and securely lock the lid. Adjust the steam release handle and press the "Manual" button. Set the timer for 5 minutes and cook on underhand.
3. When done, perform a quick pressure release and open the pot.
4. Stir in the sour cream, balsamic vinegar, and bacon. Press the "Sauté" button and cook for 2 - 3 minutes more, or until heated through. Turn over pot and transfer all to a serving plate.

GOLDEN ROSTI
Nutrition: Cal 171;Fat 15 g; Carb 3 g;Protein 5 g
Serving 8; Cook time 30 min

Ingredients
- 8 bacon slices, chopped
- 1 cup shredded acorn squash
- 1 cup shredded raw celeriac
- 2 tablespoons grated or shredded
- Parmesan cheese
- 2 teaspoons minced garlic
- 1 teaspoon chopped fresh thyme
- Sea salt
- Freshly ground black pepper
- 2 tablespoons butter

Instructions

1. In a large skillet over medium-high heat, cook the bacon until crispy, about 5 minutes.
2. While the bacon is cooking, in a large bowl, mix together the squash, celeriac, Parmesan cheese, garlic, and thyme. Season the mixture generously with salt and pepper, and set aside.
3. Remove the cooked bacon with a sloted spoon to the rosti mixture and stir to incorporate.
4. Remove all but 2 tablespoons of bacon fat from the skillet and add the buter.
5. Reduce the heat to medium-low and transfer the rosti mixture to the skillet and spread it out evenly to form a large round paty about 1 inch thick.
6. Cook until the botom of the rosti is golden brown and crisp, about 5 minutes.
7. Flip the rosti over and cook until the other side is crispy and the middle is cooked through, about 5 minutes more.
8. Remove the skillet from the heat and cut the rosti into 8 pieces.

CREAMED SPINACH
Nutrition: Cal 195;Fat 20 g; Carb 3 g;Protein 3 g
Serving 4; Cook time 40 min

Ingredients
- 1 tablespoon butter
- ½ sweet onion, very thinly sliced
- 4 cups spinach, stemmed and thoroughly washed
- ¾ cup heavy (whipping) cream
- ¼ cup Chicken Stock
- Pinch sea salt
- Pinch freshly ground black pepper
- Pinch ground nutmeg

Instructions
1. In a large skillet over medium heat, add the buter.
2. Sauté the onion until it is lightly caramelized, about 5 minutes.
3. Stir in the spinach, heavy cream, chicken stock, salt, pepper, and nutmeg.
4. Sauté until the spinach is wilted, about 5 minutes.
5. Continue cooking the spinach until it is tender and the sauce is thickened, about 15 minutes.

CELERY SPINACH STEW
Nutrition: Cal 280;Fat 28 g; Carb 5 g;Protein 2.5 g
Serving 4; Cook time 25 min

Ingredients
- 2 cups fresh spinach, chopped
- 1 small onion, chopped
- 1 cup celery leaves, chopped
- 2 cups heavy cream
- 1 tbsp. fresh lemon juice
- 2 tbsps. butter
- 1 cup celery stalks, chopped
- 2 garlic cloves, minced

- ½ tsp. black pepper, ground
- 1 tbsp. fresh mint, torn
- 1 tsp. salt

Instructions
1. In a large colander, combine spinach and celery. Rinse well under running water and drain. Transfer to a cutting board cut into bite-sized pieces. Set aside.
2. Plug with your instant pot and press the "Sauté" button. Add butter and stir constantly until melts.
3. Add celery stalks, garlic, and onions. Cook for just two minutes and add celery leaves and spinach. Sprinkle with salt and pepper. Cook for 2 - 3 minutes and pour inside the heavy cream.
4. Securely lock the lid and press the "Manual" button. Adjust the steam release handle and hang up the timer for 5 minutes. Cook on high pressure.
5. When you hear the cooker's end signal, perform a quick release with the pressure and open the pot.
6. Stir within the mint and lemon juice. Let it chill for 5 minutes before serving.

SIMPLE BASIL PESTO ZUCCHINI
Nutrition: Cal 215;Fat 17 g; Carb 8 g;Protein 5 g
Serving 4; Cook time 15 min

Ingredients
- 1 cup mozzarella cheese
- 1 large red bell pepper, cut into strips
- 2 medium-sized zucchinis, thinly sliced
- 2 tbsps. organic olive oil
- 1 medium-sized eggplant, thinly sliced
- 1 tsp. Italian seasoning
- 1 cup vegetable stock

FOR THE BASIL PESTO:
- ½ tsp garlic powder
- 2 tsps. balsamic vinegar
- ½ tsp. black pepper, freshly ground
- 2 tbsps. fresh basil, finely chopped
- 2 tbsps. sour cream
- 3 tbsps. organic olive oil
- ¼ tsp. mustard seeds

Instructions
1. Combine sliced zucchinis, stripped red bell pepper, and sliced eggplant in a large bowl. Drizzle with olive oil and Italian seasoning. Optionally, add a pinch of salt and mix well using your hands. Set aside.
2. Combine all pesto
3. Ingredients in a blender and blend until smooth and creamy. Then schedule.
4. Plug inside the Instant Pot add vegetables within the stainless-steel insert. Pour within the vegetable stock and close the lid. Adjust the steam release handle and press the "Manual" button. Set the timer for 8 minutes and cook on high pressure.
5. When done; perform a quick pressure release by moving the valve on the "Venting" position.

6. Open the pot and transfer the vegetables to a serving plate. Top with basil pesto and serve immediately.
7. Optionally, garnish with some fresh basil leaves and get!

CHEESY MASHED CAULIFLOWER
Nutrition: Cal 183;Fat 15 g; Carb 6 g;Protein 8 g
Serving 4; Cook time 20 min

Ingredients
- 1 head cauliflower, chopped roughly
- ½ cup shredded Cheddar cheese
- ¼ cup heavy (whipping) cream
- 2 tablespoons butter, at room temperature
- Sea salt
- Freshly ground black pepper

Instructions
1. Place a large saucepan filled three-quarters full with water over high heat and bring to a boil.
2. Blanch the cauliflower until tender, about 5 minutes, and drain.
3. Transfer the cauliflower to a food processor and add the cheese, heavy cream, and buter. Purée until very creamy and whipped.
4. Season with salt and pepper.

VEGETABLES À LA GRECQUE
Nutrition: Cal 326;Fat 25 g; Carb 8 g;Protein 15 g
Serving 4; Cook time 15 min

Ingredients
- 2 tablespoons organic olive oil
- 2 garlic cloves, minced
- 1 red onion, chopped
- 0.6 pounds button mushrooms, thinly sliced
- 1 eggplant, sliced
- ½ teaspoon dried basil
- 1 teaspoon dried oregano
- 1 thyme sprig, leaves picked
- 2 rosemary sprigs, leaves picked
- ½ cup tomato sauce
- ¼ cup dry Greek wine
- ¼ cup water
- 0.5 pounds Halloumi cheese, cubed
- 4 tablespoons Kalamata olives, pitted and halved

Instructions
1. Press the "Sauté" button to heat your Instant Pot; now, heat the extra virgin olive oil. Cook the garlic and red onions for one to two minutes, stirring periodically.
2. Stir in the mushrooms and then sauté a different 2 to 3 minutes.
3. Add the eggplant, basil, oregano, thyme, rosemary, tomato sauce, Greek wine, and water.
4. Secure the lid. Choose "Manual" mode and low pressure; cook for 3 minutes. Once cooking is complete, use a quick pressure release; carefully remove the lid.
5. Top with cheese and olives.

SAUTÉED CRISPY ZUCCHINI
Nutrition: Cal 94;Fat 8 g; Carb 1 g;Protein 4 g
Serving 4; Cook time 25 min

Ingredients
- 2 tablespoons butter
- 4 zucchini, cut into
- ¼-inch-thick rounds
- ½ cup freshly grated Parmesan cheese
- Freshly ground black peppe

Instructions
1. Place a large skillet over medium-high heat and melt the buter.
2. Add the zucchini and sauté until tender and lightly browned, about 5 minutes.
3. Spread the zucchini evenly in the skillet and sprinkle the Parmesan cheese over the vegetables.
4. Cook without stirring until the Parmesan cheese is melted and crispy where it touches the skillet, about 5 minutes

MUSHROOMS WITH CAMEMBERT
Nutrition: Cal 161;Fat 13 g; Carb 4 g;Protein 9 g
Serving 4; Cook time 20 min

Ingredients
- 2 tablespoons butter
- 2 teaspoons minced garlic
- 1 pound button mushrooms, halved
- 4 ounces Camembert cheese, diced
- Freshly ground black pepper

Instructions
1. Place a large skillet over medium-high heat and melt the buter.
2. Sauté the garlic until translucent, about 3 minutes.
3. Sauté the mushrooms until tender, about 10 minutes.
4. Stir in the cheese and sauté until melted, about 2 minutes.
5. Season with pepper and serve

MEXICAN-STYLE ZUCCHINI AND POBLANOS
Nutrition: Cal 250;Fat 20 g; Carb 2 g;Protein 14 g
Serving 6; Cook time 15 min

Ingredients
- 1 tablespoon vegetable oil
- 2 poblano peppers, seeded and cut lengthwise into ½-inch strips
- 2 teaspoons unsalted butter
- ½ onion, thinly sliced
- 1 tablespoon minced garlic
- 1-pound ground pork
- 1 zucchini, cut into thick rounds
- 1 yellow crookneck squash, cut into thick rounds
- ½ cup chicken broth

- ½ teaspoon ground cumin
- 1 teaspoon salt
- 1 tablespoon Mexican crema or sour cream

Instructions

1. Select "Sauté" to preheat the Instant Pot and adapt to high heat. When the hot, add the oil and invite it to shimmer. Add the poblano strips in a single layer, working in batches if necessary, and char on each side, flipping only occasionally, for around 10 minutes.
2. Add the butter for the pot. Once melted, add the onion and garlic, and sauté until soft, 2 to 3 minutes.
3. Add the soil pork and break it into chunks, mixing it well using the vegetables. Cook before lumps are finished in the meat, and it's half-way cooked, about four or five minutes.
4. Add the zucchini, squash, broth, cumin, and salt on the pot.
5. Lock the lid. Select "Pressure Cook" or "Manual" as well as set pressure to low. Cook for two main minutes. When the cooking is complete, quick-release pressure. Unlock the lid.
6. Stir inside cream, therefore it fully incorporates in the sauce.

ASPARAGUS WITH COLBY CHEESE

Nutrition: Cal 170;Fat 12 g; Carb 8 g;Protein 8 g
Serving 4; Cook time 10 min

Ingredients

- 1 ½ pounds fresh asparagus
- 2 tablespoons organic olive oil
- 4 garlic cloves, minced
- sea salt, to taste
- ¼ teaspoon ground black pepper
- ½ cup Colby cheese, shredded

Instructions

1. Add 1 cup of water as well as a steamer basket in your Instant Pot.
2. Now, put the asparagus around the steamer basket; drizzle your asparagus with olive oil. Scatter garlic in the top in the asparagus. Season with salt and black pepper.
3. Secure the lid. Choose "Manual" mode and questionable; cook for 1 minute. Once cooking is complete, work with a quick pressure release; carefully eliminate the lid.
4. Transfer the prepared asparagus to some nice serving platter and scatter shredded cheese in the top.

VEGGIE SCRAMBLE

Nutrition: Cal 200;Fat 5 g; Carb 9 g;Protein 20 g
Serving 4; Cook time 30 min

Ingredients

- 4 egg whites
- 1 egg yolk
- 2 tbsps. almond milk
- 1 cup spinach
- 1 tomato, chopped
- ½ white onion, chopped
- 3 fresh basil leaves, chopped
- salt and pepper, to taste
- ghee

Instructions

1. In a bowl, whisk the egg yolk and whites while using milk. Stir well.
2. Heat the ghee in the pan over medium heat. Add the onions and sauté until fragrant.
3. Add inside tomato to the pan with all the spinach and cook prior to the spinach is almost wilted.
4. Pour the egg mixture within the spinach and cook until firm (or before the egg sets). Stir constantly. Season with salt and pepper.

PRESSURE COOKER QUINOA AND RICE

Nutrition: Cal 100;Fat 0,6 g; Carb 0,7 g;Protein 3 g
Serving 4; Cook time 15 min

Ingredients

- Rice (white, freckled or brow, 1 ¾ cups)
- Quinoa (5 tbsp)
- Water (3 cups)

Instructions

1. Add the rinsed rice and quinoa and water inside Pressure cooker; close the top's and set to "High pressure" for 3 minutes.
2. Once the timer signalizes, the cooking ends, release pressure to succeed naturally for 10 minutes.
3. Open the lid, stir the rice and quinoa somewhat bit and serve while it's hot.

CHICKPEA CURRY AND RICE

Nutrition: Cal 290;Fat 5,6 g; Carb 50 g;Protein 9 g
Serving 4; Cook time 20 min

Ingredients

- Chickpeas (1 cup, make sure these were soaked in water overnight)
- Oil (by choice, 1 tbsp)
- Water (1 cup)
- Tomatoes pure or sauce (about 2 cups)
- Onion (1, chopped)
- Spice mix Chana Masala (2 tbsp)
- Ginger (1 tbsp, chopped)
- Garlic (1 tbsp, chopped)
- Salt (1 teaspoon)

Instructions

1. Pour water and add the rice in a very pot that's heatproof and cover it which has a foil.
2. The pressure cooker should be pre-heated if you add inside oil and also the onion. Set it to "Sauté" and cook the onion till it glazes and softens up a bit bit.
3. Add the garlic, ginger and chana masala spice mix to pressure cooker and cook for half one minute.

4. Now add the chickpeas, water, and tomatoes and mix the ingredients.
5. Place the trivet inside pressure cooker (on the
6. ingredients) and on the top than it add the heatproof pot or container (make certain they can fit inside). Close and secure the coverage and hang to "High pressure" for twenty minutes.
7. Release pressure naturally for 10 mins once it's cooked; open the lid and serve the rice as well as the chickpeas in bowls.

VEGIES, LENTILS AND MILLET PRESSURE COOKER MIX

Nutrition: Cal 300;Fat 13 g; Carb 58 g;Protein 20 g
Serving 4; Cook time 30 min

Ingredients
- Leek (1 cup)
- Asparagus (1 cup)
- Sugar snap peas (1 cup)
- Bok Choy (half cup, chopped)
- Lentils (half cup)
- Mushrooms (any kind, half cup)
- Millet (1 cup)
- Garlic (2 cloves, chopped)
- Parsley, garlic chives and onion chives mix (1/4 cup)
- Lemon juice
- Salt

Instructions
1. Set the pressure cooker to "Sauté" and add inside the mushrooms and garlic and sauté to get a short while. Then add the lentils and millet and cook for one more minute. Then add the vegetable stock.
2. Close and secure the cover and hang it to "High pressure"; allow it to go cook for 10 mins and after that release pressure naturally.
3. Open the lid and add the peas, asparagus, and bok choy (you might be free to utilize some other vegetable by choice, obviously).
4. Close the superior again and allowed this to mix sit for a little bit.
5. The millet has to be well cooked (it ought to be yellow).
6. Stir, add the parsley and chives mix and serve in a very bowl. Squeeze some lemon juice and add salt by taste.

NO-COOK FALAFEL

Nutrition: Cal 106;Fat 9 g; Carb 2,5 g;Protein 5,5 g
Serving 10; Cook time 10 min

Ingredients
- ¾ cup (120g) hulled hemp seeds
- 1 tablespoon dried parsley leaves
- 1½ teaspoons ground cumin
- 1 teaspoon granulated onion
- ½ teaspoon granulated garlic
- ¼ teaspoon cracked black pepper
- Grated zest of 1 lemon

- ¼ cup (64g) tahini, room temperature

Instructions
1. Line a rimmed baking sheet with parchment paper.
2. Using a food processor or blender, grind the hemp seeds until a coarse meal forms.
3. Transfer the hemp meal to a medium-sized mixing bowl, then add the rest of ingredients except the tahini and whisk together until combined.
4. Stir in the tahini and continue to mix until the ingredients are well combined and a somewhat crumbly dough forms. It will have the texture of pie dough and should hold together when pinched.
5. Using your hands, roll the mixture into 10 balls, about 1 tablespoon each. Place the balls on the lined baking sheet.
6. Chill in the freezer for at least 30 minutes or in the refrigerator for 2 hours so the falafel balls hold together.

LUPINI HUMMUS

Nutrition: Cal 162;Fat 15 g; Carb 4 g;Protein 5 g
Serving 2; Cook time 5 min

Ingredients
- 1½ cups (250g) jarred lupini beans (packed in brine), drained
- ½ cup (120 ml) extra-virgin olive oil
- ½ cup (120 ml) water
- ¼ cup (64g) tahini, room temperature
- Juice of 1 lemon
- 1 teaspoon crushed garlic
- 1 teaspoon ground cumin
- Paprika, for sprinkling

Instructions
1. Put the lupini beans, olive oil, water, tahini, lemon juice, garlic, and cumin in a food processor or high-powered blender and blend until smooth, 2 to 3 minutes. Transfer to a serving bowl and sprinkle with paprika.

CUCUMBER AVOCADO PINWHEELS

Nutrition: Cal 201;Fat 16 g; Carb 10 g;Protein 7 g
Serving 2; Cook time 10 min

Ingredients
- 1 medium Hass avocado (7½ ounces/212g)
- 2 sheets sushi nori
- 2 tablespoons (20g) sesame seeds
- ½ cup (50g) thinly sliced cucumbers
- ½ cup (30g) broccoli sprouts

DIPPING SAUCE SUGGESTIONS:
- Low-sodium tamari or coconut aminos with sliced scallions (green parts only)
- Tangy Avocado Mayo (here) or vegan mayo of choice

Instructions
1. Cut the avocado in half and remove the pit. Scoop the flesh into a small dish and mash with a fork.

2. Lay each sheet of nori on a flat surface and spread half of the mashed avocado on each sheet, leaving 1 inch (2.5 cm) of space at the far end of each sheet.
3. Sprinkle a tablespoon of the sesame seeds over the avocado on each sheet.
4. Lay out half of the cucumber slices on each sheet and top each with half of the broccoli sprouts.
5. Wet the far edge of each nori sheet with a little water. Starting at the edge closest to you, roll up the sheet into a roll. Press gently along the seam to make sure the wet edge of nori is sealed up against the roll.
6. Slice each roll into 6 to 8 pieces (depending on your preference), running the knife under water before each cut.
7. Serve with the dipping sauce of your choice.

CURRY TOFU SALAD BITES
Nutrition: Cal 148;Fat 10 g; Carb 6.5 g;Protein 11 g
Serving 8; Cook time 10 min

Ingredients
- 1 (14-ounce/397-g) package extra-firm tofu, drained
- ¼ cup (60 ml) Tangy Avocado Mayo (here) or vegan mayo of choice
- ¼ cup (25g) diced celery
- 2 teaspoons curry powder or chili powder
- ¼ teaspoon salt
- 32 thin slices cucumber (about 1 cup/100g)
- Cracked black pepper
- 2 scallions (green parts only), sliced

Instructions
1. In a large mixing bowl, mash together the tofu, mayo, celery, curry powder, and salt until uniformly mixed.
2. Scoop about 1 tablespoon of the tofu mixture on top of each cucumber slice.
3. Top with freshly ground pepper and sliced scallions and serve.

CARROT GINGER SOUP
Nutrition: Cal 234;Fat 20 g; Carb 8 g;Protein 20 g
Serving 4; Cook time 30 min

Ingredients
- 2 tablespoons (30 ml) extra-virgin olive oil
- 1½ cups (190g) sliced carrots
- 1 tablespoon grated fresh ginger
- 1½ cups (360 ml) vegetable broth
- 1 (13.5-ounce/400-ml) can full-fat coconut milk
- Grated zest of 1 lemon
- ¼ teaspoon freshly ground black pepper

Instructions
1. Heat the oil in a large saucepan over medium heat. Add the carrots and ginger and cook for about 5 minutes, stirring occasionally, until the carrots begin to soften.
2. Add the broth and coconut milk to the pan and cover. Continue to cook for 20 minutes, until the carrots are tender and can easily be pierced with a knife.

3. Pour the soup into a blender and blend until smooth, about 2 minutes.
4. To serve, divide the soup among 4 bowls and top with the lemon zest and freshly ground black pepper

SPICY COCONUT SOUP
Nutrition: Cal 162;Fat 15 g; Carb 5 g;Protein 7 g
Serving 4; Cook time 30 min

Ingredients
- 1 (14-ounce/397-g) block extra-firm tofu
- ½ cup (50g) sliced red bell peppers, plus extra for garnish
- ½ cup (30g) shredded red cabbage, plus extra for garnish

FOR GARNISH (OPTIONAL):
- Microgreens
- 1 stalk lemongrass, sliced
- Grated lime zest

Instructions
1. Heat the coconut milk, broth, tamari, chili paste, garlic, ginger, and lime juice in a large saucepan over medium heat, stirring just to mix the ingredients, about 5 minutes.
2. Drain, press, and cut the tofu into 1-inch (2.5-cm) cubes and add to the soup. Add the sliced peppers and shredded cabbage, cover, and continue to simmer for 15 minutes, until the peppers and cabbage are soft.
3. Remove from the heat and portion into bowls to serve. Garnish as desired.
4. To store: Refrigerate in a tightly sealed container for up to 4 days or freeze for up to a month.
5. To reheat: Warm in a covered saucepan over medium-low heat until the desired temperature is reached.

CREAMY CAULIFLOWER SOUP
Nutrition: Cal 289;Fat 20 g; Carb 10 g;Protein 16 g
Serving 4; Cook time 25 min

Ingredients
- 2 tablespoons (30 ml) extra-virgin olive oil
- 4 cups (400g) cauliflower pieces
- 3 cups (720 ml) vegetable broth
- ¾ cup (120g) hulled hemp seeds
- ¼ cup (20g) nutritional yeast
- 1 tablespoon chopped fresh chives

TOPPING SUGGESTIONS:
- Additional chopped fresh chives or sliced scallions (green parts only)
- Sauerkraut
- Freshly ground black pepper

Instructions
1. Heat the oil in a large saucepan over medium heat. Add the cauliflower and cook for about 5 minutes, stirring occasionally, until the pieces begin to soften.
2. Add the broth and continue to cook until the cauliflower is tender and can easily be pierced with a knife.

3. Carefully pour the soup into a heat-safe high-powered blender and add the hemp seeds, nutritional yeast, and chives. Blend until smooth, 2 to 3 minutes.

4. To serve, divide the soup among serving bowls and top as desired.

<u>DESSERTS</u>

COOKIES AND MUFFIN

KETO CHOCOLATE CHIP COOKIE MUFFINS

Nutrition: Cal 211; Fat 18 g; Carb 6 g; Protein 5 g
Serving 12; Cook time 30 min

Ingredients

• 4 eggs
• 1/2 cup butter, avocado oil or coconut oil
• ⅔ cup coconut flour, packed and leveled
• 1 cup super fine almond flour
• 1/2 cup sugar-free sweetener
• 1 ½ tsp baking powder
• 1/2 tsp ground cinnamon
• 1/4 tsp sea salt
• 2/3 cup chocolate chips

Instructions

1. Preheat the oven to 350 degrees F and line a muffin tray with muffin papers.
2. Crack the eggs into a mixing bowl and whisk well. Pour in the melted butter and whisk until combined (the wet ingredients).
3. In a separate mixing bowl, stir together the coconut flour, almond flour, sugar-free sweetener, baking powder, ground cinnamon, sea salt and chocolate chips (the dry ingredients).
4. Pour the flour mixture into the bowl with the wet mixture and mix until well combined. A thick dough will form - this is normal.
5. Fill the muffin holes ¾ of the way full and bake on the center rack of the preheated oven for 20 to 24 minutes, until the muffin cookies are golden-brown and baked through.
6. Allow the muffins cookies to cool for at least 30 minutes before peeling off the muffin paper and enjoying!

KETO MUFFINS CLASSIC CINNAMON

Nutrition: Cal 190; Fat 13 g; Carb 4.5 g; Protein 5 g
Serving 12; Cook time 30 min

Ingredients

• 1/2 cup heavy cream
• 5 tablespoon butter, softened
• 2 large eggs
• 1 teaspoon vanilla
• 1/2 cup powdered sweetener
• 1 ½ cups blanched almond flour
• 2 tablespoons psyllium husk powder
• 2 teaspoon baking powder
• 1/2 teaspoon nutmeg
• 1/2 teaspoon ginger
• 1/4 teaspoon allspice

FOR THE COVERING:

• 2 tablespoon butter, melted
• 1 teaspoon cinnamon
• 1/4 cup granulated sweetener

Instructions

1. Preheat oven to 350. Line a muffin pan with papers.
2. In a medium bowl using an electric mixer, cream butter, sweetener and vanilla until smooth. Beat in eggs and cream.
3. In a separate bowl, whisk together all dry ingredients (except for the topping ingredients). Slowly add to the wet ingredients, continuously mixing with the electric mixer.
4. Spoon even amounts into each muffin cup.
5. Bake 18-20 minutes or until edges are golden and set up.
6. Allow to cool completely.
7. Brush finished muffins with butter, roll in cinnamon sweetener mix. Serve!

KETO BLUEBERRY MUFFINS

Nutrition: Cal 217; Fat 19 g; Carb 6 g; Protein 7 g
Serving 12; Cook time 30 min

Ingredients

• 2 1/2 cup Wholesome Yum Blanched Almond Flour
• 1/2 cup Besti Monk Fruit Allulose Blend
• 1 1/2 tsp Baking powder
• 1/4 tsp Sea salt (optional, but recommended)
• 1/3 cup Coconut oil (measured solid, then melted; can also use butter)
• 1/3 cup Unsweetened almond milk (at room temperature)
• 3 large Eggs (at room temperature)
• 1/2 tsp Vanilla extract
• 3/4 cup Blueberries

Instructions

1. Preheat the oven to 350 degrees F (177 degrees C). Line a muffin pan with 10 or 12 silicone or parchment paper muffin liners. (Use 12 for lower calories/carbs, or 10 for larger muffin tops.)
2. In a large bowl, stir together the almond flour, Besti, baking powder and sea salt.
3. Mix in the melted coconut oil, almond milk, eggs, and vanilla extract. Fold in the blueberries.
4. Distribute the batter evenly among the muffin cups. Bake for about 20-25 minutes, until the top is golden and an inserted toothpick comes out clean.

KETO CHOCOLATE MUFFINS

Nutrition: Cal 246; Fat 16 g; Carb 8 g; Protein 6 g
Serving 12; Cook time 32 min

Ingredients

• 2 cups almond flour (or almond meal)
• 1/4 cup unsweetened cocoa
• 1/4 teaspoon salt
• 1/2 teaspoon baking powder
• 1/4 cup oil
• 1/4 cup sugar-free maple flavored syrup (we use Lakanto)
• 3 large eggs, room temperature
• 1/2 cup sugar-free, dairy-free dark chocolate chips

Instructions

1. Preheat oven to 350°F Line a cupcake pan with 12 paper liners; set aside.
2. In a large mixing bowl, whisk almond flour, cocoa, salt, and baking powder.
3. Add in the oil, maple flavored syrup, and eggs and mix until combine.
4. Stir in the chocolate chips.
5. Spoon batter evenly into your paper liners.
6. Bake for 18-20 minutes or until the center is set.
7. Remove from the oven and let cool for 5-10 minutes before serving.
8. Store in an airtight container at room temperature.

KETO LEMON MUFFINS

Nutrition: Cal 209; Fat 25 g; Carb 4.5 g;Protein 8 g
Serving 12; Cook time 40 min

Ingredients
FOR THE MUFFIN:
- 1/2 cup butter, softened
- 3/4 cup granulated erythritol sweetener
- 3 large eggs
- 3 tablespoons lemon juice
- 1 tablespoon lemon zest
- 1 1/2 cup superfine almond flour
- 1/2 cup coconut flour
- 2 teaspoons baking powder
- 1/4 teaspoon xanthan gum or arrowroot powder
- 1/2 teaspoon vanilla extract
- 1 cup full fat sour cream (or 1/2 cup unsweetened almond milk)
- pinch of salt

FOR THE STREUSEL TOPPING:
- 3 tablespoons butter, melted
- 3/4 cup superfine almond flour
- 3 tablespoons granulated erythritol sweetener
- 1 teaspoon grated lemon zest
- 1 tablespoon coconut flour

FOR THE LEMON GLAZE:
- 1/2 cup confectioners style erythritol sweetener
- 3 tablespoons lemon juice

Instructions
FOR THE MUFFIN LAYER:
1. Combine all of the muffin ingredients in a blender and blend for 2-3 minutes or until smooth. The mixture is thick so you'll have to stop a few times and scrape the sides down with a silicone spatula to get it going the first minute or so.
2. Preheat the oven to 350 degrees (F) and then start your streusel topping.

FOR THE STREUSEL TOPPING:
1. Combine the melted butter, almond flour, sweetener, lemon zest and coconut flour in a small bowl and stir well with a fork until a crumbly dough forms.
2. Spoon the muffin batter from the blender into 8 large or 12 regular muffin cups (if you're using foil or thin paper then place inside a muffin tin to support them) – or into a small loaf or cake pan.
3. Crumble the streusel topping in pea sized pieces over the top of the batter.
4. Bake on the middle rack of your oven at 350 degrees for 35 minutes (large muffins) or 25 minutes (average sized muffin) or 50 minutes (loaf or cake pan) OR until a toothpick or knife inserted in the center comes out clean.

FOR THE LEMON GLAZE:
1. Combine the erythritol and lemon juice in a cup or small bowl. Stir with a fork until smooth.
2. If too runny, add another tablespoon of erythritol (or more) until an opaque but still pourable glaze forms.
3. If too stiff to pour, add another teaspoon of lemon juice to loosen.
4. Pour the glaze over the muffins after they are baked and slightly cool. Serve warm or room temperature.
5. Store any leftovers covered in the refrigerator for up to a week.

KETO ALMOND FLOUR MUFFINS

Nutrition: Cal 197; Fat 18 g; Carb 9 g; Protein 8 g
Serving 12; Cook time 30 min

Ingredients
FOR THE MUFFINS
- 2 1/2 cups almond flour blanched almond flour, not almond meal
- 2 teaspoon baking powder
- 1/4 teaspoon salt
- 1/2 cup granulated sweetener of choice erythritol or monk fruit sweetener
- 3 large eggs
- 1/3 cup butter melted (can also use melted coconut oil)
- 6 tablespoon milk of choice I used unsweetened almond milk

FOR THE STREUSEL TOPPING
- 1/2 cup almond flour
- 2 tablespoon coconut flour
- 1/2 cup chopped nuts of choice I used chopped walnuts
- 1 tablespoon cinnamon
- 3 tablespoon granulated sweetener of choice
- 1/4 cup melted butter

ICING DRIZZLE
- 1/4 cup sugar free powdered sugar
- 1-2 tablespoon water

Instructions
1. Preheat the oven to 180C/350F. Grease a 12-count muffin tin with muffin liners and set aside.
2. Start by preparing your streusel topping. Add all the ingredients into a mixing bowl, and mix together, until a crumble remains. Set aside.
3. In a small bowl, add your almond flour, baking powder, and salt and mix well. Set aside. In a separate bowl, add the sweetener, eggs, milk, and melted butter, and whisk together, until smooth and glossy.

209

4. Gently add the dry ingredients into the wet ingredients and fold them in, until smooth and combined. Distribute the muffin batter evenly amongst the muffin tin. Sprinkle with the crumble topping over each one.
5. Bake the muffins for 22-25 minutes, or until a skewer comes out clean. Remove from the oven and let cool in the muffin pan for 10 minutes, before transferring to a wire rack to cool completely.
6. Once cooled, make your icing by whisking together the powdered sugar with water. Drizzle over the top of each muffin.

1-MINUTE KETO MUFFINS RECIPE

Nutrition: Cal 113; Fat 6 g; Carb 5 g; Protein 7 g
Serving 1; Cook time 5 min

Ingredients
• 1 eggs - medium
• 2 teaspoon coconut flour or more depending on brand used
• pinch baking powder
• pinch salt

Instructions
1. Grease a ramekin dish (or very large coffee mug) with coconut oil or butter.
2. Mix all the ingredients together with a fork to ensure it is lump free.
3. Cook the 1-minute keto muffin in the microwave on HIGH for 45 seconds - 1 minute. Alternatively, they can be baked in an oven, at 200C/400F for 12 minutes.
4. Cut in half and serve.

KETO PUMPKIN MUFFINS

Nutrition: Cal 204; Fat 13 g; Carb 7 g; Protein 6 g
Serving 12; Cook time 25 min

Ingredients
PUMPKIN SPICE MUFFINS
• 2 cups almond flour
• 1/2 cup Brown Sugar Swerve Sweetener
• 2 tablespoons coconut flour
• 1 tablespoons baking powder
• 2 teaspoons pumpkin pie spice
• 1/2 teaspoon salt
• 1 cup pure pumpkin puree
• 4 large eggs
• 1/2 cup unsweetened almond milk
PECAN CRUMB TOPPING
• 1/3 cup almond flour
• 1/4 cup Brown Sugar Swerve
• 2 tablespoons coconut flour
• 3 tablespoons crushed pecans
• 1 teaspoon cinnamon
• 3 tablespoons butter, cold

Instructions
1. Preheat the oven to 325 degrees F.

2. In a medium size mixing bowl, combine all of the pumpkin muffin ingredients until well combined.
3. Spray a muffin tin or line with paper liners.
4. Spoon the pumpkin mixture into the muffin tin until 3/4 full, set aside.
5. In a small bowl, combine the pecan crumb topping and mash with a fork until the butter is incorporated and it resembeles course crumbs.
6. Sprinkle the topping on the muffins.
7. Bake 20-22 minutes, or until a toothpick comes out clean.

KETO STRAWBERRY, ALMOND AND CHOCOLATE MUFFINS

Nutrition: Cal 244; Fat 20 g; Carb 8 g; Protein 6 g
Serving 12; Cook time 35 min

Ingredients
• 25 g (1/4 cup) coconut flour
• 3 tsp baking powder
• 200 g (2 cups) almond meal
• 50 g (1/4 cup) powdered stevia sweetener
• 250 g strawberries, hulled, chopped
• 75 g dark chocolate (85% cocoa), chopped
• 3 eggs, lightly whisked
• 2 tsp vanilla extract
• 60 ml (1/4 cup) almond milk
• 125 g unsalted butter, melted

Instructions
1. Preheat oven to 170C/150C fan forced. Line 12 holes of an 80ml (1/3 cup) capacity muffin pan with paper cases.
2. Sift the coconut flour and baking powder into a large bowl. Add the almond meal , stevia , strawberries and chocolate and stir to combine.
3. Whisk the eggs , vanilla and almond milk together in a jug. Add the egg mixture and butter to the dry ingredients and stir until just combined.
4. Divide the mixture among the prepared muffin holes. Bake for 20-25 minutes or until golden and a skewer inserted into the centre comes out clean. Set aside for 5 minutes, to cool, before transferring to a wire rack to cool completely.

KETO CHOCOLATE CREAM CHEESE MUFFINS

Nutrition: Cal 195; Fat 19 g; Carb 6 g; Protein 6 g
Serving 12; Cook time 30 min

Ingredients
• 1 1/4 cups of finely milled almond flour , measured and sifted
• 1/4 cup cocoa powder
• 1 teaspoon of instant coffee (optional for enhancing chocolate)
• teaspoons of baking powder
• 1/4 teaspoon of sea salt

•4 tablespoons of unsalted butter, room temperature

•1 cup plus 2 tablespoons of sugar substitute

•4 ounces of cream cheese, room temperature

•1 teaspoon of vanilla extract

•4 eggs , room temperature

•1 ounces of baking chocolate (melted)

Instructions

2. Preheat the oven to 400 degrees and line the muffin pan with your choice of liners.

3. In a medium-sized bowl combine all the almond flour, cocoa powder, instant coffee, baking powder, and sea salt. Set aside.

4. In a large mixing bowl beat on high the softened butter, vanilla, and sugar substitute until light and fluffy.

5. Add the cream cheese and combine well until fully incorporated.

6. Add the eggs one at a time making sure to mix well after each addition.

7. Add all the dry ingredients to the wet ingredients, mixing well until fully combined.

8. Lastly, add the melted baking chocolate in a stream and beat the mixture until fully mixed.

9. Divide the batter evenly into your prepared muffin pan filling each cup 3/4 full.

10. Bake the muffins for 5 minutes at 400 degrees temperature. Then after 5 minutes reduce your temperature to 350 and bake for another 10-15 minutes. Or until an inserted toothpick comes out clean.

11. Allow the chocolate muffins to cool on a baking rack for at least 10 minutes before enjoying.

12. Store leftovers in the refrigerator for up to 5 days or freeze for up to 3 weeks.

TRIPLE CHOCOLATE ZUCCHINI MUFFINS

Nutrition: Cal 205; Fat 17 g; Carb 4,6 g; Protein 5,5 g
Serving 35; Cook time 35 min

Ingredients

•6 oz zucchini

•1 cup classic monk fruit sweetener

•1 cup coconut flour

•1/3 cup unsweetened cocoa powder

•2 1/2 tsp cream of tartar

•1 tsp baking soda

•1/2 tsp espresso powder

•1/4 tsp salt

•1/4 tsp xanthan gum

•7 large eggs

•3/4 tsp pure vanilla extract

•oz 100% Baker's chocolate

•5 oz unsalted butter or coconut oil for dairy-free

•3 tbsp 100% cocoa chocolate chips

Instructions

1. Preheat the oven to 350 degrees and line 2 muffin pans with cupcake liners.

2. Measure and sift the almond flour and set it aside.

3. In a large bowl, using an electric mixer combine the cream cheese, butter, and beat on high until light and fluffy.

4. Add the sugar substitute and continue to mix well.

5. Add in the eggs one at a time, mixing well between each addition.

6. Next, stir in the sifted almond flour, salt, and baking powder and mix until well combined.

7. Next, add the lemon extract and lemon zest and mix.

8. Lastly, fold in 1 1/2 cups of the raspberries until fully incorporated.

9. Pour cake batter into two cupcake-lined muffin pans.

10. Sprinkle a few raspberries on the surface of each muffin.

11. Bake for 20-25 minutes or until an inserted toothpick comes out clean.

12. Muffins can be stored for up to 5 days in the refrigerator or frozen for up to 3 weeks.

KETO PECAN MUFFINS

Nutrition: Cal 270; Fat 30 g; Carb 10 g; Protein 7 g
Serving 6; Cook time 40 min

Ingredients

•3/4 cup raw pecans, toasted and chopped

•1/4 cup butter, melted

•2 large eggs

•2 tbsp heavy whipping cream

•1 tsp vanilla extract

•15-20 drops liquid stevia

•1/4 tsp Pink Himalayan Salt

•1 tsp ground cinnamon

•1 tsp allspice

•1/4 inch fresh grated ginger

•2 tsp baking powder

•1 cup almond flour

•1/4 cup Low Carb Sugar Substitute

•1/4 cup Keto Chocolate Chips optional

Instructions

1. Preheat your oven to 350 degrees. Add the pecans to a sheet pan and toast for 10-12 minutes.

2. Add the melted butter, eggs, hwc, vanilla and stevia to medium bowl and combine using a hand mixer.

3. Add the remaining ingredients, except for the pecans and chocolate chips and combine one more.

4. Fold in the chocolate chips and toasted, chopped pecans until evenly combined.

5. Grease a muffin tin and distribute the batter among 6 - it will make 6 large muffins.

6. Bake for 20-23 minutes.

7. Allow to cool for 5 minutes and enjoy! Best stored in the fridge in a zip top bag.

KETO LEMON POPPYSEED MUFFINS

Nutrition: Cal 100; Fat 12 g; Carb 2 g; Protein 4 g
Serving 12; Cook time 5 min

Ingredients

- ¾ cup almond flour
- ¼ cup golden flaxseed meal
- 1/3 cup erythritol
- 1 teaspoon baking powder
- 2 tablespoons poppy seeds
- ¼ cup salted butter, melted
- ¼ cup heavy cream
- 3 large eggs
- Zest of 2 lemons
- 3 tablespoons lemon juice
- 1 teaspoon vanilla extract
- 25 drops liquid Stevia

Instructions

1. Pre-heat oven to 350F. In a bowl, combine almond flour, flaxseed meal, erythritol, and poppy seeds together.
2. Stir in the melted butter, eggs, and heavy cream until smooth. Then add the baking powder, vanilla, stevia, lemon zest, and lemon juice. Mix again until well combined.
3. Measure the batter out equally between 12 cupcake molds. Bake for 18-20 minutes or until slight browning appears.
4. Remove from the oven and let cool for about 10 minutes on the counter. Slice and serve!

KETO PUMPKIN CHIA MUFFINS

Nutrition: Cal 211; Fat 18 g; Carb 3 g; Protein 7 g
Serving 12; Cook time 30 min

Ingredients

DRY INGREDIENTS:

- 1 1/2 cups almond flour
- 1/4 cup ground chia seeds
- 1 tbsp gluten-free baking powder
- 1 tbsp pumpkin pie spice mix
- 1/4 cup Erythritol or Swerve, powdered
- Topping: 6 tbsp pumpkin seeds (pepitas)

WET INGREDIENTS:

- 1 cup pumpkin purée (you can make your own)
- 6 large eggs, separated
- 1/2 cup butter, ghee or virgin coconut oil, melted
- 20-30 drops liquid Stevia extract
- melted coconut oil or ghee for greasing

Instructions

1. Preheat the oven to 175 °C/ 350 °F. Place all the dry ingredients - apart from the pumpkin seeds - into a bowl and combine well.
2. Separate the egg whites from the egg yolks. Using a hand beater or electric mixer, whip up the egg whites until they create soft peaks. In another bowl, place the egg yolks, melted butter, pumpkin purée and stevia.
3. The butter should be melted and cooled (don't use hot). The pumpkin purée and egg yolks should be at room temperature. If you use them straight from the fridge, the butter will clump up.
4. Process until well combined and start adding the dry mixture - a tablespoon or two at a time while mixing.
5. Add about a quarter of the whipped egg whites and mix gently. Add the remaining egg whites and fold in the batter using slow setting on your mixer or using a spatula. Be careful not to deflate the egg whites and keep the batter as fluffy as you can.
6. Line a muffin tray with 12 medium muffin paper cups.. Grease each cup with a small amount of coconut oil or ghee. Spoon the batter into the paper cups and transfer into the oven. Alternatively, you can use a silicon muffin tray or silicon muffin cups.
7. Transfer into the oven and bake for 5 minutes. After 5 minutes, sprinkle with the pumpkin seeds. Place back in the oven and bake for another 30 minutes or until the tops are golden brown.

KETO CARROT MUFFINS

Nutrition: Cal 305; Fat 27 g; Carb 8 g; Protein 7 g
Serving 12; Cook time 40 min

Ingredients

- 300 g / 3 cups grated carrot
- 5 eggs
- 180 g / ¾ cup butter, softened
- 2 very ripe medium bananas
- 150 g / 1 ¼ cup almond flour or ground almonds
- 30 g / scant ¼ cup flaxseed ground
- 50 g / ½ cup walnuts, chopped
- 2 teaspoon baking powder
- 2 teaspoon cinnamon
- 1 teaspoon mixed spice
- 2 teaspoon vanilla essence
- 1 ½ teaspoon granulated stevia
- 100 g / ½ cup cream cheese, full fat

Instructions

1. Heat your oven to 180 Celsius.
2. Blend your eggs, softened butter and bananas until thoroughly combined.
3. Mix in the ground almonds, flaxseed, spices, vanilla, 1 teaspoon stevia and baking powder.
4. Lastly, gently stir in the grated carrot and the walnuts. Make sure the carrots are grated and not ground to a pulp, which essentially separates the liquid from the fibre. This was the mistake
5. Pour the dough into a well-greased muffin tin or line your muffin tin with paper cups.
6. Bake at 180 Celsius for circa 30 minutes or until nicely browned.
7. For the icing, beat the cream cheese (should have room temperature) with ½ teaspoon of stevia and couple of

dashes of cinnamon. Spread the mixture onto to the muffins once they are cooled

KETO CRANBERRY ORANGE MUFFINS

Nutrition: Cal 144; Fat 12 g; Carb 8 g; Protein 3.5 g
Serving 12; Cook time 30 min

Ingredients
- 1 oz cream cheese, softened
- 4 eggs
- 2/3 cup (80g) powdered monk fruit sweetener or 2/3 cup (128g) classic monk fruit sweetener
- 2 tbsp (30mL) heavy whipping cream
- 2 tsp orange extract
- 1 tsp cream of tartar
- 1/2 tsp baking soda
- 1/2 tsp pure vanilla extract
- 1/4 tsp salt
- 1/2 cup (4 oz) unsalted butter
- 1/2 cup + 2 tbsp (70g) coconut flour
- 200g fresh cranberries

Instructions
1. Preheat oven to 350 degrees and line muffin tins with 12 muffin liners.
2. To a mixing bowl, add cream cheese. Using an electric mixer, whip cream cheese until creamy and fluffy. To same bowl, add eggs, monk fruit sweetener, heavy cream, orange extract, cream of tartar, baking soda, vanilla extract, and salt. Mix again with an electric mixer until ingredients are well-combined.
3. In a microwave-safe bowl, melt butter. To mixing bowl of eggs and cream cheese mixture, add melted butter and coconut flour. Mix with electric mixer until fully incorporated. Fold in cranberries.
4. Spoon dough into individual muffin liners, flattening into even layer using fingers or back of spoon, and transfer to oven to bake until muffin tops are slightly golden, about 23-25 minutes.

KETO CHEESECAKE MUFFINS

Nutrition: Cal 263; Fat 24 g; Carb 6 g; Protein 8 g
Serving 8; Cook time 30 min

Ingredients
- 1 cup almond flour
- 1 tsp baking powder
- ½ cup brown sugar substitute (we use Sukrin Gold)
- 1 tsp ground cinnamon
- ½ cup pecans (chopped)
- 1 tsp vanilla extract
- 4 eggs (large)
- 250 g cream cheese (8oz)
- salt

Instructions

1. Preheat the oven to 160C/320F and prepare your muffin moulds or cases. You will need to grease your tin. We use a silicon mould as they come out very easily and do not require any greasing
2. In a bowl combine almond flour, baking powder, cinnamon, pecans, sugar substitute and a pinch of salt
3. Chop cream cheese into small cubes
4. In a jug whisk together eggs and vanilla with a fork
5. Add the egg mixture to the dry mixture and stir to combine
6. Sprinkle the cream cheese cubes into the mixture. Take some time to do this to ensure they are all separated and not clumped together
7. Divide the mixture into your muffin moulds
8. Bake in the oven for 20-25 minutes or until they are golden brown and cooked through

KETO CHOCOLATE MUD CAKE MUF-FINS

Nutrition: Cal 180; Fat 16 g; Carb 3 g; Protein 3 g
Serving 12; Cook time 30 min

Ingredients
- 100 grams dark chocolate
- 87.5 grams butter
- 0.5 teaspoon vanilla essence
- 3 large eggs
- 0.17 cup heavy whipping cream
- tablespoons xylitol or preferred sweetener
- 1 tablespoons cocoa powder
- 4 tablespoons almond meal coarse is fine!

TO SERVE
- 0.5 cup heavy whipping cream
- 0.5 teaspoon vanilla essence
- 1 tablespoons xylitol optional
- raspberries

Instructions
1. Preheat the oven to 170C / 338F and grease a 24 cup mini muffin pan or 12 cup regular muffin pan.
2. In a small saucepan, melt the dark chocolate, butter and vanilla essence over low heat, stirring regularly. It will become a thick, glossy ganache.
3. Meanwhile, in a separate bowl, whisk together the eggs, cream and xylitol until evenly combined.
4. Once the chocolate has just melted, remove from heat and add the cocoa powder and almond meal, stirring to combine. Then stir through the egg mixture.
5. Spoon into your prepared muffin pan.
6. Cook: 12 - 15 mins for mini cakes, or 15 - 18 minutes for larger ones. Check with a toothpick - it should come out a little cakey but not wet.
7. Once cool, whip the cream with vanilla and sweetener until at stiff peaks. Pipe or spread on each cake and top with raspberries. Keep refrigerated.

CREAM CHEESE PUMPKIN MUFFINS

Nutrition: Cal 175; Fat 15 g; Carb 10 g; Protein 4 g
Serving 12; Cook time 50 min

Ingredients
- 4 eggs
- 1 egg white
- 1 cup golden monk fruit sweetener
- 1 cup pumpkin puree
- ½ cup unsalted butter, melted
- 2 tbsp coconut oil, melted
- 1 tbsp pumpkin pie spice
- 2 tsp pure vanilla extract
- 1/2 cup + 2 tbsp coconut flour
- 2 tsp cream of tartar
- 1 tsp baking soda
- ¼ tsp salt

FILLING:
- 3 oz cream cheese, softened
- 1 tbsp heavy whipping cream
- 1 tbsp powdered monk fruit sweetener
- ½ tsp pure vanilla extract

Instructions
1. Preheat oven to 350 degrees and line muffin tin with muffin liners.
2. Muffin Batter: To a mixing bowl, add eggs, egg white, golden monk fruit sweetener, pumpkin puree, melted butter, melted coconut oil, pumpkin pie spice, and vanilla extract and mix together using an electric mixer. Then, add coconut flour, cream of tartar, baking soda, and salt, and mix again with an electric mixer. Spoon mixture into muffin liners.
3. Filling: In a separate bowl, combine filling ingredients and mix with a spoon until well-combined. Spoon the filling mixture atop pumpkin batter in the muffin liners. Using a toothpick, swirl filling into pumpkin mixture.
4. Final Steps: Bake muffins until the toothpick can be poked into the center and come out cleanly about 30-35 minutes.
5. Remove muffin tin from oven and allow muffins to almost fully cool at room temperature before serving.

CHEESY CAULIFLOWER MUFFINS

Nutrition: Cal 77; Fat 5,6 g; Carb 2,7 g; Protein 4,6 g
Serving 11; Cook time 35 min

Ingredients
- 3 cups finely chopped raw cauliflower florets approximately 1/2 a head of cauliflower
- 2 large eggs
- 1 cup shredded cheddar cheese divided
- 1/4 cup almond flour
- 1/2 tsp baking powder
- 1/2 tsp dry Italian seasoning herb blend
- 1/4 tsp onion powder
- 1/4 tsp garlic powder

Instructions
1. Preheat oven to 375°F. Line a cupcake/muffin pan with cupcake liners. I prefer to use parchment cupcake liners as the muffins will not stick to them at all.
2. Combine cauliflower, eggs, 1/2 cup cheese, almond flour, baking powder, Italian seasoning, onion powder and garlic powder. Mix with a large spoon or spatula until smooth.
3. Using an ice cream scooper, scoop batter into muffin cups, about 2/3 full. You should be able to fill 11 liners. Sprinkle 1/2 cup of shredded cheese over muffins.
4. Bake for 20-25 minutes until muffins are completely cooked and no longer wet to the touch. If desired, garnish with fresh chopped parsley before serving.

DOUBLE CHOCOLATE MUFFINS

Nutrition: Cal 196; Fat 18 g; Carb 6 g; Protein 6 g
Serving 6; Cook time 30 min

Ingredients
- 48 g almond flour
- 30 g golden flaxseed meal finely ground
- 1 teaspoon baking powder
- 70 g unsalted grass-fed butter or 4 TBS coconut oil + 1 TBS coconut cream
- 1/3-1/2 cup allulose xylitol or coconut sugar if paleo (I use 1/2 cup allulose and 1/3 otherwise)
- 40 g cocoa powder
- 1/4 teaspoon kosher salt
- 1/4 teaspoon espresso powder or instant coffee (optional)
- 2 eggs at room temperature

OPTIONAL ADD-INS
- 50-80 g Lily's Sweets dark chocolate bar to taste
- 50-80 g pecans or walnuts
- flakey sea salt to garnish

Instructions
1. Position a rack in the lower third of your oven and preheat to 350°F/180°C. Line or grease and flour a muffin pan, set aside.
2. Add almond flour, flaxseed meal and baking powder to a medium bowl. Whisk until thoroughly combined, set aside.
3. Add butter (or coconut oil and cream), sweetener, cocoa powder, salt and espresso powder (optional) to a large heatproof bowl. Melt over a water bath whisking constantly (or use the microwave). You'll want to heat it up until most of the sweetener has melted and the mixture is well incorporated. Remove from heat and allow the mixture to cool slightly.
4. Add one egg at a time, whisking well after each one until completely incorporated. The texture should appear smooth, with all the sweetener dissolving into the mixture. If you used coconut oil, you want to be sure to mix it particularly well. Add the flour mixture, whisking vigorously until fully blended (about a minute). Fold in

chocolate pieces (or pecans) and spoon into prepared muffin pan.

5. Bake for 10-13 minutes if you like your keto chocolate muffins extra fudgy (they'll be set, but still jiggly), for medium fudgy-ness 14-17, and for 'normal muffin' texture 18-20 minutes. Varies a little from oven to oven, but these are good guidelines. Always keep in mind, however, that your muffins will continue to cook while cooling!

6. Sprinkle with flakey sea salt (optional) and allow to cool for at least 15-20 minutes in the muffin pan. They'll be particularly fragile right out of the oven if you made them fudgy and with xylitol, so you need to let them set.

7. Keep stored in an airtight container for 3-4 days. These guys are also best served warm.

KETO CINNAMON EGG LOAF MUFFINS
Nutrition: Cal 152; Fat 15 g; Carb 2,5 g; Protein 4
Serving 12; Cook time 30 min

Ingredients
- 4 eggs, room temperature
- 4 ounces cream cheese, room temperature
- 4 tablespoons butter, room temperature
- 1 teaspoon cinnamon
- 2 tablespoons Steviva Blends Granulated
- 1 teaspoon vanilla extract
- 1/2 cup almond flour
- 2 tablespoons butter, chilled
- 1 teaspoon cinnamon
- 2 tablespoons Steviva Blends
- 1/4 cup chopped pecans
- avocado oil spray

Instructions
1. Preheat oven to 350F
2. In a blender, combine eggs, cream cheese, butter, 1 teaspoon cinnamon, 2 tablespoons Stevia sweetener and the vanilla extract. Blended until well combined and slightly foamy, about one minute.
3. Grease your muffin cups with the avocado oil spray and pour the egg combo evenly into the muffin cups.
4. Bake for 10 minutes. While the egg loaf muffins are baking, prepare the streusel.
5. In a bowl, add the almond flour, cinnamon, Stevia sweetener, 2 tablespoon chilled butter and pecans. Using your fingertips, combine the ingredients until well mixed but crumbly.
6. After the egg loaf muffins have baked for 10 minutes, top them with the cinnamon streusel. Bake another 10 minutes.
7. Remove muffins from oven and let cool. They will appear puffy at first, but will sink back down as they cool.

CHOCOLATE CHIP BANANA BREAD MUFFINS
Nutrition: Cal 179; Fat 15 g; Carb 6 g; Protein 4
Serving 12; Cook time 35 min

Ingredients
- 1 oz cream cheese, softened
- 1 tbsp + 2 tsp banana extract
- 1/2 tsp pure vanilla extract
- 1 tsp cream of tartar
- 1/2 tsp baking soda
- 1/4 tsp salt
- 1/2 cup + 2 tbsp coconut flour
- 1/2 cup butter
- 1/3 cup chocolate chips, divided

Instructions
1. Preheat oven to 350 degrees and line muffin tins with 12 muffin liners.
2. To a mixing bowl, add eggs, classic monk fruit sweetener, heavy whipping cream, cream cheese, banana extract, vanilla extract, cream of tartar, baking soda, and salt. Mix with an electric mixer until ingredients are combined.
3. In a microwave-safe bowl, melt butter. To mixing bowl, add melted butter and coconut flour. Mix with electric mixer until fully incorporated. Fold almost all chocolate chips in to dough, saving some to top muffins with. Spoon dough into individual muffin liners. Top muffin dough with remaining chocolate chips.
4. Bake until muffin tops are slightly golden, about 23-25 minutes.

KETO CHEESY HERB MUFFINS
Nutrition: Cal 216; Fat 20 g; Carb 7,5 g; Protein 5 g
Serving 6; Cook time 40 min

Ingredients
- 6 tablespoons butter
- 1 teaspoon granulated erythritol sweetener
- 1 cup superfine blanched almond flour
- 3 tablespoons coconut flour
- 3/4 teaspoon kosher salt
- 1/4 teaspoon garlic powder
- 2 teaspoons baking powder
- ¼ teaspoon xanthan gum
- 2 eggs
- 1/2 teaspoon fresh thyme leaves
- 1/3 cup unsweetened almond milk
- 1/2 cup shredded sharp cheddar cheese

Instructions
1. Preheat the oven to 375°F.
2. Grease or line a standard cupcake pan with 8 muffin cups.
3. Place the butter in a medium-sized microwave safe bowl.
4. Microwave on high, uncovered, for 30 seconds or until melted.
5. Add the sweetener, almond flour, coconut flour, salt, garlic powder, baking powder, xanthan gum, eggs, fresh

thyme, almond milk and cheddar and mix well with a fork.

6. Spoon the batter into the muffin cups, about 2/3 full.

7. Bake for 22 minutes, or until a toothpick inserted in the center comes out clean.

KETO APPLE MUFFINS

Nutrition: Cal 221; Fat 18 g; Carb 7,5 g; Protein 5 g
Serving 6; Cook time 40 min

Ingredients

FOR THE BROWN-BUTTER 'APPLE'

- 1 tablespoon butter
- 1 large zucchini diced (about 300g)
- 1 1/2 teaspoon apple pie spice
- pinch salt
- 1-3 tablespoons golden erythritol allulose or xylitol, to taste
- 1-3 tablespoons lemon juice to taste

FOR THE 'APPLE' MUFFINS

- 64 g almond flour
- 30 g golden flaxseed meal
- 9 g psyllium husk powder
- 1 1/2 teaspoon baking powder
- 1 teaspoon apple pie spice
- 1/2 teaspoon xanthan gum
- 1/4 teaspoon kosher salt
- 1/3 cup sweetener
- 2 eggs
- 1 teaspoon vanilla extract
- 1 teaspoon apple cider vinegar
- 57 g butter
- 3 tablespoons water
- 1 cup brown-butter 'apple'

FOR THE MAPLE GLAZE (OPTIONAL)

- 2 tablespoons golden erythritol powdered
- 1 tablespoon sour or heavy cream
- 1/2 teaspoon maple extract optional

Instructions

FOR THE BROWN-BUTTER 'APPLE'

1. Heat up the butter in a skillet or pan over medium/low heat. You want to use a skillet (or wide-base pan) as opposed to a saucepan so the juices get absorbed evenly by the zucchini. Continue to cook the butter for 2-4 minutes until brown in color.

2. Add in the zucchini, spices, salt and mix everything together. Add in the lower amounts of sweetener and lemon juice, cover, lower heat to low, and let simmer for 5 minutes. Remove lid and taste for sweetness and acidity; you'll most likely need to add more of both (don't be afraid of the lemon juice, as it's acidity is what will give it that apple kick once it's thoroughly absorbed).

3. Cover once again and cook for 10 more minutes. Remove the lid, taste again, and allow to cook uncovered for 3-6 minutes longer to thicken up the juices. Allow to rest for 10 minutes and enjoy (or allow to cool and keep in the fridge for 3-4 days).

FOR THE 'APPLE' MUFFINS

1. Preheat oven to 350°F/180°C. Line (or grease and flour) a muffin pan, set aside.

2. Add almond flour, flaxseed meal, psyllium husk, baking powder, apple spice, xanthan gum and salt to a medium bowl. Whisk until thoroughly combined, set aside.

3. Add sweetener and eggs to a large bowl and beat with an electric mixer for 3-5 minutes until airy and lighter in color. With the mixer on, add in the vanilla extract, apple cider vinegar and butter.

4. Add in the dry flour mixture in two parts, alternating with the water. Continue to mix for a couple minutes until fully incor-porated and elastic, the batter will thicken as you mix. Fold in brown-butter zucchini.

5. Scoop the batter onto the prepared muffin pans, smoothing out the tops with wet fingertips.

6. Bake for 30-35 minutes, until golden and a toothpick inserted comes out clean. Watch out after minute 15, and tent with aluminum foil as soon as they begin to brown (around min 25 for me). The muffins will collapse a tad post bake as they're weighed down by the zucchini, don't sweat it!

7. To make the glaze, sift the powdered sweetener into a small bowl. Add in the cream and maple extract, and whisk to combine (adding a teaspoon of water at a time if need be).

8. Store them glazed in the fridge for 3-4 days, or unglazed at room temp (my top choice).

KETO ZUCCHINI MUFFINS

Nutrition: Cal 141; Fat 9 g; Carb 5 g; Protein 6,5 g
Serving 12; Cook time 35 min

Ingredients

- 2 cups shredded zucchini about 1 medium zucchini (196g)
- ⅔ cup coconut flour (71 g)
- ½ cup Swerve Sweetener
- ¼ cup unflavored whey protein powder or egg white protein
- 2 teaspoon baking powder
- 1 teaspoon cinnamon
- ½ teaspoon ginger
- ¼ teaspoon salt
- ⅛ teaspoon cloves
- 6 large eggs
- ¼ cup butter, melted or melted coconut oil
- 3 to 4 tablespoon water
- ½ cup chopped walnuts or pecans or chocolate chips!

Instructions

1. Set the shredded zucchini in a sieve in the sink and sprinkle lightly with salt. Let drain one hour, then squeeze as much liquid from the zucchini as possible.
2. Preheat the oven to 350F and line a muffin tin with 12 parchment or silicone liners.
3. In a large bowl, whisk together the coconut flour, sweetener, protein powder, baking powder, spices, and salt. Add the zucchini, eggs, butter, and 3 tablespoon water. Add additional water if the batter is overly thick (low carb batters tend to be quite thick as it is. This should be scoopable but not pourable).
4. Stir in the nuts, if using. Divide the batter among the prepared muffin cups and bake about 25 minutes, until the tops are lightly browned and firm to the touch.

CINNAMON ROLL MUFFINS

Nutrition: Cal 112; Fat 9 g; Carb 3 g; Protein 5 g
Serving 20; Cook time 20 min

Ingredients

- 1/2 cup almond flour
- 2 scoops vanilla protein powder 32-34 grams per scoop
- 1 teaspoon baking powder
- 1 tablespoon cinnamon
- 1/2 cup nut or seed butter of choice almond butter, peanut butter, sunflower seed butter etc.
- 1/2 cup pumpkin puree can sub for unsweetened applesauce, mashed banana or mashed cooked sweet potato
- 1/2 cup coconut oil

FOR THE GLAZE

- 1/4 cup coconut butter
- 1/4 cup milk of choice
- 1 tablespoon granulated sweetener of choice
- 2 teaspoon lemon juice

Instructions

1. Preheat the oven to 350 Fahrenheit and line a 12-count muffin tin with muffin liners and set aside. This can also be made using a mini muffin tin.
2. In a large mixing bowl, combine your dry ingredients and mix well. Add your wet ingredients and mix until fully incorporated.
3. Evenly distribute the cinnamon roll muffin batter evenly amongst the muffin liners. Bake for 10-15 minutes, checking around the 10 minute mark by inserting a skewer in the center and seeing if it comes out clean. If it does, muffins are done. Allow to cool in pan for 5 minutes, before transferring to a wire rack to cool completely.
4. Once cooled, prepare your cinnamon roll glaze by combining all ingredients and mixing until combined. Drizzle over the muffin tops and allow to firm up.

COCONUT FLOUR ZUCCHINI BREAD MUFFINS

Nutrition: Cal 125; Fat 10 g; Carb 6 g; Protein 4 g
Serving 12; Cook time 35 min

Ingredients

- 3 large eggs
- 1/4 cup coconut oil liquified
- 3/4 cup coconut flour
- 1/2 cup low carb sugar substitute or 3½ tablespoon of Truvia
- 3/4 teaspoon baking soda
- 3/4 teaspoon baking powder
- 1/4 teaspoon salt
- 1 teaspoon ground cinnamon
- 1 cup packed shredded zucchini
- 1/2 cup walnuts chopped

Instructions

1. Combine the first 8 ingredients until well blended.
2. Stir in zucchini and walnuts.
3. Spoon batter into greased muffin cups or paper liners.
4. Bake at 350 F for 20-25 minutes or until toothpick inserted in middle of muffin comes out clean.

KETO RICOTTA LEMON POPPYSEED MUFFINS

Nutrition: Cal 142; Fat 13 g; Carb 3 g; Protein 4 g
Serving 12; Cook time 50 min

Ingredients

- 1 cup (112 g) Superfine Almond Flour
- 1/3 cup (0.33 g) Swerve, or alternative sweetener
- 1 teaspoon (1 teaspoon) Baking Powder
- 1/4 cup (61.5 g) full fat ricotta cheese
- 1/4 cup (54.5 g) Coconut Oil
- 3 (3) Eggs
- 2 tablespoons (2 tablespoons) Poppy Seeds, ,
- 4 (4) True lemon packets
- 1/4 cup (59.5 g) Heavy Whipping Cream
- 1 teaspoon (1 teaspoon) Lemon Extract

Instructions

1. Mix together all ingredients and beat well until fluffy.
2. Line a muffin pan with silicone cupcake liners.
3. Pour the batter into a muffin pan, dividing equally into 12 servings.
4. Bake at 350F for 40 minutes or until a knife inserted into the center emerges clean.
5. Cool slightly before removing from liners.

CRANBERRY SOUR CREAM MUFFINS

Nutrition: Cal 241; Fat 20 g; Carb 9 g; Protein 9 g
Serving 12; Соок time 40 min

Ingredients
- ½ cup sour cream
- 4 large eggs
- 1 teaspoon vanilla extract
- 3 cups almond flour
- ½ cup Swerve Sweetener
- 2 teaspoon baking powder
- ½ teaspoon cinnamon
- ¼ teaspoon salt
- 1 cup cranberries
- ½ cup chopped pecans optional

Instructions
1. Preheat oven to 325F and line a muffin tin with parchment or silicone liners.
2. Combine sour cream, eggs, and vanilla extract in a large blender jar. Blend about 30 seconds.
3. Add the almond flour, sweetener, baking powder, cinnamon, and salt. Blend again until smooth, about 30 seconds to a minute. If your batter is overly thick, add ¼ to ½ cup of water to thin it out (different brands of almond flour can vary).
4. By hand, stir in cranberries, keeping a few for the top of the muffins, and chopped pecans if using. Divide the mixture among the prepared muffin cups and bake 25 to 30 minutes, until just golden brown and firm to the touch.
5. Remove and let cool completely.

KETO LEMON BLUEBERRY MUFFINS

Nutrition: Cal 130; Fat 10 g; Carb 7 g; Protein 2 g
Serving 12; Соок time 30 min

Ingredients
- ½ cup plain Greek yogurt
- 3 eggs
- juice of 1 lemon
- 2 teaspoons lemon zest
- ¼ cup natural Swerve sweetener
- 1 teaspoon vanilla extract
- 3 cups almond flour
- 1½ teaspoons baking powder
- ½ teaspoon baking soda
- ¼ teaspoon salt
- 1 cup blueberries fresh or frozen

Instructions
1. Preheat oven to 350°F.
2. Line a muffin tin with paper liners. Set aside.
3. Add the Greek yogurt, eggs, lemon juice, lemon zest, Swerve, and vanilla extract to a blender. Blend for about 30 seconds or until combined.
4. Add the almond flour, baking powder, baking soda, and salt. Blend on high, stopping to scrape down and stir the ingredients once or twice if necessary. Blend until the batter is smooth.
5. Fold in the blueberries. Divide the batter among the prepared muffin cups. This is very important: Fill each muffin cup ¾ full. Sprinkle with additional blueberries as desired.
6. Bake for 25-30 minutes until the tops of the muffins are set and a toothpick inserted in the center comes out clean.
7. Place the pan on a wire rack, and let the muffins cool in the pan for 10 minutes. Enjoy!

KETO BANANA NUT MUFFINS

Nutrition: Cal 183; Fat 22 g; Carb 7 g; Protein 7 g
Serving 10; Соок time 30 min

Ingredients
- 1 ¼ Cup almond flour
- ½ Cup powdered erythritol
- 2 tablespoons ground flax (feel free to omit if you don't have it...it just adds a bit more depth to the flavors)
- 2 teaspoons baking powder
- ½ teaspoons ground cinnamon
- 5 tablespoon butter, melted
- 2 ½ teaspoons banana extract
- 1 teaspoon vanilla extract
- ¼ cup unsweetened almond milk
- ¼ cup sour cream
- 2 eggs
- ¾ cup chopped walnuts
- 1 tablespoon butter, cold and cut in 4 pieces
- 1 tablespoon almond flour
- 1 tablespoon powdered erythritol

Instructions
1. Preheat oven to 350 Prepare muffin tin with 10 paper liners, and set aside.
2. In a large bowl, mix almond flour, erythritol (or preferred sweetener) flax, baking powder and cinnamon.
3. Stir in butter, banana extract, vanilla extract, almond milk, and sour cream. Add eggs to mixture and gently stir until fully combined.
4. Fill muffin tins about ½-3/4 full with mixture.

CRUMBLE TOPPING
1. Add walnuts, butter, and almond flour to food processor. Pulse a few times until nuts are chopped into small pieces. If mixture seems too dry (sometimes some walnuts are softer than others) feel free to add another tablespoon of butter.
2. Sprinkle bits of the mixture evenly over batter and gently press down. Sprinkle erythritol on top of crumble mixture.
3. Bake for 20 minutes or until golden and toothpick comes out clean. Let cool for at least 30 minutes, an hour or more if possible. This lets them firm up.

KETO SNICKERDOODLE MUFFINS
Nutrition: Cal 287; Fat 26 g; Carb 7 g; Protein 5 g
Serving 12; Cook time 35 min

Ingredients
- 2 cups (220 g) blanched finely ground almond flour
- 2/3 cup (130 g) monk fruit or erythritol
- 4 teaspoons baking powder
- 4 teaspoons ground cinnamon
- 1/2 teaspoon sea salt
- 4 large eggs
- 1/2 cup (120 ml) melted coconut oil
- 1/2 cup (120 ml) non-dairy milk
- 2 teaspoons vanilla extract
- 2/3 cup (100 g) hemp hearts
- Cinnamon Sugar Topping:
- 2 tablespoons melted coconut oil
- 1/4 cup monk fruit or erythritol
- 2 teaspoons ground cinnamon

CINNAMON SUGAR TOPPING:
- 2 tablespoons melted coconut oil
- 1/4 cup monk fruit or erythritol
- 2 teaspoons ground cinnamon

Instructions
1. Preheat oven to 350°F (177°C) and place 12 muffin liners in a 12-count muffin tin.
2. Place almond flour, erythritol, baking powder, cinnamon, and sea salt in a large bowl. Mix until combined.
3. In a separate smaller bowl, whisk eggs, melted coconut oil, milk, and vanilla extract. Then, add the egg mixture to the almond flour mixture and stir until fully combined. Then, fold in the hemp hearts.
4. Divide the batter between the prepared muffin tins and transfer to the preheated oven. Bake for 15 to 18 minutes, until the tops are golden.
5. Meanwhile, prepare the cinnamon sugar topping by placing the coconut oil in a small dish and combine the erythritol and ground cinnamon in a small bowl. Once the muffins are done, one muffin at a time, brush the top with coconut oil before placing it overtop of the cinnamon sugar bowl and sprinkling it with the cinnamon sugar. Lightly shake of excess and repeat with remaining muffins. Store in a sealed container in the fridge for up to a week, or in the freezer for up to a month.

LOW-CARB BLACKBERRY-FILLED LEMON ALMOND FLOUR MUFFINS
Nutrition: Cal 199; Fat 17 g; Carb 4 g; Protein 7g
Serving 12; Cook time 45 min

Ingredients
FOR THE BLACKBERRY FILLING:
- 3 tablespoons granulated stevia/erythritol blend (Pyure)
- 1/4 teaspoon xanthan gum
- 2 tablespoons water
- 1 tablespoon lemon juice
- 1 cup blackberries fresh or frozen

FOR THE MUFFIN BATTER:
- 2 1/2 cups super fine almond flour
- 3/4 cup granulated stevia/erythritol blend
- 1 teaspoon fresh lemon zest
- 1/2 teaspoon sea salt
- 1 teaspoon grain-free baking powder
- 4 large eggs
- 1/4 cup unsweetened almond milk original flavor
- 1/4 cup butter, ghee, or coconut oil melted
- 1 teaspoon vanilla extract
- 1/2 teaspoon lemon extract

Instructions
FOR THE BLACKBERRY FILLING:
1. In a 1 1/2 quart saucepan, whisk together the granulated sweetener and the xanthan gum. Add the water and the lemon juice one tablespoon at a time, whisking between additions.
2. Low-Carb Blackberry-Filled Lemon Almond Flour Muffins-ready for the berries.
3. Stir in blackberries. Place pan over medium low heat. Bring mixture to a simmer, stirring frequently. Turn heat to low.
4. Low-Carb Blackberry-Filled Lemon Almond Flour Muffins-adding the blackberries for the filling.
5. Simmer, stirring frequently, until berries have broken up and a thick jammy syrup has formed--about 10 minutes. Remove from heat and allow mixture to cool.
6. Low-Carb Blackberry-Filled Lemon Almond Flour Muffins-blackberry filling

FOR THE MUFFIN BATTER:
1. Preheat oven to 350° Fahrenheit. Prepare a muffin pan by lining with muffin papers.
2. In a medium bowl, whisk together the almond flour, granulated sweetener, lemon zest, sea salt and baking powder.
3. Low-Carb Blackberry-Filled Lemon Almond Flour Muffins-dry ingredients.
4. In a small bowl whisk together the eggs, almond milk, vanilla extract, and lemon extract. Stream in butter while whisking.
5. Low-Carb Blackberry-Filled Lemon Almond Flour Muffins-liquid ingredients ready to mix.
6. Slowly add liquid ingredients to dry ingredients, while stirring.
7. Low-Carb Blackberry-Filled Lemon Almond Flour Muffins-dough
8. Spoon the batter into the prepared muffin cups to partially fill about 1/3 full. Form a depression in the batter in the cups using clean fingers or a spoon.
9. Low-Carb Blackberry-Filled Lemon Almond Flour Muffins-Ready for the blackberry filling.

10. Place a spoonful of the cooled blackberry jam in each depression, dividing it equally among the cups.
11. Low-Carb Blackberry-Filled Lemon Almond Flour Muffins-adding the blackberry filling.
12. Cover the blackberry jam using the remainder of the batter until each cup is about 2/3rds full. Spread the batter to the edges of the cups to cover the jam as best you can. If cups are a little more than 2/3rds full after all of the batter is used up, that's okay.
13. Low-Carb Blackberry-Filled Lemon Almond Flour Muffins-ready for the oven
14. Bake in the preheated oven for 25-30 minutes, or until tops spring back when lightly touched.
15. Low-Carb Blackberry-Filled Lemon Almond Flour Muffins-fresh out of the oven
16. Refrigerate any extras in an airtight container. They may also be frozen if desired.

KETO COFFEE CAKE MUFFINS
Nutrition: Cal 222; Fat 18 g; Carb 9 g; Protein 7 g
Serving 12; Cook time 30 min

Ingredients
BATTER:
• 2 tablespoon butter softened
• 2 oz cream cheese softened
• 1/3 cup Joy Filled Eats Sweetener
• 4 eggs
• 2 teaspoon vanilla
• 1/2 cup unsweetened vanilla almond milk
• 1 cup almond flour
• 1/2 cup coconut flour
• 1 teaspoon baking powder
• 1/4 teaspoon salt
TOPPING:
• 1 cup almond flour
• 2 tablespoon coconut flour
• 1/4 cup Joy Filled Eats Sweetener
• 1/4 cup butter softened
• 1 teaspoon cinnamon
• 1/2 teaspoon molasses (optional)

Instructions
1. Preheat oven to 350. Line a standard muffin tin with paper liners and spray with cooking spray.
2. In a food processor combine all the batter ingredients. Mix thoroughly. Divide between the prepared muffin tin.
3. Combine topping ingredients in the food processor and pulse until crumbs form. Sprinkle on top of the batter.
4. Bake 20-25 min until golden. If the crumb topping starts to get too dark cover with foil for the last 5 minutes.

STRAWBERRY VANILLA MUFFIN
Nutrition: Cal 187; Fat 17 g; Carb 4,5 g; Protein 5,5 g
Serving 12; Cook time 30 min

Ingredients
• 2 cups Almond flour
• 2 teaspoons Baking powder
• 1/4 teaspoon Salt
• 1/2 cup Butter melted
• 1/4 cup Erythritol or sugar substitute
• 2 teaspoons Vanilla essence
• 2/3 cup Strawberries chopped
• 4 Eggs
• 1/4 Cup Water

Instructions
1. Preheat the oven to 180C/350F degrees.
2. Mix the almond flour, baking powder and salt together.
3. In another bowl mix the butter, water, eggs, erythritoll and vanilla essence.
4. Combine the wet and dry ingredients together, and stir well. Add the strawberries.
5. Pour the mixture into muffin liners in a muffin tin.
6. Bake for 15 to 20 minutes until firm.

FLAXSEED MUFFIN IN A MUG
Nutrition: Cal 283; Fat 22 g; Carb 10 g; Protein 12 g
Serving 1; Cook time 10 min

Ingredients
• 1 Egg
• 1 teaspoon Coconut Oil , melted
• 1 teaspoon Vanilla Extract
• 1/4 cup Flaxseed Meal
• 1/2 teaspoon Baking Powder
• 1/4 teaspoon Ground Cinnamon
• 1 tablespoon Erythritol or erythirtol
OPTIONAL INGREDIENTS- RASPBERRY CHOCOLATE CHIP FLAX MUFFIN
• 2 tablespoons Raspberries fresh or frozen
• 1 tablespoon Sugar-free Chocolate Chips

Instructions
1. In a bowl, whisk egg, oil, and vanilla together. Set aside.
2. Stir in the dry ingredients: flax meal, baking powder, cinnamon, and sugar-free sweetener.
3. Stir in the optional ingredients. Raspberries and chocolate chips are my favorite.
4. Transfer into a mug – mine was 2.5 inches in height. That's the minimum required to prevent the muffin from overflowing.
5. Microwave on high for 1 minute 30 seconds.
6. Wait 1 minute before eating not to burn yourself.

KETO APPLE CREAM CHEESE MUFFINS

Nutrition: Cal 254; Fat 21 g; Carb 7 g; Protein 6 g
Serving 12; Cook time 30 min

Ingredients
- 8 tablespoon butter softened
- 4 oz sour cream
- 1 teaspoon vanilla extract
- 1 cup coconut flour
- ¼ cup vanilla protein powder
- ¾ cup Sukrin Gold or low carb brown sugar sub
- 1 tsp Apple Pie Spice
- 2 teaspoon baking powder
- ½ teaspoon salt
- 1 teaspoon xanthan gum
- 6 eggs
- ¼ cup heavy cream
- ½ cup apple finely chopped
- 8 oz cream cheese softened
- 1 egg yolk
- 1 teaspoon vanilla extract
- 1 teaspoon vanilla stevia

Instructions
1. Preheat the oven to 375 degrees F.
2. Place the butter, sour cream and vanilla extract into a stand mixer and mix until smooth.
3. Whisk the next 7 dry ingredients together then add them to the mixer. Blend on low until incorporated.
4. Add in 1 egg at a time to the mixer until well absorbed.
5. Pour in the heavy cream until well absorbed.
6. Stir in the apple.
7. Set aside batter while making filling.
8. Clean your mixer then add the cream cheese, egg yolk, vanilla and stevia. Mix on high until smooth. Set aside.
9. Use cupcake liners or grease well a 12 capacity muffin pan. Fill each cup half way with batter.
10. Evenly scoop cream cheese over each muffin. Finish with remaining batter over the cream cheese on each muffin.
11. Top with a few pieces of apple if desired. Sprinkle some Sukrin Brown Sugar Sub over the top if desired.
12. Bake for 25 minutes or until a toothpick comes out clean. Best at room temperature or chilled. Keep refrigerated if making ahead for breakfast.

FLOURLESS PEANUT BUTTER MUFFINS

Nutrition: Cal 208; Fat 13 g; Carb 7,5 g; Protein 15 g
Serving 12; Cook time 35 min

Ingredients
- 1 cup peanut butter (creamy, no sugar added)
- 1 tablespoon coconut oil or butter
- ½ cup Swerve Brown
- 1 teaspoon vanilla extract
- 3 large eggs
- ½ cup collagen protein powder
- 2 teaspoon baking powder
- ¼ teaspoon salt
- ⅓ cup sugar-free chocolate chips

Instructions
1. Preheat the oven to 350°F and line a muffin pan with 12 silicone or parchment paper liners.
2. Place the peanut butter and coconut oil in a large microwave safe bowl, and microwave until they are melted and can be stirred together. Alternatively, you can melt them in a pan over low heat.
3. Whisk in the sweetener and vanilla extract until well combined, then whisk in the eggs. Add the collagen, baking powder, and salt and stir until well combined. Stir in the chocolate chips.
4. Divide the mixture evenly among the prepared muffin cups and bake 18 to 25 minutes, or until the muffins have risen, are golden brown, and firm to the touch on top.
5. Remove and let cool in the pan.

KETO GINGERBREAD MUFFINS

Nutrition: Cal 131; Fat 15 g; Carb 6,5 g; Protein 9 g
Serving 12; Cook time 40 min

Ingredients
- ½ cup sour cream
- 3 large eggs
- ¾ teaspoon vanilla extract
- ⅔ cup Swerve Brown lightly packed
- 2 ½ cups almond flour
- ⅓ cup unflavoured whey protein powder or egg white protein
- 1 tablespoon cocoa powder
- 2 teaspoon baking powder
- 2 teaspoon ground ginger
- ½ teaspoon ground cinnamon
- ⅛ teaspoon ground cloves
- ¼ teaspoon salt

VANILLA DRIZZLE
- ⅓ cup powdered Swerve Sweetener
- 1 to 2 tablespoon water
- ½ teaspoon vanilla extract

Instructions
1. Preheat the oven to 350F and line a standard metal muffin pan with 12 silicone or parchment liners.
2. In a large bowl, whisk together the sour cream, eggs, and vanilla extract. Add the sweetener and whisk until well combined, breaking up any clumps with the back of a fork.
3. Add the almond flour, protein powder, cocoa powder, baking powder, ginger, cinnamon, cloves, and salt and stir until well mixed.
4. Divide the batter evenly among the prepared muffins cups, about ¾ full. Bake 18 to 25 minutes, until golden brown and firm to the touch.
5. Remove and let cool in the pan.

VANILLA DRIZZLE

1. In a medium bowl, whisk together the sweetener and just enough water to make a drizzling consistency. Whisk in the vanilla extract.
2. Drizzle over the cooled muffins.

KETO PEACH MUFFINS
Nutrition: Cal 167; Fat 13 g; Carb 7 g; Protein 7 g
Serving 16; Cook time 50 min

Ingredients
STREUSEL TOPPING
- ½ cup almond flour
- 3 tablespoon Swerve Brown
- ¼ teaspoon salt
- 2 tablespoon melted butter

MUFFINS
- ½ cup sour cream
- 3 large eggs
- 1 teaspoon vanilla extract
- ½ teaspoon peach extract (optional)
- 2 ¼ cups almond flour
- ½ cup Swerve Granular
- ⅓ cup whey protein powder (or egg white protein powder)
- 2 teaspoon baking powder
- ¼ teaspoon salt
- 2 cups finely chopped peaches (about 2 medium peaches)

Instructions
1. In a medium bowl, whisk together the almond flour, Swerve Brown, and salt. Stir in the melted butter and toss until the mixture resembles coarse crumbs. Set aside.

MUFFINS
2. Preheat the oven to 350F and line 16 muffin cups with parchment or silicone liners.
3. In a large bowl, whisk together the sour cream, eggs, and the extracts until smooth. Stir in the almond flour, sweetener, protein powder, baking powder, and salt until well combined.
4. Stir in 1 ½ cups of the peaches and spoon into the prepared muffins cups, filling about ¾ full.
5. Top each muffin with a few additonal pieces of peach, then sprinkle with the streusel mixture. Bake 23 to 28 minutes, until golden brown and just firm to the touch

KETO JELLY DONUT MUFFINS
Nutrition: Cal 137; Fat 9 g; Carb 6 g; Protein 7 g
Serving 8; Cook time 50 min

Ingredients
"JELLY" FILLING
- ½ cup raspberries (or chopped strawberries)
- 1 tablespoon water
- ¼ cup powdered Swerve Sweetener
- ¼ teaspoon glucomannan

MINI MUFFINS
- ½ cup coconut flour
- ½ cup Swerve Sweetener
- ¼ cup unflavored whey protein powder
- 1 ½ teaspoon baking powder
- ¼ teaspoon salt
- 4 large eggs
- ¼ cup butter, melted
- ¼ cup water (more if needed)
- ¾ teaspoon vanilla extract
- Powdered sweetener for rolling

Instructions
JELLY FILLING
1. In a small saucepan over medium heat, combine the raspberries and water. Bring to a simmer, then reduce the heat to low and cook until the berries are soft enough to be mashed with a fork.
2. Mash them up, then stir in the sweetener and the glucomannan. Let cool.

MINI MUFFINS
1. Preheat the oven to 350F and grease a metal mini muffin pan well. If yours is not very non-stick, consider using silicone or parchment muffin liners.
2. In a large bowl, combine the coconut flour, sweetener, protein powder, baking powder, and salt. Add the eggs, melted butter, water, and vanilla extract and stir to combine. If the batter is very thick, add another tablespoon or two of water. It should be easily stirred but not really pourable.
3. Divide the mixture among the prepared muffin cups and bake about 15 minutes, or until the tops are firm to the touch. Remove and let cool completely in the pan.

TO ASSEMBLE
1. Once the mini muffins are cool, use a small sharp knife to cut a small cone out of the top of each. Cut off the top of the cone (the part that would be the top of the muffin) and reserve.
2. Fill the holes in the mini muffins with the raspberry filling and replace the tops. Roll the filled mini muffins in powdered sweetener.

KETO CAPPUCCINO MUFFINS
Nutrition: Cal 172; Fat 14 g; Carb 7 g; Protein 7 g
Serving 12; Cook time 45 min

Ingredients
MUFFINS:
- ½ cup sour cream
- 4 large eggs
- 1 teaspoon espresso powder
- ½ teaspoon vanilla extract
- 2 cups almond flour
- ½ cup Swerve Sweetener
- ¼ cup coconut flour
- 2 teaspoon baking powder
- 1 teaspoon cinnamon

•¼ teaspoon salt
GLAZE:
•¼ cup powdered Swerve Sweetener
•2 tablespoon heavy whipping cream
•cinnamon for garnish
Instructions
MUFFINS:
1. Preheat oven to 350F and line a muffin tin with parchment or silicone liners.
2. Combine sour cream, eggs, espresso powder, and vanilla extract in a large blender jar. Blend about 30 seconds.
3. Add the almond flour, sweetener, coconut flour, baking powder, cinnamon, and salt. Blend again until smooth, about 30 seconds to a minute. If your batter is overly thick, add ¼ to ½ cup of water to thin it out (different brands of almond flour can vary).
4. Divide the mixture among the prepared muffin cups and bake 23 to 25 minutes, until just golden brown and firm to the touch. Remove and let cool completely.
GLAZE:
1. In a small bowl, whisk together the powdered sweetener and cream. Drizzle over the cooled muffins. Sprinkle with a little cinnamon.

KETO PANCAKE MUFFINS
Nutrition: Cal 211 Fat 18 g; Carb 8 g; Protein 8 g
Serving 8; Cook time 25 min
Ingredients
•½ cup plain whole milk yogurt
•2 tablespoon unsalted butter or coconut oil melted
•3 tablespoon Swerve Sweetener or equivalent of choice (more if you like sweet muffins)
•1 teaspoon vanilla extract
•¼ teaspoon apple cider vinegar
•1 ¾ cup blanched almond flour
•½ teaspoon baking soda
•¼ teaspoon salt
•3 large eggs
•½ cup frozen blueberries and raspberries
Instructions
2. Preheat oven to 350F and line 8 muffin cups with parchment liners (or grease muffin cups very well).
3. Add yogurt, butter, sweetener, vanilla and apple cider vinegar to a blender. Then add almond flour, baking soda, and salt on top. Blend on low for 10 to 15 seconds until combined.
4. Add eggs and blend on low for another 15 to 20 seconds, then blend on high for 20 to 30 seconds, until eggs are just incorporated into the batter.
5. Add all but 2 tablespoon of the frozen berries to blender and stir in by hand (do not blend!). Divide batter among prepared muffin cups and then place a few remaining berries in the top of each.
6. Bake 15 to 18 minutes, until slightly golden brown and a tester inserted in the center comes out clean. Remove and let cool in pan for a few minutes, then transfer to a wire rack to cool completely.

KETO MOCHA MUFFINS
Nutrition: Cal 166; Fat 17 g; Carb 9 g; Protein 10 g
Serving 235; Cook time 30 min
Ingredients
•3 large eggs
•⅓ cup strong coffee
•1 teaspoon vanilla extract
•2 ¼ cups pumpkin seed flour (can sub 2 to 2 ¼ cups almond flour)
•½ cup Swerve Sweetener
•¼ cup cocoa powder
•2 tsp baking powder
•¼ teaspoon salt
•¼ cup melted butter
•⅓ cup sugar-free chocolate chips
Instructions
1. Preheat the oven to 325F and line a mini muffin pan with silicone or parchment liners.
2. In a blender or food process, combine the eggs, coffee, and vanilla extract. Blend a few seconds to combine.
3. Add the pumpkin seed flour, sweetener, cocoa powder, baking powder, and salt. Blend on high until well combined. Add the melted butter and blend again until smooth.
4. If your batter is overly thick, add a little more liquid (coffee or water) 1 tablespoon at a time. The batter should be scoopable but not pourable.
5. Stir in most of the chocolate chips by hand, reserving a few for the tops of the muffins. Fill the mini muffin cups almost to the top. You will get about 30 mini muffins so you may need to work in batches.
6. Add a few of the reserved chips to the top of each muffin. Bake 15 to 20 minutes, until the tops are set and firm to the touch. Remove and let cool in the pan.

BROWN BUTTER PECAN MUFFINS
Nutrition: Cal 250; Fat 22 g; Carb 9 g; Protein 8 g
Serving 12; Cook time 30 min
Ingredients
•1/2 cup unsalted butter
•2 1/2 cups almond flour
•1/2 cup Brown Swerve
•1/3 cup whey protein powder
•2 1/2 tsp baking powder
•1/2 tsp salt
•3 large eggs
•1/2 cup water
•1/2 tsp caramel or vanilla extract
•1/2 cup chopped, toasted pecans
Instructions
1. In a medium saucepan over medium heat, melt the butter. Continue to cook until the butter becomes a deep amber color, about 4 minutes. Let cool for 15 minutes.
2. Preheat the oven to 350F and line a muffin pan with parchment or silicone liners.

3. In a large bowl, whisk together the almond flour, Swerve, protein powder, baking, and salt. Stir in the eggs, browned butter, water, and extract until well combined. Stir in the chopped pecans, reserving a few for the top of the muffins.
4. Divide the batter among the prepared muffins cups and add a few chopped pecans to the top of each. Bake 18 to 25 minutes, until golden brown and firm to the touch.
5. Remove and let cool completely.

MAPLE WALNUT MUFFINS

Nutrition: Cal 260; Fat 23 g; Carb 7 g; Protein 8 g
Serving 12; Cook time 30 min

Ingredients
MUFFINS
- 2 cups almond flour
- 1/2 cup granulated Swerve Sweetener (more if you like things sweeter)
- 1/3 cup unflavored whey protein powder
- 1/4 cup coconut flour (or an additional cup almond flour)
- 2 tsp baking powder
- 1/4 tsp salt
- 3 large eggs
- 1/2 cup butter, melted
- 3/4 cup unsweetened almond milk
- 1 tsp maple extract
- 3/4 cup chopped walnuts, divided

GLAZE
- 1/4 cup confectioner's Swerve Sweetener
- 2 tbsp heavy cream
- 1/2 tsp maple extract
- 1 to 2 tbsp water to thin glaze

Instructions
MUFFINS
1. Preheat oven to 325F and grease 12 muffin tins well or line with paper liners.
2. In a large bowl, combine almond flour, Swerve Sweetener, protein powder, coconut flour, baking powder and salt. Stir in eggs, melted butter, almond milk and maple extract until well mixed. Stir in 1/2 cup of the walnuts.
3. Divide batter between prepared muffin cups. Sprinkle with remaining chopped nuts, pressing lightly to adhere. Bake 25 to 30 minutes, until set and golden brown. Remove and let cool.

GLAZE
1. In a small bowl, combine confectioner's Swerve, cream and maple extract. Add just enough water to thin it out to a drizzling consistency. Drizzle over cooled muffins.

PECAN CHEESECAKE MUFFINS

Nutrition: Cal 263; Fat 3 g; Carb 4 g; Protein 8 g
Serving 8; Cook time 30 min

Ingredients
- 1 cup almond flour
- 1 tsp baking powder
- 1/2 cup brown sugar substitute (we use Sukrin Gold)
- 1 tsp ground cinnamon
- 1/2 cup pecans (chopped)
- 1 tsp vanilla extract
- 4 eggs (large)
- 250 g cream cheese (8oz)
- Salt

Instructions
1. Preheat the oven to 160C/320F and prepare your muffin moulds or cases. You will need to grease your tin. We use a silicon mould as they come out very easily and do not require any greasing
2. In a bowl combine almond flour, baking powder, cinnamon, pecans, sugar substitute and a pinch of salt
3. Chop cream cheese into small cubes
4. In a jug whisk together eggs and vanilla with a fork
5. Add the egg mixture to the dry mixture and stir to combine
6. Sprinkle the cream cheese cubes into the mixture. Take some time to do this to ensure they are all separated and not clumped together
7. Divide the mixture into your muffin moulds
8. Bake in the oven for 20-25 minutes or until they are golden brown and cooked through.

BLUEBERRY LEMON MUFFINS

Nutrition: Cal 180; Fat 15 g; Carb 7 g; Protein 6 g
Serving 10; Cook time 25 min

Ingredients
- 1 ¾ cups super fine almond flour
- ¼ cup Oat Fiber , see notes
- ¾ cup of fresh blueberries
- eggs
- ⅓ cup sour cream
- ⅓ cup heavy cream
- ½ cup monk fruit/allulose
- teaspoons baking powder
- Zest and juice of 1 lemon
- 1 teaspoon vanilla extract
- Pinch of salt

Instructions
1. Preheat oven to 350F. Add the flour, baking powder, oat fiber and salt to a bowl and whisk together, then set aside.
2. In a separate bowl, add of the wet ingredients including the sweetener, and mix using a hand mixer or whisk.

3. Add the dry ingredients into the wet and mix just until combined. Gently fold in the blueberries, then scoop into silicone cupcake liners or paper liners.
4. Bake for 18-20 minutes or until a toothpick, when inserted, comes out clean. Allow to cool before serving.

CARROT CAKE ZUCCHINI MUFFINS

Nutrition: Cal 92; Fat 11 g; Carb 4 g; Protein 4 g
Serving 12; Cook time 35 min

Ingredients

- 1 egg
- 1/2 cup brown sugar packed
- 1/3 cup sugar
- 1/3 cup coconut oil melted (may sub. melted butter or vegetable oil)
- 1/4 cup sour cream
- 2 tsp vanilla extract
- 2 tsp ground cinnamon
- 1 cup all-purpose flour
- 1/2 tsp baking powder
- 1/2 tsp baking soda
- pinch of salt
- 1 cup shredded carrots
- 1 cup shredded zucchini or yellow squash
- 1/2 cup chopped pecans or walnuts

Instructions

1. Preheat oven to 350. Grease muffin tin.
2. In medium size mixing bowl, combine egg, brown sugar, sugar, coconut oil, sour cream, vanilla and cinnamon.
3. Add shredded carrots and zucchini. Mix until combined.
4. In small mixing bowl, mix dry ingredients.
5. Add dry ingredients to wet ingredients and mix until just combined.
6. Fold in chopped nuts until just combined. (optional)
7. Spoon batter into greased muffin tin and bake for 20 minutes or until toothpick comes out clean.
8. Muffins will be sticky (and delicious!).

BUTTER PECAN COOKIES

Nutrition: Cal 146; Fat 14 g; Carb 3 g; Protein 2 g
Serving 16; Cook time 30 min

Ingredients

- 4 oz cold salted butter cut into pieces
- 1 cup almond flour
- ⅓ cup coconut flour
- ⅔ cup Joy Filled Eats Sweetener
- 2 teaspoon gelatin
- 1 teaspoon vanilla
- 1 cup pecans

Instructions

1. Preheat oven to 350. Line a large cookie sheet with parchment paper.
2. Combine the butter, almond flour, coconut flour, ⅓ cup of the sweetener, gelatin, and vanilla in a food processor. Pulse until wet crumbs form. Add the

pecans. Pulse until they are chopped. The dough will come together into a ball as the pecans are chopped.
3. Divide the dough into 16 pieces. Put the remaining ⅓ cup sweetener in a shallow bowl. Roll each piece of dough into a ball. Put in the sweetener and press it into a disc. Flip it over and press again so both sides are dusted with sweetener. Put on the prepared baking sheet. Repeat.
4. Bake for 15-17 minutes or until the edges are golden. (Begin checking these around the 8-10 minute mark, they seem to bake fast in some ovens).

KETO JAM COOKIES

Nutrition: Cal 65; Fat 6 g; Carb 2 g; Protein 1 g
Serving 28; Cook time 30 min

Ingredients

- 4 oz cold salted butter cut into pieces (1 stick)
- 1 cup almond flour
- ⅓ cup coconut flour
- ⅓ cup Joy Filled Eats Sweetener
- 2 teaspoon gelatin
- 1 teaspoon vanilla
- ⅓ cup finely shredded unsweetened coconut
- about ¼ cup no sugar added or reduced carb jam

Instructions

1. Preheat oven to 350.
2. Combine the butter, almond flour, coconut flour, sweetener, gelatin, and vanilla in the food processor and pulse until it comes together in a ball of dough. Divide into 28 balls and roll each in the coconut. Put on a parchment-lined lined baking sheet and press down making a little well with your thumbs.
3. Bake for 14-17 minutes or until lightly browned around the edges. Use a small upside down measuring spoon to press down the center of each cookie. Put ½ teaspoon of jam into the well of each cookie. Cool completely. Store in the fridge.

ENGLISH TOFFEE CAPPUCCINO COOKIES

Nutrition: Cal 253; Fat 25 g; Carb 5 g; Protein 4 g
Serving 8; Cook time 45 min

Ingredients

DOUGH INGREDIENTS:

- 4 oz cold salted butter cut into pieces
- 1 cup almond flour
- 2 tablespoon cocoa powder
- 1 tablespoon instant coffee
- ⅓ cup Joy Filled Eats Sweetener
- 2 teaspoon gelatin
- 1 teaspoon vanilla

TOFFEE:

- ½ cup Joy Filled Eats Sweetener

- ⅛ cup heavy cream
- ⅛ cup salted butter

CHOCOLATE:
- ¼ cup sugar free chocolate chips
- 1 teaspoon butter

Instructions

1. Preheat oven to 350. Line 8 holes of a cupcake tin with foil liners.
2. Combine all the dough ingredients in the food processor and pulse until uniform dough forms.
3. Divide into 8 balls and put each in a foil-lined cupcake tin.
4. Bake for 18 minutes or until slightly firm to the touch. Cool completely.
5. Meanwhile, combine the sweetener, cream, and butter in a medium saucepan. Cook over medium, stirring frequently, until deep golden brown and thickened. Depending on the heat of your stovetop this can take 10-15 minutes. Watch it carefully. Cool for ten minutes.
6. Using a tart tamper or the back of a tablespoon to make an indent in each cookie cup. Fill with the caramel.
7. Melt the chocolate in the microwave or in a double boiler. I melt chocolate in the microwave stirring every thirty seconds. Spread the tops of the cookies with the chocolate.
8. The toffee center gets hard when refrigerated for more than a few hours so I recommend leaving these at room temperature. They should be fine for 2-3 days.

CRUNCHY PEANUT COOKIES

Nutrition: Cal 139; Fat 3 g; Carb 4 g; Protein 4 g
Serving 18; Cook time 27 min

Ingredients

- 1 cup unsweetened almond milk or 1% milk
- 1/2 cup fat free plain Greek yogurt
- 2 cups (9 oz) frozen strawberries
- 1 1/2 ripe medium bananas
- 1/2 cup quick oats or old fashioned oats
- 1 Tbsp honey
- 1/2 tsp vanilla extract

Instructions

1. Preheat oven to 350. Line a large cookie sheet with parchment paper.
2. Combine the butter, almond flour, ⅓ cup of the sweetener, coconut flour, gelatin, vanilla, and salt in a food processor. Pulse until wet crumbs form. Add the peanuts. Pulse until the nuts are chopped.
3. Divide the dough into 18 pieces. Put the remaining ⅓ cup sweetener in a shallow bowl. Roll each piece of dough into a ball. Put the dough in the sweetener and press it into a disc. Flip it over and press again so both sides are dusted with sweetener. Put on the prepared baking sheet. Repeat.

4. Bake for 17-19 minutes or until the edges are golden. Cool completely. These will firm up more when refrigerated.

KETO VANILLA COOKIES

Nutrition: Cal 89; Fat 8 g; Carb 2 g; Protein 1 g
Serving 20; Cook time 30 min

Ingredients

- 1 stick cold salted butter cut into pieces
- 1 cup almond flour
- ⅓ cup coconut flour
- ⅓ cup Joy Filled Eats Sweetener
- 2 teaspoon gelatin
- 2 teaspoon vanilla

ICING INGREDIENTS:
- ½ cup xylitol ground into a powder (or ⅔ cup of another powdered sweetener)
- 2 teaspoon vanilla
- 1 tablespoon almond milk
- 1 tablespoon butter melted

Instructions

1. Preheat oven to 350.
2. Combine the dough ingredients in the food processor and pulse until well combined.
3. To make round cookies: Divide into 20 balls and put on a parchment-lined baking sheet. Press down with your fingers.
4. To make cut out cookies: Roll the dough out between two sheets of parchment paper on top of a cookie sheet. Remove the top sheet. Make shapes in the dough 1-2 inches apart. Remove the dough in between the shapes. Repeat with remaining dough.
5. Bake for 14-18 minutes or until lightly browned around the edges. Cool completely.
6. Stir together the ingredients for the icing. Spread on the cooled cookies. Set them on waxed paper and refrigerate to harden the icing so they can be stacked.

MAPLE CREAM SANDWICH COOKIES

Nutrition: Cal 161; Fat 16 g; Carb 2 g; Protein 2 g
Serving 8; Cook time 27 min

Ingredients

- ¾ cup almond flour
- 3 tablespoon Joy Filled Eats Sweetener
- 3 tablespoon butter softened
- 1 teaspoon maple extract
- ½ teaspoon gelatin

MAPLE BUTTERCREAM:
- 5 tablespoon butter
- ½ cup Joy Filled Eats Sweetener
- ½ teaspoon maple extract

Instructions

1. Preheat oven to 350. Line a cookie sheet with parchment paper.

2. Combine cookie ingredients in a bowl and mix with a wooden spoon. This dough comes together pretty easily. Divide into 16 pieces. Roll each into a ball and put on a cookie sheet lined with parchment paper. OR shape the dough into a log and slice 16 pieces.
3. Using the bottom of a measuring cup or drinking glass flatten the cookies to ¼ inch thick. They might stick to the bottom but just slide the dough off and put it back on the parchment.
4. Bake for 10-12 minutes until the edges are golden. (One reader said 8 minutes was enough so if your oven runs hot start checking after 8). Cool completely.
5. While the cookies are cooling mix the butter for the icing with an electric mixer. Slowly add the sugar and mix until smooth. Add the maple extract.
6. When the cookies are completely cooled flip half upside down and divide the icing between them. Top each with a second cookie. Refrigerate for at least an hour. Otherwise the icing with ooze out when you bite them.

'APPLE' PIE COOKIES
Nutrition: Cal 192; Fat 18 g; Carb 8 g; Protein 4 g
Serving 16; Cook time 60 min
Ingredients
- 1 medium zucchini peeled and diced
- 1 tablespoon coconut oil
- 3 tablespoon Joy Filled Eats Sweetener
- 1 tablespoon cinnamon
- 1 teaspoon gluccomannan
CRUST INGREDIENTS:
- 1 ⅓ cup almond flour
- teaspoon coconut flour
- 4 tablespoon butter
- 3 tablespoon Joy Filled Eats Sweetener
- 1 tablespoon cold water
- 1 tablespoon gelatin
Instructions
1. Heat coconut oil in a large frying pan over medium heat. Saute zucchini until softened. Add the sweetener and cinnamon and cook a couple more minutes. Sprinkle the gluccomannan on top and mix well. Set aside.
2. Preheat oven to 350.
3. Combine the crust ingredients in a food processor and pulse until a dough forms. Roll it out into a large rectangle about ¼ inch thick and cut out 16 1.5-2 inch circles. (I used an upside-down cup).
4. Divide the filling between the cookies. Reroll the scraps of dough and cut thin strips of dough. Make a crisscross pattern on top of the cookies. You can gently press or crimp the strips around the edges.
5. Bake for 20-30 minutes or until golden brown.

LOW CARB LEMON COOKIES
Nutrition: Cal 70; Fat 7 g; Carb 3 g; Protein 2 g
Serving 24; Cook time 25 min
Ingredients
- 4 oz cold salted butter (1 stick) cut into pieces
- 1 cup almond flour
- ⅓ cup coconut flour
- ⅓ cup Joy Filled Eats Sweetener
- 2 teaspoon gelatin
- 1 teaspoon lemon extract or zest
ICING INGREDIENTS:
- 1 cup powdered erythritol
- 1-2 tablespoon lemon juice
- lemon zest optional
Instructions
1. Preheat oven to 350.
2. Next, combine all the dough ingredients in the food processor and pulse until a uniform dough forms. Divide into 24 balls and put on a parchment-lined baking sheet. Press down with your fingers. Sprinkle with a little more sweetener.
3. Bake for 12-15 minutes or until lightly browned around the edges. Cool for at least 10 minutes.
4. Combine the powdered sweetener with 1 tablespoon lemon juice in a small bowl. Stir until smooth. Add additional lemon juice if needed. Spread on the cooled cookies.
5. Garnish with lemon zest.

KETO FRUIT PIZZA COOKIES
Nutrition: Cal 115; Fat 9 g; Carb 5 g; Protein 4 g
Serving 10; Cook time 25 min
Ingredients
- 4 oz cold salted butter cut into pieces
- 1 cup almond flour
- ⅓ cup coconut flour
- ⅓ cup Joy Filled Eats Sweetener
- 2 teaspoon gelatin
- 1 teaspoon vanilla
TOPPING INGREDIENTS:
- 3 oz cream cheese softened
- 2 tablespoon Joy Filled Eats Sweetener
- 1-2 teaspoon half and half
- ½ teaspoon vanilla
- fresh berries
Instructions
1. Preheat oven to 350.
2. Next, combine the dough ingredients in the food processor and pulse until a uniform dough forms.
3. Divide into 10 balls and put on a parchment-lined baking sheet. Use the bottom of a glass coated with additional sweetener to press into 2.5-inch circles. Press down further with your fingers if necessary.
4. Bake for 14-16 minutes or until lightly browned around the edges. Cool completely.

5. Use an electric mixer to whip the cream cheese until fluffy. Add the powdered sweetener. Add the half and half 1 teaspoon at a time until it is spreadable. Add the vanilla and mix well. Use to top the cooled cookies. Top with fresh berries. Store in the refrigerator.

GLAZED MAPLE WALNUT COOKIES

Nutrition: Cal 132; Fat 12 g; Carb 3 g; Protein 2 g
Serving 16; Cook time 35 min

Ingredients

- 1 cup walnuts
- 4 oz cold salted butter (1 stick) cut into pieces
- ½ cup almond flour
- ⅓ cup coconut flour
- ⅓ cup Joy Filled Eats Sweetener
- teaspoon gelatin
- 1 teaspoon maple extract
- 1 teaspoon cinnamon

GLAZE INGREDIENTS:

- ½ cup powdered erythritol
- 1 tablespoon half and half
- 1 teaspoon cinnamon
- ½ teaspoon maple extract

Instructions

1. Preheat oven to 350. Line a large cookie sheet with parchment paper.
2. Pulse the walnuts in a food processor until they are finely chopped. Add the butter, almond flour, coconut flour, sweetener, gelatin, maple extract, and cinnamon. Pulse until wet crumbs form.
3. Divide the dough into 16 pieces. Roll each piece into a ball. Put on the prepared baking sheet and press down gently.
4. Bake for 18-22 minutes or until the edges are golden. Cool completely.
5. Stir together the ingredients for the glaze. Brush it on top of the cookies with a pastry brush. Put the cookies in the refrigerator to chill. The glaze will harden in the refrigerator so you can stack the cookies

CINNAMON ROLL COOKIES

Nutrition: Cal 93; Fat 13 g; Carb 2 g; Protein 2 g
Serving 1; Cook time 35 min

Ingredients

- 4 oz cold salted butter cut into pieces
- 1 cup almond flour
- ⅓ cup coconut flour
- ⅓ cup Joy Filled Eats Sweetener
- 2 teaspoon gelatin
- 1 teaspoon vanilla

FILLING INGREDIENTS:

- 2 tablespoon erythritol
- 2 teaspoon cinnamon

CREAM CHEESE DRIZZLE:

- 2 oz cream cheese
- 2 tablespoon Joy Filled Eats Sweetener

Instructions

1. Preheat oven to 350.
2. Combine all the dough ingredients in the food processor and process until the dough comes together in a ball. This takes about a minute.
3. Roll out the dough on a piece of parchment paper. Sprinkle with the erythritol and cinnamon. Roll up into a log. Slice into 20 pieces. Put on a parchment lined baking sheet and press down gently so the layers meet.
4. Bake for 12-14 minutes or until lightly browned around the edges. Cool for at least 10 minutes.
5. Meanwhile, combine the softened cream cheese and sweetener. Put in a piping bag or sandwich bag with a corner snipped off. Drizzle on top of the cooled cookies.

CHOCOLATE CHIP SHORTBREAD COOKIES

Nutrition: Cal 107; Fat 9 g; Carb 6 g; Protein 3 g
Serving 16; Cook time 30 min

Ingredients

- 4 oz cold salted butter cut into pieces
- 1 cup almond flour
- ⅓ cup coconut flour
- ⅓ cup Joy Filled Eats Sweetener
- 2 teaspoon gelatin
- 1 teaspoon vanilla
- ⅔ cup sugar-free chocolate chips

CHOCOLATE COATING:

- 3 oz sugar-free chocolate chips

Instructions

1. Preheat oven to 350.
2. Next, combine the first 6 dough ingredients in the food processor and pulse until a uniform dough forms. Stir in the chocolate chips.
3. Divide into 16 balls and put on a parchment-lined baking sheet. Press down with your fingers.
4. Bake for 16-18 minutes or until lightly browned around the edges. Cool completely.
5. Melt the chocolate in the microwave or in a double boiler. I melt chocolate in the microwave stirring every thirty seconds. Dip the cookies halfway into the chocolate. Let the excess drip off and set them on waxed paper to harden.

CRANBERRY COOKIES

Nutrition: Cal 110; Fat 9 g; Carb 4 g; Protein 2 g
Serving 16; Cook time 35 min

Ingredients

- 4 oz cold salted butter, cut into pieces
- 1 cup almond flour
- ⅓ cup coconut flour
- ⅓ cup Joy Filled Eats Sweetener
- 2 teaspoon gelatin

- 1 teaspoon vanilla
- ½ cup sugar-free dried cranberries divided

LEMON GLAZE:
- 3 tablespoon powdered erythritol such as Swerve
- 1 teaspoon lemon extract
- 1 teaspoon water
- 1 tablespoon sugar-free dried cranberries chopped

Instructions
1. Preheat oven to 350. Line a baking sheet with parchment paper.
2. Add the butter, flours, sweetener, gelatin, vanilla, and 2 tablespoons of the dried cranberries to the food processor. Pulse until the cranberries are chopped and the dough comes together in a ball. Add the remaining cranberries. Pulse just until they are mixed in.
3. Divide the dough into 2 balls. Press into 2 circles on the parchment lined baking sheet. Cut each into 8 wedges. A pizza slicer works well for this.
4. Bake for 15 minutes. Cool for 10 minutes. Separate so there is an inch or so between each wedge. Bake an additional 10 minutes until golden. Cool completely.
5. Stir together the powdered sweetener, lemon extract, and water until smooth. Drizzle the glaze over the cooled cookies. Top with chopped cranberries, if desired.

KETO MAGIC COOKIES
Nutrition: Cal 150; Fat 14 g; Carb 6g; Protein 3 g
Serving 12; Cook time 25 min

Ingredients
- 2 tablespoon coconut cream
- 2 tablespoon butter softened, not melted
- ¼ cup Joy Filled Eats Sweetener
- 2 egg yolks
- ½ cup sugar-free chocolate chips
- ½ cup walnuts (or other nuts of your choice)
- ½ cup unsweetened flaked coconut
- 1 teaspoon coconut flour optional

Instructions
1. Preheat oven to 350.
2. Stir together the butter and coconut cream until smooth. Add the sweetener and egg yolks. Mix well. Add the rest of the ingredients. Scoop onto a parchment lined baking sheet to form 12 cookies. Press down to flatten the tops.
3. Bake for 20 minutes or until golden.

SUGAR FREE LEMON BARS
Nutrition: Cal 69; Fat 4 g; Carb 7 g; Protein 4 g
Serving 24; Cook time 25 min

Ingredients
- 4 oz cold salted butter (1 stick) cut into pieces
- 1 cup almond flour
- ⅓ cup coconut flour
- ⅓ cup Joy Filled Eats Sweetener

- 2 teaspoon gelatin
- 1 teaspoon lemon extract or zest

ICING INGREDIENTS:
- 1 cup powdered erythritol
- 1-2 tablespoon lemon juice
- lemon zest optional

Instructions
1. Preheat oven to 350.
2. Next, combine all the dough ingredients in the food processor and pulse until a uniform dough forms. Divide into 24 balls and put on a parchment-lined baking sheet. Press down with your fingers. Sprinkle with a little more sweetener.
3. Bake for 12-15 minutes or until lightly browned around the edges. Cool for at least 10 minutes.
4. Combine the powdered sweetener with 1 tablespoon lemon juice in a small bowl. Stir until smooth. Add additional lemon juice if needed. Spread on the cooled cookies.
5. Garnish with lemon zest.

LOW CARB OATMEAL COOKIES
Nutrition: Cal 117; Fat 10 g; Carb 7 g; Protein 2 g
Serving 24; Cook time 22 min

Ingredients
- 4 oz butter softened
- ½ cup Joy Filled Eats Sweetener
- 1 teaspoon molasses
- 1 egg
- 1 teaspoon vanilla
- 1 cup almond flour
- 1 teaspoon baking soda
- 1 cup gluten-free oats
- 1 cup sugar-free butterscotch chips
- ½ cup unsweetened coconut flakes
- ½ teaspoon cinnamon

Instructions
1. Preheat oven to 350.
2. Cream together the butter and sweetener in a large bowl. Add in molasses, eggs, and vanilla and mix well.
3. Add the almond flour, baking soda, and cinnamon.
4. Stir in the oats, butterscotch chips, and coconut.
5. Form 24 cookies on 2 parchment-lined cookie sheets. Bake for 12 minutes. They will be soft but golden around the edges. Cool completely on the trays before transferring to a storage container.

KETO VANILLA COOKIES
Nutrition: Cal 89; Fat 8 g; Carb 2 g; Protein 1 g
Serving 20; Cook time 30 min

Ingredients
- 1 stick cold salted butter cut into pieces
- 1 cup almond flour
- ⅓ cup coconut flour

- •⅓ cup Joy Filled Eats Sweetener
- •2 teaspoon gelatin
- •2 teaspoon vanilla

ICING INGREDIENTS:
- •½ cup xylitol ground into a powder (or ⅔ cup of another powdered sweetener)
- •1 teaspoon vanilla
- •1 tablespoon almond milk
- •1 tablespoon butter melted

Instructions
1. Preheat oven to 350.
2. Combine the dough ingredients in the food processor and pulse until well combined.
3. To make round cookies: Divide into 20 balls and put on a parchment-lined baking sheet. Press down with your fingers.
4. To make cut out cookies: Roll the dough out between two sheets of parchment paper on top of a cookie sheet. Remove the top sheet. Make shapes in the dough 1-2 inches apart. Remove the dough in between the shapes. Repeat with remaining dough.
5. Bake for 14-18 minutes or until lightly browned around the edges. Cool completely.
6. Stir together the ingredients for the icing. Spread on the cooled cookies. Set them on waxed paper and refrigerate to harden the icing so they can be stacked.

KETO MOLASSES COOKIES
Nutrition: Cal 167; Fat 14 g; Carb 9 g; Protein 4 g
Serving 25; Cook time 22 min

Ingredients
- •4 oz cold salted butter, cut into pieces
- •1 cup almond flour
- •⅓ cup coconut flour
- •⅓ cup Joy Filled Eats Sweetener
- •2 teaspoon gelatin
- •1 teaspoon vanilla
- •2 teaspoon molasses
- •1 tsp fresh ginger finely grated

Instructions
1. Preheat oven to 350.
2. Combine the dough ingredients in the food processor and process until the dough comes together in a ball. This takes about a minute.
3. Divide into 25 balls and put on a parchment-lined baking sheet. Press down with your fingers. Flip them over so the flat side is up.
4. Bake for 10-12 minutes or until lightly browned around the edges. Cool completely.

KETO BROWNIE COOKIES
Nutrition: Cal 218; Fat 20 g; Carb 9 g; Protein 7 g
Serving 8; Cook time 22 min

Ingredients
- •1 cup raw sunflower seed kernels
- •½ cup xylitol (or ¼ cup of my sweetener)
- •4 tablespoon butter, softened
- •2 eggs
- •½ cup cocoa powder
- •½ cup sugar-free chocolate chips

Instructions
1. Preheat oven to 350.
2. Finely chop the sunflower seed kernels in a food processor. Add the xylitol, butter, eggs, and cocoa powder. Pulse until a dough forms. Stir in the chocolate chips.
3. Drop 8 scoops onto a parchment lined baking sheet. Bake for 12 minutes or until firm to the touch in the center. Cool for 10 minutes.

KETO TRIPLE CHOCOLATE COOKIES
Nutrition: Cal 227; Fat 23 g; Carb 6 g; Protein 4 g
Serving 6; Cook time 17 min

Ingredients
- •3 tablespoon coconut oil
- •oz bar of 85% dark chocolate chopped, divided
- •1 egg
- •⅓ cup Joy Filled Eats
- •3 tablespoon cocoa powder
- •3 tablespoon almond flour
- •2 tablespoon coconut flour
- •½ teaspoon vanilla
- •½ teaspoon baking soda
- •pinch salt
- •¼ cup sugar free chocolate chips optional
- •2 scoops Vital Proteins Collagen 40 grams

Instructions
1. Preheat oven to 350. Line a cookie sheet with parchment paper.
2. In a microwaveable bowl combine the coconut oil and half of the chopped chocolate. Microwave in 30 seconds intervals, stirring after each, until it is completely melted.
3. Whisk in the sweetener and the egg. Add the vanilla, cocoa powder, almond flour, coconut flour, baking soda, and salt. Stir until smooth. Stir in the collagen. Fold in the remaining chocolate chunks and chocolate chips.
4. Divide dough into six pieces (I used a large cookie scoop) and put on the parchment lined baking sheet. Press the cookies down a bit with your hand.
5. Bake for 12 minutes or until slightly firm to the touch.

KETO COOKIE DOUGH ICE CREAM SANDWICHES

Nutrition: Cal 257; Fat 29 g; Carb 8 g; Protein 5 g
Serving 16; Cook time 30 min

Ingredients

- 4 tablespoon butter
- 4 tablespoon cream cheese
- 2 cups almond flour
- ½ cup Joy Filled Eats Sweetener
- 1 teaspoon molasses
- 1 teaspoon vanilla
- 1 cup sugar free chocolate chips or chopped sugar free or dark chocolate

ICE CREAM INGREDIENTS:

- 2 cups heavy cream
- 1 cup half and half
- 1 cup almond milk
- 1 egg yolks
- ½ cup Joy Filled Eats Sweetener
- 1 tablespoon vanilla
- 1 tablespoon glycerin
- 1 cup sugar free chocolate chips optional

Instructions

1. Line a 8x8 square baking pan with parchment paper or foil.
2. Beat butter, cream cheese, and sweetener with an electric mixer. Add in the almond flour, sweetener, vanilla, and molasses. Mix well. Stir in the chocolate chips. Put half the cookie dough in the bottom of the pan and spread gently. Cover with another layer of parchment or foil. Spread the rest of the dough onto the second layer. (The pictures here help with this). Put this in the freezer.
3. Meanwhile, make the ice cream. Combine all the ice cream ingredients in a blender. Blend until smooth. Pour into an ice cream machine and churn according to the manufacturer's instructions. Add the additional chocolate chips during the last minute if desired. When the ice cream has gotten firm remove the cookie dough from the freezer and take out the top layer. Pour ¾ of the ice cream on top of the bottom layer of cookie dough. Save the rest in another container.
4. It is best to not top it with the top cookie dough yet. You need it to firm up a little more. So put this and the top layer of dough in the freezer separately. After an hour or two remove them from the freezer and top the ice cream with the top layer of cookie dough.
5. Freeze for an additional 3-4 hours. This is when it's nice that there was a bit of ice cream left over. It's so hard to be that patient. Eat a little of the extra while you wait.
6. Remove from the freezer and cut into squares with a sharp knife. Wrap individually with plastic wrap to store.

KETO COOKIE DOUGH BROWNIE FAT BOMBS

Nutrition: Cal 240; Fat 20 g; Carb 8 g; Protein 13 g
Serving 18; Cook time 40 min

Ingredients

- 1 cups almond flour
- ¼ cup Joy Filled Eats Sweetener
- 4 tablespoon butter softened
- 1 oz cream cheese softened
- 1 teaspoon vanilla
- ½ teaspoon molasses optional
- ¼ cup sugar-free chocolate chips

BROWNIE DOUGH:

- ¾ cup almond flour
- ¼ cup Joy Filled Eats Sweetener
- ¼ cup cocoa powder
- 4 tablespoon butter softened
- 1 oz cream cheese softened
- 1 teaspoon vanilla

COATING:

- 1 cups sugar-free chocolate chips
- 2 teaspoon refined coconut oil

Instructions

1. Combine all the ingredients for the cookie dough in a medium bowl and mix until smooth.
2. Combine all the ingredients for the brownie dough in a medium bowl and mix until smooth.
3. Scoop small balls of each dough onto a waxed paper-lined cookie sheet. You will get between 15-20 balls from each.
4. Take one ball of each dough and press together. Roll into your hands to form a ball. Repeat with the remaining dough.
5. Melt the chocolate chips and coconut oil in the microwave. Stir every 30 seconds. Once it is 75% melted stir until the chips are completely melted.
6. Cover each cookie/brownie dough ball with melted chocolate. Place back on the lined cookie sheet. Refrigerate to set the chocolate. Store in the fridge.

KETO PUMPKIN COOKIES

Nutrition: Cal 196; Fat 14 g; Carb 6 g; Protein 3 g
Serving 12; Cook time 35 min

Ingredients

- 4 oz butter
- ½ cup Joy Filled Eats Sweetener
- 1 cup almond flour
- ½ cup coconut flour
- 1 egg
- 1 cup pumpkin
- 1 teaspoon vanilla
- 1 teaspoon baking powder
- 1 teaspoon baking soda
- ½ teaspoon pumpkin spice

CREAM CHEESE FILLING:
- 4 oz cream cheese
- 1.5 tablespoon salted butter
- ½ cup powdered erythritol

Instructions
1. Preheat oven to 350. Line two cookie sheets with parchment paper.
2. Cream together the butter and sweetener in a stand mixer until light and fluffy. Add the remaining cookie ingredients. Mix well, scraping the sides as needed.
3. Scoop 24 cookies onto the prepared baking sheets. Press and smooth into a circle about ¾ inch thick.
4. Bake for 20-25 minutes. Cool completely.

CREAM CHEESE FILLING:
1. Whip the cream cheese and butter in a stand mixer until light and fluffy, scraping down the sides as needed.
2. Add the powdered erythritol. Mix for 2-3 minutes until fluffy. Scrape down the sides and mix for another minute.
3. Spread or pipe the filling between a pair of cookies. Repeat.

RASPBERRY CHEESECAKE COOKIES
Nutrition: Cal 190; Fat 18 g; Carb 5.6 g; Protein 4 g
Serving 12; Cook time 30 min

Ingredients
SHORTBREAD COOKIE
- 4 oz cold salted butter cut into pieces (1 stick)
- 1 cup almond flour
- ⅓ cup coconut flour
- ⅓ cup Joy Filled Eats Sweetener
- 2 teaspoon gelatin
- 1 teaspoon vanilla

RASPBERRY CHEESECAKE FILLING
- 4 oz cream cheese
- ¼ cup sugar free raspberry jam
- 2 tablespoon Joy Filled Eats Sweetener

TOPPING
- ¼ cup sugar free white chocolate chips
- 1 teaspoon coconut oil

Instructions
1. Preheat oven to 350.
2. Combine the butter, almond flour, coconut flour, sweetener, gelatin, and vanilla in the food processor and pulse until it comes together in a ball of dough. Divide into 12 balls. Put on a parchment-lined lined baking sheet and press down making a little well with your thumbs.
3. Combine the filling ingredients and divide between the wells.
4. Bake for 16-18 minutes or until lightly browned around the edges. Cool completely.
5. Optional: Melt the white chocolate chips and coconut oil in a small bowl in the microwave stirring every 30 seconds. Drizzle the cookies with melted white chocolate.

6. Store in the fridge in an airtight container for up to 1 week or freezer for up to 3 months.

KETO FUNFETTI COOKIE BITES
Nutrition: Cal 225; Fat 22 g; Carb 5 g; Protein 5 g
Serving 8; Cook time 20 min

Ingredients
- cups almond flour
- 4 oz butter
- ¼ cup Joy Filled Eats Sweetener
- 2 teaspoon gelatin
- ½ teaspoon vanilla
- ½ teaspoon almond extract
- ½ teaspoon butter extract
- 3 tablespoon sugar-free sprinkles

Instructions
1. Preheat oven to 350.
2. Combine the dough ingredients (except the sprinkles) in the food processor and process until a ball of dough forms. This takes 2-3 minutes at high speed. Add the sprinkles and pulse just until they are evenly distributed.
3. Press into an 8x10 inch rectangle, ½ thick, on a parchment-lined baking sheet. Cut into ½ inch squares. Separate the cookies.
4. Bake for 8-10 minutes or until lightly browned around the edges. Cool completely.

KETO COOKIE DOUGH BROWNIES
Nutrition: Cal 260; Fat 26 g; Carb 7 g; Protein 5 g
Serving 16; Cook time 50 min

Ingredients
- 4 oz dark 85% or unsweetened chocolate
- ¾ cup of butter 1.5 sticks
- ¾ cup Joy Filled Eats Sweetener
- 3 eggs
- 1 teaspoon vanilla
- ½ cup Trim Healthy Mama Baking Blend OR 2 tablespoon each coconut flour, almond flour, & golden flax meal
- ½ cup sugar-free chocolate chips

COOKIE DOUGH INGREDIENTS:
- 1 cup almond flour
- 4 tablespoon butter softened
- 1 oz cream cheese softened
- ¼ cup Joy Filled Eats Sweetener
- 1 teaspoon molasses
- 1 teaspoon vanilla
- 1 teaspoon coconut flour
- ½ cup sugar-free chocolate chips

Instructions
1. Preheat oven to 350. Spray an 8 x 8 baking dish liberally with cooking spray.

2. Melt the chocolate and butter in a glass bowl in the microwave. Add the next four ingredients and stir until smooth. Add the chocolate chips.

3. Pour into the prepared baking pan and spread evenly. Bake for 30-35 min until no longer jiggly. Cool completely.

4. To make the cookie dough stir together all the ingredients (except the chocolate chips) until smooth. Stir in the chocolate chips. Spead on top of the cooled brownies.

PIGNOLI COOKIES

Nutrition: Cal 107; Fat 10 g; Carb 2 g; Protein 3 g
Serving 26; Cook time 35 min

Ingredients
- 2 cups slivered almonds
- ½ cup Joy Filled Eats Sweetener
- ¼ cup egg whites
- 8 oz pine nuts
- powdered erythritol optional

Instructions
1. Preheat oven to 350.
2. Process the almonds and sweetener in the food processor for 5 minutes, scraping down the sides occasionally. Add the egg whites. Process until it comes together and is about the consistency of peanut butter.
3. Put the pine nuts in a shallow bowl. Drop tablespoons of the dough into the pine nuts. Roll the balls of dough around covering them with nuts. Place on a parchment lined baking sheet.
4. Bake for 20-25 minutes until slightly golden. Cool completely and dust with powdered sweetener, if desired.

PEANUT BUTTER CUP COOKIES

Nutrition: Cal 109; Fat 10 g; Carb 4 g; Protein 4 g
Serving 30; Cook time 30 min

Ingredients
- 2 large eggs
- ½ cup coconut oil
- ½ cup peanut butter
- 1 teaspoon vanilla
- ⅓ cup peanut flour
- ¾ cup Joy Filled Eats Sweetener
- 1 teaspoon salt
- ½ cup almond flour
- ¼ cup coconut flour
- 1 teaspoon aluminum-free baking powder

TOPPING INGREDIENTS:
- 3 oz sugar free chocolate chips or chopped chocolate
- 2 oz heavy cream
- ¼ cup peanuts (toasted salted)

Instructions
1. Preheat oven to 350.
2. Start by whisking the eggs and melted coconut oil with the peanut butter and vanilla.

3. Add the peanut butter powder, sweetener, salt, almond flour, coconut flour and baking powder. Mix until well combined.
4. Divide the batter between 30 mini muffin cups lined with aluminum liners.
5. Bake for 14-16 minutes or until golden around the edges. While warm and still in the pan use a tart tamper or the rounded back of a teaspoon to make a well in the center of each cookie. Cool completely.
6. To make the ganache heat the cream to just before the boiling point. Pour over the chocolate. Stir until it is smooth.
7. Fill the cooled cookies with the prepared ganache. Top with a few peanuts.

KETO TOFFEE CAPPUCCINO COOKIES

Nutrition: Cal 255; Fat 25 g; Carb 5 g; Protein 4 g
Serving 8; Cook time 45 min

Ingredients
- 4 oz cold salted butter cut into pieces
- 1 cup almond flour
- 2 tablespoon cocoa powder
- 1 tablespoon instant coffee
- ⅓ cup Joy Filled Eats Sweetener
- 2 teaspoon gelatin
- 1 teaspoon vanilla

TOFFEE:
- ½ cup Joy Filled Eats Sweetener
- ⅛ cup heavy cream
- ⅛ cup salted butter

CHOCOLATE:
- ¼ cup sugar free chocolate chips
- 1 teaspoon butter

Instructions
1. Preheat oven to 350. Line 8 holes of a cupcake tin with foil liners.
2. Combine all the dough ingredients in the food processor and pulse until uniform dough forms.
3. Divide into 8 balls and put each in a foil-lined cupcake tin.
4. Bake for 18 minutes or until slightly firm to the touch. Cool completely.
5. Meanwhile, combine the sweetener, cream, and butter in a medium saucepan. Cook over medium, stirring frequently, until deep golden brown and thickened. Depending on the heat of your stovetop this can take 10-15 minutes. Watch it carefully. Cool for ten minutes.
6. Using a tart tamper or the back of a tablespoon to make an indent in each cookie cup. Fill with the caramel.
7. Melt the chocolate in the microwave or in a double boiler. I melt chocolate in the microwave stirring every thirty seconds. Spread the tops of the cookies with the chocolate.
8. The toffee center gets hard when refrigerated for more than a few hours so I recommend leaving these at room temperature. They should be fine for 2-3 days.

CHOCOLATE THUMBPRINT COOKIES

Nutrition: Cal 73; Fat 6 g; Carb 3 g; Protein 2 g
Serving 24; Соок time 30 min

Ingredients
- 4 oz cold salted butter cut into pieces
- 1 cup almond flour
- ⅓ cup coconut flour
- ⅓ cup Joy Filled Eats Sweetener
- 2 teaspoon gelatin
- 1 teaspoon vanilla

NUT TOPPING:
- ⅔ cup sliced almonds
- 2 teaspoon Joy Filled Eats Sweetener

CHOCOLATE GANACHE:
- ⅓ cup sugar free chocolate chips
- 3 tablespoon heavy cream

Instructions
1. Preheat oven to 350.
2. Combine the ⅔ cup sliced almonds and 2 teaspoon sweetener in a food processor and pulse into chopped. Transfer to a small bowl and set aside.
3. Next, combine all the dough ingredients in the food processor and pulse until a uniform dough forms. Divide into 24 balls and roll each in the almond topping. Put on a parchment lined baking sheet and press down making a little well with your thumbs. Sprinkle a little more almond topping on each.
4. Bake for 12-15 minutes or until lightly browned around the edges. Cool for at least 10 minutes.
5. Meanwhile, put the chocolate chips and heavy cream in a microwave safe bowl and heat for 30 seconds. Stir. Heat for another 30 seconds. Stir. Repeat until the chocolate has melted. Stir until smooth.
6. Divide the chocolate ganache between the thumbprint cookies. Sprinkle with a little more of the chopped almonds.

EGGLESS CHOCOLATE CHIP COOKIES

Nutrition: Cal 180; Fat 18 g; Carb 5 g; Protein 4 g
Serving 18; Соок time 25 min

Ingredients
- 4 oz cold salted butter, cut into pieces (1 stick)
- 1 cup almond flour
- ⅓ cup coconut flour
- ⅓ cup Joy Filled Eats Sweetener
- 2 teaspoon gelatin
- 1 teaspoon vanilla
- 1 tsp molasses
- ¾ cup sugar-free chocolate chips

Instructions
1. Preheat oven to 350. Line a baking sheet with parchment paper.
2. Combine the dough ingredients (not the chocolate chips) in the food processor and process until the dough comes together in a ball. This takes about a minute.

3. Put the dough into a mixing bowl and stir in the chocolate chips.
4. Divide into 18 balls and put on a parchment-lined baking sheet. Press down with your fingers.
5. Bake for 15 minutes or until firm to the touch and golden around the edges.

EASY SAMOAS COOKIE BARS

Nutrition: Cal 154; Fat 16 g; Carb 4 g; Protein 2 g
Serving 16; Соок time 30 min

Ingredients
- 3 tablespoon butter melted
- ¾ cup almond flour
- 1 tablespoon Joy Filled Eats Sweetener

COCONUT CARAMEL LAYER:
- 3 tablespoon butter
- ⅓ cup Joy Filled Eats Sweetener
- 4 tablespoon heavy cream divided
- ¼ teaspoon vanilla
- pinch salt
- 1.5 cups unsweetened coconut flakes
- ½ cup sugar free chocolate chips

Instructions
1. Preheat the oven to 350. Spray an 8x8 pan with cooking spray. It is helpful to line with parchment paper.
2. Put the crust ingredients in a medium bowl and whisk until combined. Press into the pan. Bake for 15-20 min until the crust is golden brown.
3. Meanwhile, combine butter, sweetener, and 2 tablespoons of the cream over medium heat. Stir until the sweetener is dissolved. Add the vanilla. Cook until it is a deep golden brown. As soon as it reached that deep color (right before burning) remove from the heat and immediately add the other 2 tablespoons of heavy cream. Stir until smooth. Add the salt and coconut.
4. Gently spread the coconut on top of the crust. Drizzle with chocolate. Let cool until the chocolate is firm. Cut into 16 pieces and enjoy!

FLORENTINE COOKIES

Nutrition: Cal 275; Fat 25 g; Carb 9 g; Protein 8 g
Serving 8; Соок time 25 min

Ingredients
- 1 cup almonds coarsely ground in a food processor or almond meal
- ¼ cup Joy Filled Eats Sweetener
- 2 tablespoon butter
- ½ teaspoon molasses
- ¼ cup heavy cream
- 1 tablespoon gelatin
- 3 oz bar sugar-free chocolate

Instructions
1. Combine the sweetener, butter, molasses, and cream in a small saucepan. Bring to a boil and boil for one minute. Remove from the heat and add the chopped almonds. Cool for 20 minutes.

2. Preheat the oven to 350. Stir the gelatin into the cookie dough. Drop rounded tablespoons onto the parchment-lined baking sheets, 8 cookies per tray. Spread the dough into thin circles.
3. Bake for 10 minutes or until golden around the edges. Cool completely.
4. Melt the chocolate in the microwave or on a double boiler. (I melt chocolate by microwaving for 30-second increments and stirring after each. When it is 75% melted just stir until the rest of the chocolate melts).
5. Spread the bottom of one cookie with a little chocolate. Sandwich with another cookie. Store in the refrigerator. They are crisper after chilling.

TAGALONG COOKIES
Nutrition: Cal 84; Fat 8 g; Carb 3 g; Protein 2 g
Serving 20; Cook time 45 min
Ingredients
SHORTBREAD COOKIE LAYER:
- ¾ cups almond flour
- ¼ cup Joy Filled Eats Sweetener
- 1 teaspoon gelatin
- pinch salt
- 4 tablespoon cold butter cut into small pieces
- ½ teaspoon vanilla
- ½ tablespoon water

PEANUT BUTTER LAYER:
- ¼ cup peanut butter
- 2-3 tablespoon Joy Filled Eats Sweetener
- 1 teaspoon glucomannan (optional)
- 1 teaspoon peanut flour or almond flour

CHOCOLATE LAYER:
- ½ cup sugar free chocolate chips
- 1 teaspoon coconut oil

Instructions
SHORTBREAD COOKIES:
1. Preheat oven to 325 and line a large baking sheet with parchment paper.
2. Put the almond flour, sweetener, gelatin, and salt in a food processor and pulse to combine. Add the butter and vanilla and pulse until tiny crumbs. Add the water and pulse until a dough forms. This may take 2-3 minutes.
3. Put the dough between two sheets of waxed paper. Roll it out about ¼ inch thick. Using a 2-inch circle cookie cutter or a narrow upside down glass cut out circles. Lift gently with a spatula and put on a cookie sheet lined with parchment paper. Reroll the dough and make circles until you use it all. You will get about 20 cookies.
4. Bake 12 to 14 minutes or until golden brown. Let cool completely.

PEANUT BUTTER LAYER:
1. Put the peanut butter in a small bowl and sprinkle the glucomannan on slowly whisking between each sprinkling. Add the sweetener and peanut or almond flour. Whisk well. Spread the peanut butter filling on the cookies. Freeze until firm.

ASSEMBLY:
2. Melt chocolate in the microwave. Start with thirty seconds and then stir. Continue microwaving for thirty seconds increments and stirring after each until the chocolate is 75% melted. Then just stir until it is all melted.
3. Put one frozen peanut butter disc onto each cookie. Drizzle with melted chocolate covering as much as possible. Using a knife or offset spatula make sure the sides are covered. At this point, I lift onto a different piece of waxed or parchment paper to get cleaner edges. Refrigerate to set the chocolate. Enjoy your Tagalong cookies!

NO-BAKE COOKIE DOUGH CHEESECAKE
Nutrition: Cal 300; Fat 28 g; Carb 8 g; Protein 8 g
Serving 16; Cook time 30 min
Ingredients
COOKIE DOUGH INGREDIENTS:
- 2 cups almond flour
- 8 tablespoon butter softened
- 2 oz cream cheese softened
- ½ cup Joy Filled Eats Sweetener
- 1 teaspoon molasses
- 2 teaspoon vanilla
- 2 teaspoon coconut flour
- ½ cup sugar-free chocolate chips

CHEESECAKE INGREDIENTS:
- 8 oz cream cheese
- 1 cup cottage cheese
- ½ cup Joy Filled Eats Sweetener
- ¼ cup sour cream
- ½ teaspoon vanilla
- 2 tablespoon gelatin

GANACHE INGREDIENTS:
- 4 oz unsweetened baking chocolate
- 4 oz heavy cream
- 6 tablespoon Joy Filled Eats Sweetener

Instructions
1. To make the cookie dough stir together all the ingredients (except the chocolate chips) until smooth. Stir in the chocolate chips. Press into the bottom of a 9-inch springform pan.
2. For the cheesecake layer, process the cream cheese and cottage cheese in a food processor until smooth. Add the sour cream, sweetener, and vanilla. Process until well combined. While the machine is running slowly sprinkle in the gelatin. Spread the cheesecake mixture on top of the cookie dough.
3. To make the ganache heat the cream until bubbly in the microwave or a small saucepan. Pour over the chopped chocolate. Stir until the chocolate melts. Add the sweetener and stir until smooth. Transfer to a small blender or food processor. Process for a minute or two

until thick and shiny. This step really ensures a smooth ganache topping. Pour onto the cheesecake and spread gently.

4. Refrigerate for at least 4-6 hours. Carefully run a knife around the edge before releasing the springform pan. When serving you have to slide the pie cutter between the pan and cookie dough before lifting the slice. Since it is raw dough it is softer than a traditional graham cracker crust.

RASPBERRY AND CHOCOLATE COOKIES

Nutrition: Cal 140; Fat 13 g; Carb 5 g; Protein 3 g
Serving 15; Cook time 30 min

Ingredients

- 4 oz cold salted butter cut into pieces
- 1 cup almond flour
- ⅓ cup coconut flour
- ⅓ cup Joy Filled Eats Sweetener
- 2 teaspoon gelatin
- 1 teaspoon vanilla
- ½ cup sugar-free white chocolate chips
- ½ cup freeze-dried raspberries chopped

Instructions

1. Preheat oven to 350.
2. Next, combine the first 6 dough ingredients in the food processor and pulse until a uniform dough forms. Stir in the white chocolate chips and dried raspberries.
3. Divide into 15 balls and put on a parchment-lined baking sheet. Press down with your fingers.
4. Bake for 14-16 minutes or until lightly browned around the edges. Cool completely.

KETO NO-BAKE COOKIES

Nutrition: Cal 170; Fat 18 g; Carb 5 g; Protein 4 g
Serving 12; Cook time 25 min

Ingredients

- 2 tbsp butter
- 2/3 cup natural chunky peanut butter (or any nut butter)
- 1 cup unsweetened shredded coconut
- 1 tbsp cocoa powder
- 4 drops liquid vanilla stevia (or liquid sweetener of choice)

Instructions

1. In a microwave safe bowl, melt the butter.
2. Stir in the peanut butter and cocoa powder until smooth.
3. Add the shredded coconut and stevia; mix well.
4. Scoop 1 tbsp size spoonfuls onto a small parchment lined sheet pan, or any dish that will fit in your freezer such as a cutting board or even plate.
5. Freeze for 15 minutes.
6. Cut and separate the parchment paper while keeping the cookies in place, so that each cookie still has a piece of paper underneath (this keeps them from sticking

together). Store in a sealed container or bag in your fridge.

KETO COOKIE DOUGH FAT BOMBS

Nutrition: Cal 332; Fat 30 g; Carb 7 g; Protein 4 g
Serving 20; Cook time 20 min

Ingredients

- 1 (8oz) package cream cheese (softened)
- 6 tbsp peanut butter (no sugar added)
- 3 tbsp butter (softened)
- 1 tsp vanilla
- 1/3 cup swerve
- 1/3 cup sugar-free chocolate chips

Instructions

1. With the exception of the chocolate chips, use a mixer to cream everthing together.
2. Fold in the chocolate chips.
3. Use a small cookie scoop or spoon to scoop the dough onto a parchment paper lined cookie sheet or container small enough to fit into your freezer (you can also use sililcone molds).
4. Freeze for about 1 hour, and then store in ziplock bags in your freezer.

NO BAKE PEANUT BUTTER COOKIES

Nutrition: Cal 159; Fat 15 g; Carb 5 g; Protein 5 g
Serving 12; Cook time 20 min

Ingredients

- 1 Cup Flaked Almonds (or chopped nuts of choice)
- 1/2 Cup Shredded Coconut
- 1/2 Cup Peanut Butter
- 1/2 Cup Stevia
- 50g/1.76 ounces Unsalted Butter or 1/4 Cup Coconut Oil For Dairy Free

Instructions

1. Line a baking tray with well greased baking paper.
2. In a bowl, combine together the almonds and coconut.
3. Place the peanut butter, stevia and butter or coconut oil in a small saucepan over medium heat.
4. Heat until the butter has melted and you have a smooth, creamy, buttery sauce.
5. Pour the peanut butter mixture over the almond mixture and stir until well combined.
6. Drop a tablespoon per cookie onto the prepared baking tray.
7. Place into the fridge for a few hours for the cookies to set and harden.
8. Enjoy crisp from the fridge.

KETO CRACKERS

Nutrition: Cal 121; Fat 10 g; Carb 3 g; Protein 6 g
Serving 8; Cook time 25 min

Ingredients

- 1 cup almond flour
- 1 cup shredded cheese cheddar cheese

- 1/4 teaspoon salt
- 1-2 tablespoon water

Instructions

1. Preheat the oven to 180C/350F. Line a large baking sheet with parchment paper.
2. In a high speed blender or food processor, add your almond flour, shredded cheese, and salt, and blend well, until a dough remains. If the dough is too crumbly, add a tablespoon or two of water.
3. Line a large sheet of parchment paper on a flat kitchen surface. Transfer the dough onto it and place another sheet of parchment paper on top. Press down on the dough, before rolling it out using a rolling pin, until around 1/4 inch in thickness. Using a pizza cutter, slice up squares to form crackers.
4. Transfer the crackers onto the lined sheet. Bake for 12 minutes, flipping halfway through. Remove from the oven and allow to cool completely.

PEANUT BUTTER CRACKERS

Nutrition: Cal 17; Fat 1 g; Carb 2 g; Protein 1 g
Serving 48; Cook time 15 min

Ingredients

- 1/3 cup whole wheat flour
- 2/3 cup all purpose flour
- 1/2 teaspoon salt
- 1/4 teaspoon baking powder
- 3 tablespoons peanut butter smooth and creamy
- 5 tablespoons water
- 1 teaspoon peanut oil to brush
- 1 tablespoon sesame seeds optional

Instructions

1. In a large mixing bowl, whisk together the dry ingredients until combined. Form a well in the center then add the peanut butter and water. Stir together until a thick dough remains. Using your hands, shape the dough into a ball.
2. Transfer the dough to a lightly floured kitchen surface and knead several times. Shape the dough into a rectangle shape. wrap it in plastic wrap and refrigerate for an hour.
3. Preheat the oven to 180C/350F. Line a large baking sheet with parchment paper and set aside.
4. Remove the dough from the refrigerator and place it between two sheets of parchment paper. Roll out the dough into a large rectangle, about 12-inches down the sides and around 1/16th of an inch in thickness. Using a pizza cutter, cut out 8 rows by 6 rows, to form 48 crackers.
5. Prick each cracker with a fork. Brush the crackers with a tiny bit of peanut oil and sprinkle some sesame seeds on top.
6. Bake the crackers for 13-15 minutes, until crispy. Remove them from the oven and let them cool completely.

KETO CREAM CHEESE COOKIES

Nutrition: Cal 185,5; Fat 17,5 g; Carb 2,6 g; Protein 3 g
Serving 11; Cook time 30 min

Ingredients

DRY INGREDIENTS

- 3/4 cup blanched almond flour
- 1,5 tablespoon coconut flour
- 1/2 cup granulated sweetener
- 1 teaspoon baking powder
- 1/8 teaspoon salt

WET INGREDIENTS

- 4 ounces full fat cream cheese
- 1 large egg
- 1 teaspoon vanilla extract

Instructions

1. If using a hand mixer cream the cream cheese and add one egg at a time then go to next step. If using a blender add all wet ingredients together and blend until smooth
2. After combining egg and cream cheese add in vanilla. Set aside
3. Mix all the dry ingredients together
4. Combine dry and wet ingredients. Cover bowl then place cookie dough in refrigerator for at least an hour.
5. Preheat oven to 350°F
6. Pull cookie dough out of freezer and using a cookie scoop, scoop 11 cookies onto a baking sheet, do not flatten them. Bake 15 minutes
7. Remove and allow to cool at least 15 minutes. Dust with powdered sweetner for a nice garnish.

KETO COWBOY COOKIES

Nutrition: Cal 162; Fat 16 g; Carb 2 g; Protein 2 g
Serving 22; Cook time 25 min

Ingredients

- 10 Tbsp unsalted butter, softened, not melted
- ½ cup sugar-free brown sugar, packed
- 2 large eggs
- 1,5 teaspoons pure vanilla extract
- 1 1/3 cups finely ground almond flour, packed
- 1/3 cup oat fiber
- 2/3 cup pecans, chopped
- ⅔ cup unsweetened shredded coconut
- 1 cup sugar-free chocolate chips
- 1/2 tsp ground cinnamon
- 1 teaspoon baking powder
- 1/4 teaspoon sea salt

Instructions

1. Preheat the oven to 350 degrees F and line a baking sheet with parchment paper.
2. Add the butter and sugar-free brown sugar to a stand mixer (or mixing bowl if using an electric hand mixer) and beat on medium-high speed until combined and fluffy.
3. Use a rubber spatula to scrape the sides of the mixing bowl, then add the eggs and the vanilla extract. Beat

until combined and creamy. Again, scrape the sides of the mixer with a rubber spatula.

4. Stir together the remaining (dry) ingredients in a bowl and pour it into the mixer. Beat on medium-high until the dough is very well combined, thick, and sticky.

5. Scoop the cookie dough onto the parchment-lined baking sheet, and bake for 8 to 13 minutes, depending on the size of your cookies - for regular sized cookies, go with 8 to 11, and for larger cookies, bake for 11 to 13.

6. Remove the cookies from the oven and allow them to cool for 10 minutes before serving.

KETO NUTTER BUTTER COOKIES

Nutrition: Cal 165; Fat 15 g; Carb 4 g; Protein 4 g
Serving 10; Cook time 32 min

Ingredients

FOR THE COOKIES:
- 1 cup Low carb peanut butter or other nut butter
- 1 Egg
- ⅓ cup Swerve confectioners sugar substitute
- ½ teaspoon Vanilla extract

FOR THE FILLING:
- ¼ cup Low carb peanut butter or other nut butter
- 2 tablespoon Butter softened
- ¼ cup Swerve confectioners sugar substitute
- ½ teaspoon Vanilla extract

Instructions

1. Preheat the oven to 350 degrees.
2. In a mixing bowl, combine the ingredients for the cookies, and beat together until well blended.
3. Separate the dough into 20 equal pieces, and form each one into an oblong shape. Flat each oblong cookie, and pinch in the center to form the shape of a peanut.
4. Take the tines of a fork and press it in a criss cross design across the top of each of the cookies.
5. Bake the cookies for 10-12 minutes until browned and cooked through. Let the cookies cool to room temperature.
6. In a mixing bowl, combine the ingredients for the filling, and blend until creamy and smooth.
7. Place a thick layer of the filling on the bottom of one of the peanut shaped cookies. Place another cookie on top of the filling face down.
8. Put the cookies into the freezer for 30 minutes to chill before serving.

CRANBERRY ALMOND BISCOTTI COOKIES

Nutrition: Cal 112; Fat 9 g; Carb 6 g; Protein 5 g
Serving 14; Cook time 45 min

Ingredients

- 2 eggs
- 1 teaspoon vanilla
- ⅓ cup low carb sugar substitute
- ¼ teaspoon lemon stevia drops or plain stevia and a half teaspoon lemon extract

- 1 ½ cups almond flour
- ¼ cup coconut flour
- ½ teaspoon baking soda
- ¼ teaspoon sea salt
- ½ cup sugar free dried cranberries
- ½ cup sliced almonds
- low carb dark chocolate melted, optional

Instructions

1. Beat together the eggs, vanilla, Swerve, and stevia with an electric mixer until frothy.
2. In separate bowl, combine the almond flour, coconut flour, baking soda, and salt.
3. Add flour mixture to wet mixture and stir until dough forms.
4. Stir in the cranberries and almonds.
5. On a parchment paper lined cookie sheet, form a long rectangle of dough.
6. Bake a time 350°F for about 20 minutes or until top has browned.
7. Remove from oven and allow to cool completely.
8. Slice into thin pieces on a slight diagonal. Lay each piece on the side in baking pan.
9. Bake slices for about 15-20 minutes at 350°F until toasted.
10. Allow to cool. Drizzle with melted chocolate, if desired.

KETO SNOWBALL COOKIES

Nutrition: Cal 108; Fat 11 g; Carb 2 g; Protein 2 g
Serving 24; Cook time 27 min

Ingredients

- 2 cups Almond flour
- ½ cup Butter unsalted and softened
- ⅓ cup Swerve confectioner sugar substitute
- 1 teaspoon Vanilla extract
- ⅔ cup Chopped pecans
- pinch of salt
- ½ cup Swerve confectioners sugar substitute for coating the cookies once baked

Instructions

1. Add the butter and ⅓ cup sugar substitute to a mixing bowl and beat until creamy and smooth.
2. Add in the almond flour, salt and vanilla extract. Mix until well combined.
3. Fold in the pecans.
4. Roll the dough into 24 evenly sized balls, and freeze for 30 minutes.
5. Preheat the oven to 350 degrees and bake for 10-12 minutes until the bottoms are browned.
6. Let cool for several minutes and then roll in the remaining sugar substitute while still warm. sugar substitute for coating the cookies once baked.

KETO OREO COOKIES RECIPE

Nutrition: Cal 182; Fat 18 g; Carb 4 g; Protein 4 g
Serving 8; Cook time 25 min

Ingredients
COOKIES

• 1 cup Almond flour

• 3 teaspoon Cocoa powder unsweetened

• ¼ cup Swerve confectioners sugar substitute

• 1 teaspoon Baking powder

• 4 tablespoons Butter unsalted melted

• 1 teaspoon Vanilla extract

ICING

• 2 oz. Cream cheese softened

• 2 Tablespoons Butter unsalted softened

• 2 Tablespoons Swerve confectioners sugar substitute

• ½ teaspoon Vanilla extract

Instructions

1. Preheat the oven to 350 degrees.

2. Add the ingredients for the cookies to a mixing bowl, and blend on high until a thick dough has formed.

3. Wet your hands slightly, and form the dough into 16 even sized balls.

4. Flatten the balls of dough into the round shape of an Oreo, and place on a well greased baking sheet.

5. Bake for 8 minutes, or until cooked through.

6. Let the cookies cool to room temperature.

7. Add the ingredients for the icing to a mixing bowl, and blend on high until smooth and creamy.

8. Place a dollop of icing on the bottom of one of the cookies and spread out evenly. Top the cookie and icing with the bottom of another cookie to form a filled Oreo.

9. Repeat step 8 with the remaining cookies and icing until you have made a total of 8 Oreo cookies.

Low-Carb Cakes

SOUR CREAM CAKE

Nutrition: Cal 310; Fat 27 g; Carb 10 g; Protein 10 g
Serving 12; Cook time 70 min

Ingredients
CAKE
- 2 cups almond flour
- 1/3 cup coconut flour
- 1/3 cup unflavored whey protein powder
- 1 tbsp baking powder
- 1/4 tsp salt
- 1/2 cup butter, softened
- 1/2 cup full fat sour cream
- 3/4 cup Swerve Sweetener
- 4 large eggs, room temperature
- 1 tsp vanilla extract

PECAN STREUSEL
- 1/2 cup almond flour
- 3 tbsp Swerve Sweetener
- 1 1/2 tsp ground cinnamon
- 2 tbsp butter, melted
- 1/2 cup chopped pecans

Instructions
PECAN STREUSEL
1. In a small bowl, whisk together the almond flour, Swerve Sweetener and cinnamon. Add melted butter and toss until mixture resembles coarse crumbs. Stir in pecans.

CAKE
2. Preheat oven to 325F and grease a 9x5 loaf pan well.
3. In a medium bowl, whisk together the almond flour, coconut flour, whey protein, baking powder, and salt.
4. In a large bowl, beat butter and sour cream together until smooth. Beat in Swerve until well combined. Beat in eggs one at a time and then beat in vanilla extract.
5. Beat in almond flour mixture until dough is well combined.
6. Spread half the batter in the prepared pan and top with half of the streusel. Spread remaining batter over top and top with remaining streusel.
7. Tent cake with foil and bake 50 minutes. Remove foil and bake another 15 to 20 minutes, until golden brown and a tester inserted in the edges comes out clean.
8. Remove from oven and let cool completely.

KETO RHUBARB CAKE

Nutrition: Cal 330; Fat 29 g; Carb 9 g; Protein 12 g
Serving 10; Cook time 60 min

Ingredients
FOR THE CAKE:
- 3 cups (425g) rhubarb, sliced
- 1/2 cup (100g) plus 2 tablespoons granulated erythritol sweetener, divided
- 3 cups (288g) almond flour
- 1/3 cup (25g) unflavored whey protein powder
- 2 teaspoons baking powder
- 1/4 teaspoon salt
- 1/2 cup (113g) unsalted butter, melted
- 3 large (150g) eggs
- 1/2 cup (113g) unsweetened almond milk
- 1/2 teaspoon vanilla extract

FOR THE CRUMB TOPPING:
- 1/4 cup (24g) almond flour
- 2 tablespoons pecans, finely chopped
- 1 tablespoon granulated erythritol sweetener
- 1 tablespoon unsalted butter, room temperature

Instructions
CAKE:
1. In a medium bowl, toss together the sliced rhubarb and 2 tablespoons of the sweetener. Set aside.
2. Preheat the oven to 350F and grease a 9-inch springform pan very well.
3. In a medium bowl, whisk together the almond flour, remaining 1/2 cup of sweetener, whey protein powder, baking powder, and salt.
4. Stir in the melted butter, eggs, almond milk, and vanilla extract until well combined. Spread 2/3 of the batter in prepared pan. Sprinkle with the rhubarb and dot the remaining batter over in small spoonfuls. Bake 30 minutes.

CRUMB TOPPING:
1. While the cake is baking, combine the crumb topping ingredients in a small bowl, cutting in the room temperature butter until it resembles coarse crumbs. Sprinkle the crumb topping over the cake and cover with foil.
2. Bake another 20 to 30 minutes, until the edges are golden brown and the center is firm to the touch. Remove and let cool, then run a sharp knife around the inside of the pan to loosen. Remove the sides.

CRANBERRY ORANGE CAKE

Nutrition: Cal 227; Fat 18 g; Carb 9 g; Protein 8 g
Serving 16; Cook time 70 min

Ingredients
CAKE:
- 3 cups cranberries
- Sweetener equivalent to 1/3 cup sugar
- 1/4 cup water
- 2 1/2 cups almond flour
- 1/2 cup coconut flour
- 1/4 cup unflavored whey protein powder
- 1 tbsp baking powder
- 1/4 tsp salt
- 1/2 cup butter, softened
- Sweetener equivalent to 3/4 cup sugar
- 4 large eggs, room temperature
- 1 tbsp orange zest
- 1/2 tsp orange extract
- 2/3 cup almond milk, room temperature
- 1/2 cup chopped pecans (optional)

OPTIONAL GLAZE:
- 3 tbsp powdered sweetener (erythritol or xylitol)
- 1 tbsp water

Instructions

1. In a large saucepan, combine cranberries, sweetener, and water. Bring to a boil and then reduce heat and simmer until cranberries have popped. Mash with a fork or wooden spoon.
2. Preheat oven to 325F and grease a 9-inch springform pan (you can do this in other pans, but it may be harder to get it out nicely and the baking time may change).
3. In a large bowl, whisk together the almond flour, coconut flour, whey protein powder, baking powder, and salt.
4. In another large bowl, beat butter with sweetener until smooth and well combined. Beat in eggs, orange zest and orange extract. Beat in half of the almond flour mixture, and then beat in almond milk. Beat in remaining almond flour mixture until well combined.
5. Spread about two thirds of the batter in prepared baking pan. Spread cranberry sauce over. Stir pecans into remaining batter and spread over cranberry sauce.
6. Bake 40 to 50 minutes, until top is golden brown and firm to the touch, and a tester inserted in the center has no raw batter attached. Remove and let cool at least half an hour, then run a sharp knife around the inside edges of the pan and remove the sides.

OPTIONAL GLAZE:
1. Stir together powdered sweetener and water and drizzle over cooled cake.

BLUEBERRY CREAM CHEESE CAKE
Nutrition: Cal 230; Fat 21 g; Carb 8 g; Protein 10 g
Serving 12; Cook time 65 min

Ingredients
BLUEBERRY FILLING:
- 1 cup frozen blueberries
- ¼ cup water
- ¼ teaspoon xanthan gum

CREAM CHEESE FILLING:
- 8 oz cream cheese
- 1 large egg
- 2 tablespoon Swerve Sweetener or other granulated erythritol
- ⅛ teaspoon liquid stevia extract

CAKE:
- 2 cups almond flour
- ¼ cup Swerve Sweetener or other granulated erythritol
- ¼ cup vanilla whey protein powder
- 2 teaspoon baking powder
- 1 teaspoon xanthan gum
- ½ teaspoon baking soda
- ½ teaspoon salt
- 6 oz greek yogurt
- ¼ cup butter softened
- 3 large eggs
- ⅛ teaspoon liquid stevia extract
- ¼ cup unsweetened almond milk

Instructions
CREAM CHEESE FILLING:

2. In a medium bowl, beat cream cheese until smooth. Beat in egg until well combined, then beat in Swerve and stevia.

CAKE:
3. Preheat oven to 350F and grease a 9-inch springform pan.
4. In a medium bowl, whisk together almond flour, sweetener, vanilla protein powder, baking powder, xanthan gum, baking soda and salt.
5. In a large bowl, beat yogurt and butter together until smooth. Add eggs one at a time, beating lightly after each addition, then beat in stevia extract.
6. Beat in almond flour mixture in two additions, alternating with almond milk and scraping down beaters and sides of bowl as needed.
7. Spread batter in well-greased 9-inch springform pan with removable bottom, pushing batter up sides of pan to create center well for filling. Sides should be about 1 inch wide.
8. Spread cream cheese mixture evenly into center well, and then spread blueberry mixture over top of cream cheese.
9. Bake in 350F oven 30 to 35 minutes, or until sides are set. Center will still jiggle somewhat.
10. Let cool in pan. Run a sharp knife around cake in pan to loosen, and remove sides. Cover tightly with plastic wrap and refrigerate for at least one hour. Keep refrigerated.

BLACKBERRY CAKE RECIPE
Nutrition: Cal 204; Fat 18 g; Carb 7 g; Protein 5 g
Serving 16; Cook time 70 min

Ingredients
CAKE
- 1 ¼ cups almond flour
- ¼ cup coconut flour
- 1 teaspoon baking powder
- ½ cup Joy Filled Eats Sweetener
- ⅓ cup melted coconut oil
- ½ cup canned coconut milk
- 1 teaspoon vanilla
- 4 eggs

TOPPING
- 2 cups blackberries
- 1 cup almonds
- 2 tablespoon Joy Filled Eats Sweetener
- 2 tablespoon coconut oil

Instructions
1. Preheat oven to 350.
2. Stir together the dry cake ingredients in a medium bowl. Add all the other cake ingredients and mix well with a wooden spoon. Spread in a greased 8 x 8-inch baking dish. Sprinkle the blackberries on top of the cake batter.
3. Bake for 15 minutes.
4. Meanwhile, combine the ingredients for the topping in a food processor. Process until the nuts are chopped and

wet crumbs form. Sprinkle evenly over the partially baked cake.

5. Bake for an additional 40-55 minutes until the cake is firm to the touch, golden, and doesn't jiggle when lightly shaken. The center should feel as firm as the edge when lightly pressed with your fingertip.

CINNAMON CARROT CAKE

Nutrition: Cal 282; Fat 27 g; Carb 6 g; Protein 6 g
Serving 8; Cook time 10 min

Ingredients
- 1 large carrot
- 1/4 cup Low Carb Sugar Substitute
- 1/2 tsp liquid stevia
- 1/2 cup butter, melted
- 2 large eggs, room temperature
- 2/3 cup almond flour
- 2 tbsp coconut flour
- 1 tsp cinnamon
- 1 tsp baking soda
- pinch of salt

TOPPING
- 4 tbsp butter, room temperature
- 1/2 cup almond flour
- 1 tbsp coconut flour
- 3 tbsp Low Carb Sugar Substitute
- 1/4 tsp liquid stevia
- 1 tsp cinnamon
- pinch of salt

Instructions
1. Preheat your oven to 350°F and grease an 8-inch round cake pan with coconut oil spray or line with parchment paper.
2. Shred the carrot and set aside.
3. In a large bowl add erythritol, stevia, melted butter, and eggs. Combine using a whisk.
4. Add in the shredded carrot, almond flour, coconut flour, cinnamon, baking soda, and salt, and combine one more.
5. Spoon the batter into the greased or parchment lined round 8 inch round cake pan and set aside while you make the topping.
6. Make the topping by adding all the ingredients to a mixing bowl and combining with a spoon or your hands.
7. Sprinkle the topping over the batter and bake for 30-35 minutes.
8. Use a toothpick to test doneness. Allow to cool for 15-20 minutes prior to transferring and slicing.
9. Best stored in an air tight container int he fridge up to 10 days.

LOW CARB BLUEBERRY CHEESE DANISH CAKE

Nutrition: Cal 323; Fat 27 g; Carb 6 g; Protein 10 g
Serving 1; Cook time 50 min

Ingredients

CAKE LAYER
- 6 Tbsp butter
- 1/3 cup Swerve sweetener
- 2 eggs
- 1 Tbsp vanilla extract
- 1 cup almond flour
- 1/4 cup coconut flour
- pinch of salt
- 2 tsp baking powder
- 1/4 tsp xanthan gum
- 1/2 cup almond milk (unsweetened)
- 1 1/4 cups blueberries

CREAM CHEESE LAYER
- 3 oz cream cheese
- 1 egg
- 1 Tbsp Swerve sweetener

STREUSEL TOPPING
- 3 Tbsp butter
- 1 cup almond flour
- 3 Tbsp Swerve Sweetener
- 1/2 tsp lemon zest

Instructions
CAKE LAYER
1. Preheat your oven to 375 degrees (F)
2. Cream the butter and sweetener together in a medium bowl until smooth.
3. Add the eggs, beating well after each.
4. Add the vanilla extract and mix well.
5. Combine the almond flour, coconut flour, salt, baking powder, and xanthan gum in a separate medium bowl. Add to the wet ingredients and mix well. Pour in the almond milk and blend until smooth.
6. Grease a 9×9 (or equivalent) pan with butter. Spread the cake batter evenly over the bottom of the pan.
7. Sprinkle the blueberries evenly over the top of the batter.

CREAM CHEESE MIXTURE:
1. Heat the cream cheese for 30 seconds in the microwave until soft. Beat with a fork until smooth. Add the egg and sweetener and beat with a fork until smooth. Pour over the top of the blueberries.

STREUSEL TOPPING:
1. Melt the butter in a microwave safe bowl or on the stove. Stir in the almond flour, sweetener, and lemon zest until fully combined. Crumble over the top of the cake.
2. Bake the cake at 375 degrees (F) for 35 minutes or until a knife inserted in the center comes out clean and the top is golden brown.

ALMOND CAKE

Nutrition: Cal 231; Fat 22 g; Carb 5 g; Protein 6 g
Serving 1; Cook time 60 min

Ingredients
- 2 cups almond flour
- 1 cup granular sweetener (monk fruit is what I use)
- 1/2 cup plus 2 tablespoons olive oil
- 4 eggs

- 2 teaspoons baking powder
- 2 teaspoons cinnamon
- 1 teaspoon almond extract
- coconut oil for greasing

Instructions

1. Preheat oven to 350 degrees F and lightly grease 8x8 baking dish.
2. In a small bowl, add almond flour, sweetener and olive oil. Mix together until it becomes crumbly.
3. Set aside just barely 1 cup of mixture. Do NOT pack the measuring cup, but lightly measure.
4. In a large bowl, add the remaining crumble mixture, eggs, baking powder, cinnamon, and almond extract. Combine well with hand beaters.
5. Add mixture to baking dish.
6. Sprinkle crumble mixture that you set aside over the top of the batter and bake for 50 minutes or until center is done.

STICKY BUN COFFEE CAKE

Nutrition: Cal 272; Fat 25 g; Carb 6 g; Protein 8 g
Serving 16; Cook time 80 min

Ingredients

- 1 recipe Sugar-Free Caramel Sauce
- 3 cups almond flour
- ⅓ cup unflavoured whey protein powder
- 1 ½ teaspoon baking powder
- 1 teaspoon baking soda
- ½ teaspoon salt
- ½ cup butter softened
- ¾ cup Swerve Sweetener
- 3 large eggs
- 1 teaspoon vanilla extract
- ½ cup almond milk
- ½ cup chopped pecans

Instructions

1. Make the caramel sauce as directed in the recipe and let cool while preparing the cake.
2. Preheat oven to 325F and grease a bundt pan well (this could also be made in a 9-inch springform pan).
3. In a medium bowl, whisk together almond flour, protein powder, baking powder, baking soda and salt. Set aside.
4. In a large bowl, beat butter until smooth. Add Swerve and beat until lighter and well-combined, about 2 minutes.
5. Beat in eggs, scraping down beaters and sides of bowl with a rubber spatula as needed. Beat in vanilla extract.
6. Beat in half of the almond flour mixture, then beat in almond milk. Beat in remaining almond flour mixture until well combined.
7. Spread half the mixture in the prepared pan and use the back of a spoon to create a channel in the center of the batter, all the way around the bundt pan (if using a springform pan, simply create slightly higher sides around the edges of the pan.

8. Pour half of the caramel sauce into the channel (or spread half over the batter in the springform pan). Sprinkle with ¼ cup pecans.
9. Top with remaining batter and spread evenly with offset spatula to cover caramel and pecans.
10. Bake 35 to 45 minutes, or until cake is golden brown and just firm to the touch. A tester inserted in the center should come out clean (except for some caramel sauce!).
11. Remove and let cool 10 minutes then flip out onto a wire rack to cool completely.
12. Drizzle with remaining caramel and pecans.

SKILLET CHOCOLATE CHIP COFFEE CAKE

Nutrition: Cal 275; Fat 25 g; Carb 8 g; Protein 9 g
Serving 10; Cook time 65 min

Ingredients
CRUMB TOPPING:
- ¼ cup almond flour
- 1 tablespoon Swerve Sweetener
- 1 & ½ tsp cinnamon
- 1 tablespoon butter softened
CAKE:
- 2 cups almond flour
- ¼ cup unflavoured whey protein powder
- 2 teaspoon baking powder
- ¼ teaspoon salt
- 6 tablespoon butter softened
- ½ cup Swerve Sweetener
- 2 large eggs room temperature
- 1 teaspoon vanilla extract
- ½ cup almond milk
- ½ cup dark chocolate chips, sugar-free

Instructions

1. In a small bowl, whisk together almond flour, sweetener, and cinnamon. Cut in butter until mixture resembles coarse crumbs. Set aside.
2. For the cake, preheat oven to 325F and grease a 10 inch oven-proof skillet (does not need to be cast iron, but it's great if it is!)
3. In a medium bowl, whisk together the almond flour, whey protein powder, baking powder and salt.
4. In a large bowl, beat butter with sweetener until well combined. Beat in eggs and vanilla, then beat in half the almond flour mixture. Beat in almond milk and remaining almond flour until well combined.
5. Stir in chocolate chips and spread batter in prepared skillet. Bake 25 minutes, then remove from oven and sprinkle with topping. Return to oven and bake another 15 to 20 minutes, until sides are beginning to brown and center is just firm to the touch.
6. Remove and let cool at least 20 minutes before serving (cake will fall apart easily if you remove it while it's still very warm).

KETO PUMPKIN CRUMB CAKE

Nutrition: Cal 203; Fat 17 g; Carb 7 g; Protein 6 g
Serving 16; Соок time 60 min

Ingredients

CRUMB TOPPING:
- 1 cup almond flour
- ¼ cup coconut flour
- ½ cup Swerve Brown
- ½ teaspoon pumpkin pie spice
- ½ cup butter melted
- ¼ teaspoon salt

PUMPKIN CAKE:
- 1 cup almond flour
- ½ cup Swerve Sweetener
- ⅓ cup coconut flour
- ¼ cup unflavored egg white protein powder (can also use whey protein)
- 2 teaspoon baking powder
- ¾ tsp pumpkin pie spice
- ¼ teaspoon salt
- ½ cup pumpkin puree
- ¼ cup butter melted
- 2 large eggs
- ½ teaspoon vanilla extract

DRIZZLE (OPTIONAL):
- ¼ cup powdered Swerve Sweetener
- 2 tablespoon heavy cream
- ¼ teaspoon vanilla extract

Instructions

CRUMB TOPPING:

1. In a medium bowl, combine the almond flour, coconut flour, sweetener, pumpkin pie spice, and salt. Stir in the butter until well combined. It will be like a thick batter. Set aside

PUMPKIN CAKE:

2. Preheat the oven to 325F and grease a 9x9 inch square baking pan.
3. In a large bowl, whisk together the almond flour, sweetener, coconut flour, whey protein, baking powder, pumpkin pie spice, and salt. Stir in the pumpkin puree, butter, eggs, and vanilla extract until well combined.
4. Spread the batter in the prepared pan and smooth the top.
5. Crumble the topping mixture with your fingers into pea size pieces and sprinkle evenly overtop the cake batter. Bake 35 to 40 minutes, until the topping is golden and a tester inserted in the center comes out clean. It won't be firm to the touch because the topping is so tender.
6. Remove and let cool completely in the pan.

DRIZZLE:

1. Whisk the sweetener, cream, and vanilla extract together until smooth. Drizzle over the cooled cake.

CINNAMON ROLL CAKE

Nutrition: Cal 222; Fat 20 g; Carb 5,5 g; Protein 7 g
Serving 16; Соок time 50 min

Ingredients

CINNAMON FILLING:
- 3 tablespoon Swerve Sweetener
- 2 teaspoon ground cinnamon

CAKE:
- 3 cups almond flour
- ¾ cup Swerve Sweetener
- ¼ cup unflavoured whey protein powder
- 2 teaspoon baking powder
- ½ teaspoon salt
- 3 large eggs
- ½ cup butter melted
- ½ teaspoon vanilla extract
- ½ cup almond milk
- 1 tablespoon melted butter

CREAM CHEESE FROSTING:
- 3 tablespoon cream cheese softened
- 2 tablespoon powdered Swerve Sweetener
- 1 tablespoon heavy whipping cream
- ½ teaspoon vanilla extract

Instructions

2. Preheat oven to 325F and grease an 8x8 inch baking pan.
3. For the filling, combine the Swerve and cinnamon in a small bowl and mix well. Set aside.
4. For the cake, whisk together almond flour, sweetener, protein powder, baking powder, and salt in a medium bowl.
5. Stir in the eggs, melted butter and vanilla extract. Add the almond milk and continue to stir until well combined.
6. Spread half of the batter in the prepared pan, then sprinkle with about two thirds of the cinnamon filling mixture. Spread the remaining batter over top and smooth with a knife or an offset spatula.
7. Bake 35 minutes, or until top is golden brown and a tester inserted in the center comes out with a few crumbs attached.
8. Brush with melted butter and sprinkle with remaining cinnamon filling mixture. Let cool in pan.
9. For the frosting, beat cream cheese, powdered erythritol, cream and vanilla extract together in a small bowl until smooth. Pipe or drizzle over cooled cake.

RASPBERRY CREAM CHEESE CAKE

Nutrition: Cal 219; Fat 18 g; Carb 7 g; Protein 6 g
Serving 16; Соок time 120 min

Ingredients

CAKE BATTER:
- 2 cups almond flour
- ⅓ cup coconut flour
- 2 teaspoon baking powder
- ¼ teaspoon salt

- ½ cup butter softened
- ⅔ cup granulated Swerve Sweetener
- 3 large eggs room temperature
- ¾ teaspoon almond extract
- ½ cup unsweetened almond milk (or half heavy cream/half water)

FILLING:
- 8 oz cream cheese softened
- ½ cup granulated Swerve Sweetener (can use powdered too)
- 1 large egg
- ½ teaspoon vanilla extract
- 1 ½ cup fresh raspberries rinsed and dried

TOPPING:
- 2 tablespoon sliced almonds

Instructions
1. Preheat the oven to 325F and grease a 9-inch square baking pan (you can also use an 8x8 pan, but you will need to bake the cake for longer).
2. For the cake batter, combine the almond flour, coconut flour, baking powder, and salt in a medium bowl.
3. In a large bowl, beat the butter with the sweetener until well combined. Beat in the eggs and almond extract.
4. Beat in the almond flour mixture until combined, scraping down sides of bowl and beaters as needed. Beat in the almond milk until well combined. Set aside while making the filling.
5. For the filling, beat the cream cheese with granulated sweetener until smooth. Beat in the egg and vanilla extract until well combined.
6. To assemble the cake, spread about two thirds of the cake batter in the prepared baking pan, smoothing the top with a knife or an offset spatula.
7. Pour the cream cheese mixture over batter in pan and sprinkle with raspberries. Dot the remaining batter over the filling in small spoonfuls, allowing some of the filling to peek through. Sprinkle with sliced almonds.
8. Bake 35 to 40 minutes, or until top is light golden brown and filling is just set but still jiggles slightly in the middle. Remove and let cool completely, then transfer to refrigerator to chill for at least 1 hour.
9. Keep refrigerated until served.

KETO CAKE WITH CINNAMON AND WALNUTS

Nutrition: Cal 221; Fat 19 g; Carb 6 g; Protein 8 g
Serving 20; Cook time 75 min

Ingredients
- ¾ cup chopped walnuts
- ⅓ cup Swerve Brown
- 1 tablespoon cinnamon
- 2 ¾ cup almond flour
- 6 tablespoon coconut flour
- 6 tablespoon whey protein powder (or egg white protein powder)
- 1 tablespoon baking powder
- ½ teaspoon salt

- ¾ cup butter softened
- ¾ cup Swerve Sweetener
- 6 large eggs room temperature
- 1 tablespoon vanilla extract
- ½ to ¾ cup water

Instructions
1. Preheat the oven to 350F and grease a 9-inch tube pan (aka angel food cake pan) well. Line the bottom with parchment (see recipe notes).
2. In a medium bowl, whisk together the walnuts, Swerve Brown, and cinnamon. Set aside.
3. In a large bowl, whisk together the almond flour, coconut flour, protein powder, baking powder, and salt.
4. In a large bowl, beat the butter with the Swerve until light and fluffy, about 2 minutes. Beat in the eggs one at a time, then beat in the vanilla extract, scraping down the beaters and the sides of the bowl as needed.
5. Add the flour mixture and beat until well combined. Then beat in ¾ cup of the water. If the batter is quite thick, add additional water as necessary. The batter should be scoopable and spreadable but not quite pourable.
6. Spread about half the batter in the prepared pan, and then sprinkle with half of the walnut mixture. Spread the remaining batter in the pan and sprinkle with the remaining walnut mixture.
7. Bake 45 to 55 minutes, until golden brown and just firm to the touch. A tester inserted in the center should come out clean.
8. Remove and let cool in the pan, then run a sharp knife just around the edges to loosen and transfer to a plate.

KETO PUMPKIN CRUNCH CAKE
1. Nutrition: Cal 215; Fat 19 g; Carb 7 g; Protein 5 g
2. Serving 18; Cook time 75 min

Ingredients
- 1 ½ cups pumpkin puree
- 3 large eggs room temperature
- ⅔ cup Swerve Granular
- ½ cup heavy whipping cream
- 2 teaspoon pumpkin pie spice
- ¼ teaspoon salt
- 1 box Swerve Yellow Cake Mix divided
- 1 cup chopped pecans
- ⅓ cup Swerve Brown
- ½ cup butter melted

Instructions
1. Preheat the oven to 350°F and grease a 9×13 inch glass or ceramic baking pan.
2. In a large bowl, whisk together the pumpkin, eggs, sweetener, whipping cream, pumpkin spice, and salt. Measure out ½ cup of the cake mix and whisk into the pumpkin mixture until smooth.
3. Pour into the prepared baking pan, then sprinkle the remaining cake mix evenly overtop.

4. In a small bowl, whisk the pecans with the Swerve Brown. Sprinkle this evenly over the cake mix, then drizzle the melted butter evenly over the pecans.
5. Bake 45 to 55 minutes, until the top is just firm to the touch and a rich, deep brown. It will still be very soft underneath.
6. Remove and let cool to room temperature. You can also eat it warm, or chill it in the refrigerator to firm it up.

KETO CARAMEL APPLE COFFEE CAKE
Nutrition: Cal 232; Fat 19 g; Carb 7 g; Protein 8 g
Serving 16; Cook time 80 min

Ingredients
CINNAMON CRUMB
- ¼ cup almond flour
- 1 tablespoon Swerve Sweetener
- 1 teaspoon cinnamon
- 1 tablespoon butter

CAKE
- 3 cups almond flour
- 6 tablespoon unflavored whey protein powder
- 2 teaspoon baking powder
- 1 ½ teaspoon cinnamon
- ½ teaspoon baking soda
- ½ teaspoon salt
- ½ cup butter softened
- ½ cup Swerve Sweetener
- 3 large eggs
- ½ teaspoon apple flavoring
- ¼ teaspoon stevia extract
- ⅔ cup almond milk
- 1 medium apple peeled and cored, chopped fine
- 1 recipe Sugar-Free Caramel Sauce

Instructions
CINNAMON CRUMB
1. Whisk together almond flour, Swerve and cinnamon. Cut in butter and use your fingers to rub together until small crumbs form. Set aside.

CAKE
2. Preheat oven to 325F and grease a 9-inch springform pan.
3. In a medium bowl, whisk together almond flour, whey protein, baking powder, cinnamon, baking soda, and salt.
4. In a large bowl, beat butter with Swerve until smooth. Beat in eggs, apple flavoring and stevia extract.
5. Beat in almond flour mixture in two additions, alternating with almond milk. Stir in chopped apples.
6. Spread batter in prepared pan. Drizzle half of the caramel sauce over top and swirl into the batter with a knife.
7. Bake 25 minutes, then remove from oven and sprinkle with cinnamon crumb mixture. Bake another 25 minutes, or until golden brown and center is set (if your cake is browning too quickly, cover with foil for the last 15 minutes of baking).

8. Remove from oven and let cool. Then run a sharp knife around the inside of the pan to loosen sides. Remove sides and drizzle with remaining caramel sauce.

KETO CRANBERRY WALNUT TART
Nutrition: Cal 257; Fat 30 g; Carb 8 g; Protein 7 g
Serving 12; Cook time 75 min

Ingredients
- 1 keto pie crust
- ½ cup butter
- ⅓ cup Swerve Brown
- ⅓ cup BochaSweet or allulose
- 2 large eggs
- 1 teaspoon vanilla extract
- ¾ teaspoon cinnamon
- ¼ teaspoon salt
- 1 ½ cups walnut halves and pieces coarsely chopped
- 1 cup cranberries chopped in half if large
- 1 ½ ounces sugar-free white chocolate chips

Instructions
1. Preheat the oven to 325°F and lightly grease a 9-inch ceramic tart pan.
2. Prepare the crust according to the directions and press firmly and evenly into the bottom and up the sides of the prepared pan. Bake 10 minutes, and then let cool completely to firm up.
3. In a medium saucepan over medium low heat, melt the butter with the two sweeteners, stirring until the sweeteners have dissolved. Bring to a simmer and cook about 3 minutes, until it darkens in color and thickens slightly. Remove from the heat and let cool to room temperature.
4. Once cool, whisk in the eggs, vanilla, cinnamon, and salt. Spread the cranberries and walnuts in the prepared crust and pour the filling overtop.
5. Increase the oven heat to 350°F and bake 35 to 45 minutes, or until the filling is mostly set but the middle still jiggles slightly when shaken. Let cool completely.
6. Melt the white chocolate chips in a microwave safe bowl in short increments, stirring until smooth. Drizzle over the cooled tart.

KETO PEANUT BUTTER EARTHQUAKE CAKE
Nutrition: Cal 253; Fat 22 g; Carb 8 g; Protein 7 g
Serving 12; Cook time 60 min

Ingredients
CAKE BATTER
- 2 cups almond flour
- ½ cup Swerve Sweetener
- ¼ cup cocoa powder
- 2 teaspoon baking powder
- ¼ teaspoon salt
- 3 large eggs
- 6 tablespoon butter melted

- ⅓ cup water
- ½ teaspoon vanilla extract

FILLING
- 4 ounces cream cheese softened
- ½ cup natural peanut butter
- ¼ cup butter softened
- ⅔ cup powdered Swerve
- ⅓ cup almond milk or half water/half cream
- ½ teaspoon vanilla extract

TOPPING
- ⅓ cup dark chocolate chips, sugar-free or peanut butter chips
- ¼ cup salted peanuts chopped
- 6 sugar-free peanut butter cups chopped

Instructions
CAKE BATTER
1. Preheat the oven to 325ºF and grease a 9×13 glass or ceramic baking pan. (If using metal, the cake may bake through faster so watch it carefully).
2. In a large bowl, whisk together the almond flour, sweetener, cocoa powder, baking powder, and salt. Stir in the eggs, melted butter, water, and vanilla extract until well combined. Spread evenly in the prepared pan.

FILLING
1. In another large bowl, beat the cream cheese, peanut butter and butter together until smooth. Beat in the powdered sweetener until well combined, then beat in the almond milk and vanilla extract.
2. Dollop this mixture over the cake mixture by the spoonful, then use a knife to swirl into the cake mixture.

TOPPING
1. Sprinkle the top with the chocolate chips and chopped peanuts. Bake 35 to 45 minutes, or until the cake edges are set. The center will still be soft and slightly jiggly.
2. Sprinkle with the chopped peanut butter cups while the cake is still warm. Let cool before serving.

KETO CANNOLI SHEET CAKE
Nutrition: Cal 235; Fat 20 g; Carb 6 g; Protein 7 g
Serving 20; Cook time 25 min

Ingredients
SHEET CAKE
- 2 cups almond flour
- ⅔ cup Swerve Sweetener
- ⅓ cup coconut flour
- ⅓ cup whey protein powder (can also use egg white protein powder)
- 1 tablespoon baking powder
- ½ teaspoon salt
- 3 large eggs
- ½ cup butter (melted and cooled)
- ⅔ cup water
- 1 teaspoon vanilla extract

CANNOLI CREAM FROSTING
- ¾ cup whole milk ricotta (room temperature)
- 4 ounces cream cheese (softened)

- ½ cup powdered Swerve Sweetener
- 1 ¼ cups heavy whipping cream (divided)
- ½ teaspoon vanilla extract
- ⅓ cup sugar-free mini chocolate chips (or regular sugar-free chocolate chips)
- Additional powdered sweetener for sprinkling

Instructions
CAKE:
1. Preheat the oven to 325F and grease a 10x15 jelly roll pan very well. You can also do this in an 11x17 pan but it will be thinner and will bake faster.
2. In a large bowl, whisk together the almond flour, sweetener, coconut flour, whey protein, baking powder, and salt. Stir in the eggs, melted butter, water, and vanilla extract until well combined.
3. Spread the batter as evenly as possible in the prepared pan and bake 18 to 22 minutes, until golden brown and just firm to the touch. Remove and let cool completely.

CANNOLI FROSTING:
1. In a food processor or high powered blender, combine the ricotta and the cream cheese. Blend briefly until well combined. Add the sweetener, ¼ cup of the heavy cream, and the vanilla extract. Blend until smooth.
2. In a large bowl, beat the remaining 1 cup of cream until it holds stiff peaks. Add the ricotta mixture and fold together until well combined. Spread over the cooled cake.
3. Sprinkle with the chocolate chips and refrigerate at least 1 hour to set. Sprinkle with additional powdered sweetener just before serving.

KETO RUM CAKE RECIPE
Nutrition: Cal 245; Fat 3 g; Carb 75 g; Protein 4 g
Serving 15; Cook time 60 min

Ingredients
RUM CAKE
- 2 ¼ cups almond flour
- ¼ cup coconut flour
- ¼ cup unflavoured whey protein powder (or egg white protein powder)
- 2 ½ teaspoon baking powder
- 1 teaspoon cinnamon
- ¼ teaspoon nutmeg
- ⅛ teaspoon allspice
- ½ teaspoon salt
- ½ cup butter softened
- ¾ cup Swerve Brown
- 4 large eggs room temperature
- 1 ½ teaspoon vanilla extract
- ¾ cup dark rum

RUM GLAZE
- 2 tablespoon butter melted
- ¼ cup powdered Swerve Sweetener
- ¼ cup powdered BochaSweet or allulose
- 2 to 3 tablespoon dark rum
- ¼ cup chopped toasted pecans

Instructions
RUM CAKE
1. Preheat the oven to 350F and grease a 9×5 inch metal loaf pan well. Line with parchment paper, so that the parchment overhangs the pan (for easy removal).
2. In a medium bowl, whisk together the almond flour, coconut flour, protein powder, baking powder, cinnamon, nutmeg, and salt.
3. In a large bowl, beat the butter with the brown sweetener until creamy and well combined. Add the eggs, one at a time, beating after each addition. Beat in the vanilla extract.
4. Add the almond flour mixture in two additions, alternating with the rum and beating until well combined. Scrape down the sides of the bowl and the beaters as needed.
5. Spread in the prepared baking pan and bake 45 to 55 minutes, until the cake is golden brown and the top is just firm to the touch. Remove and let cool completely in the pan, then loosen with a knife and lift out by the parchment.

RUM GLAZE
1. Place the butter in a medium bowl and whisk in the sweeteners until combined. Drizzle in the rum, whisking until smooth, until a thick but pourable consistency is achieved.
2. Drizzle over the cooled cake and sprinkle with chopped pecans.

CAKE LAYER
1. Preheat the oven to 180C/375F degrees.
2. Grease and line an 8 inch springform cake tin with parchment paper.
3. In a bowl, mix the erythritol and butter together until soft and blended.
4. Add the egg yolks, lemon juice, lemon zest and vanilla extract and stir thoroughly.
5. Add the coconut flour, salt, baking powder and beat until combined.
6. In another bowl, whisk the egg whites until stiff.
7. Gently fold the egg whites into the cake mixture.
8. IF the mixture seems dry, add a couple of tablespoons of water.
9. Spoon the mixture into the baking tin and smooth evenly.

CREAM CHEESE LAYER
1. In a bowl, add the softened cream cheese and beat with the erythritol.
2. Add the egg, vanilla extract, lemon juice, zest and beat until smooth.
3. Spoon this mixture over the cake mixture into the cake tin and smooth evenly.

CRUMBLE TOPPING
1. For the topping, place the coconut flour and erythritol in a bowl and mix until combined.
2. Add the butter and mix with your hands, gently, so that the mixture looks like breadcrumbs.
3. Scatter the topping over the cream cheese layer
4. Bake for 40-45 minutes until firm and the top is cooked.
5. Remove from the oven, allow to cool, then place in the fridge to firm.

KETO LEMON CREAM CHEESECAKE
Nutrition: Cal 290; Fat 26 g; Carb 9 g; Protein 7 g
Serving 10; Cook time 60 min

Ingredients
CAKE
- ½ cup coconut flour
- 5 medium eggs separated
- ½ cup erythritol
- ½ cup butter, unsalted softened at room temperature
- ⅓ cup lemon juice
- 2 tablespoons lemon zest grated
- ¼ teaspoon salt
- ½ teaspoon baking powder
- 1 teaspoon vanilla extract

CREAM CHEESE LAYER
- 8 oz cream cheese softened at room temperature
- ¼ cup erythritol
- 1 medium egg
- 1 teaspoon vanilla extract
- 1 lemon - juice & zest

CRUMBLE TOPPING
- ⅓ cup coconut flour
- ⅓ cup erythritol
- ¼ cup Butter, unsalted cold, cut into small pieces

Instructions

CINNAMON SWIRL KETO CAKE
Nutrition: Cal 168; Fat 9 g; Carb 6,5 g; Protein 6 g
Serving 8; Cook time 50 min

Ingredients
CAKE
- 1 c Almond flour
- ⅓ c Coconut flour
- ½ tsp Cinnamon
- ¼ tsp Cardamom optional
- 4 Eggs room temperature
- 1/2 tsp Vanilla extract
- ⅓ c Monkfruit sweetener
- Pinch of salt
- ½ c Unsweetened nut milk
- 1 tsp Baking powder
- Coconut oil for greasing the pan

CINNAMON SWIRL
- 2 tbsp Coconut oil
- 1 tsp Cinnamon
- 1 tbsp Monkfruit sweetener

Instructions
1. Preheat the oven to 325°F (162°C) and grease your 8×8 or 8×9 baking dish with coconut oil.

2. Using two bowls, one large for mixing, one smaller for liquids. Separate the room temperature eggs, put the egg whites in the larger mixing bowl.
3. Whip the egg whites using an electric mixer. After whipping them for about 30 seconds, gradually add the 1/3 cup of monkfruit sweetener. Whip until soft peaks form when you lift the beaters. Don't overmix.
4. Combine the yolks with the unsweetened nut milk and vanilla.
5. In a separate bowl, combine the almond flour, coconut flour, 1/2 tsp of cinnamon, cardamom (optional), baking powder, and salt.
6. Combine the wet and dry ingredients thoroughly.
7. Mix half of the whipped egg whites into the flour mixture. Make sure this is thoroughly combined.
8. Gently fold in the mixture into the rest of the whipped egg whites. Only mix until this is combined. If you over-mix this, the cake won't be fluffy!
9. Pour the batter into the prepared baking dish.

PREPARE THE CINNAMON SWIRL
1. In a bowl, combine the swirl ingredients: 2 tbsp softened coconut oil, 1 tsp cinnamon, and 1tbsp monkfruit sweetener. Spoon this into a Ziploc bag and snip the corner off. Drizzle this over the cake mixture that is in the baking dish. You can drizzle in a grid-shape.
2. Use a toothpick or chopstick to swirl the cinnamon mixture into the top of the cake.
3. Bake at 325°F for 40 minutes. Check the cake with a toothpick and make sure the toothpick comes out clean. Cool and enjoy!

MACADAMIA NUT KETO CAKE
Nutrition: Cal 138; Fat 13 g; Carb 5 g; Protein 2 g
Serving 12; Cook time 45 min

Ingredients
- 2 whole eggs
- 1/4 cup butter
- 1/2 cup sour cream coconut cream
- 1/4 cup ground flax meal
- 1/4 cup coconut flour
- 1/4 cup almond flour
- 1/2 cup keto brown sugar
- 1 tbsp ground cinnamon
- 1 teaspoon baking powder
- 1 teaspoon vanilla extract
- 1 teaspoon star anise seed
- 1/2 teaspoon salt
- 1/4 teaspoon allspice powder
- 1/2 cup macadamia nuts chopped

Instructions
1. Preheat the oven to 350° F.
2. Whisk eggs in a small bowl. Add butter and cream.
3. In a second bowl, mix all dry ingredients together. Reserve the nuts to be either blended into the batter or sprinkled on top.
4. Combine the dry ingredients with the egg mixture. If desired, blend the nuts in now. Pour batter into greased

8 by 8-inch glass baking dish. If the nuts are not blended in to the dough, sprinkle them on top now.
5. Bake for 30 minutes. Test the center with a knife. If it is ready, remove from the oven and let cool. Serve warm, room temperature or cold.

RHUBARB CAKE
Nutrition: Cal 330; Fat 29 g; Carb 14 g; Protein 12 g
Serving 10; Cook time 10 min

Ingredients
- 3 cups (425g) rhubarb, sliced
- 1/2 cup (100g) plus 2 tablespoons granulated erythritol sweetener, divided
- 3 cups (288g) almond flour
- 1/3 cup (25g) unflavored whey protein powder
- 2 teaspoons baking powder
- 1/4 teaspoon salt
- 1/2 cup (113g) unsalted butter, melted
- 3 large (150g) eggs
- 1/2 cup (113g) unsweetened almond milk
- 1/2 teaspoon vanilla extract

FOR THE CRUMB TOPPING:
- 1/4 cup (24g) almond flour
- 2 tablespoons pecans, finely chopped
- 1 tablespoon granulated erythritol sweetener
- 1 tablespoon unsalted butter, room temperature

Instructions
1. In a medium bowl, toss together the sliced rhubarb and 2 tablespoons of the sweetener. Set aside.
2. Preheat the oven to 350F and grease a 9-inch springform pan very well.
3. In a medium bowl, whisk together the almond flour, remaining 1/2 cup of sweetener, whey protein powder, baking powder, and salt.
4. Stir in the melted butter, eggs, almond milk, and vanilla extract until well combined. Spread 2/3 of the batter in prepared pan. Sprinkle with the rhubarb and dot the remaining batter over in small spoonfuls. Bake 30 minutes.

TO MAKE THE CRUMB TOPPING
1. While the cake is baking, combine the crumb topping ingredients in a small bowl, cutting in the room temperature butter until it resembles coarse crumbs. Sprinkle the crumb topping over the cake and cover with foil.
2. Bake another 20 to 30 minutes, until the edges are golden brown and the center is firm to the touch. Remove and let cool, then run a sharp knife around the inside of the pan to loosen. Remove the sides.

KETO CHOCOLATE KAHLUA CAKE
Nutrition: Cal 350; Fat 32 g; Carb 7 g; Protein 10 g
Serving 12; Cook time 70 min

Ingredients
- 1 ⅔ cup almond flour
- ½ cup cocoa powder

- •⅓ cup unflavoured whey protein powder (or egg white protein powder)
- •2 teaspoon baking powder
- •1 teaspoon espresso powder
- •¼ teaspoon salt
- •½ cup butter
- •⅔ cup Swerve Granular
- •3 large eggs room temperature
- •1 teaspoon vanilla extract
- •½ cup sugar-free coffee liqueur OR ¼ cup strong coffee + 2 tablespoon vodka and 2 tablespoon rum

FROSTING
- •¼ cup sugar-free coffee liqueur OR 2 tablespoon strong coffee + 1 tablespoon vodka + 1 tablespoon rum
- •1 ½ teaspoon espresso powder
- •8 ounces mascarpone cheese softened
- •¾ cup powdered Swerve Sweetener divided
- •1 cup heavy whipping cream
- •1 teaspoon vanilla extract

GARNISH (OPTIONAL)
- •Keto chocolate sprinkles
- •Coffee beans

Instructions

CAKE

1. Preheat the oven to 350°F and grease 2 (two) 6-inch cake pans (see blog post for advice on baking in larger pans). Line the bottoms of the pans with parchment paper circles and lightly grease the parchment.
2. In a medium bowl, whisk together the almond flour, cocoa powder, protein powder, baking powder, espresso powder, and salt.
3. In a large bowl, beat the butter with the sweetener until well combined and fluffy, about 2 minutes. Beat in the eggs and vanilla extract until smooth and creamy.
4. Add the almond flour mixture in two additions, alternating with the coffee liqueur. Beat until just well combined, scraping down the sides of the bowl and the beaters as needed.
5. Divide the mixture evenly between the two baking pans, and bake 30 to 35 minutes, until risen and the tops are firm to the touch. Remove and let cool 30 minutes in the pans, then run a sharp knife around the edges and flip out onto a wire rack to cool completely.
6. Once the cakes have completely cooled, slice carefully through the middle of each with a serrated knife, to make 4 cake layers. Note: If your cakes are very domed at the top, carefully slice off the domes to even them out.

FROSTING

1. Gently warm the coffee liqueur in the microwave and stir in the espresso powder until dissolved. Let cool to room temperature.
2. In a large bowl, beat the mascarpone with ½ cup of the powdered sweetener until well combined. Beat in 2 tablespoons of the coffee mixture.
3. In another large bowl, beat the heavy cream with the remaining sweetener and the vanilla until it holds stiff peaks. Add the mascarpone mixture and beat on

medium speed until just combined. Then beat in the remaining coffee mixture until the frosting holds stiff peaks.

TO ASSEMBLE

1. Place one layer of the cake on a cake plate and top with about ½ cup of frosting, spreading to the edges. Repeat with the remaining cake layers and frosting.
2. Spread the remaining frosting over the sides of the cake, reserving a little for piping decorative accents, if desired.

GARNISH

1. Place coffee beans decoratively around the top of the cake and sprinkle with chocolate sprinkles.
2. Gently press some chocolate sprinkles into the base of the cake, all the way around.

KETO CHOCOLATE CAKE
Nutrition: Cal 366; Fat 35 g; Carb 7 g; Protein 7 g
Serving 16; Cook time 45 min

Ingredients

CAKE
- •2 cups almond flour
- •¾ cup Swerve Sweetener
- •⅔ cup cocoa powder
- •1 tablespoon baking powder
- •1 teaspoon espresso powder (optional)
- •½ teaspoon salt
- •1 cup mayonnaise
- •3 large eggs
- •⅓ cup water
- •1 teaspoon vanilla extract

DAIRY FREE CHOCOLATE FROSTING
- •2 ounces unsweetened chocolate chopped
- •¾ cup plus 1 tbsp coconut oil divided
- •4 ounces dairy free cream cheese softened
- •1 cup powdered Swerve Sweetener
- •1 teaspoon vanilla extract
- •⅓ to ½ cup full fat coconut milk

Instructions

1. Preheat the oven to 350F and grease two 8-inch round cake pans. Line the bottoms of the pans with parchment and grease the parchment.
2. In a large bowl, whisk together the almond flour, sweetener, cocoa powder, baking powder, espresso powder, and salt.
3. Stir in the mayonnaise, eggs, water, and vanilla extract until well combined. Divide the batter evenly between the prepared pans and spread to the edges and smooth the tops.
4. Bake 20 to 25 minutes, until the cakes are just firm to the touch. Remove from the oven and let cool in the pans for at least 20 minutes, then flip out onto a wire rack to cool completely. Peel off the parchment paper.

DAIRY FREE FROSTING

1. Place the chocolate and 1 tablespoon of the coconut oil in a microwave safe bowl. Melt on high in 30 second increments, stirring in between, until smooth. Allow to

cool to lukewarm. Alternatively, you can melt in a heatproof bowl over a pan of barely simmering water.

2. Place the remaining coconut oil in a large bowl. If it is very hard, microwave it for 15 seconds or so. It should be softe enough to beat without being melted. Add the cream cheese and beat until smooth. Add the sweetener and vanilla extract and beat until well combined.

3. Drizzle in the melted chocolate and beat again until smooth. Add the coconut milk a few tablespoons at a time until a spreadable consistency is achieved.

TO ASSEMBLE

1. Place one layer of cake on a large plate or cake platter. Top with one third of the frosting, spreading to the edges.

2. Gently place the second layer of cake on top and spread the top with another third of the frosting.

3. Spread the the sides with the remaining frosting.

KETO FLOURLESS CHOCOLATE CAKE

Nutrition: Cal 214; Fat 20 g; Carb 6 g; Protein 4 g
Serving 12; Cook time 50 min

Ingredients
CAKE
- 4 ounces unsweetened chocolate chopped
- ⅓ cup coconut oil
- ¾ cup Swerve Granular
- 1 teaspoon vanilla extract
- 1 teaspoon espresso powder optional
- ¼ teaspoon salt
- 3 large eggs room temperature
- ¼ cup coconut cream
- ½ cup cocoa powder

GLAZE
- ⅓ cup coconut cream
- 1 ½ ounces unsweetened chocolate chopped
- 3 tablespoon powdered Swerve Sweetener
- 1 tablespoon allulose or BochaSweet
- ½ teaspoon vanilla extract

Instructions
CAKE:

1. Preheat the oven to 350F and lightly grease an 8 inch round metal baking pan. Line the bottom with parchment paper and grease the paper.

2. In a heatproof bowl set over a pan of barely simmering water, combine the chopped chocolate and the coconut oil. Stir until melted and smooth.

3. Remove the pan from heat but keep the bowl over the warm water. Stir in the sweetener, vanilla, espresso powder, and salt until well combined.

4. Add the eggs and stir to combine. The mixture may thicken considerably so add the coconut cream quickly and keep stirring until it smooths out again. Stir in the cocoa powder until well combined.

5. Pour the batter into the prepared baking pan and smooth the top. Bake 15 to 20 minutes, until the sides are set and the top is just barely firm to the touch. Do not overbake.

6. Remove and let cool 30 minutes in the pan, then flip out onto a cake platter and remove the parchment (the bottom will become the top).

GLAZE:

1. In a small saucepan over medium heat, bring the coconut cream to just a simmer. Remove from heat and add the chopped chocolate. Let sit 5 minutes to melt.

2. Add the sweeteners and vanilla extract and whisk until smooth. Let sit a few minutes to thicken and then spread over the top of the cake.

3. Refrigerate 20 minutes to set the glaze.

KETO CHOCOLATE ORANGE CAKE

Nutrition: Cal 299; Fat 3 g; Carb 71 g; Protein 4 g
Serving 16; Cook time 70 min

Ingredients
CAKE
- ⅔ cup coconut flour (73g)
- ⅔ cup Swerve Sweetener
- 6 tablespoon dark cocoa powder
- ¼ cup unflavored whey protein powder
- 2 teaspoon baking powder
- ½ teaspoon salt
- ½ cup butter, melted and cooled
- 6 large eggs, room temperature
- 1 teaspoon orange extract
- ½ teaspoon vanilla extract
- ½ cup water more if needed

FROSTING
- 2 ½ ounces unsweetened chocolate, chopped
- 8 ounces cream cheese, softened
- ½ cup butter, softened
- ¾ cup powdered Swerve Sweetener
- 1 to 1 ½ teaspoon orange extract
- ½ teaspoon vanilla extract
- ¼ cup heavy whipping cream, room temperature

DRIP GLAZE
- 6 tablespoon heavy whipping cream
- 1 ½ ounces unsweetened chocolate, chopped
- 2 tablespoon powdered Swerve Sweetener
- 1 tablespoon powdered BochaSweet (or an additional tablespoon Swerve)

GARNISH
- Thinly sliced orange
- Long strands of orange zest

Instructions
CAKE

1. Preheat the oven to 350F and grease a 9×13 inch metal rectangular pan. Line the bottom of the pan with parchment paper (cut to fit) and grease the paper.

2. In a large bowl, whisk together the coconut flour, sweetener, cocoa powder, protein powder, baking powder, and salt.

3. Stir in the butter, eggs, orange extract, and vanilla extract. Stir in the water until the batter is smooth. If the batter is overly thick, add more water, a tablespoon at

a time, until it thins out. It should be thick but still pourable out of the bowl.

4. Spread the batter evenly in the prepared pan and bake 20 to 25 minutes, until the cake has risen and the top is firm to the touch. Remove and let cool in the pan.

5. Once the cake has cooled, run a sharp knife around the sides to loosen and flip it out onto a cutting board. Cut the cake crosswise into three even pieces.

FROSTING

1. Place the chopped chocolate in a microwave safe bowl and melt on high in 30 second increments, stirring in between, until melted.

2. In a large bowl, beat the cream cheese and butter together until smooth. Beat in the sweetener and extracts, then add the melted chocolate and beat until well combined.

3. Beat in the cream. Add more cream as necessary to achieve a spreadable consistency.

TO ASSEMBLE

1. Place one section of the cake on a cake platter. Spread the top with about ¼ of the frosting. Repeat with the remaining two layers of cake.

2. Use some of the frosting to crumb coat the sides of the cake (see the crumb coat section in blog post). Then spread the remaining frosting evenly over the sides of the cake.

3. Chocolate Drip Glaze

4. In a small saucepan over medium heat, bring the cream to a simmer. Remove from heat and add the chopped chocolate. Let sit a few minutes to melt.

5. Add the sweeteners and whisk to combine. Let cool a few minutes to thicken, and then slowly pour over the top of the cake along the edges, letting it drip down the sides.

6. Smooth the glaze over the top of the cake.

GARNISH

1. Let the glaze set for about 20 minutes, then use thinly sliced oranges and strands of orange zest to decorate as desired.

KETO LEMON BLUEBERRY MUG CAKE

Nutrition: Cal 210; Fat 23 g; Carb 8g; Protein 6 g
Serving 1; Cook time 18 min

Ingredients

- ⅓ cup coconut flour
- ⅓ cup Swerve Sweetener
- Zest from one lemon
- 1 teaspoon baking powder
- ¼ teaspoon salt
- 3 large eggs
- ⅓ cup coconut oil melted
- ⅓ cup water
- ½ teaspoon lemon extract
- ⅓ cup blueberries

Instructions

1. In a medium bowl, whisk together the coconut flour, sweetener, lemon zest, baking powder, and salt.

2. Stir in the eggs, coconut oil, water, and lemon extract. Stir in the blueberries and divide the batter between 4 mugs.

3. Cook each mug in the microwave on high for about 1 minute 30 seconds. Cook longer if desired.

KETO PUMPKIN CARAMEL LAVA CAKES

Nutrition: Cal 259; Fat 29 g; Carb 5 g; Protein 6 g
Serving 4; Cook time 45 min

Ingredients

- ½ recipe Sugar-Free Caramel Sauce
- ⅓ cup pumpkin puree
- ¼ cup butter, melted
- 2 large eggs, room temperature
- ½ teaspoon vanilla extract
- 6 tablespoon powdered Swerve Sweetener
- 6 tablespoon almond flour
- 1 teaspoon pumpkin pie spice

Instructions

1. Make the caramel sauce according to the directions, but leave out the additional water in Step 4. Let it cool completely before proceeding.

2. Preheat the oven to 350F and lightly grease 4 small (4 ounce) ramekins.

3. In a large bowl, whisk together the pumpkin puree, melted butter, eggs, and vanilla extract. Stir in the sweetener, almond flour, and pumpkin pie spice until well combined.

4. Divide about ⅔ of the batter between the ramekins to cover the bottom of each. Use a spoon to make a well in the batter (you want some batter to cover the bottom of the ramekin but raised on the sides).

5. Spoon 1 tablespoon of caramel sauce into each well. Use the remaining batter to cover the caramel in each ramekin.

6. Bake 20 to 25 minutes, until the cakes are golden brown and the tops are just barely firm to the touch. The caramel sauce may be bubbling up a bit through the top.

7. Remove and let cool 10 minutes before serving in the ramekins (these will not stand up to be flipped out of the ramekins).

8. Top with keto vanilla ice cream, if desired, and the remaining caramel sauce. If the sauce has thickened considerably, add a tablespoon of water and re-warm gently in the pan.

PUMPKIN GOOEY BUTTER CAKE

Nutrition: Cal 219 ; Fat 20; Carb 5 g; Protein 5 g
Serving 15; Cook time 80 min

Ingredients

CAKE

- 2 cups almond flour
- ½ cup Swerve Granular or other granulated eryrhritol
- 1 ½ teaspoons baking powder
- ¼ teaspoon salt

- ½ cup 1 stick unsalted butter, melted
- 1 large egg
- ½ teaspoon vanilla extract

PUMPKIN FILLING
- 8 ounces cream cheese softened
- ½ cup 1 stick unsalted butter, softened
- ⅔ cup Swerve Confectioners or other powdered erythritol
- ¼ cup Swerve Brown or other brown sugar replacement
- 1 cup pumpkin puree
- 2 large egg
- 1 teaspoon pumpkin pie spice
- ½ teaspoon vanilla extract

Instructions

CAKE

1. Preheat oven to 325F and lightly grease a 9″ x 13″ glass or ceramic baking dish (metal is not recommended).
2. In a large bowl, combine the almond flour, granulated sweetener, baking powder, and salt. Add the melted butter, egg, and vanilla extract, and stir well to combine. Transfer mixture to the prepared baking dish and press into the bottom and up the sides.
3. Press this mixture into the bottom and up the sides of the prepared baking dish.

PUMPKIN FILLING

1. In a large bowl, use an electric mixer to beat the cream cheese and softened butter until smooth. Beat in the powdered and brown sweeteners until well combined, then beat in the pumpkin, eggs, pumpkin pie spice, and vanilla until smooth.
2. Pour the filling over the crust. Bake 50-60 minutes, or until the sides are set about 2 inches from the edges of the pan, while the center is still a little jiggly.
3. Remove the cake from oven and let cool completely before cutting into squares. Top with lightly sweetened whipped cream if desired.

KENTUCKY BUTTER CAKE

Nutrition: Cal 300; Fat 27 g; Carb 5,5 g; Protein 7,4 g
Serving 16; Cook time 80 min

Ingredients

CAKE:
- 2 ½ cups almond flour
- ¼ cup coconut flour
- ¼ cup unflavoured whey protein powder
- 1 tablespoon baking powder
- ½ teaspoon salt
- 1 cup butter softened
- 1 cup Swerve Granular
- 5 large eggs room temperature.
- 2 teaspoon vanilla extract
- ½ cup whipping cream
- ½ cup water

BUTTER GLAZE:
- 5 tablespoon butter
- ⅓ cup Swerve Granular
- 2 tablespoon water

- 1 teaspoon vanilla extract

GARNISH
- 1 to 2 tablespoon Confectioner's Swerve

Instructions

1. Preheat oven to 325F. Grease a bundt cake pan VERY well and then dust with a few tablespoon of almond flour. Pro Tip: double-grease your pan to help prevent sticking. Use a solid fat first, like butter or coconut oil, and then a spray like coconut or avocado.
2. In a medium bowl, whisk together the almond flour, coconut flour, whey protein, baking powder, and salt.
3. In a large bowl, beat the butter and the sweetener together until light and creamy. Beat in the eggs and vanilla extract. Beat in the almond flour mixture and then beat in the whipping cream and water until well combined.
4. Transfer the batter to the prepared baking pan and smooth the top. Bake 50 to 60 minutes, until golden brown and the cake is firm to the touch. A tester inserted in the center should come out clean.
5. Butter Glaze:In a small saucepan over low heat, melt the butter and sweetener together. Whisk until well combined. Whisk in the water and vanilla extract.
6. While the cake is still warm and in the pan, poke holes all over with a skewer. Pour the glaze over and let cool completely in the pan.
7. Gently loosen the sides with a knife or thin rubber spatula, then flip out onto a serving platter. Dust with powdered sweetener.
8. Serve with lightly sweetened whipped cream and fresh berries.

KETO CHOCOLATE ESPRESSO MOUSSE CAKE

Nutrition: Cal 285; Fat 28 g; Carb 4 g; Protein 4 g
Serving 12; Cook time 3 hours

Ingredients

BROWNIE LAYER
- 1 recipe Ultimate Keto Brownies
- Chocolate Mousse Layer
- 2 ounces unsweetened chocolate chopped
- 1 tbsp butter
- ¼ cup water
- 1 ¼ teaspoon grassfed gelatin
- 1 cup heavy whipping cream divided
- ⅓ cup Swerve Confectioners
- ½ teaspoon vanilla extract

ESPRESSO MOUSSE LAYER
- ⅔ cup espresso or strongly brewed coffee cooled
- 1 ½ teaspoon grassfed gelatin
- ¾ cup heavy whipping cream
- ¼ cup Swerve Confectioners
- ½ teaspoon vanilla extract

GARNISH
- 1 tablespoon cocoa powder
- Fresh raspberries

Instructions
BROWNIE BASE
1. Preheat the oven to 325°F and lightly grease an 8-inch springform pan or a cake pan with a removeable bottom. Line with parchment paper and grease the paper. Set the pan on a rimmed baking sheet.
2. Prepare the brownie batter according to the directions and spread in the prepared baking pan. Bake 20 to 25 minutes, or until the edges are set but the center is still a little jiggly. Remove and let cool completely.

CHOCOLATE MOUSSE LAYER
1. In a large microwave safe bowl, melt the chocolate with the butter on high in 30 second increments, stirring in between until smooth.
2. Place the water in a small saucepan and sprinkle the gelatin over top. Let bloom 5 minutes, then place the pan over medium low heat and add ¼ cup of the heavy cream. Stir until the gelatin is dissolved, but do not let it come to a boil. Slowly whisk into the chocolate mixture.
3. In a large bowl, beat the remaining cream with the sweetener and vanilla extract until it holds stiff peaks. Stir about ¼ of the whipped cream into the chocolate to lighten it, then fold in the remaining cream until smooth.
4. Spread this mixture over the cooled cake and refrigerate while making the espresso mousse.

ESPRESSO MOUSSE LAYER
1. In the same saucepan as above, place the espresso. Sprinkle with the gelatin and let bloom 5 minutes, then place over medium low heat. Stir until the gelatin is dissolved, but do not let it come to a boil. Remove from heat and cool to lukewarm.
2. In a large bowl, beat the cream with the sweetener and vanilla extract until it holds stiff peaks. Gently fold in the cooled espresso mixture until well combined.
3. Spread over the chocolate mousse in the pan and refrigerate until firm to the touch, 1 to 2 hours.
4. Use a sifter to sprinkle the top of the cake evenly with cocoa powder.

TO UNMOLD THE CAKE
1. Warm up a small sharp knife by either running boiling water over it or holding it over a gas flame for a few seconds. Run the knife around the inside of the pan to loosen the cake.
2. Release the pan sides for a springform pan. If using a cake pan with a removeable bottom, simply push the bottom up to release the cake.
3. Serve with fresh berries.

KETO CARROT CAKE
Nutrition: Cal 320; Fat 32 g; Carb 6 g; Protein 6 g
Serving 16; Cook time 75 min
Ingredients
CARROT CAKE
- 2 cups pecan flour/almond flour See Notes
- ⅓ cup coconut flour
- ⅓ cup unflavoured whey protein powder or egg white protein powder
- 1 tablespoon baking powder
- 2 teaspoon ground cinnamon
- ½ teaspoon salt
- ¼ teaspoon ground cloves
- 4 large eggs
- ½ cup avocado oil or another neutral oil
- ½ cup Swerve Brown
- ½ cup Swerve Granular
- 1½ cups finely grated carrot lightly packed
- 1½ teaspoon vanilla extract
- ⅓ cup chopped pecans

CREAM CHEESE FROSTING
- 8 ounces cream cheese softened
- ½ cup butter softened
- ¾ cup powdered Swerve Sweetener
- 1 teaspoon vanilla extract
- ½ cup heavy whipping cream room temperature

GARNISH
- ¼ cup chopped pecans
- 1 tablespoon finely grated carrot

Instructions
CAKE
1. Preheat the oven to 350°F and grease 3 8-inch round cake pans. Line the bottoms with parchment paper and grease the paper.
2. In a medium bowl, whisk together the pecan flour, coconut flour, protein powder, baking powder, cinnamon, salt, and cloves.
3. In a large bowl, beat the eggs and oil with the sweeteners until well combined and the sweeteners are mostly dissolved. Beat in the carrots and vanilla extract.
4. Add the dry ingredients and beat on low until combined. Stir in the chopped pecans.
5. Divide the batter evenly among the baking pans and spread to the edges. Bake 18 to 25 minutes, or until golden brown and the tops are firm to the touch.
6. Remove and let cool completely in the pans, then run a sharp knife around the inside of the pans and flip out onto a wire rack.

CREAM CHEESE FROSTING
1. In a large bowl, beat the cream cheese and butter together until very smooth. Beat in the sweetener and vanilla extract until well combined.
2. Slowly beat in the heavy whipping cream until a spreadable consistency is achieved.

TO ASSEMBLE
1. Place one layer of cake on a cake stand or plate. Spread the top with one quarter of the frosting. Repeat with the remaining layers.
2. Use the final quarter of frosting to lightly crumb coat the sides, so that the cake peeks through.
3. Sprinkle the chopped pecans and shredded carrot around the outside of the top of the cake. Refrigerate 1 hour before cutting and serving.

SLOW COOKER KETO CHOCOLATE CAKE

Nutrition: Cal 205; Fat 17 g; Carb 9 g; Protein 8 g
Serving 10; Cook time 3 hours

Ingredients

- 1 cup plus 2 tablespoon almond flour
- ½ cup Swerve Granular
- ½ cup cocoa powder
- 3 tablespoon unflavoured whey protein powder can sub egg white protein powder
- 1 ½ teaspoon baking powder
- ¼ teaspoon salt
- 6 tablespoon butter melted
- 3 large eggs
- ⅔ cup unsweetened almond milk
- ¾ teaspoon vanilla extract
- ⅓ cup sugar-free chocolate chips optional

Instructions

1. Grease the insert of a 6 quart slow cooker well.
2. In a medium bowl, whisk together almond flour, sweetener, cocoa powder, whey protein powder, baking powder and salt.
3. Stir in butter, eggs, almond milk and vanilla extract until well combined, then stir in chocolate chips, if using.
4. Pour into prepared insert and cook on low for 2 to 2 ½ hours. It will be gooey and like a pudding cake at 2 hours, and more cakey at 2 ½ hours.
5. Turn slow cooker off and let cool 20 to 30 minutes, then cut into pieces and serve warm. Serve with lightly sweetened whipped cream.

KETO EASTER EGG CAKE

Nutrition: Cal 282; Fat 25 g; Carb 6 g; Protein 6 g
Serving 16; Cook time 75 min

Ingredients

CAKE

- 2 cups almond flour
- ⅓ cup coconut flour
- ⅓ cup unflavoured whey protein powder (or egg white protein powder)
- 1 tablespoon baking powder
- ½ teaspoon salt
- ½ cup butter, softened
- ¾ cup Swerve Granular
- 5 large egg whites, room temperature
- 1 teaspoon almond extract
- 1 teaspoon vanilla extract
- ⅔ cup water

FROSTING

- 6 ounces cream cheese very soft
- ½ cup butter very soft
- 1 cup powdered Swerve Sweetener divided
- 1 teaspoon almond extract
- 1 teaspoon vanilla extract
- ¾ cup plus 2 tablespoon heavy whipping cream divided, room temperature
- Natural blue food coloring

SPECKLES AND OTHER GARNISH

- ½ teaspoon cocoa powder
- 1 ½ teaspoon water
- 3 tablespoon toasted coconut
- 3 sugar free marzipan eggs

Instructions

CAKE

1. Preheat the oven to 350F and grease 2 8-inch round baking pans. Line the bottoms with parchment and grease the parchment.
2. In a medium bowl, whisk together the almond flour, coconut flour, whey protein, baking powder, and salt.
3. In a large bowl, beat the butter with the sweetener until lighter and fluffy, about 1 minute. Beat in the egg whites, almond extract, and vanilla extract until well combined.
4. Add the almond flour mixture in two additions, alternating with the water. Scrape down the sides of the bowl and the beaters as needed.
5. Divide the batter between the two prepared pans and spread evenly to the edges. Bake 25 to 30 minutes, until golden on the edges and the top is firm to the touch. Remove and let cool in the pans.
6. Run a sharp knife around the inside of the pans to loosen cake layers. Flip out onto a cooling rack and remove the parchment.

FROSTING

1. In a large bowl, beat the cream cheese and butter together until smooth. Beat in ¾ cup of the powdered sweetener, the almond extract, and the vanilla extract until well combined.
2. Beat in 2 tablespoons of the heavy whipping cream to lighten the mixture, then beat in blue food colouring until a robin's egg blue is acheived.
3. In another bowl, beat the remaining ¾ cup cream with the remaining ¼ cup powdered sweetener until it holds stiff peaks. Fold the whipped cream into the cream cheese mixture until well combined.

TO ASSEMBLE

1. Place one cake layer on a cake plate and spread the top with about ⅓ of the frosting, spreading all the way to the edges.
2. Top with another cake layer and spread the top and sides with most of the remaining frosting, reserving 2 tablespoons for the "nest" on the top.
3. In a small bowl, whisk together the cocoa powder and water until smooth and liquid. Dip a small clean paint brush into the mixture and flick it lightly over the sides and top of the cake to create brown speckles.
4. Use the remaining 2 tablespoons of frosting to create a small "nest" in the center of the top of the cake, with raised sides. Cover the nest with the toasted coconut. Place marzipan eggs in the nest.

KETO ORANGE CHEESECAKE MOUSSE
Nutrition: Cal 284; Fat 28 g; Carb 6 g; Protein 12 g
Serving 6; Cook time 30 min
Ingredients
- 1/2 Cup Water boiling
- 1 Dry Packet Sugar-Free Orange Gelatin 0.3 oz pack
- 8 oz Full Fat Cream Cheese softened
- 1 Cup Heavy Whipping Cream
Instructions
1. In a large bowl or stand mixer, beat heavy cream until it turns into whipped topping and set aside
2. Mix gelatin mix into boiling water and stir until fully dissolved. I just heated my water in a glass measuring cup in the microwave then added the mix right to the cup.
3. In a large bowl or stand mixer, beat cream cheese until smooth and creamy.
4. Slowly add in the gelatin mixture into the cream cheese and mix well.
5. Now stir in the whipped cream. Be sure not to overbeat it as you want the topping to stay airy.
6. Place in the fridge to chill for about twenty to thirty minutes before serving.
7. Top with a spoon of whipped topping, orange slice, and orange zest. (optional)

KETO PEACH CHEESECAKE FLUFF
Nutrition: Cal 277; Fat 30 g; Carb 4 g; Protein 5 g
Serving 6; Cook time 20 min
Ingredients
- 8 oz Full Fat Cream Cheese room temp
- 1 Dry Packet Sugar-Free Peach Gelatin 0.3 oz size
- 1 Cup Heavy Whipping Cream
- 1/2 Cup Water
Instructions
1. Using a mixer add your whipping cream and whisk it on medium to high speed until stiff peaks form. Set aside.
2. In another mixing bowl beat the cream cheese until it is soft.
3. Heat the water to boiling in a microwave-safe dish. It should take about a minute and a half. I just heat it right in a pyrex measuring cup.
4. Add packet of gelatin in the water and mix until fully dissolved.
5. Slowly pour about half of the gelatin mixture onto the cream cheese and mix well.
6. Then pour the other half in and a little of the whipped cream and mix well.
7. When fully mixed add the rest of the whipped cream and mix just until it is fully blended. Don't overbeat it.
8. Pour into dishes or airtight containers and store them in the fridge until you are ready to serve.

CHOCOLATE RASPBERRY CHEESECAKE FLUFF
Nutrition: Cal 300; Fat 30 g; Carb 6 g; Protein 8 g
Serving 12; Cook time 20 min
Ingredients
CHOCOLATE LAYER
- 1 Cup Heavy Whipping Cream
- 1/2 Cup Splenda
- 4 Tbsp Cocoa Powder
- 52 grams Cacao Butter
- 8 oz Full Fat Cream Cheese room temp
RASPBERRY LAYER
- 1 Cup Heavy Whipping Cream
- 8 oz Full Fat Cream Cheese room temp
- 1/2 Cup Water
- 0.30 oz Pack Of Sugar-Free Raspberry Jello
Instructions
CHOCOLATE LAYER:
1. In double boiler on the stove, you want to melt the cacao butter.
2. When melted add in the cocoa powder and mix well.
3. When fully dissolved remove the bowl from the heat.
4. Mix in the cream cheese and Splenda and blend with a hand mixer until fully blended. Set aside.
5. In a large mixing bowl with a hand mixer (or stand mixer) whip the heavy cream until it forms stiff peaks.
6. Then mix the chocolate mixture in with the whipped cream. Make sure it is fully blended but not so much that it loses its puffy/airy texture. Set in the fridge.
RASPBERRY LAYER:
1. In a microwave-safe cup heat water to boiling.
2. Dump the Jello pack into the water and mix until it is fully dissolved.
3. In large bowel or stand mixer beat heavy cream until it forms stiff peaks is looks like whipped cream.
4. In another bowl beat cream cheese until it is smooth and creamy. Then slowly add in the Jello mixture until it is fully mixed.
5. Add that mixture to the whipped cream and mix well. Make sure it is mixed well but not so much that it loses its fluffy texture.
6. Put equal portions of raspberry and chocolate mixes into dishes.

EASY KETO STRAWBERRY CHEESECAKE FLUFF
Nutrition: Cal 206; Fat 20 g; Carb 3g; Protein 2 g
Serving 8; Cook time 70 min
Ingredients
- 1/3 Cup Boiling Water needs to be 1/3 after it is boiling not before the boil as it will evaporate.
- 1 Cup Heavy Whipping Cream
- 8 oz Full Fat Cream Cheese room temp
- 1 Box Sugar Free Strawberry Gelatin Mix this will be 0.30 oz pack
- 3 Strawberries

Instructions
1. Remove strawberry stems and chop into small pieces and set aside.
2. Mix whipping cream in large bowl with mixer on high speed until it forms a whip cream texture. Set aside.
3. In another mixing bowl beat cream cheese until smooth.
4. Add about 3/4 of the whipped cream into the cream cheese and mix well. Set aside
5. In small bowl or measuring cup, mix boiling water and gelatin mix together and mix until fully dissolved.
6. Mix the gelatin mix into the cream cheese mixture. Mix well.
7. Now fold in the rest of the whip cream and strawberries.
8. Pour into loaf pan or glass food storage containers and cover. Place in fridge to chill for at least one hour.

KETO CHERRY CHEESECAKE FLUFF
Nutrition: Cal 270; Fat 26 g; Carb 7 g; Protein 4 g
Serving 6; Cook time 20 min

Ingredients
- 1/2 Cup Water
- 8 oz Cream Cheese room temp
- 1 Box Sugar-Free Cherry Gelatin 0.30 oz
- 1 Cup Heavy Whipping Cream
- 10 Fresh Cherries diced

Instructions
1. Beat the cream cheese until soft.
2. Heat half cup of water in the microwave until boiling.
3. Mix jello packet into the water. Mix well with a fork until it is fully dissolved.
4. In another bowl beat heaving whipping cream until it forms stiff peaks and looks like whipped cream.
5. Slowly add the jello mix to the cream cheese a little at a time until you have the two fully blended.
6. Add in the whipped cream to the mixture making sure it is all fully mixed.
7. Now stir in the chopped cherries.
8. Pour into a container or serving dishes and store in the fridge until you are ready to serve.

BOSTON CREAM PIE
Nutrition: Cal 315; Fat 28 g; Carb 6 g; Protein 7 g
Serving 16; Cook time 3 hours

Ingredients
PASTRY CREAM:
- (make this first and let it chill while making the other parts)
- 1 ¼ cups heavy whipping cream
- 4 egg yolks
- 6 tablespoon powdered Swerve Sweetener
- pinch salt
- 2 tablespoon butter cut into two pieces
- 1 ½ teaspoon vanilla extract
- ½ teaspoon xanthan gum
- 2 teaspoon coconut flour, sifted (only if you need it!)

CAKE:
- 2 cups almond flour (about 210g)
- ¾ cup Swerve Sweetener
- ¼ cup coconut flour
- ¼ cup unflavored whey protein powder
- 2 teaspoon baking powder
- ¼ teaspoon salt
- 3 large eggs
- ½ cup butter melted
- ½ teaspoon vanilla extract
- ½ cup water

CHOCOLATE GLAZE:
- ⅔ cup heavy whipping cream
- 2 oz unsweetened chocolate chopped
- ¼ cup powdered Swerve Sweetener
- 1 tablespoon cocoa powder
- ½ tsp vanilla extract

Instructions
PASTRY CREAM
1. Bring the whipping cream to a simmer in a medium saucepan over medium heat. In a medium bowl, whisk the egg yolks with the sweetener and salt until well combined.
2. Slowly whisk about half of the hot cream into the yolks to temper, then slowly return the yolk/cream mixture back to the saucepan and cook until thickened, about 4 to 5 minutes, whisking continuously. It thickens up very suddenly and quickly, so watch it carefully!
3. Remove from heat and whisk in the butter and vanilla extract. Sprinkle the surface with xanthan gum, whisking as you go, to combine well. Let cool to room temperature and then refrigerate at least 3 hours.

CAKE
1. For the cake, preheat the oven to 350F. Grease 2 (two) 8-inch round cake pans and line with parchment paper. Then grease the paper as well.
2. In a medium bowl, whisk together the almond flour, sweetener, coconut flour, protein powder, baking powder, and salt, breaking up any clumps with the back of a fork.
3. Stir in the eggs, melted butter, and vanilla extract until well combined. Stir in just enough water so that the batter is spreadable but not pourable. Divide the batter evenly between the prepared baking pans and spread to the edges.
4. Bake 20 to 25 minutes minutes or until edges are golden brown and the top is just firm to the touch. Cool in the pan 10 minutes and then flip out onto a wire rack to cool completely.

CHOCOLATE GANACHE
1. In a small saucepan over medium heat, bring the whipping cream to a simmer. Remove from heat and add the chopped chocolate. Let sit 3 to 4 minutes to melt.
2. Add the powdered sweetener, cocoa powder, and vanilla and whisk until smooth. Let cool 5 to 10 minutes, while assembling cake, until the glaze is thicker but still

pourable. If it's too thick, gently re-warm with an additional tablespoon or two of cream. If it's too thin, whisk in another tablespoon of cocoa powder until smooth.

TO ASSEMBLE

1. Whisk the chilled pastry cream briskly to remove any clumps. If you find it's very gooey and likely to ooze out between the layers of cake, whisk in a bit of sifted coconut flour to help thicken it.
2. Place one layer of cake on serving dish and spread with the pastry cream. Gently top with the second layer. Pour the chocolate glaze over the top of the cake and spread with a knife or offset spatula, pushing to the edges and letting it drip down over the sides.
3. Pour the chocolate glaze over the top of the cake and spread with a knife or offset spatula, pushing to the edges and letting it drip down over the sides. Refrigerate the cake 1 hour before serving.

KETO COCONUT CREAM PIE

Nutrition: Cal 365; Fat 35 g; Carb 7 g; Protein 6 g
Serving 12; Cook time 4 hours

Ingredients
FILLING:

- 1 cup heavy cream
- 1 cup coconut cream
- 2 eggs
- 1 egg yolk
- ⅔ cup powdered Swerve Sweetener
- Pinch salt
- 2 tablespoon butter
- 1 teaspoon coconut extract
- ½ teaspoon vanilla
- ¼ teaspoon xanthan gum or glucomannan
- ¾ cup shredded unsweetened coconut
- 1 almond flour pie crust Pre-baked

TOPPING:

- ⅔ cup heavy whipping cream
- ¼ cup powdered Swerve Sweetener
- ½ teaspoon vanilla extract or coconut extract
- ¼ cup shredded or flaked unsweetened coconut lightly toasted

Instructions
FILLING

1. Combine the heavy cream and coconut cream in a medium saucepan over medium heat. Bring to just a simmer.
2. In a medium bowl, whisk the eggs, egg yolk, powdered sweetener, and salt. Slowly stir in about half of the hot cream, whisking continuously, to temper the eggs. Then slowly whisk the tempered egg mixture back into pan of hot cream.
3. Cook another 4 to 5 minutes, whisking continuously, until the mixture begins to thicken.
4. Remove from heat and whisk in the butter, coconut extract, and vanilla extract. Sprinkle surface with the xanthan gum and whisk briskly to combine. Stir in the shredded coconut.
5. Pour the mixture into the baked pie crust and spread to the edges. Refrigerate at least 2 to 3 hours.

TOPPING

1. Place the whipping cream in a large bowl and add the sweetener and vanilla. Beat until the cream holds stiff peaks.
2. Spread over the top of the chilled pie and sprinkle with the toasted flaked coconut.

BOSTON CREAM POKE CAKE

Nutrition: Cal 337 Fat 30 g; Carb 8 g; Protein 9 g
Serving 1; Cook time 10 min

Ingredients
CAKE

- 3 cups almond flour
- 1/3 cup whey protein powder
- 2 tsp grain-free baking powder
- 1/4 tsp salt
- 1/2 cup unsalted butter, softened
- 3/4 cup Swerve Sweetener
- 3 large eggs, room temperature
- 1 tsp vanilla extract
- 1/2 cup almond or cashew milk, unsweetened

PASTRY CREAM

- 1 1/4 cups whipping cream
- 3 egg yolks
- 6 tbsp confectioner's Swerve Sweetener
- Pinch salt
- 2 tbsp butter, cut into two pieces
- 1 1/2 tsp vanilla extract
- 1/2 tsp xanthan gum

CHOCOLATE GANACHE

- 2/3 cup whipping cream
- 1/4 cup confectioner's Swerve Sweetener
- 2 1/2 ounces unsweetened chocolate, finely chopped
- 1/2 tsp vanilla extract

Instructions
CAKE

1. Preheat oven to 325F and grease a 9x9 square baking pan.
2. In a medium bowl, whisk together the almond flour, whey protein powder, baking powder and salt.
3. In a large bowl, beat butter with sweetener until light and fluffy. Beat in eggs, one at a time until well combined. Beat in vanilla extract.
4. Beat in half of the almond flour mixture, then beat in nut milk. Beat in the remaining almond flour mixture until well combined. Spread batter in prepared baking pan.
5. Bake 25 to 30 minutes, or until golden brown around the edges and the top is just firm to the touch. Remove and let cool in pan. Once cool, use the end of a wooden spoon to poke holes all over the cake.

PASTRY CREAM

1. Bring whipping cream to a simmer in a medium saucepan over medium heat. In a medium bowl, whisk egg yolks with sweetener and salt.
2. Slowly whisk about half of the hot cream into the yolks to temper, then return the yolk/cream mixture back to the saucepan and cook until thickened, 4 to 5 minutes more, whisking constantly. Watch it carefully and do not let it curdle.
3. Remove from heat and whisk in butter and vanilla extract. Sprinkle surface with xanthan gum and whisk vigorously to combine. Let cool about 10 minutes, then pour all over cake and tap pan firmly on counter to allow pastry cream to sink into holes.
4. Refrigerate 2 to 3 hours, until pastry cream is mostly set.

CHOCOLATE GANACHE

1. In a small saucepan over medium heat, combine cream and sweetener. Whisk until sweetener is dissolved and cream comes to just a simmer.
2. Remove from heat and add chopped chocolate and vanilla extract. Let sit 5 minutes to melt chocolate and then whisk to combine. Pour over chilled cake and refrigerate another 20 to 30 minutes, until set.

KETO ITALIAN CREAM CAKE

Nutrition: Cal 270; Fat 30 g; Carb 6 g; Protein 6 g
Serving 16; Cook time 90 min

Ingredients
CAKE

- ½ cup butter softened
- 1 cup Swerve Sweetener
- 4 large eggs room temperature, separated
- ½ cup heavy cream room temperature
- 1 teaspoon vanilla extract
- 1 ½ cups almond flour
- ½ cup shredded coconut
- ½ cup chopped pecans
- ¼ cup coconut flour
- 2 teaspoon baking powder
- ½ teaspoon salt
- ¼ teaspoon cream of tartar

FROSTING

- 8 ounces cream cheese softened
- ½ cup butter softened
- 1 cup powdered Swerve Sweetener
- 1 teaspoon vanilla extract
- ½ cup heavy whipping cream room temperature

GARNISH

- 2 tablespoon shredded coconut lightly toasted
- 2 tablespoon chopped pecans lightly toasted

Instructions
CAKE

1. Preheat the oven to 325F and grease two 8 inch or 9 inch round cake pans very well (the 8 inch pans will take a little longer to cook but the layers will be higher and I think they will look better). Line the pans with parchment paper and grease the paper.
2. In a large bowl, beat the butter with the sweetener until well combined. Beat in the egg yolks one at a time, mixing well after each addition. Beat in the heavy cream and vanilla extract.
3. In another bowl, whisk together the almond flour, shredded coconut, chopped pecans, coconut flour, baking powder, and salt. Beat into the butter mixture until just combined.
4. In another large bowl, beat the egg whites with the cream of tartar until they hold stiff peaks. Gently fold into the cake batter.
5. Divide the batter evenly among the prepared pans and spread to the edges. Bake 35 to 45 minutes (or longer, depending on your pans), until the cakes are golden on the edges and firm to the touch in the middle.
6. Remove and let cool completely in the pans, then flip out onto a wire rack to cool completely. Remove the parchment from the layers if it comes out with them.

FROSTING

1. In a large bowl, beat the cream cheese and butter together until smooth. Beat in the sweetener and vanilla extract until well combined.
2. Slowly add the heavy whipping cream until a spreadable consistency is achieved.

TO ASSEMBLE

1. Place the bottom layer on a serving plate and cover the top with about ⅓ of the frosting. Add the next layer and frost the top and the sides.
2. Sprinkle the top with the toasted coconut and pecans. Refrigerate at least half an hour to let set.

KETO NUTELLA CREAM PIE

Nutrition: Cal 337; Fat 3 g; Carb 11 g; Protein 4 g
Serving 12; Cook time 2 hours 25 min

Ingredients
CRUST

- 1 cup hazelnut flour
- ¼ cup powdered Swerve Sweetener
- 3 tablespoon cocoa powder
- Pinch salt
- ¼ cup butter, melted

HAZELNUT CREAM FILLING

- 1 recipe Sugar Free Nutella
- 8 ounces cream cheese softened
- ¾ cup powdered Swerve Sweetener divided
- ½ teaspoon hazelnut extract
- 1 cup heavy whipping cream
- ½ teaspoon vanilla extract
- ¼ cup chopped, toasted hazelnuts

Instructions
CRUST

1. In a medium bowl, whisk together the hazelnut flour, sweetener, cocoa powder, and salt. Stir in the melted butter until the mixture begins to clump together.
2. Press the mixture firmly and evenly into the bottom and up the sides of a 9 inch pie plate. Refrigerate while preparing the filling.

FILLING
1. Prepare the sugar free chocolate hazelnut spread according to the directions.
2. In a large bowl, beat the cream cheese until very smooth, about 1 minutes. Beat in ½ cup of the sweetener, then beat in the Nutella and hazelnut extract until well combined.
3. In another large bowl, beat the whipping cream with the remaining ¼ cup sweetener and the vanilla extract until it holds stiff peaks. Fold two thirds of the whipped cream into the Nutella mixture until no streaks remain.
4. Spread the filling in the prepared crust and refrigerate until firm, 2 to 3 hours.
5. Spread the remaining whipped cream over the center of the pie and sprinkle with chopped hazelnuts.

PUMPKIN ROLL WITH COFFEE CREAM
Nutrition: Cal 205; Fat 18 g; Carb 5 g; Protein 6 g
Serving 10; Cook time 3 hours

Ingredients
CAKE
- 1 cup almond flour
- 3 tablespoon coconut flour
- 1 ½ teaspoon baking powder
- 1 teaspoon xanthan gum
- 1 teaspoon cinnamon
- ½ teaspoon ginger
- ⅛ teaspoon salt
- 4 large eggs separated
- ¾ cup Swerve Sweetener divided
- ¾ cup canned pumpkin puree
- ½ teaspoon vanilla extract

FILLING:
- 1 ¼ cups whipping cream
- ⅓ cup powdered Swerve Sweetener
- 1 ½ teaspoon instant coffee
- ½ teaspoon vanilla extract
- More powdered Swerve Sweetener for dusting

Instructions
CAKE
1. Preheat oven to 350F and line an 11x17 inch baking sheet with parchment paper. Grease the paper very well.
2. In a medium bowl, whisk together the almond flour, coconut flour, baking powder, xanthan gum, cinnamon, ginger and salt. Set aside.
3. In a medium bowl, beat egg yolks on high with ¼ cup of the sweetener, until they become pale yellow and thickened. Beat in pumpkin puree and vanilla extract.

4. In large bowl, beat the egg whites until soft peaks form. Slowly add remaining sweetener, beating until stiff peaks form.
5. Fold egg yolk mixture into egg white mixture, then gently fold in the almond almond flour mixture until well combined. Spread into prepared baking pan and bake 15 to 18 minutes, or until cake just springs back when touched.
6. Remove and let cool 10 to 15 minutes, then cover with another sheet of parchment and a large cutting board or another large baking sheet. Flip everything upside down and remove the top baking sheet. Very gently peel off the parchment paper on which the cake was baked.
7. Keep the cake covered with parchment and a tea towel to keep in moisture as it cools. Let cool but don't leave too long before filling and rolling (should just be barely warm still, to avoid cracking, but too warm and it will melt the filling).

FILLING
1. Whip cream with powdered sweetener, instant coffee and vanilla extract until stiff peaks form. Do not overbeat.
2. Spread cake evenly with filling, leaving a ½ inch border. Gently roll from a short side, using the bottom parchment to lift the cake to avoid cracking as much as possible.
3. Cover and freeze until firm. Remove from freezer 15 minutes prior to serving. Dust with powdered sweetener. Return any leftover cake to the freezer.

FROZEN CHOCOLATE MOUSSE CAKE
Nutrition: Cal 320; Fat 16 g; Carb 5 g; Protein 12 g
Serving 12; Cook time 65 min

Ingredients
CAKE
- 2 large eggs
- 2 cups (200 g) almonds, ground
- 2 bitter almonds, finely ground, or 1 tsp almond extract
- ¼ cup (50 ml) coconut flour
- 1–2 tbsp cacao powder
- 1½ tbsp erythritol/stevia blend

FROSTING
- 5 ¼ (150 g) dark chocolate, 90% cacao
- 3 egg yolks
- ½ tbsp instant coffee granules (optional)
- 1 tbsp hot water
- 1 tbsp erythritol/stevia blend
- 2 cups (400 ml) whipping cream

GARNISH
- Grated chocolate
- Roasted, slivered almonds

Instructions
1. Preheat the oven to 350 °F (175 °C). Line the bottom of an 8" (21–22 cm) springform pan with parchment paper.

CAKE

2. Beat the eggs lightly. Mix the dry ingredients thoroughly and stir in the eggs. Spread the batter in the springform pan, and bake on the middle rack of the oven for about 10 minutes. Let cool completely.

FROSTING

3. Melt the chocolate over a bowl of simmering water (bain-marie). Let it cool a little. Incorporate the yolks, one at a time, into the cooled chocolate.

4. Dissolve the coffee granules in the hot water. Mix the coffee and sweetener into the chocolate mixture.

5. Whip the cream until it's thick and voluminous, and fold it carefully into the chocolate/coffee mixture. Mix to achieve a smooth blend.

6. Spread the chocolate mousse over the cooled layer of cake. Place the cake in the freezer for approximately 5 hours.

TO SERVE

1. Serve the cake partly thawed. Set it, covered, to defrost in the refrigerator for 45 minutes, and then at room temperature for 15 minutes.

2. Right before serving, decorate the cake with some grated chocolate and/or roasted, slivered almonds. You can also melt some dark chocolate and spread it in a thin layer on a sheet of parchment paper. Let the chocolate set (it will harden). Cut or break off thinpieces of chocolate to use as a garnish.

SUMPTUOUS RHUBARB PIE

Nutrition: Cal 225; Fat 22 g; Carb 12 g; Protein 10 g
Serving 12; Cook time 55 min

Ingredients
PIE CRUST
- ¾ cup (200 g) unsalted butter
- 3 large eggs
- 1—2 tbsp erythritol/stevia blend
- ½ cup (100 ml) coconut flour
- ½ cup (100 ml) almond flour or 1¾ oz (50 g) ground almonds
- 2 tsp baking powder
- ½ tsp vanilla powder or 1 tsp vanilla extract

FILLING
- 14 oz (400 g) rhubarb
- 2 cups (400 ml) almond flour or 7 oz (200 g) ground almonds
- 1—2 bitter almonds, ground, or 1 tsp almond extract
- 1½—2 tbsp erythritol/stevia blend
- 1 tbsp whipping cream
- 2 large eggs
- ⅔ cup (150 g) unsalted butter, softened

Instructions
Preheat the oven to 350°F (175°C). Melt the butter and let it cool.

PIE CRUST
1. Beat the eggs until light and airy, about 5 minutes. Add in the melted cool butter.

2. Mix the dry ingredients thoroughly, and incorporate well into the egg batter.

3. Line a pie pan with ¾ of the pastry, extending the pastry about ½"—1" (1½—2 cm) up the sides of the pan.

FILLING
1. Clean and chop the rhubarb into ½" (1 cm) chunks. Mix the almond flour with the ground bitter almonds or almond extract and sweetener; add in the whipping cream. While mixing, add in the eggs, then the butter. Stir in half the chunks of rhubarb. Spread the filling over the crust, and cover with the rest of the rhubarb; save the prettier pink chunks for the top.

2. Roll out the rest of the dough and cut it into narrow strips. Place the strips in a lattice pattern over the top of the pie filling.

3. Bake the pie on the middle rack of the oven for 20 to 25 minutes. The Mazarin almond filling should be almost set when coming out of the oven but will set further as the pie cools.

RASPBERRY PANNA COTTA PIE

Nutrition: Cal 180; Fat 8 g; Carb 4 g; Protein 10 g
Serving 8; Cook time 3 hours

Ingredients
PIE CRUST
- ½ cup (125 g) unsalted butter
- 3 large eggs
- 1½ tbsp erythritol/stevia blend
- ¾ cup (150 ml) coconut flour
- ¾ cup (150 ml) almonds, finely chopped (or slivered almonds)
- 2 tsp baking powder
- ½ tsp vanilla powder or 1 tsp vanilla extract
- Slivered almonds for the baking pan

RASPBERRY PANNA COTTA
- 4 sheets of gelatin, or equivalent amount of gelatin powder
- 1 cup (200 ml) whipping cream
- 1 cup (200 ml) crème fraîche
- 1½ tbsp erythritol/stevia blend
- 8¾ oz (250 g) raspberries; if using frozen, thawed

GARNISH
- Fresh raspberries

Instructions
1. Preheat the oven to 350°F (175°C). Melt the butter and let it cool. Line the bottom of an 8½" to 9½" (22—24 cm) springform pan with parchment paper. Butter and cover the pan with slivered almonds, at least 1¼" (3 cm) up the sides.

PIE CRUST
2. Beat the eggs until light and fluffy, and then add in the cooled butter.

3. Mix the dry ingredients thoroughly, and incorporate them in the batter to make a dough.

4. Press the dough into the prepared pan.

5. Bake on the middle rack of the oven for about 10 minutes. Let cool.
6. Raspberry panna cotta: Soak the sheets of gelatin in cold water for 5 minutes; if using gelatin powder, follow the instructions on the packet.
7. Place whipping cream, crème fraîche, and sweetener in a saucepan, stir, heat, and let simmer until the sweetener is dissolved. Squeeze out the water from the gelatin. Remove the saucepan from the heat, and mix the gelatin in with the cream mixture. Let it cool.
8. Purée the raspberries, and fold the purée into the cooled cream mixture.
9. Pour the panna cotta into the pie crust. Place the pie in the refrigerator, and let it sit for at least 3 hours or until the panna cotta has set.
10. Garnish the panna cotta pie with fresh raspberries. A dollop of lightly whipped cream pairs well with this, so why not pipe some whipped cream onto each slice?

COCONUT PIE

Nutrition: Cal 172 ; Fat 17 g; Carb 12 g; Protein 4 g
Serving 12; Cook time 50 min

Ingredients
PIE CRUST
• ½ cup (100 g) unsalted butter
• 2 large eggs
• ½ cup (100 ml) coconut flour
• ½ cup (100 ml) grated, unsweetened coconut
• 1 tbsp erythritol/stevia blend
• 1 tsp baking powder
• Grated, unsweetened coconut for the pan

FILLING
• 1 sheet of gelatin or equivalent amount of gelatin powder
• 1½ cup (300 ml) whipping cream
• ½ cup (100 ml) water
• 1½ tbsp erythritol/stevia blend
• ½ tsp vanilla powder or 1 tsp vanilla extract
• 2½ cups (500 ml) unsweetened coconut flakes
• 2 large eggs
• ⅓ cup (100 g) unsalted butter

GARNISH
• ¼–½ cup (50 ml–100 ml) grated, unsweetened coconut
• 1 cup (200 ml) whipped cream

Instructions
1. Preheat the oven to 350°F (175°C). Line the bottom of an 8" to 9" (21–22 cm) round pie pan with a sheet of parchment paper. Butter the pan and scatter grated coconut over the bottom and at least 1" (2 cm) up the sides of the pan. Melt the butter and let it cool.
2. Pie crust: Beat the eggs until light and fluffy. Add in the melted and cooled butter. Mix all the dry ingredients thoroughly and incorporate them into the batter to make a dough.
3. Press the dough into the pie pan and up the sides. Chill the dough for 30 minutes to stop the pie crust from shrinking while baking.

4. Bake on the middle rack of the oven for approximately 10 minutes.
FILLING
1. Soak the sheet of gelatin in cold water for at least 5 minutes; if using gelatin powder, follow the instructions on the packet.
2. Bring whipping cream, water, sweetener, and vanilla to a boil. Whisk in the coconut flakes and the eggs, and let simmer until mixture starts to thicken. Fold in the gelatin and then the butter. Let it cool.
3. Spread the filling in the pie crust, and set the pie in the refrigerator for several hours.
GARNISH
1. Toast grated coconut in a hot frying pan until it takes on a light color. Let cool. Pipe the whipped cream onto the pie, and right before serving, sprinkle the pie with the toasted coconut.

SPONGE CAKE WITH VARIOUS FLAVORS

Nutrition: Cal 219 ; Fat 20; Carb 5 g; Protein 5 g
Serving 12; Cook time 60 min

Ingredients
• ½ cup (100 g) unsalted butter
• 5 large eggs
• 1 cup (200 ml) crème fraîche or sour cream
• 2 tbsp erythritol/stevia blend
• 1 tsp vanilla powder or 1 tsp vanilla extract
• ½ cup (100 ml) almond flour or ½ cup (50 g) ground almonds
• ½ cup (100 ml) coconut flour
• 1 heaping tbsp whole, unflavored psyllium husk
• 2 tsp baking powder

Instructions
2. Preheat the oven to 350°F. Line a 6½ cup (1500 ml), round baking pan with parchment paper. Melt the butter and let it cool.
3. Beat the eggs for about 5 minutes until they're light and fluffy. Add in the cooled butter and the crème fraîche, and mix the batter thoroughly.
4. Mix all the dry ingredients together, and add them to the batter.
5. Pour the batter into the prepared pan, and bake on the middle rack for 35 to 40 minutes.
6. Test the sponge cake for doneness by inserting a toothpick in the center of the cake. The toothpick will come out dry if the cake is ready.

TOSCA CAKE

Nutrition: Cal 225; Fat 22 g; Carb 12 g; Protein 10 g
Serving 10; Cook time 40 min

Ingredients
CAKE
- ⅔ cup (150 g) unsalted butter
- Oat fiber or coconut flour, for dusting
- 4 large eggs
- ½ cup (100 ml) crème fraîche or sour cream
- 2 tbsp erythritol/stevia blend
- ¼ cup (50 ml) coconut flour
- ½ cup (100 ml) almond flour or ½ cup (50 g) ground almonds
- 1 heaping tbsp whole, unflavored psyllium husk
- ½ tsp vanilla powder or 1 tsp vanilla extract
- 2 tsp baking powder

TOSCA FROSTING
- ⅓ cup (75 g) unsalted butter
- 1 tbsp whipping cream
- 1½ tbsp erythritol/stevia blend
- ⅛ tsp vanilla powder or ¼ tsp vanilla extract
- 1 tsp coconut flour
- ½ cup (50 g) slivered or chopped almonds

Instructions
1. Preheat the oven to 350°F. Line the bottom of an 8½" (22 cm) springform pan with parchment paper, and butter and dust the sides with oat fiber or coconut flour. Melt and cool the butter.

CAKE
1. Beat the eggs for 5 minutes, or until light and fluffy. Add in the cooled butter and the crème fraîche, and make sure they're thoroughly mixed.
2. Mix the dry ingredients together, and stir them into the batter.
3. Pour the batter into the prepared springform pan, and bake on the middle rack for 15 minutes. Remove the cake from the oven—DO NOT turn off the oven at this point, as the cake is not yet done baking.

TOSCA FROSTING
1. Melt the butter in a heavy-bottomed saucepan. Add whipping cream, sweetener, vanilla powder, and coconut flour. Bring the mixture to a boil while you whisk. Let the mixture simmer until it has thickened. Mix in the slivered or chopped almonds.
2. Pour the frosting over the partly baked cake, and return it to the oven to continue cooking for about another 15 minutes. Let the cake cool, and then loosen it from the sides of the pan by running a sharp knife around the edge of the cake before opening the pan.

MAZARIN CAKE

Nutrition: Cal 180; Fat 10 g; Carb 17 g; Protein 4 g
Serving 10; Cook time 40 min

Ingredients
CAKE
- ⅔ cup (150 g) unsalted butter
- 5 large eggs
- ½ cup (100 ml) whipping cream
- 1½ tbsp erythritol/stevia blend
- 1 cup (200 ml) almond flour or 1 cup (100 g) ground almonds
- 4 bitter almonds, finely ground (or 2 tsp almond extract)
- ¼ cup (50 ml) coconut flour
- 2 tsp baking powder

CHOCOLATE GANACHE
1. ½ cup (100 ml) whipping cream
2. 1¾ oz (50 g) dark chocolate, 90% cacao
3. ½ tbsp erythritol/stevia blend

Instructions
1. Preheat the oven to 350°F (175°C). Line the bottom of an 8½" (22 cm) springform pan with parchment paper. Melt the butter and let it cool.

CAKE
2. Beat the eggs for about 5 minutes, or until they're light and fluffy. Add in the cooled butter and the whipping cream.
3. Mix all the dry ingredients together, and then mix them thoroughly into the batter.
4. Pour the batter into the springform pan and bake on the middle rack for approximately 25 minutes. Let the cake cool completely.

CHOCOLATE GANACHE
1. Heat the cream in a saucepan. Remove the saucepan from the heat, anmelt the chocolate in the cream while stirring. Add in the sweetener and mix thoroughly.
2. Refrigerate the ganache until it becomes spreadable. Spread the ganache over the cake, and store the cake in the refrigerator.

COCONUT SQUARES

Nutrition: Cal 165; Fat 7 g; Carb 17 g; Protein 4 g
Serving 10; Cook time 40 min

Ingredients
SPONGE CAKE
- ½ cup (100 g) unsalted butter
- Oat fiber or coconut flour, for dusting
- 5 large eggs
- 2 tbsp erythritol/stevia blend
- 1 cup (200 ml) whipping cream
- ¾ cup (150 ml) coconut flour
- 2 tbsp whole, unflavored psyllium husk
- ½ tsp vanilla powder or 1 tsp vanilla extract
- 2 tsp baking powder

COCONUT FROSTING
- ⅓ cup (75 g) unsalted butter

- 1 tbsp erythritol/stevia blend
- ½ cup (100 ml) whipping cream
- 1½ cup (300 ml) grated, unsweetened coconut
- 1 large egg

Instructions

1. Preheat the oven to 350°F (175°C). Melt the butter separately for the cake and the frosting, and let both cool. Butter a small baking pan, approx. 6" × 7¾" (15 × 20 cm) in size, and dust it with oat fiber or coconut flour.

SPONGE CAKE

2. Beat the eggs for about 5 minutes, or until light and fluffy. Add in the cooled butter and the whipping cream. Mix thoroughly.
3. Mix the dry ingredients together, and mix into the batter.
4. Spread the batter in the prepared baking pan, and bake on the middle rack for approximately 15 minutes. Remove the cake (which is only partly baked at this stage) from the oven, and leave the oven on.

COCONUT FROSTING

1. Add sweetener, whipping cream, and grated coconut to the cooled butter. Mix everything thoroughly into the butter. Stir in the egg.
2. Spread the frosting over the cake, and return the cake to the oven to continue baking for another 10 minutes or so

COCONUT AND CHOCOLATE SQUARES

Nutrition: Cal 242; Fat 24 g; Carb 11 g; Protein 8 g
Serving 12; Cook time 45 min

Ingredients

CAKE

- ½ cup (100 g) unsalted butter
- 5 large eggs
- ½ cup (100 ml) mascarpone
- 2 tbsp erythritol/stevia blend
- ¼ cup (50 ml) cacao
- ½ cup (100 ml) almond flour or ½ cup (50 g) ground almonds
- ¼ cup (50 ml) coconut flour
- 2 tbsp whole, unflavored psyllium husk
- ½ tsp vanilla powder or 1 tsp vanilla extract
- 2 tsp baking powder
- Oat fiber or coconut flour for dusting the pan

COCONUT BUTTERCREAM

- ¾ cup (175 g) unsalted butter
- 1½ tbsp erythritol/stevia blend
- 2 large eggs
- 3 cups (250 g) unsweetened coconut, grated

CHOCOLATE GANACHE

- 3½ oz (100 g) dark chocolate, 90% cacao
- ½ cup (100 ml) whipping cream
- ¼ tsp vanilla powder or ½ tsp vanilla extract
- ½ tbsp erythritol/stevia blend

Instructions

1. Preheat the oven to 350°F (175°C). Melt the butter and let it cool. Butter a small baking pan, approx. 6" × 9¾" (15 × 25 cm) in size, and dust it with oat fiber or coconut flour.

CAKE

2. Beat the eggs for about 5 minutes, or until light and fluffy. Add in the cooled butter, and then the mascarpone and the sweetener.
3. Mix all the dry ingredients together and stir them into the batter. Pour the batter into the prepared baking pan.
4. Bake on the middle rack for approximately 25 minutes. Let the cake cool completely.

COCONUT BUTTERCREAM

1. Melt butter and sweetener together, and let cool. Add in the eggs and the grated coconut, and stir to blend thoroughly. Spread the buttercream over the cake and refrigerate.

CHOCOLATE GANACHE

2. Coarsely chop the chocolate. Heat the whipping cream, and then remove the saucepan from the heat. Add the chopped chocolate, vanilla powder, and sweetener (if using) to the warm cream, and stir thoroughly to make the chocolate melt. Let it cool.
3. Spread the chocolate ganache on top of the coconut buttercream, and put the cake back in the refrigerator.

ORANGE SQUARES

Nutrition: Cal 220; Fat 19 g; Carb 11 g; Protein 10 g
Serving 12; Cook time 45 min

Ingredients

CAKE

- ½ cup (100 g) unsalted butter
- Oat fiber or coconut flour, for dusting
- 5 large eggs
- 2 tbsp erythritol/stevia blend
- Grated rind and juice from 1 organic orange
- 1 cup (200 ml) whipping cream
- ½ cup (100 ml) coconut flour
- ½ cup (100 ml) almond flour or ½ cup (50 g) ground almonds
- 2 tbsp whole, unflavored psyllium husk
- 2 tsp baking powder

ORANGE FROSTING

- 5¼ oz (150 g) cream cheese, at room temperature
- 1½ tbsp erythritol/stevia blend
- ⅔ cup (150 g) unsalted butter
- Grated rind from 1 organic orange

GARNISH

- Grated rind from 1 organic orange

Instructions

1. Preheat the oven to 350°F (175°C). Melt the butter and let it cool. Grease a small baking pan, approx. 6" × 9¾" (15 × 25 cm) in size, and dust it with oat fiber or coconut flour.

CAKE

1. Beat the eggs for 5 minutes, or until they're light and fluffy. Add in the melted butter, orange juice, grated rind, and whipping cream. Mix thoroughly.
2. Mix all the dry ingredients together and add them to the batter. Pour the batter into the prepared baking pan, and bake on the middle rack for approximately 30 minutes. Let the cake cool completely.

ORANGE FROSTING
1. Whip the cream cheese, sweetener, and butter until creamy and without any lumps. Add in the grated orange rind and stir well.
2. Spread the frosting over the cooled cake; use a dry, warm knife if you want a smooth surface.
3. A little grated orange rind makes for a pretty finish when sprinkled onto the frosting.

TIRAMISU SHEET CAKE
Nutrition: Cal 238; Fat 21 g; Carb 5 g; Protein 7 g
Serving 20; Cook time 60 min

Ingredients
- 2 cups (200g) blanched almond flour
- ¾ cup granulated erythritol-based sweetener
- ⅓ cup (37g) coconut flour
- ⅓ cup unflavored whey protein powder
- 1 tablespoon baking powder
- ½ teaspoon salt
- ¾ cup unsweetened almond milk
- ½ cup (1 stick) unsalted butter, melted but not hot
- 3 large eggs
- 1 teaspoon vanilla
- extract ¼ cup espresso or strong brewed coffee, cooled
- 1 tablespoon dark rum

MASCARPONE FROSTING
- 8 ounces mascarpone cheese, softened
- 4 ounces cream cheese (½ cup), softened
- ½ cup powdered erythritol-based sweetener
- 1 teaspoon vanilla extract
- ½ to ⅔ cup heavy whipping cream, room temperature

GARNISH
- 1 tablespoon cocoa powder
- 1 ounce sugar-free dark chocolate

Instructions
CAKE
1. Preheat the oven to 325°F and thoroughly grease an 11 by 17-inch sheet pan.
2. In a medium bowl, whisk together the almond flour, sweetener, coconut flour, protein powder, baking powder, and salt. Add the almond milk, melted butter, eggs, and vanilla extract and whisk until smooth.
3. Spread the batter in the greased sheet pan and smooth the top. Bake for 18 to 22 minutes, until the edges are golden brown and the cake is set. Remove from the oven and let cool in the pan.
4. In a small bowl, combine the espresso and rum, if using. Brush over the cooled cake.

FROSTING:
1. In a large bowl, beat the mascarpone and cream cheese with an electric mixer until smooth. Beat in the sweetener and vanilla extract.
2. Add ½ cup of the cream and beat until smooth. Add more cream as needed to thin the frosting to a spreadable consistency. Spread the frosting over the cooled cake.

GARNISH
1. Dust the top of the cake with the cocoa powder. Grate the dark chocolate over the top

FUNFETTI MUG CAKES
Nutrition: Cal 213; Fat 19 g; Carb 4 g; Protein 5 g
Serving 2; Cook time 25 min

Ingredients
- ½ cup (50g) blanched almond flour
- 2 tablespoons granulated erythritol-based sweetener
- ½ teaspoon baking powder
- Pinch of salt
- 1 large egg white
- 2 tablespoons unsalted butter, melted but not hot
- 1 tablespoon water
- ½ teaspoon vanilla extract
- 1 tablespoon Coconut Sprinkles

Instructions
2. Preheat the oven to 350°F and grease two 4-ounce ramekins or ovenproof mugs.
3. In a medium bowl, whisk together the almond flour, sweetener, baking powder, and salt. Stir in the egg white, melted butter, water, and vanilla extract until well combined.
4. Stir in the coconut sprinkles and divide the batter evenly between the ramekins. Bake for 18 to 20 minutes, until the tops are golden and the cakes are set to the touch.
5. Let cool for 5 minutes, then eat straight from the ramekins or flip each cake out onto a plate to serve.

DUTCH BUTTER CAKE
Nutrition: Cal 240; Fat 22 g; Carb 5 g; Protein 6 g
Serving 8; Cook time 60 min

Ingredients
- ⅔ cup powdered erythritol-based sweetener
- ½ cup (1 stick) unsalted butter, softened
- 1 teaspoon almond extract
- 1 large egg, lightly beaten, divided
- 1½ cups (150g) blanched almond flour
- ½ teaspoon baking powder
- ½ teaspoon salt
- 1 tablespoon sliced almonds

Instructions
1. Preheat the oven to 350°F and grease a 9-inch glass or ceramic pie pan.

2. In a large bowl, beat the sweetener, butter, and almond extract with an electric mixer until well combined. Add all but 2 teaspoons of the egg and beat in. Add the almond flour, baking powder, and salt and beat until just combined. The batter will be quite thick.
3. Spread the batter in the greased pie pan and smooth the top. Brush the remaining egg over the top. Sprinkle with the sliced almonds or arrange the almonds in a decorative pattern.
4. Bake the cake for 25 to 30 minutes, until puffed and golden brown. It will still be very soft.
5. Remove from the oven and let cool completely in the pan. Refrigerate for at least 1 hour to firm up if you want to cut the cake into proper slices. It's alsowonderful scooped out of the pan like a gooey butter cake.

CHOCOLATE HAZELNUT BROWNIE PIE
Nutrition: Cal 290; Fat 22 g; Carb 14 g; Protein 8 g
Serving 8; Cook time 2 hours
Ingredients
• 4 ounces unsweetened chocolate, coarsely chopped
• ¾ cup granulated erythritolbased sweetener
• ½ cup boiling water
• 4 large eggs
• ½ cup (1 stick) unsalted butter, cut into tablespoons
• 1 teaspoon vanilla extract
• 1 cup (100g) hazelnut meal
GARNISH:
• Whipped Cream Chopped toasted hazelnuts
Instructions
1. Preheat the oven to 350°F and grease a 9-inch glass or ceramic pie pan.
2. In a food processor, pulse the coarsely chopped chocolat and sweetener until the chocolate is finely chopped. With the machine running on high, slowly pour in the boiling water until the chocolate is melted and smooth.
3. Add the eggs, butter, and vanilla extract and pulse until well combined. Add the hazelnut meal and pulse until incorporated.
4. Pour the batter into the greased pan and bake for 25 to 30 minutes, until the edges are nicely set but the middle is still a little wet-looking. Remove from the oven and let cool to room temperature, then refrigerate for 2 hours to firm up.
5. Garnish with whipped cream and toasted hazelnuts.

ZUCCHINI-CARROT CAKE
Nutrition: Cal 180; Fat 15 g; Carb 10 g; Protein 16 g
Serving 8; Cook time 60 min
Ingredients
• 1 1/4 cups hazelnuts
• 2 eggs
• 1/2 cup oil
• 2/3 cup Splenda
• 1/2 cup yogurt

• 1/2 cup vanilla-flavored whey protein powder
• 1 teaspoon baking soda
• 1/2 teaspoon salt
• 1 1/2 teaspoons cinnamon
• 1/4 teaspoon nutmeg
• 3/4 cup shredded zucchini
• 1/4 cup shredded carrot
Instructions
1. Preheat the oven to 350°F.
2. In a food processor with the S blade in place, use the pulse control to grind the hazelnuts to a mealy consistency. (You want 1 1/2 cups of ground hazelnuts when you're done, and for some inexplicable reason they seem to actually grow a little rather than shrink a little when you grind them .) Set the ground hazelnuts aside.
3. In a large mixing bowl, whisk the eggs until well blended. Add the oil, yogurt, ground hazelnuts, protein powder, baking soda, Splenda, salt, cinnamon, and nutmeg, mixing well after each addition. (It's especially important that the baking soda be well distributed through the mixture.) Add the zucchini and carrots last, mixing well.
4. Thoroughly coat a ring mold or bundt pan with nonstick cooking spray, and turn the batter into it. If you sprayed your pan ahead of time, give it another shot just before adding the batter. And don't expect the batter to fill the pan to the rim; it fills my bundt pan about halfway.
5. Bake for 45 minutes and turn out gently onto a wire rack to cool.

PUMPKIN PIE WITH PECAN PRALINE CRUST
Nutrition: Cal 189; Fat 14 g; Carb 14 g; Protein 6 g
Serving 8; Cook time 10 min
Ingredients
CRUST
• 2 cups shelled raw pecans
• 1/4 teaspoon salt
• 2 1/2 tablespoons Splenda
• 1 1/2 teaspoons blackstrap molasses
• 4 tablespoons butter, melted
• 2 tablespoons water
PUMPKIN PIE FILLING
• 1 can (15 ounces) pumpkin
• 1 1/2 cups heavy cream
• 3 eggs
• 3/4 cup Splenda
• 1/2 teaspoon salt
• 2 teaspoons blackstrap molasses
• 1 tablespoon pumpkin pie spice
Instructions
1. Preheat the oven to 350°F.

2. Put the pecans and salt in a food processor with the S blade in place. Pulse until the pecans are chopped to a medium consistency.
3. Add the Splenda, molasses, and butter, and pulse again until well blended. Add the water and pulse again, until well combined. At this point, you'll have a soft, sticky mass.
4. Spray a 10-inch pie plate with nonstick cooking spray, or butter it well. Turn the pecan mixture into it, and press firmly in place, all over the bottom, and up the sides by 1 1/2 inches or so. Try to get it an even thickness, with no holes, and if you wish, run a finger or a knife around the top edge, to get an even, nice-looking line.
5. Bake for about 18 minutes. Cool.
6. Increase the oven temperature to 425°F.
7. Combine the pumpkin, heavy cream, eggs, Splenda, salt, molasses, and spice in a bowl, and whisk together well. Pour into the prebaked and cooled pie shell. Bake for 15 minutes, lower the oven temperature to 350°F, and bake for an additional 45 minutes. Cool, and serve with whipped cream.

PEANUT BUTTER SILK PIE
Nutrition: Cal 280; Fat 14 g; Carb 12 g; Protein 20 g
Serving 1; Cook time 10 min
Ingredients
CRUST
- 1 1/4 cup shelled raw hazelnuts
- 1/2 stick butter, melted
- 1/2 cup vanilla-flavored whey protein powder

CHOCOLATE LAYER
- 4 sugar-free dark chocolate bars (about 1.5 ounces each)
- 5 tablespoons heavy cream
- 1/4 teaspoon instant coffee crystals

PEANUT BUTTER SLIK LAYER
- 1 package (8 ounces) cream cheese, softened
- 1 cup Splenda
- 1 cup creamy natural peanut butter
- 1 tablespoon butter, melted
- 1 teaspoon vanilla extract
- 1 cup heavy cream

Instructions
1. Preheat the oven to 325°F.
2. Use the S blade in a food processor to grind the hazelnuts to a meal. Add the butter and protein powder, and pulse until well combined.
3. Spray a large pie plate with nonstick cooking spray, and press the hazelnut mixturefirmly into bottom of the pie plate (it won't build up the side very far).
4. Bake for 10 to 12 minutes, or until lightly browned. Remove from the oven to cool.
5. Melt the chocolate over the lowest possible heat, as chocolate burns very easily. (If you have a double boiler or a heat diffuser, this would be a good time to use it!) Whisk in the cream and coffee crystals, and continue

stirring until the crystals disappear. Spread this mixture evenly over the bottom of the hazelnut crust.
6. Use an electric mixer to beat the cream cheese, Splenda, peanut butter, butter, and vanilla together until creamy.
7. In a separate bowl, whip the heavy cream until stiff. Turn the mixer to the lowest setting, and beat the whipped cream into the peanut butter mixture one-third at a time.
8. Spread the peanut butter filling gently over the chocolate layer, and chill. (This is best made a day in advance, to allow plenty of time for chilling.)

LEMON SHERBET
Nutrition: Cal 180; Fat 16 g; Carb 4 g; Protein 9 g
Serving 8; Cook time 35 min
Ingredients
- 1 package (4-serving size) sugar-free lemon gelatin
- 2 cups boiling water
- 2 cups plain yogurt
- 2 teaspoons lemon extract
- 3 tablespoons Splenda
- 1/4 cup vanilla-flavored whey protein powder
Instructions
1. Put the gelatin powder in the blender, and add the water. Blend for 20 seconds, orjust long enough to dissolve the gelatin.
2. Add the other ingredients, and blend well. Put the blender container in the refrigerator and let it chill for 10 to 15 minutes. Take it out and blend it again for about 10 seconds, then chill it for another 10 to 15 minutes, and then give it another quick blend it when it's done chilling.
3. Pour the sherbet mixture into a home ice cream freezer, and freeze according to the directions for your freezer.

GRASSHOPPER CHEESECAKE
Nutrition: Cal 174; Fat 15 g; Carb 9 g; Protein 18 g
Serving 12; Cook time 40 min
Ingredients
CHOCOLATE LAYER
- 3 sugar-free dark chocolate bars (about 1.5 ounces each)
- 1/4 cup heavy cream
- 1 Almond Crust or Hazelnut Crust, prebaked in a springform pan

GRASSHOPPER FILLING
- 3 packages (8 ounces each) cream cheese, softened
- 3/4 cup Splenda
- 3/4 cup sour cream
- 3/4 teaspoon peppermint extract
- 1 1/2 tablespoons chocolate extract
- 1 or 2 drops green food coloring (optional, but pretty)
- 4 eggs
Instructions

1. Preheat oven to 325°F. In the top of a double boiler over hot water (or in a heavybottomed saucepan over the lowest possible heat), melt the chocolate and whisk in the cream until smooth. Spread this mixture evenly over the crust, and set aside.
2. In a large bowl, use an electric mixer to beat the cream cheese until smooth, scraping down the sides of the bowl often. Beat in the Splenda and the sour cream, and mix well. Beat in the peppermint and chocolate extracts, food coloring (if using), and eggs, one by one, beating until very smooth and creamy.
3. Pour the mixture into the chocolate-coated crust. Place the cake in the oven, and on the oven rack below it or on the floor of the oven place a pie pan of water. Bake for 1 hour.
4. Cool in the pan on a wire rack. Chill well before serving.

PUMPKIN CHEESECAKE
Nutrition: Cal 210 ; Fat 19 g; Carb 6 g; Protein 6 g
Serving 12; Cook time 80 min

Ingredients
- 1/2 stick butter
- 1/2 cup pecans, coarsely chopped
- 2 packages (8 ounces each) cream cheese, softened
- 1/2 to 3/4 cup Splenda sweetener
- 2 teaspoons vanilla extract
- 1 1/2 cups pure canned pumpkin
- 1/2 cup sour cream
- 4 eggs
- 1 1/2 teaspoons cinnamon
- 1 teaspoon ginger
- 1/2 teaspoon nutmeg
- 1/4 teaspoon ground cloves
- 1/4 teaspoon salt

Instructions
1. Preheat the oven to 300°F.
2. Butter the bottom and sides of a 9 1/2 -inch springform cheesecake pan. Sprinkle the bottom of the pan with chopped pecans, distributing evenly.
3. In a large mixing bowl, use an electric mixer to beat the cream cheese, Splenda, and vanilla until fluffy, stopping occasionally to scrape the sides of the bowl and beaters.
4. Add the pumpkin and sour cream, mixing thoroughly on medium speed. Add the eggs one at a time, mixing thoroughly between each one. Mix in the cinnamon, ginger, nutmeg, cloves, and salt.
5. Pour the batter over the nuts in the pan. Bake for 60 to 70 minutes, or until a knife placed in center comes out clean. Cool for 20 minutes before removing from the pan, and chill for at least 2 hours before serving.

BUTTER-PECAN CHEESECAKE
Nutrition: Cal 230; Fat 16 g; Carb 9 g; Protein 18 g
Serving 12; Cook time 80 min

Ingredients
PECAN COOKIE CRUST
- 1 stick butter, softened
- 1/2 cup Splenda
- 3/4 cups vanilla-flavored whey protein powder
- 3/4 cups chopped pecans
- 1/2 teaspoon salt

BUTTERSCOTCH FILLING
- 3 packages (8 ounces each) cream cheese, softened
- 3/4 cup Splenda
- 3/4 cup sour cream
- 2 teaspoons butter flavoring
- 1 tablespoon vanilla extract
- 1 tablespoon blackstrap molasses
- 4 eggs

Instructions
1. Preheat the oven to 325°F.
2. Beat the butter and Splenda together until light and creamy. Then beat in the protein powder, pecans, and salt. Spray a springform pan with nonstick cooking spray, and press the crust evenly and firmly into the bottom of the pan, plus just far enough up the sides to cover the seam at the bottom.
3. Bake for 12 to 15 minutes, until lightly golden. Set aside to cool while you make the filling.
4. In a large bowl, use an electric mixer to beat the cream cheese until smooth, scraping down the sides of the bowl often. Next beat in the Splenda and the sour cream, and mix well. Beat in the butter flavoring, vanilla, and molasses; add the eggs one by one, beating until very smooth and creamy.
5. Pour the mixture into the crust. Place the cake in the oven, and on the oven rack below it or on the floor of the oven place a pie pan of water. Bake for 1 hour.
6. Cool in the pan on a wire rack. Chill well before serving.

KETO RED VELVET CAKE
Nutrition: Cal 167; Fat 16 g; Carb 4 g; Protein 6 g
Serving 12; Cook time 30 min

Ingredients
- 2 cups almond flour blanched almond flour
- 1 teaspoon baking powder
- 1/4 teaspoon salt
- 4 large eggs room temperature
- 1/2 cup granulated sweetener of choice monk fruit sweetener or erythritol
- 2 tablespoon coconut oil softened
- 1 teaspoon vanilla extract
- 1 teaspoon butter extract optional
- 1-2 drops red food coloring
- 1 cup cream cheese frosting

Instructions
1. Preheat the oven to 180C/350F. Grease a 9-inch cake pan with cooking spray and set aside.
2. In a small bowl, mix together your dry ingredients. In a separate bowl, whisk together your eggs, sweetener,

coconut oil, vanilla extract, and butter extract, until combined. Add your red food coloring.

3. Gently fold through your dry ingredients into the wet and mix until combined. Transfer the batter into the greased cake pan and bake for 25-27 minutes, or until a skewer comes out clean from the center.

4. Remove from the oven and allow the cake to cool completely, before frosting.

LEMON MERINGUE PIE
Nutrition: Cal 150; Fat 11 g; Carb 16 g; Protein 4 g
Serving 8; Cook time 15 min

Ingredients
• 1 9 inch pie crust of choice
• For the vegan lemon curd
• 1/3 cup cornflour cornstarch
• 1 cup superfine sugar caster sugar
• 3/4 cup lemon juice
• 1 cup coconut milk
• 1/4 teaspoon yellow food coloring
• For the vegan meringue
• 1/2 cup Aquafaba liquid from 1 x 400 gram can of chickpea water.
• 1/2 teaspoon cream of tartar
• 1 cup powdered sugar or sugar free powdered sugar

Instructions
1. Prepare your pie crust. Either store bought, homemade or a no bake crust. Set aside.

2. Place cornflour and superfine sugar in a saucepan. Stir through the lemon juice and coconut milk. Add the yellow food coloring slowly, until nice and yellow (like a lemon meringue pie color).

3. Turn the heat on medium. Stir for 1-2 minutes, or until the sugar dissolves. Increase the heat to medium-high and cook for around 5 minutes, stirring constantly, until mixture begins to bubble and thicken.

4. Remove the lemon curd from the heat. Moving quickly, transfer the lemon curd into the pie crust. Refrigerate for at least 2 hours, to firm up.

5. Once the lemon curd has firmed up, start preparing your vegan meringue. In a large mixing bowl, add your aquafaba and beat until soft peaks form, around 5 minutes. Add the cream of tartar and continue beating, until combined. Slowly add the powdered sugar, and continue beating until stiff, glossy peaks form. Add the vanilla extract.

6. Using a rubber spatula, spread out the vegan meringue over the top of the lemon pie. Using a blow torch, gently brown the tops of the meringue.

ALMOND FLOUR BROWNIES
Nutrition: Cal 153; Fat 14 g; Carb 6 g; Protein 6 g
Serving 12; Cook time 40 min

Ingredients
• 1 1/2 cups almond flour
• 1 teaspoon baking powder
• 1/2 teaspoon salt
• 5 tablespoons butter softened
• 1 3/4 cups granulated sweetener of choice white, brown, sugar free, etc.
• 3/4 cup cocoa powder
• 3 large eggs
• 1 teaspoon vanilla extract
• 1/2 cup chocolate chips optional

Instructions
1. Preheat the oven to 180C/350F. Line an 8 x 8-inch pan with parchment paper and set aside.

2. In a small bowl, whisk together your dry ingredients. In a separate larger bowl, whisk together your softened butter, sweetener, eggs, cocoa powder, and vanilla extract, until combined.

3. Gently add in your dry ingredients and mix until fully incorporated. If using chocolate chips, fold them through at the end.

4. Transfer your brownie batter into the lined pan. Bake for 35 minutes, or until a skewer comes out just clean. Remove from the oven and allow to cool completely, before slicing.

KETO BLONDIES PIE
Nutrition: Cal 190; Fat 18 g; Carb 5 g; Protein 5 g
Serving 12; Cook time 25 min

Ingredients
• 2 cups almond flour
• 1 teaspoon baking powder
• 1 cup golden monk fruit sweetener
• 2 large eggs
• 1/2 cup butter or dairy free butter, softened
• 1 teaspoon vanilla extract
• 1/2 cup keto chocolate chips
• 1/2 cup mix ins nuts, seeds, chocolate chunks, etc.

Instructions
1. Preheat the oven to 180C/350F. Line an 8 x 8-inch pan with parchment paper and set aside.

2. In a large mixing bowl, combine your almond flour and baking powder and mix well. In a separate bowl, whisk together your golden monk fruit sweetener, eggs, softened butter and vanilla extract, until combined.

3. Combine your wet and dry ingredients, and mix until just combined. Using a rubber spatula, fold through your chocolate chips and other mix ins of choice. blondie batter with chocolate chips

4. Transfer your blondie batter into the lined pan. Bake the keto blondies for 20-25 minutes, or until a skewer comes out just clean. raw blondies

5. Remove from the oven and let cool in the pan completely.

KETO PAVLOVA WITH FRESH BERRIES

Nutrition: Cal 337; Fat 13 g; Carb 18 g; Protein 8 g
Serving 6; Cook time 25 min

Ingredients
- 3 egg whites
- ½ cup (32⁄3 oz.) erythritol
- ¼ tsp white vinegar 5%
- ½ tsp vanilla extract
- 1 pinch salt
- 1 cup heavy whipping cream
- 5 oz. (1¼ cups) fresh raspberries

Instructions
1. Preheat the oven to 400° F (200° C).
2. Prepare a baking sheet with parchment paper.
3. Whisk the egg whites until they form stiff peaks.
4. When the egg whites are ready, add the erythritol little by little and keep beating until well combined. Add the vinegar, vanilla, and salt. Mix well.
5. Using a piping bag full of the meringue mixture, or a spoon, carefully form the meringue bases on top of the parchment paper.
6. Put the baking sheet in the oven and switch the oven off.
7. Leave the meringues inside the oven until the oven cools down and the meringue bases become firm and dry. You can even leave them in the oven overnight. Set the meringues aside until it's time to assemble the pavlovas.
8. Whip the cream until it forms soft peaks.
9. Fill the meringue bases with the whipped cream and decorate with raspberries.

RASPBERRY CHEESECAKE SWIRL BROWNIES

Nutrition: Cal 230; Fat 17 g; Carb 8 g; Protein 6 g
Serving 24; Cook time 60 min

Ingredients
BROWNIE BATTER
- 4 oz. (4⁄5 cup) sugar-free baking chocolate, chopped
- 6 oz. butter
- 1 cup (7 oz.) erythritol
- 4 large eggs
- 1 cup (4 oz.) almond flour
- 2 tsp vanilla extract
- ¼ tsp salt

CREAM CHEESE FILLING
- 10 oz. (1¼ cups) cream cheese, softened
- 1⁄3 cup (1½ oz.) powdered erythritol
- 1 large egg
- 2 tsp vanilla extract
- 1 tsp raspberry extract (optional)
- 1 tbsp lemon juice
- 6 oz. (1⅓ cups) fresh raspberries

Instructions
1. Preheat the oven to 350°.
2. Line a 9" x 13" (20 x 30 cm) baking dish with parchment paper so that the sides come up over the dish and can be used to easily lift the baked brownies from the pan.
3. Use a microwave or a small saucepan to melt the chocolate and butter on low heat. When melted, add the sweetener and stir until the sweetener is dissolved.
4. In a large bowl, mix eggs, almond flour, vanilla extract and salt. When thoroughly mixed, add the melted chocolate mixture and stir to combine. Pour the mixture into the prepared pan.
5. Use a hand mixer or a stand mixer to blend the cream cheese and powdered sweetener. When creamy and smooth, add the egg and mix well.
6. Stir in the vanilla extract, raspberry extract, and lemon juice.
7. Gently fold in the fresh raspberries.
8. Drop large spoonfuls of the cheesecake mixture over the brownie batter. Use a knife to swirl the cheesecake batter into the brownie batter by dragging the tip through the batter in horizontal and vertical lines.
9. Bake for 35 to 40 minutes until set. Do not overbake. Let cool completely before serving.

KETO ESPRESSO CHOCOLATE CHEESECAKE BARS

Nutrition: Cal 232; Fat 21 g; Carb 5 g; Protein 6 g
Serving 16; Cook time 45 min

Ingredients
CHOCOLATE CRUST
- 7 tablespoons butter, melted
- 2 cups superfine, blanched almond flour
- 3 tablespoons cocoa powder
- 1/3 cup granulated erythritol sweetener

FOR THE CHEESECAKE:
- 16 ounces full fat cream cheese
- 2 large eggs
- 1/2 cup granulated erythritol sweetener
- 2 tablespoons instant espresso powder
- 1 teaspoon vanilla extract
- additional cocoa powder for dusting over the top if desired.

Instructions
FOR THE CHOCOLATE CRUST:
1. Preheat the oven to 350° F.
2. Combine the melted butter, almond flour, sweetener and cocoa powder in a medium sized bowl and mix well.
3. Transfer the crust dough to a 9 x 9 pan lined with parchment paper or foil (this will make removing the bars much easier.)
4. Press the crust firmly into the bottom of the pan.
5. Bake the crust for 8 minutes.
6. Remove from the oven and set aside to cool.

FOR THE CHEESECAKE FILLING:
1. Combine the cream cheese, eggs, sweetener, espresso powder, and vanilla extract in a blender and blend until smooth.

2. Pour over the par baked crust and spread out evenly in the pan.
3. Bake the cheesecake bars at 350° F for 25 minutes, or until set.
4. Remove from the oven and cool.
5. Dust with optional cocoa powder if using.
6. Chill for at least 1 hour, preferably longer, before cutting into four rows of squares to serve.
7. Store in an airtight container in the refrigerator for up to 5 days, or freeze for up to 3 months.

KETO AVOCADO BROWNIES
Nutrition: Cal 240; Fat 22 g; Carb 6 g; Protein 4 g
Serving 12; Cook time 40 min

Ingredients
- 1 cup (250 g) avocado (mashed)
- ½ tsp (½ tsp) vanilla
- 4 tbsp (4 tbsp) cocoa powder
- 3 tbsp (3 tbsp) refined coconut oil (or butter, ghee, shortening, lard)
- 2 (2) eggs
- ½ cup (100 g) lily's chocolate chips (melted)

DRY INGREDIENTS
- ¾ cup (90 g) blanched almond flour
- ¼ tsp (¼ tsp) baking soda
- 1 tsp (1 tsp) baking powder
- ¼ tsp (¼ tsp) salt
- ¼ cup (60 g) erythritol
- 1 tsp (1 tsp) stevia powder

Instructions
1. Preheat the oven to 180C/350F.
2. In a separate bowl, combine the dry ingredients together and whisk together.
3. Peel the avocados. Weigh or measure your avocados. Place in a food processor. Process until smooth.
4. Add each wet ingredient to the food processor, one at a time, and process for a few seconds until all of the wet ingredients have been added to the food processor.
5. Add the dry ingredients to the food processor and mix until combined.
6. Place a piece of parchment paper over a 30x20cm (12"x8") baking dish and pour the batter into it. Spoon evenly and place in the preheated oven. Bake for 30 minutes, or until a toothpick inserted in the middle comes out half clean. The top should be soft when you touch it with your fingers.
7. Take out of the oven, let it cool completely before slicing into 12 pieces.

CINNAMON ROLL COFFEE CAKE
Nutrition: Cal 174; Fat 20 g; Carb 6 g; Protein 7 g
Serving 16; Cook time 50 min

Ingredients
CINNAMON FILLING
- 3 tablespoon Swerve Sweetener
- 2 teaspoon ground cinnamon

CAKE:
- 3 cups almond flour
- ¾ cup Swerve Sweetener
- ¼ cup unflavoured whey protein powder
- 2 teaspoon baking powder
- ½ teaspoon salt
- 3 large eggs
- ½ cup butter melted
- ½ teaspoon vanilla extract
- ½ cup almond milk
- 1 tablespoon melted butter

CREAM CHEESE FROSTING:
- 3 tablespoon cream cheese softened
- 2 tablespoon powdered Swerve Sweetener
- 1 tablespoon heavy whipping cream
- ½ teaspoon vanilla extract

Instructions
1. Preheat oven to 325F and grease an 8x8 inch baking pan.
2. For the filling, combine the Swerve and cinnamon in a small bowl and mix well. Set aside.
3. For the cake, whisk together almond flour, sweetener, protein powder, baking powder, and salt in a medium bowl.
4. Stir in the eggs, melted butter and vanilla extract. Add the almond milk and continue to stir until well combined.
5. Spread half of the batter in the prepared pan, then sprinkle with about two thirds of the cinnamon filling mixture. Spread the remaining batter over top and smooth with a knife or an offset spatula.
6. Bake 35 minutes, or until top is golden brown and a tester inserted in the center comes out with a few crumbs attached.
7. Brush with melted butter and sprinkle with remaining cinnamon filling mixture. Let cool in pan.
8. For the frosting, beat cream cheese, powdered erythritol, cream and vanilla extract together in a small bowl until smooth. Pipe or drizzle over cooled cake.

LOW CARB ITALIAN CREAM CAKE
Nutrition: Cal335; Fat 30 g; Carb 6 g; Protein 6g
Serving 16; Cook time 90 min

Ingredients
CAKE
- ½ cup butter softened
- 1 cup Swerve Sweetener
- 4 large eggs room temperature, separated
- ½ cup heavy cream room temperature
- 1 teaspoon vanilla extract
- 1 ½ cups almond flour
- ½ cup shredded coconut
- ½ cup chopped pecans
- ¼ cup coconut flour

- 2 teaspoon baking powder
- ½ teaspoon salt
- ¼ teaspoon cream of tartar

FROSTING
- 8 ounces cream cheese softened
- ½ cup butter softened
- 1 cup powdered Swerve Sweetener
- 1 teaspoon vanilla extract
- ½ cup heavy whipping cream room temperature

GARNISH
- 2 tablespoon shredded coconut lightly toasted
- 2 tablespoon chopped pecans lightly toasted

Instructions
CAKE
1. Preheat the oven to 325F and grease two 8 inch or 9 inch round cake pans very well (the 8 inch pans will take a little longer to cook but the layers will be higher and I think they will look better). Line the pans with parchment paper and grease the paper.
2. In a large bowl, beat the butter with the sweetener until well combined. Beat in the egg yolks one at a time, mixing well after each addition. Beat in the heavy cream and vanilla extract.
3. In another bowl, whisk together the almond flour, shredded coconut, chopped pecans, coconut flour, baking powder, and salt. Beat into the butter mixture until just combined.
4. In another large bowl, beat the egg whites with the cream of tartar until they hold stiff peaks. Gently fold into the cake batter.
5. Divide the batter evenly among the prepared pans and spread to the edges. Bake 35 to 45 minutes (or longer, depending on your pans), until the cakes are golden on the edges and firm to the touch in the middle.
6. Remove and let cool completely in the pans, then flip out onto a wire rack to cool completely. Remove the parchment from the layers if it comes out with them.

FROSTING
1. In a large bowl, beat the cream cheese and butter together until smooth. Beat in the sweetener and vanilla extract until well combined.
2. Slowly add the heavy whipping cream until a spreadable consistency is achieved.

TO ASSEMBLE
1. Place the bottom layer on a serving plate and cover the top with about ⅓ of the frosting. Add the next layer and frost the top and the sides.
2. Sprinkle the top with the toasted coconut and pecans. Refrigerate at least half an hour to let set.

CHOCOLATE COCONUT MOUNDS PIE
Nutrition: Cal 242; Fat 21 g; Carb 12 g; Protein 5 g
Serving 8 ; Cook time 40 min

Ingredients
- 2 cups unsweetened coconut milk
- 4 eggs
- 1 tsp vanilla extract
- 1-1/2 tsp coconut stevia
- 2 cups unsweetened shredded coconut
- 1/2 cup unsweetened cocoa powder
- 1/4 cup coconut flour
- 1/2 tsp salt

COCONUT CREAM TOPPING
- 1 can (15 oz) coconut milk (opened, overnight in fridge)

OPTIONAL
- 2 ounces Lily's sugar-free coconut chocolate bar

Instructions
1. In a stand mixer with a whisk attachment blend the first 4 ingredients together.
2. Change to the paddle attachment and add the rest of the ingredients on low speed.
3. Pour mixture into a pie plate and bake for 40 minutes.
4. Allow to cool before adding coconut cream topping.
5. Keep refrigerated.

BROWNIE TRUFFLE PIE
Nutrition: Cal 370; Fat 33 g; Carb 6 g; Protein 8 g
Serving 4; Cook time 30 min

Ingredients
CRUST
- 1 1/4 cup almond flour
- 3 tbsp coconut flour
- 1 tbsp granulated Swerve Sweetener
- 1/4 tsp salt
- 5 TBSP butter chilled and cut into small pieces
- 2-4 TBSP ice water

FILLING
- 1/2 cup almond flour
- 6 TBSP cocoa powder
- 6 TBSP Swerve Sweetener
- 1 tsp baking powder
- 2 large eggs
- 5 tbsp water
- 1/4 cup melted butter
- 1 tbsP Sukrin Fiber Syrup (optional, but helps create a more gooey center)
- 1/2 tsp vanilla extract
- 3 tbsp sugar-free chocolate chips

TOPPING
- 1 cup whipping cream
- 2 tbsp confectioner's Swerve Sweetener
- 1/4 tsp vanilla extract
- 1/2 oz sugar-free dark chocolate

Instructions
CRUST

1. Preheat oven to 325°F and grease a glass or ceramic pie pan.
2. In a large bowl, combine almond flour, coconut flour, sweetener, and salt. Cut in butter using a pastry cutter or two sharp knives until mixture resembles coarse crumbs. Add two tablespoons water and mix until dough comes together. Add more water only if necessary to get dough to come together.
3. Press evenly into the bottom and up the sides of prepared pie pan, crimp edges, and prick bottom all over with a fork. Bake 12 minutes.

FILLING

1. In a large bowl, whisk together the almond flour, cocoa powder, sweetener, and baking powder. Stir in eggs, water, melted butter, and vanilla extract until well combined. Stir in chocolate chips.
2. Pour batter into crust and bake 30 minutes, covering with foil about halfway through. Remove and let cool 10 minutes, then refrigerate half an hour until cool.

TOPPING

1. Combine cream, sweetener, and vanilla extract in a large bowl. Beat until cream holds stiff peaks. Spread over cooled filling.
2. Shave dark chocolate over top. Chill another hour or two until completely set.

COCONUT KEY LIME PIE
Nutrition: Cal 460 ; Fat 42 g; Carb 6 g; Protein 11 g
Serving 9; Cook time 50 min

Ingredients
CRUST

- 2 cups raw hazelnuts
- 1 egg
- 4 tbsp chia seeds
- 4 tbsp organic butter, melted
- 1 tbsp coconut oil
- 1 tbsp Swerve

FILLING

- 1 cup coconut cream
- 1 cup sour cream
- 3 large eggs
- 1 cup fresh key lime juice
- 3 tbsp Swerve
- 1 tbsp key lime zest
- ½ cup unsweetened coconut shavings

Instructions

1. Pre heat oven to 375°F.
2. In a food processor grind the hazelnuts until they turn in to a flour, then add the chia seeds, Swerve, egg, and melted butter. Mix everything together until a dough is formed.
3. Now grease a 6 by 9 inch pyrex with coconut oil.
4. Press the crust flat into the pyrex.
5. Bake for 20 min at 375°F.

6. In the meantime, prepare the filling.
7. In a large bowl mix all the filling ingredients and blend with an immersion blender until smooth and frothy.
8. Remove the crust from the oven once done.
9. Pour filling onto crust and put back in the oven at 350°F.
10. Bake for 45 minutes.
11. Remove from the oven, and let cool, then sprinkle evenly with the coconut flakes.
12. Then refrigerate overnight.

RICOTTA CHEESE PIE
Nutrition: Cal 170; Fat 12 g; Carb 4 g; Protein 10 g
Serving 8; Cook time 50 min

Ingredients

- 1 1/2 cups almond flour, sifted
- 3 tbsp low carb sugar substitute (I used Swerve)
- 1/4 tsp salt
- 1/4 cup butter, melted
- 1 egg
- 1 tsp vanilla extract
- 4 eggs, beaten
- 1 tsp vanilla extract
- 15 oz ricotta cheese
- 1 tbsp coconut flour
- 3/4 cup Swerve (add more if desired; up to 1 cup)
- 2 tbsp low carb sugar substitute or 24 drops liquid stevia to help round out sweetness

Instructions

1. In deep dish pie plate, mix together almond flour, 3 tablespoons equivalent sugar substitute and 1/4 teaspoon salt.
2. Pour in butter, 1 egg and 1 teaspoon vanilla.
3. Mix until dough forms.
4. Press into pie plate. Bake at 350 degrees F for 10 minutes.
5. Set on rack to cool slightly.
6. In a large bowl mix 4 beaten eggs, 1 teaspoon vanilla, ricotta cheese, coconut flour, 1 cup equivalent sugar substitute and 2 tablespoons other sweetener.
7. Beat until smooth.
8. Pour into crust and bake at 350°F for 45 minutes or until lightly browned and firm.

NO-BAKE BLUEBERRY CHEESECAKE PIE
Nutrition: Cal 325 ; Fat 28 g; Carb 7 g; Protein 6 g
Serving 10; Cook time 40 min

Ingredients
CRUST

- 1 1/2 cups almond flour
- 1/4 cup powdered Swerve Sweetener
- 1/4 cup butter, melted

FILLING

- 12 oz cream cheese, softened

- 2 tbsp sour cream or Greek yogurt, room temperature
- 2 tbsp freshly-squeezed lemon juice
- 1 tsp lemon zest
- 3/4 cup powdered Swerve Sweetener
- 1/2 cup plus 2 TBSP heavy whipping cream, divided
- 1 tbsp grassfed gelatin or 1 envelope Knox gelatin

TOPPING
- Blueberry syrup no-sugar

Instructions

CRUST

1. In a medium bowl, whisk together almond flour and powdered Sweetener. Stir in butter until well combined and clumps form.
2. Press firmly into the bottom and up the sides of a 9 inch pie pan. Refrigerate until needed.

FILLING

1. In a large bowl, beat cream cheese, sour cream or yogurt, lemon juice, and lemon zest together until smooth. Beat in sweetener until well combined.
2. In a small bowl, whisk together 2 TBSP heavy cream and the gelatin. Gently warm the mixture in the microwave for about 20 to 30 seconds, and then stir until the gelatin dissolves (you can also do this in a small saucepan - do not let the cream come to a simmer). Stir into cream cheese mixture until combined.
3. In another large bowl, beat cream until it holds stiff peaks. Gently fold whipped cream into cream cheese mixture until well combined.
4. Spread filling in prepared crust, cover with plastic and refrigerate 2 to 3 hours, until set.

BLUEBERRY TOPPING

1. Pour over the cheesecake before serving.

CHAYOTE SQUASH MOCK APPLE PIE
Nutrition: Cal 190; Fat 16 g; Carb 6 g; Protein 2 g
Serving 16; Cook time 45 min

Ingredients

CRUST
- 1/2 cup butter, melted
- 1 1/2 cup almond flour
- 3/4 cup coconut flour
- 4 eggs
- 1 tbsp whole psyllium husks
- 1/2 tsp salt

FILLING
- 5 medium chayote squash
- 3/4 cup low carb sugar substitute
- 1 1/2 tsp cinnamon
- 1/4 tsp ginger
- 1/8 tsp nutmeg
- 1 tbsp xanthan gum
- 1 tbsp lemon juice
- 2 tsp apple extract (optional)
- 1/3 cup butter cut in small pieces

TOPPING

- 1 egg
- Low carb sugar substitute

Instructions

1. Mix crust ingredients to form dough.
2. Separate into two dough balls.
3. Roll each crust ball out into pie crust.
4. Transfer one crust to 9 inch pie dish. Smooth out any cracks.
5. Reserve remaining crust for pie top.

FILLING

1. Peel chayote and cut into slices.
2. Boil sliced chayote until fork tender. Drain. Return to pot.
3. Add sweetener, xanthan gum, lemon juice, and apple extract to cooked chayote squash.
4. Pour chayote mixture into prepared pie crust. Dot filling with butter.

TOPPING

1. Cover filling with reserved pie crust.
2. Flute edges of pie crust together and cut slits on pie top.
3. Brush egg on top crust and sprinkle with additional sweetener, if desired.
4. Bake at 375°F for 30-35 minutes (I took mine out after 30 minutes).

GRASSHOPPER MOUSSE PIE
Nutrition: Cal 261; Fat 25 g; Carb 55 g; Protein 3 g
Serving 12; Cook time 20 min

Ingredients

CRUST
- 3/4 cup unsweetened shredded coconut
- 1/4 cup unsweetened cocoa powder
- 1/2 cup sunflower seeds raw, unsalted
- 4 TBSP butter, softened
- 1/4 tsp salt
- 1/4 cup Swerve confectioners

FILLING
- 1/2 cup water
- 1 tsp gelatin
- 5 oz avocado, mashed
- 8 oz cream cheese, softened
- 1 tsp peppermint extract
- 1 tsp peppermint liquid stevia
- Pinch of salt
- 1 cup heavy cream

Instructions

CRUST

1. Combine all ingredients into a food processor and blend just enough to combine. Don't over blend or you will have the texture of peanut butter.
2. Taste crust to see if you need more salt or sweetness.
3. Using your fingers spread and mold crust onto bottom and sides of pie plate. Set aside.

FILLING

1. Pour the water into a small saucepan and sprinkle the gelatin on top.

2. Turn on low heat, stirring constantly until gelatin is dissolved. Let cool.
3. Place the avocado, cream cheese, peppermint extract, stevia, and salt into a stand mixer and blend on high until smooth.
4. Taste and adjust sweetness if needed.
5. Pour in heavy cream in another bowl and use an electric mixer to blend on high until soft peaks form. Fold into the cream cheese mixture.
6. Gradually pour in the cooled gelatin and stir until combined.
7. Pour filling into pie crust.
8. Refrigerate at least 2 hours, loosely covered or up to 1 day.
9. When ready to serve add optional chocolate drizzle if desired.

PEANUT BUTTER MOLTEN LAVA CAKES

Nutrition: Cal 390; Fat 35 g; Carb 8 g; Protein 6 g
Serving 4; Cook time 4 min

Ingredients
- 1/4 cup butter
- 1/4 cup peanut butter
- 2 tbsp coconut oil
- 6 tbsp powdered Swerve Sweetener
- 2 large eggs
- 2 large egg yolks
- 1/2 tsp vanilla extract
- 6 tbsp almond flour
- Low carb chocolate sauce

Instructions
1. Preheat oven to 350°F and grease 4 small (about 1/2 cup capacity each) ramekins very well. I used both butter and coconut oil spray.
2. In a medium-sized microwave safe bowl, combine butter, peanut butter, and coconut oil. Cook on high in 30 second increments until melted. Stir together until smooth.
3. Whisk in powdered sweetener until smooth. Whisk in eggs, egg yolks, and vanilla extract. Then whisk in almond flour until smooth.
4. Divide batter among prepared ramekins and bake 12 to 15 minutes, until sides are set but the center still jiggles a bit. Remove and let cool a few minutes.
5. Run a sharp knife around the inside of the ramekin to loosen the cakes. Cover each with an upside-down plate and flip over to turn the cake out onto the plate (you may need to give it one good shake, holding the plate and ramekin together tightly).
6. Drizzle with low carb chocolate sauce and serve immediately.

TEXAS SHEET CAKE

Nutrition: Cal 230; Fat 20 g; Carb 6 g; Protein 6 g
Serving 20; Cook time 30 min

Ingredients
CAKE
- 2 cups almond flour
- 3/4 cup Swerve Sweetener
- 1/3 cup coconut flour
- 1/3 cup unflavoured whey protein powder
- 1 tbsp baking powder
- 1/2 tsp salt
- 1/2 cup butter
- 1/2 cup water
- 1/4 cup cocoa powder
- 3 large eggs
- 1 tsp vanilla extract
- 1/4 cup heavy cream
- 1/4 cup water

FROSTING
- 1/2 cup butter
- 1/4 cup cocoa powder
- 1/4 cup cream
- 1/4 cup water
- 1 tsp vanilla extract
- 1 1/2 cups powdered Swerve Sweetener
- 1/4 tsp xanthan gum
- 3/4 cup chopped pecans

Instructions
CAKE
1. Preheat oven to 325°F and grease a 10x15 inch rimmed sheet pan very well.
2. In a large bowl, whisk together the almond flour, sweetener, coconut flour, protein powder, baking powder, and salt. Break up any clumps with the back of a fork.
3. In a medium saucepan over medium heat, combine the butter, water, and cocoa powder, stirring until melted. Bring to a boil and then remove from heat. Add to the bowl.
4. Add eggs, vanilla extract, cream and water and stir until well combined. Spread in prepared baking pan.
5. Bake 15 to 20 minutes, until cake is set and a tester inserted in the center comes out clean.

FROSTING
1. In another medium saucepan, combine butter, cocoa powder, cream, and water. Bring to a simmer, stirring until smooth. Stir in vanilla extract. Add powdered sweetener 1/2 a cup at a time, whisking vigorously to dissolve any clumps. Whisk in xanthan gum.
2. Pour over warm cake and sprinkle with pecans. Let cool until frosting is set, about 1 hour.

CHOCOLATE PEANUT BUTTER LAVA CAKES

Nutrition: Cal 345; Fat 30 g; Carb 7 g; Protein 8 g
Serving 3; Cook time 12 min

Ingredients
- 1/4 cup butter
- 1 oz unsweetened chocolate chopped
- 3 tbsp Swerve Sweetener
- 1 large egg
- 1 large egg yolk
- 3 TBSP almond flour
- 1/4 tsp vanilla extract
- Pinch of salt
- 2 tbsp peanut butter

Instructions
1. Preheat oven to 375°F and grease 3 small ramekins. Dust the ramekins with cocoa powder and shake out the excess.
2. In a microwave safe bowl, melt butter and chocolate together, whisking until smooth. Alternatively, you can melt it carefully over low heat.
3. Add the sweetener and whisk until combined. Then add the egg and egg yolk and whisk until smooth.
4. Whisk in the almond flour, vanilla extract, and salt until well combined.
5. Divide about 2/3 of the batter between the three ramekins, making sure to cover the bottom.
6. Divide peanut butter between the ramekins, placing in center of the batter. Cover with remaining batter. Bake 10 to 12 minutes, or until the edges of the cakes are set but the center still jiggles slightly. Remove and let cool 5 to 10 minutes. Then run a sharp knife around the edges and flip out onto plates.

PECAN PIE CHEESECAKE

Nutrition: Cal 340; Fat 30 g; Carb 5 g; Protein 6 g
Serving 10; Cook time 35 min

Ingredients
CRUST
- 3/4 cup almond flour
- 2 TBSP powdered Swerve Sweetener
- Pinch of salt
- 2 TBSP melted butter

PECAN PIE FILLING
- 1/4 cup butter
- 1/3 cup powdered Swerve Sweetener
- 1 tsp Yacon syrup or molasses optional, for color and flavor
- 1 tsp caramel extract or vanilla extract
- 2 TBSP heavy whipping cream
- 1 large egg
- 1/4 tsp salt
- 1/2 cup chopped pecans

CHEESECAKE FILLING
- 12 oz cream cheese, softened
- 5 TBSP powdered Swerve Sweetener
- 1 large egg
- 1/4 cup heavy whipping cream
- 1/2 tsp vanilla extract

TOPPING
- 2 TBSP butter
- 2 1/2 tbsp powdered Swerve Sweetener
- 1/2 tsp Yacon syrup or molasses
- 1/2 tsp caramel extract or vanilla extract
- 1 TBSP heavy whipping cream
- Whole toasted pecans for garnish

Instructions
CRUST
1. In a medium bowl, whisk together the almond flour, sweetener, and salt. Stir in the melted butter until the mixture begins to clump together.
2. Press into the bottom and partway up the sides of a 7-inch springform pan. Place in the freezer while making the pecan pie filling.

PECAN PIE FILLING
1. In a small saucepan over low heat, melt the butter. Add the sweetener and Yacon syrup and whisk until combined, then stir in the extract and heavy whipping cream.
2. Add the egg and continue to cook over low heat until the mixture thickens (this should only take a minute or so). Immediately remove from heat and stir in the pecans and salt.
3. Spread mixture over the bottom of the crust.

CHEESECAKE FILLING
1. Beat the cream cheese until smooth, then beat in the sweetener. Beat in the egg, whipping cream, and vanilla a extract.
2. Pour this mixture over the pecan pie filling and spread to the edges.

TO BAKE
1. Wrap the bottom of the springform pan tightly in a large piece of foil. Place a piece of paper towel over the top of the springform pan (not touching the cheesecake) and then wrap foil around the top as well. Your whole pan should be mostly covered in foil to keep out excess moisture.
2. Place the rack that came with your Instant Pot or pressure cooker into the bottom. Pour a cup of water into the bottom.
3. Carefully lower the wrapped cheesecake pan onto the rack (there are ways to do this with a sling made out of tin foil but I didn't bother with that).
4. Close the lid and set the Instant Pot to manual mode for 30 minutes on high. Once the cooking time is complete, let the pressure to release naturally (do not vent it).
5. Lift out the cheesecake and let it cool to room temperature, and then refrigerate for 3 or 4 hours, or even overnight.

TOPPING

1. In a small saucepan over low heat, melt the butter. Add the sweetener and Yacon syrup and whisk until combined, then stir in the extract and heavy whipping cream.
2. Drizzle over the chilled cheesecake and garnish with toasted pecans.

KENTUCKY BUTTER CAKE

Nutrition: Cal 310; Fat 27 g; Carb 6g; Protein 7 g
Serving 16; Cook time 60 min

Ingredients
CAKE
- 2 1/2 cups almond flour
- 1/4 cup coconut flour
- 1/4 cup unflavored whey protein powder
- 1 tbsp baking powder
- 1/2 tsp salt
- 1 cup butter, softened
- 1 cup Swerve Granular
- 5 large eggs room temperature.
- 2 tsp vanilla extract
- 1/2 cup whipping cream
- 1/2 cup water

BUTTER GLAZE
- 5 tbsp butter
- 1/3 cup Swerve Granular
- 2 tbsp water
- 1 tsp vanilla extract

GARNISH
- 1 to 2 tbsp Confectioner's Swerve

Instructions
1. Preheat oven to 325°F. Grease a bundt cake pan very well and then dust with a few tbsp of almond flour.
2. In a medium bowl, whisk together the almond flour, coconut flour, whey protein, baking powder, and salt.
3. In a large bowl, beat the butter and the sweetener together until light and creamy. Beat in the eggs and vanilla extract. Beat in the almond flour mixture and then beat in the whipping cream and water until well combined.
4. Transfer the batter to the prepared baking pan and smooth the top. Bake 50 to 60 minutes, until golden brown and the cake is firm to the touch. A tester inserted in the center should come out clean.
5. Butter Glaze:In a small saucepan over low heat, melt the butter and sweetener together. Whisk until well combined. Whisk in the water and vanilla extract.
6. While the cake is still warm and in the pan, poke holes all over with a skewer. Pour the glaze over and let cool completely in the pan.
7. Gently loosen the sides with a knife or thin rubber spatula, then flip out onto a serving platter. Dust with powdered sweetener.
8. Serve with lightly sweetened whipped cream and fresh berries.

CHOCOLATE WALNUT TORTE

Nutrition: Cal 340; Fat 31 g; Carb 9 g; Protein 49g
Serving 10; Cook time 30 min

Ingredients
TORTE
- 1 1/2 cup walnuts
- 3/4 cup Swerve Sweetener
- 1/4 cup cocoa powder
- 1 tsp espresso powder (optional, enhances chocolate flavor)
- 1/2 tsp baking powder
- 1/4 tsp salt
- 1/2 cup butter
- 4 oz unsweetened chocolate
- 5 large eggs
- 1/2 tsp vanilla extract
- 1/2 cup almond milk

GLAZE
- 1/2 cup whipping cream
- 2 1/2 oz sugar-free dark chocolate chopped
- 1/3 cup walnut pieces

Instructions
TORTE
1. Preheat oven to 325°F and grease a 9-inch round baking pan. Line the bottom with parchment paper and grease the paper.
2. In a food processor, process walnuts until finely ground. Add sweetener, cocoa powder, espresso powder, baking powder, and salt and pulse a few times to combine.
3. In a large saucepan set over low heat, melt butter and chocolate together until smooth. Remove from heat and whisk in eggs and vanilla extract. Add almond milk and whisk until mixture smooths out. Stir in walnut mixture until well combined.
4. Spread batter in prepared baking pan and bake about 30 minutes, until edges are set but center still looks slightly wet. Let cool 15 minutes in pan, then invert onto a wire rack to cool completely. Remove parchment paper.

GLAZE
1. In a small saucepan over medium heat, bring cream to just a simmer. Remove from heat and add chopped chocolate. Let sit to melt 5 minutes, then whisk until smooth.
2. Cool another 10 minutes, then pour the glaze over the cake, smoothing the sides. Sprinkle top with walnut pieces and chill until chocolate is firm, about 30 minutes.

CLASSIC NEW YORK KETO CHEESECAKE

Nutrition: Cal 284; Fat 24 g; Carb 3 g; Protein 8 g
Serving 12; Cook time 90 min

Ingredients

- 24 oz cream cheese, softened
- 5 tbsp unsalted butter, softened
- 1 cup powdered Swerve Sweetener
- 3 large eggs, room temperature
- 3/4 cup sour cream, room temperature
- 2 tsp grated lemon zest
- 1 1/2 tsp vanilla extract

Instructions

1. Preheat the oven to 300°F and generously grease a 9-inch springform pan. Cut a circle of parchment to fit the bottom the pan and grease the paper. Wrap 2 pieces of aluminum foil around the outside of the pan to cover the bottom and most of the way up the sides.
2. In a large bowl, beat the cream cheese and butter until smooth, then beat in the sweetener until well combined. Add the eggs, once at a time, beating after each addition. Clean the beaters and scrape down the sides of the bowl as needed.
3. Add the sour cream, lemon zest, and vanilla extract and beat until the batter is smooth and well combined. Pour into the prepared springform pan and smooth the top.
4. Set the pan inside a roasting pan large enough to prevent the sides from touching. Place the roasting pan in the oven and carefully pour boiling water into the roasting pan until it reaches halfway up the sides of the springform pan.
5. Bake 70 to 90 minutes, until the cheesecake is mostly set but still jiggles just a little in the center when shaken. Remove the roasting pan from the one, then carefully remove the springform pan from the water bath. Let cool to room temperature.
6. Run a sharp knife around the edges of the cake to loosen, the release the sides of the pan. Refrigerate for at least 4 hours before serving.

GOOEY BUTTER CAKE

Nutrition: Cal 269; Fat 24 g; Carb 5 g; Protein 6 g
Serving 12; Cook time 40 min

Ingredients
CAKE

- 2 cups almond flour
- 1/2 cup Swerve Sweetener
- 2 tbsp unflavored whey protein powder
- 2 tsp baking powder
- 1/4 tsp salt
- 1/2 cup butter, melted
- 1 large egg
- 1/2 tsp vanilla extract

FILLING

- 8 oz cream cheese, softened
- 1/2 cup butter, softened
- 3/4 cup powdered Swerve
- 2 large eggs
- 1/2 tsp vanilla extract
- Powdered Swerve for dusting

Instructions

1. Preheat the oven to 325°F and lightly grease a 9x13 baking pan.
2. In a large bowl, combine the almond flour, sweetener, protein powder, baking powder, and salt. Add the butter, egg, and vanilla extract and stir to combine well. Press into the bottom and partway up the sides of the prepared baking pan.
3. In another large bowl, beat the cream cheese and butter together until smooth. Beat in the sweetener until well combined, then beat in the eggs and vanilla until smooth.
4. Pour the filling over the crust. Bake 35 to 45 minutes, until the filling is mostly set, but the center still jiggles, and the edges are just golden-brown.
5. Remove and let cool, then dust with powdered Swerve and cut into bars.

<u>Keto Chaffle</u>

KETO CHAFFLE CHURRO

Nutrition: Cal 120; Fat 8 g; Carb 3 g; Protein 9 g
Serving 2; Cook time 10 min

Ingredients

- 1 Egg
- 1 tbsp. Almond flour
- ½ tsp. Vanilla extract
- 1 tsp. Cinnamon divided
- ¼ tsp. Baking powder
- ½ C. Shredded mozzarella
- 1 tbsp. Swerve confectioners sugar substitute
- 1 tbsp. Swerve brown sugar substitute
- 1 tbsp. Butter melted

Instructions

1. Preheat your mini waffle maker.
2. Add the egg, almond flour, vanilla extract, ½ tsp of cinnamon, baking powder, shredded mozzarella and the Swerve confectioners sugar substitute into a bowl, and mix to combine well.
3. Place an even layer of half of the mixture into the mini waffle maker, and cook for 3-5 minutes, or until your desired level of doneness has been reached. A longer cook time will give you a crispier chaffle.
4. Remove the first chaffle from the mini waffle maker, and place the second half of the batter into it. Cook the second chaffle for 3-5 minutes.
5. Cut the two chaffles into strips.
6. Place the cut strips into a bowl and cover in the melted butter.
7. Mix together the Swerve brown sugar substitute and the remaining ½ tsp of cinnamon in a bowl to combine well.
8. Pour the cinnamon sugar mixture over the churro chaffle strips in the mixing bowl, and toss to coat them well.

KETO CHAFFLE PEANUT BUTTER CHOCOLATE

Nutrition: Cal 124; Fat 12 g; Carb 3 g; Protein 2 g
Serving 2; Cook time 20 min

Ingredients

- 1 Egg
- 2 tablespoon Peanut butter butter
- 1 tablespoon Almond flour
- 1 tablespoon Swerve confectioners sugar substitute
- ½ tablespoon Cocoa powder
- ½ teaspoon Vanilla extract
- ⅓ cup Mozzarella cheese shredded
- Sugar Free whipped cream for garnish if desired
- Lily's baking chips for garnish if desired

Instructions

1. Preheat your mini waffle maker.
2. Mix together all of the ingredients except the whipped cream and the baking chips in a mixing bowl. Stir until well combined.

3. Place half of the mixture into the preheated mini waffle maker, and cook for 3-5 minutes until it is done to your liking.
4. Remove the first chaffle from the waffle maker, and place the second half of the batter into it. Cook the second chaffle for 3-5 minutes until done.
5. Let the chaffles cool slightly, and then serve topped with sugar free whipped cream and a sprinkle of Lily's baking chips for garnish if desired.

KETO CHAFFLES CARAMEL

Nutrition: Cal 125; Fat 10 g; Carb 2 g; Protein 5 g
Serving 2; Cook time 25 min

Ingredients

- 1 tbsp. Swerve confectioners sugar substitute
- 2 tbsp. Almond flour
- 1 Egg
- ½ tsp. Vanilla extract
- ⅓ C. Shredded mozzarella cheese
- For the caramel sauce:
- 3 tbsp. Butter unsalted
- 2 tbsp. Swerve brown sugar substitute
- ⅓ C. Heavy whipping cream
- ½ tsp. Vanilla extract

Instructions

1. Preheat your mini waffle maker.
2. Place the 3 tablespoons of butter and the 2 tablespoons of brown sugar substitute together in a small skillet or pan over medium heat on the stove.
3. Cook the butter and sugar substitute mixture for 4-5 minutes until it begins to brown but not burn.
4. Add the heavy whipping cream into the mixture on the stove, and whisk it in well. Cook the mixture on a low boil for 10 minutes until the mixture thickens and has the color of caramel sauce.
5. While the caramel sauce is cooking, mix together the ingredients for the chaffles in a mixing bowl.
6. Place half of the chaffle mixture into the heated mini waffle maker, and cook for 3-5 minutes until your desired level of doneness has been reached.
7. Remove the first chaffle, and cook the second half of the batter for another 3-5 minutes.
8. Take the finished caramel sauce off the heat, and add in the vanilla extract. Let cool slightly.
9. Pour the caramel sauce over the chaffles and serve.

KETO BROWNIE FRIES CHAFFLE

Nutrition: Cal 120; Fat 8 g; Carb 3 g; Protein 4 g
Serving 1; Cook time 10 min

Ingredients

- ½ C. Shredded mozzarella cheese
- 1 oz. Softened cream cheese
- 2 tbsp. Almond flour
- 2 tbsp. Swerve confectioners sugar substitute
- 1 tbsp. Unsweetened cocoa powder

- ½ tsp. Vanilla extract
- ¼ tsp. Baking powder
- 1 Egg

Instructions

1. Preheat your mini waffle maker if needed.
2. In a microwave safe bowl, combine the mozzarella and cream cheese. Microwave for 30 seconds at a time until the cheese are completely melted and combined.
3. Add the melted cheese mixture to a mixing bowl, and blend in all of the other ingredients on high until smooth and creamy.
4. Pour ⅓ of the batter into the mini waffle maker, and cook for 3-5 minutes until browned and cooked through.
5. Repeat step 4 to make two more brownie chaffles.
6. Slice the brownies chaffles into thin strips, and top with a dusting of confectioners sugar substitute if desired.

EASY KETO CHAFFLES

Nutrition: Cal 170; Fat 14 g; Carb 2 g; Protein 10 g
Serving 2; Cook time 10 min

Ingredients

- 1 egg
- 1/2 cup cheddar cheese, shredded
- 1 tbsp almond flour

Instructions

1. Preheat the waffle maker according to manufacturer instructions.
2. In a small mixing bowl, mix together egg and cheddar cheese. Stir until well combined.
3. Optionally, add the almond flour. See recipe notes for more ideas.
4. If using a mini waffle maker, pour one half of the waffle batter into the waffle maker.
5. Cook for 3-4 minutes or until it reaches desired doneness. Repeat with the second half of the batter.

KETO CHAFFLE SANDWICH

Nutrition: Cal 240 ; Fat 18 g; Carb 2 g; Protein 17 g
Serving 2; Cook time 10 min

Ingredients

FOR THE CHAFFLES

- 1 egg
- 1/2 cup Cheddar cheese, shredded

FOR THE SANDWICH

- 2 strips bacon
- 1-2 slices tomato
- 2-3 pieces lettuce
- 1 tablespoon mayonnaise

Instructions

1. Preheat the waffle maker according to manufacturer instructions..
2. In a small mixing bowl, mix together egg and shredded cheese. Stir until well combined.

3. Pour one half of the waffle batter into the waffle maker. Cook for 3-4 minutes or until golden brown. Repeat with the second half of the batter.
4. In a large pan over medium heat, cook the bacon until crispy, turning as needed. Remove to drain on paper towels.
5. Assemble the sandwich with lettuce, tomato, and mayonnaise.

KETO PIZZA CHAFFLES

Nutrition: Cal 238; Fat 18 g; Carb 2 g; Protein 17 g
Serving 2; Cook time 10 min

Ingredients

FOR THE CHAFFLES

- 1 egg
- 1/2 cup mozzarella cheese, shredded
- 1/2 tsp Italian Herb blend
- pinch garlic powder 1 tablespoon chia seeds

PIZZA TOPPINGS

- 2 tbsp tomato sauce
- 1/2 cup mozzarella cheese, shredded
- 6 pepperoni (optional)

Instructions

1. Preheat the waffle maker according to manufacturer instructions. Preheat the oven to 400.
2. In a small mixing bowl, mix together egg, cheddar cheese, garlic, and herbs. Stir until well combined.
3. If using a mini waffle maker, pour one half of the waffle batter into the waffle maker. (Use all of the batter for a large Belgian waffle maker.)
4. Cook for 3-4 minutes or until golden brown. Repeat with the second half of the batter.
5. Top the chaffle crusts with tomato sauce, cheese, and pepperoni. Place on a small baking sheet and bake in the oven until cheese is melted, about 5 minutes.

BROCCOLI AND CHEESE CHAFFLE

Nutrition: Cal 170; Fat 13 g; Carb 2 g; Protein 11 g
Serving 2; Cook time 10 min

Ingredients

- 1/2 cup cheddar cheese
- 1/4 cup fresh chopped broccoli
- 1 egg
- 1/4 teaspoon garlic powder
- 1 tablespoon almond flour

Instructions

1. In a bowl mix almond flour, cheddar cheese, egg and garlic powder. I find it easiest to mix everything using a fork.
2. Add half the Broccoli and Cheese Chaffle batter to the Dish Mini waffle maker at a time. Cook chaffle batter in the waffle maker for 4 minutes.
3. Let each chaffle sit for 1-2 minutes on a plate to firm up. Enjoy alone or dipping in sour cream or ranch dressing.

KETO BLUEBERRY CHAFFLE

Nutrition: Cal 116; Fat 8 g; Carb 3 g; Protein 8 g

Serving 5; Cook time 15 min

Ingredients

- 1 cup of mozzarella cheese
- 2 tablespoons almond flour
- 1 tsp baking powder
- 2 eggs
- 1 tsp cinnamon
- 2 tsp of Swerve
- 3 tablespoon blueberries

Instructions

1. Heat up your Dash mini waffle maker.
2. In a mixing bowl add the mozzarella cheese, almond flour, baking powder, eggs, cinnamon, swerve and blueberries. Mix well so all the ingredients are mixed together.
3. Spray your mini waffle maker with non stick cooking spray.
4. Add in a little bit less then 1/4 a cup of blueberry keto waffle batter.
5. Close the lid and cook the chaffle for 3-5 minutes. Check it at the 3 minute mark to see if it is crispy and brown. If it is not or it sticks to the top of the waffle machine close the lid and cook for 1-2 minutes longer.

PUMPKIN CHOCOLATE CHIP CHAFFLES

Nutrition: Cal 93; Fat 7 g; Carb 2 g; Protein 7 g

Serving 3; Cook time 12 min

Ingredients

- 1/2 cup shredded mozzarella cheese
- 4 teaspoons pumpkin puree
- 1 egg
- 2 tablespoons granulated swerve
- 1/4 tsp pumpkin pie spice
- 4 teaspoons sugar free chocolate chips
- 1 tablespoon almond flour

Instructions

1. Plug in your waffle maker.
2. In a small bowl mix the pumpkin puree and egg. Make sure you mix it well so all the pumpkin is mixed with the egg.
3. Next add in the mozzarella cheese, almond flour, swerve and pumpkin spice and mix well.
4. Then add in your sugar free chocolate chips
5. Add half the keto pumpkin pie Chaffle mix to the Dish Mini waffle maker at a time. Cook chaffle batter in the waffle maker for 4 minutes.
6. DO NOT open before the 4 minutes is up. It is VERY important that you do not open the waffle maker before the 4 minute mark. After that you can open it to check it and make sure it is cooked all the way, but with these chaffles keeping the lid closed the whole time is VERY important.

7. When the first one is completely done cooking cook the second one.
8. Enjoy with some swerve confectioners sweetener or whipped cream on top.

KETO CHOCOLATE CHIP CHAFFLE

Nutrition: Cal 146; Fat 10 g; Carb 7 g; Protein 6 g

Serving 1; Cook time 10 min

Ingredients

- 1 egg
- 1 tbsp heavy whipping cream
- 1/2 tsp coconut flour
- 1 3/4 tsp Lakanto monkfruit golden can use more or less to adjust sweetness
- 1/4 tsp baking powder
- pinch of salt
- 1 tbsp Lily's Chocolate Chips

Instructions

1. Turn on the waffle maker so that it heats up.
2. In a small bowl, combine all ingredients except the chocolate chips and stir well until combined.
3. Grease waffle maker, then pour half of the batter onto the bottom plate of the waffle maker. Sprinkle a few chocolate chips on top and then close.
4. Cook for 3-4 minutes or until the chocolate chip chaffle dessert is golden brown then remove from waffle maker with a fork, being careful not to burn your fingers.
5. Repeat with the rest of the batter.
6. Let chaffle sit for a few minutes so that it begins to crisp. If desired serve with sugar-free whipped topping.

CHOCOLATE CHAFFLE CAKE WITH CREAM CHEESE

Nutrition: Cal 150; Fat 13 g; Carb 5 g; Protein 6 g

Serving 2; Cook time 10 min

Ingredients
CHOCOLATE CHAFFLE

- 2 tablespoons cocoa powder
- 2 tablespoons swerve granulated sweetener
- 1 egg
- 1 tablespoon heavy whipping cream
- 1 tablespoon almond flour
- 1/4 tsp baking powder
- 1/2 tsp vanilla extract

CREAM CHEESE FROSTING

- 2 tablespoons cream cheese
- 2 teaspoons swerve confectioners
- 1/8 tsp vanilla extract
- 1 tsp heavy cream

Instructions
HOW TO MAKE CHOCOLATE CHAFFLE CAKE

1. In a small bowl, whisk together cocoa powder, swerve, almond flour, and baking powder.

2. Add in the vanilla extract and heavy whipping cream and mix well.
3. Add in the egg and mix well. Be sure to scrape the sides of the bowl to get all of the ingredients mixed well.
4. Let sit for 3-4 minutes while the mini waffle maker heats up.
5. Add half of the waffle mixture to the waffle maker and cook for 4 minutes. Then cook the second waffle. While the second chocolate keto waffle is cooking make your frosting.

HOW TO MAKE CREAM CHEESE FROSTING
1. In a small microwave safe bowl add 2 tablespoons cream cheese. Microwave the cream cheese for 8 seconds to soften the cream cheese.
2. Add in heavy whipping cream and vanilla extract and use a small hand mixer to mix well.
3. Then add in the confectioners swerve and use the hand mixer to incorporate and fluffy the frosting.

ASSEMBLING KETO CHOCOLATE CHAFFLE CAKE
1. Place one chocolate chaffle on a plate, top with a layer of frosting. You can spread it with a knife or use a pastry bag and pip the frosting.
2. Put the second chocolate chaffle on top of the frosting layer and then spread or pipe the rest of the frosting on top.

KETO CHAFFLE TACO SHELLS
Nutrition: Cal 113; Fat 10 g; Carb 3 g; Protein 8 g
Serving 5; Cook time 20 min

Ingredients
- 1 tablespoon almond flour
- 1 cup taco blend cheese
- 2 eggs
- 1/4 tsp taco seasoning

Instructions
1. In a bowl mix almond flour, taco blend cheese, eggs and taco seasoning. I find it easiest to mix everything using a fork.
2. Add 1.5 tablespoons of taco chaffle batter to the waffle maker at a time. Cook chaffle batter in the waffle maker for 4 minutes.
3. Remove the taco chaffle shell from the waffle maker and drape over the side of a bowl. I used my pie pan because it was what I had on hand but just about any bowl will work.
4. Continue making chaffle taco shells until you are out of batter. Then fill your taco shells with taco meat, your favorite toppings and enjoy!

PUMPKIN PECAN CHAFFLE
Nutrition: Cal 210; Fat 17 g; Carb 5 g; Protein 11 g
Serving 1; Cook time 10 min

Ingredients
- 1 egg
- ½ cup mozzarella cheese grated
- 1 tablespoon pumpkin puree
- ½ teaspoon pumpkin spice
- 1 teaspoon erythritol low carb sweetener
- 2 tablespoons almond flour
- 2 tablespoons pecans, toasted chopped

Instructions
1. Turn on your waffle maker and lightly grease it (I give it a light spray with olive oil)
2. In a bowl, beat the egg.
3. Add the mozzarella, pumpkin, almond flour, pumpkin spice and erythritol and mix well.
4. Stir in the pecan pieces
5. Spoon the batter into your waffle maker and spread out evenly.(If you have a smaller waffle maker use half the mixture to make one waffle, then repeat)
6. Close the lid and cook for 5 minutes.
7. Using tongs, remove the cooked waffles
8. Serve with whipped cream or low carb caramel sauce. Perhaps some pecan nuts.

PECAN WAFFLES
Nutrtion: Cal 342; Fat 28 g; Carb 14 g; Protein 12 g
Serving 6; Cook time 20 min

Ingedients
- 1 ½ cups almond flour
- ½ cup coconut flour
- 4 medium eggs
- 1 cup almond milk or coconut milk
- 2 tablespoons butter melted
- 1 teaspoon baking powder
- 3 tablespoons brown sweetener or other low carb sweetener
- 1 teaspoon cinnamon
- 1 teaspoon vanilla extract
- ½ teaspoon salt
- ½ cup pecans chopped

Instructions
1. Preheat your waffle iron to medium-high and give it a light spray with oil.
2. Place all of the ingredients except the chopped pans in a blender. Pulse until the batter is smooth.
3. Pour enough of the waffle mixture into the waffle maker to cover the base and sprinkle a handful of the chopped pecans over the mixture. Spoon more mixture to cover the pecans and cook each waffle until firm and golden.
4. Repeat until all the mixture is used.
5. Serve with sugar free syrup, whipped cream and pecans.

GRILLED CHEESE CHAFFLE

Nutrition: Cal 220; Fat 20 g; Carb 3 g; Protein 12 g
Serving 1; Cook time 10 min

Ingredients

- 1 egg
- 1/4 teaspoon garlic powder
- 1/2 cup shredded cheddar
- 2 Slices American cheese or 1/4 cup of shredded cheese
- 1 tablespoon butter

Instructions

1. Heat up your dash mini waffle maker.
2. In a small bowl mix the egg, garlic powder and shredded cheddar cheese.
3. Once the dash waffle maker is heated up add in half the chaffle mixture. Cook for 4 minutes and remove.
4. Add the remainder of the chaffle mixture to the dash mini waffle maker and cook for 4 minutes.
5. Once both chaffles are done heat a pan on the stove over medium heat.
6. Add 1 tablespoon butter and melt it. Once the butter is melted in the pan and place 1 chaffle down in the pan. Top that chaffle with the cheese of your choice and add the second chaffle on top of it.
7. Heat the chaffle for 1 minute on the first side and flip over and cook for another 1-2 minutes on the other side to finish melting the cheese.
8. Once the cheese is melted remove from the pan and enjoy!

KETO BIG MAC CHAFFLE

Nutrition: Cal 600; Fat 35 g; Carb 8 g; Protein 25 g
Serving 1; Cook time 15 min

Ingredients

CHAFFLES

- 2 Keto Burger patties
- 2 tablespoons Keto Big Mac Sauce
- 3 Garlic Cheddar chaffles
- 2 slices American cheese
- 1/4 cup iceberg lettuce
- 4 dill pickles slices
- 1/2 tablespoon onions minced
- sesame seeds optional

BIG MAC CHAFFLE

- 2 egg
- 1/2 teaspoon garlic powder
- 1 cup shredded cheddar

BIG MAC SAUCE

- 1/2 cup mayonnaise
- 1/2 tablespoon mustard
- 1/2 tablespoon relish
- 1 teaspoon vinegar
- 1/4 teaspoon onion powder
- 1/4 teaspoon garlic powder
- 1/4 teaspoon paprika

- 1/4 pound ground beef
- salt to taste
- pepper to taste

Instructions

BIG MAC CHAFFLES

1. Heat up your dash mini waffle maker.
2. In a small bowl mix the egg, garlic powder, and shredded cheddar cheese.
3. Once the dash waffle maker is heated up add in half the chaffle mixture. Cook for 4 minutes and remove. Repeat this step with the chaffle mixture two more times.

BIG MAC BURGER

1. Preheat a pan over medium heat. Divided the beef into two chaffle sized patties, season them with salt and pepper. Cook burgers for about three minutes on each side. Top the burgers with the cheese slices and remove from the heat.

KETO BIG MAC SAUCE

2. In a small bowl mix the mayonnaise, mustard, relish, vinegar, onion powder, garlic powder and paprika and set aside.

ASSEMBLE KETO BIG MAC BURGER CHAFFLE

Spread the sauce on the top of two of the chaffles. Top the first chaffle with lettuce, onion, pickles, and burger. Repeat this again with chaffle, lettuce, onion, pickles burger, and the last chaffle.
You can top the last chaffle with sesame seeds if you want to.

STRAWBERRY SHORTCAKE CHAFFLES

Nutrition: Cal 112; Fat 12 g; Carb 4 g; Protein 4 g
Serving 1; Cook time 17 min

Ingredients

- 3 Strawberries
- 1/4 cup Keto Whipped Cream
- 1/2 tablespoon granulated swerve
- 1 tablespoon Almond flour
- 1 egg
- 1/2 cup mozzarella cheese
- 1/4 teaspoon vanilla extract

Instructions

3. Heat up your waffle maker.
4. Rinse and chop up your fresh strawberries. Place the strawberries in a small bowl and add 1/2 tablespoon granulated swerve. Mix the strawberries with the swerve and set aside.
5. In a bowl mix the almond flour, egg, mozzarella cheese, granulated swerve and vanilla extract.
6. Pour 1/3 of the batter into your mini waffle maker and cook for 3-4 minutes. Then cook another 1/3 of the batter and the rest of the batter to make 3 keto chaffles.
7. While your second chaffle is cooking, make your keto whipped cream if you do not have any on hand.
8. Assemble your Strawberry Shortcake Chaffle by placing whipped cream and strawberries on top of your sweet

chaffle. Then drizzle the juice that will also be in the bowl with the strawberries on top.

PUMPKIN SPICE CHAFFLE
Nutrition: Cal 210; Fat 18 g; Carb 5 g; Protein 5 g
Serving 3; Cook time 12 min

Ingredients
- 1 cup of mozzarella cheese
- 2 tablespoons almond flour
- 1 tsp baking powder
- 2 eggs
- 1/2 tsp pumpkin pie spice
- 2 tsp of Swerve

Instructions
1. In a small bowl mix the eggs, almond flour, mozzarella cheese, baking powder, pumpkin pie spice and swerve.
2. Once it is mixed well pour into a small food processor and blend until smooth.
3. Pour 1/3 of the batter into your mini waffle maker and cook for 3-4 minutes. Then cook the more of the batter to make a second chaffle and continue on until all pumpkin spice chaffles are made.
4. Serve with Low carb syrup and butter or a sprinkle of swerve confectioners sweetener!

GINGERBREAD CHAFFLES
Nutrition: Cal 128; Fat 13 g; Carb 6 g; Protein 4 g
Serving 1; Cook time 10 min

Ingredients
- 1 cup of mozzarella cheese
- 2 tablespoons almond flour
- 1 tsp baking powder
- 2 eggs
- 1 tsp ground ginger
- 1/2 tsp cinnamon
- 1/4 tsp ground nutmeg
- 1/4 tsp ground cloves
- 2 tsp of Swerve granulated sweetener

Instructions
1. In a medium bowl add in the mozzarella cheese, almond flour, baking powder, eggs, ginger, cinnamon, nutmeg, cloves, and swerve and mix well.
2. Add 1/4 of the keto Chaffle mix to the Dish Mini waffle maker at a time. Cook chaffle batter in the waffle maker for 4 minutes.
3. DO NOT open before the 4 minutes is up. It is VERY important that you do not open the waffle maker before the 4-minute mark. After that, you can open it to check it and make sure it is cooked all the way, but with these chaffles keeping the lid closed the whole time is VERY important.
4. When the first one is completely done cooking cook the next one.
5. Enjoy with some swerve confectioners sweetener or keto whipped cream on top.

KETO CHOCOLATE WAFFLE CAKE
Nutrition: Cal 120; Fat 3 g; Carb 7 g; Protein 3 g
Serving 4; Cook time 10 min

Ingredients
- 2 Tbs Cocoa
- 2 Tbs Monkfruit Confectioner's
- 1 egg
- 1/4 Tsp Baking Powder
- 1 Tbs heavy whipping cream

FROSTING INGREDIENTS
- 2 Tbs Monkfruit Confectioners
- 2 Tbs Cream Cheese softened and room temp
- 1/4 tsp clear vanilla

Instructions
1. In a small bowl, whip up the egg.
2. Add the remaining ingredients and mix well until the batter is smooth and creamy.
3. Pour half the batter in a mini waffle maker and cook it for 2 1/2 to 3 minutes until it's fully cooked.
4. In a separate small bowl, add the sweetener, cream cheese, and vanilla. Mix the frosting until everything is well incorporated.
5. Spread the frosting on the waffle cake after it has completely cooled down to room temperature.

ITALIAN CREAM CHAFFLE CAKE
Nutrition: Cal 235; Fat 25 g; Carb 6 g; Protein 8 g
Serving 1; Cook time 20 min

Ingredients
SWEET CHAFFLE INGREDIENTS:
- 4 oz Cream Cheese softened and room temp
- 4 eggs
- 1 tablespoon melted butter
- 1 teaspoon vanilla extract
- 1/2 teaspoon cinnamon
- 1 tablespoon monkfruit sweetener or your favorite keto-approved sweetener
- 4 tablespoons coconut flour
- 1 tablespoon almond flour
- 1 1/2 teaspoons baking powder
- 1 tbs coconut shredded and unsweetened
- 1 tbs walnuts chopped

ITALIAN CREAM FROSTING INGREDIENTS:
- 2 oz cream cheese softened and room temp
- 2 tbs butter room temp
- 2 tbs monkfruit sweetener or your favorite keto-approved sweetener
- 1/2 teaspoon vanilla

Instructions
1. In a medium-size blender, add the cream cheese, eggs, melted butter, vanilla, sweetener, coconut flour, almond flour, and baking powder. Optional: Add the shredded coconut and walnuts to the mixture or save it for the frosting. Either way is great!

2. Blend the ingredients on high until it's smooth and creamy.
3. Preheat the mini waffle maker.
4. Add the ingredients to the preheated waffle maker.
5. Cook for about 2 to 3 minutes until the waffles are done.
6. Remove and allow the chaffles to cool.
7. In a separate bowl, start to make the frosting by adding all the ingredients together. Stir until it's smooth and creamy.
8. Once the chaffles have completely cool, frost the cake.

CARNIVORE CHAFFLEE
Nutrition: Cal 200; Fat 17 g; Carb 5 g; Protein 4 g
Serving 1; Cook time 12 min
Ingredients
- 1/4 cup pork panko crushed pork rinds
- 1/4 cup parmesan cheese grated
- 1 tsp GrillMates Roasted Garlic & Herb seasoning
- 1 egg beaten
Instructions
1. Combine all the ingredients in a small bowl and mix until fully combined.
2. Using a small baking sheet, layer it with parchment paper or a silicone mat.
3. Pat the mixture into a small circle with wet hands or use a silicone spatula to shape the pizza crust.
4. Oven baking time: Bake at 350 degrees in oven for 10 minutes on each side.
5. Mini Dash Waffle maker: Divide the batter into 2 and cook each portion for a minimum of 4 minutes until it forms a crust (longer if you are using a large waffle iron)
6. Air fryer baking time: Bake at 300 degrees for 8 minutes on each side.
7. Remove the carnivore pizza crust and put keto friendly sauce of choice on with any toppings you choose. She used cooked Italian sausage and black olives
8. Top with 1/3 c mozzarella cheese.
9. Put back in the oven, air fryer or microwave just long enough to melt the cheese until it's golden brown. The oven or air fryer might take 3 to 4 minutes and the microwave may only take 1 minute.

AVOCADO TOAST CHAFFLE
Nutrition: Cal 176; Fat 15 g; Carb 2 g; Protein 12 g
Serving 1; Cook time 10 min
Ingredients
- 1/2 cup mozzarella cheese, shredded
- 1 egg
- Pinch of salt
- 1/2 avocado, mashed into guacamole and spread over the chaffle
Instructions
1. Preheat mini waffle iron.
2. In a small bowl, whip the egg.

3. Add the remaining ingredients and mix until fully combined.
4. Add 1/2 the mixture to the mini waffle maker and cook for about 3 to 4 minutes until it's done and golden brown.

BAGEL CHAFFLE
Nutrition: Cal 290; Fat 23 g; Carb 3 g; Protein 20 g
Serving 2; Cook time 10 min
Ingredients
- 1 egg
- 1/2 cup sharp cheddar
- 1 tsp Everything Bagel seasoning
Instructions
1. In a small bowl, whip the egg till fluffy.
2. Add 1/2 cup sharp cheddar shredded cheese to the egg mixture and mix until it's fully combined.
3. Preheat the waffle maker.
4. Once the mini waffle iron has been heated start making the chaffles.
5. For Crispy chaffles: add 1 tsp on shredded cheese to the hot waffle iron for 30 seconds before adding the egg batter mixture.
6. Pour half the mixture into the waffle iron.
7. Sprinkle the top of the mixture with the Everything Bagel Seasoning and close the lid.
8. Cook it for about 3 to 4 minutes or until the steam stops coming up from the waffle iron. Don't open the waffle iron before 3 minutes or else you will have a melted cheese gooey mess. The cheese needs to cook long enough to form a nice crust.

KETO FLUFFERNUTTER SANDWICH
Nutrition: Cal 142; Fat 3 g; Carb 28 g; Protein 4 g
Serving 1; Cook time 10 min
Ingredients
CHAFFLE SANDWICH BREAD
- 1 tablespoons Almond Flour
- 1 teaspoon Water
- 1 tablespoon Dukes Mayonnaise
- 1/8 teaspoon baking powder
- 1 egg
- Pinch of pink Himalayan salt
MARSHMALLOW FLUFF
- 1 cup liquid allulose sweetener
- 1 teaspoon vanilla extract
- 1/4 cup water
- 1 packet of Knox unflavored gelatin
ADDITIONAL FILLING
- Sugar Free Peanut Butter
Instructions
CHAFFLE SANDWICH BREAD
1. Mix all the ingredients together in a small bowl.
2. Pour half the batter into a waffle maker and cook for about 3 1/2 to 4 minutes or until golden brown.

3. Set aside to cool.

KETO MARSHMALLOW FLUFF INSTRUCTIONS

1. In a small bowl, add the water.

2. Sprinkle the packet of unflavored gelatin over the water and let it set for about 2 minutes. Give it a little stir to help combine all the gelatin if needed.

3. Using a stand mixer, add the prepared gelatin, vanilla extract, and liquid allulose to the bowl.

4. Add the whisk attachment.

5. Turn on the mixer to level 2 (slow) until the whisk begins to move.

6. Once the mixture has begun to move, turn the mixer speed all the way up to level 10. I used the splash guard on my mixer but you may not need to if your bowl is deep enough.

7. Set a timer for exactly 20 minutes. You will see the liquid start to get texture at the 10-minute mark but to make it extra fluffy go the full 20 minutes.

8. Set aside when complete.

ASSEMBLY INSTRUCTIONS

1. After the chaffles and marshmallow fluff are made. Take one of the chaffle sandwich bread pieces and layer a good amount of sugar-free peanut butter on it.

2. Next, add a dollop of marshmallow fluff to the peanut butter layer.

3. Top with the second chaffle sandwich bread and enjoy! Your taste buds will thank you later!

KETO SWEET BREAD CHAFFLE

Nutrition: Cal 199; Fat 18 g; Carb 3 g; Protein 7 g
Serving 1; Cook time 10 min

Ingredients

- 1 tbs almond flour
- 1 egg
- 1 tbs mayo
- 1/8 tsp baking powder
- 1 tbs Allulose sweetener powdered
- 1/4 tsp cinnamon
- 1/8 tsp salt

Instructions

1. Stir all ingredients together. Let rest for 5 min.

2. Stir again.

3. Preheat the mini waffle iron

4. Put half of dough in mini waffle maker.

5. Cook 3 minutes.

6. Repeat. Let cool

LOW CARB REUBEN CHAFFLE

Nutrition: Cal 319; Fat 26 g; Carb 6 g; Protein 17 g
Serving 2; Cook time 10 min

Ingredients

RYE BREAD CHAFFLE

- 1 egg
- 2 tablespoons almond flour
- 1 tablespoon melted butter
- 1 tablespoon mozzarella cheese

- pinch salt
- pinch garlic powder
- 1/2 teaspoon baking powder
- 1/2 teaspoon of caraway seeds

REUBEN SANDWICH

- 2 tablespoons of sauerkraut
- 2 slices of swiss cheese
- 1-2 ounces thinly sliced corned beef or pastrami

RUSSIAN SAUCE

- 1 tablespoon mayo
- 1 teaspoon sugar-free ketchup
- 1 teaspoon dill relish
- pinch of monk fruit sweetener

Instructions

1. Preheat mini waffle maker.

2. Mix all rye bread chaffle ingredients in a small bowl.

3. Cook chaffles for 4 minutes in the mini waffle maker.

4. Mix together sauce ingredients in a small bowl.

5. Layer sandwich together and enjoy!

KETO LEMON CHAFFLE

Nutrition: Cal 221; Fat 20 g; Carb 5 g; Protein 6 g
Serving 4; Cook time 25 min

Ingredients

CHAFFLE CAKE:

- 2 oz cream cheese room temp and softened
- 2 eggs
- 2 tsp butter melted
- 2 tbs coconut flour
- 1 tsp monkfruit powdered confectioners blend (add more if you like it sweeter)
- 1 tsp baking powder
- 1/2 tsp lemon extract
- 20 drops cake batter extract

CHAFFLE FROSTING:

- 1/2 cup heavy whipping cream
- 1 tbs monkfruit powdered confectioners blend
- 1/4 tsp lemon extract

OPTIONAL

- Add lemon peel for extra flavor!

Instructions

1. Preheat the mini waffle maker

2. Add all of the ingredients for the chaffle cake in a blender and mix it until the batter is nice and smooth. This should only take a couple of minutes.

3. Use an ice cream scoop and fill the waffle iron with one full scoop of batter. This size of the ice cream scoop is about 3 tablespoons and fits perfectly in the mini waffle maker.

4. While the chaffles are cooking, start making the frosting.

5. In a medium-size bowl, add the chaffle frosting ingredients.

6. Mix the ingredients until the frosting is thick with peaks.

7. All the chaffles to completely cool before frosting the cake.

8. Optional: Add lemon peel for extra flavor!

COCONUT CREAM CAKE CHAFFLE
Nutrition: Cal 160; Fat 14 g; Carb 6 g; Protein 5 g
Serving 6; Cook time 25 min

Ingredients
CHAFFLES:
- 2 eggs
- 1 ounce cream cheese softened to room temperature
- 2 tablespoons finely shredded unsweetened coconut
- 2 tablespoons powdered sweetener blend such as Swerve or Lakanto
- 1 tablespoon melted butter or coconut oil
- 1/2 teaspoon coconut extract
- 1/2 teaspoon vanilla extract

FILLING:
- 1/3 cup coconut milk
- 1/3 cup unsweetened almond or cashew milk
- 2 eggs yolks
- 2 tablespoons powdered sweetener blend such as Swerve or Lakanto
- 1/4 teaspoon xanthan gum
- 2 teaspoons butter
- Pinch of salt
- 1/4 cup finely shredded unsweetened coconut

OPTIONAL GARNISHES:
- Sugar-free whipped cream
- 1 tablespoon finely shredded unsweetened coconut toasted until lightly brown

Instructions
FOR THE CHAFFLES:
1. Heat mini Dash waffle iron until thoroughly hot.
2. Beat all chaffle ingredients together in a small bowl.
3. Add a heaping 2 tablespoons batter to waffle iron and cook until golden brown and the waffle iron stops steaming, about 5 minutes.
4. Repeat 3 times to make 4 chaffles. You only need 3 for the recipe.

FOR THE FILLING:
1. Heat the coconut and almond milk in a small saucepan over medium-low heat. It should be steaming hot, but not simmering or boiling.
2. In a separate bowl, beat the egg yolks together lightly. While whisking the milk constantly, slowly drizzle the egg yolks into the milk.
3. Heat, stirring constantly until the mixture thickens slightly. Do not boil. Whisk in the sweetener.
4. While whisking constantly, slowly sprinkle in the xanthan gum. Continue to cook for 1 minute.
5. Remove from the heat and add the remaining ingredients.
6. Pour coconut cream filling into a container, cover the surface with plastic wrap and refrigerate until cool. The plastic wrap prevents a skin from forming on the filling. The mixture will thicken as is cools.

CAKE ASSEMBLY:

1. Spread 1/3 of the filling over each of 3 chaffles, stack them together to make a cake, top with whipped cream and garnish with toasted coconut.

CRANBERRY SWIRL CHAFFLES WITH ORANGE CREAM CHEESE
Nutrition: Cal 260; Fat 24 g; Carb 6 g; Protein 12 g
Serving 6; Cook time 10 min

Ingredients
CRANBERRY SAUCE:
- 1/2 cup cranberries fresh or frozen
- 2 Tbsp granulated erythritol
- 1/2 cup water
- 1/2 tsp vanilla extract

CHAFFLES:
- 1 egg
  - ounce cream cheese at room temperature
- 1 Tbsp erythritol blend such as Swerve, Pyure or Lakanto
- 1/2 tsp vanilla extract
- 1 tsp coconut flour
- 1/4 tsp baking powder

FROSTING:
- 1 ounce cream cheese at room temperature
- 1 Tbsp butter room temperature
- 1 Tbsp confectioner's sweetener such as Swerve
- 1/8 tsp orange extract OR 2 drops orange essential oil
- A few strands of grated orange zest for garnish optional

Instructions
FOR THE CRANBERRY SWIRL:
1. Combine the cranberries, water, and erythritol in a medium saucepan. Bring to a boil, then reduce heat to a gentle simmer.
2. Simmer for 10-15 minutes, until the cranberries pop and the sauce thickens.
3. Remove from heat and stir in the vanilla extract.
4. Mash the berries with the back of a spoon until a chunky sauce forms.
5. The sauce will thicken off the heat significantly.

FOR THE CHAFFLES:
1. Preheat mini Dash waffle iron until thoroughly hot.
2. In a medium bowl, whisk all chaffle ingredients together until well combined.
3. Spoon 2 tablespoons of batter into a waffle iron.
4. Add 1/2 of the cranberry sauce in little dollops over the batter of each chaffle.
5. Close and cook 3-5 minutes, until done. Remove to a wire rack.
6. Repeat for the second chaffle.

FOR THE FROSTING:
1. Mix all ingredients, except orange zest, together until smooth and spread over each chaffle.
2. Top with optional orange zest.

ALMOND JOY CAKE CHAFFLE

Nutrition: Cal 130; Fat 10 g; Carb 6 g; Protein 3 g
Serving 6; Cook time 20 min

Ingredients
CHOCOLATE CHAFFLES:
- 1 egg
- 1 ounce cream cheese
- 1 tablespoon almond flour
- 1 tablespoon unsweetened cocoa powder
- 1 tablespoon erythritol sweetener blend such as Swerve, Pyure or Lakanto
- 1/2 teaspoon vanilla extract
- 1/4 teaspoon instant coffee powder

COCONUT FILLING:
- 1 1/2 teaspoons coconut oil melted
- 1 tablespoon heavy cream
- 1/4 cup unsweetened finely shredded coconut
- 2 ounces cream cheese
- 1 tablespoon confectioner's sweetener such as Swerve
- 1/4 teaspoon vanilla extract
- 14 whole almonds

Instructions
FOR THE CHAFFLES:
1. Preheat mini Dash waffle iron until thoroughly hot.
2. In a medium bowl, whisk all chaffle ingredients together until well combined.
3. Pour half of the batter into waffle iron.
4. Close and cook 3-5 minutes, until done. Remove to a wire rack.
5. Repeat for the second chaffle.

FOR THE FILLING:
1. Soften cream to room temperature or warm in the microwave for 10 seconds.
2. Add all ingredients to a bowl and mix until smooth and well-combined.

ASSEMBLY:
1. Spread half the filling on one chaffle and place 7 almonds evenly on top of the filling.
2. Repeat with the second chaffle and stack together.

PUMPKIN CHAFFLE KETO SUGAR COOKIES

Nutrition: Cal 160; Fat 12 g; Carb 4 g; Protein 6 g
Serving 1; Cook time 10 min

Ingredients
KETO SUGAR COOKIE INGREDIENTS
- 1 T Butter melted
- 1 T Sweetener
- 1 Egg Yolk
- 1/8 tsp Vanilla Extract
- 1/8 tsp Cake Batter Extract
- 3 T Almond Flour
- 1/8 tsp Baking Powder

ICING INGREDIENTS
- 1 T Confectioners Sweetener
- 1/4 tsp Vanilla Extract
- 1-2 tsp Water

SPRINKLES INGREDIENTS
- 1 T Granular Sweetener mixed with 1 drop of food coloring. Mix well.

Instructions
1. Stir all ingredients together. Let rest for 5 min.
2. Stir again.
3. Refrigerate for 15 mins.
4. Put 1/2 of dough in pumpkin waffle maker.
5. Cook 4 minutes.
6. Repeat. Let cool.
7. Add icing and sprinkles, if desired.

OKRA FRITTER CHAFFLES

Nutrition: Cal 130; Fat 8 g; Carb 4 g; Protein 6 g
Serving 4; Cook time 10 min

Ingredients
- 1 egg
- 1 Tbsp mayo
- 2 Tbsp heavy cream
- 1/2 Tbsp Tony Chachere's Creole Seasoning
- Onion powder
- Salt and pepper to taste
- 1/4 cup almond flour
- 1 cup okra fresh or frozen, thawed
- 1/4 cup mozzarella shredded

Instructions
1. Whip together egg, mayo, heavy cream, and seasoning.
2. Add almond flour.
3. Combine well and let batter rest for 5 -10 minutes.
4. Stir in okra.
5. Add 3 tablespoons of batter to preheated waffle maker or griddle.
6. Put a little shredded mozzarella on the griddle before adding batter and a little on top after adding it.
7. Cook for 5 mins.
8. Flip and cook a couple more minutes until it reaches your desired crispiness.
9. Remove to a cooling rack and sprinkle with sea salt.

ZUCCHINI NUT BREAD CHAFFLE

Nutrition: Cal 235; Fat 22 g; Carb 13 g; Protein 4 g
Serving 4; Cook time 15 min

Ingredients
- 1 cup shredded zucchini approximately 1 small zucchini
- 1 egg
- 1/2 teaspoon cinnamon
- 1 Tbsp plus 1 tsp erythritol blend such as Swerve, Pyure or Lakanto
- Dash ground nutmeg
- 2 tsp melted butter
- 1 ounce softened cream cheese

- 2 tsp coconut flour
- 1/2 tsp baking powder
- 3 tablespoons chopped walnuts or pecans

FROSTING

- 2 ounces cream cheese at room temperature
- 2 Tbsp butter at room temperature
- 1/4 tsp cinnamon
- 2 Tbsp caramel sugar-free syrup such as Skinny Girl, OR 1 Tbsp confectioner's sweetener, such as Swerve plus 1/8 tsp caramel extract
- 1 Tbsp chopped walnuts or pecans

Instructions

1. Grate zucchini and place in a colander over a plate to drain for 15 minutes. With your hands, squeeze out as much moisture as possible.
2. Preheat mini Dash waffle iron until thoroughly hot.
3. In a medium bowl, whisk all chaffle ingredients together until well combined.
4. Spoon a heaping 2 tablespoons of batter into waffle iron, close and cook 3-5 minutes, until done.
5. Remove to a wire rack. Repeat 3 times.

FROSTING

1. Mix all ingredients together until smooth and spread over each chaffle.
2. Top with additional chopped nuts.

TURKEY BURGER WITH HALLOUMI CHEESE CHAFFLE

Nutrition: Cal 222; Fat 18 g; Carb 3 g; Protein 14 g
Serving 4; Cook time 10 min

Ingredients

- 1 lb Ground Turkey raw (no need to precook the turkey)
- 8 oz Halloumi shredded
- 1 zucchini medium, shredded
- 2 tbsp Chives chopped
- 1/2 tsp Salt
- 1/4 tsp Pepper

Instructions

1. Add all ingredients to a bowl mix thoroughly together.
2. Shape into 8 evenly sized patties
3. Preheat mini griddle.
4. Cook the patties 5-7 minutes

KETO TUNA MELT CHAFFLE

Nutrition: Cal 125; Fat 5 g; Carb 1,5 g; Protein 20 g
Serving 2; Cook time 10 min

Ingredients

- 1 packet Tuna 2.6 oz with no water I used the Jalapeno Tuna for added flavor
- 1/2 cup mozzarella cheese
- 1 egg
- pinch salt

Instructions

1. Preheat the mini waffle maker

2. In a small bowl, add the egg and whip it up.
3. Add the tuna, cheese, and salt and mix well.
4. Optional step for an extra crispy crust: Add a teaspoon of cheese to the mini waffle maker for about 30 seconds before adding the recipe mixture. This will allow the cheese to get crispy when the tuna chaffle is done cooking. I prefer this method!
5. Add 1/2 the mixture to the waffle maker and cook it for a minimum of 4 minutes.
6. Remove it and cook the last tuna chaffle for another 4 minutes.

GERMAN CHOCOLATE CHAFFLE CAKE

Nutrition: Cal 270; Fat 24 g; Carb 8 g; Protein 8 g
Serving 4; Cook time 10 min

Ingredients

CHOCOLATE CHAFFLE

- 2 eggs
- 1 tablespoon melted butter
- 1 tablespoon cream cheese softened to room temperature
- 2 tablespoons unsweetened cocoa powder or unsweetened raw cacao powder
- 2 tablespoons almond flour
- 2 teaspoons coconut flour
- 2 tablespoons Pyure granulated sweetener blend
- 1/2 teaspoon baking powder
- 1/2 teaspoon instant coffee granules dissolved in 1 tablespoon hot water
- 1/2 teaspoon vanilla extract
- 2 pinches salt

FILLING

- 1 egg yolk
- 1/4 cup heavy cream
- 2 tablespoons Pyure granulated sweetener blend
- 1 tablespoon butter
- 1/2 teaspoon caramel or maple extract
- 1/4 cup chopped pecans
- 1/4 cup unsweetened flaked coconut
- 1 teaspoon coconut flour

Instructions

CHAFFLE

1. Preheat mini Dash waffle iron until thoroughly hot.
2. In a medium bowl, whisk all ingredients together until well combined.
3. Spoon a heaping 2 tablespoons of batter into waffle iron, close and cook 3-5 minutes, until done.
4. Remove to a wire rack.
5. Repeat 3 times.

FILLING

1. In a small saucepan over medium heat, combine the egg yolk, heavy cream, butter, and sweetener.
2. Simmer slowly, stirring constantly for 5 minutes.
3. Remove from heat and stir in extract, pecans, flaked coconut, and coconut flour.

KETO "APPLE" FRITTER CHAFFLES

Nutrition: Cal 180; Fat 15 g; Carb 5 g; Protein 8 g
Serving 2; Cook time 20 min

Ingredients
"APPLE" FRITTER FILLING
- 2 cups diced jicama
- 1/4 cup plus 1 tablespoon Swerve sweetener blend
- 4 tablespoons butter
- 1 teaspoon cinnamon
- 1/8 teaspoon nutmeg
- Dash ground cloves
- 1/2 teaspoon vanilla
- 20 drops Lorann Oils apple flavoring

CHAFFLE
- 2 eggs
- 1/2 cup grated mozzarella cheese
- 1 tablespoon almond flour
- 1 teaspoon coconut flour
- 1/2 teaspoon baking powder

GLAZE
- 1 tablespoon butter
- 2 teaspoons heavy cream
- 3 tablespoons powdered sweetener such as Swerve Confectioners
- 1/4 teaspoon vanilla extract

Instructions
"APPLE" FRITTER FILLING
1. Peel the jicama and cut into small dice.
2. In a medium skillet over medium-low heat, melt the butter and add the diced jicama and sweetener.
3. Let simmer slowly for 10-20 minutes until the jicama is soft, stirring often. Do not use high heat or the sweetener will caramelize quickly and burn. It should develop a light amber color and will thicken.
4. When the jicama is soft, remove from heat and stir in the spices and flavorings.

"APPLE" FRITTER CHAFFLE
1. Preheat waffle iron until hot.
2. In a medium bowl, beat all ingredients, except cheese. Stir the jicama mixture into the eggs.
3. Place 1 tablespoon grated cheese on that waffle iron.
4. Spoon 2 heaping tablespoons of the egg/jicama mixture into the waffle iron and top with another tablespoon cheese.
5. Close the waffle maker and cook 5-7 minutes until nicely browned and crunchy.
6. Remove to a wire rack.
7. Repeat 3-4 times.

KETO "APPLE" FRITTER CHAFFLE ICING
1. Melt butter in a small saucepan and add the Swerve and heavy cream.
2. Simmer over medium heat for 5 minutes, or until slightly thickened.
3. Stir in vanilla.
4. Drizzle the hot icing over the chaffles. It will harden as it cools.

BLUEBERRY AND BRIE GRILLED CHEESE CHAFFLE

Nutrition: Cal 200; Fat 18 g; Carb 3 g; Protein 20 g
Serving 1; Cook time 10 min

Ingredients
CHAFFLE
- 1 egg beaten
- 1/4 cup mozzarella shredded
- 1 tsp Swerve confectioners
- 1 T cream cheese softened
- 1/4 tsp baking powder
- 1/2 tsp vanilla extract

BLUEBERRY COMPOTE
- 1 cup blueberries washed
- Zest of 1/2 lemon
- 1 T lemon juice freshly squeezed
- 1 T Swerve Confectioners
- 1/8 tsp xanthan gum
- 2 T water

Instructions
CHAFFLE
1. Mix everything together.
2. Cook 1/2 batter for 2 1/2- 3 minutes in the mini waffle maker
3. Repeat.
4. Let cool slightly on a cooling rack.

BLUEBERRY COMPOTE
1. Add everything except xanthan gum to a small sauce pan. Bring to a boil, reduce heat and simmer for 5-10 minutes until it starts to thicken. Sprinkle with xanthan gum and stir well. Remove from heat and let cool. Store in refrigerator until ready to use.

GRILLED CHEESE
2. Heat butter in a small pan over medium heat. Place Brie slices on a Chaffle and top with generous 1 T scoop of prepared blueberry compote.
3. Place sandwich in pan and grill, flipping once until waffle is golden and cheese has melted, about 2 minutes per side.

PECAN PIE CHAFFLE CAKE

Nutrition: Cal 270; Fat 15 g; Carb 8 g; Protein 10 g
Serving 1; Cook time 20 min

Ingredients
PECAN PIE FILLING
- 2 T butter softened
- 1 T Sukrin Gold
- 1/8 tsp blackstrap molasses optional but helps with color and flavor
- 2 T Maple Bourbon Pecan Skinny Syrup
- 2 T heavy whipping cream
- 2 large egg yolks
- Pinch salt
- 2 T pecans lightly toasted (I did it in the Airfryer)

PECAN PIE CHAFFLE

- •1 egg
- •1 T heavy whipping cream
- •2 T cream cheese softened
- •1/2 tsp maple extract Olive Nation
- •3 T almond flour
- •1 T oat fiber or another T almond flour
- •1 T Sukrin Gold
- •1/2 tsp baking powder
- •2 T pecans chopped

Instructions
PECAN PIE FILLING

1. Add butter, sweetener, heavy whipping cream and syrups to a small saucepan on low heat.
2. Whisk until well combined.
3. Remove from heat.
4. Pour 1/2 of the mixture into egg yolks and whisk well.
5. Add that mixture back into the saucepan while stirring continuously.
6. Add a pinch of salt and pecan.
7. Let simmer until it starts to thicken. Remove from heat and let cool while making the Chaffles.

PECAN PIE CHAFFLE CAKE

1. Mix all ingredients except pecans in a small blender for about 15 seconds. Stop and scrape down the sides with a spatula, and continue mixing for another 15 seconds until well blended. Mix in pecans with a spatula. Pour 3 T of batter in preheated mini waffle maker. Cook for 1 1/2 mins. Remove to cooling rack. Repeat. Will make 3 full Chaffles with a tiny one for tasting!
2. Put 1/3 of the pecan pie filling on each Chaffle and assemble as desired!

TIRAMISU CHAFFLE CAKE

Nutrition: Cal 300; Fat 27 g; Carb 12 g; Protein 8 g
Serving 4; Cook time 10 min

Ingredients

- •2 tbs Unsalted Butter melted
- •2 tsp Instant Coffee Dry Mix
- •1 oz Cream Cheese softened
- •2 Large Eggs room temp
- •1 tsp Pure Vanilla Extract
- •1/2 tsp Hazelnut Extract optional
- •1/4 c. Blanched Almond Flour fine
- •2 tbs Coconut Flour
- •1 tbs Organic Cacao Powder
- •2 tbs Powdered Monkfruit Sweetener by Lakanto
- •1 tsp Baking Powder
- •1/8 tsp Himalayan Fine Pink Salt
- •4 oz. Mascarpone Cheese by Cello
- •1/4 c. Lakanto Powdered Sweetener
- •1/2 tsp Pure Vanilla Extract
- •1/2 tbs Organic Cacao Powder
- •1/2 tsp Instant Coffee Dry Mix

Instructions

1. Melt the butter in a microwave safe dish, then stir in instant coffee.
2. In a medium mixing bowl- add cream cheese, eggs and extracts. Blend well.
3. Add all dry ingredients and mix until incorporated.
4. Scoop 2 heaping tbs of batter into waffle maker, cook 3-4 mins each.
5. Make the chaffles and let cool while making the frosting.
6. In a separate bowl- add Mascarpone, sweetener, vanilla.
7. Split cream into 2 separate bowls if you want two layers of frosting.
8. Add cacao and instant coffee into second bowl, blend well.
9. Layer the white cream over each chaffle and stack.
10. (optionallRefrigerate the cake for 20 minutes.
11. Spread the second cream over top and around the sides.
12. Put cake in the fridge for 20-30 minutes to let the frosting set up.
13. Cut into slices and enjoy!

CARROT CHAFFLE CAKE

Nutrition: Cal 180; Fat 7 g; Carb 5 g; Protein 4 g
Serving 6; Cook time 16 min

Ingredients

- •1/2 cup carrot shredded
- •1 egg
- •2 T butter melted
- •2 T heavy whipping cream
- •3/4 cup almond flour
- •1 T walnuts chopped
- •2 T powdered sweetener
- •2 tsp cinnamon
- •1 tsp pumpkin spice
- •1 tsp baking powder

CREAM CHEESE FROSTING

- •4 oz cream cheese softened
- •1/4 cup powdered sweetener
- •1 tsp vanilla extract
- •1-2 T heavy whipping cream

Instructions

1. Mix your dry ingredients - almond flour, cinnamon, pumpkin spice, baking powder, powdered sweetener, and walnut pieces.
2. Add the wet ingredients- grated carrot, egg, melted butter, heavy cream.
3. Add 3 T batter to preheated mini waffle maker. Cook 2 1/2 - 3 minutes.
4. Mix frosting ingredients together with a hand mixer with whisk attachment until well combined.
5. Stack waffles and add frosting between each layer!

BANANA PUDDING CHAFFLE CAKE
Nutrition: Cal 200; Fat 12 g; Carb 10 g; Protein 4 g
Serving 1; Cook time 20 min

Ingredients
BANANA CHAFFLE
- 1 oz cream cheese softened
- 1/4 cup mozzarella cheese shredded
- 1 egg beaten
- 1 tsp banana extract
- 2 T sweetener
- 1 tsp baking powder
- 4 T almond flour

PUDDING
- 1 large egg yolk
- 1/2 cup heavy whipping cream
- 3 T powdered sweetener
- 1/4 - 1/2 tsp xanthan gum
- 1/2 tsp banana extract

Instructions
1. Combine the heavy cream, powdered sweetener and egg yolk in a small saucepan. Whisk constantly until the sweetener dissolves and mixture thickens.
2. Simmer 1 minute. Add the xanthan gum and whisk.
3. Remove from heat and add a pinch of salt and the banana extract and stir well.
4. Transfer to a glass dish and cover surface of the pudding with plastic wrap. Refrigerate.
5. Mix all ingredients together. Cook in preheated mini waffle maker.

CAP'N CRUNCH CEREAL CHAFFLE CAKE
Nutrition: Cal 155; Fat 11 g; Carb 6 g; Protein 6 g
Serving 2; Cook time 10 min

Ingredients
- 1 egg
- 2 tablespoons almond flour
- 1/2 teaspoon coconut flour
- 1 tablespoon butter melted
- 1 tablespoon cream cheese room temp
- 20 drops Captain Cereal flavoring
- 1/4 teaspoon vanilla extract
- 1/4 teaspoon baking powder
- 1 tablespoon confectioners sweetener
- 1/8 teaspoon xanthan gum

Instructions
1. Preheat the mini waffle maker.
2. Mix or blend all of the ingredients until smooth and creamy. Allow the batter to rest for a few minutes for the flour to absorb the liquid.
3. Add about 2 to 3 tablespoons of batter to your waffle maker and cook it for about 2 1/2 minutes.
4. Top with fresh whipped cream (I added 10 drops of Captain cereal flavorinand syrup.

JICAMA LOADED BAKED POTATO CHAFFLE
Nutrition: Cal 168; Fat 12 g; Carb 5 g; Protein 10 g
Serving 4; Cook time 10 min

Ingredients
- 1 large jicama root
- 1/2 medium onion minced
- 2 garlic cloves pressed
- 1 cup cheese of choice I used Halloumi
- 2 eggs whisked
- Salt and Pepper

Instructions
1. Peel jicama and shred in food processor
2. Place shredded jicama in a large colander, sprinkle with 1-2 tsp of salt. Mix well and allow to drain.
3. Squeeze out as much liquid as possible (very important step)
4. Microwave for 5-8 minutes
5. Mix all ingredients together
6. Sprinkle a little cheese on waffle iron before adding 3 T of the mixture, sprinkle a little more cheese on top of the mixture
7. Cook for 5 minutes. Flip and cook 2 more.
8. Top with a dollop of sour cream, bacon pieces, cheese, and chives!

CHEESY GARLIC BREAD CHAFFLE
Nutrition: Cal 141; Fat 9 g; Carb 3 g; Protein 12 g
Serving 2; Cook time 10 min

Ingredients
GARLIC BREAD CHAFFLE
- 1/2 cup mozzarella cheese shredded
- 1 egg
- 1 tsp Italian seasoning
- 1/2 tsp garlic powder
- 1 tsp cream cheese I prefer to use flavored cream cheese such as chive and onion or jalapeno but you can use plain too

GARLIC BUTTER TOPPING
- 1 tbs butter
- 1/2 tsp Italian seasoning
- 1/2 tsp garlic powder

CHEESY BREAD
- 2 tbs mozzarella cheese shredded
- dash of parsley or more Italian seasoning

Instructions
1. Preheat your mini waffle maker.
2. Preheat your oven to 350F.
3. In a small bowl, mix together all of the garlic bread chaffle ingredients until it's well combined.
4. Divide the mixture in half and cook the first chaffle for a minimum of 4 minutes. If you like you chaffles a bit crunchy on the outside, I would suggest you place a tsp of shredded cheese onto the waffle maker 30 seconds

before adding the chaffle ingredients. This will create a nice, crunchy crust that's pretty amazing!

5. After you cook both of the garlic bread chaffles in the waffle maker, transfer them to a baking sheet.

6. In a separate small bowl, melt the butter in the microwave for about 10 seconds.

7. Add the garlic butter seasonings to the butter mixture.

8. Spread the butter mixture onto the warm chaffles with a basting brush.

9. Sprinkle a small amount of mozzarella on top of the garlic bread chaffles and then sprinkle with more Italian seasoning.

10. Bake for 5 minutes at 350F degrees. This is just enough time to melt the cheese on top of the Cheesy Garlic Bread Chaffles!

11. Serve warm and enjoy them with a sugar free marinara sauce such as Rao's marinara sauce!

BACON CHEDDAR BAY BISCUITS CHAFFLE

Nutrition: Cal 185; Fat 13 g; Carb 4,3 g; Protein 8 g
Serving 6; Cook time 10 min

Ingredients
- 1/2 cup Almond Flour
- 1/4 cup Oat Fiber
- 3 strips of Bacon cooked and crumbled
- 1 Egg beaten
- 1/4 cup Sour Cream
- 1 T Bacon Grease melted
- 1 1/2 T Kerrygold Butter melted
- 1/2 cup Sharp Cheddar Cheese shredded
- 1/2 cup Smoked Gouda Cheese shredded
- 1/4 tsp Swerve Confectioners
- 1/2 tsp Garlic Salt
- 1/2 tsp Onion Powder
- 1/2 T Parsley dried
- 1/2 T Baking Powder
- 1/4 tsp Baking Soda

Instructions
1. Preheat mini waffle maker.
2. Mix almond flour, baking powder, baking soda, onion powder and garlic salt to a bowl and mix using a whisk.
3. In another bowl, add the eggs, bacon, sour cream, parsley, bacon grease, melted butter and cheese. Mix until combined.
4. Add the dry ingredients into the wet and mix.
5. Scoop 2-3 T of the mix into hot waffle iron and cook for 5-6 minutes.

EASY CHICKEN PARMESAN CHAFFLE

Nutrition: Cal 205; Fat 3 g; Carb 38 g; Protein 4 g
Serving 1; Cook time 10 min

Ingredients
CHAFFLE
- 1/2 cup canned chicken breast
- 1/4 cup cheddar cheese
- 1/8 cup parmesan cheese
- 1 egg
- 1 tsp Italian seasoning
- 1/8 tsp garlic powder
- 1 tsp cream cheese room temperature

TOPPING
- 2 slices of provolone cheese
- 1 tbs sugar free pizza sauce

Instructions
1. Preheat the mini waffle maker.
2. In a medium-size bowl, add all the ingredients and mix until it's fully incorporated.
3. Add a teaspoon of shredded cheese to the waffle iron for 30 seconds before adding the mixture. This will create the best crust and make it easier to take this heavy chaffle out of the waffle maker when it's done.
4. Pour half of the mixture in the mini waffle maker and cook it for a minimum of 4 to 5 minutes.
5. Repeat the above steps to cook the second Chicken Parmesan Chaffle.

KETO CORNBREAD CHAFFLE

Nutrition: Cal 150; Fat 12 g; Carb 1 g; Protein 10 g
Serving 2; Cook time 10 min

Ingredients
- 1 egg
- 1/2 cup cheddar cheese shredded (or mozzarella)
- 5 slices jalapeno optional - picked or fresh
- 1 tsp Frank's Red hot sauce
- 1/4 tsp corn extract this is the secret ingredient that is a must!
- pinch salt

Instructions
1. Preheat the mini waffle maker
2. In a small bowl, whip the egg.
3. Add the remaining ingredients and mix it until it's well incorporated.
4. Add a teaspoon of shredded cheese to the waffle maker for 30 seconds before adding the mixture. This will create a nice and crisp crust that is absolutely fantastic!
5. Add half the mixture to the preheated waffle maker.
6. Cook it for a minimum of 3 to 4 minutes. The longer you cook it the more crispy it gets.

KETO CHOCOLATE TWINKIE COPYCAT CHAFFLE

Nutrition: Cal 105; Fat 6 g; Carb 5 g; Protein 4,5 g
Serving 6; Cook time 10 min

Ingredients
- 2 tablespoons butter melted (cooled)
- 2 ounces cream cheese softened
- 2 large eggs room temp
- 1 tsp vanilla extract
- 1/4 cup Lakanto Confectioners

- Pinch of pink salt
- 1/4 cup almond flour
- 2 tablespoons coconut flour
- 2 tablespoons cacao powder
- 1 teaspoon baking powder

Instructions

1. Preheat the Corndog Maker.
2. Melt the butter and let it cool a minute.
3. Whisk the eggs into the butter until creamy.
4. Add vanilla, sweetener, salt and then blend well.
5. Add Almond flour, coconut flour, cacao powder, and baking powder.
6. Blend until well incorporated.
7. Add ~2 tablespoons batter to each well and spread across evenly.
8. Close lid, lock and let cook 4 minutes.
9. Remove and cool on a rack.

<u>Breads</u>

CRANBERRY BREAD

Nutrition: Cal 180; Fat 15 g; Carb 7 g; Protein 7 g
Serving 12; Cook time 75 min

Ingredients

- 2 cups almond flour
- 1/2 cup powdered erythritol or Swerve, (see Note)
- 1/2 tsp Steviva stevia powder (see Note)
- 1 1/2 tsp baking powder
- 1/2 tsp baking soda
- 1 tsp salt
- 4 tbsp unsalted butter, melted (or coconut oil)
- 1 tsp blackstrap molasses (optional [for brown sugar flavor])
- 4 large eggs at room temperature
- 1/2 cup coconut milk
- 1 bag cranberries, 12 oz

Instructions

1. Preheat oven to 350°F; grease a 9-by-5 inch loaf pan and set aside.
2. In a large bowl, whisk together flour, erythritol, stevia, baking powder, baking soda, and salt; set aside.
3. In a medium bowl, combine butter, molasses, eggs, and coconut milk.
4. Mix dry mixture into wet mixture until well combined.
5. Fold in cranberries. Pour batter into prepared pan.
6. Bake until a toothpick inserted in the center of the loaf comes clean, about 1 hour and 15 minutes.
7. Transfer pan to a wire rack; let bread cool 15 minutes before removing from pan.

CHOCOLATE ZUCCHINI BREAD

Nutrition: Cal 185 Fat 17 g; Carb 6 g; Protein 5 g
Serving 12; Cook time 50 min

Ingredients

- 1 1/2 cup almond flour (170 g)
- 1/4 cup unsweetened cocoa powder (25 g)
- 1 1/2 tsp baking soda
- 2 tsp ground cinnamon
- 1/4 tsp sea salt
- 1/2 cup sugar-free crystal sweetener (Monk fruit or erythritol) (100 g) or coconut sugar if refined sugar-free

WET INGREDIENTS

- 1 cup zucchini, finely grated measure packed, discard juice/liquid if there is some - about 2 small zucchini
- 1 large egg
- 1/4 cup + 2 TBSP canned coconut cream (100 ml)
- 1/4 cup extra virgin coconut oil, melted (60ml)
- 1 tsp vanilla extract
- 1 tsp apple cider vinegar

FILLING (OPTIONAL)

- 1/2 cup sugar-free chocolate chips
- 1/2 cup chopped walnuts (or nuts you like)

Instructions

1. Preheat oven to 180°C (375°F). Line a baking loaf pan (9 inches x 5 inches) with parchment paper. Set aside.
2. Remove both extremity of the zucchinis, keep skin on.
3. Finely grate the zucchini using a vegetable grater. Measure the amount needed in a measurement cup. Make sure you press/pack them firmly for a precise measure and to squeeze out any liquid from the grated zucchini, I usually don't have any! If you do, discard the liquid or keep for another recipe.
4. In a large mixing bowl, stir all the dry ingredients together: almond flour, unsweetened cocoa powder, sugar-free crystal sweetener, cinnamon, sea salt, and baking soda. Set aside.
5. Add all the wet ingredients into the dry ingredients: grated zucchini, coconut oil, coconut cream, vanilla, egg, apple cider vinegar.
6. Stir to combine all the ingredients together.
7. Stir in the chopped nuts and sugar-free chocolate chips.
8. Transfer the chocolate bread batter into the prepared loaf pan.
9. Bake 50 - 55 minutes—you may want to cover the bread loaf with a piece of foil after 40 minutes to avoid the top to darken too much, up to you.
10. The bread will stay slightly moist in the middle and firm up after fully cooled down.
11. Transfer pan to a wire rack; let bread cool 15 minutes before removing from pan.

CINNAMON ALMOND FLOUR BREAD

Nutrition: Cal 221; Fat 15 g; Carb 10 g; Protein 9 g
Serving 8; Cook time 30 min

Ingredients

- 2 cups fine blanched almond flour (I use Bob's Red Mill)
- 2 tbsp coconut flour
- 1/2 tsp sea salt
- 1 tsp baking soda
- 1/4 cup flaxseed meal or chia meal (ground chia or flaxseed, see notes for how to make your own)
- 5 eggs and 1 egg white whisked together
- 1.5 tsp apple cider vinegar or lemon juice
- 2 tbsp maple syrup or honey
- 2–3 tbsp of clarified butter (melted) or coconut oil (divided). Vegan butter also works.
- 1 tbsp cinnamon, plus extra for topping
- Optional: Chia seeds to sprinkle on top before baking

Instructions

1. Preheat oven to 350°F. Line an 8×4 bread pan with parchment paper at the bottom and grease the sides.
2. In a large bowl, mix together your almond flour, coconut flour, salt, baking soda, flaxseed meal or chia meal, and 1/2 tablespoon of cinnamon.

3. In another small bowl, whisk together your eggs and egg white. Then add in your maple syrup (or honey), apple cider vinegar, and melted butter (1.5 to 2 tablespoons).
4. Mix wet ingredients into dry. Be sure to remove any clumps that might have occurred from the almond flour or coconut flour.
5. Pour batter into a your greased loaf pan.
6. Bake at 350°F for 30-35 minutes, until a toothpick inserted into center of loaf comes out clean. Mine came to around 35 minutes, but I am at altitude.
7. Remove from the oven.
8. Next, whisk together the other 1 to 2 tablespoons of melted butter (or oil) and mix it with 1/2 tablespoon of cinnamon. Brush this on top of your cinnamon almond flour bread.
9. Cool and serve, or store for later.
10. Transfer pan to a wire rack; let bread cool 15 minutes before removing from pan.

BLUEBERRY ENGLISH MUFFIN BREAD

Nutrition: Cal 156; Fat 13 g; Carb 4 g; Protein 5 g
Serving 12; Cook time 45 min

Ingredients
- 1/2 cup almond butter, cashew, or peanut butter
- 1/4 cup butter ghee or coconut oil
- 1/2 cup almond flour
- 1/2 tsp salt
- 2 tsp baking powder
- 1/2 cup almond milk, unsweetened
- 5 eggs, beaten
- 1/2 cup blueberries

Instructions
1. Preheat oven to 350°F.
2. In a microwavable bowl melt nut butter and butter together for 30 seconds, stir until combined well.
3. In a large bowl, whisk almond flour, salt, and baking powder together. Pour the nut butter mixture into the large bowl and stir to combine.
4. Whisk the almond milk and eggs together then pour into the bowl and stir well.
5. Drop in fresh blueberries or break apart frozen blueberries and gently stir into the batter.
6. Line a loaf pan with parchment paper and lightly grease the parchment paper as well.
7. Pour the batter into the loaf pan and bake 45 minutes or until a toothpick in center comes out clean.
8. Cool for about 30 minutes then remove from pan.
9. Slice and toast each slice before serving. 1/2 cup chopped walnuts (or nuts you like)

PUMPKIN BREAD

Nutrition: Cal 165; Fat 14 g; Carb 6 g; Protein 5 g
Serving 10; Cook time 45 min

Ingredients
- 1/2 cup butter, softened
- 2/3 cup erythritol sweetener, like Swerve
- 4 eggs, large
- 3/4 cup pumpkin puree, canned
- 1 tsp vanilla extract
- 1 1/2 cup almond flour
- 1/2 cup coconut flour
- 4 tsp baking powder
- 1 tsp cinnamon
- 1/2 tsp nutmeg
- 1/4 tsp ginger
- 1/8 tsp cloves
- 1/2 tsp salt

Instructions
1. Preheat the oven to 350°F. Grease a 9"x5" loaf pan, and line with parchment paper.
2. In a large mixing bowl, cream the butter and sweetener together until light and fluffy.
3. Add the eggs, one at a time, and mix well to combine.
4. Add the pumpkin puree and vanilla, and mix well to combine.
5. In a separate bowl, stir together the almond flour, coconut flour, baking powder, cinnamon, nutmeg, ginger, cloves, and salt. Break up any lumps of almond flour or coconut flour.
6. Add the dry ingredients to the wet ingredients, and stir to combine. (Optionally, add up to 1/2 cup of mix-ins, like chopped nuts or chocolate chips.)
7. Pour the batter into the prepared loaf pan. Bake for 45 - 55 minutes, or until a toothpick inserted into the center of the loaf comes out clean.
8. If the bread is browning too quickly, you can cover the pan with a piece of aluminum foil.

ZUCCHINI BREAD WITH WALNUTS

Nutrition: Cal 200; Fat 18 g; Carb 3 g; Protein 5 g
Serving 16; Cook time 60 min

Ingredients
- 3 large eggs
- ½ cup olive oil
- 1 tsp vanilla extract
- 2 1/2 cups almond flour
- 1 1/2 cups erythritol
- ½ tsp salt
- 1 1/2 tsp baking powder
- ½ tsp nutmeg
- 1 tsp ground cinnamon
- ¼ tsp ground ginger
- 1 cup grated zucchini
- ½ cup chopped walnuts

Instructions
1. Preheat oven to 350°F. Whisk together the eggs, oil, and vanilla extract. Set to the side.
2. In another bowl, mix together the almond flour, erythritol, salt, baking powder, nutmeg, cinnamon, and ginger. Set to the side.

3. Using a cheesecloth or paper towel, take the zucchini and squeeze out the excess water.
4. Then, whisk the zucchini into the bowl with the eggs.
5. Slowly add the dry ingredients into the egg mixture using a hand mixer until fully blended.
6. Lightly spray a 9x5 loaf pan, and spoon in the zucchini bread mixture.
7. Then, spoon in the chopped walnuts on top of the zucchini bread. Press walnuts into the batter using a spatula.
8. Bake for 60-70 minutes at 350°F or until the walnuts on top look browned.

GARLIC BUTTER KETO BREAD
Nutrition: Cal 538; Fat 36 g; Carb 10 ; Protein 43 g
Serving 7; Cook time 20 min

Ingredients
- 2 1/2 cups mozzarella, shredded
- 2 oz cream cheese
- 3 eggs
- 1 1/2 cups almond flour (super-fine)
- 1 teaspoon baking powder
- 1/3 cup cooked bacon bits
- 1/2 cup grated Parmesan
- 1 teaspoon Italian seasoning
- 1/4 cup browned butter
- 4 garlic cloves, finely minced
- 1/2 cup fresh parsley, chopped

Instructions
1. To make this garlic butter keto bread recipe – Grease a medium cast-iron skillet with oil, butter or cooking spray and set aside. In a shallow plate, combine parmesan and Italian seasoning.
2. Melt Mozzarella and cream cheese in a large bowl for one minute in the microwave. Mix well with a spatula until smooth.
3. Combine the melted cheese, eggs, baking powder, almond flour, and bacon. Mix until smooth.
4. Using a large cookie scoop, scoop dough and bread roll into the parmesan and Italian seasoning mix. Place each bread roll into the prepared cast iron skillet. Sprinkle bread roll with more parmesan cheese. Place skillet in the refrigerator for 10 minutes. In the meantime, preheat your oven to 400°F .
5. Remove the cast iron skillet from the refrigerator. Bake the garlic butter bread for 20 to 25 minutes, until golden brown.
6. In the meantime, combine minced garlic, chopped parsley, and browned butter in a small bowl.
7. Brush generously the baked garlic butter keto bread with the garlic butter sauce and serve. Enjoy!

KETO BREAD
Nutrition: Cal 135; Fat 8 g; Carb 5 g; Protein 2 g
Serving 6; Cook time 70 min

Ingredients
- 1/3 cup (1¾ oz.) ground psyllium husk powder
- 1¼ cups (5 oz.) almond flour
- 2 tsp baking powder
- 1 tsp sea salt
- 1 cup water
- 2 tsp cider vinegar
- 3 egg whites
- 2 tbsp sesame seeds (optional)

Instructions
1. Preheat the oven to 350°F.
2. Mix the dry ingredients in a large bowl. Bring the water to a boil.
3. Add vinegar and egg whites to the dry ingredients, and combine well. Add boiling water, while beating with a hand mixer for about 30 seconds. Don't over mix the dough, the consistency should resemble Play-Doh.
4. Moisten hands with a little olive oil and shape dough into 6 separate rolls. Place on a greased baking sheet. Top with optional sesame seeds.
5. Bake on lower rack in the oven for 50–60 minutes, depending on the size of your bread rolls. They're done when you hear a hollow sound when tapping the bottom of the bun.
6. Serve with butter and toppings of your choice.

KETO BAGELS
Nutrition: Cal 220 Fat 25 g; Carb 6 g; Protein 8 g
Serving 4; Cook time 35 min

Ingredients
BAGELS
- 7 oz. (1¾ cups) mozzarella cheese
- 1 oz. (2 tbsp) cream cheese
- 1½ cups (6 oz.) almond flour
- 2 tsp baking powder
- 1 egg

TOPPING
- 2 tsp flaxseed
- 1 tsp sesame seeds
- ½ tsp sea salt
- ¼ tsp poppy seeds
- 1 egg

Instructions
1. Preheat the oven to 430°F and line a large baking tray with parchment paper.
2. Place the mozzarella and cream cheese in a medium, microwave-safe bowl and microwave on high for 1 minute. Remove and stir. Repeat in 30-second bursts until the cheese has melted and can be easily combined.
3. In a separate bowl, whisk together the almond flour and baking powder, until well combined. Add the egg and almond flour mix, to the melted cheese. Mix well until

a smooth dough forms. Kneading it on a non-stick surface helps with this process!

4. Divide the dough into as many parts as portions in the recipe, and form into bun shapes. Place on your lined baking tray.
5. Use your thumb, or the handle of a wooden spoon, to push a hole through the center of each bun and then shape it further until you have bagel shapes.
6. Place the seeds and seasoning for the topping mix into a small bowl and give it a quick stir to combine.
7. Crack the second egg into a bowl and beat until combined.
8. Brush the top of each bagel liberally with the beaten egg and then sprinkle with your topping mixture.
9. Bake in the oven for 15 minutes

MEDITERRANEAN KETO FLATBREAD

Nutrition: Cal 180 Fat 12 g; Carb 3 g; Protein 4 g
Serving 6; Cook time 40 min

Ingredients
- ½ cup (1⅔ oz.) coconut flour
- 1 tbsp ground psyllium husk powder
- ¼ cup olive oil
- 1 cup boiling water
- ½ cup (1⅓ oz.) shredded Parmesan cheese or mozzarella cheese
- ½ tsp sea salt
- ¼ tsp granulated garlic
- ½ tbsp black peppercorns
- ½ tbsp dried rosemary

Instructions
1. Whisk the dry ingredients together in a mixing bowl.
2. Add olive oil and cheese.
3. Add the hot water last, stirring as it is added. Continue stirring until the psyllium fiber and coconut flour have absorbed all of the water.
4. Flatten the dough onto parchment paper on a baking sheet. Roll or press out the dough until it is thin and even. Be sure that it is a uniform thickness and less than 1/8 -inch (3mm) thick.
5. Bake at 350°F for 20 to 25 minutes. Baking time will depend on the thickness of the dough.
6. When browned, transfer to a cooling rack, peel away the parchment paper and allow the flatbread to cool. Use a pizza cutter to cut the flatbread into squares for sandwiches. Store any leftovers in the refrigerator.

LOW CARB CLOUD BREAD

Nutrition: Cal 200 Fat 16 g; Carb 4 g; Protein 4 g
Serving 4; Cook time 35 min

Ingredients
- 3 eggs
- 1 pinch salt
- 4½ oz. (9 tbsp) cream cheese
- ½ tbsp ground psyllium husk powder

- ½ tsp baking powder

Instructions
1. Separate the egg whites from the yolks into two different bowls.
2. Whip the egg whites and salt with an electric mixer or a handheld whisk until very stiff. This will take a few minutes with the electric mixer and several minutes if done by hand. They're ready when you scoop out a mound of egg white and it holds its peak. If you're using the cream of tartar (see tips below), add it as you whip the egg whites.
3. Mix the egg yolks and the cream cheese well. If you want, add the psyllium seed husk and baking powder — this makes it more bread-like.
4. Gently fold the egg whites into the egg yolk mix – try to keep the air in the egg whites.
5. Place as many dollops of the mixture as servings in the recipe on a parchment paper-lined baking tray. Spread out the circles with a spatula to about ½ inch (1 cm) thick.
6. Bake in the middle of the oven at 300° F (150° C) for about 25 minutes until golden.

NUT-FREE KETO BREAD

Nutrition: Cal 210; Fat 17 g; Carb 4 g; Protein 5 g
Serving 20; Cook time 50 min

Ingredients
- 6 large eggs
- 3 cups (12 oz.) shredded cheese
- 1 oz. (2 tbsp) cream cheese
- 2 tbsp ground psyllium husk powder
- 3 tsp baking powder
- ½ cup (1¾ oz.) oat fiber
- ½ tsp salt
- 1 tbsp butter, melted

TOPPING
- 3 tbsp sesame seeds
- 2 tbsp poppy seeds

Instructions
1. Preheat the oven to 360°F.
2. Whisk the eggs in a bowl. Add the cheese and the rest of the ingredients, except for the butter, and mix thoroughly.
3. Grease a bread pan in size 8.5" x 4.5" x 2.75" (22 x 12 x 7 cm), with butter. Spread out the dough in the bread pan with a spatula.
4. Sprinkle the dough with sesame seeds and poppy seeds. Bake the bread for 35 minutes.

KETO CORNBREAD

Nutrition: Cal 180 Fat 14 g; Carb 6 g; Protein 4 g
Serving 8; Cook time 30 min

Ingredients
- ¼ cup (¾ oz.) coconut flour
- ⅓ cup (1¼ oz.) oat fiber
- ⅓ cup (1⅕ oz.) whey protein isolate (unflavored)

- •1½ tsp baking powder
- •¼ tsp salt
- •4 oz. butter, melted
- •⅓ cup bacon fat or coconut oil, melted
- •¼ cup water
- •4 eggs
- •¼ tsp corn extract (optional)

Instructions
1. Preheat oven to 350°F .Place a greased 10" (25 cm) cast-iron skillet in the oven to heat while you make the corn-bread.
2. Combine all dry ingredients in a bowl.
3. Add the melted butter, bacon fat, eggs, and water. Beat with a hand mixer. Stir in the corn extract.
4. Pour the cornbread mixture into the hot cast iron skillet and bake for about 18 to 20 minutes or until lightly browned and firm to the touch.

KETO SEED CRACKERS
Nutrition: Cal 135 Fat 8 g; Carb 6 g; Protein 1 g
Serving 30; Cook time 75 min

Ingredients
- •⅓ cup (1⅓ oz.) almond flour
- •⅓ cup (1⅔ oz.) unsalted sunflower seeds
- •⅓ cup (1½ oz.) unsalted pumpkin seeds
- •⅓ cup (2 oz.) flaxseed or chia seeds
- •⅓ cup (1⅔ oz.) sesame seeds
- •1 tbsp ground psyllium husk powder
- •1 tsp salt
- •¼ cup melted coconut oil
- •1 cup boiling water

Instructions
1. Preheat the oven to 300°F
2. Mix all dry ingredients in a bowl. Add boiling water and oil. Mix together with a wooden fork.
3. Keep working the dough until it forms a ball and has a gel-like consistency.
4. Place the dough on a baking sheet lined with parchment paper. Add another paper on top and use a rolling pin to flatten the dough evenly.
5. Remove the upper paper and bake on the lower rack for about 40-45 minutes, check occasionally. Seeds are heat sensitive so pay close attention towards the end.
6. Turn off the oven and leave the crackers to dry in the oven. Once dried and cool, break into pieces and spread a generous amount of butter on top.

LOW CARB POPPY SEED BREAD
Nutrition: Cal 200; Fat 22 g; Carb 3 g; Protein 6 g
Serving 8; Cook time 45 min

Ingredients
LOW CARB BREAD
- •8 oz. (1 cup) cottage cheese
- •3 eggs

- •1 tbsp olive oil
- •¼ cup (1⅔ oz.) chia seeds or flaxseed
- •¼ cup (1¼ oz.) sunflower seeds
- •1 tsp baking powder
- •1 tsp ground psyllium husk powder
- •1 tsp sea salt
- •1 tbsp poppy seeds

SERVING SUGGESTIONS
- •leafy greens
- •cherry tomatoes
- •mayonnaise, flavored with curry or vegan mayonnaise
- •cooked whole chicken or deli turkey

Instructions
1. Mix all the dry ingredients. Stir in eggs, cottage cheese, and oil. Let sit for 15 minutes.
2. Spread the batter on a baking sheet lined with parchment paper. Bake in the oven at 350°F for 20–25 minutes.
3. Let dry on a rack without the parchment paper.
4. Cut into 6–8 serving pieces and enjoy with butter and toppings.
5. Put the leftover bread in the fridge or freezer, it will be like freshly baked in the toaster.
6. We have chosen to serve the bread with a filling curry chicken mayonnaise salad.

LOW CARB SESAME CRISPBREAD
Nutrition: Cal 140 Fat 8 g; Carb 2 g; Protein 3 g
Serving 30; Cook time 60 min

Ingredients
- •1¼ cups (6⅓ oz.) sesame seeds
- •½ cup (2½ oz.) sunflower seeds
- •½ cup (2 oz.) shredded cheddar cheese
- •1 tbsp ground psyllium husk powder
- •½ cup water
- •2 eggs
- •¼ tsp salt

Instructions
1. Preheat the oven to 350°F. Line a 13"x18" (33x46 cm) baking sheet with parchment paper.
2. Add all of the ingredients to a medium-sized bowl and stir to combine. Spread the mixture (about 1/8" thick or 3.1 mm) onto the parchment paper, sprinkle with sea salt, and bake for 20 minutes.
3. Remove the crispbread from the oven, and carefully cut into desired form.
4. Lower the heat to 275°F and return the crispbread to the oven for another 30-40 minutes, or until lightly golden in color.
5. Check the crispbread to make sure it is completely dry without any moist areas. Keep it in the oven with the door slightly open, until the oven is cool.
6.

LOW CARB BREAD WITH ORANGE

Nutrition: Cal 180; Fat 3 g; Carb 4 g; Protein 3 g
Serving 20; Cook time 70 min

Ingredients

- 2 cups (8 oz.) almond flour
- ½ cup (12/3 oz.) coconut flour
- 1/3 cup (12/3 oz.) sesame seeds
- 1/3 cup (2 oz.) flaxseed
- ¼ cup (11/3 oz.) ground psyllium husk powder
- 1 tbsp baking powder
- ¾ tbsp ground cloves
- ½ tbsp ground bitter orange peel
- ½ tbsp fennel seeds
- 1 tsp anise seeds
- 1 tsp ground cardamom (green)
- 1 tsp salt
- 6 eggs
- 1 cup sour cream
- 3 oz. (6 tbsp) cream cheese

Instructions

1. Preheat your oven to 400°F. Mix all dry ingredients in a medium bowl.
2. Mix eggs, sour cream, and cream cheese in a separate large bowl.
3. Add the dry mixture to the wet and stir until smooth.
4. Pour the mixture in a well-greased and paper-lined loaf pan about 9 x 5" (23 x 13 cm). Bake in the lower part of the oven for about 60 minutes or until a toothpick inserted in the center comes out clean.
5. Take the bread out of the oven, and remove it from the pan, and place on a rack to cool completely.
6. Serve the bread with butter and your favorite festive toppings.

LOW CARB TORTILLAS

Nutrition: Cal 83 ; Fat 8 g; Carb 2 g; Protein 8 g
Serving 6; Cook time 15 min

Ingredients

- 2 eggs
- 2 egg whites
- 5 oz. (2/3 cup) cream cheese
- 1½ tsp ground psyllium husk powder
- 1 tbsp coconut flour
- ½ tsp salt

Instructions

1. Preheat the oven to 400°F.
2. Beat the eggs and egg whites until fluffy. Continue to beat with a hand mixer, preferably for a few minutes. Add cream cheese and mix until the batter is smooth.
3. Mix salt, psyllium husk and coconut flour in a small bowl. Add the flour mixture to the batter one spoonful at a time and mix well. Let the batter sit for a few minutes, until it gets thick, like pancake batter. How quickly the batter swells depends on the brand of psyllium husk powder — some trial and error might be needed.
4. Bring out two baking sheets and place parchment paper on each. Using a spatula, spread the batter thinly (no more than ¼ inch thick) into 4–6 circles or 2 rectangles.
5. Bake on upper rack for about 5 minutes or more, until the tortilla turns a little brown around the edges. Carefully check the bottom side so that it doesn't burn.
6. Serve with a filling of your choice. We love them with tex-mex ground beef and salsa! And cheese is always a winner.

SPICED PUMPKIN BREAD

Nutrition: Cal 120; Fat 6 g; Carb 8 g; Protein 8 g
Serving 22; Cook time 70 min

Ingredients

- 2 tbsp pumpkin pie spice
- 1 tbsp baking powder
- 1 tsp salt
- 2 tbsp ground psyllium husk powder
- ½ cup (3 oz.) flaxseed
- 1¼ cups (5 oz.) almond flour
- ¼ cup (¾ oz.) coconut flour
- 1½ oz. (7 tbsp) walnuts, chopped
- 1½ oz. (51/3 tbsp) pumpkin seeds and extra for topping
- 3 eggs
- ½ cup unsweetened apple sauce
- 4 tbsp coconut oil melted
- 14 oz. pumpkin puree
- 1 tbsp butter or coconut oil, for greasing the pan
- 1 tbsp ground cinnamon

Instructions

1. Preheat the oven to 350°F and grease a bread pan, 8.5" (about 11 x 21 cm), with butter or oil.
2. Mix together all dry ingredients in a bowl.
3. Stir together egg, apple sauce, pumpkin puree, and oil in a bowl and mix into a smooth batter with the dry ingredients.
4. Scoop the batter into the bread pan and sprinkle a tablespoon of pumpkin seeds on top.
5. Bake on lower rack for 55-65 minutes. The bread is done when a toothpick is inserted into the center and comes out clean or when the bread feels firm to the touch in the center.
6. Let cool on a cooling rack for at least 10 minutes before slicing with a serrated knife.

LOW CARB BANANA BREAD

Nutrition: Cal 131; Fat 12 g; Carb 9 g; Protein 3 g
Serving 20; Cook time 90 min

Ingredients
- 2 (7 oz.) very ripe bananas, cut in smaller pieces
- 6 large eggs
- 6 tbsp butter melted
- 2 tsp vanilla extract
- 3 cups (12 oz.) almond flour
- 4 tsp ground cinnamon
- 2 tsp baking powder
- 1/8 tsp salt

Instructions
1. Preheat the oven to 350°F.
2. Add the banana, eggs, vanilla, and melted butter to a food processor or a medium-sized bowl if you are using an electric hand mixer. Mix until smooth.
3. Add the dry ingredients and mix until well-combined.
4. Line a loaf pan 9" x 5" (23 x 13 cm) with parchment paper and fill with the batter.
5. Bake in the oven for 50 minutes or until you insert a knife and it comes out clean. Check the loaf halfway through. If the top is getting too brown, cover loosely with tin foil.
6. Let cool on the rack for at least 30 minutes. Cut in slices and enjoy with butter or low-carb nut butter.

ZUCCHINI TORTILLAS

Nutrition: Cal 140; Fat 14 g; Carb 4 g; Protein 4 g
Serving 4; Cook time 40 min

Ingredients
- 1¼ lbs zucchini, unpeeled, and shredded
- 1½ cups (6 oz.) shredded cheese
- 2 large eggs
- 1 cup (4 oz.) almond flour
- 1 tbsp ground psyllium husk powder
- ½ tsp salt

Instructions
1. Preheat oven to 400°F. Line a large baking sheet with parchment paper.
2. Place the shredded zucchini in a tea towel or use your hands, and squeeze out any excess liquid. Add the zucchini to a large bowl, and mix together with the shredded cheese, eggs, almond flour, psyllium husk, and salt until it becomes a smooth batter.
3. Scoop equal portions of the batter onto the baking sheet, leaving space in between. Flatten each portion with moist hands, forming thin and round tortillas, approximately 10" (25 cm) in diameter.
4. Bake on the middle rack for 20-25 minutes, or until lightly browned. Set aside to cool.

CARAMELIZED ONION AND CHEESE PITA

Nutrition: Cal 160; Fat 16 g; Carb 5 g; Protein 6 g
Serving 16; Cook time 40 min

Ingredients
- 1 (4 oz.) yellow onion, minced and caramelized in butter
- 2 tbsp chia seeds, soaked in 3/4 cup boiling water
- 6 eggs at room temperature, separated yolks and whites into two bowls
- 1 cup (8 oz.) cream cheese
- 2 tbsp ground psyllium husk powder
- 1 tsp baking powder
- 1 tsp salt
- 1 cup (4 oz.) grated aged cheddar cheese
- ¾ cup (2 oz.) shredded Parmesan cheese

Instructions
1. Preheat the oven to 300°F. Chop the onion finely and fry in butter until soft, golden, and caramelized.
2. Add boiling water to chia seeds, stir well and let sit until soft and pudding-like.
3. Separate the yolks and whites into two bowls and set the whites aside.
4. Mix cream cheese and yolks until smooth, then add in baking powder, psyllium husk, and salt. Stir until evenly distributed. Add cooked onion, softened chia seeds, and shredded cheddar cheese. Mix well.
5. Beat the whites to stiff peaks. Fold into the liquid mix until you have a smooth batter.
6. Line two 9" x 13" baking sheets with parchment paper. Pour half the batter onto each sheet and spread evenly to the edges with a spatula. Sprinkle Parmesan cheese on top. Cook in the oven until golden, or for about 25 minutes.
7. Once cooked, cut into rectangles. Store in the fridge or freezer in a ziplock bag, using the parchment it was cooked on to layer in between each piece so they don't stick together. Will keep it for one week in the fridge and six months in the freezer. Reheat in the oven for warm sandwich bread or slathered with butter for a treat on its own.

THE HIGH PROTEIN BREAD

Nutrition: Cal 95; Fat 6 g; Carb 2 g; Protein 7 g
Serving 20 Cook time 30 min

Ingredients
- 6 oz. (1 cup) Greek yogurt (0% fat)
- 4 large eggs
- 1 cup (3½ oz.) whey protein isolate (unflavored)
- 1 cup (4 oz.) almond flour
- 1 tbsp ground psyllium husk powder
- 2 tsp baking powder
- ½ tsp salt
- ½ tbsp sesame seeds (optional)

Instructions
1. Preheat the oven to 350°F (175°C).

2. Line the bread pan, about 5 x 10 inches (12 x 24 cm), with parchment paper.

3. Add the yogurt and eggs to a big bowl and mix until smooth. Add the rest of the ingredients and combine until free of lumps.

4. Pour the batter into the bread pan and sprinkle it with some sesame seeds (optional). Bake for about 25 minutes or until a toothpick inserted in the center of the loaf comes out dry. Let the bread cool before slicing it.

LOW CARB ZUCCHINI BREAD

Nutrition: Cal 135; Fat 8 g; Carb 5 g; Protein 8 g
Serving 20; Cook time 90 min

Ingredients

- 14 oz. zucchini, shredded
- 6 eggs
- 1 cup (4 oz.) shredded cheese
- ½ cup (2 oz.) almond flour
- ¼ cup (1¼ oz.) sunflower seeds
- 2 tbsp ground psyllium husk powder
- 2 tsp baking powder
- ½ tsp salt
- 1 tsp paprika powder (optional)
- 1 tsp dried rosemary (optional)
- poppy seeds, for topping

Instructions

1. Preheat the oven to 350°F.

2. Rinse the zucchini but don't peel it. Finely shred it, then firmly squeeze out excess liquid from the zucchini using a cheesecloth or a clean kitchen towel.

3. In a medium-sized bowl, beat the eggs until fluffy and stir in zucchini and shredded cheese.

4. Add the rest of the ingredients, except for the poppy seeds. Combine to a smooth batter.

5. Place the batter in a 9 x 5" (23 x 13 cm) loaf pan lined with parchment paper. Sprinkle with poppy seeds.

6. Bake for 50 minutes. Allow to cool on the rack for at least 30 minutes before slicing. Enjoy with butter or your favorite low carb spread.

KETO MOZZARELLA BREAD WITH GARLIC BUTTER

Nutrition: Cal 220; Fat 19 g; Carb 3 g; Protein 6 g
Serving 17; Cook time 60 min

Ingredients

- 2 lbs (8 cups) mozzarella cheese
- 4 oz. (½ cup) cream cheese
- 4 cups (1 lb) almond flour
- 2 tbsp baking powder
- 2 tbsp white vinegar 5%
- 4 eggs

Garlic butter

- 2 oz. butter
- 2 garlic cloves, pressed
- 3 tbsp fresh parsley, finely chopped
- 2 tsp sea salt

Instructions

1. Preheat the oven to 430°F and line a large baking tray with parchment paper.

2. Place the mozzarella and cream cheese in a medium, microwave safe bowl and microwave on high for 1 minute. Remove and stir. Repeat in 30-second bursts until the cheese has melted and can be easily combined.

3. In a separate bowl, whisk together the almond flour and baking powder, until well combined. Add the eggs, vinegar and almond flour mix, to the melted cheese. Mix well until a smooth dough forms. Kneading it on a non-stick surface, helps with this process! Also, if the mixture is not combining, microwave the mixture for 30 seconds. Continue microwaving/kneading until the mixture becomes a pliable dough.

4. Roll the dough into a long "sausage shape", about 2 inch thick. Divide the dough into as many parts as portions in the recipe, and form into bun shapes. Place on your lined baking tray in the shape of a tree.

5. Bake in the oven for 15 to 20 minutes.

GARLIC BUTTER

1. Melt the butter and add the garlic.

2. Brush the newly baked bread with the garlic butter. Sprinkle with sea salt and parsley.

3. The bread hardens when it get cold so it's best served warm.

KETO DOSA

Nutrition: Cal 83; Fat 8 g; Carb 3 g; Protein 4 g
Serving 2; Cook time 25 min

Ingredients

- 1 tsp coconut oil, for frying
- ½ cup (2 oz.) almond flour
- ½ cup (2 oz.) mozzarella cheese, shredded
- ½ cup coconut milk
- ½ tsp ground cumin
- ½ tsp ground coriander seed
- salt, to taste

Instructions

1. In a bowl mix together all the ingredients.

2. Heat up and lightly oil a non-stick skillet. It's very important to use a non-stick skillet to prevent the dosa from sticking to the pan.

3. Pour in the batter and spread it around by moving the pan. You want to form a thin circular shape.

4. Cook the dosa on a low heat. The cheese will start to melt and crisp up.

5. Once it's cooked all the way through and the dosa has turned nice and golden brown on one side fold it using the spatula.

6. Remove from the pan and serve with coconut chutney.

KETO FRENCH TOAST

Nutrition: Cal 160; Fat 11 g; Carb 3 g; Protein 6 g
Serving 2; Cook time 5 min

Ingredients
MUG BREAD
- 1 tsp butter
- 2 tbsp almond flour
- 2 tbsp coconut flour
- 1½ tsp baking powder
- 1 pinch salt
- 2 large eggs
- 2 tbsp heavy whipping cream

BATTER
- 2 large eggs
- 2 tbsp heavy whipping cream
- ½ tsp ground cinnamon
- 1 pinch salt
- 2 tbsp butter

Instructions
1. Grease a large mug or glass dish with a flat bottom with butter.
2. Mix together all dry ingredients in the mug with a fork or spoon. Crack in the egg and stir in the cream. Combine until smooth and make sure there are no lumps.
3. Microwave on high (approximately 700 watts) for 2 minutes. Check if the bread is done in the middle – if not, microwave for another 15-30 seconds.
4. Let cool and remove from the mug. Slice in half.
5. In a bowl or deep plate, whisk together the eggs, cream and cinnamon with a pinch of salt. Pour over the bread slices and let them get soaked. Turn them around a few times so the bread slices absorb as much of the egg mixture as possible.
6. Fry in plenty of butter and serve immediately.

SOFT KETO TORTILLAS

Nutrition: Cal 113; Fat 8 g; Carb 3 g; Protein 4 g
Serving 6; Cook time 40 min

Ingredients
- 1 cup (3⅓ oz.) coconut flour
- ¼ tsp baking soda
- ½ tsp salt
- ¼ cup (1⅓ oz.) ground psyllium husk powder
- ½ cup avocado oil or olive oil
- 3 large egg whites
- 1½ cups hot water

Instructions
1. Heat a large cast iron skillet or griddle medium heat.
2. In a large bowl, sift together the coconut flour, baking soda and salt. Whisk in the psyllium husk.
3. Drizzle in the oil slowly as you stir the mix, it will become moist and crumbly. Fold in the egg whites.
4. Mix in the hot water half cup at a time, making sure it's completely mixed in before adding more water.

Combine until the dough looks and feels like moist play-doh.

5. Shape 12 even-sized balls. Flatten the balls between parchment paper on a tortilla press or use a 6" pot and press them down.
6. Cook 2 tortillas at a time on the large griddle by lying flat on the hot, dry cast iron and toasting 3 minutes a side, flipping once. Set aside until all the tortillas are done.

PARMESAN CHIPS

Nutrition: Cal 160; Fat 12 g; Carb 5 g; Protein 6 g
Serving 8; Cook time 50 min

Ingredients
- ¾ cup (2 oz.) freshly shredded Parmesan cheese
- 1 tbsp chia seeds
- 2 tbsp whole flaxseed
- 2½ tbsp pumpkin seeds

Instructions
1. Preheat the oven to 350°F.
2. Line a baking sheet with parchment paper.
3. Mix the Parmesan cheese and seeds in a bowl.
4. Spoon small mounds of the mixture onto the baking sheet, leaving some space between them. Do not flatten the mounds. Bake for 8 to 10 minutes. Check often. The chips should be light brown, but certainly not dark brown.
5. Remove from the oven and let cool before removing the chips from the paper and serving.

KETO SESAME BREAD

Nutrition: Cal 237; Fat 3 g; Carb 42 g; Protein 4 g
Serving 8; Cook time 50 min

Ingredients
- 4 eggs
- 7 oz. (⅘ cup) cream cheese
- 1 tbsp sesame oil
- 2 tbsp olive oil, divided
- 1 cup (4 oz.) almond flour
- 2 tbsp ground psyllium husk powder
- 1 tsp salt
- 1 tsp baking soda
- 1 tsp white vinegar 5%
- 1 tbsp sesame seeds
- sea salt (optional)

Instructions
1. Preheat oven to 350°F.
2. Beat the cream cheese, eggs, sesame oil, and half of the olive oil until fluffy with a hand mixer.
3. Add remaining ingredients except for the sesame seeds and mix until well combined.
4. Spread the batter/dough in a loaf pan (9" x 5" or 23 x 13 cm) greased with butter or lined with parchment paper. Let it rest for 5 minutes.
5. Brush with the remaining olive oil and sprinkle with sesame seeds and a touch of sea salt.

6. Bake for about 50 minutes or until golden brown on top and not doughy in the middle.

MEDITERRANEAN KETO FLATBREAD
Nutrition: Cal 115; Fat 11 g; Carb 3 g; Protein 4 g
Serving 6; Cook time 40 min

Ingredients
- ½ cup (12⁄3 oz.) coconut flour
- 1 tbsp ground psyllium husk powder
- ¼ cup olive oil
- 1 cup boiling water
- ½ cup (11⁄3 oz.) shredded Parmesan cheese or mozzarella cheese
- ½ tsp sea salt
- ¼ tsp granulated garlic
- ½ tbsp black peppercorns
- ½ tbsp dried rosemary

Instructions
1. Whisk the dry ingredients together in a mixing bowl.
2. Add olive oil and cheese.
3. Add the hot water last, stirring as it is added. Continue stirring until the psyllium fiber and coconut flour have absorbed all of the water.
4. Flatten the dough onto parchment paper on a baking sheet. Roll or press out the dough until it is thin and even. Be sure that it is a uniform thickness and less than 1/8 -inch (3mm) thick.
5. Bake at 350°F (180°C) for 20 to 25 minutes. Baking time will depend on the thickness of the dough.
6. When browned, transfer to a cooling rack, peel away the parchment paper and allow the flatbread to cool. Use a pizza cutter to cut the flatbread into squares for sandwiches. Store any leftovers in the refrigerator.

KETO COCONUT FLOUR BREAD
Nutrition: Cal 120; Fat 8 g; Carb 3 g; Protein 10 g
Serving 16; Cook time 50 min

Ingredients
- ½ cup melted coconut oil, melted (save some for greasing the pan)
- 12 large eggs
- 1 cup (31⁄3 oz.) coconut flour
- ½ tsp sea salt
- ½ tsp baking powder

Instructions
1. Preheat the oven to 350°F.
2. Grease a 9x5x3" (23x13x8cm) loaf pan and set it aside.
3. In a large bowl, whisk together the eggs, and coconut oil.
4. Add the dry ingredients, and stir until combined.
5. Spread the batter in the loaf pan. Bake on the middle rack for 40-50 minutes, or until a toothpick comes out clean, after inserting in the center of the loaf.
6. Set aside to cool for 15-20 minutes, and then slice to serve.

KETO GARLIC AND ROSEMARY FOCACCIA
Nutrition: Cal 220; Fat 22 g; Carb 2 g; Protein 5 g
Serving 8; Cook time 35 min

Ingredients
- 1½ cups (6 oz.) shredded mozzarella cheese
- 2 tbsp cream cheese
- 1 tsp white wine vinegar
- 1 egg
- ¾ cup (3 oz.) almond flour
- ½ tsp salt
- ½ tsp garlic powder

GARLIC AND ROSEMARY BUTTER
- 2 oz. butter at room temperature
- 3 garlic cloves, finely chopped
- ½ tsp sea salt
- ½ tsp fresh rosemary, chopped

Instructions
1. Preheat the oven to 400°F.
2. Heat the mozzarella and cream cheese in a small pan on medium heat or in the microwave oven. Stir occasionally.
3. Add the other ingredients and mix well. Tip: use a hand mixer with dough hooks to combine well.
4. Moisten hands with water and flatten the dough into a round crust, about 8" (20 cm) in diameter, on parchment paper.
5. Make holes in the dough with a fork and bake in the oven for about 12 minutes or until the bread has turned a golden color. Remove from the oven and let cool a little.
6. Mix together butter, garlic, salt and rosemary. Spread on top of the bread and place in a round baking dish.
7. Bake for another 10 minutes. Divide into 8–10 pieces and serve lukewarm.

KETO GARLIC BREAD
Nutrition: Cal 160; Fat 12 g; Carb 4 g; Protein 5 g
Serving 20; Cook time 70 min

Ingredients
BREAD
- 1¼ cups (5 oz.) almond flour
- 5 tbsp ground psyllium husk powder
- 2 tsp baking powder
- 1 tsp sea salt
- 1 cup water
- 2 tsp cider vinegar or white wine vinegar
- 3 egg whites

GARLIC BUTTER
- 4 oz. butter, at room temperature
- 1 garlic clove, minced
- 2 tbsp fresh parsley, finely chopped
- ½ tsp salt

Instructions

1. Preheat the oven to 350°F. Line a baking sheet with parchment paper.
2. Mix the dry ingredients for the bread, in a medium-sized bowl.
3. Bring the water to a boil and remove from heat. Add the hot water, vinegar and egg whites to the dry ingredients, while whisking with a hand mixer for about 30 seconds. Don't overmix the dough (the consistency should resemble Play-Doh).
4. Moisten hands and form the dough into 10 pieces, and then roll into hot dog buns. Place on the baking sheet, leaving space between them, as they will double in size.
5. Bake on lower rack for 40-50 minutes, remove from oven, and set aside to cool (they are done when you tap on the bottom of the bun, and hear a hollow sound). While the bread is baking, prepare the garlic butter.
6. Mix all of the garlic butter ingredients together in a small bowl. Cover, and refrigerate.
7. Remove the garlic butter from the fridge. Using a serrated knife, cut the cooled buns in half, and then spread the garlic butter on each half.
8. Increase the oven temperature to 425°F. Bake the garlic bread on the middle rack for 10-15 minutes, or until golden brown.

KETO BREAD TWISTS
Nutrition: Cal 110; Fat 10 g; Carb 3 g; Protein 4 g
Serving 10; Cook time 40 min
Ingredients
- ½ cup (2 oz.) almond flour
- ¼ cup (¾ oz.) coconut flour
- ½ tsp salt
- 1 tsp baking powder
- 1 egg, beaten
- 2 oz. butter
- 12/3 cups (6½ oz.) shredded mozzarella cheese
- ¼ cup (2 oz.) green pesto
- 1 egg, beaten, for brushing the top
Instructions
1. Preheat the oven to 350°F.
2. Mix all dry ingredients in a bowl. Add the egg and combine.
3. Melt the butter and the cheese together in a pot on low heat. Stir until the batter is smooth.
4. Slowly add the butter-cheese batter to the dry mixture bowl and mix together into a firm dough.
5. Place the dough on parchment paper that is the size of a rectangular cookie sheet. Use a rolling pin and make a rectangle, about 1/5-inch (5 mm) thick.
6. Spread pesto on top and cut into 1-inch (2.5 cm) strips. Twist them and place on a baking sheet lined with parchment paper. Brush twists with the whisked egg.
7. Bake in the oven for 15–20 minutes until they're golden brown.
8.

SOFT KETO SEED BREAD
Nutrition: Cal 170; Fat 12 g; Carb 3 g; Protein 6 g
Serving 20; Cook time 50 min
Ingredients
- 1 cup (4 oz.) almond flour
- ¾ cup (2½ oz.) coconut flour
- ⅓ cup (12/3 oz.) sesame seeds
- ½ cup (3 oz.) flaxseed
- ¼ cup (11/3 oz.) ground psyllium husk powder
- 3 tsp baking powder
- 1 tsp ground fennel seeds or ground caraway seeds
- 1 tsp salt
- 7 oz. (4/5 cup) cream cheese, at room temperature
- 6 large eggs
- ¾ cup melted butter or melted coconut oil
- ¾ cup heavy whipping cream
- 1 tbsp poppy seeds or sesame seeds, for topping
Instructions
1. Preheat the oven to 350°F.
2. Mix all dry ingredients, except the seeds for the topping, in a bowl.
3. In a separate bowl, whisk all remaining ingredients until smooth.
4. Add the wet mixture to the dry mixture and mix thoroughly. Place the dough in a greased bread pan, about 4 x 7" (10 x 18 cm), non-stick or use parchment paper. Sprinkle the top with the seeds.
5. Bake for about 45 minutes on the lower rack in the oven. Prick the bread with a knife to see if it's ready, it should come out clean. Take it out of the oven and remove the bread from the form.
6. Remove the parchment paper and let the loaf cool on a rack. If the loaf is allowed to cool in the form the crust will be soggy.
7. Serve it freshly baked with your favorite toppings.

QUICK LOW CARB BREAD
Nutrition: Cal 135; Fat 12 g; Carb 3 g; Protein 4 g
Serving 4; Cook time 20 min
Ingredients
- 2 egg whites
- 2 oz. (4 tbsp) cream cheese
- 2 tsp ground psyllium husk powder
- ½ cup (2 oz.) almond flour
- ½ cup (2½ oz.) sesame seeds
- ¼ cup (1¼ oz.) sunflower seeds
- 1½ tsp baking powder
- 2 pinches salt
Instructions
1. Preheat oven to 400°F (200°C).
2. Mix egg whites and cream cheese in a bowl.
3. Add remaining ingredients and work into the egg batter. Let rest for a few minutes.

4. Shape the batter into squares, one per serving. Sprinkle some extra sesame seeds on top if you like.
5. Bake in the oven for 10–12 minutes until golden brown.
6. Allow to cool a bit before enjoying them with your favorite topping.

90 SECOND LOW CARB KETO BREAD
Nutrition: Cal 220; Fat 21 g; Carb 4 g; Protein 4 g
Serving 1; Cook time 2 min

Ingredients
- cup frozen pineapple
- 1 banana (room temperature)
- tablespoons peanut butter
- ½ cup Greek yogurt
- ½ cup milk (or almond milk or oat milk)
- ½ teaspoon vanilla extract
- 8 ice cubes

Instructions
1. Melt butter in a microwave-safe bowl or ramekin. Add the almond flour, egg and baking powder to the butter. Beat with a fork until completely mix.
2. Microwave for about 90 seconds, until firm. Run a knife along the edge and flip over a plate to release. Slice in half, then toast in the toaster or in a skillet.
3. To Bake: Pre-heat oven to 375 F. Bake in a ramekin for 10-12 minutes or until cooked through.

KETO BREAD ROLLS
Nutrition: Cal 203; Fat 17 g; Carb 5 g; Protein 11g
Serving 10; Cook time 30 min

Ingredients
- 2 cups shredded cheese mozzarella or cheddar
- 1/4 cup cream cheese softened
- 1 1/2 cups almond flour
- 3 large eggs.
- 1 teaspoon baking powder optional

Instructions
1. Preheat the oven to 350F. Line a large baking tray with parchment paper and set aside.
2. In a large, microwave safe bowl, add your shredded cheese and cream cheese. Microwave for 30 seconds, or until the cheeses have mostly melted. Remove from the microwave and whisk together, until smooth. Let the cheese cool for several minutes.
3. When the cheese has cooled slightly, add in the almond flour and two of the eggs, and mix well, until a smooth dough remains.
4. Using your hands, form 10 balls of dough. Place them on the lined tray. Whisk the remaining egg and using a pastry brush, brush the exterior of each of the rolls.
5. Bake the rolls for 25 minutes, or until golden on the outside. Serve warm.

EASY KETO BUNS
Nutrition: Cal 250; Fat g; Carb 5 g; Protein 15 g
Serving 6; Cook time 20 min

Ingredients
- 3 cups shredded cheese mozzarella cheese
- 2 oz cream cheese
- 1 3/4 cups almond flour
- 1 tablespoon baking powder
- 2 large eggs
- For the glaze and topping
- 1 large egg
- 1 tablespoon sesame seeds

Instructions
1. Preheat the oven to 400F. Line a large baking tray with parchment paper and set aside.
2. In a microwave safe bowl, add the shredded cheese and cream cheese. Microwave in 20 second spurts, until the cheese is mostly melted. Remove and whisk together, until combined and smooth. Let the mixture cool slightly.
3. Transfer the warm cheese mixture into a food processor. Add the dry ingredients, along with the eggs, and pulse until a thick dough remains.
4. Lightly dust a kitchen surface with almond flour. Transfer the dough onto it, and, using slightly wet hands, knead it several times. Once the dough is smooth, divide it into 6 portions. Roll the portions of dough into balls and place them on the lined tray. Press down onto each one into a thinner burger bun shape. Brush the tops with the remaining egg (whisked), before sprinkling the sesame seeds on top.
5. Bake the buns for 14-17 minutes, or until golden brown on top. Remove from the oven and let cool for 5 minutes, before slicing in half and serving.

KETO CREAM CHEESE ALMOND FLOUR BREAD
Nutrition: Cal 102; Fat 5 g; Carb 2 g; Protein 3 g
Serving 12; Cook time 50 min

Ingredients
- 1 ¼ cups finely milled almond flour, measured and sifted
- 2 tsp baking powder
- 1/2 tsp of sea salt
- 4 tablespoons unsalted butter room temperature
- 1 tablespoon of sugar substitute
- 3 ½ oz full-fat cream cheese room temperature
- 4 eggs

Instructions
1. Preheat oven to 350 degrees
2. Measure and sift your almond flour.
3. In a medium-sized bowl combine the almond flour, baking powder, salt. Set aside.
4. In a large bowl using an electric mixer blend on high the butter with the tablespoon of sugar substitute until the mixture is light and fluffy and well incorporated.

5. Next, add the room temperature cream cheese and mix well with the electric mixer.
6. Add the eggs one at a time making sure to mix well after each addition with the electric mixer set to medium-low.
7. Lastly, add the dry ingredients: the almond flour, baking powder, salt and mixing well until batter is fully combined with the electric mixer setting at low.
8. In a well-greased 8 inch, loaf pan, bake the bread for 30 to 40 minutes until golden brown on top. Bread will be done once an inserted toothpick comes out clean.
9. If making rolls bake in a 12 capacity muffin tin for 20-25 minutes. This makes 12 rolls
10. Allow bread to cool in the pan for about 10 minutes and then remove the bread and allow to fully cool on a baking rack before slicing.
11. Store your keto cream cheese bread loaf in the refrigerator for up to 7 days or frozen for 30 days.

CRUNCHY NUT & SEED KETO BREAD
Nutrition: Cal 157; Fat 14 g; Carb 4 g; Protein 45g
Serving 14; Cook time 60 min

Ingredients
- 1 cup almonds or hazelnuts chopped
- ¾ cup pumpkin seeds toasted
- ¼ cup chia seeds
- 3 tablespoon sesame seeds
- ¼ cup sunflower seeds
- ¼ cup pecans or walnuts chopped
- 1 tablespoon caraway seeds
- 1 teaspoon salt
- ¼ cup flax seed powder
- ¼ cup Erythritol optional if you want a hint of sweetness
- 5 eggs
- ⅓ cup olive oil melted coconut oil is fine too.
- 1 teaspoon apple cider vinegar optional

Instructions
1. Preheat the oven to 325F. Mix the dry ingredients in a large bowl.
2. Mix all wet ingredients into dry ingredients. Mix well until incorporated.
3. Place the dough in a greased bread pan (5 x 10 inch). Bake for 50 minutes to one hour. Turn off the heat and allow the loaf to completely cool with the oven door ajar.

KETO HERB BREAD
Nutrition: Cal 220; Fat 20 g; Carb 5 g; Protein 7 g
Serving 16; Cook time 55 min

Ingredients
DRY INGREDIENTS
- 2 cups almond flour
- ¼ cup coconut flour
- 1 ½ teaspoon baking powder.
- 2 tablespoon parsley

- 1 teaspoon sage
- 1 tsp. rosemary

WET INGREDIENTS
- 8 oz. Cream Cheese 1 Package softened
- 8 eggs room temp
- ½ cup cup butter 1 Stick melted

Instructions
1. Preheat Oven to 350° F.
2. Melt a stick of butter and soften (heat slightly) an 8 oz. package of cream cheese. Microwave works for this or you can unwrap them and set them in a bowl set it on top of the pre-heating oven while you mix the dry ingredients.
3. Line the bottom of a bread pan with parchment paper.
4. In a mixing bowl combine almond flour & coconut flour. Use a fork to mix and de-clump.
5. Once the flours are thoroughly de-clumpified, add the rest of the dry ingredients, and mix completely.
6. In a separate mixing bowl - like the one on a Kitchen Aid - add the the softened cream cheese, melted butter, and mix until smooth. Add the eggs and mix until combined.
7. Add the dry ingredient mixture to the bowl with the wet ingredients and mix just until they are combined. If you are using a stand up mixture you will want to use a silicone bowl scraper to get all of the unmixed ingredients off the sides and bottom of the bowl and then mix them in again.
8. When the batter is mixed put it in the bread pan that you lined with parchment. It is pretty thick so you may need to use your silicone scraper to spread it evenly in the pan.
9. Bake at 350°F for 50-55 minutes or until it is done in the middle. (tooth-pick) test.

ALMOND FLOUR LCHF KETO BREAD
Nutrition: Cal 172; Fat 14 g; Carb 3 g; Protein 5 g
Serving 16; Cook time 60 min

Ingredients
- 7 Large Eggs room temp
- ½ cup Butter melted
- 2 tablespoon Coconut Oil melted
- ½ teaspoon Salt
- ½ teaspoon xanthan gum
- 1 teaspoon baking powder
- 2 cups Almond flour

Instructions
1. Preheat oven to 325 F
2. Whisk the eggs on high for 2 minutes until it's bubbly.
3. Pour in melted coconut oil and butter with the eggs while continuously whipping on low.
4. Add dry ingredients and mix until combined.
5. Scrape into a loaf pan that has been prepared with oil. It should look something like this.
6. Bake for 60 minutes 325 F in a glass pan. Or, 350 for 45-50 in a metal bread pan. Do the toothpick test to make sure your bread is done.

KETO LEMON BREAD

Nutrition: Cal 293; Fat 3 g; Carb 30 g; Protein 4 g
Serving 12; Cook time 50 min

Ingredients
- 2 cups almond flour
- 1/3 cup granulated sweetener
- 1 tbsp baking powder
- 1/2 tsp salt
- 2/3 cup plain yogurt or coconut cream
- 1/4 cup lemon juice
- 3 eggs or flax eggs
- 1 tbsp lemon zest

Instructions
1. Grease a 9×5 loaf pan or line it with parchment paper.
2. Preheat oven to 325 F.
3. Stir all ingredients until smooth.
4. Pour into the pan. Bake for 50 minutes.
5. I found that letting the keto lemon bread cool completely before going around the sides with a knife and popping out the loaf will ensure it doesn't break, because the recipe is super moist and soft! The lemon bread can be loosely covered and left out overnight

KETO CINNAMON ROLL BREAD

Nutrition: Cal 169; Fat 8 g; Carb 5 g; Protein 4 g
Serving 12; Cook time 40 min

Ingredients
- 1/4 cup erythritol
- 1 tbsp cinnamon

BREAD INGREDIENTS
- 1/4 cup erythritol
- 1/4 cup butter, softened
- 3 large eggs
- 1 tsp vanilla extract
- 1/4 cup heavy cream
- 2 cups almond flour
- 1 tsp ground nutmeg or cinnamon
- 1 tsp baking powder
- a pinch of salt (optional)

ICING
- 4 tbsp powdered erythritol
- 2 tbsp heavy cream

Instructions
1. Preheat the oven to 350F
2. In a small bowl, mix 1/4 cup erythritol with cinnamon and mix, set aside.
3. Beat butter with eggs and 1/4 cup erythritol. Add heavy cream and mix.
4. Add vanilla extract, almond flour, nutmeg, baking powder, salt and stir until combined, do not stir for a long time.
5. Put half the dough in the prepared greased or lined with parchment paper loaf pan. Sprinkle 3/4 of the total amount of erythritol with cinnamon mixture

6. Put the remaining dough, and sprinkle with cinnamon erythritol mixture
7. Bake from 30 to 40 minutes. Let the bread set in pan for about 15 minutes.
8. Make icing. Mix powdered erythritol and cream
9. Pour icing on the cooled bread
10. Serve and enjoy

KETO RUSTIC BREAD

Nutrition: Cal 153; Fat 12 g; Carb 7 g; Protein 6 g
Serving 16; Cook time 75 min

Ingredients
- 4 oz cream cheese softened
- ½ cup ricotta full-fat
- 5 eggs room temperature
- 2 tbsp apple cider vinegar
- 2 cups almond flour blanched
- ¼ cup coconut flour
- 1 tbsp baking powder
- 4 tbsp psyllium husk powder
- ½ tsp salt
- 1 tsp nutritional yeast optional

Instructions
1. Preheat oven to 350 °F. Prepare a baking sheet with parchment paper.
2. In a large bowl, whisk together cream cheese and ricotta until smooth. Add the eggs and whisk in well.
3. Add all the remaining ingredients and whisk until smooth. The dough will still feel sticky at this point. Let rest for 5 minutes for the moisture to be absorbed.
4. With wet hands shape the dough into roughly a 4"x7" loaf. Place on your prepared baking sheet and with a small knife, cut 3 diagonal lines on the top and pull each line a little bit apart (this will make the bread look artisan!)
5. Bake for 1 hour. The bread is done when a toothpick inserted in the center comes out clean or the center temperature has reached 201 °F. Let cool down completely and enjoy!

KETO IRISH SODA BREAD

Nutrition: Cal 188; Fat 16,5 g; Carb 5 g; Protein 6 g
Serving 12; Cook time 75 min

Ingredients
- ½ cup cream
- 1 ½ tablespoon apple cider vinegar
- 2 cups almond flour
- ¼ cup unflavoured whey protein powder (or egg white protein powder)
- 3 tablespoon Swerve Brown
- 2 tablespoon coconut flour
- 1 teaspoon baking soda
- ¼ teaspoon salt
- ¼ cup butter chilled
- ⅓ cup sugar-free dried cranberries chopped (optional)

- 2 egg whites
- 1 tablespoon melted butter to brush the top

Instructions

1. Preheat the oven to 325°F and line a baking sheet with a silicone mat.
2. In a small bowl, combine the cream and vinegar. In a large bowl, whisk together the almond flour, protein powder, sweetener, coconut flour, baking soda, and salt.
3. Grate the cold butter into the dry ingredients and stir to distribute. Stir in the dried cranberries, if using.
4. Stir in the cream mixture and the egg whites until well combined. Transfer the dough to the prepared baking sheet. With wet hands, form into a high, round loaf. Brush all over with the melted butter.
5. Use a sharp knife to cut a large X in the center of the loaf. Place the baking sheet on the second highest rack in the oven and bake 20 minutes, until the outside is turning golden brown.

Turn off the oven and let the bread sit inside until the top is firm to the touch and not spongy, another 30 to 40 minutes.

Keto Smoothites and Drinks

CREAMY CHOCOLATE MILKSHAKE

Nutrition: Cal 292; Fat 25 g; Carb 4 g; Protein 15 g
Serving 2; Cook time 10 min

Ingredients
- 16 oz. unsweetened almond milk, vanilla
- 1 packet stevia
- 4 oz. heavy cream
- 1 scoop Whey Isolate Chocolate protein powder
- ½ cup crushed ice

•Instructions
1. Place all of the ingredients in your blender, and blend until you get a creamy smoothie.

FAT BURNING ESPRESSO SMOOTHIE

Nutrition: Cal 270; Fat 16 g; Carb 2 g; Protein 30 g
Serving 1; Cook time 10 min

Ingredients
- 1 scoop Isopure Zero Carb protein powder
- 1 espresso shot
- ¼ c Greek yogurt, full fat
- Liquid stevia, to sweeten
- Pinch of cinnamon
- 5 ice cubes

Instructions
1. Place all of the ingredients in your blender, and blend until you get a creamy smoothie.

ALMOND BUTTER & BANANA PROTEIN SMOOTHIE

Nutrition: Cal 402; Fat 3 g; Carb 37 g; Protein 19 g
Serving 1; Cook time 10 min

Ingredients
- small frozen banana
- 1 cup unsweetened almond milk
- tablespoons almond butter
- tablespoons unflavored protein powder
- 1 tablespoon sweetener of your choice (optional)
- ½ teaspoon ground cinnamon

Instructions
1. Place all of the ingredients in your blender, and blend until you get a creamy smoothie.

BLUEBERRY BLISS

Nutrition: Cal 302; Fat 25 g; Carb 4 g; Protein 15 g
Serving 2; Cook time 10 min

Ingredients
- 16 oz. unsweetened almond milk, vanilla
- 1 packet stevia
- 4 oz. heavy cream
- 1 scoop Whey Isolate Vanilla protein powder
- ¼ cup frozen blueberries, unsweetened

Instructions
1. Place all of the ingredients in your blender, and blend until you get a creamy smoothie.

CINNAMON ROLL SMOOTHIE

Nutrition: Cal 165; Fat 3 g; Carb 1,6 g; Protein 15 g
Serving 1; Cook time 10 min

Ingredients
- 1 cup unsweetened almond milk
- 2 tbsp. vanilla protein powder
- ½ tsp cinnamon
- ¼ tsp vanilla extract
- 1 packet stevia
- 1 tbsp. chia seeds 1 cup ice cubes

Instructions
1. Place all of the ingredients in your blender, and blend until you get a creamy smoothie.

BLUEBERRY AVOCADO SMOOTHIE

Nutrition: Cal 377; Fat 22 g; Carb 4 g; Protein 32 g
Serving 1; Cook time 10 min

Ingredients
- 1 cup unsweetened almond milk, vanilla
- 1 tbsp. heavy cream
- ½ avocado, peeled, pitted, sliced
- 1 scoop Isopure Coconut Zero Carb protein powder
- ¼ cup frozen blueberries, unsweetened
- Liquid stevia, to sweeten

Instructions
1. Place all of the ingredients in your blender, and blend until you get a creamy smoothie.

BLACKBERRY CHOCOLATE SHAKE

Nutrition: Cal 338; Fat 34 g; Carb 4 g; Protein 4 g
Serving 2; Cook time 10 min

Ingredients
- 1 cup unsweetened coconut milk
- ¼ cup fresh blackberries
- 2 tbsp. cacao powder
- Liquid stevia, to sweeten
- 6 ice cubes
- ¼ tsp xanthan gum
- 1-2 tbsp. MCT oil

Instructions
1. Place all of the ingredients in your blender, and blend until you get a creamy smoothie.

PUMPKIN PIE BUTTERED COFFEE

Nutrition: Cal 125; Fat 12 g; Carb 2 g; Protein 4 g
Serving 1; Cook time 10 min

Ingredients

- 12 oz. hot coffee
- 2 tbsp. canned pumpkin
- 1 tbsp. regular butter, unsalted
- ¼ tsp pumpkin pie spice
- Liquid stevia, to sweeten

Instructions

1. Place all of the ingredients in your blender, and blend until you get a creamy smoothie.

CUCUMBER SPINACH SMOOTHIE

Nutrition: Cal 335; Fat 33 g; Carb 4 g; Protein 3 g
Serving 1; Cook time 10 min

Ingredients

- 2 large handfuls spinach
- ½ cucumber, peeled and cubed
- 6 ice cubes
- 1 cup coconut milk
- Liquid stevia, to sweeten
- ¼ tsp xanthan gum
- 1-2 tbsp. MCT oil

Instructions

1. Place all of the ingredients in your blender, and blend until you get a creamy smoothie.

ORANGE CREAMSICLE

Nutrition: Cal 290; Fat 25 g; Carb 4 g; Protein 15 g
Serving 2; Cook time 10 min

Ingredients

- 16 oz. unsweetened almond milk, vanilla
- 1 packet stevia
- 4 oz. heavy cream
- 1 scoop Whey Isolate Tropical Dreamsicle protein powder
- ½ cup crushed ice

Instructions

1. Place all of the ingredients in your blender, and blend until you get a creamy smoothie.

CAYENNE CHOCOLATE SHAKE

Nutrition: Cal 258; Fat 26 g; Carb 3 g; Protein 3 g
Serving 2; Cook time 10 min

Ingredients

- ¼ cup coconut cream
- 2 tbsp. unrefined coconut oil
- 1 tbsp. whole chia seeds, spectrum
- 2 tbsp. cacao
- Dash of vanilla extract
- Pinch of ground cinnamon

- ½ pinch cayenne powder
- ½ - 1 cup water
- Ice cubes, if desired

Instructions

1. Place all of the ingredients in your blender, and blend until you get a creamy smoothie.

SHAMROCK SHAKE

Nutrition: Cal 200; Fat 19 g; Carb 4,5 g; Protein 2 g
Serving 1; Cook time 10 min

Ingredients

- 1 cup coconut milk, unsweetened
- 1 avocado, peeled, pitted, sliced
- Liquid stevia, to sweeten
- 1 cup ice
- 1 tbsp. pure vanilla extract
- 1 tsp pure peppermint extract

Instructions

1. Place all of the ingredients in your blender, and blend until you get a creamy smoothie.

CHAI COCONUT SHAKE

Nutrition: Cal 233; Fat 20 g; Carb 5 g; Protein 4 g
Serving 2; Cook time 10 min

Ingredients

- 1 cup unsweetened coconut milk
- 1 tbsp. pure vanilla extract
- 2 tbsp. almond butter
- ¼ cup unsweetened shredded coconut
- 1 tsp ground ginger
- 1 tsp ground cinnamon
- Pinch of allspice
- 1 tbsp. ground flaxseed
- 5 ice cubes

Instructions

1. Place all of the ingredients in your blender, and blend until you get a creamy smoothie.

AVOCADO ALMOND SMOOTHIE

Nutrition: Cal 252; Fat 18 g; Carb 5 g; Protein 17 g
Serving 2; Cook time 10 min

Ingredients

- ½ cup unsweetened almond milk, vanilla
- ½ cup half and half
- ½ avocado, peeled, pitted, sliced
- 1 tbsp. almond butter
- 1 scoop Isopure Zero Carb protein powder
- Pinch of cinnamon
- ½ tsp vanilla extract
- 2-4 ice cubes
- Liquid stevia, to sweeten

Instructions

1. Place all of the ingredients in your blender, and blend until you get a creamy smoothie.

STRAWBERRY ALMOND DELIGHT
Nutrition: Cal 305; Fat 25 g; Carb 7 g; Protein 15 g
Serving 2; Cook time 10 min

Ingredients
- 16 oz. unsweetened almond milk, vanilla
- 1 packet stevia
- 4 oz. heavy cream
- 1 scoop Whey Isolate Vanilla protein powder
- ¼ cup frozen strawberries, unsweetened

Instructions
1. Place all of the ingredients in your blender, and blend until you get a creamy smoothie.

CREAMY BLACKBERRY
Nutrition: Cal 237; Fat 22 g; Carb 6 g; Protein 2 g
Serving 2; Cook time 10 min

Ingredients
- 1 cup fresh blackberries
- 1 cup ice cubes
- Liquid stevia, to sweeten
- ¾ cup heavy whipping cream

Instructions
1. Place all of the ingredients in your blender, and blend until you get a creamy smoothie.

PEANUT BUTTER MILKSHAKE
Nutrition: Cal 253; Fat 23 g; Carb 7 g; Protein 5 g
Serving 2; Cook time 10 min

Ingredients
- ½ cup coconut milk, regular
- 1 cup unsweetened almond milk, vanilla
- 2 tbsp. all natural peanut butter
- 1 tsp vanilla extract
- 1 cup ice cubes
- 1 packet stevia

Instructions
1. Place all of the ingredients in your blender, and blend until you get a creamy smoothie.

RASPBERRY SMOOTHIE
Nutrition: Cal 285; Fat 22 g; Carb 7 g; Protein 14 g
Serving 2; Cook time 10 min

Ingredients
- ½ cup fresh raspberries
- 1 cup unsweetened almond milk, vanilla
- 1 scoop prebiotic fibre (Pinnaclife Prebiotic Fibre)
- 1 scoop Vanilla Whey Isolate protein powder
- 2 tbsp. coconut oil
- ¼ cup coconut flakes, unsweetened

- 3-4 ice cubes

Instructions
1. Place all of the ingredients in your blender, and blend until you get a creamy smoothie.

LEPRECHAUN SHAKE
Nutrition: Cal 217; Fat 13 g; Carb 7 g; Protein 13 g
Serving 2; Cook time 10 min

Ingredients
- ½ avocado, peeled, pitted, sliced
- ¼ cup unsweetened coconut milk
- Small bunch of baby spinach
- ¼ cup fresh mint
- 1 scoop Isopure Zero Carb Whey Protein Isolate
- 1 tsp vanilla extract
- Liquid stevia, to sweeten
- Water, if desired
- 2-3 ice cubes, if desired

Instructions
1. Place all of the ingredients in your blender, and blend until you get a creamy smoothie.

BREAKFAST EGG SMOOTHIE
Nutrition: Cal 266; Fat 17 g; Carb 6 g; Protein 22 g
Serving 2; Cook time 10 min

Ingredients
- ½ cup coconut milk, unsweetened
- ½ cup Lifeway Organic Whole Milk Kefir, plain
- 4 tbsp. chia seeds
- 1 oz. egg substitute dry powder

Instructions
1. Place all of the ingredients in your blender, and blend until you get a creamy smoothie.

PEANUT BUTTER CARAMEL SHAKE
Nutrition: Cal 366; Fat 35 g; Carb 6 g; Protein 7 g
Serving 1; Cook time 10 min

Ingredients
- 1 cup ice cubes
- 1 cup coconut milk, unsweetened
- 2 tbsp. natural peanut butter
- 2 tbsp. Sugar-free Torani Salted Caramel
- ¼ tsp. xanthan gum, to thicken smoothie 1 tbsp. MCT oil

Instructions
1. Place all of the ingredients in your blender, and blend until you get a creamy smoothie.

CREAMY GREEN MACHINE
Nutrition: Cal 279; Fat 18 g; Carb 9 g; Protein 18 g
Serving 2; Cook time 10 min

Ingredients
- ½ cup unsweetened almond milk, vanilla

- ½ cup half and half
- ½ avocado, peeled, pitted, sliced
- ½ cup frozen blueberries, unsweetened
- 1 cup spinach
- 1 tbsp. almond butter
- 1 scoop Isopure Zero Carb protein powder
- 2-4 ice cubes
- 1 packet stevia

Instructions

1. Place all of the ingredients in your blender, and blend until you get a creamy smoothie.

COCONUT SUPERFOOD SMOOTHIE

Nutrition: Cal 272; Fat 22 g; Carb 8 g; Protein 15 g
Serving 2; Соок time 10 min

Ingredients

- ½ cup unsweetened almond milk, vanilla
- ½ cup coconut cream
- 1 scoop Isopure Zero Carb protein powder
- ½ cup frozen blueberries, unsweetened
- 2-4 ice cubes

Instructions

1. Place all of the ingredients in your blender, and blend until you get a creamy smoothie.

CREAMY STRAWBERRY

Nutrition: Cal 140; Fat 39 g; Carb 9 g; Protein 27 g
Serving 2; Соок time 10 min

Ingredients

- 1 cup ice cubes
- ½ cup water
- 1 scoop Isopure Zero Carb Strawberry protein powder
- 3 slices avocado, peeled, pitted
- 1 oz. MCT oil
- 1/2 cup frozen strawberries, unsweetened

Instructions

1. Place all of the ingredients in your blender, and blend until you get a creamy smoothie.

SPRING SMOOTHIE

Nutrition: Cal 263; Fat 19 g; Carb 8 g; Protein 12 g
Serving 2; Соок time 10 min

Ingredients

- 2 large handfuls mixed greens (spinach and кale)
- 1 oz. almonds, unsalted
- ¼ cup frozen blueberries, unsweetened
- 1 tbsp. chia seeds
- 1 cup raspberry tea, unsweetened

Instructions

1. Place all of the ingredients in your blender, and blend until you get a creamy smoothie.

VANILLA HEMP

Nutrition: Cal 250; Fat 20 g; Carb 9 g; Protein 7 g
Serving 2; Соок time 10 min

Ingredients

- 1 cup water
- 1 cup unsweetened hemp milк, vanilla
- 1 ½ tbsp. coconut oil, unrefined
- ½ cup frozen berries, mixed
- 4 cup leafy greens (кale and spinach)
- 1 tbsp. flaxseeds or chia seeds
- 1 tbsp. almond butter

Instructions

1. Place all of the ingredients in your blender, and blend until you get a creamy smoothie.

CACAO SUPER SMOOTHIE

Nutrition: Cal 445; Fat 14 g; Carb 9 g; Protein 16 g
Serving 2; Соок time 10 min

Ingredients

- ½ cup unsweetened almond milк, vanilla
- ½ cup half and half
- ½ avocado, peeled, pitted, sliced
- ½ cup frozen blueberries, unsweetened
- 1 tbsp. cacao powder
- 1 scoop Whey Isolate Vanilla protein powder
- Liquid stevia, to sweeten

Instructions

1. Place all of the ingredients in your blender, and blend until you get a creamy smoothie.

PEPPERMINT MOCHA

Nutrition: Cal 198; Fat 16 g; Carb 9 g; Protein 3 g
Serving 2; Соок time 10 min

Ingredients

- 1 cup cold coffee
- 1/3 Organic Chocolove Darк Chocolate, 73%
- 2 tbsp. avocado, peeled, pitted, sliced
- ½ cup half and half
- 2 tbsp. fresh mint (about 20 leaves) or 1 tsp mint extract
- 2 tsp cacao powder ¼ cup water
- Liquid stevia, to sweetener
- ¼ cup ice cubes

Instructions

1. Place all of the ingredients in your blender, and blend until you get a creamy smoothie.

HAPPY GUT SMOOTHIE

Nutrition: Cal 410; Fat 33 g; Carb 8 g; Protein 12 g
Serving 1; Соок time 10 min

Ingredients

- 2-3 cup spinach leaves
- 1 ½ tbsp. coconut oil, unrefined

- ½ cup plain full fat yogurt
- 1 tbsp. chia seeds 1 serving aloe vera leaves
- ½ cup frozen blueberries, unsweetened
- 1 tbsp. hemp hearts
- 1 cup water
- 1 scoop Pinnaclife Prebiotic Fibre

Instructions

1. Place all of the ingredients in your blender, and blend until you get a creamy smoothie.

STRAWBERRY CHEESECAKE SMOOTHIE

Nutrition: Cal 247; Fat 19 g; Carb 8 g; Protein 3 g
Serving 1; Cook time 10 min

Ingredients

- ½ cup frozen strawberries, unsweetened
- ½ cup unsweetened vanilla almond milk
- Liquid stevia, to sweeten
- ½ tsp vanilla extract
- 2 oz. cream cheese, regular
- 3-4 ice cubes
- Water, optional

Instructions

1. Place all of the ingredients in your blender, and blend until you get a creamy smoothie.

SILKEN TOFU SMOOTHIE

Nutrition: Cal 208; Fat 12 g; Carb 10 g; Protein 18 g
Serving 2; Cook time 10 min

Ingredients

- ½ cup strawberries, unfrozen
- Silken tofu
- 1 cup unsweetened almond milk, vanilla
- Pinch of cinnamon
- Liquid Stevia, to sweeten

Instructions

1. Place all of the ingredients in your blender, and blend until you get a creamy smoothie.

MANGO GREEN TEA & CARROT SMOOTHIE

Nutrition: Cal 133; Fat 9 g; Carb 10 g; Protein 6 g
Serving 2; Cook time 10 min

Ingredients

- 2 cup water
- ½ cup baby carrots
- Pinch of fresh ginger
- ½ cup frozen mango
- Liquid stevia, to sweeten
- 1 tbsp. chia seed

Instructions

1. Place all of the ingredients in your blender, and blend until you get a creamy smoothie.

PUMPKIN PARADISE

Nutrition: Cal270; Fat 10 g; Carb 10 g; Protein 30 g
Serving 1; Cook time 10 min

Ingredients

- ½ cup unsweetened almond milk, vanilla
- ½ cup water
- ½ cup canned pumpkin
- ½ tsp pumpkin pie spice
- Stevia packet
- 1 scoop Isopure Zero Carb protein powder
- 1 oz. cream cheese
- 2-3 ice cubes
- Ground cinnamon, to taste

Instructions

1. Place all of the ingredients in your blender, and blend until you get a creamy smoothie.

CREAMY GREEN SMOOTHIE

Nutrition: Cal 315; Fat 25 g; Carb 10 g; Protein 13 g
Serving 2; Cook time 10 min

Ingredients

- ¼ avocado, peeled, pitted, sliced
- 4 broccoli florets, if desired
- 1 bunch of kale and spinach
- 1 slice honeydew
- ½ cup coconut milk
- 2 tbsp. plain Greek yogurt, full fat
- 1 tbsp. almond butter
- ½ cup unsweetened almond milk, vanilla
- ¼ cup water, optional
- ½ scoop Isopure Zero Carb Protein powder

Instructions

1. Place all of the ingredients in your blender, and blend until you get a creamy smoothie.

RED VELVET SMOOTHIE

Nutrition: Cal 228; Fat 16 g; Carb 13 g; Protein 7 g
Serving 2; Cook time 10 min

Ingredients

- 2 cup unsweetened almond milk, vanilla
- 2 cup ice cubes
- 2-3 slices avocado, peeled, pitted, sliced
- 1 beet, small, cooked
- 2 tbsp. cacao
- ¼ tsp pure vanilla extract
- Liquid stevia, to sweeten

Instructions

1. Place all of the ingredients in your blender, and blend until you get a creamy smoothie.

WHIPPED SHAKE
Nutrition: Cal 238; Fat 22 g; Carb 13 g; Protein 7 g
Serving 1; Cook time 10 min
Ingredients
- 1 cup unsweetened almond milk
- 1/3 cup heavy whipping cream
- 2-4 drops liquid stevia
- ½ tsp vanilla extract
- 2 tbsp. cacao (use 1 tbsp. for lower carbohydrate)
- 3 ice cubes
Instructions
1. Place all of the ingredients in your blender, and blend until you get a creamy smoothie.

GREEN AND BLUE SMOOTHIE
Nutrition: Cal 230; Fat 4 g; Carb 12 g; Protein 38 g
Serving 1; Cook time 10 min
Ingredients
- 1/4 cup frozen blueberries
- 1/3 cup unsweetened almond milk •
- 1/2 cup Greek or Fage yogurt (plain or full-fat)
- 1 scoop vanilla isolate protein
- or 2 tablespoons gelatin plus 1 teaspoon vanilla extract
- 1 cup spinach, loosely packed
- 1/3 cup ice
Instructions
1. Place all of the ingredients in your blender, and blend until you get a creamy smoothie.

BERRY POLKA DOT DANCE
Nutrition: Cal 268; Fat 4 g; Carb 9 g; Protein 14 g
Serving 2; Cook time 10 min
Ingredients
- 1 1/2 cup unsweetened almond milk
- 1 cup spinach
- 2 tablespoons flax seeds
- 1/3 cup frozen blackberries
- 1/3 cup frozen blueberries
- 1 scoop vanilla isolate protein or 2 tablespoons gelatin plus
- 1 teaspoon vanilla extrac
Instructions
1. Place all of the ingredients in your blender, and blend until you get a creamy smoothie.

ALMOND STRAWBERRY DELIGHT
Nutrition: Cal 352; Fat 24 g; Carb 9 g; Protein 26 g
Serving 2; Cook time 10 min
Ingredients
- 16 ounces unsweetened almond milk, vanilla

- 1 packet stevia or 2 teaspoons Splenda
- 4 ounce heavy cream
- 2 scoops vanilla isolate protein or 4 tablespoons gelatin plus 1 teaspoon vanilla extract
- 1/4 cup frozen strawberries, unsweetened
Instructions
1. Place all of the ingredients in your blender, and blend until you get a creamy smoothie.

CREAMY BLACKBERRY
Nutrition: Cal 300; Fat 17 g; Carb 12 g; Protein 25 g
Serving 1; Cook time 10 min
Ingredients
- 1 cup fresh blackberries
- 1 packet stevia or 2 teaspoons Splenda
- 3/4 cup heavy whipping cream
- 2 scoops vanilla isolate protein or 4 tablespoons gelatin plus 2 teaspoon vanilla extract
- 1 cup ice cubes
Instructions
1. Place all of the ingredients in your blender, and blend until you get a creamy smoothie.

SPICY GREEN SALAD SMOOTHIE
Nutrition: Cal 267; Fat 2 g; Carb 10 g; Protein 3 g
Serving 2; Cook time 10 min
Ingredients
- 1 cup fresh white cabbage
- 1 handful fresh baby kale
- 1 handful fresh parsley
- 1 lemon juice, squeezed into the blender
- 1 medium Roma or Heirloom tomato
- 1/2 cup water
- 1/2 habanero pepper, remove seeds
- 1/2 Italian cucumber • 5–6 ice cubes
Instructions
1. Place all of the ingredients in your blender, and blend until you get a creamy smoothie.

SUPERFOOD COCONUT SMOOTHIE
Nutrition: Cal 216; Fat 15 g; Carb 9 g; Protein 13 g
Serving 2; Cook time 10 min
Ingredients
- 1/2 cup coconut cream
- 1/2 cup frozen blueberries
- 1/2 cup unsweetened almond milk, vanilla
- 1 scoop vanilla isolate protein or 2 tablespoons gelatin plus
- 1 teaspoon vanilla extract
- 2-4 ice cubes
Instructions

1. Place all of the ingredients in your blender, and blend until you get a creamy smoothie.

DAIRY-FREE GREEN SMOOTHIE
Nutrition: Cal 230; Fat 4 g; Carb 9 g; Protein 2 g
Serving 2; Cook time 10 min

Ingredients
- 1 cup raw cucumber, peeled and sliced
- 1 cup romaine lettuce
- 1 tablespoon fresh ginger, peeled and chopped
- 1/2 cup kiwi fruit, peeled and chopped
- 1/2 Half avocado (remove pit and scoop flesh out of shell)
- 1/3 cup chopped fresh pineapple
- 2 tablespoons fresh parsley
- 3 teaspoons Splenda
- 4 cups water.

Instructions
1. Place all of the ingredients in your blender, and blend until you get a creamy smoothie.

COCONUT CHAI SMOOTHIE
Nutrition: Cal 420; Fat 38 g; Carb 13 g; Protein 7 g
Serving 2; Cook time 10 min

Ingredients
- 1/4 cup unsweetened shredded coconut
- 1 cup unsweetened coconut milk
- 1 tablespoon ground flaxseed
- 1 tablespoon pure vanilla extract
- 1 teaspoon ground cinnamon
- 1 teaspoon ground ginger
- 2 tablespoons almond butter
- Pinch of allspice
- 5 ice cubes

Instructions
1. Place all of the ingredients in your blender, and blend until you get a creamy smoothie.

SPICY GREEN SALAD SMOOTHIE
Nutrition: Cal 154; Fat 3 g; Carb 10 g; Protein 2 g
Serving 1; Cook time 10 min

Ingredients
- 1 cup fresh white cabbage
- 1 handful fresh baby kale
- 1 handful fresh parsley
- 1 lemon juice, squeezed into the blender
- 1 medium Roma or Heirloom tomato
- 1/2 cup water
- 1/2 habanero pepper, remove seeds
- 1/2 Italian cucumber
- 5–6 ice cubes

Instructions

1. Place all of the ingredients in your blender, and blend until you get a creamy smoothie.

GREEN MINTY PROTEIN SHAKE
Nutrition: Cal 184; Fat 10 g; Carb 9 g; Protein 13 g
Serving 2; Cook time 10 min

Ingredients
- 1 packet stevia or 2 teaspoons Splenda
- 1/4 teaspoon peppermint extract
- 1/2 cup almond milk, unsweetened
- 1/2 avocado
- 1 scoop vanilla or
- chocolate isolate protein
- 1 cup spinach, fresh
- 1 cup ice

Instructions
1. Place all of the ingredients in your blender, and blend until you get a creamy smoothie.

PEPPERMINT PATTY
Nutrition: Cal 166; Fat 5 g; Carb 9 g; Protein 28 g
Serving 2; Cook time 10 min

Ingredients
- 1/4 teaspoon mint extract
- 1 scoop chocolate isolate protein
- 1 cup unsweetened almond milk
- 1 cup spinach
- 2 tbsp. unsweetened cocoa powder
- Ice cubes

Instructions
1. Place all of the ingredients in your blender, and blend until you get a creamy smoothie.

BLUE-RASPBERRY SMOOTHIE
Nutrition: Cal 191; Fat 6 g; Carb 12 g; Protein 26 g
Serving 1; Cook time 10 min

Ingredients
- 1/4 cup blueberries, frozen
- 1/4 cup raspberries, frozen
- 1 ½ cups unsweetened almond milk
- 1 pack gelatin or 1 scoop isolate protein

Instructions
1. Place all of the ingredients in your blender, and blend until you get a creamy smoothie

BLUEBERRY CHIA SMOOTHIE
Nutrition: Cal 160; Fat 3 g; Carb 9 g; Protein 4 g
Serving 1; Cook time 10 min

Ingredients
- cup blueberries
- 1/2 banana
- 1/2 cup nonfat milk

- 1/2 cup plain nonfat Greek Yogurt
- 1 tablespoon chia seeds
- 1/2 cup ice

Instructions

1. Place all of the ingredients in your blender, and blend until you get a creamy smoothie.

STRAWBERRY-ALMOND CRUNCH SMOOTHIE

Nutrition: Cal 135; Fat 10 g; Carb 11 g; Protein 4 g
Serving 1; Cook time 10 min

Ingredients

- 2 tablespoons almonds
- 1/2 teaspoon cinnamon
- 1/2 cup organic
- strawberries, frozen
- 1 cup unsweetened almond milk, vanilla
- 2 iced cubes

Instructions

1. Place all of the ingredients in your blender, and blend until you get a creamy smoothie.

PEACH PIE SHAKE

Nutrition: Cal 209; Fat 4 g; Carb 11 g; Protein 28 g
Serving 1; Cook time 10 min

Ingredients

- 1 peach, pitted
- 1 scoop vanilla protein powder or 2 tablespoons gelatin plus
- 1 teaspoon vanilla extract
- 1/4 cup plain Greek yogurt
- 2 pinches of cinnamon
- 2/3 cup unsweetened almond milk
- 8-10 ice cubes

Instructions

1. Place all of the ingredients in your blender, and blend until you get a creamy smoothie.

BUTTERED PUMPKIN PIE COFFEE

Nutrition: Cal 12; Fat 3 g; Carb 10 g; Protein 1 g
Serving 1; Cook time 10 min

Ingredients

- 1/4 teaspoon pumpkin pie spice
- 1 tablespoon regular butter, unsalted
- 12 ounces hot coffee
- 2 tablespoons canned pumpkin
- 1 packet stevia or 2 teaspoons Splenda

Instructions

1. Place all of the ingredients in your blender, and blend until you get a creamy smoothie.

PEANUT BUTTER CRUNCH CHOCOLATE SMOOTHIE

Nutrition: Cal 236; Fat 19 g; Carb 11 g; Protein 3 g
Serving 2; Cook time 10 min

Ingredients

- 1 cup unsweetened almond milk
- 1/3 cup heavy whipping cream
- 1 packet stevia or 2 teaspoons Splenda
- 1/2 teaspoon vanilla extract
- 1 tablespoon unsweetened cocoa powder
- 3 ice cubes

Instructions

1. Place all of the ingredients in your blender, and blend until you get a creamy smoothie.

MANGO ALMOND SMOOTHIE

Nutrition: Cal 130; Fat 3 g; Carb 12 g; Protein 25 g
Serving 2; Cook time 10 min

Ingredients

- 125 g mango, frozen
- 3/4 cup unsweetened almond milk
- 1 pack gelatin or 1 scoop isolate protein
- 1 tablespoon flax seeds
- 1/2 cup ice cubes

Instructions

1. Place all of the ingredients in your blender, and blend until you get a creamy smoothie.

ALMOND STRAWBERRY SMOOTHIE

Nutrition: Cal 162; Fat 6 g; Carb 4 g; Protein 26g
Serving 2; Cook time 10 min

Ingredients

- 16 ounces unsweetened Almond milk
- 8 almonds
- 2 large strawberry, frozen
- 1 1/2 scoop whey protein powder or 3 tablespoon gelatin
- 6 ice cubes

Instructions

1. Place all of the ingredients in your blender, and blend until you get a creamy smoothie.

CHOCOLATE AVOCADO CREAM SMOOTHIE

Nutrition: Cal 433; Fat 32 g; Carb 15 g; Protein 25 g
Serving 2; Cook time 10 min

Ingredients

- 1 avocado, frozen
- 1/2 cup heavy cream
- 1 tablespoons dark chocolate
- 1 teaspoon Splenda
- 1 pack gelatin or 1 scoop chocolate isolate protein
- 1 cup water

Instructions

1. Place all of the ingredients in your blender, and blend until you get a creamy smoothie.

BERRIES & CREAM KETO PROTEIN SMOOTHIE

Nutrition: Cal 540; Fat 50 g; Carb 7 g; Protein 10 g
Serving 1; Cook time 10 min

Ingredients

- 1 cup coconut milk
- ⅓ cup frozen raspberries
- 1 Tbsp coconut oil or MCT oil
- 1 scoop collagen
- sweetener of choice, to taste

Instructions

1. Place all of the ingredients in your blender, and blend until you get a creamy smoothie.

CUCUMBER CELERY MATCHA KETO SMOOTHIE

Nutrition: Cal 280; Fat 27 g; Carb 10 g; Protein 3 g
Serving 1; Cook time 10 min

Ingredients

- ½ cup cashew milk
- 1 baby cucumber
- 1 stalk celery
- ½ avocado
- 1 Tbsp coconut oil or MCT oil
- 1 tsp matcha powder
- sweetener of choice, to taste

Instructions

1. Place all of the ingredients in your blender, and blend until you get a creamy smoothie.

GOLDEN MILK KETO SMOOTHIE

Nutrition: Cal 420; Fat 50 g; Carb 4 g; Protein 6 g
Serving 1; Cook time 10 min

Ingredients

- 8 coconut milk ice cubes, thawed slightly (or ~1 cup coconut milk)
- 2 Tbsp additional coconut milk or water
- ½ tsp vanilla
- 1 Tbsp coconut oil or MCT oil
- ½ tsp turmeric
- ¼ tsp cinnamon
- pinch of ground ginger
- pinch of salt
- sweetener of choice, to taste

Instructions

1. Place all of the ingredients in your blender, and blend until you get a creamy smoothie.

CINNAMON ALMOND BULLETPROOF SMOOTHIE

Nutrition: Cal 500; Fat 48 g; Carb 11 g; Protein 9 g
Serving 1; Cook time 10 min

Ingredients

- 1 cup coffee
- 4 coconut milk ice cubes, or ~⅓-½ cup coconut milk
- 1 Tbsp coconut oil or MCT oil
- 2 Tbsp almond butter
- 1 Tbsp flax meal
- ½ tsp cinnamon
- sweetener of choice, to taste
- pinch of salt

Instructions

1. Place all of the ingredients in your blender, and blend until you get a creamy smoothie.

BLACKBERRY CHEESECAKE KETO SMOOTHIE

Nutrition: Cal 450; Fat 41 g; Carb 14 g; Protein 5 g
Serving 1; Cook time 10 min

Ingredients

- ½ cup blackberries, frozen
- ¼ cup 2 oz cream cheese (or full-fat coconut milk, for dairy-free)
- 1 Tbsp coconut oil or MCT oil
- ¼ tsp vanilla extract
- sweetener of choice, to taste
- pinch of salt
- ¼ cup coconut milk
- ½ cup water

Instructions

1. Place all of the ingredients in your blender, and blend until you get a creamy smoothie.

MOCHA KETO COFFEE SHAKE

Nutrition: Cal 142; Fat 3 g; Carb 28 g; Protein 4 g
Serving 1; Cook time 10 min

Ingredients

- ¾ cup coconut milk, frozen into ice cubes (~6-8 cubes)
- ½ cup cold brew coffee, or leftover cold coffee
- scoop chocolate keto meal shake, or chocolate protein powder of choice
- 1 Tbsp cashew butter

Instructions

1. Pour coconut milk into ice cube tray and freeze overnight, until set.
2. When ready to drink, add all ingredients to a blender and blend until smooth.

KETO CHOCOLATE SHAKE

Nutrition: Cal 409; Fat 39 g; Carb 10 g; Protein 6 g

Serving 1; Cook time 10 min

Ingredients
- ¾ cup unsweetened almond milk, or milk of choice
- 3 Tbsp heavy cream, or coconut cream
- 1½ tsp cocoa powder
- 10g 90%+ dark chocolate, (or keto chocolate chips)
- 1 Tbsp nut butter of choice
- 1-2 Tbsp low carb sweetener of choice, to taste, (i.e., erythritol or monk fruit)
- ⅓ cup ice
- 1-3 tsp coconut or MCT oil, (for additional fat, optional)

OPTIONAL ADDITION:
- ½-1 scoop protein powder or collagen powder

Instructions
1. Place all of the ingredients in your blender, and blend until you get a creamy smoothie.

VEGAN KETO PUMPKIN CREAM COLD BREW
Nutrition: Cal 53; Fat 3 g; Carb 5 g; Protein 3 g
Serving 1; Cook time 10 min

Ingredients
- ¾ cup cold brew or cold brew concentrate
- ½ cup water, use less water for a stronger brew

KETO PUMPKIN CREAM COLD BREW FOAM
- 1 cup milk of choice
- 1 tsp canned pumpkin puree
- ½ tsp pumpkin pie spice
- ⅛ tsp glucomannan powder
- pinch of salt

Instructions
1. Combine cold brew and water as desired. Serve over ice.
2. Separately, combine milk of choice, pumpkin puree, pumpkin pie spice, glucomannan powder, and salt. If desired, add stevia drops or sweetener of choice to taste.
3. Use a frother or immersion blender to mix ingredients together until frothy! Froth/blend for 2-3 minutes, let it sit for a minute, then continue blending for another minute until thickened and holding form.
4. Pour foam on top of cold brew, sprinkle with pumpkin pie spice, and serve.

CINNAMON DOLCE LATTE
Nutrition: Cal 235; Fat 22 g; Carb 5 g; Protein 13 g
Serving 1; Cook time 10 min

Ingredients
- 1/2 cup unsweetened milk of choice
- 6 ounces cold brewed coffee
- 1/2 tablespoon chia seeds
- 1/2 teaspoon ceylon cinnamon
- 1 scoop Perfect Keto Collagen Powder
- 1 tablespoon Perfect Keto MCT Oil
- **OPTIONAL**
- 1 handful ice

- keto friendly sweetener of choice to taste

Instructions
1. Place all of the ingredients in your blender, and blend until you get a creamy smoothie.

ENERGIZING KETO SMOOTHIE
Nutrition: Cal 250; Fat 26 g; Carb 4 g; Protein 4 g
Serving 1; Cook time 10 min

Ingredients
- 1 cup unsweetened cashew milk
- 1 tablespoon Perfect Keto MCT Oil
- 1 tablespoon Perfect Keto Nut Butter
- 2 teaspoons maca powder
- 1 handful ice

Instructions
1. Place all of the ingredients in your blender, and blend until you get a creamy smoothie.

CHOCOLATE SEA SALT SMOOTHIE
Nutrition: Cal 235; Fat 20 g; Carb 11,5 g; Protein 5,5 g
Serving 1; Cook time 10 min

Ingredients
- 1 avocado (frozen or not)
- 2 cups almond milk
- 1 tablespoon tahini
- ¼ cup cocoa powder
- 1 scoop Perfect Keto 'Chocolate' Base
- Stevia or monk fruit to taste

Instructions
1. Place all of the ingredients in your blender, and blend until you get a creamy smoothie.

ACAI ALMOND BUTTER SMOOTHIE
Nutrition: Cal 235; Fat 20 g; Carb 11,5 g; Protein 5,5 g
Serving 1; Cook time 10 min

Ingredients
- 1 100g Pack Unsweetened Acai Puree
- 3/4 cup Unsweetened Almond Milk
- 1/4 of an Avocado
- 3 tbsp Collagen or Protein Powder
- 1 tbsp Coconut Oil or MCT Oil Powder
- 1 tbsp Almond Butter
- 1/2 tsp Vanilla Extract
- 2 drops Liquid Stevia

Instructions
1. If you are using individualized 100 gram packs of acai puree, run the pack under lukewarm water for a few seconds until you are able to break up the puree into smaller pieces. Open the pack and put the contents into the blender.
2. Place the remaining ingredients in the blender and blend until smooth. Add more water or ice cubes as needed.
3. Drizzle the almond butter along the side of the glass to make it look cool.

STRAWBERRY AVOCADO KETO SMOOTHIE

Nutrition: Cal 106; Fat 7 g; Carb 10 g; Protein 1 g
Serving 1; Cook time 10 min

Ingredients

- 1 lb Frozen strawberries
- 1 1/2 cups Unsweetened almond milk
- 1 large Avocado
- 1/4 cup Besti Powdered Monk Fruit Allulose Blend

Instructions

1. Place all of the ingredients in your blender, and blend until you get a creamy smoothie.

KETO SMOOTHIE – BLUEBERRY

Nutrition: Cal 215; Fat 10 g; Carb 7 g; Protein 23 g
Serving 1; Cook time 10 min

Ingredients

- 1 cup Coconut Milk or almond milk
- 1/4 cup Blueberries
- 1 tsp Vanilla Extract
- 1 tsp MCT Oil or coconut oil
- 30 g Protein Powder

Instructions

1. Place all of the ingredients in your blender, and blend until you get a creamy smoothie.

CHOCOLATE FAT BOMB SMOOTHIE

Nutrition: Cal 240; Fat 11 g; Carb 4 g; Protein 13 g
Serving 1; Cook time 10 min

Ingredients

- 70 g avocado, frozen pieces 1/2 a cup
- 1 scoop perfect keto chocolate collagen
- 1 tbsp cacao powder
- 1 cup almond milk
- ½ – 1 cup ice

Instructions

1. Place all of the ingredients in your blender, and blend until you get a creamy smoothie.

KETO CREAMY HOT CHOCOLATE

Nutrition: Cal 183; Fat 15 g; Carb 1 g; Protein 10 g
Serving 1; Cook time 10 min

Ingredients

- 1 scoop Perfect Keto chocolate collagen
- 2 tbsp pure cream (heavy whipping cream)
- 1 cup boiling water

Instructions

1. Add chocolate collagen and cream to a cup of boiling water
2. Blend to combine. You could do this in your blender, with a milk frother or stick blender

KETO DAIRY FREE SHAMROCK SHAKE

Nutrition: Cal 137; Fat 3 g; Carb 3 g; Protein 4 g
Serving 1; Cook time 10 min

Ingredients

- ½ medium avocado
- 1 scoop dairy free vanilla protein powder (about 30g)
- ½ cup almond or coconut milk
- 8 ice cubes
- ⅛ teaspoon peppermint extract
- 5 drops natural green food coloring (optional for color)
- 2 tablespoon coconut milk whipped cream (optional)
- 1 tablespoon sugar-free dark chocolate chips

Instructions

1. Place all of the ingredients in your blender, and blend until you get a creamy smoothie.

KETO BLUEBERRY CHEESECAKE SMOOTHIE

Nutrition: Cal 311; Fat 27 g; Carb 9 g; Protein 6 g
Serving 1; Cook time 10 min

Ingredients

- ½ medium avocado
- 1 scoop dairy free vanilla protein powder (about 30g)
- ½ cup almond or coconut milk
- 8 ice cubes
- ⅛ teaspoon peppermint extract
- 5 drops natural green food coloring (optional for color)
- 2 tablespoon coconut milk whipped cream (optional)
- 1 tablespoon sugar-free dark chocolate chips

Instructions

1. Place all of the ingredients in your blender, and blend until you get a creamy smoothie.

HIGH PROTEIN KETO STRAWBERRY SMOOTHIE

Nutrition: Cal 205; Fat 14 g; Carb 8 g; Protein 13 g
Serving 2; Cook time 10 min

Ingredients

- ½ medium avocado
- 1 scoop dairy free vanilla protein powder (about 30g)
- ½ cup almond or coconut milk
- 8 ice cubes
- ⅛ teaspoon peppermint extract
- 5 drops natural green food coloring (optional for color
- 2 tablespoon coconut milk whipped cream (optional)
- 1 tablespoon sugar-free dark chocolate chips

Instructions

1. Place all of the ingredients in your blender, and blend until you get a creamy smoothie.

FAT-BURNING VANILLA SMOOTHIE

Nutrition: Cal 650; Fat 64 g; Carb 4 g; Protein 12 g
Serving 1; Cook time 10 min

Ingredients

- 2 large egg yolks
- 1/2 cup mascarpone cheese (full-fat)
- 1/4 cup water
- 4 ice cubes
- 1 tbsp coconut oil
- 1/2 pure vanilla extract
- 1 tbsp So Nourished powdered erythritol sweetener
- whipped cream

Instructions

Place all of the ingredients in your blender, and blend until you get a creamy smoothie.

Ice Cream

KETO CHOCOLATE ICE CREAM

Nutrition: Cal 200; Fat 20 g; Carb 3 g; Protein 6 g
Serving 1; Cook time 4 hours

Ingredients
- 1 Cup Heavy whipping cream
- 3 Tablespoons Granular Sweetener
- 1 Tablespoon Cocoa powder
- Splash of vanilla

Instructions
1. Add the ingredients to a large mason jar and secure with a lid.
2. Shake for 5 minutes or until the heavy cream is thick.
3. Freeze for 3-5 hours. Serve.

KETO STRAWBERRY ICE CREAM

Nutrition: Cal 200; Fat 20 g; Carb 3 g; Protein 6 g
Serving ; Cook time 4 hours

Ingredients
- 1 Cup Heavy whipping cream
- 3 Tablespoons Granular Sweetener
- ½ ounce Freeze dried strawberries - grounded to a powder
- Splash of vanilla

Instructions
4. Add the ingredients to a large mason jar and secure with a lid.
5. Shake for 5 minutes or until the heavy cream is thick.
6. Freeze for 3-5 hours. Serve.

KETO CHOCOLATE FROZEN YOGURT

Nutrition: Cal 121; Fat 6 g; Carb 10 g; Protein 10 g
Serving 4; Cook time 4 hours

Ingredients
- 2 Cups Whole Milk Greek yogurt
- ½ Cup Unsweetened Cocoa Powder
- 1 tablespoon Vanilla Extract
- ⅔ Cup Powdered Sweetener

Instructions
1. Combine all of the ingredients in a blender and blend until completely smooth.
2. Transfer the chocolate mixture into a freezer safe storage container with a lid, or a loaf pan and cover with Saran Wrap. Freeze for 1-2 hours.
3. Remove container from the freezer and stir the already frozen edges into the soft center. Cover again and place back into the freezer and let freeze for about 3 hours or until frozen. Remove from the freezer and serve. You may need to let it set out for about 10-15 minutes to soften.

KETO LAVENDER ICE CREAM

Nutrition: Cal 322; Fat 32 g; Carb 6 g; Protein 4 g
Serving 10; Cook time 4 hours

Ingredients
- 2 cups cream, heavy
- 1 cup coconut milk, canned
- 1 cup mascarpone cheese softened
- ½ cup allulose or other low carb sweetener
- 1 cup blueberries
- 1 cup raspberries
- 2 tablespoons culinary lavender

Instructions
1. Place a 1lb loaf tin (16cm long, 11cm wide and 7cm high (6 x 4 x 3 inches) in the freezer.
2. In a medium saucepan add the cream, coconut milk and lavender buds and place this on a medium heat. When it looks like the mixture is about to boil, remove it from the heat.
3. Let the mixture steep for 15 minutes.
4. Place the blueberries and raspberries into a blender and blitz until smooth.
5. Strain the liquid into a medium bowl to remove the lavender buds.
6. In another medium bowl add the mascarpone and allulose and whisk until smooth.
7. Pour in the coconut mixture and whisk to combine.
8. Add the blended berry mixture and stir until you have an even colour.
9. Remove the tin/container from the freezer and pour the mixture into it. Cover with clingfilm and freeze for at least 4 hours.

KETO COFFEE ICE CREAM

Nutrition: Cal 265; Fat 26 g; Carb 2 g; Protein 2 g
Serving 8; Cook time 1 hour 15 min

Ingredients
- 2 ¼ cups heavy whipping cream divided
- ½ cup unsweetened almond milk (or hemp milk for nut-free)
- ½ cup powdered Swerve Sweetener divided
- ¼ cup BochaSweet
- 2 tablespoon butter
- ¼ teaspoon xanthan gum
- 1 to 1 ½ tablespoon instant coffee
- ¾ teaspoon vanilla extract

Instructions
1. In a medium saucepan over medium heat, combine 1 cup of the cream and the almond milk. Whisk in ¼ cup of the Swerve and the BochaSweet. Bring to a boil, then reduce the heat and simmer 40 minutes, whisking occasionally.
2. Remove from heat and add the butter. Whisk to combine, until the butter is melted. Then sprinkle the

surface with xanthan gum and whisk vigorously to combine.

3. Whisk in the instant coffee and vanilla extract, until the coffee granules have dissolved. Let cool to room temperature.

4. Whip remaining 1 ¼ cups whipping cream with the remaining Swerve sweetener until it just holds stiff peaks. Gently fold in the cooled coffee mixture until well combined.

5. Transfer to a container and freeze until firm, about 5 or 6 hours.

ALMOND FUDGE – KETO ICE CREAM

Nutrition: Cal 310; Fat 28 g; Carb 5 g; Protein 5 g
Serving 8; Cook time 6 hours

Ingredients
CUSTARD BASE
- 1 ½ cups heavy whipping cream
- ¾ cup almond milk
- ⅓ cup Swerve Sweetener
- ⅓ cup BochaSweet or allulose
- 2 teaspoon espresso powder or 1 to 2 tablespoon instant coffee
- 3 large egg yolks
- ¼ teaspoon xanthan gum
- 1 ½ tablespoon vodka optional
- ½ teaspoon vanilla extract

FUDGE SWIRL
- ⅓ cup heavy whipping cream
- 3 tablespoon confectioner's Swerve Sweetener
- 1 ½ ounces unsweetened chocolate finely chopped
- ½ teaspoon vanilla extract
- ½ cup toasted almonds chopped

Instructions
1. For the ice cream, combine the cream, almond milk, sweeteners, and espresso powder in a medium saucepan over medium heat, stirring until the sweetener and coffee dissolve.

2. Heat the mixture until it's steaming and it reaches 165F on an instant read thermometer.

3. In a medium bowl, whisk the egg yolks until smooth. Slowly whisk in 1 cup of the hot cream mixture to temper the yolks. Then slowly whisk the tempered yolks back into the remaining cream mixture in the pan. Cook, whisking continuously until it reaches 170F to 175F.

4. Sprinkle the surface with the xanthan gum and whisk vigorously to combine.

5. Pour the custard into a bowl set over an ice bath and let cool 10 minutes. Then wrap tightly in plastic wrap and refrigerate until fully chilled, at least 3 hours.

KETO MAPLE WALNUT ICE CREAM

Nutrition: Cal 318; Fat 32 g; Carb 3 g; Protein 3 g
Serving 8; Cook time 5 hours 45 min

Ingredients
- ½ cups heavy whipping cream divided
- ¼ cup Swerve Brown
- ¼ cup Bocha Sweet
- 2 tablespoon butter
- ½ teaspoon maple extract
- ¼ teaspoon xanthan gum
- ⅓ cup chopped walnuts

Instructions
1. In a medium saucepan over medium heat, bring 1 ¼ cups of the whipping cream and the two sweeteners to a simmer. Reduce the heat and simmer gently for 30 minutes. Watch carefully as you want it to simmer but not continue to boil. There should be little bubbles along the edges the whole time.

2. Remove from heat and whisk in the butter and maple extract. Sprinkle the surface with xanthan gum, whisking vigorously to combine. Let the mixture cool to room temperature and then refrigerate until chilled, about 2 hours.

3. In a large bowl, beat the remaining whipping cream until it holds stiff peaks. Fold in the chilled maple/cream until well combined. Stir in the chopped walnuts.

4. Transfer the mixture to an airtight container and freeze until firm, about 5 hours.

KETO CANNOLI ICE CREAM

Nutrition: Cal 242; Fat 20 g; Carb 7 g; Protein 6 g
Serving 8; Cook time 6 hours 10 min

Ingredients
- 1 cup heavy whipping cream
- ⅓ cup powdered Swerve Sweetener
- ⅓ cup BochaSweet (can sub allulose or xylitol)
- ¾ cup ricotta cheese
- 3 ounces cream cheese room temperature
- 1 teaspoon vanilla extract
- ⅓ cup dark chocolate chips, sugar-free
- ¼ cup chopped pistachios or other nuts (optional)

Instructions
1. In a large bowl, beat the cream with the Swerve until it holds stiff peaks.

2. In a blender or food processor, combine the ricotta, cream cheese, vanilla extract and the BochaSweet. Blend until smooth and the sweetener has dissolved.

3. Fold the ricotta mixture into the whipped cream. Then gently fold in the chocolate chips.

4. Spread in an airtight container and freeze until firm, 6 to 8 hours.

BLUEBERRY PIE ICE CREAM

Nutrition: Cal 283; Fat 27 g; Carb 6 g; Protein 2 g
Serving 10; Cook time 9 hours 20 min

Ingredients

CRUMBLE:
- ¼ cup almond flour
- 2 tablespoons shredded coconut
- 1 tablespoons Swerve Granular
- 1½ tablespoons butter melted

BLUEBERRY SAUCE:
- 1½ cups fresh Oregon blueberries
- ¼ cup water
- 2 tablespoons Swerve Granular
- t2 ablespoons allulose or BochaSweet
- 1 teaspoon lemon zest
- ½ teaspoon glucomannan or xanthan gum

NO CHURN VANILLA ICE CREAM:
- 2½ cups heavy whipping cream divided
- ½ cup almond milk
- ½ cup Swerve Confectioners divided
- ¼ cup allulose or BochaSweet
- 2 tablespoons butter
- 1 teaspoon vanilla extract
- ¼ teaspoon glucomannan or xanthan gum

Instructions

CRUMBLE:
1. Preheat the oven to 325°F and line a baking sheet with parchment paper.
2. In a medium bowl, whisk together the almond flour, coconut, and sweetener. Stir in the melted butter until the mixture begins to clump together.
3. Transfer to the mixture to the prepared baking sheet and spread out into a thin layer. Top with another piece of parchment and press down to help it stick together.
4. Remove the top piece of parchment and bake 18 to 25 minutes, until the crumble is golden brown. Remove from the oven and let cool completely to crisp up, then break into small pieces with your fingers.

BLUEBERRY SAUCE:
1. Combine the blueberries, the sweeteners, and the water in a medium saucepan over medium heat. Bring to a boil, then lower the heat to a simmer and cook until the berries are soft enough to be mashed, about 7 minutes.
2. Remove from heat and stir in the lemon zest. Sprinkle the glucomannan overtop and whisk to combine. Let cool completely.

VANILLA ICE CREAM:
1. Prepare the condensed milk: In a medium saucepan over medium heat, combine 1 cup of the cream, the almond milk, ¼ cup of the Swerve, the allulose, and the vanilla extract. Bring to a simmer, then reduce the heat and simmer 20 minutes.
2. Remove from heat and add the butter. Let melt, then stir in the vanilla extract. Sprinkle the surface with the glucomannan and whisk to combine. Let cool to room temperature.
3. In a large bowl, beat the remaining 1 ½ cups cream with the remaining powdered sweetener until it holds stiff peaks. Gently fold in the cooled cream/almond milk mixture until no streaks remain.

TO ASSEMBLE:
1. Spread half of the vanilla ice cream in a freezer-safe container and dollop half of the blueberry sauce overtop. Sprinkle with half of the crumble and swirl with a knife to combine.
2. Repeat with the remaining ice cream, the sauce, and the crumble. Swirl until well mixed but still streaky.
3. Cover tightly and freeze until firm. Depending on what sweetener you use, this can take 8 to 24 hours.

PEANUT BUTTER ICE CREAM CAKE

Nutrition: Cal 264; Fat 23 g; Carb 7 g; Protein 6 g
Serving 16; Cook time 5 hours 20 min

Ingredients

BROWNIE BASE:
- ⅓ cup creamy peanut butter
- ⅓ cup softened butter
- ⅓ cup cocoa powder
- ⅓ cup powdered Swerve Sweetener
- ½ teaspoon vanilla extract
- 1 cup almond flour
- 1 to 3 tablespoon water

No Churn Peanut Butter Ice Cream:
- 1 cup sour cream
- ¾ cup creamy peanut butter
- ½ cup confectioner's Swerve Sweetener divided
- 1 cup whipping cream
- ½ teaspoon vanilla extract

Instructions

BROWNIE BASE:
1. In a medium bowl, stir peanut butter and butter together until smooth. Stir in the cocoa powder, sweetener, and vanilla extract until well combined.
2. Stir in the almond flour. The dough will become very stiff and hard to mix. Add water, 1 tablespoon at a time, until you have a cohesive but stiff dough.
3. Press evenly into the bottom of a 9-inch springform pan. Top with a layer of waxed paper and smooth with a flat-bottomed glass or measuring cup. Refrigerate while preparing the ice cream.

NO CHURN PEANUT BUTTER ICE CREAM:
1. In a large bowl, beat together the sour cream, peanut butter, and ¼ cup of the sweetener. In another large bowl, beat the whipping cream with the remaining ¼ cup sweetener and the vanilla extract until stiff peaks form.
2. Gently fold whipping cream into peanut butter mixture until well combined and no streaks remain. Spread ice cream over brownie base and freeze until firm, 4 to 6 hours.
3. Before serving, drizzle with a little low carb chocolate sauce, if desired

CHOCOLATE PEANUT BUTTER ICE CREAM

Nutrition: Cal 294; Fat 26 g; Carb 7 g; Protein 6 g
Serving 10; Cook time 5 hours 35 min

Ingredients
- 1 ¾ cups heavy cream
- ¾ cup unsweetened almond milk
- ½ cup Swerve Sweetener
- ¼ cup BochaSweet or allulose
- ¼ cup cocoa powder
- 3 egg yolks
- 2 ounces unsweetened chocolate finely chopped
- 2 tablespoon vodka
- ½ teaspoon xanthan gum
- ½ cup peanut butter

Instructions
1. Set a medium bowl in a large container of ice water.
2. Whisk cream, almond milk, sweeteners and cocoa powder in a medium saucepan until cocoa powder is mostly dissolved. Over medium heat, stir occasionally and heat until mixture is steaming but not simmering, or 170F on a candy thermometer.
3. Whisk egg yolks in a small bowl until smooth. Very slowly whisk in 1 cup of the hot cream mixture to temper the yolks. Then slowly whisk tempered yolks back into cream mixture, stirring constantly. Continue to cook until very hot, 175 – 180F.
4. Add chopped chocolate and let sit 1 minute to melt, then whisk to combine.
5. Pour mixture into bowl in ice bath and let cool 10 minutes then wrap tightly with plastic wrap and refrigerate at least 3 hours.
6. When ready to churn, remove custard from fridge and add vodka, stirring to combine. Sprinkle with xanthan gum and whisk vigorously to combine.
7. Pour mixture into canister of an ice cream maker and churn according to manufacturer's directions. When ice cream is about the consistency of soft serve, transfer half to an airtight container.
8. Working quickly, add about half the peanut butter by spoonfuls. Add the remaining ice cream and the remaining peanut butter and swirl with a knife to spread evenly.
9. Press plastic wrap flush to the surface and freeze until firm, 1 to 2 hours.
10. Leftovers will freeze hard but not unscoopable.

KETO BLACKBERRY HAZELNUT SEMI-FREDDO

Nutrition: Cal 254; Fat 22 g; Carb 6 g; Protein 4 g
Serving 1; Cook time 8 hours 30 min

Ingredients
- 4 large egg yolks
- 1 large egg
- ¼ cup BochaSweet (or allulose)
- 1 ⅓ cup whipping cream
- ¼ cup powdered Swerve Sweetener
- 1 teaspoon hazelnut extract (or vanilla extract)
- 1 cup blackberries divided
- ¾ cup toasted chopped hazelnuts divided

Instructions
1. Grease a 9x5 inch loaf pan and line with two pieces of parchment paper so that the pan is covered and the edges of parchment overhang the sides.
2. Set a heatproof bowl over a pan of barely simmering water. Add the egg yolks, egg, and the BochaSweet, whisking continuously, until thickened, 5 to 7 minutes. Remove the bowl from over pan and cool the egg mixture to lukewarm, whisking frequently. Whisk in the extract.
3. In a large bowl, whip the cream with the powdered sweetener until stiff peaks form. Fold one large scoop of whipped cream into the egg mixture to lighten. Then gently fold egg mixture back into whipped cream until no streaks remain.
4. Stir in ¾ cup of the blackberries and ½ cup chopped hazelnuts. Spread the mixture in the prepared loaf pan and freeze until firm, at least 8 hours or overnight.
5. Run a spatula between pan and parchment paper. Invert the semifreddo onto serving platter and peel off parchment. Top with remaining blackberries and hazelnuts and cut into 1 inch slices.

NEAPOLITAN ICE CREAM CAKE

Nutrition: Cal 354; Fat 33 g; Carb 6 g; Protein 5 g
Serving 16; Cook time 7 hours

Ingredients
CAKE:
- 1 cup almond flour
- ¼ cup Swerve Sweetener
- ¼ cup cocoa powder
- 1 ½ teaspoon baking powder
- ¼ teaspoon salt
- 2 large eggs, room temperature
- ½ cup butter, melted
- ½ teaspoon vanilla extract
- 2 to 4 tablespoon cold coffee or water

ICE CREAM:
- 2 cups heavy whipping cream
- ½ cup Bocha Sweet divided (or allulose or xylitol)
- 6 tablespoon powdered Swerve Sweetener
- 3 tablespoon butter
- 1 teaspoon vanilla extract
- ½ teaspoon xanthan gum
- 1 cup chopped fresh strawberries
- 12 ounces cream cheese softened

CHOCOLATE GLAZE:
- ½ cup heavy whipping cream
- 2 ounces unsweetened chocolate chopped and cut into chunks
- ¼ cup powdered Swerve Sweetener
- ½ teaspoon vanilla extract

Instructions
CAKE:
1. Preheat the oven to 325F and grease a 9-inch springform pan well. Line the bottom with parchment paper and grease the parchment.
2. In a medium bowl, whisk together the almond flour, cocoa powder, baking powder, and salt. Add the eggs, melted butter, and vanilla extract and stir to combine. Add the coffee or water 1 tablespoon at a time until a spreadable consistency is achieved. The batter should not be pourable.
3. Spread the batter evenly in the prepared baking pan and bake 30 minutes or until just firm to the touch. Remove and let cool completely. Once it's completely cool, run a sharp knife around the edges of the pan and loosen the sides. Then tighten the sides back on (this is just to ensure the cake does not stick to the pan sides after freezing).

ICE CREAM:
4. In a large heavy saucepan over medium heat, combine the whipping cream with 6 tablespoons of the Bocah Sweet and all of the powdered Swerve. Bring to just a boil, then reduce the heat and simmer gently for 30 minutes. Watch carefully as you want it to simmer but not continue to boil. There should be little bubbles along the edges the whole time.
5. Remove from heat and whisk in the butter until melted. Sprinkle the surface with the xanthan gum and whisk vigorously to combine. Let cool to room temperature, about 20 minutes.
6. Meanwhile, place the strawberries in a blender with the remaining 2 tablespoons of Bocha Sweet. Puree and set aside.
7. In a large food processor, combine the cream cheese and the cream mixture. Blend until very smooth. Taste for sweetness and if you want it a bit sweeter, add more powdered Swerve. Add more vanilla if desired.
8. Spread about ⅔ of this mixture evenly over the cooled cake.
9. Add the strawberry puree to the remaining mixture in the food processor and blend to combine, scraping down the sides of the food processor to ensure it all mixes in. Again, taste for sweetness.
10. Spread this mixture over the vanilla in the pan, smoothing the top. Freeze until firm, about 6 hours.

CHOCOLATE GLAZE:
11. In a small saucepan over medium heat, bring the cream to just a simmer. Remove from heat and add the chopped chocolate. Let sit a few minutes to melt and then whisk in the sweetener and vanilla.
12. Let thicken about 5 minutes, then pour over the top of the cake and let drizzle down the sides. It will harden quickly on the frozen cake.
13. To serve, heat a sharp knife briefly in hot water or over the flame of gas stove (this is what I do!). Slice straight down, making sure to cut through the bottom cake layer. Work a spatula under the cake but over the parchment paper.

NO CHURN MINT CHIP ICE CREAM
Nutrition: Cal 340; Fat 21 g; Carb 24 g; Protein 8 g
Serving 6; Cook time 6 hours

Ingredients
- 1/2 cups whipping cream
- 1/2 cup Swerve, Confectioners, divided
- 1 cup sour cream
- 1 to 2 tsp mint extract (depending on how minty you want it)
- 1 tsp matcha powder OR a few drops green food coloring (optional)
- 3 ounces sugar-free dark chocolate, chopped

Instructions
1. In a large bowl, beat the whipping cream with 1/4 cup of the Swerve until stiff peaks form.
2. In another bowl, stir together the sour cream, remaining Swerve, and mint extract. If you want a green color, whisk in the matcha powder or green food coloring.
3. Fold in the whipped cream until well combined. Stir in the chocolate. Transfer to a container and freeze until firm, 4 to 6 hours.

COCONUT CARAMEL ICE CREAM
Nutrition: Cal 342; Fat 30 g; Carb 6 g; Protein 10 g
Serving 8; Cook time 4 hours 15 min

Ingredients
- Caramel Sauce
- ¼ cup butter
- ¼ cup brown erythritol or other low carb sweetener
- ½ cup heavy cream
- Ice Cream
- 2 cups heavy cream
- ½ cup allulose
- 1 cup coconut, shredded or unsweetened desiccated coconut
- ½ cup caramel sauce as per above

Instructions
CARAMEL SAUCE
1. Melt the butter in a small pan and let it cook, stirring every so often, until fully browned (about 5 minutes) This will give the sauce a deeper caramel flavour.
2. Pour in heavy cream and stir until combined. Lower the heat and simmer for a minute.
3. Add in your brown erythritol and stir until dissolved.
4. Cook until you see it getting thicker and stir the sauce intermediately to ensure it does not stick. This should take about 15 minutes.
5. Set aside to cool before use.

ICE CREAM
1. In a large bowl, pour the cream, coconut extract and add the allulose. Whisk until you have firm peaks.
2. Stir in the shredded coconut.

3. Pour the mixture into a container with a lid. Gently spoon the caramel sauce into the ice cream mixture and swirl.
4. With the lid firmly on, place the ice cream in the freezer to firm for at least 4 hours.
5. Serve with more caramel sauce and toasted coconut.

RASPBERRY KETO ICE CREAM

Nutrition: Cal 230; Fat 29 g; Carb 7 g; Protein 4 g
Serving 6; Cook time 30 min

Ingredients
- 12 ounce bag frozen raspberries
- 8 ounces mascarpone cheese
- 1 cup heavy cream, cold
- ⅔ cup allulose confectioners
- ½ teaspoon vanilla extract
- ¼ teaspoon xanthan gum

Instructions
1. Add the raspberries to the bowl of a food processor. Pour the heavy cream and mascarpone over the top. Blend until well combined.
2. Add in the rest of the ingredients and continue mixing until you have a smooth creamy mixture. You can leave it a little chunky or even add in a few more raspberries towards the end if you'd like.
3. Pour the mixture into an airtight container, and chill 20 minutes for a soft-serve consistency and 2-3 hours for ice cream.

KETO STRAWBERRY CHEESECAKE ICE CREAM

Nutrition: Cal 213; Fat 18 g; Carb 3 g; Protein 1 g
Serving 10; Cook time 5 hours 20 min

Ingredients
FOR THE KETO STRAWBERRY CHEESECAKE ICE CREAM:
- 225 g strawberries
- 225 g cream cheese softened
- 1 13.5-ounce can full fat coconut milk
- 135-150 g allulose xylitol
- 1/4 teaspoon kosher salt
- 1/4 teaspoon xanthan gum
- 2 teaspoons vanilla extract
- 240 g sour cream or heavy cream, whipped

FOR THE LAZY (NO-BAKE!) GRAHAM CRACKER CRUMBS (OPTIONAL)
- 96 g almond flour or meal
- 2-4 tablespoons powdered xylitol or sweetener of choice, to taste
- 1/2 teaspoon cinnamon
- 1/8 teaspoon kosher salt
- 28 g unsalted grass-fed butter

FOR THE KETO GRAHAM CRACKER TOPPING (OPTIONAL)
- 1/2 batch keto graham crackers optional

Instructions
FOR THE STRAWBERRY CHEESECAKE ICE CREAM
1. Make a puree by simply blending strawberries with the cream cheese in a food processor or blender and sieve it. Feel free to set aside (or add!) a handful of diced strawberries if you like 'fruity bits' in your ice cream! Set aside.
2. Add coconut milk, sweetener, and salt to a saucepan over medium heat. Whisk until all the solids from the coconut milk have the dissolved and the mixture is smooth.
3. Sprinkle xanthan gum little by little and whisk (or blend with an immersion blender) until fully combined. You will likely have some air bubbles, but be sure to check there are no lumps. Any lumps will be resolved by mixing with an immersion blender (or in an actual blender).
4. Sieve the mixture to a bowl, stir in vanilla extract, cover with a layer of cling film (saran wrap) laid directly over the mixture (to avoid a 'skin' forming), and allow the mixture to cool completely. The texture will be thick and jelly-like (don't worry, your ice cream won't have this texture!).
5. Add heavy whipping cream or cold coconut cream to a large chilled bowl and whip until soft peaks form. Mix in the chilled vanilla mixture, followed by the strawberry cream cheese mixture.
6. Transfer ice cream to a sealable container and place in the freezer until frozen (4-6 hours to overnight). And note that you can still use your ice cream machine if you wish (roughly 15 minutes to churn).
7. If you're adding in graham crackers or crumbs, fold them in once the ice cream is semi-hard (either right after churning or about 2-3 hours after freezing).

FOR THE GRAHAM CRACKER CRUMBS (OPTIONAL)
1. Lightly toast almond flour in a skillet or pan over medium heat, until fully golden and fragrant (2-4 minutes). This is very important taste-wise, so don't skip!
2. Transfer toasted almond flour to a medium bowl, and mix in sweetener, cinnamon and salt. Add in butter and mix until thoroughly combined. Form into clumps using your fingertips, transfer to a plate and allow to come to room temperature and freeze for 15-20 minutes before folding into the ice cream.

KETO SALTED CARAMEL ICE CREAM

Nutrition: Cal 267; Fat 18 g; Carb 3 g; Protein 22 g
Serving 8; Cook time 4 hours 20 min

Ingredients
- 6 tablespoon butter
- ⅓ cup Swerve Brown
- ⅓ cup BochaSweet or allulose
- ½ teaspoon vanilla extract
- ¾ teaspoon kosher or sea salt
- ¼ teaspoon xanthan gum
- 1 ½ cups whipping cream

- 1 cup unsweetened almond milk (or hemp milk)
- 3 large egg yolks
- 2 tablespoon vodka (optional, helps reduce iciness)

Instructions

1. Set a medium bowl over an ice bath and set aside.
2. In a large saucepan, combine the butter and sweeteners. When the butter has melted, whisk to combine well. Bring to a boil and cook 3 to 5 minutes, being careful not to burn it.
3. Remove from heat and stir in the vanilla and salt. Sprinkle the surface with the xanthan gum and whisk vigorously to combine.
4. Slowly add the cream, whisking constantly; the mixture may bubble vigorously. Stir in the almond milk. Set over medium low heat and cook, whisking frequently, until the mixture reaches 165F on an instant read thermometer.
5. In a medium bowl, whisk the egg yolks until smooth. Slowly add about 1 cup of the hot cream mixture, whisking constantly. Then slowly return the egg yolks to the hot cream in saucepan, whisking constantly. Continue to cook until mixture reaches 175F on an instant read thermometer.
6. Pour the custard into the bowl set over ice bath and cool 10 minutes. Then wrap tightly in plastic wrap and chill at least 2 hours.
7. Whisk in the vodka, if using. Pour the mixture into the canister of an ice cream maker and churn according to manufacturer's directions.
8. Once churned, transfer the ice cream to an airtight container. Freeze until firm, about 2 hours.

HAZELNUT ICE CREAM

Nutrition: Cal 260; Fat 22 g; Carb 8 g; Protein 4 g
Serving 8; Cook time 5 hours 30 min

Ingredients

- 1 cup / 8 fl oz. hemp milk, unsweetened
- 1 ½ cups / 12 fl oz. heavy cream
- 2 TBSP vegetable glycerin
- 3 ½ oz. / 100g xylitol (NO substitutes!)
- ½ tsp. sea salt
- 7 oz. / 195g roasted hazelnuts, skins removed
- 1 tsp. vanilla extract
- 2 oz. / 55g cream cheese (full fat)
- ½ tsp. guar gum

Instructions

1. Warm the hemp milk, cream, glycerin, xylitol, and sea salt in a medium pan until it just starts to boil. Remove from the heat, add the roasted hazelnuts, cover and leave for 2 hours to soak.
2. Soaking your nuts is important!
3. Carefully pour the soaked hazelnuts and cream in a blender and blend for 4 – 5 minutes until the nuts are completely smooth. I mean completely smooth. Test it. They gotta be smooth.
4. Add the cream cheese and vanilla extract and blend until the cheese is completely mixed in. It will be super

thick. While the blender is still running, add the guar gum by tapping it through the opening in the lid, and blend for 30 seconds.

5. Pour the ice cream custard into a bowl or jar, cover, and place in the 'fridge for at least 8 hours, but preferably overnight. Don't skip the chillin', no matter which type of churner you have.
6. Stir the chilled custard well – this one will take a lot of stirring!
7. Freeze the custard in your churner according to the manufacturer's instructions. It typically takes between 15 - minutes to freeze to a soft-serve consistency.
8. Once the ice cream has frozen to a soft-serve consistency, quickly transfer it from the churning bowl into your pre-chilled container and quickly stir in the Chocolate Chunks evenly through the custard.
9. Place in the freezer for at least 8 hours, preferably overnight.

KETO VANILLA ICE CREAM

Nutrition: Cal 240; Fat 22 g; Carb 6 g; Protein 6 g
Serving 8; Cook time 5 hours 30 min

Ingredients

- 1 ½ cups / 12 fl oz. almond milk, unsweetened
- vanilla 1 whole vanilla pod, split lengthwise, seeds scraped out
- 100 g xylitol (NO substitutes!)
- 1 tsp. sea salt
- 1 cup / 8 fl oz. heavy cream
- 1 ½ cups / 12 fl oz. thick coconut milk
- 1 tsp. vanilla extract
- 1 tsp. guar gum

Instructions

1. Warm the almond milk, vanilla seeds and pod, xylitol, sea salt, and cream in a medium pan until it just starts to boil.
2. Simmer for one minute and then remove from the heat, cover, and leave for an hour to steep.
3. Pour the vanilla-infused milk through a sieve to remove the vanilla pod.
4. Place the thick coconut milk in a blender with the vanilla-infused milk, and the vanilla extract, and blend for 10 seconds.
5. Turn the blender to low speed, and while the blender is running, add the guar gum by tapping it through the opening in the lid, and blend for 30 seconds.
6. Pour the ice cream custard into a bowl or jar, cover, and place in the 'fridge for at least 8 hours, but preferably overnight. Don't skip the chillin', no matter which type of churner you have.
7. Freeze the custard in your churner according to the manufacturer's instructions. It typically takes between 15 – 25 minutes to freeze to a soft-serve consistency.
8. Once the ice cream has frozen to a soft-serve consistency, quickly transfer it from the churning bowl into your pre-chilled container, and place in the freezer for at least 8 hours, preferably overnight.

KETO PECAN ICE CREAM

Nutrition: Cal 240; Fat 24 g; Carb 8 g; Protein 6 g
Serving 8; Cook time 5 hours 30 min

Ingredients

- 1 oz. / 30g butter
- 5 ¼ oz. / 150g pecan halves
- ¼ tsp. sea salt
- 1 ½ cups / 12 fl oz. almond milk, unsweetened
- 1 cup/8 fl oz. heavy cream
- 3 ½ oz. / 100g xylitol (NO substitutes!)
- 1 tsp. sea salt
- 1 tsp. vanilla extract
- 1 cup / 8 fl oz. thick coconut milk
- 2 oz. / 55g butter, softened
- 1 tsp. guar gum

Instructions

1. Preheat the oven to 350F. Melt the butter in a small pan. Remove from the heat, add the pecans and salt, and stir until the nuts are well coated with butter.
2. Spread evenly on a baking sheet and toast in the oven for 10 minutes, stirring occasionally, until golden brown. Remove from the oven. Try not to eat them all.
3. Once the nuts are completely cooled, chop them roughly and store in an airtight container in the freezer.
4. Place the almond milk, cream, xylitol, sea salt, vanilla extract, thick coconut milk, and butter in a blender and blend for 10 seconds.
5. Turn the blender to low speed, and while the blender is running, add the guar gum by tapping it through the opening in the lid, and blend for 30 seconds.
6. Pour the ice cream custard into a bowl or jar, cover, and place in the 'fridge for at least 8 hours, but preferably overnight. Don't skip the chillin', no matter which type of churner you have.
7. Freeze the custard in your churner according to the manufacturer's instructions. It typically takes between 15 – 20 minutes to freeze to a soft-serve consistency.
8. Once the ice cream has frozen to a soft-serve consistency in the churner, add the chopped frozen buttered pecan pieces and churn until mixed through.
9. Quickly transfer the ice cream from the churning bowl into your pre-chilled container, cover and place in the freezer for at least 8 hours, preferably overnight

PISTACHIO ROSE ICE CREAM

Nutrition: Cal 280; Fat 28 g; Carb 4 g; Protein 12 g
Serving 8; Cook time hours 30 min

Ingredients

- 1 ¼ cups / 10 fl oz. heavy cream
- 3 ½ oz. / 100g xylitol (NO substitutes!)
- ½ tsp. sea salt
- 4 tbsp rose water
- 1 tsp. rose extract
- 1 cup / 8 fl oz. thin coconut milk
- 7 ½ oz. / 210g crème fraiche
- 1 tsp. guar gum

- 3 oz. / 85g pistachio pieces, toasted and frozen

Instructions

1. Warm the cream, xylitol, sea salt, rose water, and rose extract in a medium pan until it just starts to boil. Simmer for 1 minute and then remove from the heat and cool for 15 minutes.
2. Carefully pour the warm cream mixture into a blender, add the thin coconut milk and crème fraiche and blend for 10 seconds.
3. Turn the blender to low speed, and while the blender is running, add the guar gum by tapping it through the opening in the lid, and blend for 30 seconds.
4. Pour the ice cream custard into a bowl or jar, cover, and place in the 'fridge for at least 8 hours, but preferably overnight. Don't skip the chillin', no matter which type of churner you have.
5. Freeze the custard in your churner according to the manufacturer's instructions. It typically takes between 15 – 20 minutes to freeze to a soft-serve consistency.
6. Once the ice cream has frozen to a soft-serve consistency in the churner, pour the frozen pistachio pieces through the opening in the top of the churner and churn until mixed through.
7. Quickly transfer it from the churning bowl into your pre-chilled container and place in the freezer for at least 8 hours, preferably overnight.

KETO AVOCADO ICE CREAM

Nutrition: Cal 340; Fat 36 g; Carb 10 g; Protein 12 g
Serving 6; Cook time 8 hours 30 min

Ingredients

- 1 cup / 8 fl oz. almond milk, unsweetened vanilla
- ½ cup / 4 fl oz. heavy cream
- 4 oz. / 110g sour cream
- 3 ½ oz. / 100g xylitol (NO substitutes!)
- ½ tsp. sea salt
- 1 tbsp white wine vinegar
- 2 tbsp vegetable glycerin
- 12 oz. / 335g avocado flesh (approx. 3 medium)
- 1 tsp. guar gum

Instructions

1. Place the almond milk, cream, sour cream, xylitol, sea salt, white wine vinegar, and vegetable glycerin in a blender and blend for 10 seconds.
2. With the blender running on low, add the avocado flesh and guar gum through the hole in the blender lid and blend until smooth. It will be very thick and you might have to stop the blender and scrape down the sides a time or two.
3. This custard needs to be churned immediately! It typically takes between 10 - minutes to freeze to a soft-serve consistency.
4. Once the ice cream has frozen to a soft-serve consistency, quickly transfer it from the churning bowl into your pre-chilled container, and place in the freezer for at least 8 hours, preferably overnight.

CHAI ICE CREAM

Nutrition:cal 220; Fat 18 g; Carb 6 g; Protein 6 g
Serving 1; Cook time 10 min

Ingredients

- 1 ¾ cups / 14 fl oz. thin coconut milk, unsweetened
- 3 ½ oz. / 100g xylitol (NO substitutes!)
- 4 chai teabags
- 1 ¾ cups / 14 fl oz. heavy cream
- 1 ½ tbsp espresso powder
- ½ tsp. sea salt
- 1 tsp. guar gum

Instructions

1. Warm the thin coconut milk and xylitol in a medium pan until it just starts to boil. Remove from the heat, add the chai teabags, stir well and leave for an hour to steep.
2. Pour the chai-infused milk through a sieve to remove the teabags, and then return the infused milk to the pan over a low heat.
3. Add the cream, espresso powder, and sea salt and stir well until the espresso powder is dissolved, and then remove from the heat.
4. Carefully pour the espresso chai mixture into a blender and blend for 10 seconds.
5. Turn the blender to low speed, and while the blender is running, add the guar gum by tapping it through the opening in the lid, and blend for 30 seconds.
6. Pour the ice cream custard into a bowl or jar, cover, and place in the 'fridge for at least 8 hours, but preferably overnight. Don't skip the chillin', no matter which type of churner you have.
7. Freeze the custard in your churner according to the manufacturer's instructions. It typically takes between 15 – 20 minutes to freeze to a soft-serve consistency.
8. Once the ice cream has frozen to a soft-serve consistency, quickly transfer it from the churning bowl into your pre-chilled container, and place in the freezer for at least 8 hours, preferably overnight.

WHITE RUSSIAN ICE CREAM

Nutrition: Cal 220; Fat 17 g; Carb 4 g; Protein 4 g
Serving 1; Cook time 10 min

Ingredients

- 1 ¼ cups / 10 fl oz. almond milk
- 1 ¾ oz. / 50g xylitol (NO substitutes!)
- 5 TBSP Kahlua
- 1 ¾ cups / 14 fl oz. heavy cream
- ½ cup / 4 fl oz. avocado oil
- 1 tsp. vanilla extract
- 1 tsp. guar gum

Instructions

1. Warm the almond milk, xylitol, and Kahlua in a medium pan until it just starts to boil. Simmer for 1 minute and remove from the heat.
2. Place the cream, avocado oil, and vanilla extract in a blender with the warm Kahlua milk, and blend on low for 30 seconds.

3. With the blender still on low speed, and while the blender is running, add the guar gum by tapping it through the opening in the lid, and blend for 30 seconds.
4. Pour the ice cream custard into a bowl or jar, cover, and place in the 'fridge for at least 8 hours, but preferably overnight. Don't skip the chillin', no matter which type of churner you have.
5. Freeze the custard in your churner according to the manufacturer's instructions. It typically takes between 15 – 20 minutes to freeze to a soft-serve consistency.
6. Once the ice cream has frozen to a soft-serve consistency, quickly transfer it from the churning bowl into your pre-chilled container, and place in the freezer for at least 8 hours, preferably overnight.

CINNAMON ICE CREAM

Nutrition: Cal 220; Fat 20 g; Carb 8 g; Protein 7 g
Serving 8; Cook time 8 hours 30 min

Ingredients

- 1 ½ cup / 12 fl oz. almond milk
- 1 cup / 8 fl oz. heavy cream
- 3 ½ oz. / 100g xylitol (NO substitutes!)
- ½ tsp. sea salt
- 1 cup / 8 fl oz. thick coconut milk
- 1 ½ tsp. ground cinnamon
- ¼ tsp. vanilla extract
- 1 tsp. guar gum

Instructions

1. Place the almond milk, cream, xylitol, sea salt, thick coconut milk, ground cinnamon, and vanilla extract into a blender and blend for 10 seconds.
2. Turn the blender to low speed, and while the blender is running, add the guargum by tapping it through the opening in the lid, and blend for 30 seconds.
3. Pour the ice cream custard into a bowl or jar, cover, and place in the 'fridge for at least 8 hours, but preferably overnight. Don't skip the chillin', no matter which type of churner you have.
4. Freeze the custard in your churner according to the manufacturer's instructions. It typically takes between 15 – 20 minutes to freeze to a soft-serve consistency.
5. Once the ice cream has frozen to a soft-serve consistency, quickly transfer it from the churning bowl into your pre-chilled container, and place in the freezer for at least 8 hours, preferably overnight.

LEMON POP ICE CREAM

Nutrition: Cal 280; Fat 24 g; Carb 10 g; Protein 14 g
Serving 1; Cook time 10 min

Ingredients

- 1 ¼ cup / 10 fl oz. thin coconut milk
- 4 oz. / 110g xylitol (NO substitutes!)
- ½ tsp. sea salt
- ¾ cup / 6 fl oz. heavy cream
- Zest of 3 whole lemons

- 8 oz. / 225g crème fraiche
- ½ cup / 4 fl oz. thick coconut milk
- 1 tbsp lemon juice
- ½ oz. / 15g poppy seeds
- 1 tsp. guar gum

Instructions

1. Warm the thin coconut milk, xylitol, sea salt, and cream in a medium pan until it just starts to boil.
2. Remove from the heat, add the lemon zest, cover and leave for an hour to steep.
3. Pour the lemon-infused milk through a sieve to remove the zest.
4. Place the crème fraiche and thick coconut milk in a blender with the lemoninfused milk, and the lemon juice, and blend for 10 seconds.
5. Turn the blender to low speed, and while the blender is running, add the poppy seeds followed by the guar gum by tapping them through the opening in the lid, and blend for 30 seconds.
6. Pour the ice cream custard into a bowl or jar, cover, and place in the 'fridge for at least 8 hours, but preferably overnight. Don't skip the chillin', no matter which type of churner you have.
7. Freeze the custard in your churner according to the manufacturer's instructions. It typically takes between 15 – 20 minutes to freeze to a soft-serve consistency.
8. Once the ice cream has frozen to a soft-serve consistency, quickly transfer it from the churning bowl into your pre-chilled container, and place in the freezer for at least 8 hours, preferably overnight.

VANILLA GREEN TEA ICE CREAM

Nutrition: Cal 230; Fat 20 g; Carb 3 g; Protein 4 g
Serving 4; Cook time 8 yours 20 min

Ingredients

- 1 ¼ cup / 10 fl oz. thin coconut milk
- 1 ¼ cup / 10 fl oz. heavy cream
- 3 ½ oz. / 100g xylitol (NO substitutes!)
- ½ tsp. sea salt
- 2 TBSP green tea powder / matcha powder
- 1 cup / 8 fl oz. thick coconut milk
- 3 tsp. vanilla extract
- 1 tsp. guar gum

Instructions

1. Warm the thin coconut milk, cream, xylitol, and sea salt in a medium pan until it just starts to boil. Simmer for 1 minute, then remove from the heat and cool for 5 minutes.
2. Vigorously whisk the green tea powder into the hot cream mixture until it is completely dissolved.
3. Carefully pour the warm green tea cream into a blender, add the thick coconut milk and vanilla extract and blend for 10 seconds.
4. Turn the blender to low speed, and while the blender is running, add the guar gum by tapping it through the opening in the lid, and blend for 30 seconds.

5. Pour the ice cream custard into a bowl or jar, cover, and place in the 'fridge for at least 8 hours, but preferably overnight. Don't skip the chillin', no matter which type of churner you have.
6. Freeze the custard in your churner according to the manufacturer's instructions. It typically takes between 15 – 20 minutes to freeze to a soft-serve consistency.
7. Once the ice cream has frozen to a soft-serve consistency, quickly transfer it from the churning bowl into your pre-chilled container, and place in the freezer for at least 8 hours, preferably overnight.

ORANGE CREAMSICLE ICE CREAM

Nutrition: Cal 106; Fat 3 g; Carb 28 g; Protein 4 g
Serving 1; Cook time 10 min

Ingredients

- Zest of 4 oranges
- 1 cup / 8 fl oz. almond milk
- ½ cup / 4 fl oz. heavy cream
- 3 ½ oz. / 100g xylitol (NO substitutes!)
- ½ tsp. sea salt
- 1 cup / 8 fl oz. thick coconut milk
- ½ tsp. vanilla extract
- 1 tsp. orange extract
- 1 tsp. guar gum

Instructions

1. Zest the oranges directly into a small pan.
2. Add the almond milk, cream, xylitol, and sea salt to the pan with the zest, stir well, and bring just to the boil. Remove from the heat, cover, and leave to cool.
3. Pass the orange milk through a sieve to remove the zest. Discard the zest.
4. Place the orange milk in a blender with the thick coconut milk, vanilla extract, and orange extract, and blend for 10 seconds.
5. Turn the blender to low speed, and while the blender is running, add the guar gum by tapping it through the opening in the lid, and blend for 30 seconds.
6. Pour the ice cream custard into a bowl or jar, cover, and place in the 'fridge for at least 8 hours, but preferably overnight. Don't skip the chillin', no matter which type of churner you have.
7. Freeze the custard in your churner according to the manufacturer's instructions. It typically takes between 15 – 20 minutes to freeze to a soft-serve consistency.
8. Once the ice cream has frozen to a soft-serve consistency in the churner, quickly spoon a layer of ice cream into the bottom of your cold storage container.

LIME IN THE COCONUT ICE CREAM

Nutrition: Cal 240; Fat 21 g; Carb 6 g; Protein 7 g
Serving 1; Cook time 10 min

Ingredients

- 3 oz. / 85g flaked or desiccated coconut
- unsweetened Zest of 2 limes
- ¾ cup / 6 fl oz. thin coconut milk

- ¾ cup / 6 fl oz. heavy cream
- ½ tsp. sea salt
- 3 ½ oz. / 100g xylitol (NO substitutes!)
- 1 ½ cups / 12 fl oz. thick coconut milk
- 1 tsp. guar gum

Instructions

1. Spread the coconut on a baking sheet and toast under a broiler (grill) until lightly browned. Browning happens very quickly – do not walk away! Remove from under the broiler (grill) and leave to cool.
2. Zest the limes directly into a small pan.
3. Add the thin coconut milk, cream, sea salt, and xylitol to the lime zest in the pan and bring just to the boil. Remove from the heat, cover, and leave to cool.
4. Pass the lime milk through a sieve to remove the zest. Set zest to one side and reserve. You will use it at the churning stage.
5. Place the lime milk in a blender with the thick coconut milk and toasted coconut, and blend for seconds. It will NOT be smooth. Don't try to make it be smooth!
6. Turn the blender to low speed, and while the blender is running, add the guar gum by tapping it through the opening in the lid, and blend for 30 seconds.
7. Pour the ice cream custard into a bowl or jar, cover, and place in the 'fridge for at least 8 hours, but preferably overnight. Don't skip the chillin', no matter which type of churner you have.
8. Freeze the custard in your churner according to the manufacturer's instructions. It typically takes between 15 – 20 minutes to freeze to a soft-serve consistency.
9. Once the ice cream has frozen to a soft-serve consistency in the churner, add the lime zest to the churner through the opening in the top, and churn until mixed through.
10. Quickly transfer the ice cream from the churning bowl into your pre-chilled container, cover, and place in the freezer for at least 8 hours, preferably overnight.

BEER FLOAT ICE CREAM

Nutrition: Cal 320; Fat 28 g; Carb 10 g; Protein 8 g
Serving 1; Cook time 10 min

Ingredients

- 1 cup / 8 fl oz. thick coconut milk
- 1 ¼ cup / 10 fl oz. almond milk
- ½ cup / 4 fl oz. heavy cream
- ¼ cup / 2 fl oz. avocado oil
- 3 ½ oz. / 125g xylitol (NO substitutes!)
- ½ tsp. sea salt
- 1 tsp. vanilla extract
- 4 tsp. root beer extract
- 1 tsp. guar gum

Instructions

1. Place all ingredients EXCEPT the guar gum in a blender and blend for 10 seconds.
2. Turn the blender to low speed, and while the blender is running, add the guar gum by tapping it through the opening in the lid, and blend for 30 seconds.

3. Pour the ice cream custard into a bowl or jar, cover, and place in the 'fridge for at least 8 hours, but preferably overnight. Don't skip the chillin', no matter which type of churner you have.
4. Freeze the custard in your churner according to the manufacturer's instructions. It typically takes between 15 – 20 minutes to freeze to a soft-serve consistency.
5. Once the ice cream has frozen to a soft-serve consistency, quickly transfer it from the churning bowl into your pre-chilled container, and place in the freezer for at least 8 hours, preferably overnight

BASIL ICE CREAM

Nutrition: Cal 192; Fat 16 g; Carb 5 g; Protein 4 g
Serving 6; Cook time 8 hours 30 min

Ingredients

- 1 cup / 8 fl oz. heavy cream
- ¾ cup / 6 fl oz. almond milk, unsweetened vanilla
- 4 oz. / 100g xylitol (NO substitutes!)
- ¾ tsp. sea salt
- 2 oz. / 55g fresh basil leaves
- ½ cup / 4 fl oz. thick coconut milk
- 8 oz. / 225g ricotta cheese
- 1 tbsp lemon juice
- 1 tsp. guar gum

Instructions

1. Warm the cream, almond milk, xylitol, sea salt, and basil leaves in a medium pan until it just starts to boil. Remove from the heat, cover and leave for an hour to steep.
2. Pour the basil-infused milk through a sieve to remove the leaves. Press down hard on the leaves to extract as much flavor as possible. DO NOT DISCARD THE LEAVES.
3. Place the thick coconut milk, ricotta, and lemon juice in a blender with the strained basil-infused milk, and blend on low for 30 seconds. Add 1 packed tbsp of the soggy basil leaves from earlier and blend until the custard is flecked with little basil pieces. So pretty!
4. With the blender still on low speed, and while the blender is running, add the guar gum by tapping it through the opening in the lid, and blend for 30 seconds.
5. Pour the ice cream custard into a bowl or jar, cover, and place in the 'fridge for at least 8 hours, but preferably overnight. Don't skip the chillin', no matter which type of churner you have.
6. Freeze the custard in your churner according to the manufacturer's instructions. It typically takes between 15 – 20 minutes to freeze to a soft-serve consistency.
7. Once the ice cream has frozen to a soft-serve consistency, quickly transfer it from the churning bowl into your pre-chilled container, and place in the freezer for at least 8 hours, preferably overnight.

BACON CRAZY ICE CREAM

Nutrition: Cal 280; Fat 24 g; Carb 3 g; Protein 6 g
Serving 6; Cook time 8 hours 30 min

Ingredients

- 1 cup / 8 fl oz. heavy cream
- 1 ¼ cups / 10 fl oz. hemp milk
- 4 oz. / 110g xylitol (NO substitutes!)
- 2 ½ tbsp caramel extract
- 1 tsp. sea salt
- ½ cup / 4 fl oz. thick coconut milk
- ¼ cup / 2 fl oz. avocado oil
- 2 oz. / 55g full fat cream cheese
- 1 tsp. guar gum
- 8 oz. / 225g bacon, cooked (but NOT hard and crispy), chopped into small pieces and chilled

Instructions

1. Warm the cream, hemp milk, xylitol, caramel extract, and sea salt in a medium pan until it just starts to boil. Simmer for 1 minute and then remove from the heat.
2. Place the thick coconut milk, avocado oil, and cream cheese in a blender with the warm caramel cream, and blend on low for 30 seconds.
3. With the blender on low speed, and while the blender is running, add the guar gum by tapping it through the opening in the lid, and blend for 30 seconds.
4. Pour the ice cream custard into a bowl or jar, cover, and place in the 'fridge for at least 8 hours, but preferably overnight. Don't skip the chillin', no matter which type of churner you have.
5. Freeze the custard in your churner according to the manufacturer's instructions. It typically takes between 15 – 20 minutes to freeze to a soft-serve consistency.
6. Once the ice cream has frozen to a soft-serve consistency, quickly transfer it from the churning bowl into your pre-chilled container and stir in the chopped bacon thoroughly. Be quick so the ice cream doesn't start to melt. Cover and place in the freezer for at least 8 hours, preferably overnight.

KETO RASPBERRY ICE CREAM

Nutrition: Cal 190; Fat 12 g; Carb 8 g; Protein 4 g
Serving 6; Cook time 8 hours 30 min

Ingredients

- 12 oz. / 500g fresh or frozen raspberries
- 1 cup / 8 fl oz. thick coconut milk
- ½ cup / 4 fl oz. almond milk, unsweetened vanilla
- 1 cup / 8 fl oz. heavy cream
- 3 ½ oz. / 100g xylitol (NO substitutes!)
- ½ tsp. sea salt
- 1 ½ tbsp lemon juice
- 1 tsp. guar gum

Instructions

1. Heat raspberries in a pan over a medium heat until they are very soft – about 15 minutes.
2. Press the raspberry pulp through a sieve to remove all the seeds. This will take a little while, but will be SO worth the effort! DO NOT puree the raspberries before you sieve them to save you a few minutes. You will end up with a "dusty" taste in the final ice cream.
3. Place the raspberry puree, thick coconut milk, almond milk, cream, xylitol, sea salt, and lemon juice into a blender and blend for 10 seconds.
4. Turn the blender to low speed, and while the blender is running, add the guar gum by tapping it through the opening in the lid, and blend for 30 seconds.
5. Pour the ice cream custard into a bowl or jar, cover, and place in the 'fridge for at least 8 hours, but preferably overnight. Don't skip the chillin', no matter which type of churner you have.
6. Freeze the custard in your churner according to the manufacturer's instructions. It typically takes between 15 – 20 minutes to freeze to a soft-serve consistency.
7. Once the ice cream has frozen to a soft-serve consistency, quickly transfer it from the churning bowl into your pre-chilled container, and place in the freezer for at least 8 hours, preferably overnight.

CRANBERRY ICE CREAM

Nutrition: Cal 180; Fat 14 g; Carb 8 g; Protein 4 g
Serving 6; Cook time 8 hours 30 min

Ingredients

- 10 oz. / 280g cranberries
- 4 ½ oz. / 125g xylitol (NO substitutes!)
- ½ cup / 4 fl oz. almond milk
- 1½ cups / 12 fl oz. heavy cream
- 1 tsp. cinnamon extract
- 2 tsp. orange extract
- ½ tsp. sea salt
- ½ cup / 4 fl oz. thick coconut milk
- 1 tsp. guar gum

Instructions

1. Place the cranberries and xylitol in a pan over medium heat and cook for 15 minutes until the cranberries are very soft.
2. Blend the cooked cranberries until they are very smooth and then press through a fine mesh sieve to remove any remaining seed and skins.
3. Return the cranberry puree to the pan and add the almond milk, cream, cinnamon and orange extracts, and sea salt. Heat until the mixture just starts to boil. Simmer for 1 minute and then remove from the heat.
4. Place the thick coconut milk in a blender with the cranberry cream and blend for 10 seconds.
5. Turn the blender to low speed, and while the blender is running, add the guar gum by tapping it through the opening in the lid, and blend for 30 seconds.
6. Pour the ice cream custard into a bowl or jar, cover, and place in the 'fridge for at least 8 hours, but preferably overnight. Don't skip the chillin', no matter which type of churner you have.
7. Freeze the custard in your churner according to the manufacturer's instructions. It typically takes between 15 – 20 minutes to freeze to a soft-serve consistency.

8. Once the ice cream has frozen to a soft-serve consistency, quickly transfer it from the churning bowl into your pre-chilled container, and place in the freezer for at least 8 hours, preferably overnight

KETO BLACKBERRY ICE CREAM

Nutrition:Cal 260 Fat 22 g; Carb 10 g; Protein 8 g
Serving 8; Cook time 8 hours 30 min

Ingredients

- 20 oz. / 560g fresh blackberries
- 2 TBSP water
- 3 ½ oz. / 100g xylitol (NO substitutes!)
- ½ tsp. sea salt
- 2 tsp. lemon juice
- 1 tbsp kirsch (cherry liqueur)
- ½ cup / 4 fl oz. heavy cream
- ½ cup / 4 fl oz. thick coconut milk
- 7 ½ oz. / 210g crème fraiche
- ½ tsp. guar gum

Instructions

1. Place blackberries and water in a pan over medium heat and cook, stirring occasionally, until the berries are very soft – about 10 minutes.

2. Carefully pour the cooked berries into a blender and blend on high until the fruit is pureed. Rinse out the pan you used, place a sieve on it, and press the puree through the sieve. Use a clean spatula to scrape the puree from the underside of the sieve when finished.

3. Put the pan back over medium heat, add the xylitol, sea salt, lemon juice, kirsch, and cream. Stir well and bring just to a boil. Reduce heat and simmer for 1 minute. Remove and let cool for minutes before carefully pouring the warm puree into a clean blender. Add the thick coconut milk and crème fraiche and blend for 10 seconds.

4. Turn the blender to low speed, and while the blender is running, add the guar gum by tapping it through the opening in the lid, and blend for 30 seconds.

5. Pour the ice cream custard into a bowl or jar, cover, and place in the 'fridge for at least 8 hours, but preferably overnight. Don't skip the chillin', no matter which type of churner you have.

6. Freeze the custard in your churner according to the manufacturer's instructions. It typically takes between 20 – 30 minutes to freeze to a soft-serve consistency.

7. Once the ice cream has frozen to a soft-serve consistency, quickly transfer it from the churning bowl into your pre-chilled container, and place in the freezer for at least 8 hours, preferably overnight.

KETO BLUEBERRY ICE CREAM

Nutrition: Cal 240; Fat 18 g; Carb 8 g; Protein 4 g
Serving 4; Cook time 8 hours 30 min

Ingredients

- ¾ cup / 6 fl oz. almond milk, unsweetened vanilla
- 3 ½ oz. / 100g xylitol (NO substitutes!)
- ½ tsp. sea salt
- 1 ½ tsp. cinnamon extract
- ¾ cup / 6 fl oz. heavy cream
- 8 oz. / 225g fresh blueberries
- ½ cups / 4 fl oz. thick coconut milk
- 4 oz. / 110g cream cheese
- 1 tsp. guar gum

Instructions

1. Warm the almond milk, xylitol, sea salt, cinnamon extract, and cream in a medium pan until it just starts to boil.

2. Remove from the heat and carefully pour into a blender.

3. Immediately add the fresh blueberries and blend until smooth.

4. Add the thick coconut milk and cream cheese to the warm blueberry cream and blend on low until completely smooth.

5. With the blender still on low speed, and while the blender is running, add the guar gum by tapping it through the opening in the lid, and blend for 30 seconds.

6. Pour the ice cream custard into a bowl or jar, cover, and place in the 'fridge for at least 8 hours, but preferably overnight. Don't skip the chillin', no matter which type of churner you have.

7. Freeze the custard in your churne according to the manufacturer's instructions. It typically takes between 15 – 2 minutes to freeze to a soft-serve consistency.

8. Once the ice cream has frozen to a soft-serve consistency, quickly transfer it from the churning bowl into your pre-chilled container, and place in the freezer for at least 8 hours, preferably overnight.

APRICOT CARDAMOM ICE CREAM

Nutrition: Cal 280; Fat 17 g; Carb 12 g; Protein 6 g
Serving 1; Cook time 10 min

Ingredients

- 8 oz. / 225g fresh apricots, stoned
- 1 cup / 8 fl oz. almond milk, unsweetened vanilla
- ½ cup / 4 fl oz. heavy cream
- 3 ½ oz. / 100g xylitol (NO substitutes!)
- ½ tsp. sea salt
- 1 cup / 8 fl oz. thick coconut milk
- ¾ tsp. ground cardamom
- 1 tsp. guar gum
- 8 oz. / 225g fresh apricots, stoned and chopped into small pieces
- 1 oz. / 30g xylitol

Instructions

1. Simmer 8 oz. 225g apricots, almond milk, cream, 3 ½ oz. 100g xylitol and salt over medium heat until apricots are very soft.
2. Blend the apricot mixture on high until completely smooth and then press through a fine mesh sieve.
3. Place the thick coconut milk and ground cardamom in the blender, add the apricot puree and blend for 10 seconds.
4. Turn the blender to low speed, and while the blender is running, add the guar gum by tapping it through the opening in the lid, and blend for 30 seconds.
5. Pour the ice cream custard into a bowl or jar, cover, and place in the 'fridge for at least 8 hours, but preferably overnight. Don't skip the chillin', no matter which type of churner you have.
6. At least an hour before churning, mix the remaining 8 oz. 225g chopped apricots in a bowl with oz. 30g xylitol and stir well. Leave to marinate, stirring often.
7. Freeze the custard in your churner according to the manufacturer's instructions. It typically takes between 15 – 20 minutes to freeze to a soft-serve consistency.
8. Once the ice cream has frozen to a soft-serve consistency, carefully pour the chopped apricots into the churner and continue churning until mixed through.
9. Quickly transfer it from the churning bowl into your pre-chilled container, cover, and place in the freezer for at least 8 hours, preferably overnight

PEACHES ICE CREAM

Nutrition: Cal 270; Fat 13 g; Carb 8 g; Protein 4 g
Serving 1; Cook time 10 min

Ingredients

- ½ cup / 4 fl oz. hcmp milk
- 10 oz. / 280g fresh peaches, stones removed
- 1 cup / 8 fl oz. heavy cream
- ¾ tsp. sea salt
- 3 ½ oz. / 100g xylitol (NO substitutes!)
- 1 cup / 8 fl oz. thick coconut milk
- 1 tsp. guar gum
- 7 oz. / 200g fresh peaches, stones removed and chopped into small pieces
- 1 oz. / 30g xylitol

Instructions

1. Place hemp milk, 10oz 280g peaches, cream, sea salt, and ½ oz. 100g xylitol in a pan and simmer over a medium heat until peaches are very soft – about minutes.
2. Place the peach mixture in a blender and blend until completely smooth.
3. Pass through a fine sieve to remove any peach fibers.
4. Place the peach puree and thick coconut milk in the blender and blend for 10 seconds.
5. Turn the blender to low speed, and while the blender is running, add the guar gum by tapping it through the opening in the lid, and blend for 30 seconds.
6. Pour the ice cream custard into a bowl or jar, cover, and place in the 'fridge for at least 8 hours, but preferably overnight. Don't skip the chillin', no matter which type of churner you have.
7. Meanwhile, place the remaining 7 oz. 200g chopped peaches in a bowl with 1 oz. 30g xylitol and mix well. Cover and leave to marinate for at least an hour, stirring often.
8. Freeze the custard in your churner according to the manufacturer's instructions. It typically takes between 15 – 20 minutes to freeze to a soft-serve consistency.
9. Once the ice cream has frozen to a soft-serve consistency in the churner, add the marinated peach pieces to the churner and churn until mixed through.

Quickly transfer it from the churning bowl into your pre-chilled container, cover, and place in the freezer for at least 8 hours, preferably overnight.

Conclusion

I hope this book helps those women out there that are looking for a diet that will help them change their entire lifestyle. The ketogenic diet has helped me in so many ways to recover from the diseases that I had to face due to the growing age. Females, unlike males, have to go through a lot in a lifetime. Menopause is one of the biggest changing factors that is the start of the decline in our health. Just like how we first encounter our first period, stopping the menstrual cycle can have a huge impact on our body. With that comes a lot of issues such as obesity, joint problems (arthritis), fatigue, hormonal imbalances, mood swings, insomnia, acne, and so much more that you have read about in this book. It doesn't only talk about the problems women over 50 faces but how the keto diet can help fight those problems more healthily. No diet only benefits, just like how trying out a new workout can be hard on your body and in the beginning, starting a new diet can have some problematic impact on your body as well. Some problems that come alongside the ketogenic diet have been discussed in this book as well. Like the keto flu (ugh! don't get me started on that one), keto rash, keto cramps, and more. But, unlike other books, you will find solutions alongside every problem enlisted in this book. And not only solutions but a handful of some delicious recipes for your beginner keto-friendly meal and all the ingredients you might need to start this diet. Hopefully, this will help you grasp the technicalities of the keto diet and help you make a healthier you.

Sandra Grant

2023

Made in the USA
Las Vegas, NV
11 July 2023

74534829R00188